Istanbul

Verity Campbell
Tom Brosnahan

LONELY PLANET PUBLICATIONS
Melbourne • Oakland • London • Paris

Istanbul
3rd edition – February 2002
First published – April 1997

Published by
Lonely Planet Publications Pty Ltd ABN 36 005 607 983
90 Maribyrnong St, Footscray, Victoria 3011, Australia

Lonely Planet offices
Australia Locked Bag 1, Footscray, Victoria 3011
USA 150 Linden St, Oakland, CA 94607
UK 10a Spring Place, London NW5 3BH
France 1 rue du Dahomey, 75011 Paris

Photographs
Many of the images in this guide are available for licensing from Lonely Planet Images.
email: lpi@lonelyplanet.com.au
Web site: www.lonelyplanetimages.com

Front cover photograph
A view of the Blue Mosque (Sultan Ahmet Camii) in Old İstanbul (Grant V Faint, Getty Images)

ISBN 1 74059 044 9

Printed by Craft Print International Ltd, Singapore

Although the authors and Lonely Planet try to make the information as accurate as possible, we accept no responsibility for any loss, injury or inconvenience sustained by anyone using this book.

Contents – Text

THE AUTHORS 4

THIS BOOK 5

FOREWORD 6

INTRODUCTION 9

FACTS ABOUT İSTANBUL 10

History 10
Geography 17
Geology 17
Climate 18
Ecology & Environment 18
Government & Politics 19
Economy 19
Population & People 20
Arts 21
Society & Conduct 26
Religion 27
Language 28

ARCHITECTURE 29

FACTS FOR THE VISITOR 36

When to Go 36
Itineraries 36
Orientation 36
Maps 36
Responsible Tourism 37
Tourist Offices 37
Travel Agencies 40
Documents 40
Embassies & Consulates 41
Customs 42
Money 42
Post & Communications 45
Digital Resources 47
Books 47
Films 48
Newspapers & Magazines 48
Radio & TV 49
Photography & Video 49
Time 50
Electricity 50
Weights & Measures 50
Laundry 50
Toilets 50
Left Luggage 50
Health 50
Women Travellers 53
Gay & Lesbian Travellers 53
Disabled Travellers 54
Senior Travellers 54
İstanbul for Children 54
Cultural Centres & Libraries 54
Universities 55
Dangers & Annoyances 55
Emergencies 57
Legal Matters 57
Business Hours 57
Public Holidays & Special Events 57
Doing Business....59
Work 60

GETTING THERE & AWAY 61

Air 61
Bus 64
Train 66
Car & Motorcycle 69
Hitching 70
Boat 70

GETTING AROUND 72

Atatürk Airport 72
To/From Atatürk Airport 72
Bus 73
Train 73
Metro 74
Trams 74
Tünel 74
Car 75
Taxi 75
Dolmuş 76
Boat 76
Organised Tours 77

THINGS TO SEE & DO 78

Byzantine Sultanahmet 79
Great Palace Mosaics Museum 79
Aya Sofya 80
Sunken Cistern 83
Hippodrome 83
The Sphendoneh 84
Küçük Aya Sofya Camii 85
Sea Walls & Bucoleon Palace 85
Ottoman Sultanahmet 85
İstanbul Archaeology Museums....86
Gülhane Park & Sublime Porte 88
Soğukçeşme Sokak 88

Caferağa Medresesi 88
Baths of Lady Hürrem 88
Blue Mosque 89
Carpet & Kilim Museum 90
Hamamzade İsmail Dede Efendi Evi Müzesi 90
Sokollu Mehmet Paşa Camii 90
Museum of Turkish & Islamic Arts 90
Palace of the Sultans 91
Topkapı Palace 91
Path of Empires 99
Divan Yolu 99
Çemberlitaş 100
Beyazıt Camii 101
Beyazıt Square 101
İstanbul University 101
Museum of Turkish Calligraphic Art 101
Süleymanıye Camii 102
Şehzade Mehmet Camii 102
Aqueduct of Valens 102
Fatih Anıtı Parkı 103
Cartoon & Humour Museum 103
The Bazaar District 103
Nuruosmaniye Camii 103
Kapalı Çarşı 104
Mahmut Paşa Yokuşu 105
Büyük Yenı & Büyük Valıde Han 105
Uzunçarşı Caddesi 106
Rüstem Paşa Camii 106
Tahtakale 106
Hasırcılar Caddesi................107
Mısır Çarşısı 107
Yeni Cami 107
Galata Bridge 108
Beyoğlu 108
Taksim Square 109
North of Taksim 109
Around Taksim Square 110
İstiklal Caddesi 110
Tünel 113
Karaköy (Galata) 114
Dolmabahçe Palace to Ortaköy 116
Dolmabahçe Palace 117
Deniz Müzesi 118
Ihlamur Kasrı 119
Çırağan Sarayı 119
Yıldız Şale & Park 119
Ortaköy 121
Sights on the Asian Shore .121
Crossing to Üsküdar 122
Üsküdar 122
Crossing to Kadiköy 124
Kadiköy 125
Western Districts 125
Mihrimah Sultan Camii 125
Kariye Müzesi 126
Tekfur Sarayı 127
Fethiye Camii......................127
Sultan Selim Camii 128
Fener 128
Church of St Stephen of the Bulgars 129
Balat 129
Zeyrek Camii 130
Fatih Camii 130
The Walls & Eyüp 130
Hasköy 133
Aynalıkavak Kasrı 133
Rahmi M Koç Müzesi 134
Activities 134
Billiards, Bowling & Backgammon 134
Golf 134
Nargıleh 134
Hamams 134
Swimming & Gyms 134
Bosphorus Night Cruises 135
Courses 135

PLACES TO STAY 138

Where to Stay 138
Types of Accommodation ..138
Booking 139
Places to Stay – Budget 139
Places to Stay – Mid-Range 141
Places to Stay – Top End 145

PLACES TO EAT 148

Restaurants 148
Self-Catering 150
Breakfast 150
Sweets & Desserts 150
Drinks 150
Places to Eat – Budget 151
Places to Eat – Mid-Range 159
Places to Eat – Top End 163

ENTERTAINMENT 164

Venues 164
Classical Music 165
Art Galleries 165
Folk Dance & Music 166
Belly Dance 167
Ballet & Opera 167
Theatre 167
Cinema 167
Bars 168
Discos & Rock Clubs 171
Gay & Lesbian Venues 172
Jazz 173
Entertaining the Kids 174
Shadow Puppet Theatre 175
Spectator Sports 175

TURKISH CARPETS 176

SHOPPING **180**

Carpets 180
Leather 181
Silk 183
Handicrafts 183
Antiques 183
New & Second-hand Books 184
Old Books, Maps & Prints 185
Copper 186
Inlaid Wood 186
Jewellery 186
Meerschaum 187
Clothes 188
Spices, Potions & Turkish Delight 189
Glassware 190
Ceramics 190
Music & Musical Instruments 191

EXCURSIONS **192**

The Bosphorus 192
Touring the Bosphorus 193
Sights on the European Shore 195
Sights on the Asian Shore ..199
Kızıl Adalar 202
Edirne 204
Gallipoli & Troy 209
Gallipoli 209
Çanakkale 214
Troy 216

LANGUAGE **219**

GLOSSARY **225**

THANKS **227**

INDEX **234**

METRIC CONVERSION **inside back cover**

Contents – Maps

THINGS TO SEE & DO

Map 1 – Aya Sofya 81
Map 2 – İstanbul Archaeology Museum 86
Map 3 – Topkapi ....*opposite* 97
Map 4 – Kapali Çarşı ....*opposite* 105

EXCURSIONS

Map 5 – Excursions 192
Map 6 – Bosphorus 193
Map 7 – Edirne 205
Map 8 – Gallipoli 211
Map 9 – Anzac Battlefields..212
Map 10 – Çanakkale 215

İSTANBUL MAP SECTION (COLOUR) **see back pages**

Map 11 – Greater İstanbul
Map 12 – İstanbul
Map 13 – Sultanahmet Area
Map 14 – Fatih, Aksaray & Laleli
Map 15 – Around Sultanahmet
Map 16 – İstiklal Caddesi
Map 17 – Elmadağ, Harbiye & Nistansı
Map 18 – Western Districts
Map 19 – Üsküdar

MAP LEGEND **back page**

The Authors

Verity Campbell

When her security blanket was scrunched under the wheel of a dolmuş, Verity knew she was fated to be dragged round the world by an intrepid mother. Struggling to fight the travel bug, she went to university and studied landscape architecture. A year later she quit her graduate job and landed a job at Lonely Planet in Melbourne. Five years on she swapped her padded office chair for an air-cushioned author's life. Verity lived in İstanbul in 1990 and 1991, so she was delighted to get the chance to practise her Turkish, tramp through İstanbul's history once again and give her belly dancing a work-out. Verity is also the co-author of *Sri Lanka* and the Turkey chapters in *Mediterranean Europe* and *Europe*.

Tom Brosnahan

A native of Pennsylvania, Tom went to college in Boston, then set out on the road. His first two years in Turkey were spent as a US Peace Corps Volunteer. He studied Middle Eastern history and the Ottoman Turkish language for eight years, but abandoned the writing of his PhD dissertation in favour of travelling and writing guidebooks. Tom has written over 30 books for different publishers and has sold over two million copies in 12 languages.

FROM VERITY

Firstly, *çok teşekkürler* to the İstanbullus whose charm, sense of humour and generosity made research thoroughly enjoyable. Thanks to expats Janet and Kay for their advice, suggestions and insider tips on *the* places to be and see. Thanks also to David for his incredible generosity and teşekkürler to old friends Murat, Metin and Mehmet. Pat Yale, fellow İstanbul devotee, gave her time and knowledge as usual – cheers Pat.

In Australia, I'm grateful to the eagle eyes of Julia and Anna at Lonely Planet and for their time spent sweating over the manuscript and maps. Thanks also to the extremely helpful folk at the Turkish embassy and tourist offices. I won't mention Micky because he gets embarrassed. Finally, I'm especially grateful to my beloved, tireless mother.

This Book

Tom Brosnahan researched and wrote the first and second editions of *Istanbul*. Verity Campbell researched and extensively updated this third edition.

From the Publisher

This edition of *Istanbul* was edited at Lonely Planet's Melbourne office by Julia Taylor and proofed by Anne Mulvaney and Liz Filleul. Anna Judd designed the book and took care of the mapping. Maria Vallianos designed the cover; Emma Koch produced the Language chapter; Annie Horner from LPI coordinated the photographic images; Matt King coordinated the illustrative content; and Martin Harris drew the chapter end. Thanks to the senior editors Michelle Glynn and Brigitte Ellemor and senior designer Brett Moore, assisted by Maree Styles, who guided the book through all stages of production.

THANKS
Many thanks to the travellers who used the last edition and wrote to us with helpful hints, advice and interesting anecdotes. Your names appear in the back of this book.

Foreword

ABOUT LONELY PLANET GUIDEBOOKS

The story begins with a classic travel adventure: Tony and Maureen Wheeler's 1972 journey across Europe and Asia to Australia. Useful information about the overland trail did not exist at that time, so Tony and Maureen published the first Lonely Planet guidebook to meet a growing need.

From a kitchen table, then from a tiny office in Melbourne (Australia), Lonely Planet has become the largest independent travel publisher in the world, an international company with offices in Melbourne, Oakland (USA), London (UK) and Paris (France).

Today Lonely Planet guidebooks cover the globe. There is an ever-growing list of books and there's information in a variety of forms and media. Some things haven't changed. The main aim is still to help make it possible for adventurous travellers to get out there – to explore and better understand the world.

At Lonely Planet we believe travellers can make a positive contribution to the countries they visit – if they respect their host communities and spend their money wisely. Since 1986 a percentage of the income from each book has been donated to aid projects and human rights campaigns.

Updates Lonely Planet thoroughly updates each guidebook as often as possible. This usually means there are around two years between editions, although for more unusual or more stable destinations the gap can be longer. Check the imprint page (following the colour map at the beginning of the book) for publication dates.

Between editions up-to-date information is available in two free newsletters – the paper *Planet Talk* and email *Comet* (to subscribe, contact any Lonely Planet office) – and on our Web site at www.lonelyplanet.com. The *Upgrades* section of the Web site covers a number of important and volatile destinations and is regularly updated by Lonely Planet authors. *Scoop* covers news and current affairs relevant to travellers. And, lastly, the *Thorn Tree* bulletin board and *Postcards* section of the site carry unverified, but fascinating, reports from travellers.

Correspondence The process of creating new editions begins with the letters, postcards and emails received from travellers. This correspondence often includes suggestions, criticisms and comments about the current editions. Interesting excerpts are immediately passed on via newsletters and the Web site, and everything goes to our authors to be verified when they're researching on the road. We're keen to get more feedback from organisations or individuals who represent communities visited by travellers.

Lonely Planet gathers information for everyone who's curious about the planet – and especially for those who explore it first-hand. Through guidebooks, phrasebooks, activity guides, maps, literature, newsletters, image library, TV series and Web site we act as an information exchange for a worldwide community of travellers.

Research Authors aim to gather sufficient practical information to enable travellers to make informed choices and to make the mechanics of a journey run smoothly. They also research historical and cultural background to help enrich the travel experience and allow travellers to understand and respond appropriately to cultural and environmental issues.

Authors don't stay in every hotel because that would mean spending a couple of months in each medium-sized city and, no, they don't eat at every restaurant because that would mean stretching belts beyond capacity. They do visit hotels and restaurants to check standards and prices, but feedback based on readers' direct experiences can be very helpful.

Many of our authors work undercover, others aren't so secretive. None of them accept freebies in exchange for positive write-ups. And none of our guidebooks contain any advertising.

Production Authors submit their manuscripts and maps to offices in Australia, USA, UK or France. Editors and cartographers – all experienced travellers themselves – then begin the process of assembling the pieces. When the book finally hits the shops, some things are already out of date, we start getting feedback from readers and the process begins again …

WARNING & REQUEST

Things change – prices go up, schedules change, good places go bad and bad places go bankrupt – nothing stays the same. So, if you find things better or worse, recently opened or long since closed, please tell us and help make the next edition even more accurate and useful. We genuinely value all the feedback we receive. A well-travelled team reads and acknowledges every letter, postcard and email and ensures that every morsel of information finds its way to the appropriate authors, editors and cartographers for verification.

Everyone who writes to us will find their name listed in the next edition of the appropriate guidebook. They will also receive the latest issue of *Planet Talk*, our quarterly printed newsletter, or *Comet*, our monthly email newsletter. Subscriptions to both newsletters are free. The very best contributions will be rewarded with a free guidebook.

We may edit, reproduce and incorporate your comments in all Lonely Planet products, such as guidebooks, Web sites and digital products, so let us know if you don't want your comments reproduced or your name acknowledged.

Send all correspondence to the Lonely Planet office closest to you:

Australia: Locked Bag 1, Footscray, Victoria 3011
USA: 150 Linden St, Oakland, CA 94607
UK: 10a Spring Place, London NW5 3BH

Or email us at: talk2us@lonelyplanet.com.au

For news, views and updates see our Web site: www.lonelyplanet.com

HOW TO USE A LONELY PLANET GUIDEBOOK

The best way to use a Lonely Planet guidebook is any way you choose. At Lonely Planet we believe the most memorable travel experiences are often those that are unexpected, and the finest discoveries are those you make yourself. Guidebooks are not intended to be used as if they provide a detailed set of infallible instructions!

Contents All Lonely Planet guidebooks follow roughly the same format. The Facts about the Destination chapters or sections give background information ranging from history to weather. Facts for the Visitor gives practical information on issues like visas and health. Getting There & Away gives a brief starting point for researching travel to and from the destination. Getting Around gives an overview of the transport options when you arrive.

The peculiar demands of each destination determine how subsequent chapters are broken up, but some things remain constant. We always start with background, then proceed to sights, places to stay, places to eat, entertainment, getting there and away, and getting around information – in that order.

Heading Hierarchy Lonely Planet headings are used in a strict hierarchical structure that can be visualised as a set of Russian dolls. Each heading (and its following text) is encompassed by any preceding heading that is higher on the hierarchical ladder.

Entry Points We do not assume guidebooks will be read from beginning to end, but that people will dip into them. The traditional entry points are the list of contents and the index. In addition, however, some books have a complete list of maps and an index map illustrating map coverage.

There may also be a colour map that shows highlights. These highlights are dealt with in greater detail in the Facts for the Visitor chapter, along with planning questions and suggested itineraries. Each chapter covering a geographical region usually begins with a locator map and another list of highlights. Once you find something of interest in a list of highlights, turn to the index.

Although inclusion in a guidebook usually implies a recommendation we cannot list every good place. Exclusion does not necessarily imply criticism. In fact there are a number of reasons why we might exclude a place – sometimes it is simply inappropriate to encourage an influx of travellers.

Maps Maps play a crucial role in Lonely Planet guidebooks and include a huge amount of information. A legend is printed on the back page. We seek to have complete consistency between maps and text, and to have every important place in the text captured on a map. Map key numbers usually start in the top left corner.

Introduction

Founded six centuries before Christ as Byzantium, refounded in AD 330 as Constantinople, and conquered by the Ottomans in 1453, İstanbul was the great eastern European imperial capital for almost 16 centuries. Known to its ancient inhabitants as simply 'The City', it remained enclosed within its mighty walls for 1500 years. However, in the last few decades it has grown ferociously, spreading westward beyond Atatürk Airport (23km from the city centre), northward almost to the Black Sea and eastward deep into Anatolia.

With this growth has come industry, enterprise and increased wealth for many of its people. And much of İstanbul's character has been forged by this juxtaposition of wealth: Although the Ottoman Empire is over, its gold-dripping ways are alive among the modern elite in the Bosphorus-side *yalıs* (villas), gourmet shops and sleek restaurants and bars; while other suburbs are in a time warp, living with ramshackle wooden houses, manic street markets and cobbled lanes crisscrossed with clotheslines.

In this sprawling city you can tramp the streets where Crusaders and janissaries once marched; admire mosques that are the most sublime architectural expressions of Islamic piety; peer into the sultan's Harem; and hunt for bargains in the 4000 shops of the Kapalı Çarşı (Grand Bazaar). Side by side with Old İstanbul you'll find hip bars and clubs, dot com executives, malls and haute cuisine. And then there is a rich arts culture – opera, music, cinema – which nods its head to the Ottoman and Byzantine ways while taking cues from Europe.

All this beauty, culture and bustle coexists around the spine of the Bosphorus, a constantly busy, heaving mass, dotted with ships and ferries, and providing the link between Europe and Asia.

Whatever your interest – architecture, art, nightlife, cuisine, history, religion, shopping – İstanbul has more than enough of it, at prices which are among the lowest in Europe. It's so good that some visit for a holiday and end up staying for years – will you be next?

Facts about İstanbul

HISTORY

Early Times

The Mediterranean region was inhabited as early as 7500 BC, during Palaeolithic (Old Stone Age) times. Turkey has some of the world's oldest 'cities', including Çatal Höyük, 50km south-east of Konya. These early Anatolian communities developed fine wall paintings, statuettes and domestic architecture during the Stone and Copper Ages.

The Bronze Age, starting in 2600 BC, saw the rise of the Hittite civilisation in central Anatolia, followed by those of the Phrygians, Urartians, Lydians and others.

Semistra, the earliest-known settlement on the site of İstanbul, was probably founded around 1000 BC, a few hundred years after the Trojan War and in the same period that kings David and Solomon ruled in Jerusalem.

Semistra was followed by a fishing village named Lygos, which occupied Seraglio Point (Seray Burnu) where Topkapı Palace stands today. Later, around 700 BC, colonists from Megara (near Corinth) in Greece settled at Chalcedon (now Kadıköy) on the Asian shore of the Bosphorus.

Byzantium

The first settlement here to have historic significance was founded, according to legend, by a Megarian colonist named Byzas. Before leaving Greece, he asked the oracle at Delphi where he should establish his new colony. The enigmatic answer was 'Opposite the blind'. When Byzas and his fellow colonists sailed up the Bosphorus, they noticed the colony on the Asian shore at Chalcedon. Looking west, they saw the superb natural harbour of the Golden Horn (Haliç) on the European shore. Thinking, as legend has it, 'Those people in Chalcedon must be blind', they settled in 657 BC on the opposite shore at Lygos, and their new town came to be called Byzantium after its founder.

The legend might as well be true. İstanbul's location on the waterway linking the Sea of Marmara and the Black Sea, and on the Thracian 'land bridge' linking Europe and Asia, is still of tremendous importance today, 26 centuries after the oracle spoke.

In 512 BC, Darius, emperor of Persia, captured the town during his campaign against the Scythians. Following the retreat of the Persians in 478, the town came under the influence and protection of Athens, Sparta, Samos and other forces.

Around 400 BC, Xenophon led the remnants of the Ten Thousand (the Greek army in the service of Cyrus the Younger) back to Greece from the battle of Cunaxa by way of the Bosphorus.

Byzantium submitted willingly to the armies of Alexander the Great, victor in the Battle of the Granicus (334 BC; near present-day Biga, north-west of Balıkesir). In 179 BC it was captured and became part of the Kingdom of Pergamum. When the last Pergamene king died in 133 BC, he willed his entire kingdom to Rome, and Byzantium became part of the Roman province of Asia.

Except for some tussles between Rome and the king of Pontus, Byzantium enjoyed peace and prosperity under Roman rule until it picked the wrong side in a civil war. When the emperor Septimius Severus emerged victorious over his rival Pescennius Niger, he massacred Byzantium's citizens, razed its walls and burned the disloyal city.

Realising, however, the importance of the city's strategic position, he soon set about building a new, wider circuit of walls (which stretched roughly from the Yeni Cami to the Cankurtaran lighthouse) and named it Augusta Antonina.

Founding of Constantinople

Emperor Diocletian retired in AD 305 and left government of the Roman Empire to co-emperors Licinius in the east (Augusta Antonina) and Constantine in the west (Rome). This resulted in a civil war, which was won by Constantine in 324 when he defeated Licinius at Chrysopolis (Üsküdar).

With his victory, Constantine became sole emperor (r. 324–37) of a reunited empire. To solidify his power he summoned the First Ecumenical Council at Nicaea (İznik) in 325, which established the precedent of the emperor's supremacy in church affairs.

He also decided to move the capital of the empire to the shores of the Bosphorus. He built a new, wider circle of walls around the site of Byzantium and laid out a magnificent city within. The city was dedicated on 11 May 330 as New Rome, but was soon called Constantinople. The place which had been first settled as a fishing village over 1000 years earlier was now the capital of the Eurasian world, and would remain so for almost another 1000 years.

Constantine the Great died in Nicomedia (İzmit, Kocaeli) seven years after the dedication of his new capital. On his deathbed he formally adopted Christianity, though he had been governing its affairs for over a decade.

The city continued to grow. Emperor Theodosius II (r. 408–50) came to the throne as a boy, heavily influenced by his sister Pulcheria. Threatened by the forces of Attila the Hun, he ordered an even wider, more powerful circle of walls to be built around the city. Completed in 413, they were brought down by an earthquake in 447 and hastily rebuilt in a mere two months – the rapid approach of Attila and the Huns acting as a powerful stimulus. The Theodosian walls successfully held out invaders for the next 757 years, and still stand today.

Theodosius also built a new cathedral, the Sancta Sophia (Aya Sofya or Church of the Divine Wisdom; 415), to replace an earlier church of the same name, which had been burned during a riot in 404.

Justinian & Theodora

During the 5th and 6th centuries, as the barbarians of Europe captured and sacked Rome, the new eastern capital grew in wealth and strength. The emperor Justinian (r. 527–65) brought the Eastern Roman Empire to the height of its strength. A few years after taking the throne, he married Theodora, a devout, strong-willed former courtesan who is credited with having great influence over her husband. During the Nika riots of 532, the greatest threat to his reign, Justinian was reportedly ready to flee the capital, but the empress persuaded him to stand and fight, thus saving his throne.

Under Justinian, Byzantium's great general Belisarius reconquered Anatolia, the Balkans, Egypt, Italy and North Africa.

The emperor further embellished Constantinople with great buildings. His personal triumph was a new Sancta Sophia (today known as the Aya Sofya), built to replace Theodosius II's church, which had been burned in the Nika riots. When finished, in 537, this architectural masterpiece was the most splendid church in Christendom, and remained so for almost 1000 years, after which it became the most splendid mosque.

Justinian's ambitious building projects and constant wars of reconquest exhausted his treasury and his empire, however. Following his reign, the Byzantine Empire would never again be as large, powerful or rich.

İstanbul Time Line

1000–657 BC
Ancient fishing villages on this site.

657 BC–AD 330
Byzantium, a Greek city-state, later subject to Rome.

AD 330
Constantine the Great founds Constantinople, the 'New Rome', capital of the Eastern Roman (Byzantine) Empire.

MARTIN HARRIS

Emperor Justinian

413
Emperor Theodosius II completes a new, much wider ring of mighty walls around the city.

527–65
Reign of Justinian, the height of eastern Roman power and influence.

669
Arab Muslim armies lay siege to the city for the first time but cannot penetrate its walls.

Later Emperors

From 610 to 1025, a succession of warrior emperors kept the 'barbarians' at bay. The Arab armies of the nascent Islamic empire reached the walls of Constantinople in 669, but couldn't penetrate them. Again in 717 they tried, and again failed. The powerful emperors of the Bulgarian empire besieged the city in 814, 913 and 924, never conquering it. Under Emperor Basil II (r. 976–1025), the Byzantine armies drove the Arab armies out of Anatolia and completely annihilated the Bulgarian forces.

After Basil, the empire was virtually ruled by the ambitious Empress Zoe (r. 1028–50). She was 50 years old when she married the aged emperor Romanus III Argyrus. He died mysteriously in his bath in 1034, and Zoe quickly married her youthful, virile companion, who joined her on the throne as Michael IV. Eight years later, after Michael died from an illness contracted while on campaign, Zoe and her sister Theodora ruled as empresses in their own right, but they were not able to dominate the fractious nobles. At the age of 64 Zoe wed an eminent senator who became the third Mr Zoe, Constantine IX Monomachus. He outlived the empress, but did no better a job at ruling. After his death, Theodora ruled as empress again.

In 1071, Emperor Romanus IV Diogenes led his army to eastern Anatolia to do battle with the Seljuk Turks who had been forced out of Central Asia by the encroaching Mongols. However, at Manzikert (Malazgirt) the Byzantines were disastrously defeated, the emperor captured and imprisoned, and the former Byzantine heartland of Anatolia thus thrown open to Turkish invasion and settlement. Soon the Seljuks had built a thriving empire of their own in central Anatolia, with their capital first at Nicaea, and later at Konya.

As Turkish power was consolidated in Anatolia to the east of Constantinople, the power of Venice – always a maritime and commercial rival to Constantinople – grew in the west.

The Crusades

The convoluted, treacherous imperial court politics of Constantinople have given us the word 'Byzantine'. Rarely blessed with a simple, peaceful succession, Byzantine rulers were always under threat from members of their own families as well as would-be tyrants and foreign powers.

In 1195 Alexius III deposed and blinded his brother, Emperor Isaac II. Isaac's oldest son, Prince Alexius, escaped to Rome and pleaded to the pope for help in restoring his father to the Byzantine throne. At the time, the Fourth Crusade was assembling in Venice to sail to Egypt and attack the Infidel. When Prince Alexius offered to pay richly to be put on the throne, Enrico Dandolo, Doge of Venice, led the crusaders to his rival in Constantinople, arriving in 1203.

Alexius III fled with the imperial treasury, and the crusaders restored Isaac II to the throne and made Prince Alexius his co-emperor. However, the new co-emperors had no money to pay their allies so they im-

İstanbul Time Line

717–18
A further Arab siege of Constantinople is unsuccessful.

814–924
Armies of the Bulgarian empire besiege the city unsuccessfully.

976–1025
Reign of Basil II, Byzantium's most illustrious emperor.

1071
Emperor Romanus IV Diogenes defeated and captured by the Seljuk Turks at Manzikert.

SARAH JOLLY

1204
Armies of the Fourth Crusade capture the city, sack it, and put a Latin emperor on the throne; Theodore I Lascaris founds the Empire of Nicaea to wait out the Latin occupation.

1261
Michael VIII Palaeologus, emperor of Nicaea, recaptures

posed a crushing tax burden on their people. Rising in revolt, the Byzantine people killed both of them. Within months, impatient for his money, Dandolo ordered the conquest of the city. On 13 April 1204 the crusaders succeeded in breaking through the walls; and then proceeded to sack and pillage the rich capital of their Christian ally.

When the smoke cleared, Dandolo took control of three-eighths of the city, including Aya Sofya, leaving the rest to his co-conspirator Count Baldwin of Flanders. The Byzantine nobility fled to what was left of their estates and fought among themselves in best Byzantine fashion for control of the shreds of the empire.

Count Baldwin had Aya Sofya converted to a Roman Catholic cathedral, and there had himself crowned emperor of Romania, his name for his new kingdom.

Never a strong or effective state, Baldwin's so-called empire steadily declined until, just over half a century later in 1261, it was easily recaptured by the soldiers of Michael VIII Palaeologus, formerly the emperor of Nicaea, now emperor of a restored Byzantine Empire.

Birth of the Ottoman Empire

Two decades after Michael re-established Byzantine rule in its traditional capital, a Turkish warlord named Ertuğrul died in the village of Söğüt not far east of Nicaea. He left to his son Osman a small territory and a band of followers which in 1326 Osman would leave to his son, Orhan (r. 1324–60), as the nascent Ottoman Empire.

Orhan captured Bursa and made it his capital, then captured Nicaea as well, and sent his forces further afield, conquering Ankara to the east and Thrace to the west. His son Murat I (r. 1360–89) took Adrianople (Edirne) in 1362 and pursued his conquests to Kosovo, where he defeated the Serbs and Bosnians, though he was assassinated by a treacherous Serb.

Though temporarily checked by the armies of Tamerlane and by fratricidal civil war within the Ottoman ruling family, the empire continued to grow in power and size. By 1440 the Ottoman armies had laid siege to Constantinople and Belgrade (unsuccessfully), and had battled Christian armies for Transylvania.

The Conquest

What Europeans refer to as 'the fall of Constantinople' is to Turks 'the Conquest'.

By 1450, the Byzantine emperor had effective control over little more than Constantinople itself and a few small territories in what is now Greece.

When Sultan Mehmet II (r. 1451–81) came to the Ottoman throne as a young man, his 150-year-old empire needed a firm hand. He provided it, establishing central governmental control and battling troublesome Turkish emirs into submission. To solidify his power, he decided on the obvious: the conquest of the great city his territories already surrounded.

Mehmet ordered construction of the fortress of Rumeli Hisarı to be completed in four months. Miraculously, it was. He also

Constantinople and re-establishes the Byzantine Empire.

1288
Osman Gazi, a Turkish warlord on the Byzantine frontier near Bursa, founds the Ottoman state.

1326–31
Orhan Gazi, son of Osman, captures Bursa and Nicaea for the Ottomans; Bursa becomes the Ottoman capital.

TOM BROSNAHAN

Monument to Sultan Mehmet II (the Conqueror) in Fatih Anıtı Parkı

1362
The Ottomans take Adrianople (Edirne).

1391–94
Sultan Beyazıt I blockades Constantinople, but is forced to withdraw to do battle with Crusaders.

1453
Sultan Mehmet II (the Conqueror) builds Rumeli Hisarı and conquers Constantinople.

had Anadolu Hisarı, Beyazıt's fortress on the Asian shore, repaired. Between them, the two great fortresses could close the Bosphorus at its narrowest point, blockading the imperial capital from the north.

The Byzantines had closed the mouth of the Golden Horn with a heavy chain (on view today in İstanbul's Askeri Müzesi, or Military Museum) to prevent Ottoman ships from sailing in and attacking the city walls on the north side. Mehmet outsmarted them by marshalling his boats at a cove where Dolmabahçe Palace now stands and having them transported by night overland on rollers and slides up the valley (where the İstanbul Hilton now stands) and down the other side into the Golden Horn at Kasım Paşa. As dawn broke, his fleet attacked the city, catching the Byzantine defenders completely by surprise. Soon the Golden Horn was under Ottoman control.

As for the mighty Theodosian land walls to the west, a Hungarian cannon founder named Urban had come to offer his services to the Byzantine emperor for the defence of Christendom. Finding that the emperor had no money, he went to Mehmet, who paid him richly to cast an enormous cannon capable of firing a huge ball up to 1.5km – or, more to the point, right through the city walls.

Despite the inevitability of the Conquest, Emperor Constantine XI Palaeologus refused the surrender terms offered by Mehmet on 23 May 1453, preferring to wait in hope that Christendom would come to his rescue. On 28 May the final attack began: The mighty walls were breached between the gates now called Topkapı and Edirnekapı, the sultan's troops flooded in and, by the evening of the 29th, they were in control of every quarter. The last emperor of Byzantium died in battle fighting on the walls.

The areas of the city that did not resist Mehmet's troops were spared and their churches guaranteed to them. Areas that resisted were sacked for the customary three days, and the churches turned into mosques. As for Aya Sofya, the greatest church in Christendom, it was immediately converted into a mosque.

Ottoman Greatness

Mehmet the Conqueror saw himself as the legitimate successor to the imperial throne of Byzantium by right of conquest. He began at once to rebuild and repopulate the city. He built a mosque, the Fatih (Conqueror) Camii, on one of the city's seven hills, repaired the city walls and made İstanbul, as it would soon be called, the administrative, commercial and cultural centre of his growing empire. In Byzantine times it was informally known as the city *(polis)*. İstanbul probably derives its name from 'to the city' *(eis ten polin)*. Constantinople was officially changed to İstanbul by Atatürk at the same time he proclaimed Ankara would be the capital (October 1923).

Süleyman the Magnificent (r. 1520–66) was perhaps İstanbul's greatest builder. Blessed with the services of Mimar Sinan (c. 1497–1588), Islam's greatest architect, the sultan and his family, court and grand viziers crowded the city with great build-

İstanbul Time Line

1520–66
Reign of Sultan Süleyman the Magnificent.

1566–1687
The 'Rule of the Women', when powerful princesses and queen mothers ruled Topkapı Palace.

1789–1807
Reign of Sultan Selim III, who adopted Western-style systems of politics and defence.

Süleyman the Magnificent

1826
Sultan Mahmut II destroys the corrupt janissaries with a massacre in the Hippodrome.

1839
Sultan Abdül Mecit implements the Tanzimat (Reorganisation) political and social reforms.

1876
The Tanzimat movement ends with the promulgation of the first Ottoman constitution.

ings. Süleyman's mosque, the Süleymaniye (1550), is İstanbul's largest. Many of the other 300 buildings attributed to Sinan are also in İstanbul.

During his reign, Süleyman had the support of his wife, Hürrem Sultan, known in the west as Roxelana. Though allowed four legal wives and as many concubines as he could support by Islamic law, this sultan was devoted to Hürrem alone. A decisive and forceful woman, she mastered the art of palace intrigue. She even convinced the sultan to have İbrahim Paşa, Süleyman's lifelong companion and devoted grand vizier, strangled when he objected to her influence. Unfortunately, she also made sure that her drunken son, Selim the Sot, would succeed to the throne by having the able heir apparent, Prince Mustafa, strangled. Her machinations began the period known as the Rule of the Women (1566–1687).

Selim and his successors, under the influence of the powerful palace women, were encouraged to lose themselves in the pleasures of the harem and the bottle. Luckily for them, external and military affairs were dealt with by a succession of exceptionally able grand viziers.

Among the most fascinating of the harem leaders was Kösem Sultan, the favourite of Sultan Ahmet I. She influenced the course of the empire through Ahmet, then through her sons Murat IV and İbrahim, and finally through her grandson Mehmet IV – a reign extending from 1617 to 1651. She was finally strangled at the command of the *valide sultan* (queen mother) Turhan Hatice, Mehmet IV's mother, who was jealous and perhaps frightened of grandma's power.

Ottoman Decline

The motor that drove the Ottoman Empire was military conquest, and when the sultan's armies reached their geographical and technological limits, decline set in for good. In 1687 the Ottomans laid siege for the second time to Vienna, but failed again to take the city. With the Treaty of Karlowitz in 1699, the Austrian and Ottoman emperors divided up the Balkans, and the Ottoman Empire went on the defensive.

By this time Europe was well ahead of Turkey in politics, technology, science, banking, commerce and military development. Sultan Selim III (r. 1789–1807) initiated efforts to catch up to Europe, but was overthrown in a revolt by *janissaries* (the sultan's personal bodyguards). The modernisation efforts were continued under Mahmut II (r. 1808–39). He founded a new army along European lines, provoked a riot among the janissaries, then in 1826 sent his new force in to crush them, which it did. The bodies of janissaries filled the Hippodrome, and the ancient corps, once the glory of the empire, was no more.

Sultan Abdül Mecit (r. 1839–61) continued the catch-up, implementing the Tanzimat (Reorganisation) political and social reforms. But these efforts were too little, too late. During the 19th century, ethnic nationalism, a force more powerful even than Western armies, penetrated the empire's domain and proved its undoing.

1876–1909

Sultan Abdül Hamit II abrogates the constitution and rules the empire with an iron hand.

1909–18

The 'Young Turks' depose Abdül Hamit II and rule as a virtual military junta.

1922–23

The Grand National Assembly, led by Mustafa Kemal (Atatürk), abolishes the Ottoman sultanate and proclaims the Turkish Republic.

1973

The first Bosphorus Bridge, joining Europe and Asia, is opened on the 50th anniversary of the republic's founding.

1988 to the Present

The Fatih Bridge across the Bosphorus is opened. İstanbul enjoys a renaissance as 'capital of the east'.

Atatürk

Ethnic Nationalism

For centuries, the non-Turkish ethnic and non-Muslim religious minorities in the sultan's domains had lived side by side with their Turkish neighbours, governed by their own religious and traditional laws. The head of each community – chief rabbi, Orthodox patriarch etc – was responsible to the sultan for the community's wellbeing and behaviour.

But Ottoman decline and misrule provided fertile ground for the growth of ethnic nationalism. The subject peoples of the Ottoman Empire rose in revolt, one after another, often with the direct encouragement and assistance of the European powers who coveted parts of the sultan's vast domains. After bitter fighting in 1831, the Kingdom of Greece was formed; the Serbs, Bulgarians, Romanians, Albanians, Armenians and Arabs would all seek their independence soon after.

As the sultan's empire broke up, the European powers (Britain, France, Italy, Germany, Russia) hovered in readiness to colonise or annex the pieces. They used religion as a reason for pressure or control, saying that it was their duty to protect the sultan's Catholic, Protestant or Orthodox subjects from misrule and anarchy.

The Russian emperors put pressure on the Turks to grant them powers over all Ottoman Orthodox Christian subjects, whom the Russian emperor would thus 'protect'. The result was the Crimean War (1853–56), with Britain and France fighting on the side of the Ottomans against the growth of Russian power.

During the war, wounded British soldiers were brought to İstanbul for treatment. Florence Nightingale, a young nurse sent out to tend to them, was appalled at the unsanitary conditions in the military hospitals. She and her fellow nurses established standards for care that served as the foundation for modern nursing.

Even during the war, the monarch in İstanbul continued in the imperial building tradition. Vast Dolmabahçe Palace and its mosque were finished in 1856, and the palaces at Beylerbeyi, Çırağan and Yıldız would be built before the end of the century. Though it had lost the fabulous wealth of the days of Süleyman the Magnificent, the city was still regarded as the Paris of the East. It was also the terminus of the *Orient Express,* which connected İstanbul and Paris, the world's first great international luxury express train.

Abdül Hamit II & the Young Turks

In the midst of imperial dissolution, Mithat Paşa, a successful general and powerful grand vizier, brought the young crown prince Abdül Hamit II (r. 1876–1909) to the throne along with a constitution in 1876. But the new sultan did away both with Mithat Paşa and the constitution, and established his own absolute rule.

Abdül Hamit modernised without democratising, building thousands of kilometres of railways and telegraph lines and encouraging modern industry. However, the empire continued to disintegrate with nationalist insurrections in Armenia, Bulgaria, Crete and Macedonia.

The younger generation of the Turkish elite – particularly the military – watched bitterly as their country fell apart, then organised secret societies bent on toppling the sultan. The Young Turk movement for Western-style reforms gained enough power by 1908 to force the restoration of the constitution. In 1909, the Young Turk–led Ottoman parliament deposed Abdül Hamit and put his hopelessly indecisive brother Mehmet V (Vahdettin) on the throne.

In its last years, though a sultan still sat on the throne in İstanbul, the Ottoman Empire was actually ruled by three members of the Young Turks' Committee of Union & Progress: Talat, Enver and Jemal. Their rule was vigorous but overly harsh and misguided, and it only worsened an already completely hopeless situation.

When WWI broke out, the Ottoman rulers made the fatal error of siding with Germany and the Central Powers. With their defeat, the Ottoman Empire collapsed, İstanbul was occupied by the British, and the sultan became a pawn in the hands of the victors.

Republican İstanbul

The situation looked very bleak for the Turks as their armies were being disbanded and their country was taken under the control of the Allies, but a catastrophe provided the impetus for rebirth.

Ever since gaining independence in 1831, the Greeks had entertained the Megali Idea (Great Plan) of a new Greek empire encompassing all the lands which had once had Greek influence – in effect, the refounding of the Byzantine Empire, with Constantinople as its capital. On 15 May 1919, with Western backing, Greek armies invaded Anatolia in order to make the dream a reality.

Even before the Greek invasion, however, an Ottoman general named Mustafa Kemal, the hero of Gallipoli, had decided that a new government must take over the destiny of the Turks from the powerless sultan. He began organising resistance to the sultan's captive government on 19 May 1919.

The Turkish War of Independence, in which the Turkish Nationalist forces led by Mustafa Kemal fought off Greek, French and Italian invasion forces, lasted from 1920 to 1922. Victory in the bitter war put Mustafa Kemal (1881–1938) in command of the fate of the Turks. The sultanate was abolished in 1922, as was the Ottoman Empire soon after. The republic was born on 29 October 1923.

The nation's saviour, proclaimed Atatürk (Father Turk) by the Turkish parliament, decided to move away, both metaphorically and physically, from the imperial memories of İstanbul. He established the seat of the new republican government in a city (Ankara) that could not easily be threatened by foreign gunboats. Robbed of its importance as the capital of a vast empire, İstanbul lost much of its wealth and glitter in succeeding decades. Its title 'Paris of the East' was assumed first by Beirut, then by Athens.

Atatürk had always been ill at ease with Islamic traditions and he set about making the Republic of Turkey a secular state. The fez (Turkish brimless cap) was abolished, along with polygamy, Friday was replaced by Sunday as the day of rest, surnames were introduced, the Arabic alphabet was replaced by a Latin script, and civil (not religious) marriage became mandatory.

The first opposition party in Turkey's history – the Democratic Party – won elections in 1950. But the next few decades were tumultuous with military coups, governments dogged by corruption charges, and constitutional violations and amendments. İstanbul continued its downward turn amid the political turmoil, but in 1983 the economist Turgut Özal was elected. Özal was the catalyst for Turkey's economic and tourism boom, and the next decade saw tourism infrastructure blossom in inner İstanbul, though the outskirts groaned under the weight of the growing tide of immigrants from the Turkish countryside. Since the 1990s İstanbul's vigorous municipal leadership has poured money into the restoration of much of the city's historic infrastructure, while also improving public transport. The city has won back its wealth and is once again the pride of the country.

GEOGRAPHY

İstanbul is at latitude 41° north, and near longitude 29° east, putting it at about the same latitude as Beijing, Madrid, Naples and New York. The low hills on which the city is built border the Golden Horn, a freshwater estuary, and the busy Bosphorus, a saltwater strait connecting the Black and Marmara Seas and the junction between Europe and Asia. The Sea of Marmara joins the Aegean Sea via the Dardanelles, the strait made famous by the battles of WWI. The region around İstanbul has fertile soil – excellent for producing fruit such as grapes, peaches and apricots, as well as vast crops of sunflowers.

GEOLOGY

İstanbul, and the northern part of Turkey, lie over the North Anatolian Fault, which runs for about 1500km between the Anatolian (to the south) and Eurasian (to the north) tectonic plates. As the Arabian and African plates to the south push northward, the Anatolian plate is shoved into the Eurasian plate, and squeezed west towards Greece. This movement creates stress along the North Anatolian Fault, which accumulates, and then releases as earthquakes. Thirteen major quakes have been recorded since 1939, with the latest in August 1999 devastating İzmit and Adapazarı, about 90km east of İstanbul, and leaving thousands dead. İstanbul remained relatively unscathed although the suburb of Avcılar, in the west of the city, had hundreds of deaths due to collapsed dwellings.

This pattern of earthquakes leaves İstanbul in an unenviable position. The city has been hit four times by major earthquakes in the last 500 years. Experts predict that the strain placed by İzmit's earthquake on nearby stress segments along the fault could lead to another major quake within the next few decades. As the destruction at Avcılar illustrated, much of the city's urban development in the last few decades has been jerry-built. Although the authorities have produced glossy pamphlets aimed to dispel fears, an earthquake will be the judge.

CLIMATE

Turkey has seven climatic regions. İstanbul is situated in the Marmara region, which includes eastern Thrace and Edirne. It's a countryside of rolling steppeland and low hills with an average yearly rainfall of 668mm. Rainfall is highest (between 80mm and 100mm per month) from November to February; July and August have the least rainfall. Humidity follows the same pattern, with the lowest humidity (under 30%) in July, August and September, and the highest (over 60%) a bone-chilling damp in December and January.

Temperatures in July and August peak at around 30°C (86°F), with lows around 20°C (68°F). In December and January, temperatures can fall as low as 2°C (36°F), with daily highs only about 9°C (48°F). April, May, September and October are the best times to visit, with daytime highs usually around 16°C to 25°C (61°F to 77°F), and lows from around 9°C to 18°C (48°F to 64°F).

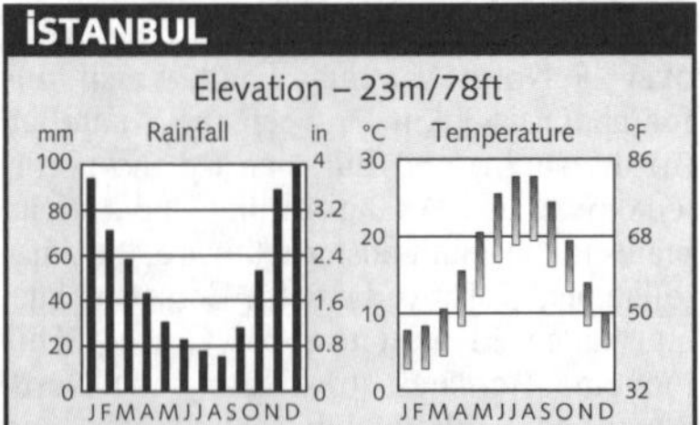

ECOLOGY & ENVIRONMENT

İstanbul has been plagued by hyper-growth during the last few decades as villagers move to the city by the tens of thousands in search of a better life. Air and water pollution are big problems. The moving and rebuilding of the 19th-century Galata Bridge along the Golden Horn, coupled with recent rubbish removal programs, have cleaned up the Golden Horn and Bosphorus waters considerably – though they are both still polluted.

Clean-burning Russian natural gas has replaced dirty lignite (soft coal) as the preferred winter heating fuel, and İstanbul's winter air is now cleaner, though it's still far from country-fresh. As for indoor pollution, cigarette smoking is a national passion. Although more and more areas are being declared nonsmoking zones, the rules are often ignored.

The 'Green' conservation movement is well under way in İstanbul. Although there are a few protected areas around İstanbul – Kızıl Adalar (Princes' Islands) and the Beykoz Nature Forests near Polonezköy, for example – a low average of just over 1 sq metre of forest reserve is put aside per person; conservationists say the average in Europe is about 40 sq metres per person. Many of the freshwater lakes around the city have been inadvertently protected due to their status as water catchments, though the protected areas around them are shrinking as government policies bend to developers. Some of these have even made their way onto the list of endangered flora and fauna sites identified by conservationists: Büyükçekmece Lake in the west of European İstanbul, and the Ömerlı Reservoir on the Asian side, for example.

You may see the occasional green recycling bin in the city, but there are few home recycling collections. Instead, enterprising recyclers scour the streets after dark, collecting aluminium and other recyclables to sell on to collecting depots.

Ship traffic along the Bosphorus, to and from Russia and other countries bordering the Black Sea, is another major headache for environmentalists and the Turkish government. The number of tankers carrying oil and other hazardous cargo through the strait is increasing, along with the threat of more collisions and oil spills. Adding salt to the wound, in July 2001 Russia approved a bill allowing the import of spent nuclear waste, which would, no doubt, arrive via the thin Bosphorus strait.

Two environmental groups in İstanbul are:

Doğal Hayatı Koruma Derneği (The Society for the Protection of Nature; Map 15, #15; ☎ 212-528 2030, fax 528 2040, W www.dhkd.org) Floor 5–6, Büyük Postane Caddesi 43–45, Eminönü. This is a member of the Worldwide Fund for Nature (WWF).

TEMA (W www.tema.org.tr) This is a Turkey-based organisation that runs tree planting campaigns.

GOVERNMENT & POLITICS

Though the Turks are firm believers in democracy, the tradition of popular rule is relatively short. Real multiparty democracy came into being only after WWII, and has been interrupted several times by military control, though the military has always returned government to civilians.

İstanbul is actually two political entities: the city and the province. The city is organised as a *büyükşehir belediyesi,* or metropolitan municipality, with several large submunicipalities under the overall authority of a metropolitan city government. The boundaries of the province of İstanbul extend almost to Çorlu in the west and to Gebze in the east.

Until electoral reforms became law in the 1980s, municipal governments in Turkey were largely controlled by the national government. Now, however, İstanbullus elect their own local government, and complain that, whoever may be in power, the problems of corruption and cronyism persist.

The municipal elections of March 1994 were a wake-up call against politics-as-usual, however. The upstart religious-right Refah Partisi (Welfare Party) won elections across the country, including those in İstanbul and Ankara. Its victory was seen in part as a protest vote against the corruption, ineffective policies and tedious political wrangles of the traditional parties.

In the national elections of December 1996, the Refah polled more votes than any other party (23%), and eventually formed a government vowing moderation and honesty.

Emboldened by political power, however, Prime Minister Necmettin Erbakan and other Refah politicians tested the boundaries of Turkey's traditional secularism. Erbakan made triumphant visits to Iran and other aggressively Islamist countries, and reputedly received financial subsidies from them. Local politicians made Islamist gestures and statements that alarmed the powerful National Security Council, the most visible symbol of the centrist military establishment's role as the caretaker of secularism and democracy.

In 1997 the council let it be known that Refah's time was up. Erbakan was forced to resign and his party was dissolved for having flouted the constitutional ban against religion in politics. Recep Tayyip Erdogan, the Refah mayor of İstanbul elected in 1994, was ousted by the secularist forces in the national government in late 1998.

National elections in April 1999 brought in a coalition government led by Bülent Ecevit's left-wing Democratic Left Party. After years under the conservative right of the Refah party, the election result heralded a shift towards European-style social democracy. When Turkey was accepted as a candidate to the European Union optimism skyrocketed – despite the government's bungling of the August 1999 earthquake aftermath. In 2001 the economy crash and the loss of the city's Olympic bid brought everyone back to earth – where they remain, watching prices soar and the politicians shifting uneasily in their seats.

ECONOMY

Though Turkey has traditionally been a net exporter of food (one of the few such countries in the world), its strong agricultural sector has now been superseded by even stronger commercial and manufacturing activity, much of which is centred in İstanbul. Turkey produces motor vehicles, appliances and consumer goods, and has undertaken many large engineering projects. The country's products are exported throughout the region. İstanbul's commercial centre is north of the historic city on the western side of the Bosphorus. Industrial plants are to the west and east of the city centre.

The crash of the Turkish lira in February 2001 seriously dented the government's economic initiatives, which are backed by the International Monetary Fund (IMF). At the time of the crash, the government had been implementing privatisation schemes and aiming for a three-year plan to reduce inflation to 7% by the end of 2002 (in 1999 inflation stood at 62.9%, in 2000 at 34%), but this figure now seems unrealistic. Gross National Product (GNP) growth stands at around 5%.

Tourism is now among the most important sectors of the Turkish economy. In 1999, nearly 7.5 million visitors came to Turkey (this figure was down on the 9.7 million of the previous year due to the 1999 earthquake and terrorism). The government hopes for tourist numbers to increase each year by around 5.5%.

POPULATION & PEOPLE

Turkey has a population of approximately 70 million, the great majority being Sunni Muslim Turks. Though İstanbul's population is given officially as some nine million, estimates of the true size of the urban agglomeration reach as high as 13 million.

Turks

The Turkic peoples originated in Central Asia, where they were a presence to be reckoned with as early as the 4th century AD. The Chinese called them Tu-küe, which is perhaps the root of our word 'Turk'. They were related to the Hiung-nu, or Huns.

The normally nomadic Turks ruled several vast but short-lived empires in Central Asia before being pushed westward by the Mongols. Various tribes of the Oğuz Turkic group settled in Azerbaijan, northern Iran and Anatolia, finally overrunning Constantinople in 1453, and going on to conquer much of Eastern Europe.

Early Turks followed each of the great Asian and Middle Eastern religions, including Buddhism, Nestorian Christianity, Manichaeism and Judaism. During their western migrations they became more familiar with Islam, and it stuck.

Kurds

Turkey has a significant Kurdish minority estimated at 10 million or more. Some ethnologists believe that the Kurds, who speak an Indo-European language, are closely related to the Persians, and that they migrated here from northern Europe centuries before Christ. There are significant Kurdish populations in neighbouring Iraq, Iran and Syria as well. İstanbul numbers many Turkish Kurds among its citizens.

Over the centuries the Kurds have struggled for autonomy from the various majority governments that have ruled them. In 1924 Kemal Atatürk banned any expression of Kurdishness in an attempt at assimilation. Major battles and atrocities ensued throughout the 1920s and 1930s and over the past few decades nearly 30,000 people have died.

In 1999, the Kurdistan Workers Party's (PKK) leader Abdullah Öcalan was captured and tried for treason and murder. He received the death sentence but his appeal is under way.

Jews

İstanbul's Jewish community of around 24,000 forms the majority of Turkey's Jewish population of some 27,000. The Turkish Jewish community is the remnant of a great influx that took place in the 16th century when the Jews of Spain (Sephardim) were forced by the Spanish Inquisition to flee their homes. They were welcomed into the Ottoman Empire, and brought with them knowledge of many European scientific and economic discoveries and advancements. Though in 1992 they celebrated 500 years of peaceful life among the Turks, many Turkish Jews have emigrated to Israel since the founding of the Jewish state in 1948. The Galata area in Beyoğlu, and Balat on the Golden Horn, were the centres of the community in İstanbul and both areas still have buildings commissioned by Jewish merchants and synagogues.

Greeks

Turkey's community of ethnic Greeks was in the millions during the Ottoman Empire, but most fled to Greece or abroad during the cataclysm of WWI and the Turkish War of Independence. Many others left as part of the League of Nations' exchange of populations between Turkey and Greece after the war. The conflict with Cyprus in the 1960s raised tensions between Turkey and Greece, causing another exodus of Turkish Greeks to Greece and Greek Turks to Turkey. It is estimated that ethnic Greeks in Turkey now number fewer than 100,000, many of whom live in İstanbul's Fener district surrounding the Ecumenical Orthodox Patriarchate.

Armenians

The Armenians are thought by some to be descended from the Urartians (518–330 BC) of eastern Anatolia, but others think they arrived from the Caucasus area after the Urartian state collapsed.

Armenians have lived in eastern Anatolia for millennia, almost always as subjects of some greater state. They lived with their Kurdish and Turkish neighbours in relative peace and harmony under the Ottoman *millet* system of distinct religious communities. But when this system was destroyed by modern ethnic nationalism, their community was decimated by emigration, conflict, massacre and deportation.

Though many Armenians remained loyal to the Ottoman sultan, others organised guerrilla bands in pursuit of an independent Armenian state on Ottoman soil. The resultant outrage of terrorism (new at the time, though all too familiar to us now) set off a powerful anti-Armenian backlash, resulting in widespread massacres of innocent Armenians in İstanbul and elsewhere.

With the support of the Imperial Russian army, a short-lived Armenian Republic was proclaimed in north-eastern Anatolia in the closing years of WWI, and the victorious Armenians repaid defeated local Muslims with massacres in kind. On 3 December 1920, the Ankara government concluded a peace treaty with the Armenian government in Yerevan, by then a Soviet republic. By the end of the war, the Armenian population of Anatolia had been reduced to insignificant numbers. The centre of İstanbul's Armenian community is in Kumkapı where it has its own schools, churches and cultural organisations.

ARTS

Islam prohibits as idolatry the depiction of any being 'with an immortal soul' (meaning any human or animal). This prohibition determined the course of Islamic art: it would be very rich in architecture, calligraphy, stained glass, manuscript illumination, glass-blowing, marquetry, metalwork and other geometric design, but would have little painting or sculpture as those arts are understood in non-Islamic countries.

Likewise, the Islamic tradition of sequestering women would hamper performance of arts such as dance, theatre and music. These arts were refined within the households of the Ottoman nobility, but performances by family members were private.

With the founding of the secular Turkish Republic in 1923, the Turkish art scene underwent a revolutionary change. All at once women were encouraged to perform in public, and artists of both genders were encouraged to create paintings, sculptures, plays, films and musical scores portraying the entire range of human activity and emotion. The government in Ankara oversaw the founding and subsidising of opera and dance companies, symphony and chamber music ensembles, and the establishment of fine arts academies and museums.

Today İstanbul is the cosmopolitan artistic heart of the Turkish Republic, with lively schools of painting, sculpture, film, music, literature, dance and theatre.

Calligraphy

Proportion of line and stroke, and felicity of design and execution are the strong points of

Islamic calligraphy, an ancient and highly esteemed art.

The conquest of İstanbul in 1453 provided the impetus for the Ottoman Empire to develop its own calligraphic styles and by the 17th century the art had reached its zenith. The *tuğra,* or monogram, of the sultans is the most conspicuous calligraphic art from this time, and you'll see many examples in the city's museums. The gilded, elaborate seals, unique to each sultan, were used to stamp all imperial edicts. These were painted by the best calligraphers in the empire.

Many of İstanbul's museums, especially Topkapı Palace, the Museum of Turkish & Islamic Arts and the Museum of Turkish Calligraphic Art, have fine examples.

Faience

The making of coloured tiles is an ancient art form in the Middle East. Its high point was reached during the 16th and 17th centuries in Anatolia when the workshops of İznik (Nicaea) and Kütahya turned out exquisitely designed and crafted tiles to be used on the walls of palaces, mosques, Turkish baths, fountains and many other structures, both public and private. Many of İstanbul's mosques are covered in these tiles but unfortunately some have been damaged or stolen, which is one of the reasons some mosques are locked outside prayer time. Some of the very best faience examples are found at Rüstem Paşa Camii in Eminönü, the Çinili Cami in Üsküdar on the Asian side and the Tiled Kiosk (Çinili Köşk) at the İstanbul Archaeology Museums complex in Sultanahmet.

Other tiles from this period are now treasured antiquities, but the master tilemakers of Kütahya, and to a lesser extent İznik, continue the tradition offering fine work for sale in İstanbul (see Ceramics in the Shopping chapter).

Textiles

With portraiture prohibited during much of the Ottoman period, stylised and geometric design prevailed. Turkish textiles are among the world's finest, from the exquisitely designed sultans' kaftans of the Topkapı Palace workshops to the vigorous, lively patterns of traditional Turkish carpets woven by village women. Several modern Turkish couturiers, such as Hussein Chalayan, show fashion ranges to a worldwide following.

Painting

Miniature painting was popular during the early Seljuk empire (AD 1037–1109), but it wasn't until the late empire of the 12th and 13th centuries that depictions of daily life (idolatry was forbidden in Islam) appeared in miniature. Mehmet the Conqueror fostered miniature painting, especially portraiture, but it was during Süleyman's reign in the 15th century that Ottoman miniature painting reached its height. At this time, and into the 16th century, depictions of historic events were common subjects. After this classic age, the art went into decline as the empire began to look to Europe for artistic inspiration. The best places to see miniature paintings are the Museum of Turkish & Islamic Arts and Topkapı Palace. Today few artisans paint miniatures, but if you're interested in buying a piece, see Handicrafts in the Shopping chapter.

European-style painting developed in the late 18th century in Turkish military academies. Painting continued to mirror movements in the West until the foundation of the Republic in 1923, which allowed artists to fully abandon Islamic restrictions and explore portraiture (prohibited in Islam) and other movements – in the 1930s Fauvism and cubism were all the rage. Contemporary Turkish painting has unlimited boundaries, but much of it looks to Europe and the US for inspiration, and reinterprets those themes within a Turkish context.

Sculpture

İstanbul's wonders of sculpture are not modern works but the masterpieces created during the Hellenic, Hellenistic and Roman periods. You can see them in İstanbul's Archaeological Museums complex.

Architecture

Architecture was the glory of Islamic art, and it thrived during the Ottoman centuries when painting and sculpture were prohibited. The great buildings of the Ottomans, such as mosques, *medreses* (theological schools), *hamams* (steam baths), *hans* (caravanserais) and palaces, are worthy descendants of the masterpieces produced by the Greeks, Romans, Persians, Arabs and Byzantines. A surprisingly large number of Byzantine buildings remain as well. And then there is the huge body of architecture built during the 18th and 19th centuries, much of it inspired by Europe. (See the special section 'Architecture' pp29–35.)

Traditional Turkish Music

There are many kinds of Turkish music, almost all of them unfamiliar to foreign ears. Ottoman classical, religious (particularly Sufi Mevlevi) and some types of folk and popular music use a system of *makams* (modalities), an exotic-sounding series of notes similar in function to the familiar Western scales of whole and half-tone intervals. Much Turkish music also uses quarter tones, which can be perceived as flat until the ear becomes accustomed to their sound.

Traditional Musical Instruments

Both folk and classical instruments play an integral part in the creation of Turkish music. If you're interested in buying one of these instruments, shops are listed under Music & Musical Instruments in the Shopping chapter.

Stringed Instruments

Kemençe This narrow, three-stringed fiddle has a short neck. It is held vertically, with the player sitting and the lower part of the fiddle resting on his/her knee, and played with a bow.

Oud The lute, popular in the 15th and 16th centuries, evolved from the oud. The bellies of earlier ouds were constructed of skin.

Saz The saz, or *bağlama,* has a long, unfretted neck, four strings and a bulbous, melon-shaped body that has no sound hole.

ANNA JUDD

Traditional Turkish instruments displayed in a music shop on Beyoğlu

Wind Instruments

Ney This bamboo flute, difficult to master, is the principal instrument in the Mevlevi music that accompanies the dance of whirling dervishes. It makes a breathy, plaintive sound.

Zurna A cylindrical wooden oboe with a double reed, this is often played with the *davul*.

Percussion Instruments

Davul A large, two-headed drum that is slung from the shoulders, the davul is a folk instrument usually played in combination with the zurna. The davul became fashionably exotic in the 18th century, and Mozart included sections reminiscent of it in his compositions.

Kaşık These are wooden spoons, played either as the sole accompaniment for dancing or with wind or stringed instruments.

Kudum A small double kettledrum, usually played with two sticks called *zahme*, the kudum is an essential element of Mevlevi music.

Turkish Crescent Otherwise known as a 'jingling Johnny', this instrument doubled as a standard carried by Ottoman soldiers. Crescent and hat-shaped ornaments bearing horsetail plumes and numerous bells are spaced along its length.

Trudi Canavan

Though Ottoman classical music sounds ponderous and lugubrious to the uninitiated, Turkish folk music as played in the countryside can be sprightly and immediately appealing. *Türkü,* of which you'll hear lots on the radio, falls somewhere in between: traditional folk music as performed by modern city-based singers. You'll hear this type of music at the nightly 'Turkish Shows' at places such as Kervansaray (see Folk Dance & Music in the Entertainment chapter). Your best chance of catching Ottoman classical music is during the International İstanbul Music Festival (see Festivals under Classical Music in the Entertainment chapter).

The 1000-year-old tradition of Turkish troubadours *(aşık),* still very much alive as late as the 1960s and 1970s, is now all but dead in its pure form, killed off by radio, TV, video and CDs. But the songs of the great troubadours Yunus Emre (who died in the early 14th century), Pir Sultan Abdal (16th century) and more recently Aşık Veysel (who died in 1974) are still popular.

The Turkish music most easily comprehensible to foreign ears is the energetic *fasıl* or *taverna* style, which you can hear at *meyhanes* (taverns) throughout the city (see Meyhanes in the Places to Eat chapter for venue details).

Popular Music

İstanbul's music scene (jazz, pop, rock) is jumping and live music is played at many bars and clubs around town. Though the music of Europe and the USA played a predominant role in Turkish musical life for most of the 20th century, the phenomenal growth and sophisticated development of local Turkish artists and recording studios (mostly in İstanbul) has pushed Western pop music into the background. A good place to find out about latest releases is on the US-based Web site W www.turkishmusic.com. If you're keen to buy CDs look up Music & Musical Instruments in the Shopping chapter for retail outlets.

Symphony & Chamber Music

The İstanbul Symphony Orchestra, visiting orchestras and chamber ensembles give

Turkish Top of the Pops

Rock music in Turkey is as faddy and ephemeral as anywhere else. The flavour of the moment is Tarkan, the teenybop idol, who rocketed to fame on the back of his 1994 *Acayıpsın* (You're Weird) album, and is still riding high thanks to his latest release, *Karma*.

But alongside the shooting stars there are also many well-established artists whose back catalogues remain as popular as those of the Rolling Stones. Queen of 1990s pop, Sezen Aksu, whose memorable melodies were typified by the 1991 album *Gülümse* (Smile), is still going strong. As is left-leaning singer and musician Zülfü Livaneli. Since Livaneli's music often incorporates Western instrumentation, it's fairly accessible to non-Turkish audiences. His songs are often covered by other musicians, not least by his daughter Aylin, and he has recorded with Greek musicians Maria Farandouri and Mikis Theodorakis in an effort to heal one set of Turkey's political wounds.

More alien to Western ears is the style of music known as arabesque which, as its name implies, puts an Arabic spin on home-grown Turkish traditions. The mournful themes (if not the melodies) of this music have led to its being compared to Greek *rembetika* and until the advent of independent radio and TV in the 1990s, the authorities kept arabesque off the airwaves, even conjuring up their own, more cheerful version in an attempt to undermine its power. The Kurdish singer İbrahim Tatlıses is a burly, moustached former construction worker from Şanlıurfa who has become hugely successful with his arabesque tunes. Ebru Gündes is also popular, and tours internationally. Arabesque also attracts a gay audience and diva Bülent Ersoy's name keeps cropping up. In 1980 Ersoy's music was banned following his sex-change operation. Once the ban was lifted, Ersoy started performing live again – only to be shot at by a member of the reactionary, neo-fascist Grey Wolves militia group for refusing to sing a nationalist anthem. Ersoy wed a 19-year-old, divorced him and was last seen flitting about enjoying the profits of her latest release, *Alaturka 2000*.

concerts during the winter season and during the International İstanbul Music Festival from early June to early July.

Opera & Ballet

The İstanbul State Opera's season runs from October to May. Mozart's *Abduction from the Seraglio* is one of its outstanding performances.

The İstanbul State Ballet usually performs classic ballets such as the *Nutcracker* at the Atatürk Cultural Centre. The International İstanbul Dance Festival, held in early March, also has performances.

The International İstanbul Music Festival brings Turkish and foreign opera and ballet to perform in the city (see Festivals under Classical Music in the Entertainment chapter).

Theatre

Prohibited to Muslims during Ottoman times, Turkish theatre shared in the explosion of creativity that followed the establishment of the Turkish Republic. Today İstanbul is the centre of Turkish drama. Though vibrant, Turkish theatre has been strongly challenged by the temptations of TV and video, which reduce audiences.

Turkish theatre troupes, some subsidised by the government, stage traditional and contemporary dramas and comedies as well as the works of giants such as Brecht, Ibsen, Molière and Shakespeare.

For the foreign visitor, the major barrier to enjoying Turkish theatre is the obvious one of language. Your best chance to see theatre you understand is during the International İstanbul Theatre Festival (see Festivals under Theatre in the Entertainment chapter).

Cinema

Cinema appeared in Turkey just a year after the Lumière brothers presented their first cinematic show in 1895. At first it was only foreigners and non-Muslims who watched movies, but by 1914 there were cinemas run by and for Muslims as well.

The War of Independence inspired actor Muhsin Ertuğrul, Turkey's cinema pioneer, to establish a film company in 1922 and make patriotic films. Comedies and documentaries followed. Within a decade Turkish films were winning awards in international competitions, even though a mere 23 films had been made.

After WWII the industry expanded rapidly with new companies and young directors. Lütfi Akad's *Kanun Namına* (In the Name of the Law, 1952), Turkey's first colour film, brought realism to the screen in the place of melodrama.

By the 1960s, Turkish cinema was delving deeply into social and political issues. Metin Erksan's *Susuz Yaz* (Dry Summer, 1964) won a gold medal at the Berlin Film Festival, and another award in Venice. Yılmaz Güney, the fiery actor-director, directed his first film *At, Avrat, Silah* (Horse, Woman, Gun) in 1966, and starred in Lütfi Akad's *Hudutların Kanunu* (The Law of the Borders) after he had written the script.

The 1970s brought the challenge of TV, dwindling audiences, political pressures, and unionisation of the industry, but the quality of films continued to improve, and social issues such as Turkish workers in Europe were treated with honesty, naturalism and dry humour. By the early 1980s, several Turkish directors were well recognised in Europe and the USA, and the movie industry has continued to blossom thanks partly to the International İstanbul Film Festival. Recent movies set in İstanbul include *Journey to the Sun* by Yeşim Ustaoğlu, which won the top prize at the International İstanbul Film Festival in 1999, and *Hamam* by Ferzan Özpetek. Another recent movie worth catching is *Byzantium the Perfidious* by Gani Müdje.

Film can be an enriching way to explore the culture and politics of a country – which is exactly why the government keeps close tabs on the Turkish industry. Yılmaz Güney's *Yol* was banned for 15 years and only released in 1999, and other films have been banned if they might 'encourage crime against the Republic'. These films are still often showcased at İstanbul's film festival before skipping on to the international film festival circuit.

İstanbul has a lively cinema culture centred in the movie houses along İstiklal

Caddesi (see Cinema in the Entertainment chapter for listings).

Literature

Literature before the republic was bound up with Islam. Treatises on history, geography and science were cast in religious terms. Ottoman poets, borrowing from the great Arabic and Persian traditions, wrote sensual love poems of attraction, longing, fulfilment and ecstasy in the search for union with God.

By the late 19th century some Ottoman writers were adapting to European forms. With the foundation of the republic, the ponderous cadences of Ottoman courtly prose and poetry gave way to use of the vernacular. Atatürk decreed that the Turkish language be 'purified' of Arabic and Persian borrowings. This, and the introduction of the new Latin-based Turkish alphabet, brought literacy within the reach of many more citizens.

In the second half of the 20th century some of Nazım Hikmet and Yashar Kemal's work was translated into other languages; it met with critical and popular acclaim abroad. Nazım Hikmet focuses on poetry (see his collection *Poems of Nazım Hikmet*), while Yashar Kemal has written over 30 novels. Kemal's stories are often set around the lives of Kurds in Turkey, and his famous *Memed, My Hawk* and *Salman the Solitary* are good examples. İstanbul novelist Orhan Pamuk has also gained a worldwide following. *The White Castle* and *The Black Book* are his two best-known works in English.

SOCIETY & CONDUCT

Traditional Culture

Under the Ottoman Empire (from the 14th century to 1923), Turkish etiquette was highly organised and very formal. When Atatürk founded the new Republic, he wanted to do away with the rigid Ottoman societal codes. This symbolic modernisation was set into laws requiring men to give up the fez and women to give up veils. Although Atatürk's reforms have instilled plenty of liberal Western dress and attitude in İstanbul, glimpses of traditional attitudes and behaviour often come through.

In general, you may find your dealings with Turks to be more formal than you're used to at home. Though Turks have abandoned the stiff formality of Ottoman society and adapted to the informality of 21st-century life, you'll still notice vestiges of the courtly Ottoman state of mind. Were you to learn Turkish, you'd find dozens of polite phrases – actually rigid formulas – to be repeated on cue in many daily situations: upon meeting or leaving someone, upon picking up a drink or sitting down to a meal or even emerging from a Turkish bath.

Hospitality is an honoured tradition in Turkey, from the shopkeeper who plies you with tea or coffee and sweets to the family

Turkish Body Language

When Turks say *'evet'* and nod their head forward and down it means 'yes'.

Saying *'hayır'* and nodding your head up and back while lifting your eyebrows at the same time – or just raising your eyebrows – means 'no'.

Another way of saying 'no' is *'yok'*, literally, 'It doesn't exist (here)', or 'We don't have any (of it)' – the same head upward, raised eyebrows applies.

Remember, when a Turkish person seems to be giving you an arch look, they're only saying 'no'. They may also make the sound 'tsk', which also means 'no'. There are lots of ways to say 'no' in Turkish.

By contrast, wagging your head from side to side doesn't mean 'no' in Turkish; it means 'I don't understand'. So if a Turkish person asks you, 'Are you looking for the bus to Sultanahmet?' and you shake your head, they'll assume you don't understand English, and will probably ask you the same question again, this time in German.

If someone – a shopkeeper or restaurant waiter, for instance – wants to show you the stockroom or the kitchen, they'll signal 'Come on, follow me' by waving a hand downward and towards themselves in a scooping motion. Waggling an upright finger would never occur to them, except perhaps as a vaguely obscene gesture.

that invites you to share their home and meals for the customary three days.

Commercialism has begun to corrupt traditional hospitality. You will find the shady carpet merchant who lays on the friendliness only to sell you shoddy goods at inflated prices, as well as the Turks who greet you with excessive informality, tailoring their behaviour to your expectations, in the hope of selling you something.

Don't, however, let this make you lose sight of true Turkish hospitality, which is wonderful.

Dos & Don'ts

Turks are very understanding of foreigners' different customs, but if you want to behave in accordance with local feelings, bear in mind a few things. It's looked upon as impolite to point your finger directly towards any person. Don't show the sole of your foot or shoe towards anyone (ie, so they can see it). Don't blow your nose openly in public, especially in a restaurant; instead, turn or leave the room and blow quietly. Don't pick your teeth openly, but cover your mouth with your hand. Kissing or hugging in public is not acceptable in the more conservative parts of the city such as Sultanahmet, Fatih and Eminönü; if you're unsure of the appropriateness of such behaviour, do as the locals do.

Mosque Etiquette Always remove your shoes before stepping on the clean area just in front of the mosque door, or on the carpets inside. This is not a religious law but a practical one. Worshippers kneel and touch their foreheads to the carpets, and they like them to be clean. If there are no carpets, as in a saint's tomb, it is OK to leave your shoes on.

Wear modest clothes when visiting mosques, as you would when visiting a church or synagogue. Don't wear shorts. Women should have head, arms and shoulders covered, and wear modest dresses or skirts, preferably reaching to the knees.

Headscarves can be borrowed at most mosques, and at some of the most visited mosques, attendants will lend you long robes if your clothing doesn't meet a minimum standard. The loan of a scarf and robe is free, though the attendant will probably indicate where you can give a donation to the mosque. If you donate, chances are that the money will actually go to the mosque.

The best time to visit mosques is mid-morning on any day but Friday. Avoid entering mosques at prayer time (ie, at the call-to-prayer at dawn, noon, mid-afternoon, dusk and evening, or 20 minutes thereafter). Mosques are crowded with worshippers at noon on Friday, and sightseeing visits are inappropriate then.

When you're inside a mosque, even if it is not prayer time, there may be a few people praying. Don't disturb them in any way, don't walk directly in front of them, and don't take flash photos.

RELIGION

The Turkish population is 99% Muslim, mostly of the orthodox Sunni creed. There are groups of Shiites in the east and south-east of the country and small populations in İstanbul. The Büyük Valide Han, north of the Grand Bazaar, has one of the few Shiite mosques in the city.

Principles of Islam

The Torah and Bible are sacred books to Muslims. Adam, Noah, Abraham, Moses, Jesus and other Jewish and Christian saints and prophets, their teachings and revelations, are accepted by Muslims, except for Jesus' divinity and his status as saviour. Jews and Christians are called 'People of the Book', meaning those with a revealed religion that preceded Islam.

However, Muslims believe that Islam is the 'perfection' of this earlier tradition, and Mohammed is the last and greatest of the prophets, in fact *the* Prophet. Mohammed is not a saviour, nor is he divine, nor even an object of worship or a figure of intercession. He is God's messenger, deliverer of the final, definitive message.

Muslims worship only God. In fact, Muslim in Arabic means 'one who has submitted to God's will'; Islam is 'submission to God's will'. It's all summed up in the *ezan,* the phrase called out from the minaret five times a day and said at the beginning of Muslim prayers: 'There is no god but God, and Mohammed is his Prophet' (*'La il-laha illa Allah Mohammud rasul Allah'*).

The Quran

God's revelations to Mohammed are contained in the Kur'an-i Kerim, the Holy Quran. Mohammed recited the *suras* (verses or chapters) of the Quran in an inspired state. They were written down by followers, and are still regarded as the most beautiful, melodic and poetic work in Arabic literature, sacred or secular. The Quran, being sacred, cannot be translated. It exists truly only in Arabic.

Religious Duties & Practices

To be a Muslim, one need only submit in one's heart to God's will and perform a few simple religious duties:

- One must say, understand and believe, 'There is no god but God, and Mohammed is his Prophet'.
- One must pray five times daily: at dawn, noon, mid-afternoon, dusk and after dark.
- One must keep the fast of Ramazan, if capable of doing so.
- One must make a pilgrimage to Mecca once during one's life if possible.

Muslim prayers are set rituals. Before praying, Muslims wash hands and arms, feet and ankles, head and neck in running water; if no water is available, in clean sand; if there's no sand, the motions suffice. Then they cover their head, face Mecca and perform a series of gestures and genuflections. If they deviate from the pattern, they must begin again.

In daily life, a Muslim must not touch or eat pork, or drink 'wine' (interpreted as any alcoholic beverage), and must refrain from fraud, usury, slander and gambling. No 'being with an immortal soul' (ie, human or animal), or its image or effigy, may be revered or worshipped in any way.

Though Islam has evolved a complex theology, and has been split (like Christianity) into many sects, these tenets are still the basic ones shared by all Muslims.

LANGUAGE

The national language of Turkey is Turkish, though you'll hear snippets of German, French, English and other foreign languages as you stroll through the Grand Bazaar and other tourist haunts. In return, by learning a few Turkish phrases you'll do your bit to charm the locals; see the Language chapter in the back of this book for tips.

ARCHITECTURE

The classic buildings of the Ottomans, such as mosques, *medreses* (theological schools), baths and palaces line the Bosphorus and dot İstanbul's hills, while a surprisingly large number of Byzantine buildings remain as well. Add to this mix the huge body of architecture inspired by Europe (the palaces, embassies and kiosks), pop in İstanbul's stark modernist pieces, and you have a hectic but scenic variety of architectural styles.

Byzantine Architecture

Much remains of Constantinople's 1123 years spent as a Christian city within the Roman Empire.

Religious

Byzantine churches in Constantinople were built in two styles: as T-shaped basilicas or as centralised polygons (or octagons). The basilica plan had a central nave, columns down either side and two side aisles. At the opposite end to the entry was the apse, a semicircle, where the sermons were held. The entry was via a narthex (courtyard). All this was topped off by a long, flat roof supporting a spire or two. Only one structure of this type of design survives in İstanbul, the church of **St John of Studius** (c. 462) in Kocamustafa Paşa (Map 12).

Constantinople blossomed during Justinian's reign from 527 to 565. He encouraged architects to aspire to buildings worthy of his Byzantine

İstanbul's Must-See Architecture

Byzantine

Aya Sofya Big is best, the dome aficionados gave handshakes all round for this incredible achievement (page 80)

Küçük Aya Sofya Camii Fading fast, but still a beautiful relic of original Byzantine architectural design (page 85)

Yedikule A little rough around the edges but these walls have had to put up with a lot for the last 1551 years! (page 130)

Sunken Cistern The largest surviving Byzantine cistern is now a wet and wonderful tourist attraction (page 83)

Kariye Müzesi Stunning Byzantine mosaics makes the short venture out west towards the city walls well worthwhile (page 126)

Ottoman

Central Post Office Ottoman meets European architecture (page 45)

Church of St Stephen of the Bulgars Not representative of any one style but it's not every day you get to see a church made almost entirely of cast iron! (page 129)

Dolmabahçe Palace The best kitsch in town (page 117)

Süleymaniye Camii Sinan's classic Ottoman mosque and *külliye* (complex; page 102)

Selimiye Camii Sinan gave himself top marks for this Ottoman opulence in Edirne (page 207)

Inset: Art Nouveau doors in İstanbul; Art Nouveau was one of the influences in the creation of the Turkish baroque style that appeared in the late 19th and early 20th centuries.

Empire. They dabbled by adding the dome to the basilica plan, aiming to create interior space of mammoth proportions. Few would say **Aya Sofya** (Sancta Sophia; Map 1), built in 537 and with a dome diameter of over 30m, missed the mark.

The other Byzantine design was the centralised polygonal plan with supporting walls and a dome set on top, wrapped inside square or rectangular external walls. There was still an entrance narthex. The musty, but lovely **Küçük Aya Sofya Camii** (Map 13, #113), built around 530, is a surviving example of this trend.

Later, a mixed basilica and centralised polygonal plan developed. This plan took a polygonal form with a series of smaller domes and half domes that surround and support a central dome, while four large columns provide further support. The T-shape basilica ground plan was squashed into a squarish shape. This design was the foundation for church design in İstanbul from the 11th century until the Conquest (1453); many classic Ottoman mosques were inspired by this plan. The **Zeyrek Camii** (Church of the Pantocrator; Map 14), built in 1130, is a good example of this style. The **Kariye Müzesi** (Chora Church; Map 18), with its stunning mosaics, is another example though it has undergone major remodelling over the years.

When Mehmet the Conqueror took İstanbul in 1453 many churches were converted into mosques, but despite the minarets, you can usually tell a church-cum-mosque by the giveaway distinctive red bricks, characteristic of all İstanbul's Byzantine churches.

Secular

Looking at İstanbul today, it's easy to forget that civic planning was once alive and well here. Take the **Milion** (Map 13), for example: that seemingly useless rubble poking out from a park in Sultanahmet was the reference point for Constantine's city planning. Divan Yolu was one of the major Roman thoroughfares. The **Çemberlitaş** (Map 13, #3), originally crowned with a statue of Constantine, is one of the monuments that lined the length of the way; **Beyazıt Square** (Map 15), formerly the Forum of Theodosius, is another. The **Hippodrome**, close by, was a jousting space and civic square.

Constantine (r. 324–37) built a set of walls around his new capital, but it is Theodosius II's (r. 408–50) **walls** that still stand today. **Yedikule** (Fortress of the Seven Towers; Map 11) is a fine sample.

Water was needed for the masses and it came via aqueducts, such as the **Aqueduct of Valens** (Map 14), to be stored in cisterns, such as the **Sunken Cistern** (Yerebatan Sarnıçı; Map 13, #43) in Sultanahmet built by Justinian.

The Great Byzantine Palace, built at the founding of Constantinople (c. AD 320), was renovated and added to by successive Byzantine leaders. Much of it exists as substructure under Sultanahmet and Cankurtaran, though some areas have been excavated. The **Bucoleon Palace** (Map 13, #121), along the sea walls, and **Tekfur Sarayı** (Map 18), along the city walls near Edirnekapı, are remnants of Byzantine palaces.

VERITY CAMPBELL

Ottoman Architecture

After the conquest of Constantinople in 1453, Ottoman architects had full liberty to admire and examine the Aya Sofya. They incorporated parts of its genius into the great Ottoman mosques.

Religious

Before Ottoman times (that is, before the 14th century), the most common form of mosque in Islam was the vaulted pier type, a large square or rectangular space sheltered by a series of small domes resting on pillars, as in Edirne's **Eski Cami**.

When the Ottomans took Bursa and İznik in the early 14th century they were exposed to Byzantine architecture, particularly ecclesiastical architecture. From this exposure, blended with that of Sassanian Persia, sprang a completely new style: the T-shape plan. The **Üçşerefeli Cami** in Edirne became the model for other mosques not only because it was one of the first forays into this T plan, but also because it was the first Ottoman mosque to have a wide dome and a forecourt with an ablutions fountain.

The classic Ottoman mosque was perfected by the great Mimar Sinan (c. 1497–1588), architect to Sultan Süleyman the Magnificent (r. 1494–1566). **Selimiye Camii**, in Edirne, is considered by many to be the finest example. Each mosque has a large forecourt with an ablutions fountain at its centre and domed arcades on three sides. On the fourth side of the court is the mosque, with a two-storey porch. The main prayer hall is covered by a large central dome rising considerably higher than the two-storey facade and surrounded by smaller domes and semidomes. Lattice or grillework partitions off an area at the back for use by female worshippers, while men occupy the

DONALD C & PRISCILLA ALEXANDER EASTMAN

Top: Begun as a triumphal arch in the late 4th century, Yedikule (Fortress of the Seven Towers) is near the southern walls of the city. Over time it has been variably used as a prison, a repository for the imperial treasury, an execution place and for defence.

Bottom: Layer upon layer: View of the ablutions fountain in the central internal courtyard of the Blue Mosque (Sultan Ahmet Camii). A work of classic Ottoman design, the fountain is surrounded by the domes and cupolas of this 17th-century masterpiece.

central space. The *mihrab* (niche indicating the direction of Mecca) is in the far wall of the prayer hall.

When a sultan decided to build an imperial mosque, he did it in style and it quickly became the centre of a new quarter. Workers poured in, and residences, workshops and shops popped up. The building of a mosque took years, at the end of which time the quarter would be fully populated.

Each imperial mosque had a *külliye* (collection of charitable institutions) clustered around it. These might include a hospital, asylum for the insane, orphanage, *imaret* (soup kitchen), hospice for travellers, medrese, library, baths and a cemetery in which the mosque's imperial patron, his or her family and other notables could be buried. Over time, many of these buildings were demolished or altered, but the **Süleymaniye Camii** complex (see the diagram below) still has many of its buildings – tombs, theological college etc – intact. The **Yeni Cami** complex (Map 15, #7) in Eminönü is also fairly intact. The **Mısır Çarşisi** (Egyptian Market; Map 15) was built to provide funds for the upkeep of the mosque complex, while the tomb and even a water fountain *(sebil)* still exist.

The mosque design developed during the reign of Süleyman the Magnificent proved so durable that it is still being used, with variations, for modern community mosques all over Turkey.

Bottom: The Süleymaniye Camii, surrounded by its *kulliye* (complex), is an impressive example of the classic Ottoman mosque. It was completed in 1557 and built by the great architect, Mimar Sinan.

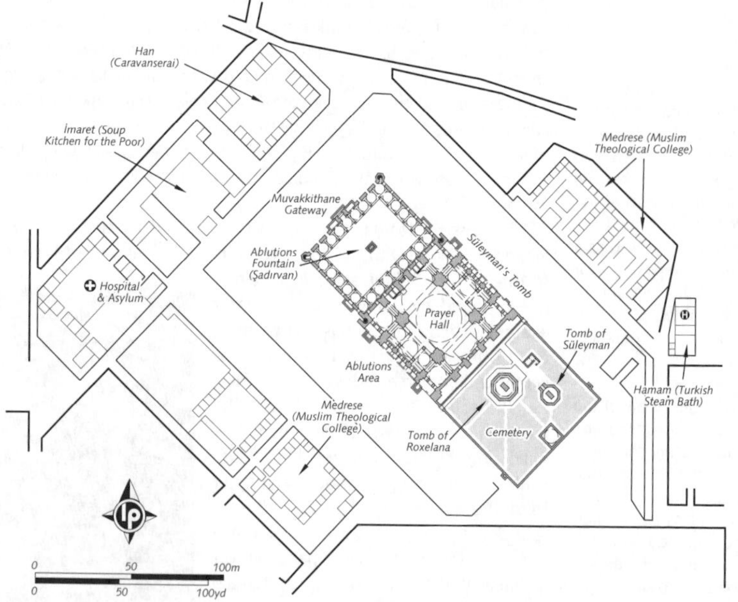

CHARLOTTE HINDLE

VERITY CAMPBELL

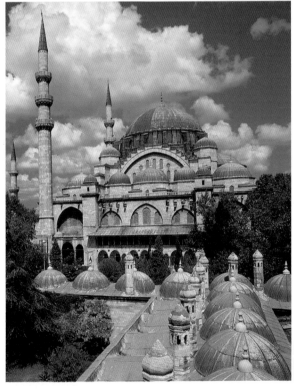

IZZET KERIBAR

Top Left: In the midst of Old İstanbul's traffic and in need of a clean, the Valide Camii was built in 1871 and is an example of the highly decorative architecture created in the final years of the Ottoman Empire.

Top Right: Bucoleon Palace, on the sea walls near Cankurtaran, is the only above-ground remnant of the Great Byzantine Palace built by Theophilos c. AD 830.

Bottom: Süleymaniye Camii, completed in 1557 during the reign of Süleyman the Magnificent, is İstanbul's grandest and largest mosque. It represents the flowering of Ottoman architecture under the great architect Sinan.

VERITY CAMPBELL

EDDIE GERALD

VERITY CAMPBELL

EDDIE GERALD

Top Left: The highly unusual Church of St Stephen of the Bulgars, built in 1871, is made completely of cast iron.

Top Right: Built in AD 532 by Emperor Justinian, the Sunken Cistern (Yerebatan Sarnıçı) is a Byzantine water-storage tank that was rediscovered in the 16th century. Today the cool underground cavern is a tourist attraction with great appeal on hot days.

Middle: *Yali*, lavish timber villas built towards the end of the Ottoman period, can still be found along the Bosphorus shore.

Bottom: The opulent Dolmabahçe Palace, on the banks of the Bosphorus, was completed in 1856 and is an example of the excesses of the Turkish baroque period.

Secular

The Ottoman Empire's military defeats in the 17th century became a catalyst for the empire's decline. Europe shot well ahead of Turkey in societal sophistication and, when Sultan Ahmet III (1703–30) sent ambassadors to Europe, European ways took off in Ottoman society with a vengeance. This was a time of Frenchified indulgence, poetry, outdoor living and literature. Architecturally, this period was characterised by floral, colourful embellishments. The **Fountain of Sultan Ahmet III** (Map 13, #58), just outside the gate to the first court of Topkapı, is a good example, as is the **Dining Room of Ahmet III** (Map 3, #26) in the Harem. The tulip, popular in Holland and with the sultan and his upper-crust cronies, began to symbolise the time, hence the well-worn name of this era: the Tulip Period.

From the mid-18th century onwards, rococo and baroque influences hit Tulip Period architecture resulting in a pastiche of hammed-up curves, frills, scrolls, murals and fruity excesses. This mess came under the rather indefinable title of Turkish baroque. The period's best – or worst, depending on your point of view – archetype is the extravagant **Dolmabahçe Palace** (Map 12). Although building mosques was passé, the **Valide Camii** in Aksaray snuck through. It's a fine illustration of Turkish baroque Islamic architecture. Kiosks built to enjoy the outdoors were popular during this period, and **Küçüksu Kasrı** (Map 15), on the Asian side of the Bosphorus, is a good example.

Bottom: View of the facade and entrance of the central post office, part of Istanbul's early-20th-century heritage. The building is a comparatively restrained work, combining Ottoman flourishes with European symmetry.

VERITY CAMPBELL

In the 19th and early 20th centuries foreign or foreign-trained architects began to unfold a neoclassical blend of European architecture alongside Turkish baroque, with some concessions to classic Ottoman style. Pera, nowadays Beyoğlu, was the scene of colonial arm wrestles: Many lavish embassies were built as vehicles for the great colonial powers to cajole and pressure the Sublime Porte into concessions of territory, trade and influence. The vogue Swiss Fossati brothers were responsible for the **Netherlands** (Map 16, #107) and **Russian** (Map 16, #113) consulates general along İstiklal Caddesi.

Over in Old İstanbul things were less heated. In Eminönü, Vedat Tek, a Turkish architect who had studied in Paris, built the **central post office** (Map 15, #16), a mix of Ottoman elements such as arches and faience, and European symmetry. **Sirkeci train station** (Map 15), by a German called Jachmund, is another example of this eclectic neoclassicism. Even Art Nouveau came to İstanbul, fostered by the Italian architect Raimondo D'Aronco; the **Egyptian consulate** in Bebek (Map 6) is a good example.

Post-Republic Architecture

When Atatürk proclaimed Ankara the capital of the new republic in 1923, İstanbul immediately lost much of its glamour and investment capital. Modernism was played out on the

Glossary of Architecture

arasta – row of shops near a mosque, the rent from which supports the mosque; the Arasta Bazaar (Map 13) near the Blue Mosque, and Mısır Çarşısı (Map 15) close by Yeni Cami are good examples
bedesten – vaulted, fireproof market enclosure or warehouse where valuable goods are kept; look out for the Sandal and İç Bedesten in Kapalı Çarşı
cami(i) – mosque
hamam(ı) – a Turkish steam bath; Haseki Hürrem Hamamı (Map 13, #64), designed by Sinan in 1556 as part of Aya Sofya's *külliye*, is considered to be the most refined Ottoman *hamam*
han – caravanserai; a place where traders could bring goods from all parts of the empire, unload and trade right in the bazaar's precincts; check out the pretty Zincirli Han (Map 4) at the Kapalı Çarşı
hünkar mahfili – see *imperial loge*
imaret – soup kitchen for the poor
imperial loge – an elevated pavilion, screened from public view so the Sultan could come, pray and go unseen, preserving the imperial mystique; see the one at Aya Sofya (Map 1)
kasri – imperial lodge; these were designed as getaway palaces for the rich; the Aynalıkavak Kasrı (Map 12) in Hasköy is a fine example
kilise(si) – church
köşk(ü) – pavilion, villa, kiosk; these were picnic pavilions set in parkland; the kiosks of Yıldız Park (Map 12) are worth checking out
kule(si) – tower
külliye(si) – mosque complex including *medrese*, hospital, *hamam*, *imaret* etc

KELLI HAMBLET

new canvas of Ankara, while İstanbul's dalliances went little further than the **İstanbul City Hall** (Map 14), built in 1953, near Fatih and the **Atatürk Cultural Centre** (Map 16, #4), built in 1956, on Taksim Square.

Architecture over the last few decades in İstanbul can hardly be called inspiring. The **Akmerkez Shopping Centre** is an example of the genre: skyscrapers aping the stark functionalist architecture of the 1980s. The city's apartment blocks are also lessons in what not to do: the further out they are the taller and uglier they become (look out near Atatürk Airport if you dare). Illegal housing or *gecekondus*, built by immigrants from Turkey's countryside, is an ongoing headache for urban developers – especially since planning regulations are difficult to enforce in these areas.

But the earthquake in 1999 has led many to reassess architectural prototypes and building materials. Those who can afford to are now in-

Glossary of Architecture

medrese – Muslim theological seminary providing a secular education taught in a series of rooms surrounding a courtyard; the Caferağa Medresesi (Map 13, #50) near Aya Sofya is a good example

mihrab – the niche in a mosque indicating the direction of Mecca (see illustration opposite); Süleymaniye Camii and Fatih Camii (Map 14) each have a fine mihrab

mimber – the pulpit in a mosque (left); one of the most ornate examples is in the Blue Mosque (Map 13)

minare(si) – minaret; the tall fluted towers from which Muslims are called to prayer

şadırvan – fountains where Muslims perform ritual ablutions; usually found in a mosque's forecourt

saray(ı) – palace

sebil – public fountain or water kiosk; the Fountain of Sultan Ahmet III (Map 13, #58) outside Topkapı Palace is a particularly fine example

MELISSA KIRKBY

tekke(si) – dervish lodge(s); these ceremonial halls usually have a central area for the whirling *sema* (Sufic religious ceremony), and galleries above for visitors to observe; the Museum of Court Literature (Galata Mevlevihanesi; Map 16, #134) in Tünel, Beyoğlu, has one of the few remaining *tekkesi* in the city

türbe(si) – tomb or mausoleum; these are usually built in the cemetery of the *külliye* for the patron of the mosque complex; the Süleymaniye Camii complex has exquisite tombs

yalı – seaside villa; these wooden palatial dwellings were built as summer retreats along the shores of the Bosphorus (Map 6) in the early 19th century; you'll see many at Sarıyer and Yeniköy, and a fine example is the Sadberk Hanım Müzesi at Büyükdere

creasingly moving out of apartment blocks and into housing developments; the land around Beykoz and Paşabahçe on the Asian side is one area where these 'villages' are blossoming. Although İstanbul has not had a strong architectural identity since the Republic was formed, it does seem to have an ongoing desire to reclaim and rejoice in its architectural heritage. Ottoman relics – and even Byzantine buildings – are being restored and reinterpreted. The **Sarnıç** (Map 13, #53), a restaurant in Sultanahmet (see Places to Eat), is built in a Byzantine cistern, while the **Caferağa Medresesi** (Map 13, #50) near Aya Sofya is a workshop/cafe in a restored Ottoman theological seminary (see under Ottoman Sultanahmet in the Things to See & Do chapter). Similarly, anyone who's anyone is restoring an Ottoman yalı on the Bosphorus if they can afford to, and the many Ottoman-style hotels attest to the popularity of these old Ottoman dwellings for tourists and locals alike.

Facts for the Visitor

WHEN TO GO

Spring and autumn, roughly from April to May and from September to October, when the climate is perfect, are the best seasons to visit. But at these times accommodation prices tend to go up by around 25% and the main sights are packed. During July and August it is hot and steamy; a lot of İstanbullus head for the west and south coasts. (For more details see Climate in the Facts about İstanbul chapter, and Public Holidays & Special Events later in this chapter.)

ITINERARIES

The top sights are mostly in Old İstanbul so you could see them in a single day. Two to three days is the minimum time required for a meaningful visit (see the boxed text 'İstanbul in 48 Hours' over the page). With a week you can see most of the city's sights and take an overnight excursion; 10 days is even better if you plan to take an excursion further afield to Gallipoli, Troy or Edirne.

ORIENTATION

İstanbul is divided from north to south by the Bosphorus (the wide strait connecting the Black and Marmara Seas) into European (Avrupa) and Asian (Asya) portions. European İstanbul is further divided by the Golden Horn (Haliç) into Old İstanbul (Eski İstanbul, sometimes called the Old City) to the south and Beyoğlu (**Bey**-oh-loo; formerly Pera and Galata) and other modern districts to the north. The *otogar* (main bus station) is 10km south-west of Old İstanbul, while Atatürk Airport is about 23km west. The main train station on the European side, Sirkeci Gari, sits at the southern side of the Golden Horn in Old İstanbul. Haydarpaşa train station (Haydarpaşa Gari), between Üsküdar and Kadıköy on the Asian side, is the terminal for Anatolian trains.

Old İstanbul

The Old City has gone by many different names: Byzantium, Constantinople, İstanbul (and 19th-century travellers called it Stamboul). It's in the Old City, stretching from Seraglio Point (Saray Burnu) on the Bosphorus to the mammoth land walls some 7km westward, that you'll find the great palaces and mosques, hippodromes and monumental columns, ancient churches and the Kapalı Çarşı (Grand Bazaar). The best selection of budget and mid-range hotels is also found here, with a few top-end places as well.

Beyoğlu

North of the Golden Horn is Beyoğlu, the Turkish name for the Ottoman districts of Pera and Galata, or roughly all the land from the Golden Horn to Taksim Square. Here you'll find luxury hotels, bars, banks, the European consulates, hospitals and Taksim Square itself, the hub of 21st-century İstanbul.

Old İstanbul and Beyoğlu are connected by the Galata Bridge (Galata Köprüsü) at the mouth of the Golden Horn. Just east of the bridge are the docks for Bosphorus ferryboats.

Asian İstanbul

The Asian part of the city, on the eastern shore of the Bosphorus, is of less interest to tourists, being mostly dormitory suburbs such as Üsküdar and Kadıköy. If you have time, however, this untouristy part of the city is worth exploring.

The Bosphorus

The Bosphorus is lined with more suburbs, some of which are charming, for example, Çengelköy and Anadolu Kavağı, and good for a day's excursion.

MAPS

Lonely Planet produces a handy, laminated *İstanbul* city map that includes a walking tour, Topkapı Palace map, a Greater İstanbul map, a complete index and more.

The Ministry of Tourism offices usually provide a free and useful *İstanbul City*

Plan, although at the time of research this practice had unfortunately been temporarily suspended. There are editions in the languages of all major tourist groups. For more detailed guidance, including all minor streets, the *İstanbul A-Z Rehber-Atlas*, widely available in foreign-language and tourist-oriented bookshops for about US$7, is the most reliable source.

RESPONSIBLE TOURISM

İstanbul was hit by the tourism boom of the 1980s and 1990s, which saw a mushrooming of hotels and guesthouses, particularly in and around Sultanahmet. Akbıyık Caddesi in Cankurtaran is one of the streets which has suffered most: Houses have been turned over to guesthouses and hostels, with the residents squeezed out to make way for thumping bars and gaudy facades.

Consider staying instead in one of the guesthouses or hotels that blends in with its streetscape: Küçük Aya Sofya is a good spot to start looking. If you're after carousing nightlife, head to Beyoğlu which is littered with bars and, unlike Sultanahmet, not surrounded by mosques and other holy sites.

A very tight watch is kept on the city's valuable antiquities (see Customs later in this chapter).

TOURIST OFFICES

Local Tourist Offices

The Ministry of Tourism offices usually hand out free maps but little else. The most helpful tourist office is in Sultanahmet, but some of the others are hopeless. Be mindful that hotel, entertainment and other recommendations from tourist offices may not be impartial as commissions may be involved; it's best to receive tips from other travellers.

There are tourist offices at Atatürk Airport (Map 11; ☎ 212-573 4136, fax 663 0793) in the international arrivals area; at the northeastern end of the Hippodrome in Sultanahmet (Map 13, #36; ☎ 212-518 8754, fax 518 1802), open 9am to 5pm daily; at Sirkeci train station (Map 15, #18; ☎ 212-511 5888); and in Beyazıt Square (Hürriyet Meydanı; Map 15, #40; ☎ 212-522 4902).

In Beyoğlu, there is a tourist office in Karaköy at the Karaköy Yolcu Salonu (Karaköy International Maritime Passenger Terminal; Map 16, #154; ☎ 212-249 5776). There is another office in Elmadağ (Map 17, #22; ☎ 212-233 0592) in the İstanbul Hilton Hotel arcade, just off Cumhuriyet Caddesi, open 9am to 5pm, closed on Sunday. There is also an office (Map 16, #17; ☎ 212-245 6876) at the Taksim end of İstiklal Caddesi; it's open 9am to 5pm Monday to Friday.

Tourist Offices Abroad

There are Turkish tourist offices in the following countries:

Australia
(☎ 02-9223 3055, fax 9223 3204, **e** turkish@ozemail.com.au) Room 17, Level 3, 428 George St, Sydney, NSW 2000

Canada
(☎ 613-230 8654, fax 230 3683, **e** toturcan@magi.com) Constitution Square, Suite 801, 360 Albert St, Ottawa, Ontario K1R 7X7

France
(☎ 01 45 62 78 68, fax 01 45 63 81 05, **e** turizm@imaginet.fr) 102, avenue des Champs-Elysées, 75008 Paris

Germany
Berlin: (☎ 30-214 3752, fax 214 3952) Tauentzienstrasse 7, 10789
Frankfurt: (☎ 69-23 30 81, fax 23 27 51) Baselerstrasse 35–37, 60329
München: (☎ 89-59 49 02, fax 550 4138) Karlsplatz 3/1, 80335
w www.tuerkei-ferien.de

Israel
(☎ 3-517 6157, fax 517 6303, **e** turktrsm@netvision.net.il) 1 Ben Yehuda St, 63801 Tel Aviv

Italy
(☎ 6-487 1190, fax 488 2425) Piazza della Repubblica 56, 00185 Roma

Netherlands
(☎ 70-346 9998, fax 364 4468, **e** ttoinfo@euronet.nl) 5th floor, Waldeck Pyrmontkade 872 G, 2518 JS, The Hague

UK
(☎ 020-7629 7771, fax 7491 0773, **e** tto@turkishtourism.demon.co.uk) 1st floor, 170–173 Piccadilly, London W1V 9EJ

USA
(☎ 212-687 2194, fax 599 7568, **w** www.tourismturkey.org) 821 UN Plaza, New York, NY 10017

İstanbul in 48 Hours

If you live in the UK or continental Europe you may want to consider İstanbul for a weekend pitstop: Fly in Friday night ready for a sightseeing frenzy.

Friday Night: Arrival
Let's assume you're staying in the Sultanahmet area, where most travellers stay.

10pm At İstanbul's Atatürk Airport you'll have to go through the usual ho-hum red tape (customs, immigration/visa), collect your baggage, change money (carefully count what you're given) etc. Don't fuss around with the airport bus: Jump straight in a taxi and ask to be taken to Sultanahmet. It'll cost US$10.

11pm Check in at the hotel and head out to the **Cafe Meşale** (page 153), open 24 hours from March to August, for your first introduction to the **Blue Mosque** (Mosque of Sultan Ahmet; page 89) and **Aya Sofya** (Sancta Sophia; page 80), both lit at night. On a balmy evening there should be a few people around, many birds circling the minarets and, hopefully, no carpet-shop touts circling you.

Saturday
7am You can't sleep away this weekend. Enjoy your breakfast at the hotel and get ready to head out.

8am Start with an early morning ferry jaunt over the Bosphorus from Eminönü to Üsküdar (and back) to enjoy the views and get your bearings.

9am Back at Eminönü, head through the **Yeni Cami** (page 107) on your way to check out the spices at the **Mısır Çarşisi** (page 107). Watch out for the pigeons' missiles at the steps of the mosque.

9.30am Goodies abound at the Mısır Çarşişi and many hopefuls get sucked into buying the Royal love potions – if you're satisfied in that department at least try Turkish Delight. Then head west through the streets to marvel at the tiles at the exquisite **Rüstem Paşa Camii** (page 106).

11am Next, head south up bustling **Uzunçarşı Caddesi** (page 106), watching out for stray elbows and the occasional wandering hand.

11.30am The **Kapalı Çarşı** (Grand Bazaar; page 104) will keep you entertained for hours and this is the place to shop for souvenirs. Stop for a tea break at the quaint **Şark Kahvesi** (page 155), and for lunch at the **Subaşı Restaurant** (page 154). Alternatively, if you're an architecture buff and you want to see Sinan's **Süleymaniye Camii** (page 102), spin through the Kapalı Çarşı and then head north along Fuat Paşa Caddesi to find it.

4pm By this time you've hopefully staggered out of the bazaar (and Süleymaniye) and dumped your bags of goodies back at the hotel.

4.30pm The **Cağaloğlu Hamamı** (page 137) will teach you how to relax your shopper's feet Ottoman-style. Sweat, enjoy your massage (let's hope it's not painful) and take your time – you've got a big night ahead of you.

6.30pm After your pamper, pop into the Blue Mosque – if you can fight your way through the touts outside.

8pm You've been back to the hotel, donned gear for a night out on the town, crossed the Golden Horn (Haliç) and you're now standing in Taksim Square starving. Start 'promenading' along İstiklal

İstanbul in 48 Hours

Caddesi, past the groomed teens, glitzy shops, packed bars and restaurants. If you're after a quiet meal head to **Hacı Abdullah** (page 162), otherwise continue down İstiklal. For an eyeful, walk through the **Çiçek Pasajı** (page 111), into the **Balık Pazar** (page 111) and past **Ney'le Mey'le** (page 161) and other rowdy *meyhanes* (taverns) lining Nevizade Sokak. Pick a restaurant or end up for a meal at manic **Pano** wine bar (page 157). Try Turkish *rakı* (aniseed brandy; beware, it's strong stuff), and an assortment of Turkey's mouth-watering meze.

11pm Club time. No visit to İstanbul would be complete without greasing shoulders with the grunge folk at **Kemancı** (page 171), or try **Andon** (page 171) close by. Both places are back near Taksim Square.

2am Grab your newly found love (just joking) and head to the *büfes* (snack bars; page 155) close by to gorge with the throngs of swaying post-revellers. Coming here to line one's stomach after a night on the town is an İstanbul tradition.

2.30am If you haven't finished yet you may be disappointed to hear that İstanbul's clubs usually don't run till dawn. But don't panic: It's time to sip strong Turkish coffee and suck on a *nargileh* (water pipe) at the **Amerikan Pazar** (page 134) in Tophane. A taxi can take you there via Sıraselviler Caddesi for about US$1.50.

4am Back over to Sultanahmet where you can continue at **Cafe Meşale** (page 153) or get to bed ready for another full day tomorrow.

Sunday

9.15am What better way to wake up in the morning than with beautiful Aya Sofya – the church, not the saint. Don't miss the murals in the galleries, or trying your luck with the 'weeping' column.

10am Exit Aya Sofya, and follow the road, Caferiye Sokak, which runs along the west side. At the end of this road you come to cobbled **Soğukçeşme Sokak** (page 88). Turn right and walk up to the Imperial Gate of the first court of **Topkapı Palace** (page 91). Buy your ticket and head straight to the Harem ticket office to buy a ticket for the 10.30am or 11am tour. While you're waiting for the tour to start, you may want to explore the kitchens and the second court. For lunch, enjoy the views of the Bosphorus at the **Konyalı Restaurant** (page 153).

2pm Head back to the first court of Topkapı and turn right to the **İstanbul Archaeology Museums** (page 86). The highlights here are the Tiled Kiosk, the panels from the Ishtar gate of ancient Babylon in the Museum of the Ancient Orient and the sarcophagi in the Archaeology Museum.

3.30pm At the exit of the Archaeology Museums, head right down the hill and out through the gates of **Gülhane Park** (page 88) to Alemdar Caddesi. Follow this road south for a few minutes.

4pm You'll only need 20 minutes to go through the **Sunken Cistern** (page 83). Let's hope the drip-dripping from the ceilings doesn't bring on a bout of tears about your impending departure from İstanbul.

4.30pm If you've got a bit of time to spare before your flight home consider walking down to **Küçük Aya Sofya Camii** (page 85) or along the **Hippodrome** (page 83).

Home time You'll need to get to the airport at least 75 minutes before your plane departs. Bundle your tired bones into a taxi. Let's hope you're not too tired to work tomorrow!

TRAVEL AGENCIES

Sultanahmet, in Old İstanbul, has many small travel agencies, all of them selling air and bus tickets and tours, sometimes at a big mark-up; shop around for the best deals. Most also offer speedy (but expensive) foreign-exchange facilities and can arrange minibus transport to the airport. For information about İstanbul city tours turn to Organised Tours in the Getting Around chapter.

Right on the main drag of tourist town (Sultanahmet), Marco Polo (Map 13, #23; ☎ 212-519 2804, fax 513 1781) at Divan Yolu 54/11 has maintained a good reputation for a decade or more. It provides on-the-spot air tickets, gives advice on local tours and so on.

Backpackers (Map 13, #78; ☎ 212-638 6343, fax 638 3922, W www.backpackers travel.net) at Akbıyık Caddesi 22, Cankurtaran, has a good following. It specialises in tours around Turkey – Gallipoli, Ephesus etc – but it also has İstanbul city tours.

About 2km north of Taksim, Orion-Tour (☎ 212-248 8437, e orion@oriontour.com.tr, W www.orion-tour.com), at Halaskargazi Caddesi 284/3, Marmara Apartımanı, Şişli, can arrange flights, cruises (including private or group yacht charters), city tours of İstanbul and other major cities.

DOCUMENTS

Visas

Nationals of the following countries (among others) may enter Turkey for up to three months with only a valid passport (no visa is required): Denmark, Finland, France, Germany, Greece, Iceland, Japan, Liechtenstein, Luxembourg, Monaco, New Zealand, Norway, Singapore, Sweden, Switzerland, Tobago and Trinidad. Make sure your passport has at least three months' validity remaining, or you may not be admitted.

Citizens of the Republic of South Africa may enter with a passport (no visa needed) for up to one month.

Nationals of Australia, Austria, Belgium, Canada, Holland, Ireland, Israel, Italy, Portugal, Spain, UK and USA may enter for up to three months upon purchase of a visa sticker at their point of arrival (ie, not at an embassy in advance). If you arrive at İstanbul's Atatürk Airport, make sure you obtain your visa from the booth to the left of customs before you line up. Exact cash is required. Major foreign currencies such as pounds sterling or US dollars are accepted, as is Turkish lira. No credit cards or travellers cheques are accepted. The fees change, but at the time of writing Australians paid US$20, Canadians US$45, Italians US$5, Spaniards US$10, Britons UK£10 and Americans US$100.

Visa Extensions Depending on your nationality, you may be permitted to extend your visa for a longer stay. Most visitors wanting to extend their stay for a few months avoid bureaucratic tedium by taking a quick overnight trip to Greece (Thessaloniki or Rhodes), returning to Turkey the next day with a new three-month stamp in their passports.

Work Visas It's best to obtain a *çalışma vizesi* (work visa) from the Turkish embassy or consulate in your home country before you leave. You'll need to have a job lined up before a work visa will be issued and your employment must be approved by the relevant Turkish ministry (eg, the Ministry of Education for a teaching job). Your prospective employer will organise this approval and provide you with the permission letter. You must submit this letter as part of your work visa application along with the completed visa form, your passport and two photos of yourself. If your visa is granted (most are), you then need to pay the required fee. Your passport will be returned with the visa stamped inside; it usually takes six to eight weeks.

If you're not at home and you want a work visa, you must apply for it outside Turkey. The Turkish consulate in Komotini, Greece (see Embassies & Consulates opposite), a 10-hour overnight bus ride from İstanbul is accustomed to such requests. It usually grants the visa within a few hours. If you plan to make a special trip, ring to make sure the consulate will be open when you arrive.

Once you arrive in Turkey on a work visa, you must obtain an *ikamet tezkeresi* (residence permit or most commonly known as a 'pink book'). Contact the tourism police (Map 13, #44) in Sultanahmet or a tourist office to find out where to get one. Your employer may organise it for you. If not, apply with your passport, two more photos and the US$40 processing fee. The permit should be ready in two or three days. The pink book is renewable every year, as long as you show proof of continued employment.

For information on the main types of jobs available, see Work later in this chapter.

Travel Insurance

A travel insurance policy to cover theft, loss and medical problems is a good idea. There is a wide variety of policies available, so check the small print. Check that the policy covers ambulances or an emergency flight back to your home.

Driving Licence & Permits

Drivers must have a valid driving licence. An International Driving Permit (IDP) is required for stays of more than three months, or if your licence is from a locality that a Turkish police officer is likely to find obscure.

Third-party insurance, valid for driving in Turkey, is obligatory; otherwise, you will be required to purchase a Turkish policy at the border.

The Türkiye Turing ve Otomobil Kurumu (Turkish Touring & Automobile Association; ☎ 212-282 8140, e turing@turing.org.tr), Oto Sanayi Yanı, Çamlık Caddesi, 4. Levent, about 7km north of Taksim, has information on how to bring your own vehicle into the country.

Hostel Cards

A Hostelling International (HI) card will get you almost nothing in İstanbul. The very few HI-affiliated hostels usually offer the same rates to all comers, and their rates are little different from those at comparable cheap guesthouses.

Student & Youth Cards

Holders of an International Student Identity Card (ISIC) should get good discounts at most museums and historic buildings, though sometimes the ticket sellers may insist the student price is only for Turkish students; stand your ground. You'll also get at least a 20% discount on Turkish State Railways and Turkish Maritime Lines fares – of little good within İstanbul proper. Apply for an ISIC card before you get to İstanbul.

Copies

All important documents (passport data page and visa page, credit cards, travel insurance policy, air/bus/train tickets, driving licence, travellers cheque numbers etc) should be photocopied before you leave home. Leave one copy with someone at home and keep another with you, separate from the originals.

EMBASSIES & CONSULATES

Turkish Embassies & Consulates

Turkey has the following embassies and consulates around the world:

Australia (☎ 02-6295 0227, fax 6239 6592, e turkembs@ozemail.com.au) 60 Mugga Way, Red Hill, ACT 2603
Bulgaria (☎ 02-980 2270, fax 981 9358) Blvd Vasil Levski No 80, 1000 Sofia
Canada (☎ 613-789 4044, fax 789 3442) 197 Wurtemburg St, Ottawa, Ontario KIN 8L9
France (☎ 01 56 33 33 33, fax 01 42 27 58 18, e tcparbsk@world.net.fr) 184, boulevard Malesherbes, 75017 Paris
Germany (☎ 30-27 58 50, fax 27 59 09 15) Rungestrasse 9, 10179 Berlin
Greece (☎ 01-724 5915, fax 722 9597) Vasilissis Georgiou B Street 8, 10674 Athens
Consulate in Komotini: (☎ 531-22713, 31823, fax 32761) Odos Ionon 14
Ireland (☎ 1-668 5240, fax 668 5014, e turkemb@iol.ie) 11 Clyde Rd, Dublin 4
Netherlands (☎ 70-360 4912, fax 361 7969, e turkije@dataweb.nl) Jan Everstraat 2514 BS, The Hague
New Zealand (☎ 4-472 1290, fax 472 1277, e turkem@xtra.co.nz) 15–17 Murphy St, Level 8, Wellington
UK (☎ 020-7393 0202, fax 7393 0066, e info@turkishembassy-london.com) 43 Belgrave Square, London SW1X 8PA
USA (☎ 202-612 6700, fax 612 6744, e info@turkey.org) 2525 Massachusetts Ave NW, Washington, DC 20036

Consulates in İstanbul

Embassies *(büyükelçiliği)* are in Ankara, the national capital. İstanbul has consulates *(konsolosluğu)* from many countries.

Australia (☎ 212-257 7050, fax 257 7054) Tepecik Yolu 58, Etiler
Canada (☎ 212-272 5174, fax 272 3427) Büyükdere Caddesi 107/3, Bengün Han, Gayrettepe
France (Map 16, #24; ☎ 212-293 2461, fax 293 9764) İstiklal Caddesi 8, Taksim
Georgia (Map 16, #8; ☎ 212-292 8111, fax 292 8112) İnönü Caddesi 55, Taksim
Germany (Map 16, #8; ☎ 212-334 6100, fax 249 9920) İnönü Caddesi 16, Gümüşsuyu, Taksim
Greece (Map 16, #64; ☎ 212-245 0596, fax 252 1365) Turnacıbaşı Sokak 32, Ağahamam, Kuloğlu, Beyoğlu
Iran (☎ 212-513 8230, fax 511 5219) Ankara Caddesi 1, Cağaloğlu
Ireland (Map 17, #24; ☎ 212-246 6025, fax 248 0744) Cumhuriyet Caddesi 171/3, Elmadağ
Israel (☎ 212-225 1040, fax 317 6555) Yapı Kredi Plaza, Block C, Apt 7, Levent
Italy (☎ 212-243 1024, fax 252 5879) Palazzo di Venezia, Tomtom Kaptan Sokak 15, Galatasaray, Beyoğlu
Netherlands (Map 16, #107; ☎ 212-251 5030, fax 292 5031) İstiklal Caddesi 393, Tünel, Beyoğlu
Spain (☎ 212-225 2153, fax 225 2088) Cumhuriyet Caddesi 233, Harbiye
Syria (Map 17, #9; ☎ 212-232 6721, fax 230 2215) Maçka Caddesi 59, Ralli Apt 3, Teşvikiye
UK (Map 16, #82; ☎ 212-293 7540, fax 245 4989) Meşrutiyet Caddesi 34, Tepebaşı, Beyoğlu
USA (Map 16, #118; ☎ 212-251 3602, fax 251 3632) Meşrutiyet Caddesi 104–108, Tepebaşı, Beyoğlu

CUSTOMS

İstanbul's Atatürk Airport uses the red and green channel system, spot-checking passengers' luggage at random. Items valued over US$15,000 should be declared, and may be entered in your passport to guarantee that you take the goods out of the country. You are allowed to bring in 5L of liquor, 1.5kg of coffee, one carton (200) of cigarettes and 50 cigars. If you buy cigarettes from the duty-free shops at Atatürk Airport upon entry, you can bring in two cartons.

Antiquities

It is illegal to buy, sell, possess or export antiquities. Only true antiquities well over a century old are off limits, not newer items or the many artful fakes (but will the customs officer know genuine from fake?). Penalties for breaking the antiquities law are severe, and may land you in jail.

MONEY

Currency

The unit of currency is the Turkish *lira,* or TL. Coins come in amounts of 25,000, 50,000 and 100,000. Banknotes come in 250,000, 500,000, one million, five million and 10 million lira etc.

With all those zeroes, it's often difficult to make sure you're trading the correct notes. Beware! Shopkeepers and taxi drivers may sometimes try to give you a 500,000 lira note in place of a five million, or one million note instead of a 10 million.

When the government undertakes the inevitable elimination of some zeroes on the currency, the confusion will be far greater, as old lira notes with all the zeroes will remain in circulation with new notes for a time. Take your time and be sure of amounts.

Exchange Rates

Despite the government's recent attempts to bring the inflation rate down, the value of the lira drops daily. An exchange rate table

Turkish Lira Crash

A dispute between President Sezer and Prime Minister Ecevit in mid-February 2001 (amid an already tenuous economic climate) was the catalyst for sending the İstanbul Stock Exchange into mayhem and the Turkish lira into free fall. The central bank was forced to refloat the lira on the world currency market. Before the dispute, one US dollar was worth about 600,000 TL, a few months later the same US dollar was worth 1,300,000 TL. As the government, aided by fresh International Monetary Fund (IMF) money, gets back on the road to recovery expect more currency fluctuations and a few headaches with prices in this book.

is therefore not provided: it would be prehistoric by the time you arrive.

Exchanging Money

Wait until you arrive in Turkey to change your home currency (cash or travellers cheques) into Turkish liras. Exchange bureaus in other countries usually offer terrible rates of exchange for Turkish liras. There are a couple of 24-hour exchange bureaus in the arrivals hall at Atatürk Airport. Count the money you're given carefully.

Don't change large amounts of money all at once. With constant devaluation, tomorrow you'll almost certainly get even more liras for your money. Save your currency exchange receipts *(bordro)*. You may need them to reconvert Turkish liras at the end of your stay.

As Turkish liras are fully convertible, there is no black market.

Cash US dollars and pounds sterling are easily changed anywhere, and are often accepted as payment without being changed. Other currencies such as French francs, Australian, Canadian or New Zealand dollars are fairly easily changed too, though it's better to stick with the major currencies. You will usually need to show your passport when changing cash.

Travellers Cheques Banks, shops and hotels often see it as a burden to change travellers cheques (including Eurocheques), and may ask you to go elsewhere. You may have to insist. Generally, it's better to change cheques to Turkish liras at a bank, although most banks charge fees. Moneychangers usually won't change travellers cheques.

ATMs Automated teller machines (ATMs, cashpoints) are common in İstanbul. Virtually all of them offer instructions in English, French and German and will pay out Turkish liras when you insert your bank debit (cash) card. This is the fastest and cheapest way to get Turkish money, though remember that you will be charged about US$2 per transaction (taken directly from your home account).

ATMs will also pay cash advances on most major credit cards (especially Visa). The limit on cash advances is generally the equivalent of about US$250 per day. Remember that you will pay a steep rate of interest on the cash advance (and usually a fee of US$2) from the day you use the ATM until the day you pay off your credit card.

All of the major Turkish banks and some smaller banks have ATMs but Akbank ATM (Map 19, #27) and Yapı Kredi ATM (Map 13, #11) are the most convenient and reliable. The specific machine you use must be reliably connected to the major ATM networks' computers via telephone lines. Look for stickers with the logos of these services (Cirrus, Maestro, Plus Systems etc) affixed to the machine. If the connection is not reliable, you may get a message saying that the transaction was refused by your bank (which may not be true), and your card will (hopefully) be returned to you.

Credit Cards Big hotels, car rental agencies and the more expensive shops will accept major credit cards, but check in advance. The commonly used cards are Access, American Express, Diners Club, Eurocard, MasterCard and Visa, with Visa heading the pack.

Moneychangers İstanbul continues to sprout currency exchange bureaus *(döviz bürosu)*. They offer faster service than banks, longer opening hours, and may not charge a commission. The rates are worse at offices heavily used by tourists, such as those in Sultanahmet. Better rates are offered outside the Kapalı Çarşı, in Taksim, Şişli, Eminönü and other areas where Turks change money.

Costs

All costs in this guide are given in US dollars only, as prices in Turkish liras would be laughably out of date before the book even emerged from the printer.

Accommodation rates quoted in this guide all include taxes, but restaurant prices don't. See the boxed text 'Turkish Lira Crash' earlier for more information about the costs quoted in this book.

Turkey is Europe's low-price leader, and you can visit İstanbul for as little as US$25 to US$40 per person per day staying in a hostel or pension, getting around by city bus and *dolmuş* (shared taxi), and eating two cheap restaurant meals daily.

If you plan to spend US$50 to US$70 per person per day then you can stay in fancier guesthouses, and eat most meals in average restaurants.

For US$75 to US$100 per day you can move up to the gourmet guesthouses and three-star hotels, take taxis everywhere, and dine in restaurants all the time.

For top-end style you'll need at least US$170 per person, although if you stay and eat at the top hotels and have a car and driver at your disposal each day you can easily drive the cost of an İstanbul stay up to US$250 to US$400 per person per day.

Outside İstanbul and the major resorts, costs are substantially lower.

The following table lists some average costs for İstanbul:

Single room	US$15–US$75
Double room	US$25–US$100
Loaf of bread	US$0.40
Bottle of beer	US$1 (shop)
	US$2–US$3.50 (bar)
Litre of petrol/gasoline	US$0.90–US$0.97
US gallon	US$2.56–US$3.31
Local telephone call	US$0.10
Turkish Daily News	US$0.80

Price Adjustments Government entities such as the Ministry of Culture (which administers many of the city's museums) and the Turkish State Railways may set prices at the beginning of the year, and then adjust them every three or four months – if at all – throughout the year. Thus a museum admission fee or train fare might cost you US$6 in January, but only US$4 or even US$3 later in the year. For this reason, many prices in this guide must be looked upon as approximate.

Private enterprises tend to adjust their prices more frequently and many in the travel industry such as airlines, rental car firms and the more expensive hotels quote prices in US dollars.

Tipping & Bargaining

When haggling, you can often get a discount by offering to buy several items at once; or by paying in US dollars or another strong major currency; or by not requesting a receipt (see Taxes & Refunds). If shopkeepers don't supply a receipt, they can fiddle the books around tax time.

For other bargaining tips see the boxed text 'Bagging a Bargain' in the Shopping chapter.

Restaurants Some places will automatically add a service charge of 10% or 15% to your bill – the bill may say *servis dahil* (service included) – but this does not absolve you from the tip, oddly enough. The service charge goes into the pocket of the *patron* (owner). Turks will give 5% to 10% to the waiter directly; many don't tip at the cheapest restaurants, but at these restaurants the waiters probably need tips most. Only in the fancy, foreign-operated hotels will waiters expect those enormous 15% to 20% US-style tips.

If you're at a meyhane with musicians, you should give at least US$5 per table; so if there are two of you at a table tip US$5, if there are three US$5 is still OK and so on. The same goes for a bellydancer – she's not shaking it for nothing!

Hotels In the cheapest hotels tips are not expected. In the better hotels, a porter will carry your luggage and show you to your room. For doing this he'll expect US$2 or US$3.

Taxis Turks don't tip taxi drivers, but they often round up the metered fare to a convenient amount. A driver of a dolmuş gets only the standard fare.

Hamams If staff in a nontourist *hamam* (Turkish steam bath) approach you as you are leaving, share out 20% of the bath fees among them. In the touristy baths, you sometimes pay a tip as part of your entrance fee, which is supposed to go to the masseur or masseuse – ensure that it does. If a tip isn't included, tip 20% of the bath fees.

Taxes & Refunds

Turkey has a value-added tax (VAT), the *katma değer vergisi* (KDV), added to most goods and services. All prices quoted in this guide, except for restaurant prices, include taxes.

If you buy an expensive item such as a carpet or leather garment and take it out of the country soon afterwards, in principle you are entitled to a refund of the KDV, which may be as high as 15% or 20% of the purchase price. Not all shops participate in the scheme, so you must ask if it is possible to get a *KDV iade özel fatura* (special VAT refund receipt). Ask for this during the haggling, rather than after you've bought.

The receipt can in principle be converted to cash at a bank in the international departures lounge at the airport (if there is a bank open, which there may not be); or, if you submit the form to a customs officer as you leave the country, the shop will (one hopes) mail a refund cheque to your home after the government has completed its procedures. Don't hold your breath.

To increase your chances of actually getting the refund, make a photocopy or two of the KDV iade özel fatura in advance and, when you're leaving Turkey, take along a stamped envelope addressed to the shop where you bought the goods. Have your KDV form stamped by the customs officer at the airport to show that you've exported the goods, then mail it right from the airport to the shop. Enclose a note requesting refund of the tax and giving the address to which the refund cheque should be sent. In some cases it can take as long as four months for the cheque to arrive.

POST & COMMUNICATIONS

Post

Post offices, marked by black-on-yellow signs, are traditionally known as PTTs (peh-teh-teh; Posta Telefon, Telegraf). İstanbul's central post office (*merkez postane;* Map 15, #16) is several blocks south-west of Sirkeci train station on Mevlana Caddesi. It has a section open 24 hours a day where you can make phone calls, buy stamps and send and receive faxes. Other services, such as the poste restante, are open 8.30am to 12.30pm and 1pm to 4.30pm daily.

There's a PTT booth (Map 13, #63) outside Aya Sofya on Aya Sofya Meydanı, in Sultanahmet, which is open 9am to 4pm Tuesday to Sunday. There are PTT branches in the law courts (Map 13, #18) on İmran Öktem Caddesi in Sultanahmet; in Taksim Square (Map 17, #64) near the McDonald's on Cumhuriyet Caddesi; just off İstiklal Caddesi (Map 16, #87) in Galatasaray; and in the south-western corner of the Kapalı Çarşı (Map 4, #21) near the Havuzlu Lokantası on Gani Çelebi Sokak.

The *yurtdışı* slot is for mail to foreign countries, *yurtiçi* is for mail to other Turkish cities, and *şehiriçi* is for mail within İstanbul. Mail delivery is fairly reliable. A standard letter to Australia will take about 10 days and cost US$0.70. Letters to the UK and USA cost US$0.65. Stamps for postcards, irrespective of where they're going, cost US$0.45.

Parcels To mail packages out of the country you must have your package opened for customs inspection, and you will probably have to endure a bit of frustrating officialdom. You may be directed by postal officials to the special Paket Postane (Parcel Post Office) near Karaköy. Have paper, box, string, tape and marker pens with you when you go.

If you want to make certain that a parcel will get to its destination intact and quickly, send it by Federal Express (FedEx; ☎ 212-549 0404), DHL (☎ 212-444 0040), by the post office's express mail service *(acele posta servisi)* or at least by registered mail *(kayıtlı)*.

Telephone

Türk Telekom has a monopoly on phone services. You'll find most public phones in clusters, often near PTTs. International calls can be made from most of these phones. You pay for calls with a *telekart* debit card or a major credit card, depending upon the phone; a few old phones require a *jeton* (token). Telekarts usually come in denominations of 30, 60 and 100 usage units and cost US$1, US$2 and US$3.50. You can buy them from booths near clusters of phones or from PTTs. In general, a 30-unit card is sufficient for local calls; 60 units for a short, domestic intercity call; and 100 units for longer domestic or international calls. Rates for local and intercity domestic calls are moderate. European İstanbul's area code is ☎ 212; Asian İstanbul's area code is ☎ 216.

eKno Communication Service Lonely Planet's eKno global communication service provides low-cost international calls – for local calls you're usually better off with a local phonecard. eKno also offers free messaging services, email, travel information and an online travel vault, where you can securely store all your important documents. You can join online at W www.ekno.lonelyplanet.com, where you will find the local-access numbers for the 24-hour customer-service centre. Once you have joined, always check the eKno Web site for the latest access numbers for each country and updates on new features.

Long-Distance Calls International calls can cost (per minute) almost £1 to the UK, US$2 to the USA and US$2 to Australia. Reduced rates are in effect from midnight to 10am, and on Sunday. Beware of hotel surcharges, which can double your bill.

Omit İstanbul's area codes if you're calling in the same area. Press '0' (zero) and the area code to make an intercity call within Turkey, or '00' to make an international call. Turkey's country code is ☎ 90.

Fax

Most PTTs will send and hold faxes for you. The central post office in Sirkeci has a fax centre open all the time. It usually costs (per A4 page) £2 to the UK, US$3.50 to the USA, and US$3.50 to Australia. Many private communication bureaus around town also send faxes. In Beyoğlu, Pirdaloğlu (☎ 212-292 3512), at Mis Sokak 4, off İstiklal Caddesi near Taksim Square, has decent rates. It's open 8am to 2am Monday to Saturday.

Email & Internet Access

There are heaps of Internet cafes in İstanbul. The untouristy cafes are mostly filled with truant pimply adolescents playing games – but these are the cheapest cafes. Many of the guesthouses and hotels also have Internet service that you can use for a fee. The best time to log on is before breakfast, especially on Sunday; at other times access points can be frustratingly slow.

You'll usually pay around US$1 to US$2 per hour; some places charge this as a minimum rate which can be annoying if you only want to use the Internet for a short while. Look elsewhere.

Anatolia Internet Cafe (Map 13, #42; ☎ 212-511 8349) İncili Çavuş Sokak 37/2. Near the Sultan Pub, in Sultanahmet, this cafe has more computers but it's a bit pricier than Backpackers.

Backpackers (Map 13, #78; ☎ 212-636 6343) Akbıyık Caddesi 22, Cankurtaran. Near Sultanahmet, this travel agency has a small, good Internet room downstairs.

Cafenet (☎ 216-330 7752) Osmanağa Mah, Piri Çavuş Sokak 50. Over in Kadıköy on the Asian side, Cafenet has a good set-up and cheap access.

Sinera Internet (Map 16, #31; ☎ 212-292 6899) Mis Sokak 6/1. Just off İstiklal Caddesi, Sinera is less classy than Yağmur, but is well run.

Yağmur Cybercafe (Map 16, #120; ☎ 212-292 3020) 2nd floor, Çitlembik Apartıman building, Şeyh Bender Sokak 18, Asmalımescit, Beyoğlu. This is well run and also has waffles (from US$1) and good coffee.

CompuServe (access number ☎ 212-234 6100; W www.compuserve.com) and America Online (access number ☎ 212-234 6100; W www.aol.com) have nodes in İstanbul. You will need to download and install supplementary CCL files in your CompuServe or AOL software to access these networks, and pay US$6 per hour while you're online. Contact those companies for information.

In four- and five-star hotels, most telephone connections are made using the American-style small clear plastic RJ11 plug. In cheaper hotels the phones often use a larger white or beige three-prong Turkish plug. Many electrical shops sell these plugs and also phone cords with RJ11 plugs on them, so if you're handy with a screwdriver you can easily make your own phone line adaptor for a laptop computer. For more information on travelling with a portable computer, see W www.teleadapt.com or W www.warrior.com.

DIGITAL RESOURCES

There's no better place to start your Web explorations than the Lonely Planet Web site (W www.lonelyplanet.com). Here you'll find succinct summaries on travelling to most places on earth, postcards from other travellers and the Thorn Tree bulletin board, where you can ask questions before you go or dispense advice when you get back. You can also find travel news and updates to many of our most popular guidebooks, and the subWWWay section links you to the most useful travel resources elsewhere on the Web.

There are many Web sites dealing with İstanbul:

W **www.exploreistanbul.com** Advertisements are laid on heavy here but if you can be bothered wading through them, the touristy sights are well covered. The pretty photographs are the main drawcard.
W **www.istanbulcityguide.com** Fairly up-to-date listings on what's happening in the city, though there's not much detail about each event. Covers weather, arts, galleries, hotels and more.
W **www.theguideistanbul.com** Produced by the same crew that does the magazine, this Web site has general information about the city's famous and less glamorous sights as well as feature articles.
W **www.turkishdailynews.com** This is the dull-as-dishwater Internet edition of the daily English-language newspaper *Turkish Daily News*, but it's worth checking out for the latest news (no classifieds). No freeloaders are allowed in the archive section.
W **www.turkey.org/turkey** This site has information about the whole country, but there's still some useful, if a bit dated, practical İstanbul information and good links.

BOOKS

Everyone from Mark Twain to Agatha Christie has written about İstanbul. Most books are published in different editions by different publishers in different countries. As a result, a book might be a hardcover rarity in one country while it's readily available in paperback in another. Fortunately, bookshops and libraries search by title or author, so your local bookshop or library is best placed to advise you on the availability of the following recommendations.

For bookshop recommendations, see Bookshops in the Shopping chapter.

Lonely Planet

As well as this guide to İstanbul, a good companion is Lonely Planet's *Turkish phrasebook*, or if you're enjoying Turkish food, you may want to check out *World Food Turkey*. Lonely Planet also covers the entire country in detail in *Turkey*. And if you're taking the children, Lonely Planet's *Travel with Children* will help to make the trip an interesting and enjoyable one for all the family.

Guidebooks

The classic walking guide to the great buildings of İstanbul is the excellent *Strolling Through İstanbul* by Hilary Sumner-Boyd & John Freely.

For the literary-minded, *Istanbul – a traveller's companion* by Laurence Kelly is a delight. The editor has combed through the writings of two millennia and collected the choicest bits of history, biography, diary and travellers' observations relating to Byzantium, Constantinople and İstanbul.

Travel

The published diaries and accounts of earlier travellers in Turkey provide fascinating glimpses of Ottoman life. Of the many Europeans who lived in Ottoman İstanbul and wrote about it, the most interesting and revealing is Lady Mary Wortley Montagu, who published her *Letters* in 1789, followed in 1837 by Miss Julia Pardoe with her *City of the Sultan and Domestic Manners of the Turks*.

One of the more familiar 19th-century accounts of a visit to imperial İstanbul is Mark Twain's *Innocents Abroad*.

Jeremy Seal's *A Fez of the Heart* is the account of the author's journeys throughout Turkey in search of Turks who still wear the fez. It's a witty, entertaining inquiry into resurgent Islam and what it means to be a 'modern' Turk.

History

The city's two millennia of history have inspired countless writers to describe Byzantium, Constantinople and İstanbul, and the events that took place there. Procopius (died circa 565), Byzantine chronicler and one-time prefect of Constantinople, left us his scurrilous *Secret History* of court life in the capital during the reign of Justinian.

Kritovoulos's *History of Mehmet the Conqueror* is a chronicle of the conquest of Constantinople, by an astute Byzantine observer of the time.

Peter Gilles (Petrus Gyllius) left us his *Antiquities of Constantinople,* published in an English edition in 1729.

For a fascinating look into the final years of the Ottoman Empire and the early years of the Turkish Republic, read İrfan Orga's *Portrait of a Turkish Family.*

General

Anthropology For a good overview of life during the great days of the empire, look in a library for *Everyday Life in Ottoman Turkey* by Raphaela Lewis.

Carpets Everything you need to know about buying carpets is contained in *Oriental Carpets: A buyer's guide,* by Essie Sakhai. It includes full-colour photographs of each style of carpet as well as information on the origins of design, how they are made and tips on what buyers should look for.

Cuisine The definitive guide to Turkish cookery is *Eat Smart in Turkey,* by Joan & David Peterson. More than just an aid in deciphering menus, recognising foodstuffs in the marketplace, and enjoying Turkish cooking, this book provides amusing and informative historical notes on Turkish dishes as well.

Fiction Everybody knows about Agatha Christie's *Murder on the Orient Express.* Though it has some scenes in Turkey, most of the train's journey was through Europe and the Balkans. However, it demonstrates the importance of the Ottoman Empire in the 19th century.

Detective-novel junkies might like Barbara Nadel's *Belshazzar's Daughter* and *A Chemical Prison.* Set in İstanbul, the novels, inspired by Ottoman excesses, send detective İkmen into plots thick with intrigue.

FILMS

For a list of films produced by local filmmakers see Cinema in the Facts about İstanbul chapter. Many international filmmakers have used İstanbul merely as a picturesque backdrop, rarely allowing the city to inform the story or plot.

Oliver Stone's infamous *Midnight Express* is a film the government would like to forget. It's an anti-Turkish diatribe in which a convicted drug smuggler is magically transformed into a suffering hero. The classic suspense-comedy *Topkapi,* with Peter Ustinov and Melina Mercouri, is much more fun to watch. Later, James Bond turns on the wiles in *From Russia with Love,* a typical Bond boy-charms-girl thriller with İstanbul as the backdrop. Sean Connery also stars in the 1974 classic *Murder on the Orient Express.* This film adaptation of Agatha Christie's novel also stars Ingrid Bergman and Lauren Bacall.

NEWSPAPERS & MAGAZINES

Local daily newspapers are in full lurid colour featuring scantily clad women squeezed between the advertisements. The journalistic content is best left unmentioned. Of prime interest to visitors is the *Turkish Daily News,* an English-language daily newspaper published in Ankara and sold for US$0.80 in İstanbul. The *Turkish News* is another English-language daily.

The guide is out every two months and covers listings of restaurants, shopping and sightseeing. It's a bit dry and features consistently glowing reviews. *İstanbull...* is more like it. Produced by expats for expats, it has witty and insightful warts-and-all anecdotes about the city as well as unsolicited venue reviews. Check out the Web site (W www.istanbullshit.net) or pick it up from many of the cafes in Beyoğlu.

You can also buy the big international papers such as the *International Herald Tribune, Le Monde, Corriere della Sera, Die Welt* etc but they're much more expensive (US$2 for the *Herald Tribune*). Check the date on any international paper before you buy it. High-circulation magazines, including *The Economist, Newsweek, Time, Der Spiegel* and the like, are also available. Most foreign-language bookshops and the newsagent booths around Aya Sofya sell these newspapers and magazines; otherwise try the five-star hotel newsstands.

RADIO & TV

Türkiye Radyo ve Televizyon (TRT) is a quasi-independent government broadcasting service modelled on the BBC. TRT Tourism (Holiday) Radio broadcasts travel-oriented features in English, French and German on 101.6 Mhz FM in İstanbul daily from 7.30am to 12.45pm and 6.30pm to 10pm. Listen for news from 8.30am to 12.30pm and at 9.30pm. TRT's Radio 3 (88.2 Mhz FM) also presents short news broadcasts in English at 9am, noon, 5pm and 9pm.

The BBC World Service is often receivable on AM as well as on short-wave. The 'Voice of America' broadcasts in English on AM, relayed from Rhodes, each morning.

TRT broadcasts on four TV channels from breakfast time till midnight. Independent Turkish-language stations carry the familiar Los Angeles–made series and films dubbed in Turkish. Occasionally you'll catch a film in the original language. In addition to the Turkish channels, many of the larger and more expensive hotels have satellite hook-ups to receive Turkey's Digiturk. Its standard subscription package has French, Italian and German channels, BBC World and more.

PHOTOGRAPHY & VIDEO

Many museums and historical sites impose hefty fees (above the admission charge) for photography and video usage. Payment of such a fee entitles you to take photos *without* a flash and/or tripod; to use these 'professional' accessories you must obtain official written permission from the Ministry of Culture or the official body in charge of the museum or site – a difficult, tedious and time-consuming process.

Film is moderately expensive in Turkey (24 Kodacolor print film costs about US$8, plus developing). Both major- and minor-brand colour print film is readily available and easily developed in İstanbul. The E-6 process slide (diapositive, transparency) films such as Ektachrome, Fujichrome and Velvia are also easily found. A 36 roll of Velvia costs about US$12 per 36 shots; developing – without mounting – costs about US$10 per 36. Kodachrome slide film is difficult to find, and cannot be developed.

If you are from North America, remember that Turkey uses the European PAL TV-video system, not the NTSC system.

Photo shops (selling film, accessories and with processing facilities) are concentrated in the narrow streets just west of Sirkeci train station. Try Özgül (Map 15, #22; ☎ 212-519 3680) at Hüdavendigar Caddesi 60–61, Sirkeci. Over near Taksim, Refo Color (Map 17, #32; ☎ 212-240 3285) at Cumhuriyet Caddesi 53, Elmadağ, has one-hour print and slide processing. It stocks slide and colour print film too.

For camera repair, one reader recommends Nazmi Kılıçer (☎ 212-511 4259), Babiali Caddesi, Başmusahip Sokak 19/2, Cağaloğlu. Although he is a Hasselblad specialist, he repairs all sorts of cameras. Alternatively, try the photo shops west of Sirkeci train station.

Research and planning are the keys to taking good photos. For comprehensive information you may want to pick up *Travel Photography: A Guide to Taking Better Pictures* by Richard I'Anson and published by Lonely Planet, or you could start by following these tips:

- The best time to take photographs is around sunrise and sunset.
- Always carry a skylight or UV filter.
- Don't buy cheap equipment. The quality of your lens is the most important thing.
- Take a tripod and faster film (at least 400 ASA/ISO) rather than use flash.

Don't take photos of military subjects. It's also polite to ask (sign language will suffice) before taking pictures of people who are not obviously used to such exposure.

TIME

İstanbul time is East European Time, two hours ahead of Coordinated Universal Time (UTC, alias GMT), except in the warm months, when clocks are turned ahead one hour. Daylight saving (summer) time usually begins at 1am on the last Sunday in March, and ends at 2am on the last Sunday in September.

ELECTRICITY

Electricity in İstanbul is supplied at 220V, 50Hz, as in Europe. Plugs *(fiş)* are of the European variety with two round prongs. Electricity shops have adaptors for European and North American plugs, though it's not a bad idea to bring your own to avoid wasting time finding a Turkish electrical shop.

WEIGHTS & MEASURES

Turkey uses the metric system. For those who are used to imperial or US measurements, see the metric conversion table inside the back cover.

LAUNDRY

If you don't want to wash your own crusty laundry, ask for prices at your hotel or go to one of the cheaper options listed below. By the way, the word for laundry *(çamasır)* also means 'underwear' in Turkish, which could be confusing at times.

Can Laundry (Map 16, #55; ☎ 212-252 9360) Bakraç Sokak 32/C, Cihangir, Beyoğlu. Open 8.30am to 8pm Monday to Friday, 8.30am to 4pm Saturday, Can also charges US$1.50 per 1kg to wash and dry.

Star Laundry (Map 13, #75; ☎ 212-638 2302) Akbıyık Caddesi 18, Cankurtaran. Star charges US$1.50 per 1kg to wash and dry, and it's open 8am to 8pm daily.

İstanbul has numerous dry-cleaners. You'll pay about US$3.50 for a suit, US$1.50 for a skirt. The following two places are open 8am to 7pm Monday to Saturday.

Doğu Expres (Map 13, #106; ☎ 212-518 2154) Peykhane Sokak 57, Sultanahmet

Pertek (Map 16, #100; ☎ 212-292 7327) Meşrutiyet Caddesi 131, Beyoğlu

TOILETS

In most public toilets you must pay a fee of US$0.10 to US$0.20. Turkish loos are equipped with facilities for washing 'private parts' (always with the left hand): A tap, or spigot, with a can on the floor nearby or, much more conveniently, a little copper tube pointing right to the spot where it's needed. As washing is the accustomed method of hygiene, toilet paper – used by Turks mostly for drying – is considered a dispensable luxury and may not be provided. If you want to use paper, it's a good idea to carry it with you at all times.

You will also probably meet the infamous flat 'elephant's feet', or squat toilet, a porcelain or concrete rectangle with two oblong foot-places and a sunken hole. Though somewhat daunting for first-timers, it has much to recommend it: It's said that the squatting position aids in the swift and thorough accomplishment of your daily duty; and since only your feet contact the vessel, it is more sanitary than bowl toilets.

Serviceably clean public toilets can be found near the big tourist attractions. In other places, it depends. Look first. Every mosque has a toilet, often smelly and very basic, but it may be better than nothing, depending upon the urgency of nature's call.

LEFT LUGGAGE

Atatürk Airport has a left-luggage facility *(emanet)* in the arrivals hall. It's open 24 hours and charges US$3.50 per suitcase or backpack per 24-hour period. Both Sirkeci and Haydarpaşa train stations have places to leave luggage, too.

HEALTH

İstanbul has the best medical services in Turkey, including hospitals under American, French and German administration.

For minor problems, it's customary to ask at a chemist/pharmacy *(eczane)* for advice. Sign language usually suffices to communicate symptoms, and the pharmacist will prescribe treatment on the spot. Drugs requiring a prescription in Western countries are often sold over the counter (except for the most dangerous or addictive ones). Most pharmacies have both male and female staff, so if you need to explain embarrassing problems you can usually find a sympathetic soul of your own gender. See the Language chapter later in this book for a short list of medical terms; for a more comprehensive list get a copy of Lonely Planet's *Turkish phrasebook*.

Though Turkey manufactures many medicines, avoid the risk of running out of a drug taken regularly by bringing your own supply. If your medicine is available in Turkey, it may be less expensive than at home. Make sure you know the generic name of your medicine; the commercial name may not be the same.

Predeparture Preparations

Health Insurance Make sure that you have adequate health insurance.

Medical Kit It is wise to carry a small, straightforward medical kit with analgesics and bandages, but the many pharmacies/chemists in İstanbul have most of what you're likely to need.

Vaccinations You need no special inoculations before entering Turkey unless you're coming from an endemic or epidemic area. However, do discuss your requirements with your doctor. Vaccinations you should consider if you plan to travel off the beaten track in Turkey include hepatitis A and B, and typhoid fever; also make sure that your tetanus/diphtheria and polio vaccinations are up to date (boosters are necessary every 10 years).

A rabies vaccination should be considered for those who plan to stay for a month or longer in Turkey where rabies is common. Rabid dogs were a problem in İstanbul in 2000 but the council now vaccinates dogs (the yellow tag on the ear shows they've been vaccinated) and the worry seems to have been alleviated.

Food & Water

Travellers in Turkey experience a fair amount of travellers' diarrhoea ('the sultan's revenge'), and you may pick up a bout in İstanbul.

Dining Precautions In restaurants serving ready-cooked food (see the Places to Eat chapter), choose dishes that look freshly prepared and sufficiently hot. As for grilled meats, if they look pink, send them back for more cooking (no problem in this).

Beware of milk products and dishes containing milk that have not been properly refrigerated. If you want a rice pudding *(sütlaç)* or some such dish with milk in it, choose a shop that has lots of them in the window, meaning that a batch has been made recently. In general, choose things from trays, pots etc that are fairly full rather than almost empty. Eating some fresh yogurt every day helps to keep your digestive system in good condition.

Drinking Precautions Tap water in İstanbul is chlorinated, but is still not guaranteed to be safe (most locals don't drink it), and bottled spring water tastes better. Spring water is sold everywhere in .33L, 1.5L and 3L plastic bottles.

Alternatives to spring water include naturally fizzy mineral water *(maden suyu)* and artificially carbonated mineral water *(maden sodası* or just *soda)*. Packaged fruit juice *(meyva suyu)*, soft drinks, beer and wine are reliably pure, except in rare cases.

Illnesses

Food Poisoning & Travellers' Diarrhoea Food poisoning symptoms are headaches, nausea and/or stomachache, diarrhoea, fever and chills. If you get food poisoning, go to bed and stay warm. Drink lots of fluids, preferably hot tea without sugar or milk. Chamomile tea *(papatya çay)*, can ease a queasy stomach.

Simple things like a change of water, food or climate can all cause a mild bout of diarrhoea, but a few rushed toilet trips with no other symptoms is not indicative of a major problem.

Dehydration is the main danger with any diarrhoea, particularly in children or the elderly as dehydration can occur quite quickly.

Gut-paralysing drugs such as loperamide or diphenoxylate can be used to bring relief from the symptoms, although they do not actually cure the problem. Only use these drugs if you do not have access to toilets, eg, if you *must* travel. Note that these drugs are not recommended for children under 12 years.

In certain situations antibiotics may be required: Diarrhoea with blood or mucus (dysentery), any diarrhoea with fever, profuse watery diarrhoea, persistent diarrhoea not improving after 48 hours and severe diarrhoea. These suggest a more serious cause of diarrhoea and in these situations gut-paralysing drugs should be avoided. A stool test may be necessary to diagnose what bug is causing your diarrhoea, so you should seek medical help urgently.

Remember *fluid replacement* (at least equal to the volume being lost) is really important. Weak black tea with a little sugar, soda water, or soft drinks allowed to go flat and diluted 50% with clean water are all good. You need to drink at least the same volume of fluid that you are losing in bowel movements and vomiting. Urine is the best guide to the adequacy of replacement – if you have small amounts of concentrated urine, you need to drink more. Keep drinking small amounts often. Stick to a bland diet as you recover.

Sexually Transmitted Infections

HIV/AIDS and hepatitis B can be transmitted through sexual contact. Other STIs include gonorrhoea, herpes and syphilis; sores, blisters or rashes around the genitals and discharges or pain when urinating are common symptoms. In some STIs, such as wart virus or chlamydia, symptoms may be less marked or not observed at all, especially in women. Chlamydia infection can cause infertility in men and women before any symptoms have been noticed. Syphilis symptoms eventually disappear completely but the disease continues and can cause severe problems in later years. While abstinence from sexual contact is the only 100% effective prevention, using condoms is also effective (you can buy condoms in chemists and supermarkets in İstanbul). The treatment of gonorrhoea and syphilis is with antibiotics. The different STIs each require specific antibiotics.

Women's Health

Gynaecological Problems Antibiotic use, synthetic underwear, sweating and contraceptive pills can lead to fungal vaginal infections, especially when travelling in hot climates. Fungal infections are characterised by a rash, itch and discharge and can be treated with a vinegar or lemon-juice douche, or with yogurt. Nystatin, miconazole or clotrimazole pessaries or vaginal cream are the usual treatment. Maintaining good personal hygiene and wearing loose-fitting clothes and cotton underwear may help prevent these infections.

Sexually transmitted diseases are a major cause of vaginal problems. Symptoms include a smelly discharge, painful intercourse and sometimes a burning sensation when urinating. Medical attention should be sought and male sexual partners must also be treated. For more details see the previous paragraph, Sexually Transmitted Infections. Besides abstinence, the best thing is to practise safer sex using condoms.

Medical Care

Contact your country's consulate in İstanbul or embassy in Ankara for advice about suitable doctors, dentists, hospitals and other medical care. You'll need to have payment (preferably cash) ready at all of these services.

Half of all the physicians in İstanbul are women. If a woman visits a male doctor, it's customary to have a companion present during any physical examination or treatment as there is not always a nurse available to serve in this role.

For dentistry, Neşem Güreralp (Diş Doktoru, tooth doctor) has been recommended. Her consultation (Map 16, #56; ☎ 212-244 2574) is at Defterdar Yokuşu Safir Apt 129/2, Cihangir, Beyoğlu. The American Hospital also has a special dental clinic (see the following list).

Don't discount public hospitals, which are busier and not as fancy as private hospitals, but the consultation can be just as good. Although English is not widely spoken, the doctors usually know enough to get by. You could try Taksim İlk Yardım Hastanesi (Emergency Hospital; Map 16, #53; ☎ 212-252 4300) in Sıraselviler Caddesi, Cihangir, Beyoğlu. This hospital has been recommended by some expats living in İstanbul. It's basic but well run.

İstanbul has several private hospitals that provide quality care often at premium prices, though not prohibitively so:

Alman Hastanesi (Map 16, #52; ☎ 212-293 2150) Sıraselviler Caddesi 119, Cihangir, Beyoğlu. This hospital is a few hundred metres south of Taksim Square on the left-hand side. It has a German administration.

American Hospital (Map 11; ☎ 212-311 2000) Güzelbahçe Sokak 20, Nişantaşı. About 2km north-east of Taksim Square, this hospital has a US administration and a dental clinic.

La Paix (Lape) Hastanesi (Map 11; ☎ 212-246 1020) Büyükdere Caddesi 22–24, Şişli. La Paix, about 4km north of Taksim Square, has a French administration.

WOMEN TRAVELLERS

As in most Muslim countries, Western women often attract the sort of attention they (thankfully) never would at home. Most of this attention will be innocent and friendly. Inevitably, however, some of it won't be. Though serious assault is far less common in İstanbul than in London, Paris or New York, harassment such as rude noises and touching are more common – especially in the more conservative sections of the city such as Old İstanbul.

You may often find men have a conversation with your breasts, instead of your face, burst into song as you pass, or throw a pathetic handful of foreign words your way. Much of these embarrassing attempts at seduction are due to cultural misunderstandings bred by European and American films and different cultural norms. In general, keep your dealings with Turkish men formal and polite, not friendly. Avoid casual eye contact. Ignore noises or advances on the street. Avoid walking around on your own at night, especially in Karaköy and the back streets of Beyoğlu. It's also a good idea to sit in the back seat of taxis. If you are approached by a Turkish man in circumstances that upset you, try saying *Ayıp!* (ah-**yuhp**), which means 'Shame on you!'.

Whatever happens, try not to get paranoid and don't let these hassles ruin your trip. Provided you dress modestly and behave appropriately with local attitudes in mind, most men will treat you hospitably, with kindness and respect.

By the way, you'll have no trouble finding tampons, sanitary napkins and condoms in pharmacies and supermarkets in İstanbul.

Aile Salonu

Women are welcomed in all public establishments, but the overwhelmingly male clientele of many places makes some Turkish women uncomfortable. Therefore, many restaurants have rooms set apart for use only by women, couples and mixed groups. Called the *aile salonu* (family room), it is the place for women to go to escape unwanted attention. Look for the sign *Aile Salonumuz Vardır* (We Have a Family Room) in the front windows of cheap and mid-range restaurants. Sitting in the aile salonu is optional, of course. If you'd rather sit in the main dining room, feel free to do so.

Organisations

Pazartesi (☎ 212-292 0739, ⓔ pazartesidergi@superonline.com), at Abdullah Sokak 9, Beyoğlu, is an organisation working towards equal rights for women in Turkey. The Women's Library (see Cultural Centres & Libraries later in this chapter) is another source of information.

GAY & LESBIAN TRAVELLERS

While not strictly illegal, laws prohibiting 'lewd behaviour' are often used to suppress homosexuality in İstanbul. Even so, it exists openly at a small number of gay bars and clubs. At other places be discreet.

The place to start looking for information is on Lambda İstanbul's Web site: Ⓦ www.qrd.org/qrd/www/world/europe/turkey.

Lambda is a Gay, Lesbian, Bisexual and Transgender liberation group that's been around since 1993. It organises weekly meetings, monthly parties and has its sights firmly set upon seeing a homophobia-free Turkey. You can contact Lambda (☎ 212-233 4966, fax 224 3792, e lambda@lambdaistanbul.org) by post at PK 162, 80050 Beyoğlu. Other organisations such as Kaos GL, which produces a magazine, and Saphonun Kızları, for lesbians, provide services and Web sites – but just in Turkish.

For entertainment options see Lambda's Web site and also Gay & Lesbian Venues in the Entertainment chapter.

DISABLED TRAVELLERS

İstanbul has severely limited accessibility for disabled travellers. Roads are potholed, pavements are crooked and cracked – if they exist at all! Though local people will go out of their way to help a disabled traveller get around, you will have trouble getting around unaided.

Airlines and some top hotels have meagre provisions for wheelchair access. Ramps are beginning to appear (ever so slowly) in a few buildings and streets though most are dangerously steep and narrow. Some tourist sights have adequate wheelchair access (Topkapı Palace, Aya Sofya) but you will have a problem visiting many of the palaces (lots of stairs and no ramps). Public toilets throughout the city aren't wheelchair friendly.

For good information on accessible travel, contact the Royal Association for Disability & Rehabilitation (Radar; ☎ 020-7250 3222, fax 7250 0212, w www.radar.org.uk), 12 City Forum, 250 City Rd, London EC1V 8AF, UK.

The Turkish tourist offices in your home country (see Tourist Offices Abroad earlier in this chapter) have some information to help with planning. Access-Able is a Web site (w www.access-able.com) with a small list of tour operators and transport servers specialising in disabled travel to İstanbul.

SENIOR TRAVELLERS

Seniors (*altın yaş,* golden age) are welcomed and age is respected in Turkey. Seniors sometimes receive discounts at hotels, especially if you sweet-talk the receptionist. Upon presentation of a passport, seniors may be granted reduced-price admission to some museums and historical sites. If you have a seniors' card, bring it.

İSTANBUL FOR CHILDREN

For loads of practical advice on hassle-free family travel (an oxymoron?), Lonely Planet's *Travel with Children* is a valuable resource.

Your child *(çocuk)* or children *(çocuklar)* will be showered with kisses in İstanbul and, given the high Turkish birth rate, they'll have lots of company. The larger hotels can arrange for daycare *(kreş)* and baby-sitting services.

The market for childhood products and services is not as elaborately developed in Turkey as in Europe or America, but Turks are handy at improvising anything that may be needed for a child's safety, health or enjoyment.

Disposable nappies, or baby diapers *(bebek bezi),* are readily available for infants *(bebek).* The best brand is Ultra Prima, sold in pharmacies/chemists and supermarkets according to the baby's weight in kilograms. A packet of 24 costs about US$6. Ultra-pasteurised milk is sold everywhere. Some baby foods in individual jars may also be found, but it's usually better to rely on the willingness and ingenuity of hotel and restaurant staff to make up special dishes for small children. If you have an infant, you might also want to carry a small portable food mill to puree vegetables, fruits and meats.

Child safety seats are available from all large and many small car rental companies at an extra daily charge. It's best to request a child seat in advance when you reserve your car.

For information on things to do with the children see the Entertainment chapter.

CULTURAL CENTRES & LIBRARIES

İstanbul has numerous cultural centres and libraries catering largely to the expatriate population.

American Library (Map 16, #118; ☎ 212-251 2675) Meşrutiyet Caddesi 108, Tepebaşı. Next to the US consulate, the library is only open by appointment between 10am and 3.30pm Monday to Friday.

British Council (Map 12; ☎ 212-327 2716, fax 327 2717, Ⓦ www.britishcouncil.org.tr) Barbaros Bulvarı, Akdoğan Sokak 43, Beşiktaş. The council has a library that is open 10.30am to 7.30pm Tuesday and Wednesday, 10.30am to 5pm Thursday to Saturday.

Goethe Institut (Map 16, #90; ☎ 212-249 2009, fax 252 5214, Ⓦ www.goethe.de/istanbul) Yeni Çarşı Caddesi 52, Beyoğlu. Near Galatasaray Square, the institute has regular theatre, films and concerts.

Institut Français d'Istanbul (Map 16, #24; ☎ 212-244 4495, fax 249 4895, ⓔ institut@infist.org) İstiklal Caddesi 8. Near Taksim Square, the institute has a library (closed Sunday and Tuesday), theatre, regular films and music performances.

İstanbul Library (Map 13, #54; ☎ 212-512 5730) Soğukçeşme Sokak. The library is small and quiet with a surprising number of books available in foreign languages about the architecture, history and arts of the city. You can't borrow, but you can sit, read and photocopy. It's open 10am to noon and 1.30pm to 4.30pm Monday and Friday only.

Women's Library (Kadın Eserleri Kütüphanesi ve Bilgi Merkezi Vakfı; Map 18; ☎ 212-534 9550). Just south-east of Church of St Stephen of the Bulgars (the cast-iron church) on the south-west side of the Golden Horn, the library is open 9.30am to 6pm Monday to Friday. Housed in a historic building, the library acts as a women's resource centre, with a program of cultural and special events aimed at women. If you call ahead they'll organise an English-speaking volunteer to help you out.

UNIVERSITIES

İstanbul is quite popular with foreigners on university exchanges or here for summer programs.

Bilgi Üniversitesi (Map 12; ☎ 212-293 5010, Ⓦ www.bilgi.edu.tr) İnönü Caddesi 28, Kuştepe, Şişli. This university teaches in English and has a summer school.

Boğaziçi Üniversitesi (Bosphorus University; ☎ 212-358 1500, fax 265 6357, Ⓦ www.boun.edu.tr) This university is out near Bebek along the Bosphorus. The courses are held in English and there's also a summer school program running for seven weeks.

DANGERS & ANNOYANCES

İstanbul is quite a safe city compared with others of its size. If you live in a large European or US city, you may feel safer here than at home. However, due to its position over the North Anatolian Fault, there is a risk of earthquakes. See Geology in Facts about İstanbul for information.

Police

Blue-clad officers are part of a national force designated by the words *polis* or *emniyet* (security). Under normal circumstances you will have little to do with them. If you do encounter them, they will judge you partly by your personal appearance. If you look tidy and 'proper', they'll be on your side. If you're dressed carelessly, they may not be as helpful.

Other blue-clad officers with peaked caps are market inspectors *(belediye zabıtası)*. You won't have much to do with them.

Theft & Robbery

Theft is not generally a big problem, and robbery (mugging) is comparatively rare, but don't let İstanbul's relative safety lull you. Take normal precautions.

Keep close track of your wallet (don't ever put it in your back pocket), handbag or other valuables at all times but especially on crowded buses, trains and in markets. Don't leave valuables in your hotel room, or at least not in view, and don't walk in unknown parts of town when nobody else is around, especially at night. There are isolated reports of bags or bag straps being quietly slashed in the Kapalı Çarşı, and of distract-bump-and-grab thefts. You should wear a discreet moneybelt around your waist with a stash of cash in case something does happen.

See the Entertainment chapter for information on a common nightclub rip-off.

Lese-Majesty

There are laws against insulting, defaming or making light of Atatürk, the Turkish flag, the Turkish people or the Turkish Republic. Any difficulty will probably arise from misunderstanding. At the first sign that you've

Warning!

There have been cases of theft via drugging in İstanbul. The cases vary, but usually a traveller (usually a man on his own) is approached by two or three people who offer a drink or meal. Often one of the thieves is a woman, and they may claim to be Moroccan or from some other country. The drinks or snacks contain drugs that cause the victims to lose consciousness quickly. When the victim awakes hours later, they have been stripped of everything they own, and in some cases they have also been beaten up. This scheme can be difficult to defeat as Turks are generally very hospitable, and it is a Turkish custom to offer visitors drinks. Here are some things you can do to protect yourself:

- If you are a single male traveller, be suspicious of pairs or trios of other males (usually aged 18 to 28 years) who befriend you, whether Turkish or foreign. Be especially suspicious if they ask you where you are going, then travel with you.
- If you are at all suspicious of new-found friends, eat and drink only from your own supplies or those brought fresh in sealed containers from the hand of a waiter or shopkeeper. (It's possible to inject drugs into a sealed container using a syringe through the seal.) The Turkish friends may offer to pay for drinks to satisfy the requirements of traditional hospitality. They needn't deliver the drinks themselves.

inadvertently been guilty of lese-majesty, be sure to make your apologies, which should be readily accepted.

The Imperial Auto

As a pedestrian, give way to cars and trucks in all situations, even if you have to jump out of the way. The sovereignty of the pedestrian is recognised in law, but not out on the street. If a car hits you, the driver (if not the law courts) will blame *you,* a pedestrian, merely an annoyance composed of so much worthless protoplasm. This does not apply, however, on a recognised crossing controlled by a traffic officer or a traffic signal, where if you've got a 'walk' light, you have the right of way. Watch out, all the same. A dispute with a driver will get you nowhere.

Traffic Accidents

It's worth mentioning that Turkey has one of the world's highest motor-vehicle accident rates. Drive very defensively. A massive safety campaign is under way, but its full effects will not be felt for some years.

Racial Discrimination

The Ottoman Empire was not a colonial power, and so the country's ethnic diversity is not of a wide scope. Turkey's racial mix is mostly among sub-groups of the Caucasian group, with admixtures (sometimes ancient) of Asian races.

Although blacks sent as slaves from Africa sometimes rose through the imperial palace hierarchy to positions of very great importance in the government, most who did so were eunuchs, and thus they left no legacy of prominent families.

With a relatively homogeneous population and no great history of foreign travel or colonisation, most Turks have little or no experience in dealing with people of other races. Racial prejudice and discrimination root easily in such soil.

If you are of Asian ancestry, Turks will probably assume that you are a Japanese tourist even if you carry an American or Australian passport; you may have an amusing time convincing them that you are a 'real' American or Aussie.

If you are of African ancestry, you should anticipate some hassles. The least of it will be people staring at you on the street, simply because they have seen few black people and are curious. The worst of it may be finding that hotels with plenty of vacant rooms are mysteriously and suddenly 'full' when you request lodging. This may happen more frequently in the cheapest places, less frequently or hardly at all in the more expensive places. There is no organised or institutionalised racism, so any instances of it will depend on the actual persons involved. The best plan is usually to withhold your patronage from such people and to find a more fair and open-minded establishment to patronise.

Cigarette Smoke

If you're offended by cigarette smoke, you will have some unpleasant moments in İstanbul. Though the local cancer prevention society fields a brave effort to stop smoking, Turkey is the land of aromatic Turkish tobacco, and smoking is well and truly a national passion. Smoking is – supposedly – not permitted on city buses, intercity buses, aeroplanes, in museums and mosques, and in similar public spaces.

Noise

İstanbul is an intense, crowded, noisy city. In the 'good old days' it must have been beautiful to hear the clear voices of the müezzins calling from a hundred minarets, even before dawn, when the first of the five daily calls is given. Now the call comes through microphones – you'll get used to it, but it may take a while. When considering a hotel room, ask *'Sakin mi?'* 'Is it quiet here?' – if there's a minaret right outside your hotel window, you'll know it.

Air Pollution

In summer there is pollution from cars, but it's no worse than in other big cities. In winter the air is dirtier, but far better than it used to be in the days before clean Russian natural gas replaced lignite (soft brown coal) as the heating fuel of choice. The heating season lasts from 15 October to 1 April.

EMERGENCIES

If you have a personal crisis, the multilingual blue line (☎ 212-638 2626) should be able to give advice. Pharmacies (eczane) are plentiful, but are only open from about 8am to 6pm daily. The address for the tourism police (Map 13, #44) is Yerebatan Caddesi 6, Sultanahmet. For dentist and hospital contact details, see Medical Care under Health earlier in this chapter.

Ambulance	☎ 112
Fire	☎ 110
Tourism police	☎ 212-527 4503

LEGAL MATTERS

Foreign travellers are subject to Turkish law. If arrested, telephone your embassy, though they won't be very helpful in emergencies if the trouble you're in is remotely your own fault. Steer well clear of dealing, using and possessing illegal drugs in Turkey. Antiquity smuggling is also illegal.

BUSINESS HOURS

Some small one-person shops in traditional markets may close for 20 minutes or so at prayer time so the owner can worship. Otherwise, İstanbul's opening hours are:

Banks From 8.30am to noon and 1.30pm to 5pm, Monday to Friday.
Grocery shops From 6am or 7am to 7pm or 8pm daily.
Offices Government and business offices may open at 8am or 9am, close for lunch, and reopen around 1.30pm, remaining open until 5pm Monday to Friday. However, during the holy month of Ramazan (see Religious Holidays) the work day is shortened.
Shops From 9am to 6pm or 7pm Monday to Saturday; some shops close for lunch (noon to 1.30pm or 2.30pm).

PUBLIC HOLIDAYS & SPECIAL EVENTS

The official Turkish calendar is the Gregorian (Western) one. Friday is the Muslim holy day, but it is not a holiday. The day of rest, a secular one, is Sunday.

Religious Holidays

Religious festivals, two of which (Şeker Bayramı and Kurban Bayramı) are public holidays, are celebrated according to the Muslim lunar Hejira calendar. As the lunar year is about 11 days shorter than the Gregorian one, Muslim festivals occur 11 days earlier each year.

Muslim days, like Jewish ones, begin at sundown. Thus a Friday holiday will begin on Thursday at sunset and last until Friday at sunset.

For major religious and civic holidays there is also a half-day vacation for preparation, called *arife,* preceding the start of a festival; shops and offices close about noon, and the festival begins at sunset.

Ramazan During the Holy Month, called Ramadan in other Muslim countries, a good Muslim lets *nothing* pass the lips during daylight hours: no eating, drinking, smoking, or even licking a postage stamp.

The fast is broken traditionally with flat *pide* (bread). Lavish dinners are given and may last far into the night. Before dawn, drummers circulate throughout the town to awaken the faithful so they can eat before sunrise occurs.

Although many İstanbullus observe the fast, most restaurants and cafes are open as usual to serve non-Muslims and locals who are not observing the fast. It's polite to avoid ostentatious public smoking, eating, drinking and drunkenness during Ramazan.

The 27th day of Ramazan is Kadir Gecesi (Night of Power) when the Quran was revealed and Mohammed was appointed to be the Messenger of God.

Şeker Bayramı Called Eid es-Seghir in Arabic countries, this is a three-day festival at the end of Ramazan. *Şeker* (shek-**ehr**) is sugar or candy. During this festival children traditionally go door to door asking for sweet treats, Muslims exchange greeting cards and pay social calls, and everybody enjoys drinking lots of tea in broad daylight after fasting for Ramazan. The festival is a national holiday when banks and offices are closed, and hotels, buses, trains and aeroplanes are heavily booked.

Kurban Bayramı Called Eid al-Adha in Arabic countries, this is the most important religious holiday of the year. Meaning Sacrifice Holiday, it is a four-day festival commemorating Abraham's near-sacrifice of his son on Mt Moriah (Genesis 22; Quran, Sura 37). Right after the early morning prayers on the actual day of Bayram, the head of the household sacrifices a sheep. A feast is prepared, with much of the meat going to charity. Almost everything closes, including banks. Transport may be packed.

Annual Holidays & Special Events

January

New Year's Day 1 January.

March

International İstanbul Dance Festival A few days in early March. Ballet and modern dance are the features (see Festivals under Ballet & Opera in the Entertainment chapter).

April

National Sovereignty & Children's Day 23 April. This holiday commemorates the day the first republican parliament met in Ankara in 1920. It's also Children's Day, and a parade is often held along İstiklal Caddesi, Beyoğlu.

International İstanbul Film Festival Last two weeks of April. This excellent arthouse film festival showcases local films, plus has some international flicks (see Festivals under Cinema in the Entertainment chapter).

Anzac Day 25 April. It's not a public holiday, but a day when mostly Australians and New Zealanders gather at Gallipoli, the site of the Anzac landing on this day in 1915 (see Gallipoli in the Excursions chapter).

May

International İstanbul Puppet Festival Beginning of May. This eight-day festival highlights Turkish Karagöz plus international puppetry (see Festivals under Shadow Puppet Theatre in the Entertainment chapter).

Youth & Sports Day 19 May. A holiday commemorating Atatürk's birthday.

Conquest of Constantinople 29 May. On this day in 1453 Constantinople was captured by Mehmet the Conqueror. It's not a public holiday, but there are festivities and celebrations throughout the city.

Major Islamic Holidays

Hejira Year	New Year	Prophet's Birthday	Ramazan Begins	Şeker Bayramı	Kurban Bayramı
1423	15.03.02	25.05.02	10.11.02	5.12.02	12.02.03
1424	04.03.03	14.05.03	30.10.03	24.11.03	31.01.04
1425	22.02.04	03.05.04	19.10.04	13.11.04	20.01.05

June/July

Kırkpınar Oil Wrestling Festival Middle of June to early July. Hundreds of leather-clad hulks gather in Edirne, 2½ hours west of İstanbul, and battle it out during the week-long festival (see Edirne in the Excursions chapter).

International İstanbul Music Festival Early June to early July. This top-class festival has classic music, ballet and theatre (see Festivals under Classical Music in the Entertainment chapter).

July

International İstanbul Jazz Festival Two weeks from the beginning of July. This festival is a weird hybrid of conventional jazz, electronica, drum'n'bass, world music and rock (see Festivals under Jazz in the Entertainment chapter).

August

Victory Day 30 August. This national holiday commemorates the victory over invading Greek armies at Dumlupınar in 1922 during the War of Independence.

September/October

International İstanbul Biennial The biennial runs for about six weeks starting in mid-September (every two years). International and local artists explore themes contextualised in this city (see Fesitvals under Art Galleries in the Entertainment chapter).

Republic Day 29 October. This holiday celebrates the proclamation of the republic by Atatürk in 1923.

Akbank Jazz Festival Ten-day event in October. This festival attracts local musicians (see Festivals under Jazz in the Entertainment chapter).

November

Atatürk's Death 10 November. Not a holiday, but special ceremonies are held and a moment of silence is undertaken at the time of his death (9.05am, 1938).

Tüyap Book Fair 3–11 November. Tüyap holds many different kinds of fairs throughout the year, but this is one of its biggest. It's at the Tüyap İstanbul Exhibition Palace, Tepebaşı, near Pera Palas. (Check out W www.tuyapfair.com for details.)

DOING BUSINESS

Despite the many public-sector holdovers from the 1930s to the 1970s, Turkey has a vibrant private-sector business community and newly prominent stock market.

Turkish offices have a gloss of Western-style business manners and practices, but doing business here can be different from what you may be used to in Western Europe or North America. Most risks are greater, but as a rapidly developing country, the rewards may be greater as well. Government, traditionally a capricious and stubborn obstacle to business development, has been actively more cooperative with business endeavours since the late president Turgut Özal introduced reforms and innovations.

Even so, government cooperation cannot be assumed until the project is completed and actively operating. In part, this is because of frequent changes in the endless succession of fairly weak ruling coalitions, and the subsequent uncertainty among the ministries regulating business and financial activity. An astute Turkish business partner is usually essential; finding a suitably ethical one is important.

Getting Started

The first person to contact is the commercial attache at the nearest Turkish embassy or consulate. The attache can put you in touch with local trade and business groups in your home country, and can suggest useful government contacts in Turkey.

The *Executive's Handbook Turkey Almanac* is a useful book published yearly in İstanbul. It has a collection of articles about the economy, markets and policies for the previous year, and other general information about Turkey's business world. You can buy it at bookstores in İstanbul or contact the publishers Intermedia (☎ 212-279 6402, fax 264 5209, e info@intermedia.com.tr). A similar book is the quarterly *Doing Business in Turkey,* which details regulations and the climate of the Turkish business world. Order it online at the publisher's Web site W www.ibsresearch.com – which also has heaps of useful information – or try ☎ 212-252 2460, fax 252 2430.

The monthly *Turkish Business World* is available in bookstores and newspaper stands around the city. It has a collection of articles and ads though its professionalism is somewhat dented by the many irrelevant photographs of attractive women! Check out W www.turkishbusinessworld.com.

DEİK (Dış Ekonomik İlişkiler Kurulu; ☎ 212-243 4180, fax 243 4184, e info@deik.org, w www.deik.org.tr), at İstiklal Caddesi 286/9, Odakule İş Merkezi, Beyoğlu, is the Foreign Economic Relations Board. Its Web site has many useful links, as well as economic and business information.

In North America, the American Turkish Council (☎ 202-783 0483, fax 783 0511, e atctr@aol.com, w www.americanturkishcouncil.org), 915 15th St NW, Suite 700, Washington, DC 20005, will help you to set up business contacts. ATC hosts the major annual conference of government, business, cultural and military leaders early each year in Washington, DC.

For guidance in personal interaction with Turks, you may wish to read *Turkish Culture for Americans* by Hasan Dindi, Maija Gazur, Wayne M Gazur & Ayşen Kırkköprü-Dindi.

WORK

Many come for a short holiday only to wind up working in İstanbul. Most teach English at one of the many private colleges or schools, though others pick up nannying, or journalist work at the *Turkish Daily News*, for example. There are other work opportunities, but they'll be harder to sniff out.

Looking for Jobs

If you want to get a job at one of the well-paid private schools you'll need to have a Teaching English as a Foreign Language (TEFL) certificate, or an equivalent, and a graduate degree (it doesn't matter what it's in). These schools can pay between US$1000 to US$2000 per month for full-time work. Native English speakers with a TEFL (or equivalent) but no graduate degree can find jobs paying around US$750 to US$1000 per month. You'll have more difficulty finding a job if English isn't your native language; your best bet is to contact your embassy/consulate in İstanbul or Ankara for advice.

The library at the British Council (see Cultural Centres & Libraries earlier in this chapter) has a list of English-language teaching institutions in İstanbul. Check the *Turkish Daily News* for advertisements about other employment possibilities.

This list of schools is a starter; you'll probably need to shop around to find a school you're happy with.

Berlitz (Map 16, #84; ☎ 212-293 7400, fax 293 7699) Tütüncü Çıkmazı 1/1, Beyoğlu
English Fast (☎ 212-542 5627, fax 516 3231) Zuhuratbaba Caddesi 41, Bakırköy
Gök Dil (☎ 212-274 9366) Musryi Sokak 1, Mecidiyeköy

Accommodation

For information about long-term accommodation, check out Apartments & Long-Term Rentals in the Places to Stay chapter.

Work Visas

If you get a teaching job at one of the large private schools it will often organise a work visa. The smaller schools usually won't organise the visa for you (see Work Visas under Documents earlier in this chapter).

Getting There & Away

AIR

İstanbul's Atatürk Airport is Turkey's largest and busiest. See the Getting Around chapter for details on the airport, and ground transportation to and from it.

Departure Tax

Turkey's airport departure tax of approximately US$12 is usually included in the price of your air ticket.

Other Parts of Turkey

Türk Hava Yolları (THY; Turkish Airlines; airline code: TK) is Turkey's national carrier, though a few smaller airlines have started to compete. THY hubs are İstanbul and Ankara, and it services most cities and larger towns. Check details at Ⓦ www.thy.com.tr.

The USA

Discount travel agents in the USA are known as consolidators (although you won't see a sign on the door saying Consolidator). San Francisco is the ticket consolidator capital of America, although some good deals can be found in Los Angeles, New York and other big cities.

Council Travel (☎ 800-226 8624, Ⓦ www.counciltravel.com), America's largest student travel organisation, has around 60 offices in the USA. Call it for the office nearest you. STA Travel (☎ 800-781 4040, Ⓦ www.statravel.com) has offices in Boston, Chicago, Miami, New York, Philadelphia, San Francisco and other major cities. Phone for office locations.

Ticket Planet (Ⓦ www.ticketplanet.com) is a leading ticket consolidator in the USA and is recommended.

Turkish Airlines operates daily nonstop flights on the New York–İstanbul route in summer, and a service from Chicago (nonstop five days per week). Delta Air Lines also flies nonstop daily. The major European airlines offer one-stop service.

Turkish Airlines coach-class New York–İstanbul excursion fares sometimes dip below US$600 in the wintertime, and even Los Angeles–İstanbul fares can get as low as US$700 or so; November and early January are particularly cheap times to travel. Summer excursion fares are more like US$1000 to US$1200.

Warning

The information in this chapter is particularly vulnerable to change: Prices for international travel are volatile, routes are introduced and cancelled, schedules change, special deals come and go, and rules and visa requirements are amended. Airlines and governments seem to take a perverse pleasure in making price structures and regulations as complicated as possible. You should check directly with the airline or a travel agent to make sure you understand how a fare (and ticket you may buy) works. In addition, the travel industry is highly competitive and there are many lurks and perks.

The upshot of this is that you should get opinions, quotes and advice from as many airlines and travel agents as possible before you part with your hard-earned cash. The details given in this chapter should be regarded as pointers and are not a substitute for your own careful, up-to-date research.

Canada

Canadian discount air ticket sellers are also known as consolidators and their air fares tend to be about 10% higher than those sold in the USA. Travel Cuts (☎ 866-246 9762, Ⓦ www.travelcuts.com) is Canada's national student travel agency and has offices in all major cities.

Flying from Toronto to İstanbul starts at C$2300 for fixed-date return (excursion) fares during the high season, and can be as low as C$1200 in the low season.

The UK

Discount air travel is big business in London. Advertisements for many travel agencies appear in the travel pages of the weekend newspapers, *Time Out,* the *Evening Standard* and in the free magazine *TNT*.

For students or travellers under 26 years, popular travel agencies include STA Travel (☎ 0870-160 0599; northern call centre ☎ 0161-830 4713, W www.statravel.co.uk), which has offices across the country; and Usit Campus (☎ 0870-240 1010, W www.usitcampus.co.uk), which also has branches throughout the UK.

Turkish Airlines' summer one-way fare from London to İstanbul is £300 and up, but there are fixed-date return (excursion) fares for as low as £270. British Airways and Turkish Airlines fly the route daily nonstop.

Continental Europe

Turkish Airlines flies to many points in Europe, but don't neglect the European charter lines. (Turkish charter lines tend not to stay in business for long.) Note: Prices in former European currencies were calculated on November 2001 exchange rates.

Germany Recommended agencies include STA Travel and Usit Campus. STA Travel (☎ 030-311 0950), Goethesttrasse 73, 10625 Berlin also has branches in major cities across the country. Usit Campus (call centre ☎ 01805-788336, Cologne ☎ 0221-923990, W www.usitcampus.de) has several offices in Germany, including one at 2a Zuelpicher Strasse, 50674 Cologne.

Turkish Airlines' fixed-date return (excursion) high-season fare from Frankfurt to İstanbul starts at €357.

France Recommended travel agencies include OTU Voyages (☎ 01 40 29 12 12, W www.otu.fr), which has an office at 39 ave Georges-Bernanos, 75005 Paris, plus branches across the country; and Nouvelles Frontières (nationwide number ☎ 08 25 00 08 25; Paris ☎ 01 45 68 70 00, W www.nouvelles-frontieres.fr), which has an office at 87 blvd de Grenelle, 75015 Paris, plus branches across the country.

Fixed-date return (excursion) high-season tickets from Paris to İstanbul start at €350 with Turkish Airlines.

Spain Recommended agencies include Usit Unlimited (☎ 91-225 25 75, W www.usitunlimited.es) with an office at 3 Plaza de Callao, 28013 Madrid, and branches in major cities; and Nouvelles Frontières (☎ 91-547 42 00, W www.nouvelles-frontieres.es), which has an office at Plaza de España 18, 28008 Madrid, plus branches in major cities.

Expect to pay around €379 for a Turkish Airline return (excursion) high-season fare from Madrid to İstanbul.

Greece Olympic Airlines and Turkish Airlines share the Athens-İstanbul route. Turkish Airlines offers daily flights in summer; prices for the 70-minute flight from Athens start at €220 one way, or €229 for a round-trip excursion (fixed-date) ticket.

Italy Recommended travel agencies include CTS Viaggi (☎ 06-462 0431), 16 Via Genova, Rome, a student and youth specialist with branches in major cities; and Passagi (☎ 06-474 0923), Stazione Termini FS, Galleria Di Tesla, Rome.

Turkish Airlines return (excursion) high-season fares from Rome to İstanbul should start at €309.

Australia

For flights to Europe from Australia, there are a lot of competing airlines and a wide variety of air fares. Think about a round-the-world (RTW) ticket if you plan more travel after İstanbul.

Quite a few travel offices specialise in discount air tickets. Some travel agencies, particularly smaller ones, advertise cheap air fares in the travel sections of weekend newspapers.

Two well-known agents for cheap fares are STA Travel and Flight Centre. STA Travel (☎ 03-9349 2411, W www.statravel.com.au) has its main office at 224 Faraday St, Carlton, in Melbourne, with offices in all major cities and on many university campuses. Call ☎ 131 776 Australia-wide for the location of your nearest branch. Flight Centre (☎ 131 600 Australia-wide, W www.flightcentre.com.au) has a central office at

82 Elizabeth St, Sydney, and there are dozens of offices throughout Australia.

Flights from Australia to İstanbul by Malaysian Airlines or Singapore Airlines cost about A$1800 in the low season or A$2500 in the peak season for round-trip fares. Cheaper are Emirates, Gulf Air and EgyptAir with round-trip fares costing about A$1600 in the low season or A$2150 in the high season. There are also connecting flights via Athens, London, Rome, Amsterdam or Singapore on Thai International, British Airways, Olympic, Alitalia, KLM, Turkish Airlines and Qantas.

All these airlines regularly have specials (usually during the European low season of mid-January to the end of February and the start of October to mid-November) with most offering fares for A$1400 or less. Usually these specials must be booked and paid for reasonably quickly.

If you can get a cheap fare to London, you might do well once you're there to look for a cheap flight to Turkey.

New Zealand

RTW tickets for travel from New Zealand could be the best value, especially if you are planning onward travel from İstanbul. Flight Centre (☎ 09-309 6171, Ⓦ www.flightcentre.co.nz) has a large central office in Auckland at National Bank Towers, 205–225 Queen St and many branches throughout the country. STA Travel (☎ 09-309 0458, Ⓦ www.statravel.co.nz) has its main office at 10 High St, Auckland, and has other offices around the country.

Turkish Airlines has open-return fares between Auckland and İstanbul starting at NZ$3800 in the high season; from NZ$2100 for a one-way flight.

Azerbaijan & Georgia

Turkish Airlines runs flights from İstanbul nonstop to Baku (five per week) from US$479 for a round-trip excursion, and nonstop to Tblisi (three per week).

Middle East

Usually the best travel deal you will manage in the Middle East is an airline's official excursion fare. Some travel agencies will knock down the price by up to 10% if you're persistent, but they may then tie you into fixed dates or flying with a less popular airline.

Details of the most popular services to İstanbul from various Middle Eastern countries follow.

Cyprus (Turkish Side) Turkish Airlines operates one-stop flights connecting Cyprus' Ercan airport (ECN) in Nicosia (Lefkoşa in Turkish) and İstanbul daily from US$200 for a round-trip excursion.

Egypt The area around Midan Tahrir in Cairo is teeming with travel agencies, but don't expect any amazing deals.

EgyptAir and Turkish Airlines have at least one flight per day between them, charging from E£1300 to E£1575 one way. Cairo to İstanbul flights start at E£1425 for a round-trip excursion ticket on the nonstop, two-hour flight.

Israel In Tel Aviv, the Israel Student Travel Association (ISSTA; ☎ 03-524 6322, 725 1800, Ⓦ www.issta.co.il) is at 128 Ben Yehuda St. In Jerusalem (☎ 02-625 2799) it is situated at 31 HaNevi'im St.

El-Al and Turkish Airlines have six nonstop flights per week from Tel Aviv to İstanbul from US$330 for a round-trip excursion.

Jordan Turkish Airlines and Royal Jordanian share the traffic, with about three flights per week. The nonstop 2½-hour flight from Amman costs around JD220 one way. A round-trip high-season excursion ticket costs about JD215.

Syria Syrian Arab Airlines and Turkish Airlines make the 2½-hour flight from Damascus to İstanbul two days per week and charge from S£12,300 one way, or S£13,400 for a round-trip excursion.

Asia

Most Asian countries offer fairly competitive air fare deals with Bangkok, Singapore and Hong Kong the best places to shop around for discount tickets. Hong Kong's travel market can be unpredictable, but some excellent bargains are available if you are lucky.

In Singapore, STA Travel (☎ 65-737 7188, W www.statravel.com.sg) has its head office at 35a Cuppage Road, Cuppage Terrace. STA offers competitive fares for Asian destinations and beyond. Singapore, like Bangkok, has hundreds of travel agencies, so you can compare prices on flights. Chinatown Point shopping centre on New Bridge Rd has a good selection of travel agencies.

Hong Kong has a number of reliable travel agencies and some not-so-reliable ones. A good way to check on a travel agency is to look it up in the phone book: Fly-by-night operators don't usually stay around long enough to get listed. Phoenix Services (☎ 2722 7378, fax 2369 8884), Room B, 7th floor, Milton Mansion, 96 Nathan Rd, Tsimshatsui, is recommended.

Flights on Turkish Airlines from Tokyo to İstanbul should start at US$1080 for a round-trip excursion ticket.

Airline Offices

Most of İstanbul's offices are on Cumhuriyet Caddesi between Taksim Square and Harbiye, in the Elmadağ district, but Turkish Airlines has offices around the city. Travel agencies can also sell tickets and make reservations. Some addresses follow:

Aeroflot (Map 17, #66; ☎ 212-243 4725, fax 252 3998) Mete Caddesi 30, Taksim

Air France (Map 17, #59; ☎ 212-254 4356, fax 254 7614) Cumhuriyet Caddesi 1, Taksim; (☎ 212-663 0600) Atatürk Airport

Alitalia (☎ 212-231 3391, fax 231 5586) Valikonağı Caddesi 73, Nişantaşı; (☎ 212-663 0577) Atatürk Airport

American Airlines (Map 17, #33; ☎ 212-219 8223, fax 219 8227) Cumhuriyet Caddesi 6, Elmadağ

British Airways (Map 17, #30; ☎ 212-234 1300, fax 234 1308) Cumhuriyet Caddesi 10, Elmadağ; (☎ 212-663 0574) Atatürk Airport

Delta Air Lines (Map 17, #23; ☎ 212-233 3820, fax 231 2346) Hilton arcade, Cumhuriyet Caddesi, Elmadağ; (☎ 212-663 0752) Atatürk Airport

El-Al Israel Airlines (☎ 212-246 5303, fax 230 3705) Rumeli Caddesi 4/1, Nişantaşı; (☎ 212-663 0810) Atatürk Airport

Iberia (☎ 212-237 3105, fax 250 5478) Topçu Caddesi 2/2, Elmadağ; (☎ 212-663 0826) Atatürk Airport

Japan Airlines (Map 17, #28; ☎ 212-233 0841, fax 234 2209) Cumhuriyet Caddesi 107/2, Elmadağ

KLM–Royal Dutch Airlines (☎ 212-230 0311, fax 232 8749) Valikonağı Caddesi 73/7, Nişantaşı; (☎ 212-663 0604) Atatürk Airport

Lufthansa Airlines (☎ 212-315 3434, fax 275 6961) Maya Akar Centre, B Blok floor 3, Büyükdere Caddesi 100–102, Esentepe; (☎ 212-663 0594) Atatürk Airport

Malev–Hungarian Airlines (☎ 212-241 0909, fax 230 2034) Cumhuriyet Caddesi 141, Elmadağ; (☎ 212-465 4344) Atatürk Airport

Olympic Airways (☎ 212-246 5081, fax 232 2173) Cumhuriyet Caddesi 171/A, Harbiye; (☎ 212-663 0820) Atatürk Airport

Qantas Airways (Map 17, #33; ☎ 212-219 8223, fax 219 8227) Cumhuriyet Caddesi 6, Elmadağ

Sabena (Map 17, #33; ☎ 212-231 2844, fax 246 4646) Cumhuriyet Caddesi 6, Elmadağ; (☎ 212-663 6676) Atatürk Airport

Singapore Airlines (☎ 212-232 3706, fax 248 8620) Halaskargazi Caddesi 113, Harbiye; (☎ 212-663 0710) Atatürk Airport

Turkish Airlines (reservations ☎ 212-663 6363, fax 240 2984, W www.thy.com.tr); (Map 17, #57; ☎ 212-249 4446) Cumhuriyet Caddesi, Taksim Gezi Dükkanları 7, Taksim

BUS

Other Parts of Turkey

The bus and the *dolmuş* (minibus) are the most widespread and popular means of transport in Turkey. Buses go literally everywhere, all the time. Virtually every first-time traveller in Turkey comments on the convenience of the bus system.

The bus service runs the gamut from plain and inexpensive to comfortable and moderately priced. It is so cheap and convenient that many erstwhile long-distance hitchers opt for the bus. The cost of bus travel in Turkey usually works out to be around US$2.75 to US$4.50 per 100km.

Fares & Travel Times The following chart shows some examples of bus fares and travel times to/from İstanbul. Fares vary

ALL PHOTOS BY GREG ELMS

Freshly prepared food is one of İstanbul's major delights and you will find many tempting morsels, including grilled meat (top left), corn on the cob (top right), spices and nuts (middle left), *simits* (sesame rolls; middle right), delicious sweets (bottom right) and lots of tea (bottom left).

GREG ELMS

GREG ELMS

IZZET KERIBAR

İstanbul has a picturesque location on the Bosphorus, as seen here from the minaret of Rüstem Paşa Camii (bottom). The Bosphorus also supplies a large part of the İstanbullu diet (top right). Try a fish sandwich direct from the boats that are often berthed at the ferry terminal in Eminönü (top left).

Buses to/from İstanbul

destination	distance (km)	duration (hrs)	price (US$)
Alanya	840	13	14–20
Ankara	450	6	11–24
Antakya	1115	20	23–31
Antalya	725	12	13–20
Artvin	1352	24	34–40
Ayvalık	570	9	13–21
Bodrum	830	14	15–24
Bursa	230	4½	6–9
Çanakkale	340	5½	9–12
Denizli (for Pamukkale)	665	13	13–20
Edirne	235	2½	6
Erzurum	1275	18	18–30
Fethiye	980	12-15	18–23
Gaziantep	1136	16	18–21
Göreme (Cappadocia)	725	11	13–15
İzmir	610	9½	12
Kaş	1090	15	15–20
Konya	660	10	16
Kuşadası	700	11	11–15
Marmaris	900	15	15–24
Side	790	13	13–24
Trabzon	1110	18	20–30

among companies, and sometimes can be reduced by haggling or by showing a student card. Departures to major cities and resorts are very frequent.

Bus Ticket Offices Travel agencies in Sultanahmet will sell you bus tickets, though often at inflated prices, so it's better to go straight to the bus ticket offices. Many are in Beyoğlu near Taksim Square on Mete and İnönü Caddesis.

Bosfor Turizm (Map 16, #6) İnönü Caddesi
Kamil Koç (Map 16, #7; ☎ 212-257 7223) İnönü Caddesi 35/B
Nev Tur (Map 17, #65; ☎ 212-252 6373) Mete Caddesi 18. Nev Tur has buses to Cappadocia.
Pamukkale (Map 16, #2; ☎ 212-249 2791) Mete Caddesi 16
Uludağ (Map 16 #9; ☎ 212-244 0822) İnönü Caddesi 33
Ulusoy (Map 16, #6; ☎ 212-249 4373) İnönü Caddesi 59
Varan (Map 16, #10; ☎ 212-251 7474, W www.varan.com.tr) İnönü Caddesi 29/A. Varan is a premium line with routes to major Turkish cities and to several points in Europe, including Athens.

Main Intercity Bus Station The International İstanbul Bus Station (Uluslararası İstanbul Otogarı; Map 11; ☎ 212-658 0505, fax 658 2858), called simply the 'otogar', is in the western district of Esenler, just south of an expressway and about 10km west of Sultanahmet. With 168 ticket offices, restaurants, mosques and shops, it is a town in itself, and one of the world's largest bus terminals. For Turkish travellers, this is the domestic equivalent of London-Heathrow or New York-JFK.

Buses depart the otogar for virtually all cities and towns in Turkey and to neighbouring countries including Azerbaijan, Bulgaria, Greece, Iran, Romania, Saudi

Arabia, Syria and other destinations in Eastern Europe and the Middle East. The top national lines, giving premium service at somewhat higher prices, are Kamil Koç (office 146–7), Bosfor Turizm (127), Pamukkale (43–44), Uludağ (120), Ulusoy (128) and Varan (15–16). Other bus companies are smaller regional or local lines; these may have more frequent, less polished services at lower prices.

Except in busy holiday periods, you can usually just come to the otogar, spend 30 minutes shopping for tickets, and be on your way to your destination at a good price within the hour. There is no easy way to find the best bus company and the best fare; you've got to go from one office to another asking for prices and times, and looking at the buses parked at the *perons* (gates) at the back.

Metro, buses and taxis connect the otogar with the city centre and the airport. See the Getting Around chapter for details. Many bus companies also run free *servis* buses (to/from the otogar) – see the boxed text 'Hassle-Free Service Buses' in the Getting Around chapter.

Harem Bus Station There is another bus station on the Asian shore of the Bosphorus at Harem (Map 12; ☎ 216-333 3763), 2km north-west of Haydarpaşa train station. If you're arriving in İstanbul by bus from anywhere on the Asian side of Turkey it's much quicker to get out at the Harem bus station and take the car ferry (every half-hour from 7am to 9.30pm, US$0.55) to Sirkeci/Eminönü; if you stay on the bus until the otogar (İstanbul's main bus station in Esenler), you'll add at least an hour to your journey.

If you're going the other way and heading off through Asian İstanbul, you may want to *catch* your bus from here, instead of going to the otogar; ask if this is possible when you buy your ticket in town.

Greece

Buses to İstanbul depart from the Peloponnese train station (Hellenic Railways Organisation, Plateia Peloponisu) in Athens. Varan and Ulusory operate daily buses to İstanbul via Thessaloniki. The trip takes about 22 hours. A one-way ticket to İstanbul costs about US$65 from Athens and US$40 from Thessaloniki. Going the other way, Varan buses leave İstanbul at 8am every Friday and cost US$60 to Athens, via Thessaloniki.

Western Europe

Turkish bus companies operate frequent passenger services between Western Europe and İstanbul, but the bus trip takes days, the flight only hours; and a cheap air fare is usually cheaper than the bus fare, especially when you add the cost of bus-trip meals and incidentals. Going by bus, however, is often faster and more comfortable than the now-neglected trains, and comparable in price.

Several Turkish bus lines, including Ulusoy, Varan and Bosfor Turizm, offer service between the İstanbul otogar and some central European cities such as Frankfurt, Munich and Vienna; the trip may take 35 to 47 hours. One-way tickets range from US$60 to US$130. Round-trip fares are discounted about 20%.

Eastern Europe

Marmaris (☎ 212-658 2065, fax 658 1268), office 132 at the İstanbul otogar, has daily buses to Sofia leaving at 4pm (US$18), daily buses to Bucharest leaving at 1pm (US$25), and three buses per week heading to Skopje.

Middle East

Iğdırlı (☎ 212-658 2676), office 166 at the İstanbul otogar, has daily buses to Tehrān leaving at 1pm. The 30-hour trip costs US$30. Buses regularly head to Damascus, Amman and Jerusalem.

TRAIN

Buying Tickets

Most seats on the best trains, and all sleeping compartments, must be reserved. You should make your reservation and buy your ticket as far in advance as possible. A few days will usually suffice, except at holiday times (see Public Holidays & Special Events in the Facts for the Visitor chapter). Weekend trains seem to be the busiest. If you can't buy in advance, check at the station anyway; there may be cancellations, even at the last minute.

Though Turkish State Railways now has a computerised reservations system, it is usually impossible to book sleeping-car space except in the city from which the train departs. You can buy tickets for most trains departing from İstanbul from the Sirkeci train station between 8.30am and 7pm daily.

Classes of Travel Coaches on the top trains *(süper expresi* or *mavi trens)* such as the *Başkent Ekspresi* and *Fatih Ekspresi* have Pullman reclining seats; most of the normal expresses have 1st- and 2nd-class Pullman seats, but some also have sleeping compartments.

Sleeping accommodation is of three classes. A *kuşetli* (couchette) wagon has six-person compartments with seats that rearrange into six shelf-like beds at night; you sleep with strangers. *Örtülü kuşetli* means the couchettes have bedding (sheets, pillows, blanket) and there are four beds per compartment, so two couples travelling together can get an almost private compartment. A *yataklı* wagon has European-style sleeping compartments (with bedding supplied) capable of sleeping two people (three on the *Bosfor Expresi*). Price depends upon the number of occupants: per-person cost is lowest when two share; you'll pay the double rate listed if you want a compartment all to yourself.

Discounts & Passes Inter-Rail passes are valid on the Turkish State Railways' entire network; Eurail passes are not valid on any of it.

Full fare is called *tam*. Round-trip (return) fares, called *gidiş-dönüş,* are discounted by 20%. Student *(öğrenci* or *talebe)* fares discounted by 20% are offered on most routes (show your ISIC). Teachers get 20% discount, disabled persons get 40% off, while press card holders 50% off. If you are under 27 years of age or over 55, you can buy a Seyahat Kartı for US$40 which allows you one month's unlimited rail travel on all trains (even suburban lines) except the top trains *(süper expresi)*. Other specials are available such as the monthly card: for 150km travel per month, you pay US$32. Ask at Sirkeci station in İstanbul for details.

Cancellation Penalties If you decide not to travel and you seek a refund for your rail ticket up to 24 hours before the train's departure, you must pay a cancellation fee of 10% of the ticket price. Less than 24 hours before departure the fee rises to 20%. After the train has departed you'll receive no refund.

Other Parts of Turkey

Turkish State Railways (TC Devlet Demiryolları, TCDD or DDY) runs services to many parts of the country. Check details at W www.tcdd.gov.tr. Alas, TCDD trains are the poor cousins in Turkey's transport mix. In the past few decades millions have been poured into highways and airports, but very little into the railway network. Passenger equipment has a distinctly 1960s look to it, with many holes, patches and cigarette burns since then.

It's not a good idea to plan a train trip all the way across Turkey in one stretch as the country is large, and the cross-country trains are slower than the buses. For example, the *Vangölü Ekspresi* from İstanbul to Lake Van (Tatvan), a 1900km trip, takes around 32 hours – and that's an express! The bus would take less than 24 hours, the plane under two hours. Train travel between Ankara and İstanbul is fast and pleasant, however.

Whenever you take an intercity train in Turkey, you'd do well to take only süper expresi, *mavi tren* (blue train), *ekspres* or *mototren* trains. These are fairly fast, comfortable, and often not too much more expensive than the bus. On *yolcu* (passenger) and *posta* (mail) trains, however, you could grow old and die before reaching your destination.

Note that Turkish train schedules indicate *stations,* not cities; the station name is usually, but not always, the city name. Thus you may not see İstanbul on a schedule, but you will see Haydarpaşa and Sirkeci, the Asian and European stations in İstanbul.

Trains to European Turkey All trains to and from Europe terminate at Sirkeci train station (Map 15; ☎ 212-527 0051), next to Eminönü in the shadow of Topkapı Palace. The station has a small post office and currency exchange booth, as well as a restaurant, cafe and tourist office (☎ 212-511 5888).

The northern facade of the building was where passengers entered to board the fabled *Orient Express* to Paris. The new main (western) door is a boring modern structure.

Destinations from Sirkeci train station include Edirne (the *Edirne Ekspresi* departs at 3.50pm) and Uzunköprü, near the Greek border (the *Uzunköprü Ekspresi* departs at 8.30am).

Trains to Asian Turkey Haydarpaşa (☎ 216-336 0475), on the Asian shore of the Bosphorus, is the terminus for trains to and from Anatolia and points east and south.

Haydarpaşa has an *emanet* (left-luggage room), a restaurant serving alcohol, snack shops, bank ATMs and a small PTT.

Destinations from Haydarpaşa include the following.

Ankara The nightly *Anadolu Ekspresi* between Ankara and İstanbul via Eskişehir hauls Pullman (US$8) and kuşetli (US$10) cars. It departs İstanbul at 10pm and arrives in Ankara at 7am. Private compartments on the similar yataklı *Ankara Ekspresi* between İstanbul and Ankara cost US$26/47 a single/double. It departs İstanbul at 10.30pm and arrives in Ankara at 8am.

The fastest train to Ankara is the *Başkent Ekspresi* (Capital Express), pride of the Turkish State Railways. It departs İstanbul at 10am and makes the run to Ankara in six hours and 50 minutes. It's an air-conditioned, super-1st-class day train with Pullman seats. The fare is US$10. Named after Mehmet the Conqueror (Mehmet Fatih), the *Fatih Ekspresi* is a night train departing İstanbul and Ankara at 11.30pm, arriving in the opposite city at 7.20am, otherwise similar to the *Başkent* in comfort, speed and price.

The *Boğaziçi Ekspresi* (Bosphorus Express) is a comfortable, if faded, 1st-class Pullman-car train between İstanbul and Ankara, departing each city at 1.30pm, and arriving in the other at 10.27pm. The fare to Ankara is US$8.

Denizli The night-time *Pamukkale Ekspresi* departs İstanbul daily at 5.35pm, via Burdur and Eğirdir, arriving in Denizli at 8.20am. İstanbul to Denizli fares are US$6.50/8.50 for 1st-/2nd-class Pullman seats; US$9/11 for 1st-/2nd-class kuşetli; for yataklı compartments, total fares are US$22/40 for singles/doubles.

Kars Though the *Doğu Ekspresi* departs from İstanbul on time at 8.35am, it is usually late thereafter on its long trip via Ankara, Sivas, Erzincan and Erzurum to Kars, near the Armenian border. It is a long, slow trip (about 38 hours) and far from pleasant, but it is certainly cheap. It only has Pullman seats which cost US$6.50/9 1st/2nd class to Kars.

Tatvan & Diyarbakır or Kurtalan The *Güney-Vangölü Ekspresi* stops in Ankara, Kayseri, Sivas and Malatya before arriving at Elazığ Junction. East of the junction, the train continues as the *Vangölü* (Lake Van) *Ekspresi* to Tatvan, or the *Güney* (Southern) *Ekspresi* to Diyarbakır and Kurtalan (east of Diyarbakır), depending upon the day. For the *Vangölü* eastbound, board in İstanbul on Monday (9.05pm), Wednesday (8.05pm) or Saturday (8.05pm). For the *Güney*, board in İstanbul at 8.05pm on Tuesday, Thursday, Friday or Sunday.

Konya The *Meram Ekspresi* departs İstanbul daily at 7.20pm via Kütahya and Afyon, arriving in Konya at 8.20am. The İstanbul to Konya fare is US$6/8.50 in 1st-/2nd-class Pullman seats; for yataklı compartments, fares are US$21/40 a single/double.

Gaziantep The *Toros Ekspresi* departs İstanbul on Tuesday, Thursday and Sunday at 8.55am and heads for the south-east, stopping in Eskişehir (Enveriye), Afyon, Konya, Adana and finally Gaziantep (11.35am the following day). A Pullman seat between İstanbul and Gaziantep costs US$6.50/9.50

The *Orient Express*

The fabled *Orient Express*, which first ran between Paris and Constantinople in 1883, was removed from the timetables and the rails in 1977 and replaced by the *İstanbul Express* to Munich, though this service has also retired.

In the 1960s and 1970s, there was little romance left on the famed *Orient Express* route from Paris (Gare de l'Est) via Lausanne, Milan, Venice, Trieste, Belgrade, Sofia and Edirne to İstanbul. The trains were not well kept, and were always many hours – even days – late.

When armed conflict does not make rail travel through the Balkans impossible, the *Orient Express* lives on in special excursion trains with various names, but the fares for these deluxe tours cost between US$4200 and US$5500 one way. These packages include transportation from European points to İstanbul aboard restored railway coaches, with lectures and optional side trips. By the way, the train that now bears the name *Venice-Simplon Orient Express* goes nowhere near İstanbul on its run between London and Venice.

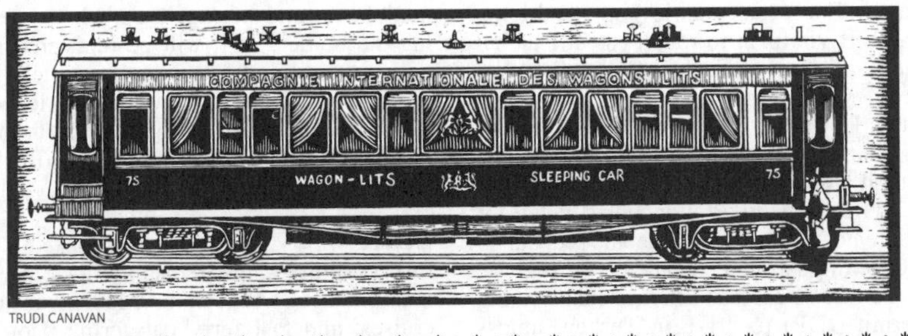

TRUDI CANAVAN

1st/2nd class; a yataklı berth costs US$22/42 a single/double.

Greece

A passenger train with Pullman reclining seats only leaves from İstanbul daily. It takes 16 to 18 hours to get to Thessaloniki (US$35) and 24 hours to Athens (US$51).

Central/Eastern Europe

At the time of research there were no direct trains between Western Europe and Turkey. To travel from Munich to İstanbul, for example, you must change trains in Vienna and again in Budapest.

The *Bosfor Expresi* departs İstanbul daily at 8.35pm for Budapest (32 hours) with örtülü kuşetli cabins only costing US$95 per person. The same train travels to Bucharest in 18 hours and costs US$26 for örtülü kuşetli cabins or US$29/58 per single/double for yataklı cabins. Going the other way, daily trains depart for İstanbul from Budapest at 7.30pm and from Bucharest at 2.05pm.

Middle East

The *Vangölü-Tehrān Ekspresi* departs at 9.05pm on Monday from Haydarpaşa train station travelling to Tehrān after Tatvan. It takes 50 hours to get to Tehrān and costs US$47 per person in örtülü kuşetli cabins. Trains heading to İstanbul from Tehrān leave at 8.25pm on Tuesday. Trains to Damascus depart at 8.55am on Thursday and cost US$68 each in örtülü kuşetli cabins for the 30-hour trip.

CAR & MOTORCYCLE

Don't plan to get around İstanbul by private vehicle. The traffic is horrendous. If you arrive in Turkey by car or motorcycle, park your vehicle in a safe place for the duration of your stay in İstanbul.

The major routes from Europe to İstanbul are usually heavily trafficked by trucks and buses. It's not a pleasant drive. However the final stretch from Edirne to İstanbul is a breeze on the *otoyol* (multi-lane divided toll highway).

Do not drive someone else's car into Turkey. The car will be entered in the driver's passport as imported goods, and must be driven out of the country by the same visitor within the time period allowed. If you want to leave your car in Turkey and return for it later, the car must be put under customs seal, usually a tedious process.

Normally, you cannot rent a car in Europe and include Turkey (or many other Eastern European countries) in your driving plans. If you plan to rent a car in İstanbul for excursions to Edirne, Gallipoli and/or Troy, you might want to pick it up at Atatürk Airport. This saves you the hassle of fighting your way out of the city centre, plus it's easy to get on the highway westward from the airport. For contact details of car rental agencies in İstanbul, see Car in the Getting Around chapter.

You don't need an International Driving Permit (IDP) to drive in Turkey, unless you're staying over three months. Your home driving licence, unless it's something unusual (say, from Burkina Faso), will be accepted by traffic police and by car rental firms. If you'd feel more secure against bureaucratic hassle by carrying an IDP, you can get one through your automobile club in your home country. Always carry your normal licence as well.

For stays longer than three months, or for information regarding car travel in Turkey, contact the Turkish Touring & Automobile Association (see under Car in the Getting Around chapter for contact details).

HITCHING

Hitching is never entirely safe in any country in the world, and we don't recommend it. Travellers who decide to hitch should understand that they are taking a small but potentially serious risk. Women in particular should not hitch in Turkey. People who do choose to hitch will be safer if they travel in pairs and let someone know where they are planning to go.

Long-distance hitching in Turkey, though possible, is uncommon. When you hitch *(otostop),* Turkish custom requires that you offer to pay for your ride. The bus and minibus network is so elaborate and cheap that most people opt for that, figuring that if bus fares must be paid, bus comforts might as well be enjoyed.

The signal used in hitching is not an upturned thumb; in Turkey you face the traffic, hold your arm out towards the road, and wave your hand and arm up and down as though bouncing a basketball.

If you hitch in from another country, don't be the one driving the car when crossing the border, or it will be registered in your passport and you will have to take it out or pay a huge duty when you leave. Also, if contraband (drugs etc) is found hidden in the car, customs officers will assume that it's yours.

BOAT

Luxury cruise ships frequently dock at İstanbul during Aegean or Mediterranean cruises, and fast ferryboats bring people here from other parts of Turkey.

Other Parts of Turkey

Turkish Maritime Lines (TML), also called Turkish Maritime Administration (Türkiye Denizcilik İşletmeleri), operates car and passenger ferries from İstanbul eastward along the Black Sea coast and southward through the Aegean to İzmir, as well as car and passenger ferry services in the Sea of Marmara.

The main TML office is in İstanbul, and there's an agent in İzmir:

İstanbul (Map 16, #156; ☎ 212-249 9222, fax 251 9025) Rıhtım Caddesi, Karaköy. Open 9am to 6pm Monday to Friday.
İzmir (☎ 232-464 8864, fax 464 7834) Denizyolları Acentesi, Yeni Liman, Alsancak. Open 9am to 5pm Monday to Friday, 9am to 2pm Saturday and Sunday.

Car Ferry Car and passenger ferries save you days of driving. Even if you have no car, they offer the opportunity to take mini-cruises along the Turkish coasts. Room on these ships is usually in hot demand, so reserve as far in advance as possible through the İstanbul office by fax.

İstanbul to İzmir The İstanbul-İzmir car-ferry service operates each weekend. From 1 September to 18 June it departs İstanbul's Seraglio Point (Saray Burnu) dock each Friday at 3pm, arriving in İzmir on Saturday at 9am. Departure from İzmir is on Sunday at 2pm, arriving in İstanbul on Monday at 9am. From 19 June to 31 August it leaves İstanbul at 5.30pm Friday, arriving at İzmir at 12.30pm on Saturday; it departs İzmir at 2pm on Sunday to arrive in İstanbul at 9am on Monday.

One-way fares for Pullman seats are US$17 (per person), while a two-berth, B-class cabin costs US$64 a double and deluxe cabins cost US$164 a double. Should you want to use your cabin as a hotel room on Saturday night in İzmir, the cost starts at US$16 a double for the cheapest cabin, while a two-berth, B-class cabin costs US$23 and a deluxe cabin costs US$40 a double.

If you're travelling in the Pullman seats meals are extra (US$3 for breakfast, US$7 for lunch or dinner); if you're in the cabins, breakfast and dinner is included in the fare. The ticket for a car costs US$28 one way or US$14 for a motorcycle.

İstanbul to Trabzon Car ferries operate each week from 18 June to 31 August, departing from İstanbul on Monday at 2pm, stopping briefly in Zonguldak, Sinop, Samsun and arriving in Trabzon on Wednesday at 8.30am. The boat continues to Rize, then returns to Trabzon where it departs on the return voyage to İstanbul at 6pm on Wednesday. The returning ferry stops briefly at Samsun, Sinop and Zonguldak arriving back in İstanbul on Friday at 12.30pm.

One-way fares between İstanbul and Trabzon cost US$11 (per person) for Pullman seats, while a two-berth, B-class cabin costs US$68 a double, and a deluxe cabin costs US$107 a double. Meals cost US$3 for breakfast, US$7 for lunch or dinner. Cars cost US$53, motorcycles US$20.

Catamaran & Fast Car-Ferries The drive (or bus ride) east around the Sea of Marmara, via the Bay of İzmit, is long, congested and the scenery's ugly. Take a short cut by ferry instead.

İstanbul Deniz Otobüsleri (İDO; Map 15; **W** www.ido.com.tr) has fast catamaran passenger and car ferries connecting İstanbul's Yenikapı seabus port with Yalova and Bandırma (both on the south side of the Sea of Marmara). You can pick up a timetable at any of the seabus stops in İstanbul.

There is also a traditional (meaning slow) car-ferry service to Yalova leaving Sirkeci at 9.15am, 2pm and 6.15pm daily. Another leaves every half-hour between Gebze (Eskihisar docks), about 50km south-east of Üsküdar on the Marmara coast, and Topçular, east of Yalova on the Sea of Marmara's southern shore.

Other Countries

Comfortable TML car-ferry services operate between Venice and İzmir; and Brindisi, Italy and Çeşme (nearby İzmir). Other ferries run between Greek ports and several Turkish ports. However there are no direct ferry connections with İstanbul. If you're interested in these services contact the TML office in İstanbul (see contact details under Other Parts of Turkey opposite).

Getting Around

İstanbul has a decent dirt-cheap public transport network which you'll appreciate once you get the hang of prebuying tickets, jumping on half-moving vehicles, and avoiding armpits in tram jams. And if it all gets too much, a mad taxi driver is never far away to race you to your destination at half the time your heart travelled – you won't pay much for the thrill either. But all public transport slows to a crawl around peak hours and, if you haven't already, this is the time to take to your feet: Walking is the best way to see İstanbul – though the ferry rides rate a close second.

Transport maps are hard to get your hands on, though you will usually find maps and timetables pasted up inside bus, metro, tram and train stops.

ATATÜRK AIRPORT (Map 11)

As a first peek at İstanbul, you'd have to be impressed by its US$300 million airport. Situated 23km west of Sultanahmet (the heart of Old İstanbul), the international terminal (Dış Hatlar; flight information ☎ 212-663 6300) is polished and organised. Close by, the domestic terminal (İç Hatlar) is smaller. Another airport, Sabiha Gokçen International Airport at Kurtköy on the Asian side of the city, opened in early 2001, though most flights still arrive and depart from Atatürk Airport.

TO/FROM ATATÜRK AIRPORT

Airport to City

A cheap but slow option is the Havaş airport bus (☎ 212-243 3399) which departs from outside the arrivals hall, then goes to Yenikapı (30 minutes) and on to Taksim Square (45 to 60 minutes). Buses leave every half-hour from 5am to 11.30pm. Tickets cost US$2 – irrespective of where you get off. If you're heading to Sultanahmet, get out at the Yenikapı stop under the overpass. Catch the train (US$0.50) from the nearby Yenikapı station, east to the Cankurtaran station for Sultanahmet hotels. Another Havaş airport bus runs from the airport to Etiler (Akmerkez shopping centre), every half-hour from 7am to 9pm.

The similar and cheaper (if there's more than one of you) option is to catch a taxi (US$2) from the airport to the suburban train station *(banliyö tren istasyonu)* at Yeşilköy. You may get taken to Yeşilyurt train station instead. It doesn't matter – both are equally close to the airport. You'll find the taxi driver may insist there are no trains, the stations are closed, or he'll come up with some other sob story to get you to go all the way into the centre of town. Ignore him. From either Yeşilköy or Yeşilyurt, battered trains (US$0.50) run every half-hour or less to Sirkeci train station. Get off at Cankurtaran for Sultanahmet hotels, or at Sirkeci (end of the line) for Beyoğlu and Taksim.

The fastest and most convenient way to get into town from the airport is by taxi. Outside the arrivals hall there's a board, near the row of waiting taxis, which lists flat rate taxi charges. It costs US$10 (20 minutes) to Sultanahmet, around US$12 (30 minutes) to Taksim, and US$8 (20 minutes) to the *otogar* (bus station). If it's between midnight and 6am or there's heavy traffic, you'll pay US$3 to US$5 on top of these fares. You don't need to tip the driver.

City to Airport

You must check in *at least* 45 minutes before departure time for domestic flights. For international flights, you should be in line at the check-in counter at least 1½ hours before take-off.

If you're staying in Old İstanbul, you can get on a suburban train (US$0.50) at Sirkeci, Cankurtaran or Yenikapı, and get out at Yeşilköy or Yeşilyurt, then take a taxi (US$2) to the airport.

Your guesthouse or hotel can book 24-hour minibus transport from your hotel door to the airport for US$4. Allow lots of time for the trip as the minibus may spend an hour circulating through the city collecting all the other passengers (yawn) before heading out to the airport (30 to 45 minutes). Some guesthouses and hotels also offer a free pick-up and drop-off service.

If you're staying in Beyoğlu, the most convenient way to the airport is by Havaş bus (Map 17, #48; ☎ 212-243 3399; US$2), which departs from near the DHL office on Cumhuriyet Caddesi just north of Taksim Square. Daily departures are at 5am, 6am, 7am, 7.30am then every half-hour until 11.30pm. The trip takes about an hour.

BUS

International Bus Station (Map 11)

The International İstanbul Bus Station (Uluslararası İstanbul Otogarı; ☎ 212-658 0505, fax 658 2858) is the city's main bus station for both domestic and international routes. Called simply the 'otogar', it's in the western district of Esenler, just south of the expressway and about 10km west of Sultanahmet or Taksim.

See the boxed text 'Hassle-Free Service Buses' for information about a convenient way to get to and from the otogar. Otherwise, if you're heading to Sultanahmet, take the metro (US$0.50) east towards Aksaray. In Aksaray, leave the station, turn right and go through the underpass to cross the road, then take the side turn-off beside the mosque to the main road. Here you'll see a tramway (tram) stop; head east for Sultanahmet. For Taksim, buses No 83E or 83O leave from the centre of the otogar and take about an hour (US$0.50) to finish up right in Taksim Square.

Harem Bus Station (Map 12)

There is a much smaller, older, more confusing bus station on the Asian shore of the Bosphorus at Harem (☎ 216-333 3763), south of Üsküdar and north of Haydarpaşa train station. If you're arriving in İstanbul by bus from anywhere on the Asian side of Turkey it's much quicker to get out at Harem and take the car ferry (every half-hour from 7am to 9.30pm, US$0.55) to Sirkeci/Eminönü; if you stay on the bus until the otogar, you'll add at least an hour to your journey. If you're going the other way, you may want to *catch* your bus here, instead of going to the otogar; ask if this is possible when you buy the ticket in town.

Hassle-Free Service Buses

Many bus companies offer a free *servis* bus to or from İstanbul's otogar. If you're booking a ticket out of İstanbul from a bus office in Taksim (or elsewhere), ask about this service. You'll be asked to return to the same office around an hour before your bus is due to leave and a dinky minibus will pick you up – hassle free – and take you from the office to your bus at the otogar.

If you've just arrived by bus in İstanbul at the otogar, ask your bus driver about the service bus. One should be waiting close by to drop you at Sultanahmet or Taksim Square.

City Buses

Destinations and main stops on city bus routes are shown on a sign on the right (kerb) side of the bus. Ubiquitous red-and-beige or green İstanbul Elektric Tramvay ve Tünel (İETT) buses are run by the city, and you must have a ticket (US$0.50) before boarding. You can buy tickets from the white booths near major stops or from some nearby shops for a small mark-up (look for 'İETT otobüs bileti satılır'). Stock up in advance. Running the same routes there are also private buses regulated by the city called Özel Halk Otobüsü, which are usually green-and-blue or double-decker; they accept cash (US$0.50) or Akbil (see the boxed text 'Akbil Fare Savings') only, so have change on you.

TRAIN

The suburban train line *(banliyö treni)* rattles along the Sea of Marmara shore from Sirkeci train station, around Seraglio Point to Cankurtaran, Kumkapı, Yenikapı, and out near Atatürk Airport by the south-western suburbs. The trains are a bit decrepit but reliable (nearly every half-hour) and cheap (US$0.50). Don't confuse this train with the metro lines described later in this chapter.

Akbil Fare Savings

If you're staying in the city for a week or more you may want to buy an Akbil pass, a computerised debit fare card. Get one at the Akbil Sales Point (Akbil Satıi Noktası) booths at Sirkeci, Eminönü, Aksaray or Taksim Square bus stations for US$6 deposit and load fares from US$2. Press the card's metal button into the fare machine on a bus, ferry or tram and – beep – the fare is automatically deducted. Akbil fares are 20% lower than cash or ticket fares but unfortunately there are usually huge queues at the sales booths and you can't use an Akbil pass on dolmuşes. You'll get your US$6 deposit back when you return the device.

Sirkeci Train Station (Map 15)

All trains from Europe terminate at Sirkeci train station (☎ 212-527 0051), right next to Eminönü. Outside the station's main door there's a tram up the hill to Sultanahmet, Beyazıt and Aksaray. A taxi to Sultanahmet costs US$1.50, or it's a 10-minute walk.

A taxi to Taksim will cost only US$2.50, but if you want a cheaper option try the bus. Go out the station door and turn right. Walk towards the sea, then follow the shore (west) past the ferry terminals. Continue through the underpass under Galata Bridge and you'll see the Eminönü bus station ahead, with departures to many parts of the city including Taksim.

Haydarpaşa Train Station (Map 12)

Haydarpaşa train station (☎ 216-336 0475), on the Asian shore of the Bosphorus south of Üsküdar, is the station for trains to and from the Asian side of Turkey and points east and south.

From Eminönü, ferries to Kadıköy (Map 15; dock two), which run every 20 minutes between 7.30am and 8.35pm for US$0.60, often stop at Haydarpaşa train station on the way – but double-check before you board. Ferries also run about every 30 minutes from 7am to 10.45pm between Karaköy (at the northern end of the Galata Bridge) and Kadıköy. These usually stop at Haydarpaşa train station – but, again, double-check before you board.

Ignore anyone who suggests you should take a taxi to Haydarpaşa. The ferry is cheap, convenient, pleasant and speedy. Taxis across the Bosphorus are expensive and slow.

Haydarpaşa has a left-luggage room *(emanet)*, a restaurant serving alcoholic beverages, numerous snack shops, bank ATMs and a small PTT.

METRO

İstanbul's underground metro system will be under construction for a few years yet, but several useful lines are already in service. The fare is US$0.40, and trains usually run every 10 to 20 minutes.

The main metro line goes from the western side of Aksaray, north-westward under Adnan Menderes Bulvarı through the Bayrampaşa and Kartatepe districts. Then it turns south past the otogar in Esenler, and terminates at Yenibosna.

The 7.8km-long slick Taksim metro passes through Şişli and Gayrettepe to terminate at 4. Levent. It won't be overly useful to tourists.

TRAMS

A street tram runs from Eminönü to Gülhane, Sultanahmet, and then along Divan Yolu to Çemberlitaş, Beyazıt (for Kapalı Çarsi) and Aksaray, then out through the city walls to Zeytinburnu. Trams run every 15 to 20 minutes, and the fare costs US$0.40. Watch out for this tram in Sirkeci, where it runs dangerously close to the skinny footpaths.

In Beyoğlu, a restored early 20th-century tram squeaks along İstiklal Caddesi between Taksim and Tünel Squares. Trams run about every half-hour, and tickets cost US$0.40. There are only three stations on the line, the upper, lower and outside the Ağa Camii, so there's no getting lost.

TÜNEL

İstanbul's little underground train, the Tünel, runs between Karaköy and the southern end of İstiklal Caddesi called Tünel

Square. The fare is US$0.30. Trains run every five to 10 minutes from 7am (7.30am on Sunday) to 9pm.

CAR

It makes no sense to drive in İstanbul. If you have a car, park it (if you can find a spot) and use public transport, except perhaps for excursions out of the city. The Türkiye Turing ve Otomobil Kurumu (Turkish Touring & Automobile Association; ☎ 212-282 8140, ⓔ turing@turing.org.tr) is at Oto Sanayi Yanı, Çamlık Caddesi, 4. Levent – about 7km north of Taksim. It has licence and other information you'll need to know if you want to hire a car or bring your own vehicle into the country.

Rental

You need to be at least 21 years old, with a year's driving experience, to be able to rent a car. You must pay with a major credit card, or you will be required to make a large cash deposit. Most rental cars have standard gearshift; you'll pay more to have automatic transmission and air-conditioning.

Costs Rental cars are moderately expensive in Turkey, partly due to huge excise taxes paid when the cars are purchased. Total costs of a rental arranged on the spot in Turkey during the busy summer months, for a week with unlimited kilometres, including full insurance and tax, will be from US$300 to US$600 – excluding petrol.

The mandatory Collision Damage Waiver (CDW; around US$5 per day) covers for damage to the rented car, or another, and for rental revenue lost while the car is being repaired or, in the case of a stolen car, until the car is recovered. The normal CDW does not cover damage to the car's glass (windscreen, side windows, head and tail lamps etc) nor to its tyres – yet another charge of US$2 to US$4 per day is required to pay for this insurance.

Note that many travellers do not need the personal injury insurance proffered by the rental company. Your health insurance from home may cover any medical costs of an accident.

Any traffic fines you incur will be charged to you. Normally, the company charges your credit card.

Safety & Accidents Child safety seats are usually available for about US$5 per day.

If your car incurs any accident damage, or if you cause any, do not move the car before finding a police officer and asking for a *kaza raporu* (accident report). The officer may ask you to submit to a breath-alcohol test. Contact your car-rental company within 48 hours. Your insurance coverage may be void if it can be shown that you were operating under the influence of alcohol or other drugs, were speeding, or if you did not submit the required accident report within 48 hours.

Rental Agencies All the agencies listed have 24-hour booths at the arrivals hall in Atatürk Airport's international terminal:

Avis (Map 17, #26; ☎ 212-246 5256, emergency ☎ 663 0646, fax 231 6244, ⓦ www.avis.com.tr) Hilton Hotel Arcade, Cumhuriyet Caddesi, Elmadağ

Budget (Map 17, #29; ☎ 212-296 3196, emergency ☎ 238 8280, fax 296 3188, ⓦ www.budgettr.com) Cumhuriyet Caddesi 12, Seyhan Apartımanı, 4th floor, Elmadağ

Europcar (Map 17, #39; ☎ 212-254 7799, emergency ☎ 216-663 2587, fax 212-255 5928), Topçu Caddesi 1, Taksim

Sixt (Sun Rent a Car; Map 17, #25; ☎ 212-291 1055, emergency ☎ 0542-232 3324, fax 212-291 1058, ⓦ www.sunrent.com) Hilton Hotel Arcade, Cumhuriyet Caddesi, Elmadağ. A local firm with a good reputation and offices in major cities.

TAXI

İstanbul is full of yellow taxis. Some drivers are lunatics, others are con artists and about half are neither. If you get caught with the first category and you're about to go into meltdown, say *yavaş gidin!* (slow down!). We receive many letters from travellers who have been snared by the second category: con artists. All taxis have digital meters and are required to run them but some drivers ask for a flat fare, or pretend the meter doesn't work so they can gouge you at the end of the run. No meter? No ride – find another taxi. Other drivers take advantage of the many zeros on Turkish currency to charge you 10 times what the meter reads, to short-change you, or to try this common scam:

You give a five million bill to your taxi driver, and he turns and gives you back a 500-thousand bill, saying you didn't give him enough. You think you've just made a mistake with the bills and pay him...We had one that did this once, then I gave him ANOTHER five million bill, and he turned around AGAIN with another 500-thousand bill as if I'd done it again!

Laura Claycomb

The base rate (drop rate, flag fall) is about US$0.50 during the daytime *(gündüz);* the night-time *(gece)* rate, from midnight to 6am, is 50% higher. Meters, with LCD displays, flash 'gündüz' or 'gece' when they are started. Some drivers try to put the night-time (gece) rate on during the day, so watch out. You don't need to tip taxi drivers. A daytime trip between Aksaray and Sultanahmet costs about US$1.25; between Taksim and Karaköy about US$2.25; between Taksim and Sultanahmet about US$3; and between Sultanahmet and Atatürk Airport about US$10.

DOLMUŞ

A *dolmuş* is a shared minibus; it waits at a specified departure point until it has a full complement of passengers, then follows a given route to its destination. Fares (pay on board) are slightly more than the bus, but a dolmuş is almost as comfortable as a taxi, yet considerably cheaper. Useful routes are mentioned in the text.

BOAT

Without doubt the nicest – and cheapest – way to travel any considerable distance in İstanbul is by ferry. The familiar white İstanbul ferries have been replaced on many routes by fast, modern catamarans called *deniz otobüsü* which charge up to several times as much.

The major ferry docks are at the mouth of the Golden Horn (Eminönü, Sirkeci and Karaköy) and at Kabataş, 2km north-east of the Galata Bridge, just south of Dolmabahçe Palace. Short ferry rides (under 30 minutes) cost US$0.50 or US$0.60, most longer ones (up to an hour) cost US$1.30. Buy your token or ticket from the agent in the booth.

Ferries to Üsküdar

Ferries depart from Eminönü (Map 15; dock one) every 15 minutes between 6.30am and 8pm, and then every half-hour until 11.30pm. From Kabataş, just south of Dolmabahçe Palace, ferries run to Üsküdar around every 30 minutes from 7.15am to 8.45pm (every hour from 10.30am to 3.30pm). A ferry service also operates between Beşiktaş (catch it from beside the Deniz Müzesi) and Üsküdar. Ferries start at 6.30am and run every half-hour until 10.30pm, and tokens cost US$0.50.

Ferries to Haydarpaşa/Kadıköy

To get to Haydarpaşa train station, or for a little cruise around Seraglio Point and across the Bosphorus (good for photos of Topkapı Palace, Aya Sofya and the Blue Mosque), catch a Kadıköy ferry from Eminönü (Map 15; dock two); they run every 20 minutes between 7.30am and 8.35pm. Another to Kadıköy also operates from Karaköy running every half-hour until 10.45pm. Some ferries go only to Kadıköy, 1km south of Haydarpaşa, so check your boat's itinerary. The round trip to Haydarpaşa and/or Kadıköy (US$1.20) takes about an hour.

Ferries to Harem Bus Station

A car ferry runs from Sirkeci to Harem daily from 7am, then every half-hour until 9.30pm. Passenger tickets cost US$0.55, cars cost US$1.30.

Ferries to Eyüp

Ferries run from Üsküdar, to Eminönü, then head up the Golden Horn (Haliç) stopping by Kasımpaşa, Fener, Balat and a few other stops until they reach Eyüp. The first ferry leaves Eminönü at 7.20am, then 8.15am, then hourly until 6.15pm, 6.55pm and the last leaves at 8pm. Going the other way, the first from Eyüp leaves at 7.05am, 8am,

8.50am, then every hour thereafter until 6.50pm and finally one leaves at 7.30pm.

Bosphorus Excursion Ferries

The Bosphorus excursion most tourists do is on the special government-run ferries. For times, costs and more, see the Bosphorus Excursion Ferries section in the Excursions chapter.

Cross-Bosphorus Ferries

Ferries cross at various points up the Bosphorus, for example Kanlıca (Asian side) to Bebek (European side) and Sarıyer to Anadolu Kavağı. For more information see Cross-Bosphorus Ferries in the Excursions chapter.

Seabus

Seabuses *(deniz otobüsü)* are fast catamarans that run on commuter routes between the European and Asian shores of İstanbul, and up the Bosphorus. Major docks on the European side are at Yenikapı and Kabataş, with less frequently served docks at Eminönü, Karaköy and several Bosphorus docks such as İstinye and Sarıyer. On the Asian side, major docks are at Bostancı and Kartal, and minor docks at Büyükada and Heybeliada.

Fares for the catamarans are US$1 to US$2.50. Except for the route up the Bosphorus, you may find that you rarely use the intracity catamarans on touristic excursions. The İstanbul Deniz Otobüsleri (İDO; Map 15; W www.ido.com.tr) has fare and timetable information or you can pick up a timetable at any of the seabus docks.

ORGANISED TOURS

The quality of any tour depends greatly on the competence, character and personality of your particular guide; but it's difficult to pick a tour by guide rather than company, so you must go by the tour company's reputation. The best course of action is to ask for recommendations at your hotel and from other travellers.

Watch out for the following rip-offs: A tour bus that spends the first hour or two of your 'tour' circulating through the city to various hotels, picking up tour participants; or a tour that includes an extended stop at some particular shop (from which the tour company or guide gets a kickback).

It is always a lot cheaper (and often quicker) to see things on your own by public transport. The day tour offered by companies to the Princes' Islands for example, is a rip-off at US$60; if you go yourself, eat lunch and organise the horse carriage ride yourself, you'll pay US$25 tops.

Kirkit Voyage (Map 13, #91; ☎ 212-518 2282, fax 518 2281, e kirkit@kirkit.com) Kutlugün Sokak 24, Cankurtaran. Kirkit organises off-the-beaten-path walking tours focusing on architecture (Art Nouveau, hans), neighbourhoods (Balat, Fener) and Kilyos, or bike riding on Büyükada (Princes' Islands). It charges from US$15 to US$20 for half-day walks, US$25 to US$30 for a full day.

Plan Tours (☎ 212-230 2272, W www.plantours.com) Cumhuriyet Caddesi 131/1, Elmadağ. Plan has tours from US$30 (half-day) to US$110. The touristy sites are well covered but Plan also has special Christian and Jewish heritage tours. These are very pricey at US$60 per half-day or US$110 a full day but it'll save you getting to these out-of-the-way sites on your own. Other tours include a day trip to Bursa, and another to Troy and Gallipoli.

İstanbul Vision (Map 13, #61; ☎ 212-230 2272) İstanbul Vision runs a cheesy hop-on-hop-off double-decker bus, which leaves from Aya Sofya Meydanı 1, Sultanahmet, and heads via Eminönü, over to Beyoğlu and back via Fener and the city walls. There's really only one spot to get off and on (Taksim Square); the rest of the time you're in the bus, whizzing past the sights, with your brain plugged into an audio guide. You're going to get little chance to explore the sights, but it may be a good trip to get your bearings. Tickets cost US$15. It's managed by Plan Tours.

For travel agent recommendations (these often run city tours too) see Travel Agencies in the Facts for the Visitor chapter.

Things to See & Do

The heart of historical İstanbul is Sultanahmet, the district centred on the Byzantine Hippodrome in the oldest part of the city. The top sights are grouped within a few minutes' stroll of one another. Other top sights in the old city are a walk or a short bus, tram or taxi ride away. In Beyoğlu, on the north side of the Golden Horn (Haliç), don't miss a stroll past the grand 19th-century buildings along İstiklal Caddesi or a visit to Dolmabahçe Palace on the shores of the Bosphorus.

What better way to see this city than by tramping the cobbled, winding streets? Most sights are within easy walking distance of each other, so you should barely raise a sweat. If the pace does get too much, a tea garden *(çay bahçe)* is never too far away.

You may need to use ferries, buses, taxis, and trams to reach the start of the tours. Sights not structured into walking tours are mentioned in this chapter too.

Most of the city's principal sights can be seen on nine walking tours:

- Byzantine Sultanahmet (page 79)
- Ottoman Sultanahmet (page 85)

İstanbul's Highlights

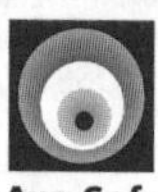

Shamelessly biased and by no means exhaustive, here is a list of İstanbul's delights:

Aya Sofya (page 80)
This church-cum-mosque-cum-museum is probably İstanbul's most famous resident; the enormity of the dome in this will take your breath away – if you haven't already lost it fighting through the crowds

Sunken Cistern (page 83)
With 336 columns and a high, vaulted ceiling, this Byzantine relic was primarily used to store the city's water.

Hippodrome (page 83)
Imagine chariots furiously racing and angry crowds wildly cheering – this is one of İstanbul's oldest civic relics.

İstanbul Archaeology Museums (page 86)
Well presented and extensive, they're loaded with superb Roman sarcophagi, Turkish faience, Hittite artefacts and more.

Blue Mosque (page 89)
'Blue' because of its stunning interior decorated with İznik tiles, this mosque is one of the city's largest and busiest.

Museum of Turkish & Islamic Arts (page 90)
Set in a palace, the well-presented museum houses some superb samples of calligraphy, miniatures, antique carpets and more.

Topkapı Palace (page 91)
Most flock to the Harem to see the stunning interior in which women reigned, but the palace has umpteen splendidly tiled rooms, hundreds of exhibits and beautiful grounds too.

Süleymaniye Camii (page 102)
Architecture buffs will enjoy İstanbul's largest, and one of its most famous, mosques.

Kapalı Çarşı (page 104)
Monstrous, labyrinthine and totally manic, the bazaar's selection of goodies should satiate shoppers – though the touts may annoy.

Dolmabahçe Palace (page 117)
A symbol of the last throes of the Ottoman Empire, this palace is revoltingly decadent – some of the best kitsch in town.

Kariye Müzesi (page 126)
This small church has the richest collection of Byzantine mosaics in the city, while the suburbs around it are rich with Greek and Jewish temples.

The Bosphorus (page 135)
Integral to an İstanbul adventure is a boat trip to appreciate the expanse of the city – its architecture, greenness and beauty. Take one of the day trips to the Black Sea or just a trip to the Asian side.

- Palace of the Sultans (page 91)
- Path of Empires (page 99)
- The Bazaar District (page 103)
- Beyoğlu (page 108)
- Dolmabahçe Palace to Ortaköy (page 116)
- Üsküdar (page 122)
- Western Districts (page 125)

If you're after old-world İstanbul start at Sultanahmet. With bits of Byzantium, layered with Constantinople and chockers with Ottoman past, this one district could keep you busy for days. We've divided it into two walking tours: The first walk, Byzantine Sultanahmet, will introduce you to the remnants of Byzantium and Constantinople, while the second walk, Ottoman Sultanahmet, will show you the Ottoman city.

Byzantine Sultanahmet

Ever since 657 BC when Byzas first sailed up to where the Golden Horn, the Bosphorus and the Sea of Marmara meet, the promontory at the junction has held a city: Byzantium (after Byzas), Constantinople, then İstanbul. For over 1500 years the Great Byzantine Palace adorned the top; there's little to show for it now, but there are plenty of other sights to help you imagine the vibrant empire. Although many Byzantine buildings were adapted to fit the Muslim world after the Conquest – Aya Sofya (Sancta Sophia) and the Küçük Aya Sofya Camii, for example – try to imagine these as they once were.

> **Byzantine Sultanahmet**
>
> 
>
> The Byzantine Sultanahmet walk will take three to four hours. (Red trail: Map 13)
>
> 1. Great Palace Mosaics Museum
> 2. Aya Sofya
> 3. Sunken Cistern
> 4. Hippodrome
> 5. Sphendoneh
> 6. Küçük Aya Sofya Camii
> 7. Sea Walls & Bucoleon Palace
>
> 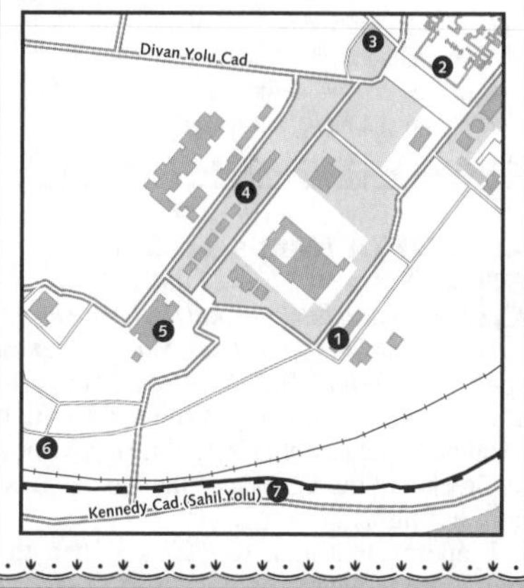
>

GREAT PALACE MOSAICS MUSEUM (Map 13, #101)

When archaeologists from the University of Ankara and the University of St Andrew's (Scotland) dug at the back of the Blue Mosque in the mid-1950s, they uncovered a stunning mosaic dating from early Byzantine times, c. AD 500. It is now preserved in the Great Palace Mosaics Museum (*Büyük-saray Mozaik Müzesi; ☎ 212-518 1205, Torun Sokak; adult/student US$1.50/0.50; open 9.15am-4.30pm Tues-Sun*). The mosaic pavement, said to have been added by Justinian to the Great Byzantine Palace, is estimated to have measured from 3500 to 4000 sq metres. The dust and rubble of 1500 years have left the excavated pavement considerably lower than ground level.

The pavement is filled with intricate hunting and mythological scenes and emperors' portraits. Note the ribbon border with heart-shaped leaves surrounding the mosaic. In the westernmost room is the most colourful and dramatic picture, that of two men in leggings carrying spears and holding off a raging tiger.

Other 5th-century mosaics were saved providentially when Sultan Ahmet had shops built on top of them. A row of shops, called the **Arasta**, was intended to provide revenue for the upkeep of the mosque. Now it houses carpet shops and the exit from the museum.

Great Byzantine Palace

The Great Byzantine Palace was built at the founding of Constantinople (c. AD 320) by Constantine the Great, and renovated and added to by successive Byzantine leaders. The opulent palace was a series of buildings set in parklands and terraces, stretching from the Hippodrome over to Aya Sofya and down the slope, ending at the sea walls and the Bucoleon Palace. In the 13th century it was abandoned, and the ruins of the palace were filled in after the Conquest to become mere foundations to much of Sultanahmet and Cankurtaran. The mosaics in the Great Palace Mosaics Museum were part of the complex. In 1998 archaeologists unearthed frescoes in structures to the south-east of Aya Sofya, which are still being excavated today.

AYA SOFYA (Maps 13 & 1)

Aya Sofya *(☎ 212-522 0989, Aya Sofya Meydanı; adult/student US$10/5; church open 9.15am-4.30pm Tues-Sun; galleries open 9.15am-4pm Tues-Sun)* was not named after a saint; its name means holy wisdom. It is called Sancta Sophia in Latin, Hagia Sofia in Greek and the Church of the Divine Wisdom in English.

Emperor Justinian (r. 527–65) had the church built as yet another effort to restore the greatness of the Roman Empire. It was constructed on the site of Byzantium's acropolis, which had also been the site of an earlier Aya Sofya destroyed in the Nika riots of 532. Justinian's church was completed in 537 and reigned as the greatest church in Christendom until the conquest of Constantinople in 1453. Justinian, on entering his great creation for the first time almost 1500 years ago, exclaimed, 'Glory to God that I have been judged worthy of such a work. Oh Solomon! I have outdone you!'

There are bigger buildings, and bigger domes, but not without modern construction materials such as reinforced concrete and steel girders. The achievement of the architects is unequalled. The sense of air and space in the nave, the 30 million gold mosaic tiles *(tesserae)* which covered the dome's interior, and the apparent lack of support for the dome, made the Byzantines gasp in amazement. Indeed, it almost was impossible, because the dome lasted only 11 years before an earthquake brought it down in 559.

The dome is supported by 40 massive ribs constructed of special hollow bricks made in Rhodes from a unique light, porous clay, resting on huge pillars concealed in the interior walls. (Compare them with the Blue Mosque's four huge freestanding pillars to appreciate the genius of Aya Sofya.)

It was through the Imperial Door that Mehmet the Conqueror came in 1453 to take possession for Islam of the greatest religious edifice in the world. Before he entered, historians tell us, he sprinkled earth on his head in a gesture of humility. Aya Sofya remained a mosque until 1935, when Atatürk proclaimed it a museum.

Over the centuries it was necessary for succeeding Byzantine emperors and Ottoman sultans to rebuild the dome several times, to add buttresses and other supports and to steady the foundations. Current restoration research shows that the original 6th-century mosaic work was extremely fine, but that later 14th-century repairs were done quickly and poorly. Ignore, if you can, the clutter of buttresses and supports, kiosks, tombs and outbuildings which hug its massive walls, and the renovations (partly Unesco funded) which are filling the interior with scaffolding.

Mosaics

Justinian filled his church with fine mosaics. The Byzantine church and state later endured a fierce civil war (726–87) over the question of whether images were biblically correct or not. The debated passage was Exodus 20:4:

> Thou shalt not make unto thee any graven image or any likeness of anything that is in heaven above, or that is in the earth beneath, or that is in the water under the earth: Thou shalt not bow down thyself to them, nor serve them.

Though the Bible seems clear, images (icons, mosaics, statues) were very popular

JONATHAN SELIG

WES WALKER

PETER PTSCHELINZEW

ompleted in AD 537, Aya Sofya (Sancta Sophia) was the largest church in the world. After the ttoman Conquest in 1453 it was turned into a mosque: four minarets were added and the marvel-us mosaics, such as this 14th-century figure of Christ (top right), were plastered over.

VERITY CAMPBELL

ANNA JUDD

STUART WASSERMAN

The magnificent 17th-century Blue Mosque (Mosque of Sultan Ahmet), still a popular place of worship for İstanbullus (top right), is at its most spectacular under the floodlights at night (bottom). It acquired its English nickname from the blue İznik tiles that line the interior walls.

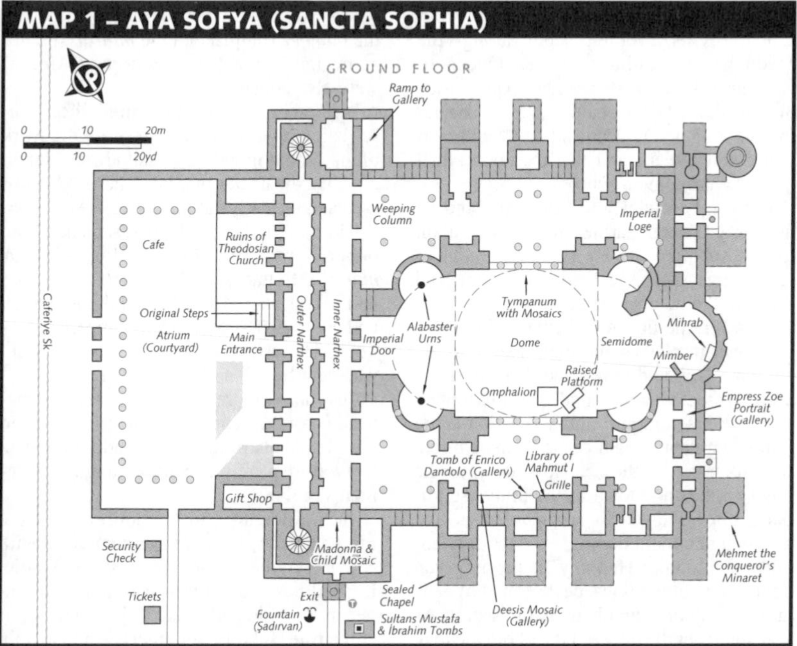

and the iconoclasts (image-breakers) were ultimately defeated. It's interesting to speculate whether iconoclastic Islam, militant and triumphant at this time, had any influence on Byzantine theology.

When the Turks took Constantinople there was no controversy. The Quran repeatedly rails against idolatry, as in Sura 16:

> We sent a Messenger into every nation saying, Serve God and give up idols.

Islamic art isn't supposed to depict people, animals, fish or fowl, nor anything else with an immortal soul, and the mosaics had to go. Luckily they were covered with plaster rather than destroyed, and some have been successfully uncovered.

From the floor of Aya Sofya, 9th-century mosaic portraits of St Ignatius the Younger (c. 800), St John Chrysostom (c. 400) and St Ignatius Theodorus of Antioch are visible high up at the base of the northern tympanum (semicircle) beneath the dome (though these were obscured by scaffolding at the time of writing). Even better mosaics are in the galleries reserved for female worshippers in Byzantine times.

Ground Floor

In Justinian's time, a street led uphill from the west straight to the main door. Today the ticket kiosk is at the south-west side. To experience the church as its architects, Anthemius of Tralles and Isidorus of Miletus, intended, walk to the atrium (courtyard) before the main entrance. Here are the sunken ruins of a Theodosian church (404–15), and the low original steps. Enter through the main entrance slowly, one step at a time, looking ahead: at first there is only darkness broken by the brilliant colours of stained-glass windows. As your eyes adjust to the dark, two massive doorways appear within, in the **outer narthex** and **inner narthex**, and far beyond them in the dim light, a semidome blazing with gold mosaics (presently obscured by scaffolding) portraying the Madonna and Child – she as Queen of Heaven. Take a few steps and stop just inside the threshold of the main entrance: the far mosaic is clear and beautiful (or would be if you could see it), and the apse beneath it makes a harmonious whole.

Look up from where you are standing now in the outer narthex to see a brilliant mosaic of *Christ as Pantocrator* (Ruler of All) above the largest door (the imperial door) in the inner narthex.

Stand in the doorway between the outer and inner narthexes and look deep into the church again, and you'll see that the semidome of the Madonna and Child is topped by another semidome, and above that is the famous, gigantic main dome of the church.

Walk through the second door into the inner narthex and towards the immense **imperial door**, and you are surprised to see that the 'gigantic main dome' is in fact only another semidome: Halfway to the imperial door, a row of windows peeks out above the larger semidome and betrays the secret. As you approach the imperial threshold the real, magnificent main dome soars above you and seems to be held up by nothing. During its years as a church (almost 1000), only imperial processions were permitted to enter through the central, imperial door. You can still notice the depressions in the stone by each door just inside the threshold where imperial guards stood.

The Ottoman chandeliers, hanging low above the floor, combined their light with rows of glass oil lamps lining the balustrades of the gallery and the walkway at the base of the dome. Imagine them all lit to celebrate some great state occasion, with the smell of incense and the chants of the Orthodox liturgy reverberating through the huge interior space.

The Byzantine emperor was crowned while seated in a throne placed within the **omphalion**, the square of inlaid marble in the main floor. The nearby raised **platform** was added by Sultan Murat III (r. 1574–95), as were the large **alabaster urns** so that worshippers could perform their ritual ablutions before prayer. During the Ottoman period the *mimber* (pulpit) and the *mihrab* (prayer niche indicating the direction of Mecca) were also added.

The large 19th-century **medallions** inscribed with gilt Arabic letters are the work of master calligrapher Mustafa İzzet Efendi, and give the names of God (Allah), Mohammed and the early caliphs Ali and Abu Bakr.

The curious, elevated kiosk, screened from public view, is the **imperial loge** *(hünkar mahfili)*. Sultan Abdül Mecit (r. 1839–61) had it built in 1848 so he could come, pray and go unseen, preserving the imperial mystique. The ornate **library**, on the west wall, was built by Sultan Mahmut I in 1739.

Justinian ordered the most precious materials for his church. Note the matched marble panels in the walls, and the breccia (a type of rock made up of angular fragments) columns.

In the side aisle to the north-east of the imperial door is the **weeping column**, with a worn copper facing pierced by a hole. Legend has it that those who put their finger in the hole and make a wish will see it come true if the finger emerges moist. Join the queue of hopefuls.

The Galleries

The galleries (where the best mosaics are found) are reached by a switchback ramp at the northern end of the inner narthex.

The striking *Deesis Mosaic,* in the south gallery, dates from the early 14th century. Christ is at the centre, with the Virgin Mary on the left, and John the Baptist on the right.

At the eastern (apse) end of the south gallery is the mosaic portrait of the Empress Zoe (r. 1028–50). When her portrait was done she was 50 years old and newly married to the aged Romanus III Argyrus. Upon Romanus' death in 1034, she had his face excised from the mosaic and that of her virile new husband, Michael IV, put in its place. Eight years later, with Michael dead from an illness contracted on campaign, Zoe and her sister Theodora ruled as empresses in their own right, but did it so badly that it was clear she had to marry again. At the age of 64, Zoe wed an eminent senator, Con-

Dandolo the Doge

Enrico Dandolo (c. 1108–1205), buried in Aya Sofya, came from the prominent Venetian family that supplied Venice with four doges, numerous admirals and a colonial empire. Dandolo became doge in 1192. During the Fourth Crusade of 1203–04, he diverted the Crusader armies from their goal of an assault on the infidels to an assault on the friendly but rival Christian city of Constantinople. Venice got the better part of the rich spoils, as well as numerous Byzantine territories. Dandolo ruled three-eighths of conquered Constantinople, including Sancta Sophia, until his death in 1205, when he was buried here. Look for his tomb, marked by a marble slab inscribed DANDOLO in the floor of the south gallery towards its eastern wall.

Tradition tells us that Dandolo's tomb was broken open after the Conquest of the city in 1453, and his bones thrown to the dogs.

stantine IX Monomachus, whose portrait remains only because he outlived the empress. The inscription reads, 'Constantine, by the Divine Christ, Faithful King of the Romans'. To the right of it is another mosaic depicting a less saucy story: the Virgin holding Christ, centre, with Emperor John II (the Good) to the left and Empress Eirene (also known for her charity) to the right.

Back on the ground floor, as you leave the inner narthex and enter the passage to the outside, turn and look up to see the Madonna and Child, one of the church's finest late 10th-century mosaics, above the door. Constantine the Great, on the left, offers Mary the city of Constantinople; Emperor Justinian, on the right, offers her Aya Sofya.

As you exit the museum, the fountain *(şadırvan)* to the right was for ablutions. To your left is the church's baptistry, converted after the Conquest to a tomb for sultans Mustafa and İbrahim. Other tombs are clustered behind it, including those of Murat III, Selim II and Mehmet III. The minarets were added by Mehmet the Conqueror (r. 1451–81), Beyazıt II (r. 1481–1512) and Selim II (r. 1566–74). To the south-east of Aya Sofya, a wall hides excavations on a section of the Great Byzantine Palace.

SUNKEN CISTERN (Map 13, #43)

Built in AD 532, the Sunken Cistern *(Yerebatan Sarnıçı; ☎ 212-522 1259, Yerebatan Caddesi 13; adult/student US$3.50/2.50; open 9am-4.30pm Nov-Mar, 9am-5.30pm Apr-Oct)* is the largest surviving Byzantine cistern in İstanbul.

It's an enormous water storage tank constructed by Justinian, who was incapable of thinking in small terms. Columns, capitals and plinths from ruined buildings were used in its construction. Two columns in the north-western corner are supported by two blocks carved into Medusa heads.

The cistern is 70m wide and 140m long and its roof is supported by 336 columns. It once held 80,000 cubic metres of water which was pumped and delivered through nearly 20km of aqueducts from a reservoir near the Black Sea. The water was used to support part of the city during lengthy sieges.

Unfortunately the cistern became a dumping ground for all sorts of junk, as well as corpses. Since it was built the cistern has undergone a number of facelifts, most notably in the 18th century and then between 1955 and 1960. The cistern was cleaned and renovated between 1985 and 1988 by the İstanbul Metropolitan Municipality.

Water drips from the vaulted ceiling onto the lamp-lit walkways and you may spot ghostly carp in the water.

THE HIPPODROME (Map 13)

The Hippodrome (Atmeydanı) was the centre of Byzantium's life for 1000 years and of Ottoman life for another 400 years. It was the scene of countless political dramas during the long life of the city.

History

In Byzantine times, the rival chariot teams of 'Greens' and 'Blues' had separate political connections. Support for a team was akin to membership of a political party, and a team victory had important effects on policy. A Byzantine emperor might lose his throne as the result of a post-match riot.

Ottoman sultans kept an eye on activities in the Hippodrome. If things were going badly in the empire, a surly crowd gathering here could signal the start of a disturbance, then a riot, then a revolution. In 1826, the slaughter of the debased janissary corps (the sultan's personal bodyguards) was carried out here by the reformer Sultan Mahmut II. In 1909, there were riots here which caused the downfall of Abdül Hamit II and the repromulgation of the Ottoman constitution.

Though the Hippodrome might be the scene of their downfall, Byzantine emperors and Ottoman sultans outdid one another in beautifying it. Many of the priceless statues carved by ancient masters have disappeared. The soldiers of the Fourth Crusade sacked Constantinople, a Christian ally city, in 1204, tearing all the bronze plates from the stone obelisk at the Hippodrome's southern end in the mistaken belief that they were gold. The crusaders also stole the famous *quadriga,* or team of four horses cast in bronze, a copy of which now sits atop the main door of the Basilica di San Marco in Venice (the original is in the museum inside).

Kaiser Wilhelm's Fountain (Map 13, #37)

Near the northern end of the Hippodrome, the little gazebo in beautiful stonework is actually Kaiser Wilhelm's fountain. The German emperor paid a state visit to Abdül Hamit II in 1901 and presented this fountain to the sultan and his people as a token of friendship. According to the Ottoman inscription, the fountain was built in the Hejira (Muslim lunar calendar) year of 1316 (AD 1898–99). The monograms in the stonework are those of Abdül Hamit II and Wilhelm II, and represent their political union.

Obelisk of Theodosius (Map 13, #102)

The impressive granite obelisk with hieroglyphs was carved in Egypt around 1450 BC. According to the hieroglyphs, it was erected in Heliopolis (now a Cairo suburb) to commemorate the victories of Thutmose III (r. 1504–1450 BC). The Byzantine emperor, Theodosius, had it brought from Egypt to Constantinople in AD 390. He then had it erected on a marble pedestal engraved with scenes of himself in the midst of various imperial pastimes. Theodosius' self-promoting marble billboards have weathered badly over the centuries. However, the magnificent obelisk, spaced above the pedestal by four bronze blocks, is as crisply cut and shiny as when it was carved in Upper Egypt some 3500 years ago.

Spiral Column (Map 13, #103)

South of the obelisk is a strange column coming up out of a hole in the ground. It was once much taller and was topped by three serpents' heads. Originally cast to commemorate a victory of the Hellenic confederation over the Persians, it stood in front of the temple of Apollo at Delphi from 478 BC until Constantine the Great had it brought to his new capital city around AD 330. Though badly bashed up in the Byzantine struggle over the place of images in the church, the serpents' heads survived until the early 18th century. Now all that remains of them is one upper jaw, housed in İstanbul's Archaeology Museum.

The level of the Hippodrome rose over the centuries, as civilisation piled up its dust and refuse here. The Obelisk of Theodosius and the Spiral Column were cleaned out and tidied up by the British troops who occupied the city after the Ottoman defeat in WWI.

Rough-Stone Obelisk (Map 13, #104)

All we know about the rough-stone obelisk at the southern end of the Hippodrome is that it was repaired by Constantine VII Porphyrogenitus (r. 913–59), and that its bronze plates were ripped off during the Fourth Crusade.

THE SPHENDONEH (Map 13, #118)

At the end of the Hippodrome, turn left, then right, then right again onto Nakilbent Sokak. You'll be able to recognise the filled-in arches of the Byzantine Sphendoneh on your right, with a small bare park in front of it. The Sphendoneh supported the southern end of the Hippodrome.

KÜÇÜK AYA SOFYA CAMİİ (Map 13, #113)

Turn left onto Aksakal Sokak and right onto Kaleci Sokak. Look for an old *hamam* (steam bath) called Çardaklı Hamamı at the intersection with Şehit Mehmet Paşa Sokak; turn left to find the Küçük Aya Sofya Camii *(Little Aya Sofya; SS Sergius & Bacchus Church; ☎ 212-458 0776, Küçük Aya Sofya Caddesi; admission free)*. Justinian and Theodora built this little church sometime between 527 and 536 (just before Justinian built Aya Sofya) and you can still see their monogram worked into some of the frilly white capitals (check the south-west of the church). The church is run-down, but beautiful, and the layout and decor are typical of an early Byzantine church. The building was repaired and expanded several times during its life. It was converted into a mosque by the chief white eunuch Hüseyin Ağa around 1500; his tomb is to the north of the building. Photos are for sale; if the mosque is not open, the guardian is sure to appear with the key.

The *medrese* (theological school) cells, arranged around the mosque's forecourt, are now used by craftspeople. The leafy forecourt also has a tea garden.

SEA WALLS & BUCOLEON PALACE (Map 13, #121)

After you've finished with Küçük Aya Sofya Camii, turn right onto Küçük Aya Sofya Caddesi, and right again onto Aksakal Sokak. Head south towards the Sea of Marmara, pass under the train line, and turn left (east) at busy Kennedy Caddesi (Sahil Yolu). After about 200m you'll come to what's left of the Bucoleon Palace, built by Theophilos (c. AD 830), one of the buildings of the Great Byzantine Palace. This is the palace's only above-ground structure left standing. This stretch of sea walls was built around AD 300. The building jutting out to the east of the Bucoleon Palace was the **Pharos lighthouse**.

The Byzantine tour is now finished. From the palace, you could continue east, along Kennedy Caddesi beside the sea walls, and up through Gülhane Park.

Ottoman Sultanahmet

In 1453, Mehmet the Conqueror, living up to his name, barged into Constantinople and converted most churches into mosques. As the Ottoman Empire flourished, so did the architecture, and most of it is still around, complemented by a rich collection of relics housed in the many museums. It is not difficult to imagine the sometimes decadent, gold-dripping ways of the empire.

Ottoman Sultanahmet

This full-day walking tour takes you into museums and examples of Ottoman architecture including hamams mosques and dwellings. (Blue trail: Map 15, then Map 13)

1. İstanbul Archaeology Museums
2. Gülhane Park & Sublime Porte
3. Soğukçeşme Sokak
4. Caferağa Medresesi
5. Baths of Lady Hürrem
6. Blue Mosque
7. Carpet & Kilim Museum
8. Hamamzade İsmail Dede Efendi Evi Müzesi
9. Sokollu Mehmet Paşa Camii
10. Museum of Turkish & Islamic Arts

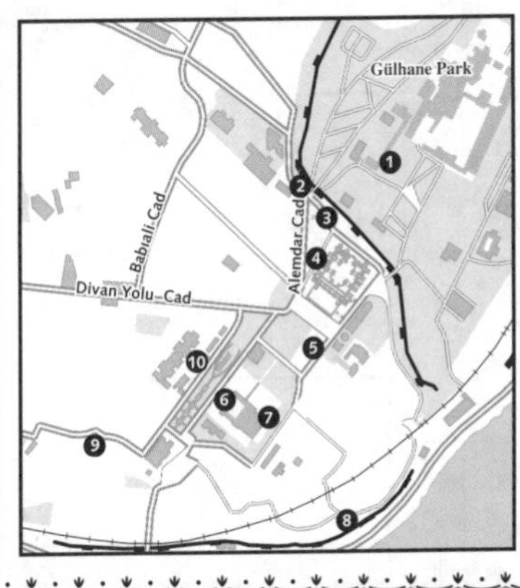

İSTANBUL ARCHAEOLOGY MUSEUMS (Maps 15 & 2)

İstanbul's Archaeology Museums complex *(Arkeoloji Müzeleri; ☎ 212-520 7740, Osman Hamdi Bey Yokuşu; adult/student US$3.50/2; open 10am-4.30pm Tues-Sun Nov-Mar, 10am-6.30pm Tues-Sun Apr- Oct),* located between Gülhane Park and Topkapı, can be easily reached by walking down the slope from Topkapı's Court of the Janissaries (first court).

The complex is divided into three buildings: the Archaeology Museum (Arkeoloji Müzesi, though at the time of research only the ground floor was open for viewing); the Museum of the Ancient Orient (Eski Şark Eserler Müzesi); and the Tiled Kiosk (Çinili Köşk). These museums house the palace collections, formed during the 19th century by Osman Hamdi Bey and added to greatly since the **republic**. While not immediately as dazzling as Topkapı, they contain a wealth of artefacts from the 50 centuries of Anatolia's history. Signs are in both Turkish and English.

Museum of the Ancient Orient (Map 15, #30)

This is the first building on your left as you enter the museum complex. It houses Anatolian pieces (from Hittite empires) as well as pre-Islamic items collected from the expanse of the Ottoman Empire. You can't miss the series of large glazed-brick panels depicting various animals such as lions and bulls. These beautiful blue-and-yellow panels lined the processional street and the Ishtar gate of ancient Babylon from the time of Nebuchadnezzar II (605–563 BC). Another treat here is the oldest surviving political treaty: a copy of the Kadesh Treaty drawn up in the 13th century BC between the Egyptians and Hittites. Other exhibits include clay tablets bearing Hammurabi's famous law code (in cuneiform, of course), ancient Egyptian scarabs and Assyrian reliefs.

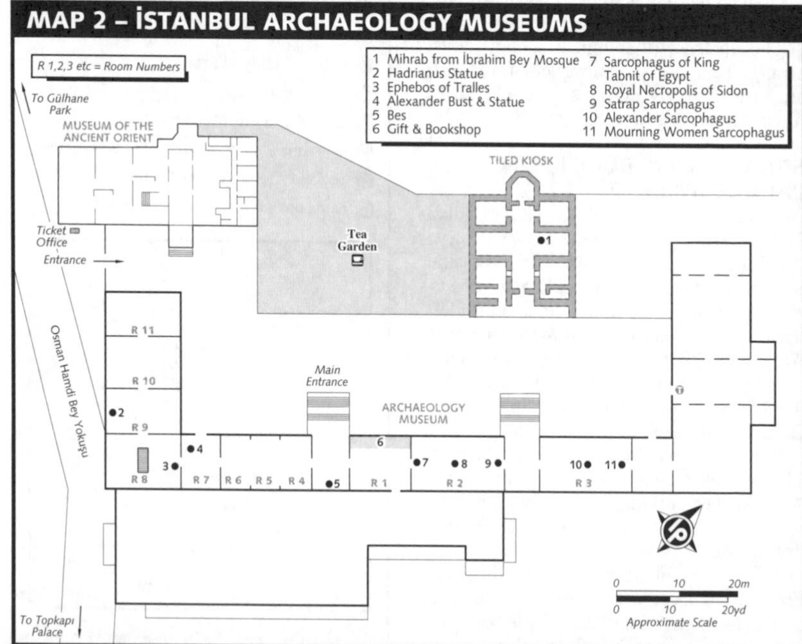

Archaeology Museum (Map 15, #29)

This neoclassical building houses an extensive collection of Hellenic, Hellenistic and Roman statuary and sarcophagi.

A Roman statue of the daemonic god Bes greets you as you enter. Turn left into Room 1, and walk past the **book and gift shop (Map 2, #6)** to the dimly lit rooms beyond. Room 2 is filled with sarcophagi from the **Royal Necropolis of Sidon (Map 2, #8)**. You will also find the monolithic basalt **sarcophagus of King Tabnit of Egypt (Map 2, #7)**, as well as its former occupant in a neighbouring glass case. Up the end are everyday scenes featuring the provincial governor in the **Satrap sarcophagus (Map 2, #9)**. Pass into Room 3 to see the famous marble **Alexander sarcophagus (Map 2, #10)**, now known not to have been Alexander's, but it's nonetheless an exquisite work of art. One side shows the Persians (long pants, material headwear) battling with the Greeks. Alexander, on horseback, has a lion's head as a headdress. Remarkably, the sculpture has remnants of its original red-and-yellow paintwork. At the end of this room the **Mourning Women sarcophagus (Map 2, #11)** was thought to have been created for a king fond of women. At this stage retrace your steps to Bes.

Continue past Bes through to Room 4. Here start the statuary galleries. In ancient Greece and Rome, sculpture was an important element in the decoration of building facades and public spaces. Rooms 5 and 6 exhibit a selection of fine works. **Alexander (Map 2, #4)** makes a genuine appearance (Room 7) – you'll see his bust and statue. In Room 8 the **Ephebos of Tralles (Map 2, #3)** is a young boy, wrapped in a cape, leaning against a pillar.

Room 9 is crowded with busts. The **Hadrianus statue (Map 2, #2)**, resting his foot on a boy on the ground, is a fine example. Artisans at Anatolia's three main sculpture centres – Aphrodisias, Ephesus and Miletus – turned out thousands of beautiful works, some of which have been collected in Room 10. There's a beautiful relief showing the struggle of Athena and the Giants from Aphrodisias, and a statue from Miletus showing Apollo wearing ornate sandals and playing a lyre. The lazy River God, from Ephesus, tries to block your way to Room 11. The last room has examples of sculpture from throughout the Roman Empire. Look out for the delicately carved statue of Tyche; you won't miss the statue of Zeus from Gaza.

The museum's 2nd and 3rd floors were closed for renovation at the time of research. Also unavailable for viewing (though it may be open by the time you read this) is a mock-up of the facade of the Temple of Athena at Assos (Behramkale) in a long room behind Room 1. Erected in 525 BC, it was the first and only temple of the Archaic Period designed in the Doric order. On the mezzanine level above the Temple of Athena is an exhibition called 'İstanbul Through the Ages', tracing the city's entire history, concentrating on its most famous buildings and public spaces: Archaic, Hellenistic, Roman, Byzantine and Ottoman. It was also closed at the time of research.

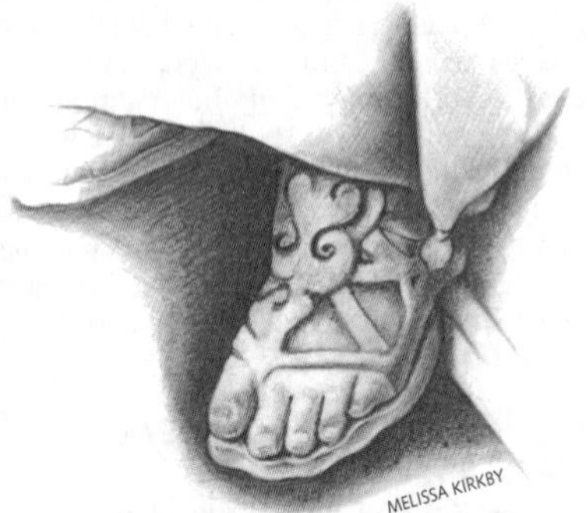

Detail from a 2nd-century statue of Apollo, found in Miletus, Anatolia and now in İstanbul's Archaeology Museum

Tiled Kiosk (Map 15, #28)

The Tiled Kiosk of Sultan Mehmet the Conqueror is the oldest surviving nonreligious Turkish building in İstanbul, constructed in 1472 not long after the Conquest. It was built as an outer pavilion of Topkapı Palace, to be used for watching sporting events.

The recessed doorway area is covered with tiles – some with white calligraphy *(sülüus)* on blue. The geometric patterns and colour of the tiles – turquoise, white, black – on the facade show obvious Seljuk influence.

Much of the interior of the kiosk is covered with triangular and hexagonal tiles of brown, green, yellow and blue. The excellent collection of Turkish faience (tin-glazed earthenware tiles) highlights İznik tiles from the period in the 17th and 18th centuries when that city produced the finest coloured tiles in the world. When you enter the first room you can't miss the stunning mihrab from the İbrahim Bey Mosque, built in 1432. Head towards the back of the kiosk. In the room on your left you'll find a pretty fountain recessed into the wall; the room on the right has ceramics from Kütahya.

Leaving the İstanbul Archaeology Museums

After you've finished, you may want to have a restful cup of tea between the antiquities in the tea garden beside the Tiled Kiosk. Otherwise, exit and head to the right down the hill.

GÜLHANE PARK (Map 15) & SUBLIME PORTE (Map 15, #32)

Gülhane Park was once the palace park of Topkapı. Crowds pack it at weekends to enjoy its shade, street food and the occasional live concert. It has a wretched little **zoo (Map 15, #24)** *(admission free; open 10am-4pm daily)* with a peculiar selection of inmates: budgies, pigeons, goats, cats, rabbits (we kid you not). Because you're in the area (and only for this reason) you may as well pop into the decaying **Tanzimat Müzesi (Map 15, #25)** *(☎ 212-512 6384; open 8.30am-4.30pm daily)*. 'Tanzimat' (Reorganisation) was the name given to the political and societal reforms planned by Sultan Abdül Mecit in 1839 and carried out through the middle of the 19th century.

At the far (north) end of the park, up the hill, is a series of terraces with a tea garden, the **Set Üstü Çay Bahçesi (Map 15, #27)**, where you get superb views over the Bosphorus.

Retrace your steps and leave the park by the south end. As you exit look to the right. That bulbous little kiosk built into the park walls at the next street corner is the **Alay Köşkü (Map 15, #31)** *(Parade Kiosk)*. The sultan would sit in there and watch the periodic parades of troops and trade guilds, which commemorated great holidays and military victories.

Across the street from the Alay Köşkü (not quite visible from the Gülhane gate) is a gate leading into the precincts of what was once the grand vizierate, or Ottoman prime ministry, known in the West as the **Sublime Porte (Map 15, #32)**. Today the buildings beyond the gate hold various offices of the İstanbul provincial government.

SOĞUKÇEŞME SOKAK (Map 15)

Soğukçeşme Sokak, or Street of the Cold Fountain, to your left, runs between the Topkapı Palace walls and Aya Sofya. This picturesque street has many prim Ottoman-style houses which were restored by the Turkish Touring & Automobile Association and turned into the Aya Sofya Pansiyonları (Aya Sofya Pensions).

CAFERAĞA MEDRESESİ (Map 13, #50)

The Caferağa Medresesi *(☎ 212-513 3601, Caferiye Sokak; admission free; open 9am-11pm daily)* was designed by Sinan on the orders of Cafer Ağa, the Chief Black Eunuch. A medresesi is a school for Islamic and secular education, and today it continues to perform part of the function for which it was built in 1560. There are workshops, with regular classes teaching traditional Ottoman crafts (many are for sale here). There is also a busy tea garden in the centre, so if you can move the weighty chairs, sit down and have a tea (US$0.50) – avoid the food.

BATHS OF LADY HÜRREM (Map 13, #64)

Every mosque had a steam bath nearby. Aya Sofya's is across the road on Aya Sofya Meydanı. The Baths of Lady Hürrem *(Haseki Hürrem Hamamı; ☎ 212-638 0035,*

Aya Sofya Meydanı 4; admission free; open 9am-5pm daily) were commissioned by Süleyman for his wife Hürrem Sultan (Roxelana). It's another of Sinan's works, built in 1556 on the site of earlier Byzantine baths. Unfortunately it's now a carpet shop (run by the Ministry of Culture) but you can go in for a wander around without getting hassled. See the Shopping chapter for more information about the shop.

Designed as a 'double hamam' with identical baths for men and women, the centre wall dividing the two has now been breached by a small doorway. Both sides have the three traditional rooms: first the square *frigidarium* for disrobing (on the men's side, this has a pretty marble fountain and stained-glass windows); then the long *tepidarium* for washing; and finally the octagonal *caldarium* for sweating and massage. In the caldarium, note the four *eyvan* (niches) and the four semiprivate washing rooms. The *göbektaşı* (hot platform) in the men's bath is inlaid with coloured marble.

BLUE MOSQUE (Map 13)

Sultan Ahmet I (r. 1603–17) set out to build a mosque that would rival and even surpass the achievement of Justinian. He came close to his goal. The Blue Mosque *(Sultan Ahmet Camii; ☎ 212-518 1319, Hippodrome; closed during prayer times)* is a triumph of harmony, proportion and elegance. Its architect, Mehmet Ağa, achieves the sort of visual experience on the exterior that Aya Sofya has on the interior. There's a sound-and-light show after dusk daily from May to September – see the board for languages. Admission is by donation.

You must approach the Blue Mosque properly in order to appreciate its architectural mastery. Don't walk straight from Sultanahmet Park through the crowds. Rather, go out to the middle of the Hippodrome and approach the mosque from its front.

The layout of the Blue Mosque is classic Ottoman design. Walk towards the mosque through the gate in the peripheral wall. Note the small dome atop the gate: this is the motif Mehmet Ağa uses to lift your eyes to heaven. As you walk through the gate, your eyes follow a flight of stairs up to another gate topped by another dome; through this gate is yet another dome, that of the ablutions fountain in the centre of the mosque courtyard. As you ascend the stairs, semidomes come into view: first the one over the mosque's main door, then the one above it, and another, and another. Finally the **main dome** crowns the whole, and your attention is drawn to the sides, where forests of smaller domes reinforce the effect, completed by the **minarets**, which lift your eyes heavenward.

The Blue Mosque is such a popular tourist sight that admission is controlled so as to preserve its sacred atmosphere. Only worshippers are admitted through the main door; tourists must use the north door and are not admitted at prayer times. At the door an attendant will take your shoes; women will be lent a headscarf; if your clothing is immodest by local standards, you'll be lent a robe. There's no charge for this, but you may be asked to make a donation for the mosque.

Though the stained-glass windows are replacements, they still create the luminous effects of the originals. The semidomes and the dome are painted in graceful arabesques. The 'blue' of the mosque's English nickname comes from the **İznik tiles** that line the walls, particularly in the gallery (which is not open to the public).

You can see immediately why the Blue Mosque, constructed between 1606 and 1616, over 1000 years after Aya Sofya, is not as daring as Aya Sofya. Four massive pillars hold up the less ambitious dome, a less elegant but sturdier solution.

Note also the imperial loge, covered with marble latticework, to the left; the piece of the sacred Black Stone from the Kaaba in Mecca, embedded in the mihrab; the grandfather clock, useful as prayers must be made at exact times; and the high, elaborate chair *(mahfil)* from which the imam (teacher) gives the sermon on Friday. The mimber is the structure with a curtained doorway at floor level, a flight of steps and a small kiosk topped by a spire. From this mimber, of fine marble skilfully carved, the destruction of the janissary corps was proclaimed in 1826.

Mosques built by the great and powerful usually included numerous public-service institutions. Clustered around the Blue Mosque were a medrese; a soup kitchen *(imaret)* serving the poor; a hamam so that the faithful could bathe on Friday, the holy day; and shops (the Arasta Bazaar), the rent from which supported the upkeep of the mosque. The tomb *(türbe)* of the mosque's great patron, Sultan Ahmet I *(donation expected; open 9.30am-4.30pm daily),* is on the north side facing Sultanahmet Park. Buried with Ahmet are his brothers, Sultan Osman II and Sultan Murat IV.

CARPET & KILIM MUSEUM (Map 13, #100)

Up the stone ramp on the Blue Mosque's north side is the Carpet & Kilim Museum *(Halı ve Kilim Müzesi; ☎ 212-528 5332; admission US$1; open 9am-4pm Tues-Sat),* with displays of some of the country's finest. After you've finished here, head through the arched gateway (watch out for the dangling chain) to Arasta Bazaar and along to the end of Mimar Mehmet Ağa Caddesi. Turn right, then first left under the train line. To the right you'll see the modest **Akbıyık Camii (Map 13, #123)**, dating from 1453, one of the oldest mosques in the city; go straight on to see an Ottoman dwelling.

HAMAMZADE İSMAİL DEDE EFENDİ EVİ MÜZESİ (Map 13, #124)

This museum *(☎ 212-516 4314, Ahırkapı Sokak 17; admission US$0.50; open 11am-5pm Tues, Thur, Sat & Sun)* is the restored home of Dede Efendi (1778–1846), a famous Ottoman musical composer of the Mevlevi (whirling) dervish order. The house gives you a good idea of living conditions among the Ottoman intelligentsia of the 18th and 19th centuries.

SOKOLLU MEHMET PAŞA CAMİİ (Map 13, #110)

This mosque *(Şehit Çeşmesi Sokak 20-22; open 7am-8.30pm daily)* was built in 1571 during the height of Ottoman architectural development by the empire's greatest architect, Sinan. Though named after the grand vizier of the time, it was really sponsored by his wife Esmahan, daughter of Sultan Selim II. Besides its architectural harmony, typical of Sinan's greatest works, the mosque is unusual because the medrese is not a separate building but actually part of the mosque structure, built around the forecourt (compare it to the similar plan of the Mihrimah Camii, described in the Western Districts walk later in this chapter). If the mosque is not open, wait for the guardian to appear; he may offer photos for sale.

When you enter, notice the harmonious form, the coloured marble and the spectacular İznik tiles – some of the best ever made. The mosque contains four fragments from the sacred Black Stone in the Kaaba at Mecca: one above the entrance framed in gold, two in the mimber and one in the mihrab. Interestingly, the marble pillars by the mihrab revolve if the foundations have been disturbed by an earthquake – an ingenious early warning device – though they didn't move during the earthquake of 1999 as one is 'out of order'!

Surrounding the mosque are several religious buildings, including a pile of rubble which was once a mosque, and an **Özbekler** *tekke* (lodge) for Nakşibendi dervishes. The tekke was built in 1692 and was used for dervish ceremonies until the Turkish Republic was born, then it became a shelter for the homeless until it was boarded up.

MUSEUM OF TURKISH & ISLAMIC ARTS (Map 13, #19)

The Palace of İbrahim Paşa (1524), on the western side of the Hippodrome, houses the ritzy Museum of Turkish & Islamic Arts *(Türk ve İslam Eserleri Müzesi; ☎ 212-518 1805, Hippodrome 46; adult/student US$2/1; open 10am-5pm Tues-Sun Nov-Mar; 10am-6pm Tues-Sun Apr-Oct)*. It gives you a glimpse into the opulent life of the Ottoman upper class in the time of Süleyman the Magnificent. İbrahim Paşa was Süleyman's close friend, son-in-law and grand vizier. His wealth, power and influence on the monarch became so great that others wishing to influence the sultan became envious. After a rival accused İbrahim of disloyalty, Süleyman's favourite, Haseki Hürrem Sultan (Roxelana), convinced her husband that İbrahim was a threat. Süleyman had him strangled.

Labels are in Turkish and English. The coffee shop in the courtyard of the museum is a welcome refuge from the press of crowds and touts in the Hippodrome.

Exhibits date from the 8th and 9th centuries up to the 19th century. Highlights include the superb calligraphy exhibits, including writing sets, imperial edicts *(fermans)* with monograms *(tuğras)* and illuminated manuscripts. In the largest room (and last room on the 1st floor) have a look at the wooden inlaid Quran stands and chests from the 16th century and the colourful Turkish miniatures. This room also has some enormous antique carpets.

The lower floor of the museum houses ethnographic exhibits. First up is a village loom on which carpets and kilims are woven. Next you'll see the insides of a *yurt* (Central Asian felt hut). An exhibit of the plants and materials used to make natural dyes for the textiles follows, then there's a black tent *(kara çadır)*, made of goat hair, like those used by nomads in eastern Turkey. Henceforth the exhibits travel up the 'civilised' ladder, with domestic scenes acted by stuffed-sack people: a village house from Yuntdağ; a late 19th-century house from the Bursa region; while the last scene, an İstanbul house in the early 20th century, looks like a European tea party.

The buildings behind and beside İbrahim Paşa's palace are İstanbul's law courts and legal administration buildings.

Palace of the Sultans

Mehmet the Conqueror built the first Topkapı Palace shortly after the Conquest in 1453, and lived here until his death in 1481. Sultan after sultan played out the drama of the Ottoman sovereign here until the 19th century. Mahmut II (r. 1808–39) was the last emperor to occupy the palace. After him, the sultans preferred to live in grand and ostentatious European-style palaces such as Dolmabahçe, Çırağan and Yıldız which they built on the shores of the Bosphorus.

Topkapı Palace

It will take you more than half a day to explore Topkapı Palace. In the busy summer months, if you start early (at 9am) you can avoid the worst of the crowds. The following is a list of Topkapı's must-see exhibits in order of importance. (A walking tour through the Harem is shown on Map 3 opposite page 97.)

1. Harem
2. Imperial Council Chamber
3. Imperial Treasury
4. Sacred Safekeeping Rooms
5. Baghdad Kiosk
6. Tower of Justice

TOPKAPI PALACE (Maps 15 & 3)

Buy your ticket to Topkapı Palace *(Topkapı Sarayı; ☎ 212-512 0480, Soğukçeşme Sokak; adult/student US$10/5; open 9am-5pm Wed-Mon Nov-Mar, 9am-6pm Wed-Mon Apr-Oct)* just outside the gate to the second court. If you wish to tour the Harem, you will need to buy another ticket from the office outside it. There are usually lengthy queues at the Harem ticket office, so it's a good idea to head there as soon as you enter Topkapı.

Fountain of Sultan Ahmet III (Map 13, #58)

Before you enter the Imperial Gate (Bab-ı Hümayun) of Topkapı, take a look at the ornate structure in the cobbled square near the gate. It's the Fountain of Sultan Ahmet III, built in 1728 by the sultan who so favoured tulips. It replaced a Byzantine fountain at the same spring. Typical of architecture built during the Tulip Period, it features Turkish rococo decorations (note the floral carvings).

Court of the Janissaries (First Court) (Map 13)

Topkapı grew and changed with the centuries, but its basic four-courtyard plan remained the same. As you pass through the Imperial Gate behind Aya Sofya, you enter the first court, the Court of the Janissaries.

On your left is the former **Aya İrini Kilisesi (Map 13, #56)** *(Church of Divine Peace; ☎ 212-522 0989; only opened for concerts)*. There was a Christian church here from earliest times and, before that, a pagan temple. The early church was replaced by the present one during the reign of Justinian, in the 540s, so the church you see is as old as Aya Sofya. When Mehmet the Conqueror began building his palace, the church was within the grounds. It was used as an arsenal for centuries, then as an artillery museum and now as a concert hall (especially during the International İstanbul Music Festival). Upcoming concerts are posted on a board outside the church.

Janissaries, merchants and tradespeople could circulate as they wished in the Court of the Janissaries, but the second court was restricted. The same is true today as you must buy your admission ticket for the palace at the gate to the second court. The ticket windows are on your right as you approach the gate. Just past the ticket windows is a little fountain where the imperial executioner used to wash the tools of his trade after decapitating a noble or rebel who had displeased the sultan. The head of the unfortunate victim was put on a pike and exhibited above the gate you are about to enter.

Second Court (Map 3)

The **Middle Gate (Map 3, #73)** (Ortakapı or Bab-üs Selâm) led to the palace's second court, used for the business of running the empire. Only the sultan and the *valide sultan* (queen mother) were allowed through the Middle Gate on horseback. Everyone else, including the grand vizier, had to dismount. The gate was constructed by Süleyman the Magnificent in 1524, utilising architects and workers he had brought back from his conquest of Hungary.

To the right after you enter are models and a map of the palace. Beyond them, in a nearby building, you'll find imperial carriages made in Paris, Turin and Vienna, for the sultan and his family.

The second court has a beautiful, park-like setting. Topkapı is not based on a typical European palace plan – one large building with outlying gardens – but is a series of pavilions, kitchens, barracks, audience chambers, kiosks and sleeping quarters built around a central enclosure.

The great **palace kitchens (Map 3, #69)**, on your right, hold a small portion of Topkapı's vast collection of Chinese celadon porcelain, valued for its beauty but also because it was reputed to change colour if touched by poisoned food. In a building close by are the collections of European, Russian and Ottoman porcelain, silverware and glassware. The last of the kitchens, the Helvahane, in which all the palace sweets were made, is now set up as a kitchen, and you can easily imagine what went on in these rooms as the staff prepared food for the 5000 inhabitants of the palace.

On the left (west) side of the second court is the ornate **Imperial Council Chamber (Map 3, #63)**, also called the Divan Salonu. It's beneath the squarish Tower of Justice, the palace's highest point. The Imperial Divan (council) met in the Imperial Council Chamber to discuss matters of state while the sultan eavesdropped through a grille high on the wall. During the great days of the empire, foreign ambassadors were received on days when the janissaries were to get their pay. Huge sacks of silver coins were brought to the Imperial Council Chamber. High-court officers would dispense the coins to long lines of the tough, impeccably costumed and faultlessly disciplined troops as the ambassadors looked on in admiration.

North of the Imperial Council Chamber is the **Inner Treasury (Map 3, #49)** which today exhibits Ottoman and European armoury.

Though closed for renovation, the **Imperial Stables (Map 3, #71)** are entered from the second court, just to the north-west of the Middle Gate. Go down the cobbled slope.

Harem (Map 3)

The entrance to the Harem *(adult/student US$10/5; open 10am-noon & 1pm-4pm; tours every half-hour starting at 10am),* open by guided tour only, is beneath the **Tower of Justice (Map 3, #64)** (Adalet Kulesi). A visit to the Tower of Justice is not part of the Harem tour, but if you're interested in seeing the tower, at the end of the tour head back to the Harem ticket office. Ignore the queue (at your own risk) and knock at the side of the ticket booth. You'll be sold a separate ticket (adult/student US$3.50/1.50). A guard will be assigned to escort you up to the top, past the gilded grille through which the sultan eavesdropped on the meetings of his ministers of state. The view from the top is truly splendid.

Legend vs Reality Fraught with legend and romance, the Harem is usually imagined as a place where the sultan could engage in debauchery at will. In fact, these were the imperial family quarters, and every detail of Harem life was governed by tradition, obligation and ceremony.

Every traditional Muslim household had two distinct parts: the *selamlık* (greeting room) where the master greeted friends, business associates and tradespeople; and the *harem* (private apartments), reserved for himself and his family. The Harem, then, was something akin to the private apartments in Buckingham Palace or the White House.

The women of the Harem had to be foreigners, as Islam forbade enslaving Muslims, Christians or Jews (although Christians and Jews could be enslaved in the Balkans: see the boxed text 'The Janissaries' later in this section). Girls, too, were bought as slaves (often having been sold by their parents at a good price) or were received as gifts from nobles and potentates. A favourite source of girls was Circassia, north of the Caucasus Mountains in Russia, as Circassian women were noted for their beauty.

Upon entering the Harem, the girls would be schooled in Islam and Turkish culture and language, the arts of make-up, dress, comportment, music, reading and writing, embroidery and dancing. They then entered a meritocracy, first as ladies-in-waiting to the sultan's concubines and children, then to the sultan's mother and finally, if they were the best, to the sultan himself.

Ruling the Harem was the valide sultan, the mother of the reigning sultan. She often owned large landed estates in her own name and controlled them through black eunuch servants. She was allowed to give orders directly to the grand vizier. Her influence on the sultan, on the selection of his wives and concubines and on matters of state, was often profound.

The sultan was allowed by Islamic law to have four legitimate wives, who received the title of *kadın* (wife). If a wife bore him a son she was called *haseki sultan; haseki kadın* if it was a daughter. The Ottoman dynasty did not observe primogeniture (the right of the first-born son to the throne), so in principle the throne was available to any imperial son. Each lady of the Harem contrived mightily to have her son proclaimed heir to the throne, to thus assure her own role as the new valide sultan.

As for concubines, Islam permits as many as a man can support in proper style. The Ottoman sultans had the means to support many, sometimes up to 300, though they were not all in the Harem at the same time. The domestic thrills of the sultans were usually less spectacular, however. Mehmet the Conqueror, builder of Topkapı, was the last sultan to have four official wives. After him, sultans did not officially marry, but instead kept four chosen concubines without the legal encumbrances, thereby saving themselves the embarrassments and inconveniences suffered by another famous Renaissance monarch, King Henry VIII.

The Harem was much like a village with all the necessary services. About 400 or 500 people lived in this section of the palace at any one time. Not many of the ladies stayed in the Harem all their lives: The sultan might grant them their freedom, after which they would often marry powerful men who wanted the company of these well-educated women, not to mention their connections with the palace. And the relationship was twofold: The sultan was also happy to have the women, educated to be loyal, spread throughout the empire to help keep tabs on political affairs via their husbands.

The chief black eunuch, the sultan's personal representative in administration of the Harem and other important affairs of state, was the third-most powerful official in the empire, after the grand vizier and the supreme Islamic judge.

Many of the 400-odd rooms in the Harem were constructed during the reign of Süleyman the Magnificent (r. 1520–66), but much more was added or reconstructed thereafter. In 1665 a disastrous fire destroyed much of the complex, which was rebuilt by Mehmet IV and later sultans.

Life in the Cage

As children, imperial princes were brought up in the Harem, taught and cared for by its women and servants.

In the early centuries of the empire, Ottoman princes were schooled as youths in combat and statecraft by direct experience: They practised soldiering, fought in battles and were given provinces to administer. But as the Ottoman dynasty did not observe primogeniture (succession of the firstborn), the death of the sultan regularly resulted in a fratricidal bloodbath as his sons battled it out among themselves for the throne. In the case of Beyazıt II (r. 1481–1512), his sons began the battles even before the sultan's death, realising that to lose the battle for succession meant death for themselves. The victorious son, Selim I (r. 1512–20), not only murdered his brothers but even forced Sultan Beyazıt to abdicate, and may even have had him murdered as he went into retirement.

Fratricide was not practised by Ahmet I (r. 1603–17), who could not bring himself to murder his mad brother Mustafa. Instead, he kept him imprisoned in the Harem, beginning the tradition of cage life *(kafes hayatı)*. This house arrest, adopted in place of fratricide by later sultans, meant that princes were prey to the intrigues of the women and eunuchs, ignorant of war and statecraft, and thus usually unfit to rule if and when the occasion arose. Luckily for the empire in this latter period, there were able grand viziers to carry on.

In later centuries the dynasty adopted the practice of having the eldest male in the direct line assume the throne.

Touring the Harem Although the Harem is built into a hillside and has six levels, the standard tour takes you through or past only a few dozen rooms on one level, but these are among the most splendid. Most Harem tours are given in Turkish and English, and in other languages in summer. Informative plaques in Turkish and English have been placed in the Harem, though you won't get much time on the tour to read them.

The tour route may vary from time to time, as various rooms are closed for restoration and others are finished and opened to view. Following is a description of the tour at the time of research.

You enter the Harem by the **Carriage Gate (Map 3, #67)**, through which Harem ladies would enter in their carriages. Inside the gate is the **Dome with Cupboards**. Beyond it is the **Hall with Şadırvan (Map 3, #65)**, a guard room decorated with fine İznik faience; the green colours are unusual in İznik tiles. To the left is a doorway to the **Black Eunuchs' Mosque (Map 3, #61)**, on the right the doorway to the Tower of Justice which rises above the Imperial Council Chamber.

Beyond the Hall with Şadırvan is the narrow **Black Eunuchs' Courtyard (Map 3, #55)**, decorated in Kütahya tiles from the 17th century. Behind the marble colonnade on the left are the **Black Eunuchs' Dormitories (Map 3, #56)**. In the early days white eunuchs were used, but black eunuchs sent as presents by the Ottoman governor of Egypt later took control. As many as 200 lived here, guarding the doors and waiting on the women.

Near the far end of the courtyard on the left, a staircase leads up to the rooms in which imperial princes were given their primary schooling. On the right is the **Chief Black Eunuch's Room (Map 3, #50)**.

At the far end of the courtyard, safely protected by the eunuchs, is the **Main Gate**

(Map 3, #48) into the Harem proper, and another **guard room** with two gigantic gilded mirrors. From this, the **Concubines' Corridor (Map 3, #47)** on the left leads to the **Concubines' & Consorts' Courtyard (Map 3, #51)**. A concubine came by gift or purchase; the more talented and intelligent rose in the palace service to hold offices in the administration of the Harem; the less talented waited on the more talented.

Next you'll go through the **Sultan Ahmet's Kiosk (Map 3, #46)** to the **Valide Sultan's Quarters (Map 3, #45)**, the very centre of power in the Harem. These rooms include a large salon, a small bedroom, a room for prayer and other small chambers. From these ornate rooms the valide sultan oversaw and controlled her huge 'family'. After his accession to the throne, a new sultan came here to receive the allegiance and congratulations of the people of the Harem.

The sultan, as he walked these corridors, wore slippers with silver soles. As no woman was allowed to show herself to the sultan without specific orders, the clatter of the silver soles warned residents of the sultan's approach allowing them to disappear from his sight. This rule no doubt solidified the valide sultan's control, as *she* got to choose the most beautiful, talented and intelligent of the Harem girls to be her personal servants, and thus introduced them to her son, the sultan.

The tour passes through the private hamams and toilets of the valide sultan to the **Emperor's Chamber (Map 3, #28)**, decorated in Delft tiles. This grand room was where the sultan and his ladies gathered for entertainment, often with musicians in the balcony. Designed perhaps by Sinan during the reign of Murat III (r. 1574–95), it was redecorated in baroque style by Osman III (r. 1754–57). The smaller part of the room remains baroque; the larger part has had its 16th-century decor restored.

The tour enters the **Privy Chamber of Murat III (Map 3, #24)** (1578), one of the most sumptuous rooms in the palace. Virtually all of the decoration is original, and is probably the work of Sinan. Besides the gorgeous İznik tiles and a fireplace, there is a three-tiered fountain to give the sound of cascading water and, perhaps not coincidentally, to make it difficult to eavesdrop on the sultan's conversations.

Adjoining the Privy Chamber to the west is the **Library of Ahmet I (Map 3, #25)** (1609), with small fountains by each window to cool the summer breezes as they enter the room. Perhaps Ahmet I retired here to inspect plans of his great building project, the Blue Mosque. The adjoining **Dining Room of Ahmet III (Map 3, #26)** (1706), with wonderful painted panels of flowers and fruit, was built by Ahmet I's successor.

East of the Privy Chamber of Murat III is the **Double Kiosk (Map 3, #22)**, two rooms dating from around 1600. Note the painted canvas dome in the first room, and the fine tile panels above the fireplace in the second. Fireplaces and braziers – which give off toxic carbon monoxide – were the palace's winter heating system.

North and east of the Double Kiosk is the **Favourites' Courtyard & Apartments (Map 3, #20)** The Turkish word for 'favourite', *gözde,* literally means 'in the eye' (of the sultan). Over the edge of the courtyard you'll see a swimming pool. Just past it is the **Private Prison (Map 3, #21)** (*kafes,* cage) where the unwanted brothers or sons of the sultan were kept (see the boxed text 'Life in the Cage' earlier in this section).

A corridor leads east to the **Golden Road (Map 3, #39)**, a passage leading south. A servant of the sultan's would toss gold coins to the women of the Harem here, hence the name.

The tour re-enters the guardroom with the huge gilded mirrors, then exits through the **Birdcage Gate** into the palace's third courtyard.

Third Court (Map 3)

If you enter the third court through the Harem, and thus by the back door, you should head for the main gate into the court. Get the full effect of entering this holy of holies by going out through the gate, and back in again.

This gate, the **Gate of Felicity (Map 3, #36)**, also sometimes called the Gate of the White Eunuchs, was the entrance into the

The Janissaries

The word 'janissary' comes from the Turkish *yeni çeri*, 'new levies'. These soldiers were personal servants of the sultan, fed and paid regularly by him, and subject to his will. They were full-time soldiers, an innovation in an age when most soldiers – and all soldiers in Europe – were farmers in spring and autumn, homebodies in winter and warriors only in summer.

In a process termed *devşirme*, which was begun shortly after the conquest of Constantinople, government agents went out from İstanbul into the towns and villages of the Balkans rounding up 10-year-old boys from Christian families for the sultan's personal service. Having one's son taken was undoubtedly a blow to the family, who would probably lose his love and labour forever; but it was the road to ultimate advancement. The boy would be instructed in Turkish, converted to Islam, and enrolled in the sultan's service.

The imperial service was a meritocracy. Those of normal intelligence and capabilities went into the janissary corps, the sultan's imperial guard. The brightest and most capable boys went into the palace service, and many eventually rose to the highest offices, including that of grand vizier. This ensured that the top government posts were always held by personal servants of the sultan. These top government and military officers would often remember their birthplaces, and would lavish benefits such as public works projects (mosques, bridges, schools etc) upon them.

By the early 19th century, the janissary corps had become unbearably corrupt and self-serving, and a constant threat to the throne. The reforming sultan Mahmut II, risking his life, his throne and his dynasty, readied a new, loyal, European-style army, then provoked a revolt of the janissaries in the Hippodrome and brought in his new army to wipe them out, ending their 350-year history in 1826.

sultan's private domain. As is common with oriental potentates, the sultan preserved the imperial mystique by appearing in public very seldom. The third court was staffed and guarded by white eunuchs, who allowed only a few very important people in. As you enter the third court, imagine it alive with the movements of imperial pages and white eunuchs scurrying here and there in their palace costumes. Every now and then the chief white eunuch or the chief black eunuch would appear, and all would bow. If the sultan walked across the courtyard, all activity stopped until the event was over.

An exception to the imperial seclusion was the ceremony celebrating a new sultan's accession to the throne. After girding on the sword of Osman, which symbolised imperial power, the new monarch would sit enthroned before the Gate of Felicity and receive the obeisance, allegiance and congratulations of the empire's high and mighty.

Before the annual military campaigns in summertime, the sultan would also appear before this gate bearing the standard of the Prophet Mohammed to inspire his generals to go out and win one for Islam.

Audience Chamber (Map 3, #35) Just inside the Gate of Felicity is the **Audience Chamber**, constructed in the 16th century, but refurbished in the 18th century. Important officials and foreign ambassadors were brought to this little kiosk to conduct the high business of state. An ambassador, frisked for weapons and held on each arm by a white eunuch, would approach the sultan. At the proper moment, he knelt and kowtowed; if he didn't, the eunuchs would urge him ever so forcefully to do so.

The sultan, seated on the divans whose cushions are embroidered with over 15,000 seed pearls, inspected the ambassador's gifts and offerings as they were passed through the small doorway on the left. Even if the sultan and the ambassador could converse in the same language (sultans in the later years knew French, and ambassadors often learned Turkish), all conversation was with the grand vizier. The sultan would not deign to speak to a foreigner, and only the very highest Ottoman officers were allowed to address the monarch directly.

Library of Ahmet III (Map 3, #33) Right behind the Audience Chamber is a

VERITY CAMPBELL

GREG ELMS

IZZET KERIBAR

EDDIE GERALD

Topkapı Palace, residence of the sultans for nearly four centuries, has a splendid location overlooking the Bosphorus (top left). The decoration is exquisite, from the İznik tiles found throughout (top right) to the Emperor's Chamber (bottom) in the Harem and the gates of the Imperial Council Chamber (middle left).

MAP 3 – TOPKAPI PALACE (TOPKAPI SARAYI)

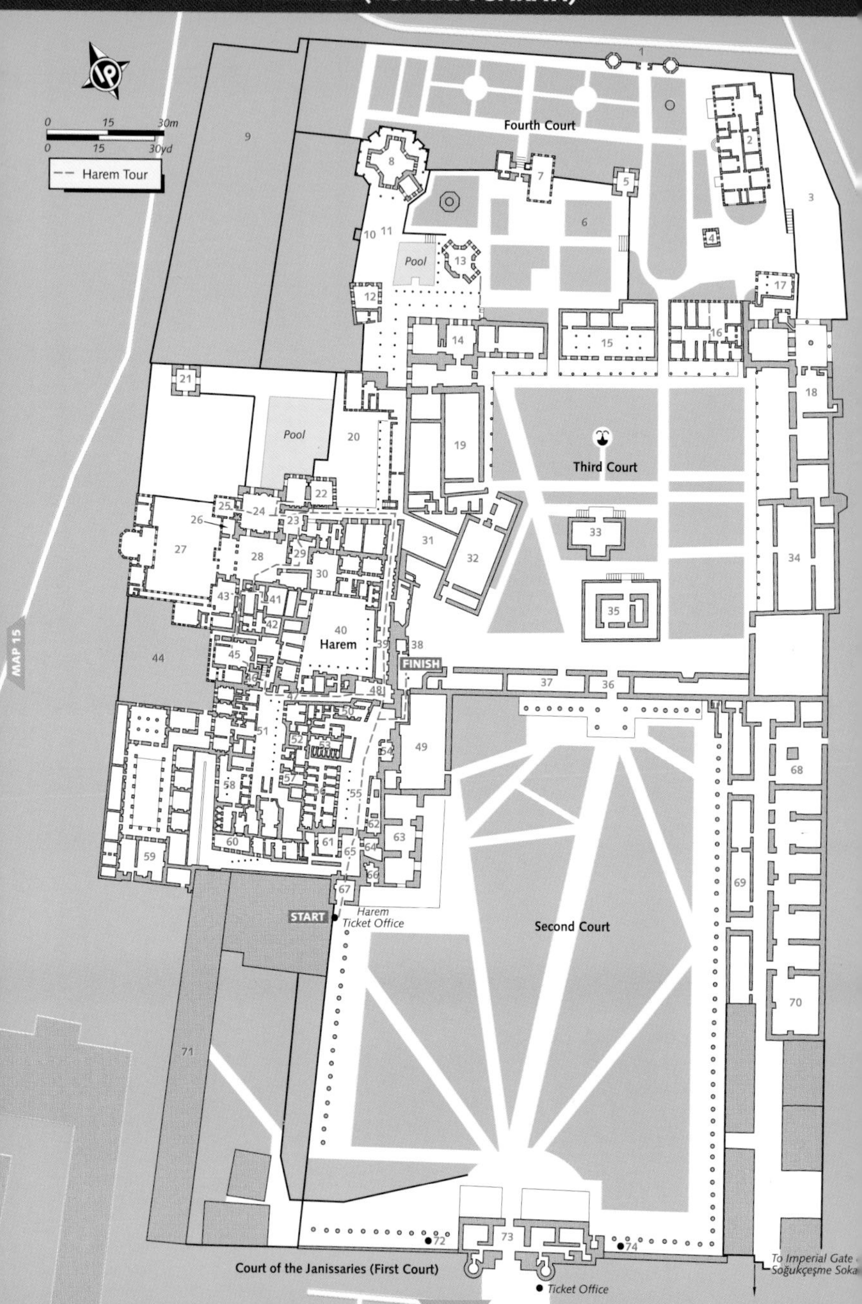

MAP 3 – TOPKAPI PALACE (TOPKAPI SARAYI)

SECOND COURT

49 Inner Treasury
63 Imperial Council Chamber
66 Kiosk
68 Restored Confectionery
69 Palace Kitchens
70 Chinese & Japanese Porcelain
71 Imperial Stables
72 Book & Gift Shop
73 Middle Gate
74 Imperial Carriages

THIRD COURT

14 Sacred Safekeeping Rooms
15 Treasury Dormitory
16 Museum Directorate
18 Imperial Treasury
19 Quarters of Pages in Charge of the Sacred Safekeeping Rooms
32 Mosque of the Eunuchs & Library
33 Library of Ahmet III
34 Dormitory of the Expeditionary Force
35 Audience Chamber
36 Gate of Felicity
37 White Eunuchs' Quarters

FOURTH COURT

1 Gate of the Privy Gardens
2 Mecidiye Köşkü; Konyalı Restaurant
3 Konyalı Restaurant & Cafe Terraces
4 Bookshop
5 Chief Physician's Room
6 Tulip Garden
7 Kiosk of Mustafa Pasha
8 Baghdad Kiosk
9 Lower Gardens of the Imperial Terrace
10 İftariye Baldachin
11 Marble Terrace & Pool
12 Circumcision Room
13 Erivan Kiosk
17 Sofa or Terrace Mosque

HAREM

20 Favourites' Courtyard & Apartments
21 Private Prison
22 Double Kiosk
23 Beautifully Tiled Antechamber
24 Privy Chamber of Murat III
25 Library of Ahmet I
26 Dining Room of Ahmet III
27 Terrace of Osman III
28 Emperor's Chamber
29 Room with Hearth; Room with Fountain
30 Consultation Place of the Genies
31 Harem Mosque
38 Birdcage Gate
39 Golden Road
40 Courtyard of the Valide Sultan
41 Valide Sultan's Hamam
42 Sultan's Hamam
43 Chamber of Abdül Hamit I
44 Harem Garden
45 Valide Sultan's Quarters
46 Sultan Ahmet's Kiosk
47 Concubines' Corridor
48 Main Gate; Second Guard Room
50 Chief Black Eunuch's Room
51 Concubines' & Consorts' Courtyard
52 Harem Kitchen
53 Imperial Princes' School
54 Harem Chamberlain's Room
55 Black Eunuchs' Courtyard
56 Black Eunuchs' Dormitories
57 Women's Hamam
58 Women's Dormitory
59 Harem Hospital
60 Laundry Room
61 Black Eunuchs' Mosque
62 Harem Eunuchs' Mosque
64 Tower of Justice
65 Hall with Şadırvan
67 Carriage Gate; Dome with Cupboards

pretty little library built in 1719 by Sultan Ahmet III. Light-filled, it has comfy reading areas and stunning inlaid woodwork.

Dormitory of the Expeditionary Force (Map 3, #34) Walk to the right as you are leaving the Audience Chamber, and enter the rooms of the Dormitory of the Expeditionary Force, which now house the rich collections of imperial robes, kaftans and uniforms worked in silver and gold thread. Textile design reached its highest point during the reign of Süleyman the Magnificent, when the imperial workshops produced cloth of exquisite design and work.

Imperial Treasury (Map 3, #18) At the time of research the Imperial Treasury was undergoing renovation. Should the new-look Treasury have similar displays to the old, you can expect to find an incredible number and variety of objects made from or decorated with gold, silver, rubies, emeralds, jade, pearls and diamonds. The tiny figurine of a sultan sitting under a canopy, his body one enormous pear, is well worth seeking out.

The Spoonmaker's Diamond is an 86-carat rock surrounded by several dozen smaller stones. First worn by Mehmet IV at his accession to the throne in 1648, it is the world's fifth-largest diamond. There is also an uncut emerald weighing 3.26kg, and the golden dagger set with three large emeralds which was the object of Peter Ustinov's criminal quest in the movie *Topkapi*. Hunt down the gold throne given by Nadir Shah of Persia to Mahmud I (r. 1730–54).

Next door to the Imperial Treasury is the **Balcony of Life**. From here the breeze is cool and there's a marvellous view of the Bosphorus and the Sea of Marmara.

Mad about Tulips

Tulips, originally from Central Asia, were introduced to Ottoman gardens throughout the empire at a very early age. But it wasn't until the 16th century that tulips first made their debut in Europe and catapulted to unsuspecting stardom. Tulip-mania was born, with the Dutch in particular committing finances (a new variety of the flower earned its creator fame and money) until bulbs eventually became a currency. The market crashed, the speculators lost, but the modest tulip endured in Europe. In the 18th century Sultan Ahmet III caught on to the tulip craze and the Tulip Period in Turkey was born. The flowers were planted in abundance while their form influenced carvings, paintings, embroideries and architecture throughout the empire. The Fountain of Sultan Ahmet III, just outside the Court of the Janissaries (first court), is a good example of Tulip Period architecture.

Sacred Safekeeping Rooms (Map 3, #14) Opposite the Imperial Treasury is another set of wonders, the holy relics in the Suite of the Felicitous Cloak, nowadays called the Sacred Safekeeping Rooms. These rooms, sumptuously decorated with İznik faience, constitute a holy of holies within the palace. Only the chosen could enter the third court, but entry into these special rooms was for the chosen of the chosen, and even then only on ceremonial occasions. During the empire, this suite of rooms was opened only once a year so that the imperial family could pay homage to the memory of the Prophet on the 15th day of the holy month of Ramazan. Even though anyone, prince or commoner, faithful or infidel, can enter the rooms now, you should respect the sacred atmosphere by observing decorous behaviour, as this is still a place of pilgrimage for Muslims.

Notice in the entry room the carved door from the Kaaba in Mecca and, hanging from the ceiling, gilded rain gutters from the same place. Don't miss the harmonious dome above.

To the right (north) a room contains a hair of Prophet Mohammed's beard, his footprint in clay, his sword, tooth and more. Sometimes an imam is seated in a glass booth, chanting passages from the Quran. The 'felicitous cloak' itself resides in a golden casket in a small adjoining room along with the battle standard.

On the opposite side (south) of the entry room are more relics including a letter from Mohammed to the governor of Al-Aksa mosque in Jerusalem, Caliph Omar's sword and even Moses' walking stick!

Other Exhibits The third court holds buildings of the Enderun or palace school for pages or janissaries. The **Quarters of Pages in Charge of the Sacred Safekeeping Rooms (Map 3, #19)** these days has exhibits of Turkish miniature paintings, calligraphy, and portraits of the sultans. Notice the graceful, elaborate *tuğra* (monogram) of the sultans. The tuğra, placed at the top of any imperial proclamation, contains elaborate calligraphic rendering of the names of the sultan and his father, eg, 'Abdül Hamit Khan, son of Abdül Mecit Khan, Ever Victorious'.

Other buildings in the third court include the **Mosque of the Eunuchs** and a little **library (Map 3, #32)**.

Fourth Court

Examples of the pleasure pavilion occupy the north-easternmost part of the palace, sometimes called the tulip gardens or fourth court. The **Mecidiye Köşkü (Map 3, #2)** was built by Abdül Mecit (r. 1839–61) according to 19th-century European models. Beneath it is the **Konyalı Restaurant (Map 3, #2 & #3)** (see the Places to Eat chapter for details).

In the other direction (north-west) is the sultan's **Chief Physician's Room (Map 3, #5)**, who was always one of the sultan's Jewish subjects. Nearby, you'll see the **Kiosk of Mustafa Pasha (Map 3, #7)**, sometimes called the Sofa Köşkü. Outside the kiosk, during the reign of Sultan Ahmet III, the **Tulip Garden (Map 3, #6)** was filled with the latest varieties of the flower. Little lamps would be set out among the tulips at night. See the boxed text 'Mad about Tulips' above.

Up the stairs at the end of the Tulip Garden are two of the most enchanting kiosks joined by a marble terrace with a beautiful pool. Sultan Murat IV (r. 1623–40) built the **Erivan Kiosk (Map 3, #13)** in 1635 after reclaiming the city of Yerevan (now in Armenia) from Persia. He also constructed the **Baghdad Kiosk (Map 3, #8)** in 1639 to commemorate his victory over that city. Notice the superb İznik tiles, the inlay and woodwork.

Enjoy the views from under the onion-shaped roof of the **İftariye Baldachin (Map 3, #10)** which juts out from the terrace. Sultan İbrahim built this small structure in 1640 as a picturesque place to break the fast of Ramazan.

On the west end of the terrace is the **Circumcision Room (Map 3, #12)**, used for the ritual that admits Muslim boys to manhood. (Circumcision is usually performed when the boy is nine or 10.) The outer walls of the chamber are graced by particularly beautiful tile panels.

Path of Empires

Divan Yolu, the Road to the Imperial Council, is the main thoroughfare of the old city. Starting from the Hippodrome on the city's first of seven hills, it heads west, up another hill, past the Kapalı Çarşı, through Beyazıt Square and past İstanbul University to Aksaray Square. Turning north a bit, it continues to the Topkapı (Cannon Gate) in the ancient city walls. In its progress through the city, its name changes from Divan Yolu to become Yeniçeriler Caddesi, Ordu Caddesi and Turgut Özal (formerly Millet) Caddesi.

This thoroughfare, dating from the early times of Constantinople, was laid out by Roman engineers to connect the city with Roman roads heading west. The street held its importance in Ottoman times, as Mehmet the Conqueror's first palace was in Beyazıt Square.

DİVAN YOLU (Map 13)

Start the walk at the **Milion**, the great marble milestone from which all distances in Byzantium were measured, on the south side of the park near the Sunken Cistern. Head west along Divan Yolu to the little **Firuz Ağa Camii (Map 13, #22)** built in 1491. It was commissioned during the time of Beyazıt II (r. 1481–1512). The style is the simple one of the early Ottomans: a dome on a square base with a plain porch in front.

Just behind Firuz Ağa Camii is the **Palace of Antiochus (Map 13, #21)** (5th century), now mere ruined foundations.

The first major intersection is that with Babıali Caddesi. Turn right onto this street until you reach Nuruosmaniye Caddesi; a few blocks north is **Cağaloğlu Square (Map 13)**, once the centre of İstanbul's newspaper

Path of Empires

This full-day walk will travel along Divan Yolu Cad, via Çemberlitaş, Süleymaniye Camii and finish at the Cartoon & Humour Museum. A few recreational options are thrown in too, so you may want to visit the following over a couple of days. (Purple trail: Starts Map 13, then Map 4, Map 15 & Map14)

1. Divan Yolu
2. Çemberlitaş
3. Beyazıt Camii
4. Beyazıt Square
5. İstanbul University
6. Museum of Turkish Calligraphic Art
7. Süleymaniye Camii
8. Şehzade Mehmet Camii
9. Aqueduct of Valens
10. Fatih Anıtı Parkı
11. Cartoon & Humour Museum

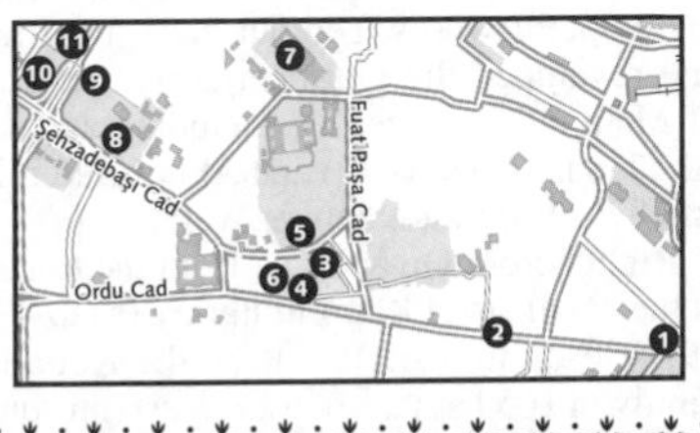

and book publishing industry. Most of the newspaper publishers have now moved to large, modern buildings outside the city walls, though some of the smaller book publishers survive here. The **Cağaloğlu Hamamı (Map 13, #28)** is nearby, along Yerebatan Caddesi (see the boxed text 'Hamams' at the end of this chapter for more details).

If instead you turn left (south) from Divan Yolu, you'll be on Klodfarer Caddesi, named after the Turcophile French novelist Claude Farrère. It leads to a small park beneath which lies the 4th-century Byzantine Philoxenes cistern now called **Binbirdirek (Map 13, #16)**, or '1001 Columns'. Unfortunately it's closed indefinitely.

Back on Divan Yolu, the impressive enclosure right at the corner of Babıali Caddesi is filled with **tombs (Map 13, #10)** *(admission free; open 9am-5pm daily)* of the Ottoman high and mighty, including several sultans. The first to be built was for Sultan Mahmut II (r. 1808–39), the reforming emperor who wiped out the janissaries and revamped the Ottoman army. Several of Mahmut's successors, including sultans Abdülaziz (r. 1861–76) and Abdül Hamit II (r. 1876–1909), are here as well.

Right across Divan Yolu from the tombs is the small stone **Köprülü library (Map 13, #9)** (closed to visits) built by the Köprülü family in 1659 as part of a *külliyesi* (mosque complex). The Köprülüs rose to prominence in the mid-17th century and furnished the empire with viziers, generals and grand admirals for centuries. They administered the empire during a time when the scions of the Ottoman dynasty fell well below the standards of Mehmet the Conqueror and Süleyman the Magnificent.

Running south downhill beside the library is Piyer Loti Caddesi, named after another French Turcophile author. Follow this street for a short distance. Just round the bend look for the large Eminönü Belediye Başkanlığı (Eminönü Municipal Presidency) building on the right. To the right of the main entrance is a doorway with **Şerefiye Sarnıçı (Map 13, #13)** *(Theodosius Cistern; admission free; open 9am-5pm)*, carved into its lintel. Wander in, ask the guard to turn on the lights and you can see what the Sunken Cistern looked like before it was tarted up for tourism.

Back on Divan Yolu, at the corner of Türbedar Sokak is the **Basın Müzesi (Map 13, #8)** *(Press Museum; ☎ 212-513 8458, Divan Yolu 84; admission free; open 10am-6pm Mon-Sat)*. The old printing presses may interest some. Others may want to visit the amateur art gallery on the 1st floor or the handicrafts shop on the ground floor.

ÇEMBERLİTAŞ (Map 13)

Stroll a bit further along Divan Yolu and into the Çemberlitaş district where Divan Yolu changes name to Yeniçeriler Caddesi. On the left are some more buildings from the Köprülü külliyesi **(Map 13, #5)**: The **tomb** is that of Köprülü Mehmet Paşa (1575–1661), and the octagonal **mosque**, on the corner, was a lecture and study room. Across the street, that strange building with a row of streetfront shops is actually an ancient Turkish bath, the **Çemberlitaş Hamamı (Map 13, #6)** (1580; see the boxed text 'Hamams' at the end of this chapter). Part of this building has been converted to a restaurant, **Cennet (Map 13, #7)** (see the Places to Eat chapter).

The derelict column rising up from the pigeon-packed plaza close by is surprisingly one of İstanbul's most ancient and revered monuments. Called **Çemberlitaş (Map 13, #3)** (The Banded Stone or Burnt Column), it was erected by Constantine the Great (r. 324–37) to celebrate the dedication of Constantinople as capital of the Roman Empire in 330. This area was the grand Forum of Constantine, and the column was topped by a statue of the great emperor himself. In an earthquake zone erecting columns can be a risky business. This one has survived, though it needed iron bands for support within a century after it was built. The statue crashed to the ground in a quake almost 1000 years ago.

If you wish, at this point of the walking tour you could head along Vezir Hanı, to the Nuruosmaniye Camii and Kapalı Çarşı to start the Bazaar District walking tour. See that section later in this chapter.

SMOKERS' BREAK (Maps 13 & 4)

The little **mosque (Map 13, #2)** close to Çemberlitaş is that of Atik Ali Paşa, a eunuch and grand vizier of Beyazıt II. Built in 1496, it's one of the oldest in the city.

Beyond Atik Ali Paşa Camii on the right (north) side is the **Koca Sinan Paşa Medresesi (Map 4, #26)**. Here lies Grand Vezir Koca Sinan Paşa. His **tomb** *(admission free; open 9.30am-4.30pm Tues-Sun)* is finely carved, complete with coloured stonework. After you've seen the tomb, head past the cemetery and to the right. Here's the quiet gardens of the **İlesam Lokalı** *(☎ 212-511 2618, Yeniçeriler Caddesi 84)*, a club formed by the enigmatically named Professional Union of Owners of the Works of Science & Literature. Consider trying a *nargileh* (water pipe; US$1) with a tea or coffee.

Just on the other side of Bileyciler Sokak from İlesam is a similar place, the **Erenler Nargile Salonu (Map 4, #25)**, in the courtyard of the Çorlulu Ali Paşa Medresesi. This place is smaller, a bit cheaper, but more cramped. There's a row of carpet shops down the side. It's a university students' hang-out.

BEYAZIT CAMİİ (Map 15, #38)

Continue along Yeniçeriler Caddesi until you see the Beyazıt Camii *(Mosque of Sultan Beyazıt II; ☎ 212-519 3644, Yeniçeriler Caddesi)*, built in 1501–06, on your right. Beyazıt used an exceptional amount of fine stone in his mosque: marble, porphyry, verd antique and rare granite. The mihrab is simple, except for the rich stone columns framing it.

This was the second imperial mosque to be built in the city after Mehmet the Conqueror's Fatih Camii (see the Western Districts walking tour later in this chapter), and was the prototype for other imperial mosques. In effect, it is the link between Aya Sofya, which obviously inspired its design, and the great mosques such as the Süleymaniye, which are realisations of Aya Sofya's design fully adapted to Muslim worship.

Some of the other buildings of Beyazıt's külliyesi have been well utilised. The soup kitchen has been turned into a library, while the medrese is now the Museum of Turkish Calligraphic Art (see that entry). Unfortunately the once-splendid hamam is still waiting to be restored.

BEYAZIT SQUARE (Map 15)

Beyazıt Square, officially called Hürriyet Meydanı (Freedom Square), though everyone knows it simply as Beyazıt, is out the front of Beyazıt Camii. Under the Byzantines it was called the Forum of Theodosius. Emperor Theodosius rebuilt it in AD 393 to become the largest of the city's many forums, endowing it with a monumental arch and other decorative structures heralding the wonders of himself. Today it's packed with cars and pigeons, and a few policemen who like to keep an eye on student activities. Sections of **columns (Map 15, #41)**, decorated with stylised oak-knot designs, which were dug up from the square during the 1950s, can be seen on the other side of Yeniçeriler Caddesi.

İSTANBUL UNIVERSITY (Map 15)

Beyazıt Square is backed by the impressive portal of İstanbul University. After the Conquest, Mehmet the Conqueror built his first palace here, a wooden structure, which burnt down centuries ago. After he built Topkapı, he used the old palace as a home for harem women. The frilly gates and main building of the university were originally built in the mid-19th century for the Ottoman War Ministry, which explains their grandiose and martial aspect. The stone **tower**, visible from most of Old İstanbul, was built as a lookout for fires. Both the university and tower are off limits.

MUSEUM OF TURKISH CALLIGRAPHIC ART (Map 15, #39)

The small building at the western side of Beyazıt Square is the Museum of Turkish Calligraphic Art *(Türk Vakıf Hat Sanatları Müzesi; ☎ 212-527 5851, Hürriyet Meydanı; adult/student US$1.70/0.90, camera US$4.50; open 9am-4pm Tues-Sat)*. The museum has a good collection of wall hangings and manuscripts, many from the 13th century. Most examples illustrate cursive calligraphic styles. Exhibits are protected by glass boxes with push-button lighting, but unfortunately the signs are in Turkish. The building, once the medrese or theological college of Beyazıt Camii, is a series of rooms surrounding a leafy courtyard.

SÜLEYMANİYE CAMİİ (Map 15, #2)

If you are facing the İstanbul University in Beyazıt, go to the right, and head through a denim-selling district, Fuat Paşa Caddesi, following the university's walls. First left up Prof Sıddık Sami Onar Caddesi will bring you to the famous Süleymaniye Camii *(Mosque of Sultan Süleyman the Magnificent; ☎ 212-514 0139, Prof Sıddık Sami Onar Caddesi)*. The Süleymaniye Camii, İstanbul's largest mosque, crowns one of İstanbul's hills, dominating the Golden Horn and providing a magnificent landmark for the entire city. This, the grandest of all Turkish mosques, was built between 1550 and 1557 by the greatest, richest and most powerful of Ottoman sultans, Süleyman I (1520–66), 'The Magnificent' (see the special section 'Architecture' pp29–35).

Süleyman, the patron of Mimar Sinan, Turkey's greatest architect, was a prolific builder who restored the mighty walls of Jerusalem (an Ottoman city from 1516) and built countless other monuments throughout his empire. Though the smaller Selimiye Camii in Edirne is generally counted as Sinan's masterpiece, the Süleymaniye is without doubt his grandest work.

Inside, the mosque is breathtaking in its size and pleasing in its simplicity. There is little decoration except for some very fine İznik tiles in the mihrab, gorgeous stained-glass windows done by one İbrahim the Drunkard, and four massive columns, one from Baalbek, one from Alexandria and two from Byzantine palaces in İstanbul. The painted arabesques on the dome are 19th-century additions, recently renewed. Sinan, ever challenged by the technical accomplishments of Aya Sofya, took the floor plan of that church, and here perfected its adaptation to the requirements of Muslim worship.

The külliye of the Süleymaniye is particularly elaborate, with the full complement of public services: soup kitchen, hostel, hospital, theological college etc. Near the south-east wall of the mosque is the cemetery, with the tombs of Süleyman and his wife Haseki Hürrem Sultan (Roxelana). The tilework in both is superb. In Süleyman's tomb, little jewel-like lights in the dome are surrogate stars. In Hürrem's tomb, the many tile panels of flowers and the delicate stained glass produce a serene effect.

Looking for Lunch?

There are several little eateries in the row of souvenir shops outside the mosque enclosure to the south-west, including the restaurants **Beydağı** and **Kanaat Lokantası (Map 15, #3)**. Or if you are looking for something more substantial, try **Darüzziyafe (Map 15, #1)** (see the Places to Eat chapter).

ŞEHZADE MEHMET CAMİİ (Map 14)

After lunch, walk along Süleymaniye Caddesi, which goes south-west from the mosque, and turn right onto Şehzadebaşı Caddesi. After about 200m you'll come to Şehzade Mehmet Camii *(Mosque of the Prince; Şehzadebaşı Caddesi; open 7am-8.30pm daily)*. Süleyman had it built between 1544 and 1548 as a memorial to his son Mehmet, who died in 1543 at the age of 22. It was the first important mosque to be designed by Mimar Sinan, who spent the first part of his long career as a military architect. Among the many important people buried in tile-encrusted **tombs** here are Prince Mehmet, his brothers and sisters, and Süleyman's grand viziers, Rüstem Paşa and İbrahim Paşa. Admission is free, though you may be hassled for a US$1 donation.

AQUEDUCT OF VALENS (Map 14)

Continue along Şehzadebaşı Caddesi. On the left you'll see the 1950s **İstanbul City Hall** (Belediye Sarayı). On the right, you can't miss the remnant of the high Aqueduct of Valens (Bozdoğan Kemeri). It's not certain that the aqueduct was constructed by the Emperor Valens (r. 364–78), though we do know it was repaired in 1019, in later times by several sultans, and in the late 1980s. It's thought that it carried water over this valley to a cistern at Beyazıt Square, to finally end up at the Great Byzantine Palace.

FATİH ANITI PARKI (Map 14)

Cross the manic junction of Atatürk Bulvarı to moth-eaten Fatih Anıtı Parkı (Conqueror Monument Park), so named after the obvious monument to the mounted Mehmet II.

South of the park across Macar Kardeşler Caddesi are a few bits of marble ruin and foundation, all that remains of the gigantic **Byzantine Church of St Polyeuchtos**. The church was built during the reign of Justinian by one of the immensely powerful noble families which the emperor sought to control. Larger and grander than Aya Sofya, it was the nobles' way of one-upping the head of state. Earthquakes ruined it utterly, however, while Justinian's great church still exists to this day.

CARTOON & HUMOUR MUSEUM (Map 14)

Head along Atatürk Bulvarı, through an arch of the Bozdoğan Kemeri to the former medrese of Gazanfer Ağa (1599), now the Cartoon & Humour Museum *(İstanbul Karikatür ve Mizah Müzesi; ☎ 212-521 1264; Kovacılar Sokak 12; admission free; open 10am-6pm)*. Turkish cartoon artistry has been lively and politically important since Ottoman times, as the changing exhibits show. All exhibits and signs are in Turkish so you may have difficulty getting the in-jokes, but you can still enjoy the pictures and the pleasant courtyard, with its fountain and grapevines.

All sane folks should finish the walking tour now. Jump in a taxi, catch a bus to Eminönü along Macar Kardeşler Caddesi or stroll back up bus-choked Atatürk Bulvarı for a tram along Ordu Caddesi (and Divan Yolu) to Sultanahmet. If you opt for the latter option, while you're down at the spaghetti junction of Atatürk Bulvarı and Ordu Caddesi, you may as well check out the **Valide Camii**. It's a frilly late Ottoman work built in 1871 by Valide Sultan Pertevniyal, mother of Sultan Abdülaziz. Although it once looked like a white wedding cake among the drab box-buildings of Aksaray, exhaust fumes have left it sooty and traffic flyovers block a full view, but it's an indicative building of its period.

Further along Ordu Caddesi **Laleli Camii** is an Ottoman baroque mosque built from 1759 to 1763 by Sultan Mustafa III. The ornate baroque architecture houses a most sumptuous interior. Underneath the mosque are shops and a plaza with a fountain, the former producing rent for the upkeep of the mosque.

The Bazaar District

The Kapalı Çarşı is the southern anchor of a vast market district that spills northward downhill to the Golden Horn, including the exquisite Rüstem Paşa Camii, and ending at Eminönü's Mısır Çarşısı (Egyptian Market, also known as Spice Bazaar). Eminönü is the transport nerve centre of the city: Bosphorus and Marmara ferries dock here, Galata Bridge traffic passes through, and the Sirkeci train station is nearby.

NURUOSMANİYE CAMİİ (Map 13, #1)

The Nuruosmaniye Camii *(Light of Osman Mosque; Vezir Hanı Caddesi; open 7am-8.30pm)* was built in Ottoman baroque style between 1748 and 1755 by Mahmut I and finished by his successor Osman III. Though meant to exhibit the sultans' 'modern' taste, the Nuruosmaniye has very strong echoes of Aya Sofya: the broad, lofty dome, colonnaded mezzanine galleries, windows topped with Roman arches, and the broad band of calligraphy around the interior.

The courtyard of the mosque is peaceful and green, but with a constant flow of pedestrian traffic heading to and from the bazaar.

On the other side of the courtyard you face Nuruosmaniye Kapısı, one of several doorways into the bazaar. The gold emblem above the doorway is the Ottoman armorial emblem with the sultan's monogram.

The Bazaar District

To start this half-day walk turn right off Yeniçeriler Caddesi (the continuation of Divan Yolu) at the Çemberlitaş and walk down Vezir Hanı Caddesi. (Light green trail: Map 4, then Map 15)

1. Nuruosmaniye Camii
2. Kapalı Çarşı
3. Mahmut Paşa Yokuşu
4. Büyük Yeni & Büyük Valide Han
5. Uzunçarşı Caddesi
6. Rüstem Paşa Camii
7. Tahtakale
8. Hasırcılar Caddesi
9. Mısır Çarşısı
10. Yeni Cami
11. Galata Bridge

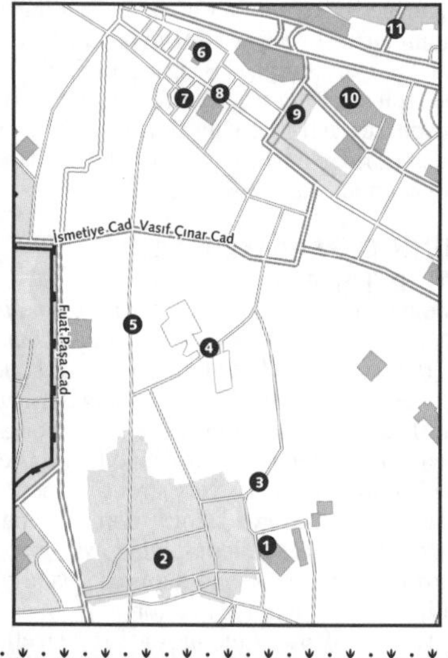

KAPALI ÇARŞI (Map 4)

Tonnes of tourist wares meet ancient shopping mall – this is İstanbul's **Kapalı Çarşı** *(Covered Market; Grand Bazaar; open 8.30am-6.30pm Mon-Sat Nov-Mar, 8.30am-7.30pm Mon-Sat Apr-Oct)*. With over 4000 dazzling shops and several kilometres of lanes, as well as mosques, banks, police stations, restaurants and workshops, this is a covered world. These days it's all tourists and touts – get used to inane comments like, 'Madam, are you looking for me?'. Despite this, most of the streets around the bazaar still cater to locals, and the bazaar itself is well worth strolling through. Beware of the occasional pickpocket or bag slasher.

Starting from a small masonry *bedesten* (warehouse) built in the time of Mehmet the Conqueror, the bazaar grew to cover a vast area as neighbouring shopkeepers decided to put up roofs and porches so that commerce could be conducted comfortably in all weather. Finally, a system of locked gates and doors was provided so that the entire minicity could be closed up tight at the end of the business day. Street names refer to trades and crafts: Jewellers St, Pearl Merchants St, Fez-Makers St. Though many trades have died out or moved on, there are still areas worth seeing.

The gold-glittery street inside the Nuruosmaniye Kapısı (doorway) is called **Kalpakçılarbaşı Caddesi** and it's the closest thing the bazaar has to a main street. Most of the bazaar is on your right (north) in the crazy maze of tiny streets and alleys. If you're hopeless with directions stay on the walking tour outlined below – though the best way to enjoy the bazaar is to explore, and inevitably get lost. If you're here to shop, check out what to buy, and where to buy it, under Kapalı Çarşı in the Shopping chapter.

Pop into the **Sandal Bedesten**, a rectangle hall with a domed roof supported by 12 large pillars. This is also called the Yeni Bedesten or New Warehouse as it was built after Mehmet's central bedesten some time in the 17th century. It was once the city's auction place for used and antique goods, but today it has a pricey restaurant, **Colheti Cafe & Restaurant (Map 4, #7)** (see the Places to Eat chapter), and cheap clothes for sale.

Back on Kalpakçılarbaşı Caddesi, the first street on the left, and up a few steps, will lead you to the **Kürkçüler Çarşısı** (Furriers

GREG ELMS

WAYNE WALTON

CHRISTINA DAMEYER

EDDIE GERALD

CHRISTINA DAMEYER

Kapalı Çarşı, İstanbul's 500-year-old Grand Bazaar, is a maze of streets in Old İstanbul where you will find everything from Turkish slippers (top right) and hats (bottom left) to brass and copper kitchenware (bottom right). Stroll among the tea drinkers and be entertained by the vendors, young and old.

MAP 4 – KAPALI ÇARŞI (GRAND BAZAAR)

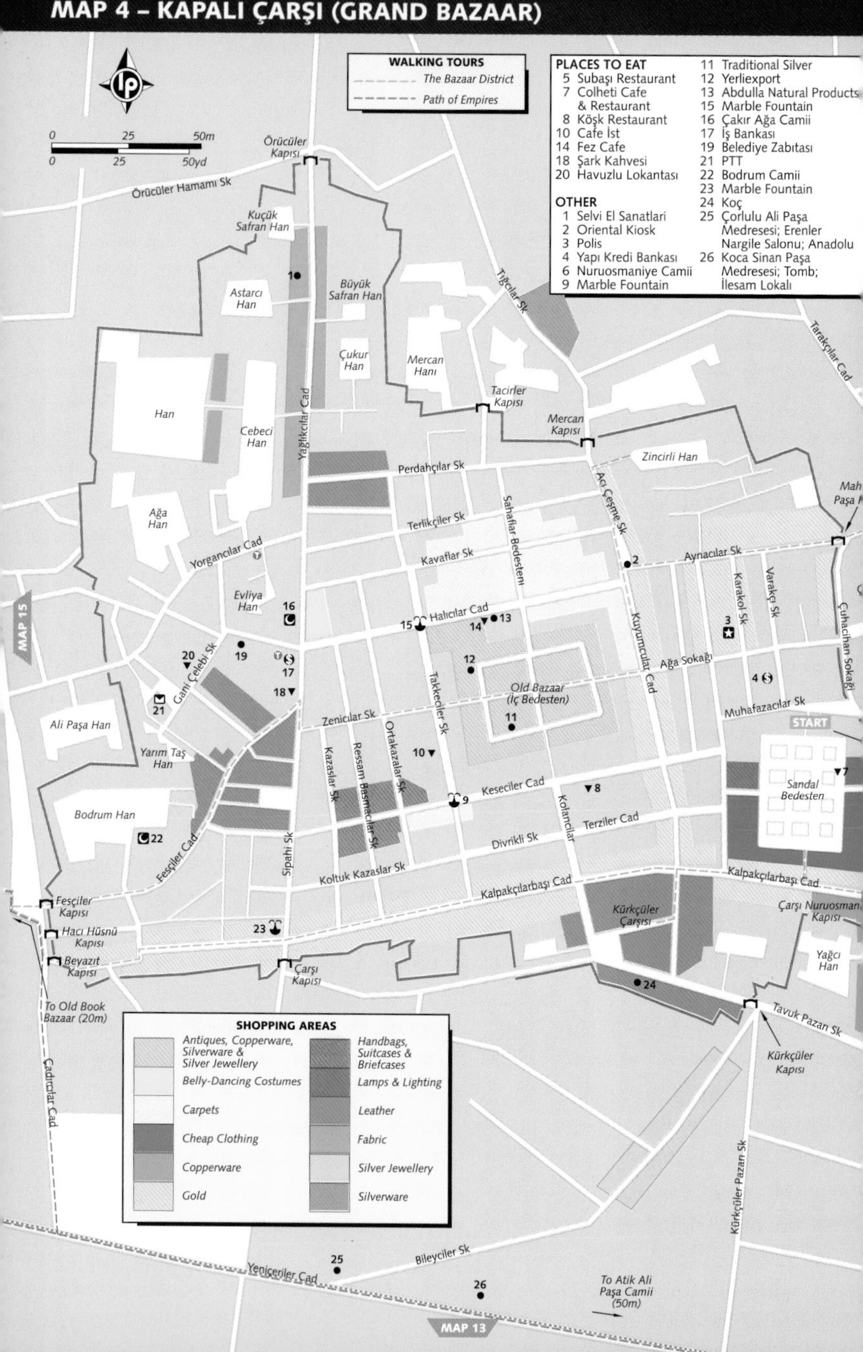

Bazaar). It houses shops selling leather clothing.

Head west and exit the bazaar at the end of Kalpakçılarbaşı Caddesi. Once outside, turn right onto Çadırcılar Caddesi, then left through a doorway to the **Old Book Bazaar** (Sahaflar Çarşısı; see the boxed text 'Old Book Bazaar'). When you're done, head back into the Kapalı Çarşı and take a well-earned rest at **Şark Kahvesi (Map 4, #18)** (see the Places to Eat chapter) – a worn-out, but charming relic of Old İstanbul.

The **Old Bazaar** (İç Bedesten), also known as Cevahir Bedesteni, at the centre of the market, is probably the first building Mehmet the Conqueror built. Its structure is similar to the Sandal Bedesten, but this hall is crammed with small shops selling silver jewellery, silverware, antique jewellery, copper vessels and more.

Exit via the eastern doorway to **Kuyumcular Caddesi** (Jewellers St), aglitter with gold and gems. Turn left to find the crooked **Oriental Kiosk (Map 4, #2)**, which was built as a coffee house. Continue north, up Acı Çeşme Sokak as far as the right turn, into the gorgeous, pink **Zincirli Han** – you'll see other *hans* (caravanserais) on the rest of the walk.

Time to leave the shelter of the bazaar and head out, via Mahmut Paşa Kapısı, into the streets where locals shop.

Old Book Bazaar

The bulk of the Old Book Bazaar *(Sahaflar Çarşısı; open 8.30am-6.30pm Mon-Sat Nov-Mar, 8.30am-7.30pm Mon-Sat Apr-Oct)* surrounds a shady little courtyard. Actually, the wares in the shops here are both new and old. It's unlikely that you'll uncover any underpriced antique treasures, but you can certainly find books on İstanbul and Turkish culture in several languages, old engravings and a curiosity or two.

The book bazaar dates from Byzantine times. Today, many of the booksellers are members of a dervish order called the Halveti after its founder, Hazreti Mehmet Nureddin-i Cerrahi-i Halveti. Their *sema* (religious ceremony) includes chanting from the Quran, praying, and rhythmic dancing and breathing to the accompaniment of classical Turkish liturgical music. As with all dervish orders, the sema is an attempt at close knowledge of and communion with God. The Mevlevi dervishes attempt it by their whirling dance, the Halveti through their circular dance and hyperventilation. Don't, however, expect to wander into a den of mystics – dervishes, unlike Christian monks, live and work in the 'secular' world.

Just beyond the northern gate of the Sahaflar Çarşısı is a **daily flea market** specialising in old coins, stamps, watches, jewellery and Ottoman knick-knacks. On Sunday the flea market expands into Beyazıt Square with hawkers selling everything from pirated software to electric-blue socks.

MAHMUT PAŞA YOKUŞU (Map 15)

Mahmut Paşa Yokuşu is where Turkish shoppers hunt down tizzy white-meringue wedding dresses, shoes, buttons, sewing materials, luggage – you name it. Bursting shops line the cobbled street, spruikers fill most of the roadway, and the good-natured throng of shoppers elbow-jostle and lurch through the maze, frequently parting (under duress) to allow an overloaded pick-up truck to squeeze through.

Head downhill along the street. You'll soon pass the **Mahmut Paşa Hamamı (Map 15, #34)** on the left. Built in 1476, it's one of the oldest hamams in the city. Today it houses enough circumcision robes to clothe an army.

Walk another 250m, then turn left into Çakmakçılar Yokuşu.

BÜYÜK YENİ (Map 15, #35) & BÜYÜK VALİDE HAN (Map 15, #36)

Just off Çakmakçılar Yokuşu are two hans worth popping into (see the boxed text 'Hans' later in this chapter). The large blue doors, just after the first street on the left, hide one of İstanbul's Ottoman baroque caravanserais, the Büyük Yeni Han (Big New Han). The only han that's bigger is the Büyük Valide Han. To find it, continue another 150m up Çakmakçılar Yokuşu and you'll see the entrance on the right.

Maşallah!

You can't miss the white outfits decking out some shops. These are the robes boys wear on the day (usually Sunday) of their circumcision *(sünnet)*. The white suit is supplemented with a spangled hat and red satin sash emblazoned with the word Maşallah ('What wonders God has willed!').

Circumcision, or the surgical removal of the foreskin on the penis, is performed on a Turkish Muslim lad when he is nine or 10 years old, and marks his formal admission into the faith.

On the day of the operation the boy is dressed in the special suit, visits relatives and friends, and leads a parade – formerly on horseback, now in cars – around his neighbourhood or city, attended by musicians and merrymakers. You may come across these boys while visiting the Eyüp Sultan Camii, one of Islam's holiest places, where they often stop on their way to circumcision.

The simple operation, performed in a hospital or in a clinic during the afternoon, is followed by a celebration with music and feasting. The newly circumcised boy attends, resting in bed, as his friends and relatives bring him special gifts and congratulate him on having entered manhood.

MARTIN HARRIS

Pass through the first small courtyard and stand in the gateway of the huge courtyard; you should see steps on either side leading to the grimy 1st floor of the han. A friendly 'guide' may materialise to take you up to the roof (excellent 360 degree views) – watch your step. He'd appreciate a tip. The mosque you see in the main courtyard is used by Shiite members of Islam. The shops around this car-filled courtyard mainly sell suits; the next grubby courtyard to the north supplies the material. The Büyük Valide Han was the biggest han in İstanbul, built in 1651 by Sultan İbrahim's mother. It's grimy and faded, but it's still an interesting example of its kind. Back on Çakmakçılar Yokuşu, turn right into Uzunçarşı Caddesi to continue our walk.

UZUNÇARŞI CADDESİ (Map 15)

Uzunçarşı Caddesi or 'Longmarket St' lives up to its name: One long market of woodturners' shops, luggage merchants, shops selling guns and hunting equipment, plastic toys, freshly baked sesame rolls *(simits)*, backgammon sets and more.

At the foot of the hill, Uzunçarşı Caddesi runs straight to the small, exquisite Rüstem Paşa Camii.

RÜSTEM PAŞA CAMİİ (Map 15, #5)

This mosque *(Mosque of Rüstem Pasha; ☎ 212-526 7350, Hasırcılar Caddesi; open 7am-8.30pm)* is easy to miss because it's not at street level; look out for a stone doorway, a plaque above it, and a flight of steps leading up.

At the top of the steps there's a terrace and the mosque's colonnaded porch. You'll notice at once the panels of İznik faience set into the mosque's facade. The interior is covered in similarly gorgeous tiles, so take off your shoes (women should also cover head and shoulders) and venture inside. This particularly beautiful mosque was built by Sinan for Rüstem Paşa, son-in-law and grand vizier of Süleyman the Magnificent. Ottoman power, glory, architecture and tilework were all at their zenith when the mosque was built in 1561. A donation is requested upon admission.

TAHTAKALE (Map 15)

After your visit to the mosque, you might want to spend some more time wandering the streets of this fascinating market quarter. Tahtakale, as it's called, is synonymous with buying and selling anything and everything, including the bizarre and the illegal.

HASIRCILAR CADDESİ (Map 15)

Going south-east from the Rüstem Paşa Camii is Hasırcılar Caddesi (Mat-Makers' St). Shops along it sell spices, nuts, condiments, knives, bowls and tea. The colours, smells, sights and sounds make this one of the liveliest and most interesting streets in the city. A 10-minute stroll brings you right to the Mısır Çarşısı.

MISIR ÇARŞISI (Map 15)

The Mısır Çarşısı *(Spice Bazaar; open 8.30am-6.30pm Mon-Sat)* is so named because of its many spice shops. It's also known as the Egyptian Market.

The market was constructed in the 1660s as part of the Yeni Cami mosque complex, the rents from the shops going to support the upkeep of the mosque and its charitable activities. These included a school, baths, hospital and public fountains.

Strolling through the market, the number of shops selling tourist trinkets is increasing annually, though there are still some shops that sell spices *(baharat)* and even a few that specialise in the old-time folk remedies, such as love potions. More to the point for anyone on a walking tour are the shops selling nuts, dried and candied fruits, chocolate and other snacks. Try some figs *(incir)* or Turkish delight *(lokum)*. Fruit pressed into sheets and dried is called *pestil* – it looks like leather. It's often made from apricots or mulberries, and is delicious and relatively cheap.

Between the Mısır Çarşısı and the Yeni Cami is the city's major outdoor market for flowers, plants, seeds and songbirds. There's a toilet *(tuvalet)* down a flight of stairs, subject to a small fee. Across the courtyard near the mosque is the **tomb of Valide Sultan Turhan Hatice (Map 15, #10)**, the woman who completed construction of the Yeni Cami. Buried with her are no fewer than six sultans, including her son Mehmet IV, plus dozens of imperial princes and princesses.

YENİ CAMİ (Map 15, #7)

Only in İstanbul would a 400-year-old mosque be called 'New'. The Yeni Cami *(New Mosque; ☎ 212-527 8505, Yeni Cami Meydanı Sokak)* was begun in 1597, commissioned by Valide Sultan Safiye, mother of Sultan Mehmet III (r. 1595–1603). The site was earlier occupied by a community of Karaite Jews, radical dissenters from orthodox Judaism. When the valide sultan decided to build her grand mosque here, the Karaites were moved to Hasköy, a district further up the Golden Horn that still bears traces of their presence.

The valide sultan lost her august position when her son the sultan died, and the mosque was completed six sultans later in 1663 by Valide Sultan Turhan Hatice, mother of Sultan Mehmet IV (r. 1648–87).

In plan, the Yeni Cami is much like the Blue Mosque and the Süleymaniye Camii, with a large forecourt and a square sanctuary surmounted by a series of semidomes crowned by a grand dome. The interior is richly decorated with gold, coloured tiles and carved marble.

Both the mosque and its tiles were created after Ottoman architecture had reached its peak. The tilemakers of İznik were turning out slightly inferior products by the late 17th century. Compare these tiles with the exquisite examples found in the Rüstem Paşa Camii, which are from the high period of İznik tilework.

Hans

Hans (caravanserais) were built by rich merchants at the edges of a bazaar so that caravans could bring goods from all parts of the empire, unload and trade right in the bazaar's precincts. They are typically two- to three-storey arcaded buildings surrounding a courtyard that could be locked at night. The arcades are backed by small rooms that provided accommodation and offices to the traders. Today, many of these rooms have been taken over by industry.

By the way, no-one will mind if you wander into any of these hans for a look around. In fact, you may well be invited to rest your feet, have a glass of tea and exchange a few words.

GALATA BRIDGE (Map 15)

In Byzantine times the Golden Horn provided a perfect natural harbour for the city's commerce. Suppliers of fresh vegetables and fruits, grain and staple goods set up shop in the harbour. Until a decade ago, their successors in İstanbul's wholesale vegetable, fruit and fish markets performed the same services in the same area – to the west of the Galata Bridge in Eminönü. With the drive to clean up and beautify the Golden Horn, the wholesale markets have been moved to the outskirts of the city.

Until June 1992 the Galata Bridge, which crosses the mouth of the Golden Horn and marks the end of this tour, was a 19th-century structure that floated on pontoons. Ramshackle fish restaurants, teahouses and nargileh joints filled the dark recesses beneath the roadway, while an intense stream of pedestrian and vehicular traffic passed above.

The pontoon bridge blocked the natural flow of water and kept the Golden Horn from flushing itself of pollution, so it was replaced by a new bridge which allows the water to flow. (The old bridge was moved further up the Golden Horn and reinstalled without its flow-blocking pontoons.)

Beyoğlu

Across the Galata Bridge from Eminönü lies Beyoğlu. The easiest way to tour Beyoğlu is to start from its busy nerve centre, Taksim Square. To get to the square from Sultanahmet, catch the street tram to Eminönü, and jump on bus 69E at the Eminönü bus station. Alternatively, the T4 İETT bus leaves from near the Sultanahmet tourist office and gets to Taksim Square in around half an hour, but the timetable is so erratic that waiting for it may have you frothing at the mouth.

Beyoğlu (**bey**-oh-loo), the 'new' section of İstanbul on the northern side of the Golden Horn, is not really new. There's been a settlement here almost as long as there has been a city on Seraglio Point (Saray Burnu). But new ideas, brought from Europe by traders and diplomats, walked into Ottoman daily life down the streets of Pera and Galata.

The Europeans who lived in Pera brought new fashions, machines, arts and manners, and rules for the diplomatic game. Old İstanbul, on the south bank of the Golden Horn, was content to continue living in the Middle Ages with its oriental bazaars, great mosques and palaces, narrow streets and traditional values. But Pera was to have telephones, underground trains, tramways, electric light and modern municipal government.

Eventually the sultans followed Pera's lead, and the upper classes followed the sul-

Pera in History

Sometimes called the New City, Beyoğlu is 'new' only in a relative sense. There was a settlement on the northern shore of the Golden Horn, near Karaköy Square, before the birth of Christ. By the time of Theodosius II (r. 408–50), it was large enough to become an official suburb of Constantinople. Theodosius built a fortress here, no doubt to complete the defence system of his great land walls, and called it Galata, as the suburb was then the home of many Galatians.

The word 'new' actually applied more to Pera, the quarter above Galata that ran along the crest of the hill from the Galata Tower to Taksim Square. This was built up only in later Ottoman times.

In the 19th century, the European powers were waiting eagerly for the 'Sick Man of Europe' (the decadent Ottoman Empire) to collapse so that they could grab territory and spheres of influence. All the great colonial powers – the British, Russian, Austro-Hungarian and German empires, France and the kingdom of Italy – maintained lavish embassies and tried to cajole and pressure the Sublime Porte into concessions of territory, trade and influence.

The embassy buildings, as lavish as ever, still stand. Ironically, most of the great empires that built them collapsed along with that of the Ottomans. Only the British and French survived to grab any of the spoils. Their occupation of Middle Eastern countries under League of Nations 'mandates' has given us the Middle East we have today.

tans. From the reign of Abdül Mecit (r. 1839–61) onwards, no sultan lived in Mehmet the Conqueror's palace at Topkapı. Rather, they built opulent European-style palaces in Pera and along the shores of the Bosphorus to the north.

Beyoğlu holds the architectural evidence of the Ottoman Empire's frantic attempts to modernise and reform itself, and the evidence of the European powers' attempts to undermine and subvert it. As the Ottomans struggled to keep their sprawling, ramshackle empire together, the European diplomats in the great embassies of Pera were jockeying for domination of the entire Middle East. They wanted to control its holy places, its sea lanes through the Suez Canal to India, and especially its oil, already important at that time.

Later in this section, a walking tour will lead you through the highlights of Beyoğlu, beginning on İstiklal Caddesi.

TAKSİM SQUARE (Map 16)

A 'taksim' in Turkish is a dividing point. Taksim Square takes its name from a reservoir in the city's old water-conduit system. The main water line from the Belgrade Forest, north of the city, was laid to this point in 1732 by Sultan Mahmut I (r. 1730–54). Branch lines then led from the taksim to other parts of the city.

The prominent modern building at the eastern end of the plaza is the **Atatürk Cultural Centre (Map 16, #4)** (Atatürk Kültür Merkezi; sometimes called the Opera House). In the summertime, during the International İstanbul Music Festival, tickets for the various concerts are on sale in the ticket kiosks here, and numerous performances are staged in the centre's halls.

At the western end of the square is the **Cumhuriyet Anıtı (Map 16, #15)** (Republic Monument), one of the Turkish Republic's earliest monuments, executed by Canonica, an Italian sculptor, in 1928. Atatürk, his assistant and successor İsmet İnönü and other revolutionary leaders appear prominently on the monument set in a circular garden circumnavigated by the İstiklal Caddesi tram. The monument's purpose was not only to commemorate revolutionary heroes, but also to break down the Ottoman-Islamic prohibition against the making of 'graven images'.

To the south of the square is the luxurious Marmara hotel. To the north is the **Taksim Gezi Yeri (Map 17)** (Taksim Park or Promenade) with the Ceylan Inter-Continental İstanbul hotel at its northern end. Beneath Taksim Park is the southern terminal of the city's newest metro line which runs north under Cumhuriyet Caddesi to the business and residential districts of Etiler and Levent.

Before leaving Taksim on your walking tour of old Pera along İstiklal Caddesi, consider taking a detour north of the square.

NORTH OF TAKSİM (Map 17)

From the roundabout, Cumhuriyet Caddesi (Republic Ave) leads north past banks, travel agencies, airline offices, nightclubs and the Divan, İstanbul Hilton and Hyatt Regency hotels to the districts of Harbiye, Nişantaşı and Şişli. Harbiye holds the Turkish war college and its military museum. Nişantaşı is an upmarket shopping district. Şişli is a district of offices, shops and apartments.

Askeri Müzesi (Map 17, #11)

A kilometre north of Taksim in Harbiye is the Askeri Müzesi *(Military Museum; ☎ 212-233 2720, Valikonağı Caddesi; adult/student US$0.50/0.20, camera US$1, video US$2; open 9am-5pm Wed-Sun)*. Concerts by the Mehter, the medieval Ottoman Military Band, are held between 3pm and 4pm.

The large museum is spread over two floors. On the ground floor are displays of weapons, a 'martyrs' gallery *(şehit galerisi)* with artefacts from fallen Turkish soldiers of many wars, displays of Turkish military uniforms through the ages, and glass cases holding battle standards, both Turkish and captured. The captured ones include Byzantine, Greek, British, Austro-Hungarian, Italian and Imperial Russian. Perhaps the most interesting of the exhibits are the imperial pavilions *(sayebanlar)*. These luxurious cloth shelters, heavily worked with fine silver and gold thread, jewels, precious silks and elegant tracery, were the battle headquarters for sultans during the summer campaign season.

Amazingly, there is also a portion of the great chain which the Byzantines stretched across the mouth of the Golden Horn to keep out the sultan's ships during the battle for Constantinople in 1453; and a tapestry woven by Ottoman sailors (who must have had lots of time on their hands) showing the flags of all of the world's important maritime nations.

The upper floor has more imperial pavilions, and a room devoted to Atatürk (featuring his socks and other clothing) who was, of course, a famous Ottoman general before he became founder and commander-in-chief of the republican army, and first president of the Turkish Republic.

This floor is where you really feel the spirit of the Ottoman Empire. It has exhibits of armour (including cavalry), uniforms, field furniture made out of weapons (eg, chairs with rifles for legs), and a Türk-Alman Dostluk Köşesi (Turco-German Friendship Corner) with mementos of Turkish and German military collaboration before and during WWI.

Outside the museum, to the east of the building, you'll find cannons, including Gatling guns cast in Vienna, bearing the sultan's monogram. More of the Golden Horn's great chain is here as well.

Perhaps the best reason to visit this museum is for a short **concert by the Mehter**. According to historians, the Mehter was the world's first true military band. Its purpose was not to make pretty music for dancing, but to precede the conquering Ottoman paşas into vanquished towns, impressing upon the defeated populace their new, subordinate status. Marching in with steady, measured pace, turning all together to face the left side of the line of march, then the right side, looking formidable in their long moustaches, tall janissary headdresses, brilliant instruments and even kettledrums – they were the musical representatives of Ottoman conquest.

AROUND TAKSİM SQUARE (Map 16)

To the south-west, two streets meet before entering the square. Sıraselviler Caddesi goes south and İstiklal Caddesi goes south-west.

Nestled in the small triangle formed by these two streets, rising above the shops and restaurants which hide its foundations, is the **Aya Triyada Kilisesi (Map 16, #22)**, or Greek Orthodox Church of the Holy Trinity, dating from 1882. It's open daily for services, and you can visit.

Now head down İstiklal Caddesi for a look at the vestiges of 19th-century Ottoman life. The restored tram from the turn of the century runs from Taksim via Galatasaray to Tünel for US$0.40. It's fun, but runs too seldom to be very useful, and is always crowded.

İSTİKLAL CADDESİ (Map 16)

Stretching between Taksim Square and Tünel Square, İstiklal Caddesi (Independence Ave) was formerly the Grande Rue de

Beyoğlu

This walk will take four to five hours and lead you along İstiklal Caddesi though the main sights. (Orange trail: Map 16)

1. Galatasaray Square
2. Çiçek Pasajı
3. Balık Pazar
4. Tünel
5. Galipdede Caddesi
6. Karaköy (Galata)

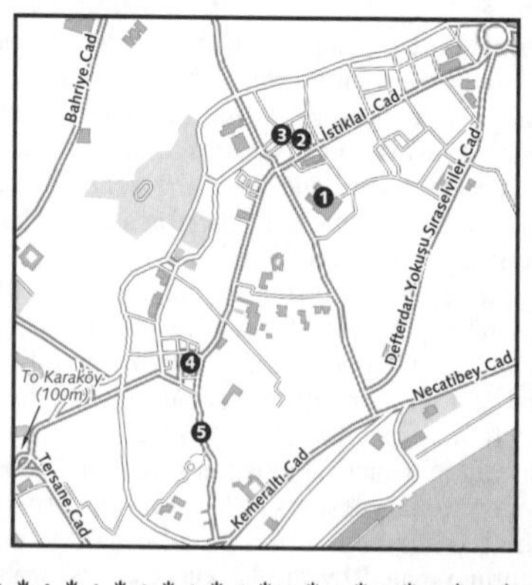

Péra. It was the street with all the smart shops, several large embassies and churches, many impressive residential buildings and a scattering of teashops and restaurants. Renovation has restored much of its appeal. It's now a pedestrian way, which in Turkey means that there are fewer cars.

As you stroll along İstiklal, try to imagine it during its heyday a century ago, peopled by frock-coated merchants and Ottoman officials, European officers in uniform, lightly veiled Turkish women, and European women in the latest fashions.

Just out of Taksim Square, the first building on the right is the former French plague hospital (1719), now the **French Consulate General (Map 16, #24)** and cultural centre.

As you stroll along, take detours down the narrow side streets with intriguing names such as Büyükparmakkapı Sokak, 'Gate of the Thumb St'; Sakızağacı Sokak, 'Pine-Gum Tree St'; and Kuloğlu Sokak, 'Slave's Son St'. The Places to Eat and Entertainment chapters have heaps of suggestions for cafes, restaurants and clubs in this area.

A few streets before coming to Galatasaray Square, turn left onto Turnacıbaşı Sokak. At its end is the **Tarihi Galatasaray Hamamı (Map 16, #63)**, one of the city's best (see the boxed text 'Hamams' at the end of this chapter). Down behind the hamam are Faikpaşa and Çukurcuma Caddesis, lined with **antique shops** (see Antiques in the Shopping chapter).

Galatasaray Square (Map 16)

The small square's prominent feature is its namesake, the **Galatasaray Lycée (Map 16, #89)**, established in 1868 by Sultan Abdülaziz who wanted a place where students could listen to lectures in both Turkish and French. Today it's a prestigious public school.

Çiçek Pasajı (Map 16, #77)

A little way back (east) up İstiklal, turn left into Çiçek Pasajı (Flower Passage). This is the inner court of the 19th-century 'Cité de Pera' building, which symbolised Pera's growth as a 'modern' European-style city. For years the courtyard held a dozen cheap little restaurant-taverns. In good weather, beer barrels were rolled out onto the pavement, marble slabs were balanced on top, wooden stools were put around, and enthusiastic revellers filled the stools as soon as they hit the ground.

In the late 1980s parts of the Cité de Péra building collapsed. In rebuilding, the venerable Çiçek Pasajı was 'beautified', its makeshift barrel heads and stools replaced with comfortable, solid wooden tables and benches, and the broken pavement with smooth tiles, all topped by a glass canopy to keep out foul weather. The clientele is better behaved now, but its smattering of adventurous tourists has become a significant proportion. The Çiçek Pasajı (see the Places to Eat chapter) is still good for an evening of beer drinking, food and conversation.

Balık Pazar (Map 16)

Walk through the Çiçek Pasajı to neighbouring Sahne Sokak, turn right, then look for a little passage off to the left. This is the **Avrupa Pasajı** (European Passage), a small gallery with marble paving and shops selling tourist wares and some antique goods. In Pera's heyday it was elegant, a state which recent restoration has done much to re-create.

Sahne Sokak is the heart of Beyoğlu's Balık Pazar (Fish Market), though it's actually a general-purpose market with a good number of fish merchants. Small stands sell *midye* (skewered mussels) fried in hot oil (get a skewer that's been freshly cooked), and *kokoreç* (grilled lamb intestines packed with more lamb intestines).

At 24A Sahne Sokak, look for the huge black doors to the courtyard of the **Üç Horan Ermeni Kilisesi (Map 16, #76)** (Armenian Church of Three Altars). You can visit if the doors are open.

Leading off to the right of Sahne Sokak is Nevizade Sokak, lined with *meyhanes* (taverns) where the old-time life of the Çiçek Pasajı continues, untrammelled by touristic İstanbul. On Thursday, Friday and Saturday nights, this place buzzes. Feel free to wander in and have a meal and a drink.

Unless you want to continue down the slope among the fishmongers, turn back and then right into Duduodaları Sokak, and stroll down this little street past fancy food shops, bakers' and greengrocers' shops.

At the end of the market street you will emerge into the light. Straight ahead of you is Meşrutiyet Caddesi, and on the corner here are the huge gates to the **British Consulate General (Map 16, #82)**, an Italian palazzo built in 1845 to plans by Sir Charles Barry, architect of London's Houses of Parliament. Head along Meşrutiyet Caddesi, which makes its way down to the Pera Palas Oteli and the US Consulate General.

Just past the British Consulate General, watch for an iron gate and a small passage on the left, leading into a little courtyard, the Hacopulo Pasajı, with a derelict lamppost in the centre. Enter the courtyard, turn right up the stairs, and you'll discover the Greek Orthodox **Church of Panaya Isodyon (Map 16, #97)**. It's tidy and quiet, hidden away in the midst of other buildings. It's usually locked, but the custodian, if he's around, is happy to open it so you can have a look inside.

When you've seen the church, go down the stairs to the east of it (not the stairs you came up). Turn right, and just past the church property on the right-hand side you will see the entrance to the **Rejans Lokantası (Map 16, #98)** (Regency Restaurant). Founded apparently by three White Russian dancing girls who fled the Russian Revolution, the restaurant is still operated by their Russian-speaking descendants.

This area of Beyoğlu was a favourite with Russian emigrés after the 1917 revolution. The Rejans, by the look of it, was a cabaret complete with orchestra loft and grand piano. Lunch and dinner are still served daily, except Sunday. Though in vogue with İstanbul's intelligentsia, service is far from good and prices are quite high for what you get.

When you go out the restaurant door, go down the steps, turn right, and then left along the narrow alley called Olivia Han Pasajı, which brings you back to İstiklal Caddesi.

Back on İstiklal Caddesi (Map 16)

Turn right and continue walking along İstiklal. You'll soon notice, on the left, a large Italian Gothic church behind a fence. The Franciscan **Church of San Antonio di Padua (Map 16, #93)** *(☎ 212-244 0935, İstiklal Caddesi 327)* was founded here in 1725; the red-brick building dates from 1913.

Past the church is Eskiçiçekçi Sokak on the left, then Nuruziya Sokak. The third street, a little cul-de-sac, ends at the gates of the **Palais de France (Map 16, #104)**, once the French embassy to the Ottoman sultan. The grounds are extensive and include the chapel of St Louis of the French, founded here in 1581, though the present chapel building dates from the 1830s.

A few steps along İstiklal Caddesi brings you to the pretty **Netherlands Consulate General (Map 16, #107)**, built as the Dutch embassy in 1855 by the Swiss Fossati brothers, formerly architects to the Russian tsar. The first embassy building here dates from 1612. Past the consulate, turn left down the hill into Postacılar Sokak. The **Dutch Chapel (Map 16, #108)** *(☎ 212-244 1075, Postacılar Sokak 11; admission by appointment),* on the left, is now the home of the Union Church of İstanbul, a multinational English-speaking Protestant congregation.

The narrow street turns right, bringing you face to face with the **former Spanish embassy (Map 16, #112)**. The little chapel, which was founded in 1670, is still in use.

The street then bends left and changes names to become Tomtom Kaptan Sokak. At the foot of the slope, on the right, is the **Palazzo di Venezia (Map 16, #111)**, once the embassy for Venice, now the Italian consulate. Continuing along İstiklal Caddesi, the **Church of St Mary Draperis (Map 16, #109)**, built in 1678 and extensively reconstructed in 1789, is behind an iron fence and down a flight of steps.

Past the church, still on the left-hand side, is the grand **Russian Consulate General (Map 16, #113)**, once the embassy of the tsars, built in 1837 to designs by the Fossati brothers. After designing several embassies, they were employed by the sultan to do extensive restorations of Aya Sofya.

Turn right (north-west) off İstiklal Caddesi along Asmalımescit Sokak, a narrow, typical Beyoğlu street that holds some fusty antique shops, little eateries and some suspect hotels. After 200m the street intersects Meşrutiyet Caddesi. To the left of the intersection is the American Library & Cultural Center (once the Constantinople Club), and just beyond it the Palazzo Corpi (1880), a pretty marble palace built by an Italian shipping magnate and later rented, then sold, to the USA for use as the US embassy to the Sublime Porte. It is now the **US Consulate General (Map 16, #118)** and heavily fortified.

To the right of the intersection is the grand old **Pera Palas Oteli (Map 16, #117)** (see the boxed text 'Pera Palas Oteli' below), built for passengers arriving on the *Orient Express*.

Once you've taken a turn through the Pera Palas, and perhaps had a drink in the bar or tea in the salon (not for the budget-minded), walk back up Asmalımescit Sokak towards İstiklal Caddesi.

Christ Church (Map 16, #139)

Back on İstiklal Caddesi, you will notice, on your left, the **Royal Swedish Consulate (Map 16, #129)**, once the Swedish embassy. Across İstiklal, the large pillared building called the Narmanlı Han was formerly the Russian embassy.

> **Pera Palas Oteli**
>
> The Pera Palas was built by Georges Nagelmackers, the Belgian entrepreneur who founded the Compagnie Internationale des Wagons-Lits et Grands Express Européens in 1868. Nagelmackers, who had succeeded in linking Paris and Constantinople by luxury train, found that once he got his esteemed passengers to the Ottoman imperial capital, there was no suitable place for them to stay.
>
> The hotel opened in the 1890s and advertised itself as having 'a thoroughly healthy situation, being high up and isolated on all four sides', and 'overlooking the Golden Horn and the whole panorama of Stamboul'.
>
> With its spacious salons, atmospheric bar, precious and pricey pastry shop, and birdcage lift, the Pera Palas is a living memory of what life was like in İstanbul a century ago.

Beside the Swedish consulate, turn left downhill on Şahkulu Bostanı Sokak. At the base of the slope turn left, then right, onto Serdarı Ekrem Sokak to find the Anglican sanctuary of **Christ Church (Map 16, #139)** *(☎ 212-244 4228, Serdarı Ekrem Sokak 82-84; admission free; open 9am-10am & 6pm-7pm daily, 10am Sun for services)*. Designed by CE Street (who did London's Law Courts), its cornerstone was laid in 1858 by Lord Stratford de Redcliffe, known as 'The Great Elchi' (*elçi*: ambassador) because of his paramount influence in mid-19th century Ottoman affairs. The church, dedicated in 1868 as the Crimean Memorial Church, is the largest of the city's Protestant churches. It was restored and renamed in the mid-1990s.

Back up on İstiklal Caddesi, the road curves to the right into Tünel Square.

TÜNEL (Map 16)

İstanbul's short underground railway, the Tünel, was built by French engineers in 1875. It allowed European merchants to get from their offices in Galata to their homes in Pera without hiking up the steep hillside. The fare is US$0.35. Trains run from 7am to 9pm daily (from 7.30am on Sunday), every five or 10 minutes.

Head towards Karaköy along Galipdede Caddesi, which is lined with shops selling books, Turkish and European musical instruments, plumbing and cabinet-making supplies.

Museum of Court Literature (Map 16, #134)

After a short walk along Galipdede Caddesi you'll find the Museum of Court Literature *(Divan Edebiyatı Müzesi; ☎ 212-245 4141, Galipdede Caddesi 15; adult/student US$1/0.60; open 9.30am-4.30pm Wed-Mon)*. The museum was originally a Galata Mevlevihanesi (Whirling Dervish Hall) and a meeting place for Mevlevi (whirling) dervishes. The dervishes still whirl here, every Sunday at 5pm from May to September, and 3pm from October to April. Tickets cost US$6.50 (no student fee). It's a good idea to buy tickets a few days beforehand as the shows get booked up.

The Whirling Dervishes

The whirling dervishes took their name from the great Sufi mystic and poet, Celaleddin Rumi (1207–73), called Mevlana (Our Leader) by his disciples. Sufis seek mystical communion with God through various means. For Mevlana, it was through a *sema* (ceremony) involving chants, prayers, music and a whirling dance. The whirling induced a trance-like state which made it easier for the mystic to seek spiritual union with God.

The Mevlevi *tarikat* (order), founded in Konya during the 13th century, flourished throughout the Ottoman Empire. Like several other orders, the Mevlevis stressed the unity of humankind before God regardless of creed.

Dervish orders were banned in the early days of the republic because of their ultraconservative religious politics. Although the ban has been lifted, only a handful of functioning *tekkesi* (dervish lodges) remain in İstanbul. Konya remains the heart of the Mevlevi order.

MICK WELDON

In Ottoman times, the Galata Mevlevihanesi was open to all who wished to witness the sema (ceremony), including foreign, non-Muslim visitors.

This modest tekke (dervish lodge) was restored between 1967 and 1972, but the first building here was erected by a high officer in the court of Sultan Beyazıt II in 1491. Its first *şeyh* (sheik) was Mohammed Şemai Sultan Divani, a grandson of the great Mevlana. The building burned in 1766, but was repaired that same year by Sultan Mustafa III.

In the midst of the city, this former monastery is an oasis of flowers and shady nooks. As you approach the building, notice the graveyard on the left and its stones with graceful Ottoman inscriptions. The shapes atop the stones reflect the headgear of the deceased, each hat denoting a different religious rank. Note also the tomb of the sheik by the entrance passage, and the ablutions fountain.

Inside the tekke, the central area was for the whirling sema, while the galleries above were for visitors. Separate areas were set aside for the orchestra and for female visitors (behind the lattices). In the display cases surrounding the central area, there are exhibits of calligraphy, writing and musical instruments and other paraphernalia associated with this highly developed Ottoman art.

Leaving the Museum of Court Literature, turn left down Galipdede Caddesi. A few minutes' walk along Galipdede Caddesi will bring you to İstanbul's old Genoese business district.

KARAKÖY (GALATA) (Map 16)

In order to avoid 'contamination' of their way of life, both the later Byzantine emperors and the Ottoman sultans relegated Genoese traders to offices and residences in Galata, now called Karaköy. The traders built a triangular-shaped fortification which stretched from a point near the Galata Bridge, over to where the Atatürk Bridge is today, and up to a higher point on the slope, where they built the Galata Tower.

From the 16th century onwards, Galata had a largely Jewish population. In the 19th century European emigrés moved into the area, and it still has many 'Frankish' houses giving a glimpse of what life was like for other emigrés who came to make their fortunes centuries ago. Scattered throughout this neighbourhood are Greek and Armenian churches and schools and synagogues, reminders of the time when virtually all of the empire's businesspeople were non-Muslims.

Today Karaköy still harbours some commercial offices and banks, as well as small traders. Down by the Golden Horn and the

Bosphorus you'll find the busy ferry and shipping docks and also the docks for Mediterranean cruise ships. Karaköy has busy bus stops, dolmuş queues and the lower station of the Tünel underground railway.

Galata Tower (Map 16, #147)

The cylindrical Galata Tower *(Galata Kulesi; ☎ 212-293 8180, Galata Kulesi Sokak; admission US$3.50, US$3 on Mon; open 9am-8pm daily)* was the high point in the Genoese fortifications of Galata, and has been rebuilt many times. Today it holds a forgettable restaurant/nightclub, and a memorable **panorama balcony** with superb views.

In the shadow of the tower are wood-working shops, turners' lathes, plus workshops making veneer and other materials for interior decoration. If you are ready for a break, try **Cafe Enginar (Map 16, #145)** (see the Places to Eat chapter).

Neve Shalom Synagogue (Map 16, #146)

During the 19th century, Galata had a large Sephardic Jewish population, but most of this community has now moved to more desirable residential areas. A block north-west of the Galata Tower is the Neve Shalom Synagogue *(☎ 212-244 1576, Büyük Hendek Caddesi 67-69)*. If you want to visit, you must ring the Chief Rabbinate of Turkey (☎ 212-243 5166 between 9.30am and 5pm Monday to Thursday or 9.30am and 1pm on Friday) at least 24 hours before your intended visit. You'll need to fax through a copy of the identification papers of your passport.

The synagogue was the site of a brutal massacre by Arab gunmen during the summer of 1986. Now restored, it is used by İstanbul's Jewish community for weddings, funerals and other ceremonies.

Head back to the Galata Tower and continue downhill on the street called Galata Kulesi Sokak.

Church of SS Peter & Paul (Map 16, #148)

Along Galata Kulesi Sokak, on the right, you'll see the small blue doorway to the courtyard of the Church of SS Peter and Paul *(☎ 212-249 2385, Galata Kulesi Sokak; admission free, ring the bell)*. A Dominican church originally stood on this site, but the building you see today dates from the mid-19th century. It's the work of the Fossati brothers who also designed the Netherlands and Russian consulates (both in Beyoğlu). The building was built as a French parish, but today it serves the Maltese community. The church backs onto a section of the Genoese fortifications.

Continue down Galata Kulesi Sokak and turn left into Kart Çınar Sokak.

Kamondo Stairs (Map 16, #151) & Schneidertemple Art Centre (Map 16, #152)

The Kamondo Stairs run south from Kart Çınar Sokak (you'll see them on your right) down to Voyvoda Caddesi. Built at the end of the 18th century, these simple but stylish steps are the work of the Jewish merchant family Kamondo, who also built many buildings in this area, including the Galata Konutları Apart Hotel (Map 16, #153; see the Places to Stay chapter).

Before you go down the stairs you may be interested in seeing what's showing at the Jewish art gallery, the Schneidertemple Art Centre *(Schneidertempel Sanat Merkezı; ☎ 212-252 5157, Felek Sokak 1; admission free; open 10.30am-6.30pm Tues-Sat, noon-6.30pm Sun)*.

VERITY CAMPBELL

The 18th-century Kamondo Stairs were built in Karaköy (Galata) by the Jewish community's most prosperous family.

Voyvoda Caddesi (Map 16)

At the bottom of the Kamondo Stairs, Voyvoda Caddesi (also called Bankalar Caddesi) leads up a slope towards Şişhane Square. This street was the heart of the banking centre during the days of the empire, and many merchant banks still have headquarters or branches here. The biggest building was that of the Ottoman Bank, now a branch of the Turkish Republic's Central Bank. On 26 August 1896, Armenian revolutionaries seized the Ottoman Bank building and threatened to blow it up if their demands were not met. They were not, and the terrorists surrendered, but anti-Armenian riots following the incident caused many Armenian casualties.

Arap Camii (Map 16, #150)

Turn right at Voyvoda Caddesi and walk for around 100m until you see Perşembe Pazari Caddesi (Thursday Market St) on your left. Take this road, and the first right, Galata Mahkemesi Sokak, will lead you to the Arap Camii *(Arab Mosque; Galata Mahkemesi Sokak)*. This church was built by the Genoese in the 14th century, and later converted to a mosque by Spanish Moors in the 16th century. It has a simple plan – long hall, tall square belfry-cum-minaret – with ornate flourishes such as the galleries added in the 20th century. Ask for an attendant if the mosque is locked.

Azapkapı Sokollu Mehmet Paşa Camii & Fountain (Map 16, #149)

Continue along Galata Mahkemesi Sokak to the intersection with Abdül Selah Sokak. Turn left and head to the end of the street to busy Tersane Caddesi. Head right to find, after five minutes' walk, another of the architect Sinan's works, the Azapkapı Sokollu Mehmet Paşa Camii *(Tersane Caddesi, beside Atatürk Bridge)*. Built in 1577, the pretty mosque is unusual in that it and the minaret are raised on a platform. Don't miss the attractive fountain *(sebil)* close by. Ask for the attendant if the mosque is locked.

You've now finished the walk. Retrace your steps along manic Tersane Caddesi or weave through the warren of little streets closer to the Golden Horn on your way to the north end of Galata Bridge where you can walk over to the transport hub of Eminönü.

Dolmabahçe Palace to Ortaköy

This walking tour will catapult you to the high and mighty world of brash Ottoman-European fantasy palaces, take you through parks, and plop you back down to earth with the grunge crowd at picturesque Ortaköy. The best day to do this tour is on Sunday, as Ortaköy has an arts and crafts market. Bus No 25E follows the Bosphorus from Eminönü, past Dolmabahçe Palace and the other shore-side sights all the way to Ortaköy and beyond. If you get sick of walking between the sights, you can always jump on this bus.

To get to Dolmabahçe Palace from Sultanahmet, catch the T4 İETT bus (which leaves from near the tourist office) and get

Dolmabahçe Palace to Ortaköy

Follow this day-long walking tour along the Bosphorus. (Peach trail: Map 12, then Map 11)

1. Dolmabahçe Palace
2. Deniz Müzesi
3. Ihlamur Kasrı
4. Çırağan Sarayı
5. Yıldız Şale & Park
6. Ortaköy

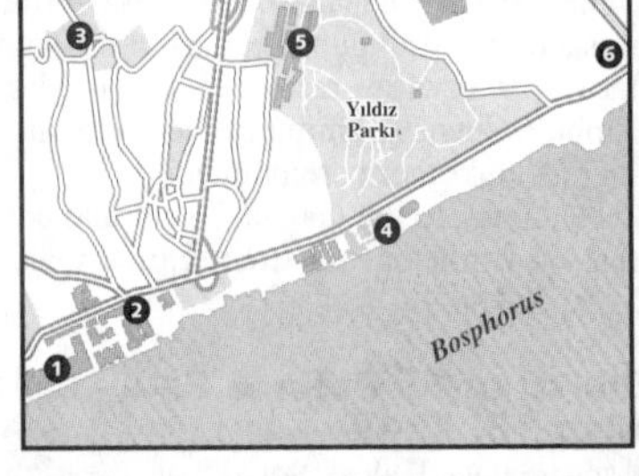

out at the Kabataş ferry bus stop; you'll see the frilly gates of Dolmabahçe about 200m ahead. If you're coming from Taksim Square, you can walk here in 10 minutes along İnönü Caddesi.

DOLMABAHÇE PALACE (Map 12)

This palace *(Dolmabahçe Sarayı; ☎ 212-236 9000, Dolmabahçe Caddesi; admission US$4.50-7 depending on ticket type; open 9am-4pm Tues, Wed & Fri-Sun)* was built between 1843 and 1856, when the homeland of the once-mighty Ottoman Empire had become the 'Sick Man of Europe'. His many peoples, aroused by a wave of European nationalism, were in revolt; his wealth was mostly under the control of European bankers; his armies, while still considerable, were obsolescent. The European, Christian way of life had triumphed over the Asian, Muslim one. Attempting to turn the tide, 19th-century sultans turned to European models, modernising the army and civil service, granting autonomy to subject peoples and adopting European ways.

Sultan Abdül Mecit decided he wanted a grandiose palace that would give the lie to talk of Ottoman decline. For a site he chose the *dolma bahçe* (filled-in garden) where his predecessor Sultan Ahmet I (1607–17) had filled in a little cove in order to build an imperial pleasure kiosk surrounded by gardens. Other wooden buildings succeeded the original kiosk, but all burned to the ground in 1814. Abdül Mecit's imperial architects, Nikogos and Karabet Balyan, concocted this dripping-with-wealth, totally overdecorated Ottoman-European palace that did more to precipitate the empire's bankruptcy than to dispel rumours of it.

Admission

The palace is divided into two sections, the **Selamlık** (Ceremonial Suites) and the **Harem-Cariyeler** (Harem & Concubines' Quarters). You must take a guided tour to see either section; the Selamlık tour takes about an hour, the Harem-Cariyeler takes half that. Only 1500 people are allowed into each section each day, so it's not a bad idea to reserve your space on a tour in advance. Entrance to the Selamlık costs US$4.50, to the Harem-Cariyeler the same; a ticket good for both sections costs US$7. The charge for a camera is US$4.50, for a video camera US$9; flash and tripod are not allowed. If you only have enough time for one tour, make it the Selamlık.

The tourist entrance to the palace is near the ornate clock tower, north of the mosque.

Touring the Selamlık (Ceremonial Suites)

The tour starts by passing through opulent salons and halls to a room with glass cabinets displaying gaudy crystal and tea sets. After visiting the palace mosque and ablutions room, things really start to get extravagant at the staircase with a French crystal balustrade. Here the Bohemian chandelier weighs close to 1000kg. The hallway at the top of the stairs has two Russian bearskins, a 2000kg chandelier and candelabras standing about 3m tall.

If your eyes are popping out of your head, you haven't seen anything yet: The tour continues past exquisite parquetry floors, Sèvres vases, Czechoslovakian meringue-like tiled fireplaces, through an exquisite hamam and past more monster candelabras. But even these extravagances are a mere prelude to the magnificent Grand Hall. Used in 1877 for the first meeting of the Ottoman Chamber of Deputies, feast your eyes on this lavishly painted hall, complete with fake columns and a chandelier that weighs over 4000kg. There are grated windows from which the resident women could watch the goings-on.

Touring the Harem-Cariyeler (Harem & Concubines' Quarters)

The pink building houses the Harem & Concubines' Quarters, which are not as lavish as the Selamlık but are still worth touring. The tour passes through a post-circumcision resting hall, a couple of hamams and the blue Harem's reception room. One room off the side was used by the fat Sultan Abdülaziz who needed an enormous bed.

Don't set your watch by any of the palace clocks, all of which are stopped at 9.05am, the moment at which Kemal Atatürk died in Dolmabahçe on 10 November 1938. You will be shown the small bedroom he used during his last days. Each year on 10 November, at 9.05am, the country observes a moment of silence in commemoration of the leader.

On to Deniz Müzesi

After you've finished at Dolmabahçe you may want to stop by the cafe near the clock tower, pull up one of the rocking fleet of picnic tables and enjoy the premium Bosphorus views.

When you're ready, head east along the treed Dolmabahçe Caddesi (which then morphs into Beşiktaş Caddesi). You'll soon come to the **İstanbul Museum of Painting & Sculpture (Map 12)** *(Resim ve Heykel Müzesi; ☎ 212-261 4298, open 10am-4pm Wed-Sun)*. Established by Atatürk in 1937 in a building once part of Dolmabahçe Palace, this museum holds over 2500 paintings and 550 sculptures from the early 19th century onwards.

Continue on for another 10-minute walk and you'll come to the Deniz Müzesi on the right, just after a pedestrian overpass. Beside the shore is the Beşiktaş İskelesi (Beşiktaş ferry terminal); ferries go from here to Üsküdar and Kadıköy (for timetables and costs see Crossing to Üsküdar and Crossing to Kadıköy under Sights on the Asian Shore later in this chapter).

DENİZ MÜZESİ (Map 12)

The Deniz Müzesi *(Maritime Museum; ☎ 212-261 0040, cnr Cezayir & Beşiktaş Caddesis; adult/student US$0.60/0.20, camera US$1.10, video US$2; open 9am-12.30pm & 1.30pm-5pm Wed-Sun)* is on the Bosphorus shore, just south of the flyover in Beşiktaş. Although there are some interesting exhibits (don't miss the imperial barges), the three floors of the main building are a tad musty and dull.

History

Though the Ottoman Empire is most remembered for its conquests on land, its maritime power was equally impressive. During the reign of Süleyman the Magnificent (r. 1520–66), the eastern Mediterranean was virtually an Ottoman lake. The sultan's navies cut a swathe in the Indian Ocean as well. Sea power was instrumental in the conquests of the Aegean coasts and islands, Egypt and North Africa. Discipline, well-organised supply and good ship design contributed to Ottoman victories.

However, during the later centuries the navy, like the army and the government, lagged behind the West in modernisation. The great battle that broke the spell of Ottoman naval invincibility was fought in 1571 at Lepanto, in the Gulf of Patras off the Greek coast. Though the Turkish fleet was destroyed, the sultan quickly produced another, partly with the help of rich Greek shipowners who were his subjects.

Exhibits

The sleek, swift imperial *caïques* (long, thin rowboats) in which the sultan would speed up and down the Bosphorus from palace to palace are over 30m in length but only 2m wide. With 13 banks of oars, the caïques were the speed boats of their day. Those with latticework screens were for the imperial women. There's also a war galley with 24 pairs of oars.

You may also be curious to see a replica of the *Map of Piri Reis,* an early Ottoman map (1513), which purports to show the coasts and continents of the New World. It's assumed that Piri Reis (Captain Piri) got hold of the work of Columbus for his map. The original map is in Topkapı Palace.

There's an outdoor display of cannons (including Selim the Grim's 21-tonne monster) and a statue of Barbaros Hayrettin Paşa (1483–1546), the famous Turkish admiral known also as Barbarossa who conquered North Africa for Süleyman the Magnificent. The admiral's tomb, designed by Sinan, is in the square opposite the museum.

TO IHLAMUR KASRI OR ONWARDS (Map 12)

When you've finished at the Deniz Müzesi you may want to visit Ihlamur Kasrı. The gardens are pretty and the kiosk pleasant, but you won't be missing out too much if you skip it. To get there from the Deniz Müzesi, you could walk (25 minutes uphill), catch a taxi (US$1.30) or bus No 26 or 26A which run from Eminönü to Karaköy, Dolmabahçe and Beşiktaş before heading inland via the Ihlamur stop.

If you're missing Ihlamur, continue walking east along Beşiktaş Caddesi (which turns into Çırağan Caddesi) to Çırağan Sarayı – 20 minutes all up. If you're catching bus No 25E get out at the Yahya Efendi stop to reach the entrance to the Çırağan complex.

If you want to head straight to Ortaköy (the end of this walking tour) a ferry heads to Bebek, via Ortaköy, from the Beşiktaş ferry terminal at 5.30pm and every half-hour until 8pm (Monday to Friday only).

IHLAMUR KASRI (Map 12)

Sheltered in a narrow valley about 1.2km inland and to the north of the Deniz Müzesi is a park containing the two pavilions of the Ihlamur Kasrı *(Kiosk of the Linden Tree; ☎ 212-259 5086, Ihlamur Teşvikiye Yolu; admission adult/student US$1.80/0.60, camera US$4.50, video US$9; open 9.30am-5pm Tues & Wed, Fri-Sun)*. If you've come from the floral excesses of Turkish baroque at its worst – Dolmabahçe Palace – you may want to give this place a miss, because it's more of the same, having been built by the same architects (Nikogos and Karabet Balyan).

If you're still keen, buy your ticket – a guide will approach to take you on the (mandatory) free tour.

Try to imagine what it must have been like when these two miniature hunting palaces stood here alone, in the midst of a forest. Near the entry gate the park is open and formal, with grassy lawns, ornamental trees and a quiet pool.

Look across the pool to find the **Merasim Köşkü** (Sultan's Kiosk) built on the orders of Sultan Abdül Mecit between 1849 and 1855.

Up the marble stairway and through the ornate door is the Hall of Mirrors, with crystal from Bohemia and vases from France. The music room, to the right of the entrance, has precious Hereke fabrics on the chairs and an enamelled coal-grate fireplace painted with flowers. The main appliance in the Imperial Water Closet is of the traditional flat Turkish type, demonstrating that in here even the sultan was dethroned. The room to the left of the entrance was a reception salon.

The **Maiyet Köşkü**, or Retinue Kiosk, was for the sultan's suite of attendants, guests or harem. Make yourself welcome too: it's now a teahouse serving tea, coffee and snacks (for around US$2).

ÇIRAĞAN SARAYI (Map 12)

Not satisfied with the architectural exertions of his predecessor at Dolmabahçe, Sultan Abdülaziz (r. 1861–76) built his own grand residence at Çırağan, on the Bosphorus shore only 1.5km away from Dolmabahçe. The architect of the moment was Balyan, who also designed Dolmabahçe.

The sultan was deposed, however, and later died in Çırağan under mysterious circumstances. His mentally unstable nephew Murat came to the throne, but was deposed within a year by his brother Abdül Hamit II, who kept Murat a virtual prisoner in Çırağan. Much later (1909) it was the seat of the Ottoman Chamber of Deputies and Senate, but in 1910 it was destroyed by fire under suspicious circumstances.

The palace has been restored (the interior in lurid lollypop colours) as part of the ritzy Çırağan Palace Hotel Kempinski İstanbul, and is now used for conferences. If you're decently dressed, they won't mind if you enter the plush marbled hotel foyer, wander around the immaculate grounds and admire the Bosphorus view, but don't step on the toes of the glitterati. Perhaps have a drink, though you'll pay US$10 minimum.

Just a minute's walk east of Çırağan is the entrance, on the left, to Yıldız Park.

YILDIZ ŞALE & PARK (Map 12)

Sultan Abdül Hamit II (r. 1876–1909) also had to build his own fancy palace. He added considerably to the structures built by earlier sultans in Yıldız Park *(☎ 212-261 8460, Çırağan Caddesi; admission cars/pedestrians US$1.70/free; open 6am-9.30pm)*. If you come to the park by taxi, have it take you up the steep slope to Yıldız Şale. You can visit the other kiosks on the walk down. (A taxi from Taksim Square to the top of the hill might cost around US$5 or US$6.)

The park began life as the imperial reserve for Çırağan Sarayı, but when Abdül Hamit built Yıldız Şale, largest of the park's surviving structures, the park served that palace. Under Abdül Hamit, the park was planted with rare and exotic trees, shrubs and flowers, and was provided with carefully tended paths and superior electric lighting and drainage systems.

The park, with its kiosks, had become derelict, but was beautifully restored by the Turkish Touring & Automobile Association (Turing) in the 1980s, under lease from the city government. In 1994 the newly elected city government declined to renew the lease, and took over operation of the park. Today it's a pretty, leafy retreat alive with birds and picnickers. Couples enjoy the park as well – avert your eyes from the rustling bushes!

As you toil up the hill along the road, near the top of the slope to the left you'll see the **Çadır Köşkü**. Built between 1865 and 1870, the ornate kiosk is nestled beside a small lake, with a leafy outdoor cafe. The views are nothing special.

To the right (north) as you hike up the road from the gate are two greenhouses hidden by vegetation, the **Kış Bahçesi** (Winter Garden) and the **Yeşil Sera** (Green Nursery).

When you get to the top of the slope, at the T-intersection, take the road to the right. You'll pass the turn-off on the left for the Yıldız Şale (see that entry following) but keep going for another 500m to find the **Malta Köşkü** (see the Places to Eat chapter).

If you continue walking past the Malta Köşkü for 10 minutes you'll arrive at the **Yıldız Porselen Fabrikası** *(Yıldız Porcelain Factory; ☎ 212-260 2370; free guided tour; open 9am-6pm Mon-Fri)*. The factory was constructed to manufacture dinner services for the palace. It still operates and is open to visitors for half-hour tours. You don't need to book for a tour, just turn up. There is a small ceramics shop at the entrance.

Yıldız Şale

At the very top of the hill, enclosed by a lofty wall, is the Yıldız Şale *(Yıldız Chalet; ☎ 212-259 4570; admission US$4, camera US$4.50, video US$9; open 9.30am-5pm Tues & Wed, Fri-Sun)*. It's a 'guesthouse' put up in 1882 and expanded in 1898 by Abdül Hamit for use by Kaiser Wilhelm II of Germany during a state visit. As you enter the palace, a guide will approach and give you the half-hour tour, which is required. Although the chalet isn't as plush as Dolmabahçe, it's a lot less crowded so you get more time to ask questions and to feast your eyes on the exhibits.

It would seem the kaiser had enough space to move in, as the chalet has 64 rooms. After his imperial guest departed, the sultan became quite attached to his 'rustic' creation, and decided to live here himself, forsaking the palaces on the Bosphorus shore.

Abdül Hamit was paranoid, and for good reason: Fate determined that his fears would come true. When eventually deposed, he left this wooden palace in April 1909 and boarded a train that took him to house arrest in Ottoman Salonika (today Thessaloniki, in Greece). He was later allowed by the Young Turks' government to return to İstanbul and live out his years in Beylerbeyi Sarayı, on the Asian shore of the Bosphorus.

Yıldız Şale was to be associated with more dolorous history. The last sultan of the Ottoman Empire, Mehmet V (Vahideddin), lived here until, at 6am on 11 November 1922, he and his first chamberlain, bandmaster, doctor, two secretaries, valet, barber and two eunuchs accompanied by trunks full of jewels, gold and antiques, boarded two British Red Cross ambulances for the secret journey to the naval dockyard at Tophane. There they boarded the British battleship HMS *Malaya* for a trip into exile, ending the Ottoman Empire forever. On the way to the quay one of the tyres on the sultan's ambulance went flat; while it was being changed, the 'Shadow of God on Earth' quaked, fearing that he might be discovered.

In the republican era, the Yıldız Şale has served as a guesthouse for visiting heads of state, including Charles de Gaulle, Pope Paul VI and the Empress Soraya of Iran.

The first section you visit was the original chalet, built in 1882. The first room on

IZZET KERIBAR

JONATHAN SELIG

IZZET KERIBAR

VERITY CAMPBELL

CHRISTINA DAMEYER

Top: The interior of Rüstem Paşa Camii (left) and an entrance to Dolmabahçe Palace (right)
Middle: Lively İstiklal Caddesi (left) hosts the National Sovereignty and Children's Day on 23 April (right).
Bottom: The elaborate Çırağan Sarayı was built in 1874 and is now an expensive hotel.

VERITY CAMPBELL

VERITY CAMPBELL

GREG ELMS

VERITY CAMPBELL

VERITY CAMPBELL

The ancient streets of Old İstanbul support colourful street markets, such as this in Eminönü (bottom left), and the ancient sites such as the 12th-century Fethiye Camii (top left), the venerable Great School of Fener (top right) and the sacred Eyüp Sultan Camii and its cemetery (middle and bottom right).

the tour was used by Abdül Hamit's mother for her religious devotions, the second was her guest reception room with a very fine mosaic tabletop. Then comes a women's resting room, and afterwards a tearoom with furniture marked with a gold star on a blue background, which reminds one that this is the 'star' *(yıldız)* chalet.

In 1898 the chalet was expanded, and the older section became the harem (with steel doors), while the new section was the selamlık. In the selamlık are a bathroom with tiles from the Yıldız Porcelain Factory, and several reception rooms, one of which has furniture made by Abdül Hamit himself, an accomplished woodworker. The grand hall of the selamlık is vast, its floor covered by a 7½-tonne Hereke carpet woven just for this room. So huge is the rug that it had to be brought in through the far (north) wall before the building was finished.

İstanbul Şehir Müzesi & Yıldız Şale Müzesi

Yıldız has two more sights but to get to them you'll have to exit the park and make your way along Müvezzi Caddesi, which follows along the west side of the park, or the larger Barbaros Bulvarı, which follows a similar course.

The Merasim Köşkü (Ceremonial Kiosk and barracks) was restored in 1988 and opened as the İstanbul Şehir Müzesi *(İstanbul City Museum; ☎ 212-258 5344, Ihlamur Yıldız Caddesi; admission US$1; open 9am-4pm Tues-Sat)*. It was closed for renovations at the time of research but it apparently houses objects from the Conquest (1453) onwards. In the same complex, the carpentry shop *(marangozhane)* at Yıldız, where Abdül Hamit II liked to lay down the burdens of rank and office, pick up chisel and mallet and make furniture, is now also the Yıldız Şale Müzesi *(Yıldız Chalet Museum; ☎ 212-259 4570; admission US$2; open 9am-5pm Wed-Mon)*. It houses rare Yıldız porcelain vases and urns.

ORTAKÖY (Map 11)

Back on Çırağan Caddesi, catch bus No 25E east to Ortaköy. Literally 'middle village', this Bosphorus suburb has an interesting ethnic history in which church, synagogue and mosque coexist peacefully in its narrow streets. Today it is a trendy gathering place for the young and hip, with art galleries, chic cafe-bars, and boutiques selling antiques, carpets and jewellery. On warm Sundays, artisans display their wares (silver and costume jewellery, hats, books and more) in the narrow streets from around noon to midnight.

Get out of the bus at Osmanzade Sokak, near the doorway to the **Etz Ahayim Synagogue**. The synagogue has been here since 1660, though the current building dates from 1941, when the old one was destroyed by a disastrous fire. The **Church of Hagios Phocas** (1856) is a short distance north of it.

At the water's edge by the ornate mosque called the **Ortaköy Camii** are terrace cafes, their open-air tables enjoying views of the Bosphorus and the mosque. Officially named the Büyük Mecidiye Camii, the eclectic-baroque mosque is the work of Nikogos Balyan, architect of Dolmabahçe Palace, who designed it for Sultan Abdül Mecit III in 1854. Within the mosque hang several masterful examples of Arabic calligraphy executed by the sultan, who was an accomplished calligrapher.

For suggestions for places to eat, drink and be merry (now that you've finished the walking tour), see the Places to Eat and Entertainment chapters.

Sights on the Asian Shore

The Asian shore of the Bosphorus has a number of possibilities for interesting excursions, with the added bonus that you will meet far fewer tourists than in European İstanbul. Üsküdar and Kadıköy are easy to get to from Eminönü, and the ferry ride over is a very pleasant way to start the day. Üsküdar is an ancient part of İstanbul with loads of character, and the walking tour will help you absorb it. Kadıköy was the site of the first settlement in the area – it's not as pretty as Üsküdar, but on Tuesday the open-air market hums, and there are plenty of cafes, bars, restaurants and good clothes and antique shopping. Bus No 12H (US$0.50) runs between Kadıköy and Üsküdar.

CROSSING TO ÜSKÜDAR

If you're coming from Sultanahmet, hop on the ferry from Eminönü (dock one), which runs every 15 minutes between 6.30am and 8pm, and then every half-hour until 11.30pm. Tokens cost US$0.50.

A ferry service also operates between Beşiktaş (catch it from beside the Deniz Müzesi) and Üsküdar. Ferries start at 6.30am and run every half-hour until 10.30pm; tokens cost US$0.50. From Kabataş, just south of Dolmabahçe Palace, ferries run to Üsküdar every half-hour from 7.15am to 8.45pm (every hour from 10.30am to 3.30pm).

Another alternative is to catch the small boat from Seraglio Point that goes directly to the Kız Kulesi. Boats leave at 12.30pm, 2.30pm and 4.30pm Wednesday to Sunday for US$3.50 one way including a drink (nonalcoholic). From Kız Kulesi you can catch another small boat across to Salacak (within walking distance to Üsküdar).

There are also buses and dolmuşes departing from Taksim for Üsküdar, but forget them – the ferries are faster and far more enjoyable.

ÜSKÜDAR (Map 19)

Üsküdar (**er**-sker-dar) is the Turkish form of the name Scutari. The first colonists lived in Chalcedon (modern-day Kadıköy), to the south, and Chrysopolis (now Üsküdar) became a suburb of it; both towns existed about two decades before Byzantium was founded. The harbour at Chrysopolis was superior to Chalcedon, and as Byzantium blossomed, Chrysopolis outgrew Chalcedon to become the largest suburb on the Asian shore. Unfortunately this busy Asian hub was unwalled and therefore vulnerable – it became part of the Ottoman Empire at least 100 years before the Conquest of 1453.

İskele Camii (Map 19, #1)

As you leave the ferry dock in Üsküdar, the **Demokrasi Meydanı** (main square), is right before you. North-east of the square behind the dolmuş ranks and near the ferry landing is the İskele Camii *(Dock Mosque; Demokrasi Meydanı; open 7am-8.30pm daily)*. Sometimes called the Mihrimah Sultan Camii, it was built in 1547 by Sinan for Süleyman the Magnificent's daughter. It's imposing on the outside, but inside it's a bit claustrophobic and dull.

Üsküdar

Üsküdar is still a busy suburb, and you will enjoy browsing through its streets, markets and mosques. on this two- to three-hour walk. (Pink trail: Map 19)

1. İskele Camii
2. Kız Kulesi
3. Yeni Valide Camii
4. Mimar Sinan Çarşısı
5. Çinili Cami

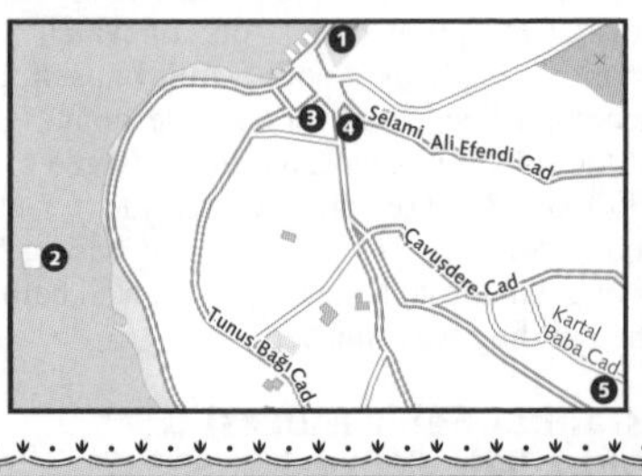

Heading Around the Bend

Head back to the shore road, Sahil Yolu, and west along the path that edges the Bosphorus. You'll pass ferry docks on the right, dolmuş stops on the left, and a flotilla of bobbing fish restaurant boats dishing up fish sandwiches for US$0.70. Overlooking the Bosphorus is the delightful **Şemsi Paşa Camii (Map 19, #3)** *(Sahil Yolu)*, designed by Sinan and built in 1580 for grand vizier Şemsi Paşa. It's a simple, charming mosque; the vizier's tomb, alongside, has an opening into the mosque.

After visiting the mosque, continue around the bend following the shore for about 1.5km (it's a pleasant walk as the views over to European İstanbul are superb) until you come to the district of Salacak and the closest land point to the Kız Kulesi. You'll see a small white ticket office, and a cluster of wind-blown tourists.

Kız Kulesi (Map 19, #18)

If you take the ferry to Üsküdar, you'll notice to the south, just off the Asian mainland, the Kız Kulesi *(Maiden's Tower; ☎ 216-342 4747; open 11.30am-11pm Wed-Sun)*. The tower was a toll booth and defence point in ancient times; the Bosphorus could be closed off by means of a chain stretching from here to Seraglio Point. Although also known as Leander's Tower in English, the tower has nothing to do with Leander, who was no maiden, and who swam not the Bosphorus but the Hellespont (Dardanelles), 340km from here.

The tower is subject to the usual legend: oracle says maiden will die by snakebite; concerned father puts maiden in snake-proof tower; fruit vendor comes by boat, sells basket of fruit (complete with snake) to maiden, who gets hers. The legend seems to crop up wherever there are offshore towers and maidens, and then we have to repeat them in guidebooks.

In September 2000, the tower was stylishly renovated and it's now open to the public as a cafe and restaurant. Unfortunately it hasn't escaped the cheesier aspects of tourism – you can get your photograph taken in 'maiden' costume for US$4.50 – but it's still worth visiting for the views alone. Small boats run from Salacak to the tower every 15 minutes from 11.30am to 7pm Wednesday to Sunday for adult/student US$3.50/2.70 return, including a drink. For details about the food, see Üsküdar in the Places to Eat chapter.

When you're back on dry land, you may want to stop for lunch at the fine **Huzur Restaurant (Map 19, #20)** (see the Places to Eat chapter). Otherwise, retrace your steps to Demokrasi Meydanı to continue the inland.

Yeni Valide Camii (Map 19, #14)

To the south of Demokrasi Meydanı is the Yeni Valide Camii *(New Queen Mother's Mosque; Demokrasi Meydanı)*, built by Sultan Ahmet III in 1710 for his mother Gülnuş Emetullah. Built late in the period of classical Ottoman architecture, it is not as fine as earlier works. The odd wooden additions to the side that faces Demokrasi Meydanı were added as the entrance to the imperial loge.

Mimar Sinan Çarşısı (Map 19, #13)

If you head along Hakimiyet-i Milliye Caddesi on the left you'll pass the Mimar Sinan Çarşısı *(Hakimiyet-i Milliye Caddesi; admission free; open 9am-6pm)*, thought to have been the first hamam designed by Sinan. Built by Nurbanu Sultan, mother of Sultan Murat III, in 1574–83, it was a double hamam. Having fallen into ruins, part of it was torn down to accommodate construction of the avenue; the remaining half was restored in 1966 and is now cramped and crowded with shops.

Heading Towards Çinili Cami (Map 19)

If you walk through the Çarşısı, you'll come out into a little square where the small Kara Davut Paşa Camii (Map 19, #12) (1495) faces onto one side. Continue walking along Hakimiyet-i Milliye Caddesi for another 250m to a busy intersection. Near the Akbank you'll find the **Niyazibey İskender Kebapçı (Map 19, #26)** (see the Places to Eat chapter), if you are hungry.

The Çinili Cami is Üsküdar's jewel, a small and unassuming building harbouring a wealth of brilliant İznik faience on its interior walls. It's a neighbourhood mosque in the quarter called Tabaklar, up the hillside away from Üsküdar's main square. It can be tricky to find on your own (a 30-minute walk); a taxi costs less than US$2, and is well worth it.

If you're intent on walking you'll pass by some quaint old houses, and many bland apartment blocks. It's not a particularly scenic walk, but it gives you a glimpse into local neighbourly life. From the Niyazibey İskender Kebapçı intersection, bear left and walk along busy Dr Fahri Atebay Caddesi for a few minutes; turn left onto Eski Toptaşı Caddesi. You'll immediately see the Kentbank on the left side; on the right side is the **Hacı Bedel Mustafa Efendi Camii (Map 19, #29)**. Follow the small road running to the left, Sansar Sokak, which then widens into Çavuşdere Caddesi. Walk for six or seven minutes uphill until you come to a fork in the road with Balçelievler Sokak; take the unmarked road to the right for another six minutes uphill.

Approaching the Çinili Cami, you first come to the **Çinili Hamam (Map 19, #31)** *(wash-only US$3, with massage US$6; open 8am-5pm daily),* the mosque's Turkish bath, which, because it gets virtually no foreign visitors, is cheap and friendly.

Çinili Cami (Map 19, #32)

The Çinili Cami *(Tiled Mosque; Çinili Mescit Sokak),* uphill from the bath, is unprepossessing from the outside: just a shady little neighbourhood mosque with the usual collection of bearded old men sitting around. Take a moment to greet them pleasantly and they will respond with fulsome welcomes, gratified that someone has come so far to see their historic mosque. Admission is free though a donation of US$1 is appreciated. It's only open at prayer times, but a friendly warden should appear to open it at other times.

Inside, the mosque is brilliant with İznik faience, the bequest of Mahpeyker Kösem (1640), wife of Sultan Ahmet I (r. 1603–17) and mother of sultans Murat IV (r. 1623–40) and İbrahim (r. 1640–48). As it is used heavily by local people for prayer, be properly dressed and on your best behaviour when you visit, and avoid visiting on Friday.

As the walk is now finished, retrace your steps back to the heart of Üsküdar. Alternatively, you may wish to head south-west through the maze of streets to another interesting mosque, the prominent **Atik Valide Camii (Map 19, #30)** *(Tabaklar Camii Sokak),* one of the grandest of Sinan's İstanbul mosques, second only to his Süleymaniye. It was built for Valide Sultan Nurbanu, wife of Selim II and mother of Ahmet III, in 1583.

Büyük Çamlıca

The hilltop park *(☎ 216-443 2198; Turistik Çamlıca Caddesi; admission free; open 9am-11pm daily),* the highest point in İstanbul at 261m, has long been enjoyed by İstanbul's nobility, poets and everyday folk. It's well worth a visit.

Once it was favoured by Sultan Mahmut II (r. 1808–39), but by the late 1970s it was a dusty (or muddy), unkempt car park threatened by illegal and unplanned construction. In 1980 the municipal government leased the land to the Turing group, which landscaped the hilltop and built a cafe and restaurant such as Mahmut might have enjoyed. The municipal government took over management of the park in 1995.

To reach the hilltop from Üsküdar's main square, you can take a taxi (US$2.50) all the way to the summit, or a dolmuş (US$0.50) most of the way. For the latter, walk to the dolmuş ranks in front of the İskele Camii, take a dolmuş headed for Ümraniye, and ask for Büyük Çamlıca. The dolmuş will pass the entrance to Küçük Çamlıca and drop you off shortly thereafter in a district called Kısıklı. The walk uphill (pleasant, but no great views) following the signs to the summit takes from 30 to 40 minutes, depending on your speed and stamina.

Once at the top you can rest and marvel at the view (and the crowds, if it's a weekend) and the pretty gardens. From Büyük Çamlıca the Bosphorus is laid out like a map, with its twists and turns, and the minaretted skyline of Old İstanbul looks just like the picture postcards. Enjoy a meal at the **Çamlıca Restaurant** (see the Places to Eat chapter).

The neighbouring hilltop, Küçük Çamlıca, is not quite as fancy as its loftier sibling but with its tea garden it's equally pleasant.

CROSSING TO KADIKÖY (Map 12)

If you're coming from Sultanahmet, hop on the ferry from Eminönü (dock two), which runs every 20 minutes between 7.30am and 8.35pm. Tokens cost US$0.60.

A ferry service also operates from Beşiktaş (catch it from beside the Deniz Müzesi), starting at 7.15am, running every half-hour until 10.45pm; tokens cost US$0.50. A similar service starts from Karaköy ferry.

Bus No 110 (US$1) runs from Taksim Square to Kadıköy, and there are frequent dolmuşes (US$1.30) that take the same route from 7am to 1am.

If you take the ferry, you will notice the large **Selimiye Kışlası** *(Selimiye Barracks; Kavak İskele Caddesi)*, a square building with towers at the corners. It dates from the early 19th century, when Selim III and Mahmut II reorganised the Ottoman armed forces along European lines. Not far away is the **Selimiye Camii** (1805) and the Ottoman rest-home for ageing palace ladies, which is now used by Marmara University.

The ferry will probably make a stop at the conspicuous German-style **Haydarpaşa station** *(☎ 216-336 0475 for train bookings; Haydarpaşa İstasyon Caddesi)*, the city's terminal for Asian trains. During the late 19th century, when Kaiser Wilhelm was trying to charm the sultan into economic and military cooperation, he gave him the station as a little gift.

KADIKÖY (Map 11)

Legend has it that the first colonists established themselves at Chalcedon, now modern Kadıköy. Byzas, bearing the oracle's message to found a colony 'Opposite the blind', thought the Chalcedonites blind to the advantages of Seraglio Point as a town site, and founded his town on the European shore. Today Kadıköy has little to show for its historic beginnings, but it's a busy suburb, popular with expats and locals alike. It has good shopping, eating and bars.

The two ferry docks – Eminönü and Karaköy & Kızıl Adalar – face a plaza along the south side of Kadıköy's small harbour; Haydarpaşa station is to the north. The main street, Söğütlüçeşme Caddesi, runs eastward from the docks into Kadıköy proper; another main road, Serasker Caddesi, runs parallel to it. A pedestrian way, Bahariye Caddesi, runs perpendicular to both of them, around 300m inland. Buses and dolmuşes leave from Deniz Sokağı, the road that runs beside the plaza near the harbour.

The **market** on Tuesday (8am to 6pm) has clothing, homeware, toys – no tourist gear, but plenty of shopping bargains. To get there, head along Söğütlüçeşme Caddesi for about 500m until you come to a busy intersection, Altıyol Meydanı. Cross over and continue eastward along Kuşdili Caddesi for another 250m. At Hasırcıbaşı Caddesi turn left and you'll see the tent-city market spread out before you.

Kadıköy has plenty of **antique** shops without inflated prices for tourists. Try the shops along Tellalzade Sokak, south of Serasker Caddesi, which are open daily except Sunday.

The bustling pedestrian precinct, Bahariye Caddesi, has many clothing shops, and a busy cheap outdoor eatery, Nail Bey Sokak, which is popular with students. Nightlife in Kadıköy is centred around Kadife and Halil Efendi Sokak.

If you'd like to head to Üsküdar after you've taken a turn around town, take bus No 12H (US$0.50).

Western Districts

From early times the heart of this ancient city has been near the tip of Seraglio Point. As the city grew over the centuries, its boundaries moved westward and a series of successive city walls were put up to wall the city.

West of Atatürk Bulvarı in Old İstanbul, out towards the city walls, are many interesting and under-visited things to see, including the Fatih Camii, Kariye Müzesi (once the Chora Church), Tekfur Sarayı (Palace of Constantine Porphyrogenetus), and a number of other churches and mosques.

MİHRİMAH SULTAN CAMİİ (Map 18)

Start the day by catching a bus or dolmuş headed north-west from Sultanahmet along Fevzi Paşa Caddesi towards Edirnekapı. Get out just before the city walls at the Mihrimah Sultan Camii *(Ali Kuşçu Sokak)*, a mosque built by Süleyman the Magnificent's favourite daughter, Mihrimah, in the

Western Districts

This day-long walking tour takes you from old-fashioned Edirnekapı to Fener. The mosques of Zeyrek and Fatih are included at the end of the tour; they are easily accessible by taxi. (Green trail: Map 18)

1. Mihrimah Sultan Camii
2. Kariye Müzesi
3. Tekfur Sarayı
4. Fethiye Camii
6. Sultan Selim Camii
7. Great School
8. St Mary of the Mongols
9. Ecumenical Orthodox Patriarchate
10. Church of St Stephen of the Bulgars

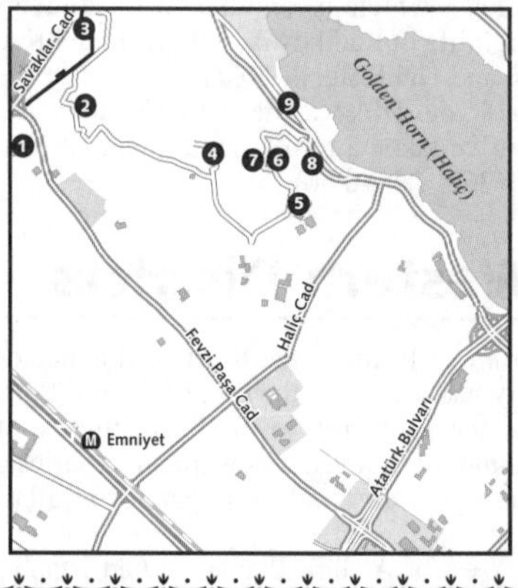

1560s. Mihrimah married Rüstem Paşa, Süleyman's brilliant and powerful grand vizier (his little tile-covered mosque is down by the Mısır Çarşısı).

The architect of the Mihrimah Camii was Sinan, and the mosque, a departure from his usual style, is among his best works. Visit in the morning to get the full effect of the light streaming through the delicate stained-glass windows on the east side. The interior space is very light, with 19 windows in each arched tympanum. Virtually every other surface is painted in arabesques, creating a very delicate effect.

Cross the road from the Mihrimah Camii and, still inside the walls, head north towards the Golden Horn. You'll see signs, and children pointing the way, to the Kariye Müzesi.

KARİYE MÜZESİ (Map 18)

If we translate the original name, Chora Church, of this building, it would be called 'Church of the Holy Saviour Outside the Walls' or 'in the Country', because the first church on this site was indeed outside the walls built by Constantine the Great. But just as London's church of St Martin-in-the-Fields is hardly surrounded by bucolic scenery these days, the Church of the Holy Saviour was soon engulfed by Byzantine urban sprawl. It was enclosed within the walls built by the Emperor Theodosius II in 413, less than 100 years after Constantine. So the Holy Saviour in the Country was 'in the country' for about 80 years, and has been 'in the city' for over 1580 years.

It was not only the environs of the church that changed: For four centuries it served as a mosque (Kariye Camii), and is now a museum, the **Kariye Müzesi** (*☎ 212-523 3009, Kariye Camii Sokak; adult/student US$4.50/2; open 9.30am-4pm Thur-Tues Nov-Mar, 9.30am-6pm Thur-Tues Apr-Oct*).

The building you see is not the original church-outside-the-walls. Rather, this one was built in the late 11th century, with repairs and restructuring in the succeeding centuries. Virtually all of the interior decoration – the famous mosaics and the less-renowned but equally striking mural paintings – dates from about 1320. Between 1948 and 1959 the decoration was carefully restored under the auspices of the Byzantine Society of America.

The **mosaics** are breathtaking, and follow the standard Byzantine order. The first ones are those of the dedication, to Christ and to the Virgin Mary. Then come the offertory ones; Theodore Metochites, builder of the church, offering it to Christ. The two small domes of the inner narthex have portraits of all Christ's ancestors back to Adam. A series outlines the Virgin Mary's life, and another, Christ's early years. Yet another series concentrates on Christ's ministry. Various saints and martyrs are depicted in the interstices.

In the nave are three mosaics: of Christ, of the Virgin as Teacher, and of the Dormition (Assumption) of the Blessed Virgin – turn around to see this, it's over the main door you just entered. The 'infant' in the painting is actually Mary's soul, being held by Jesus, while her body lies 'asleep' on its bier.

South of the nave is the parecclesion, a side chapel built to hold the tombs of the church's founder and his relatives, close friends and associates. The frescoes appropriately deal with the theme of death and resurrection. The striking painting in the apse shows Christ breaking down the gates of Hell and raising Adam and Eve, with saints and kings in attendance.

If you are feeling peckish, you have a choice of cheap eats in the **Kariye Pembe** Köşk, or pricier fare in **Asitane Restaurant** which is under the **Kariye Oteli** (see the Places to Eat chapter).

TEKFUR SARAYI (Map 18)

From Kariye, head west to the city walls, then north again, and you'll soon come to the Tekfur Sarayı *(Palace of Constantine Porphyrogenetus; Hocaçakır Caddesi; open 9am-5pm Wed, Thur & Sun)*. It's nominally open on the listed days, but you can usually just wander around the back via the sportsground and have a look. The caretaker may appear and sell you a ticket for US$0.25.

Though the building is only a shell these days, it is remarkably preserved for a Byzantine palace built in the 14th century. Sacred buildings often survive the ravages of time because they continue to be used, even though they may be converted for use in another religion. Secular buildings, however, are often torn down and, once their owners die, they are used as quarries for building materials. The Byzantine palaces that once crowded Sultanahmet Square are all gone; so is the great Palace of Blachernae, which adjoined the Tekfur Sarayı. Only this one remains.

For information about the city walls see The Walls & Eyüp later in this chapter.

HEADING EAST (Map 18)

After you've finished at Tekfur Sarayı, retrace your steps to the Kariye Müzesi. To walk to the Fethiye Camii from the Kariye Müzesi (about 20 minutes), head south and, just past the Kariye Oteli, turn left downhill on Neşler Sokak. Turn left at the bottom of the hill around a little pink mosque, then head straight on along a level street and uphill on Fethiye Caddesi. At the top of the slope most traffic goes right, but you go left towards the mosque, which is visible from this point.

FETHİYE CAMİİ (Map 18)

Fethiye Camii (Mosque of the Conquest) was built in the 12th century as the Church of the Theotokos Pammakaristos or Church of the Joyous Mother of God. It is usually closed so if you want to enter you'll have to organise a time with the caretaker at Aya Sofya (☎ 212-522 0989).

The original monastery church was added to several times over the centuries, then converted to a mosque in 1591 to commemorate Sultan Murat III's victories in Georgia and Azerbaijan. Before its conversion it served as the headquarters of the Ecumenical Orthodox Patriarch (1456–1568); Mehmet the Conqueror visited to discuss theological questions here with Patriarch Gennadios, not long after the conquest of the city. They talked things over in the side chapel known as the parecclesion, which has been restored to its former Byzantine splendour; the rest of the building remains a mosque. Unfortunately, the church itself is something of a disappointment inside, though the exterior still bears some inscriptions in Greek on the south side.

From the Fethiye Camii you can continue your explorations by walking south-east to the Sultan Selim Camii. Continue uphill along Manyasizade Caddesi for 10 minutes through the colourful Çarşamba district, then turn sharp left around the police station *(polis karakolu)* onto Sultan Selim Caddesi, with the mosque visible ahead.

Approaching the mosque along Sultan Selim Caddesi, you pass the huge, open Roman **Çukur Bostan** (Cistern of Aspar) built by a general in the Roman army in the AD 400s. After it ceased being used as a cistern, a Turkish village grew up sheltered in its depths. That was recently swept away to make room for spacious sportsgrounds and parkland.

SULTAN SELİM CAMİİ (Map 18)

This mosque *(Mosque of Yavuz Selim; tomb open 9.30am-4.30pm Tues-Sun)* was built by Süleyman the Magnificent for his father, Selim I. The simple building is a bit rundown, but it's a loved part of the neighbourhood; picnickers enjoy the views of the Golden Horn from the terrace surrounding the mosque. Selim's tomb is here too.

FENER (Map 18)

Fener (from *Phanar,* Greek for lantern or lighthouse) was the centre of Greek life in Ottoman İstanbul, and is still the seat of the Ecumenical Orthodox patriarchate.

Selim 'the Grim'

Sultan Selim I, Selim 'the Grim' (r. 1512–20), laid the foundations of Ottoman greatness for his son and successor, Süleyman the Magnificent.

Though he ruled for a very short time, Selim greatly expanded the empire's territory, solidified its institutions and filled its treasury. He came to power by deposing his father, Beyazıt II (r. 1481–1512), who died 'mysteriously' soon after.

To avoid any threat to his power, and thus the sort of disastrous civil war that had torn the empire apart in the days before Mehmet the Conqueror, Selim had all his brothers put to death, and in the eight years of his reign he had eight grand viziers beheaded.

But his violence was in the interests of empire-building, at which he was a master. He doubled the empire's extent during his short reign, conquering part of Persia and all of Syria and Egypt. He took from Egypt's decadent, defeated rulers the title Caliph of Islam, which was borne by his successors until 1924. In his spare time he wrote poetry in Persian, the literary language of the time.

From the Sultan Selim Camii turn right and head down Camcı Çeşme Yokuşü Sokak. Take the first street on the left, Mesnevihane Sokak, and walk along it until you see a large red-brick tower ahead. This is the **Great School** (Greek Lycee of Fener), the oldest learning institution in İstanbul, founded long before the Conquest. The present building dates from 1881. Walk up and around the school to find **St Mary of the Mongols**. This is the only Byzantine church in İstanbul which has not, at some stage or another, been in Ottoman hands. The caretakers will happily show you through; consider placing a donation in the box. After you've visited the church, head left (downhill), take the first right and go down the flight of steps. When you reach the bottom turn left, and take the first right again. Continue through the Akçin Sokak intersection (you'll see the Golden Horn on your left) for another 500m or so along Sadrazam Ali Paşa Caddesi.

ECUMENICAL ORTHODOX PATRIARCHATE (Map 18)

The Ecumenical patriarch *(Patrikhane; ☎ 212-531 9673, Sadrazam Ali Paşa Caddesi)* is a ceremonial head of the Orthodox churches, though most of the churches in Greece, Cyprus, Russia and other countries have their own patriarchs or archbishops who are independent of İstanbul. Nevertheless, the 'sentimental' importance of the patriarchate, here in the city that saw the great era of Byzantine and Orthodox influence, is considerable.

In the eyes of the Turkish government, the patriarch is a Turkish citizen of Greek descent nominated by the church and appointed by the government as an official in the Directorate of Religious Affairs. In this capacity he is the religious leader of the country's Orthodox citizens and is known officially as the Greek Patriarch of Fener (Fener Rum Patriği).

The patriarchate has been in this district since 1601. It's a good idea to phone in advance if you want to enter, but it's usually open from 9am to 4pm daily; there's a service between 9am and noon Sunday.

The **Church of St George**, within the patriarchate compound, is a modest place, built in 1720, but the ornate patriarchal throne may date from the last years of Byzantium. In 1941 a disastrous fire destroyed many of the buildings but spared the church.

After you've seen the patriarchate compound, retrace your steps to Akçin Sokak and turn left on the main road, Balat Vapur İskelesi Caddesi. Head north-west, past the Women's Library, to the conspicuous church ahead.

CHURCH OF ST STEPHEN OF THE BULGARS (Map 18)

The Church of St Stephen of the Bulgars *(Balat Vapur İskelesi Caddesi)* is made completely of cast iron, as is most of its interior decoration. The building is unusual, and its history even more so.

The church is not normally open for visits, but if you offer to tip (say, US$3) the caretaker who lives on the grounds, he may open the gate to let you in – it's well worth the effort.

During the 19th century, ethnic nationalism swept through the Ottoman Empire. Each of the empire's many ethnic groups wanted to rule its own affairs. Groups identified themselves on the basis of language, religion and racial heritage. This sometimes led to problems, as with the Bulgars.

The Bulgars, who were originally a Turkic-speaking people, came from the Volga in about AD 680 and overwhelmed the Slavic peoples living in what is today Bulgaria. They adopted the Slavic language and customs, and founded an empire that threatened the power of Byzantium. In the 9th century they were converted to Christianity.

The Orthodox Patriarch, head of the Eastern church in the Ottoman Empire, was an ethnic Greek; in order to retain as much power as possible, the patriarch was opposed to any ethnic divisions within the Orthodox church. He put pressure on the sultan not to allow the Bulgarians, Macedonians and Romanians to establish their own religious groups.

The pressures of nationalism became too great, however, and the sultan was finally forced to recognise some sort of autonomy for the Bulgars. He established not a Bulgarian patriarchate, but an 'exarchate', with a leader supposedly of lesser rank, yet independent of the Greek Orthodox patriarch. In this way the Bulgarians would achieve their desired ethnic recognition and would get out from under the dominance of the Greeks, but the Greek Patriarch would allegedly suffer no diminution of his glory or power.

St Stephen's is the Bulgarian exarch's church. The Gothic structure was cast in Vienna, shipped down the Danube on 100 barges, and assembled in İstanbul in 1871. A duplicate church erected in Vienna, the only other copy, was destroyed by aerial bombing during WWII.

This is where the walking tour finishes; jump in a taxi to visit Zeyrek Camii and Fatih Camii (over the page).

BALAT (Map 18)

The quarter on the Golden Horn called Balat used to house a large portion of the city's Jewish population. Spanish Jews, driven from their country by the judges of the Spanish Inquisition, found refuge in the Ottoman Empire in the late 15th and early 16th centuries. As the sultan recognised, they were a boon to his empire: They brought news of the latest Western advances in medicine, clock making, ballistics and other means of warfare. These refugees set up the first printing presses in Turkey. Like all other religious 'nations' within the empire, the Jewish community was governed by its supreme religious leader, the Chief Rabbi, who oversaw their adherence to biblical law and who was responsible to the sultan for their good conduct.

Balat used to have dozens of **synagogues**; two remain for worship: the recently restored **Ahrida** and the nearby **Yanbol**. Visits must be organised with the Chief Rabbinate of Turkey (☎ 212-243 5166) at least 24 hours before your visit. You'll need to fax a copy of your passport identification papers. Call between between 9.30am and 5pm Monday to Thursday, 9.30am and 1pm Friday.

ZEYREK CAMİİ (Map 14)

Zeyrek Camii (Church of the Pantocrator) is actually three buildings in one – all built within about 15 years of each other around AD 1130. The northernmost building is derelict, but the southern church, built by Empress Eirene (she features in a mosaic at Aya Sofya with Emperor John II), still has some features intact, including a magnificent marble floor. This monastery was once one of the most important religious complexes in İstanbul, containing a hospital, asylum and a hospice. The church now functions as a mosque. Though it has undergone some restoration, it has recently been earmarked for more; you can visit, though you may be asked for a US$4.50 'donation'.

The area surrounding the mosque is also steeped in history: Many wooden Ottoman houses – some decrepit, some recently restored – line the streets. The Ottoman building to the east has been poshed up into a restaurant, the **Zeyrekhane** (see the Places to Eat chapter).

After you've finished at Zeyrek, you could catch a taxi to Fatih Camii. It's not one of the most beautiful mosques in the city, but it is the mosque of the Conqueror.

FATİH CAMİİ (Map 14)

This mosque *(Mosque of the Conqueror; Fevzi Paşa Caddesi)* is 750m north-west of the Aqueduct of Valens. The Fatih Camii was the first great imperial mosque to be built in İstanbul following the Conquest. For its location, Mehmet the Conqueror chose the hilltop site of the ruined Church of the Apostles. The mosque complex, finished in 1470, was enormous, set in extensive grounds, and included in its külliye 15 charitable establishments – religious schools, a hospice for travellers, a caravanserai etc. The mosque you see, however, is not the one he built. The original stood for nearly 300 years before toppling in an earthquake in 1766. It was rebuilt, but destroyed by fire in 1782. The present mosque dates from the reign of Abdül Hamit I, and is on a completely different plan. The exterior still bears some of the original decoration; the great doors have been beautifully restored; the interior is of less interest, though there is a simple but beautiful mihrab and plentiful fine stained glass.

Directly behind (south-east of) the mosque are two tombs, the tomb of Mehmet the Conqueror and that of his wife Gülbahar, who is rumoured to have been a French princess.

To get back to Taksim, walk five blocks south-east and catch a dolmuş from İstanbul City Hall (Belediye Sarayı) near the aqueduct. For Sultanahmet catch any bus that has 'Eminönü' listed on its itinerary board, get off at Eminönü and hop on the tram or walk.

The Walls & Eyüp

THE WALLS (Map 12)

Since being built in the 5th century, the city walls have been breached by hostile forces only twice. The first time was in the 13th century, when Byzantium's 'allies', the armies of the Fourth Crusade, broke through and pillaged the town, deposing the emperor and setting up a king of their own. The second time was in 1453 under Mehmet the Conqueror. Even though Mehmet was ultimately successful, he was continually frustrated during the siege as the walls admirably withstood even the heaviest bombardments by the largest cannon in existence.

The walls were kept defensible and in good repair until about a century ago, when the development of mighty naval guns made such expense pointless: If İstanbul was going to fall, it would fall to ships firing from the Bosphorus, not to soldiers advancing on the land walls.

During the late 1980s, the city started to rebuild the major gates and walls. Debates raged in the Turkish newspapers over the style of the reconstruction. Some said the restorations were too theatrical, while others said that if the walls never actually did look like that, perhaps they should have. The gates that have been completed include the Topkapı, Mevlanakapı and Belgratkapı.

Yedikule (Map 11)

If you arrived in İstanbul by train from Europe, or if you rode in from the airport along the seashore, you've already had a glance at Yedikule *(Fortress of the Seven Towers; Yedikule Caddesi; adult/student US$1/0.50; open 9.30am-5pm Thur-Tues),* looming over the southern approaches to the city.

History Theodosius I built a triumphal arch here in the late 4th century. When the next Theodosius (r. 408–50) built his great land walls, he incorporated the arch. Four of the fortress' seven towers were built as part of Theodosius II's walls; the other three, inside the walls, were added by Mehmet the Conqueror. Under the Byzantines, the great arch became known as the **Golden Gate**, and was used for triumphal state processions into and out of the city. For a time, its gates were indeed plated with gold. The doorway was sealed in the late Byzantine period.

In Ottoman times the fortress was used for defence, as a repository for the imperial treasury, a prison and a place of execution. Ambassadors of 'enemy' countries were chucked in prisons; for foreign ambassadors to the Sublime Porte, Yedikule was that prison. Latin and German inscriptions still visible in the Ambassadors' Tower bring the place's eerie history to light. It was also here that Sultan Osman II, a 17-year-old youth, was executed in 1622 during a revolt of the janissary corps. The kaftan he was wearing when he was murdered is now on display in Topkapı Palace's costumes collection.

Visiting Yedikule & the Walls Yedikule is surrounded by a quiet local district. The walls protect a green, if somewhat weedy, park that has the odd tethered sheep and clutch of picnickers. It's well worth making the effort out here if you have time. As it's an under-visited site, single women should take care. The best view of the city walls and of the fortress is from the **Tower of Sultan Ahmet III**, near the Golden Gate in the city wall. It is possible to walk along the land walls from the Sea of Marmara past Yedikule, even making some of the walk atop the walls. The district is not the safest, however, and we know of at least one robbery attempt, so it's best to go in a group and to take the normal precautions.

Right down at the shoreline, where the land walls meet the Sea of Marmara, you will find the **Marble Tower**, once part of a small Byzantine imperial seaside villa.

Getting There & Away Yedikule is a long way from most other sights in İstanbul and involves a special trip. Situated where the great city walls meet the Sea of Marmara, it's accessible by cheap train from Sirkeci. Take any suburban train *(banliyö tren)* and hop off at Yedikule. Turn left as you come out of the station and walk about 500m to the entrance in the north-east. You can also take bus No 80 (Yedikule) from Eminönü, which will drop you at Yedikule's gate – but the ride may take over an hour.

EYÜP (Map 12)

The district of Eyüp, once a village outside the city walls, is named after the standard-bearer of the Prophet Mohammed. Ayoub al-Ansari (Eyüp Ensari) had been a friend of the Prophet and a revered member of Islam's early leadership. His tomb and the adjoining **Eyüp Sultan Camii** *(Mosque of the Great Eyüp; Camii Kebir Sokak)* are sacred places for most Muslims, ranking after Mecca, Medina and Jerusalem.

As the Eyüp Sultan Camii is so sacred, many important people, including lots of grand viziers, wanted to be buried in its precincts. Between the mosque-and-tomb complex and the Golden Horn lies a virtual 'village' of octagonal tombs. Even those who were not to be buried here left their marks. The Valide Sultan Mihrişah, Queen Mother of Selim III, built important charitable institutions such as schools, baths and soup kitchens. Sokollu Mehmet Paşa, among the greatest of Ottoman grand viziers, donated a hospital, which still functions as a medical clinic to this day.

Eyüp Sultan Camii & Tomb (Map 12)

Mehmet the Conqueror had a mosque built here within five years of his victory. His mosque was levelled by an earthquake in 1766, and a new mosque was built on the site by Sultan Selim III in 1800.

Ayoub al-Ansari

Ayoub al-Ansari (Eyüp Ensari in Turkish), a friend of the Prophet's and a revered member of Islam's early leadership, fell in battle outside the walls of Constantinople while carrying the banner of Islam during the Arab assault and siege of the city in 674–78. He was buried outside the walls and, ironically, his tomb later came to be venerated by the Byzantine inhabitants of the city.

When Mehmet the Conqueror besieged Constantinople in 1453, Eyüp's tomb was no doubt known to him. He undertook to build a grander and more fitting structure to commemorate it.

A legend persists, however, that the tomb had been lost and was miraculously rediscovered by Mehmet's Supreme Islamic Judge, an event seen by the Turkish armies as a sign from heaven that they would be victorious.

Perhaps both stories are true. If the tomb was known to Mehmet and his leadership, but not to the common soldiers, its 'rediscovery' may well have inspired the troops for the holy war in which they were engaged.

From the plaza outside the complex, enter the great doorway to a large courtyard, then to a smaller court shaded by a huge ancient plane tree. Note the wealth of brilliant İznik tilework on the walls. To the left, behind the tiles and gilded grillework, is Eyüp's tomb *(open 9.30am-4.30pm daily);* to the right is the mosque. Be careful to observe the Islamic proprieties when visiting: decent clothing (no shorts), and modest dresses for women, who should also cover head, shoulders and arms. Take your shoes off before entering the small tomb enclosure, rich with silver, gold, crystal chandeliers and coloured tiles. Try not to stand in front of those at prayer; be respectful; don't use a camera (and especially not a flash!). The mosque opens long hours every day but avoid visiting on Friday or on other Muslim holy days.

The mosque is the place where, for centuries, the Ottoman princes came for the Turkish equivalent of coronation: to gird on the Sword of Osman, signifying their power and their title as *padişah* (king of kings), or sultan.

During your visit you may see boys dressed up in white satin suits with spangled caps and red sashes emblazoned with the word 'Maşallah'. These lads are on the way to their circumcision and have made a stop beforehand at this holy place. For more information about circumcision see the boxed text 'Maşallah!' under The Bazaar District earlier in this chapter.

For a snack or lunch, there are little pastry shops and snack stands on Kalenderhane Caddesi across from the mosque. Try **Karadeniz Lahmacun, Pide ve Kebap Salonu** (see the Places to Eat chapter).

Pierre Loti Café (Map 12)

Up the hill to the north of the Eyüp mosque is the **Pierre Loti Café** (see the Places to Eat chapter), where French novelist Pierre Loti is said to have come for inspiration.

Loti loved İstanbul, its decadent grandeur, and the fascinating late-medieval customs of a society in decline. When he sat in this cafe, under a shady grapevine sipping tea, he saw a Golden Horn busy with caiques, schooners and a few steam vessels. The water in the Golden Horn was still clean enough to swim in, and the vicinity of the cafe was given over to pasture.

The rustic cafe, which today bears his name, may not have any actual connection to Loti, but it occupies a similar spot and offers superb views that he must have enjoyed. It's in a warren of little streets on a promontory surrounded by the Eyüp Sultan Mezarlığı (Cemetery of the Great Eyüp), just north of the Eyüp mosque. The surest way to find it is to walk out of the mosque complex to the plaza, turn right, and walk around the mosque complex (keeping it on your right) to the north side of the mosque until you see a cobbled path going uphill into the cemetery marked by a small marble sign, 'Maraşal Fevzi Çakmak'. Hike up the steep hill for 15 minutes to reach the cafe. If you take a taxi (US$1.50 from near the mosque), it will follow a completely different route because of one-way streets. The cafe serves drinks only.

Pierre Loti

Louis-Marie Julien Viaud (1850–1923), aka Pierre Loti, pursued a distinguished career in the French navy, and at the same time became his country's most celebrated novelist. Though a hard-headed mariner, he was also an inspired and incurable romantic who fell in love with the graceful and mysterious way of life he discovered in Ottoman İstanbul.

Loti set up house in Eyüp for several years and had a love affair, fraught with peril, with a married Turkish woman whom he called Aziyadé (the title of his most romantic and successful novel). He was transferred back to France and forced to leave his mistress and his beloved İstanbul, but he decorated his French home in Ottoman style and begged Aziyadé to flee and join him. Instead, her infidelity was discovered and she 'disappeared'.

Pierre Loti's romantic novels about the daily life of İstanbul under the last sultans introduced millions of European readers to Turkish customs and habits, and helped to counteract the politically inspired Turkophobia then spreading through Europe.

Getting There & Away

The nicest way to get to Eyüp is by ferry from Eminönü. Ferries run from Üsküdar, to Eminönü, then head up the Golden Horn stopping by Kasımpaşa, Fener, Balat and a few other stops until they reach Eyüp. The first ferry leaves Eminönü at 7.20am, then 8.15am then hourly until 6.15pm, 6.55pm and the last leaves at 8pm. Going the other way, the first from Eyüp leaves at 7.05am, 8am, 8.50am, then every hour thereafter until 6.50pm and finally one leaves at 7.30pm.

Alternatively, take bus No 55T (Taksim to Eyüp Üçşehitler) or bus No 99 (Eminönü to Alibeyköyü) and get off at the 'Eyüp' stop.

Hasköy

About 6km north-west of Karaköy on the Golden Horn in Hasköy, the early 19th-century imperial hunting lodge at Aynalıkavak is rarely visited by foreign tourists, which makes it all the more appealing. Also here is a fine museum chronicling İstanbul's industrial history.

AYNALIKAVAK KASRI (Map 12)

Several centuries ago an imperial naval arsenal was established at Kasımpasa, southeast of Hasköy, and near it a shipyard *(tersane)*. The collection of imperial hunting lodges and pleasure kiosks at Hasköy became known as the Tersane Sarayı or Aynalıkavak Kasrı *(☎ 212-250 4094; admission US$1; open 9.30am-4pm Tues & Wed, Fri-Sun)*. İstanbul's *kasrs* (imperial lodges) are less outwardly impressive than its many palaces. However, they are designed on a more human scale; kasrs were built not to impress visitors but to please the monarchs themselves.

A wooden kasr was built on this site by Sultan Ahmet III (r. 1703–30), and restored by Selim III (r. 1789–1807). What you see today is mostly the work of Sultan Mahmut II (r. 1808–39). With its Tulip Period decoration and Ottoman furnishings, the pavilion is a splendid if dusty place giving a vivid impression of the lifestyle of the Ottoman ruling class at the turn of the 19th century, when Hasköy was a thriving Jewish neighbourhood. Some rooms – much the most comfortable – are furnished in Eastern style, others in the less commodious European style then penetrating the sultan's domains.

Selim III composed poetry and music in one of its eastern rooms; futon-like beds were tucked away into cabinets during the day. The waiting room *(bekleme salonu)* has the only extant Tulip Period ceiling. One of the European-style rooms is filled with sumptuous mother-of-pearl furniture. There's also the small **Museum of Turkish Musical Instruments** on the lower level.

The pavilion's gardens and grounds provide a welcome respite from the city's concrete landscape.

Getting There & Away

The only practical way to reach Aynalıkavak is by taxi (US$3.50 from Beyoğlu). Tell the driver to take you to the Hasköy police station (polis karakolu) or to the athletic facilities (Şükrü Urcan Spor

Tesisleri) which are well known. A minute's walk south-east of the Hasköy police station along Kasımpaşa-Hasköy Yolu brings you to Aynalıkavak Kasrı.

RAHMİ M KOÇ MÜZESİ (Map 12)

This museum *(Rahmi M Koç Industrial Museum; ☎ 212-256 7153, Hasköy Caddesi 27, Sütlüce; admission US$2; open 10am-5pm Tues-Sun)* was founded by the current head of the Koç industrial group, one of Turkey's most prominent conglomerates, to exhibit artefacts from İstanbul's industrial past.

Exhibits include engines and anything to do with them: Bosphorus ferry parts and machinery; Hotchkiss guns; ship and train models; cars (how about that 1936 Austin roadster!); jet engines; soda machines; and even much of the fuselage of 'Hadley's Harem', a US B-24D Liberator bomber that crashed off Antalya in August 1943. **Café du Levant**, in the museum's grounds, is a surprisingly elegant French bistro with tasty, gourmet food (see the Places to Eat chapter).

The museum is near the northern end of the old Galata Bridge (near where Hasköy Caddesi changes into Kumbarahane Caddesi) about 1km north-west of Aynalıkavak Kasrı.

Activities

BILLIARDS, BOWLING & BACKGAMMON

Turks have perfected the art of socialising, and game playing is an important ingredient. Any tea garden should be able to come up with a backgammon board (for free) if you ask, though if you want to play billiards or bowling you'll need to head to Beyoğlu.

Bab Bowling Cafe (Map 16, #70; ☎ 212-251 1595) Yeşilçam Sokak 24, Beyoğlu. Bab is open from 10am to midnight daily. Bowling costs US$2 to US$2.50 per game between 10am and 7pm Monday to Friday, and US$3 up until midnight Monday to Friday. On weekends you'll pay US$3 per game irrespective of the time. There's also darts (US$0.50), air hockey (US$0.70), overpriced billiards (US$3.50 per hour) and a cafe for snacks.

Demir Billiard Salon (Map 16, #32; ☎ 212-245 4550) Mis Sokak 20, Beyoğlu. Demir is open from 7am to midnight daily. It serves locals tea (US$0.50) to drink during its backgammon *(tavla)* tournaments. Downstairs in the echoey marble basement, others play billiards or pool at US$3 per table per hour. There are a few other places along this street with similar deals.

GOLF

İstanbul isn't known for its golfing facilities, but it does have a few courses close by if you're keen.

Kemer Golf & Country Club (☎ 212-239 7010) Kemerburgaz. Around 12km north-west of Taksim, Kemer takes visitors on its nine- and 18-hole course if you book ahead.

Klassis Golf Country Club (☎ 212-748 4600, W www.lux-hotels.com/tr/klassis-club) Seymen Köyü, Altıntepe Mevkii, Silivri. It's 100km from İstanbul, but it's a world-class course with a nine- and18-hole course and a putting range.

NARGİLEH

Sitting and yakking around a nargileh is a quintessential Middle Eastern experience. Even if you're not a smoker you may be lured by the fruity and flowery tobacco concoctions. The water in the bottom of the nargileh filters out at least some of the harmful tar and nicotine, or so they say. Try the following places:

Amerikan Pazar (Map 16, #144) Salı Pazarı Sıra Mağazalar, Tophane

Cafe Meşale (Map 13, #97; ☎ 212-518 9562) Arasta Çarşısı 45 (near the Arasta Bazaar, Sultanahmet)

Erenler Nargile Salonu (Map 4, #25) Çorlulu Ali Paşa Medresesi, Beyazıt

İlesam Lokalı (Map 4, #26; ☎ 212-511 2618) Yeniçeriler Caddesi 84, Beyazıt

HAMAMS

See the boxed text 'Hamams' at the end of this chapter for hamam information.

SWIMMING & GYMS

Swimming in the Bosphorus is an ugly option though you will see the occasional local braving the current, oil slicks and floaties between Seraglio Point and Kumkapı. Those with more sense head to the beaches at Yeşilköy and Florya (you can get to these by train from Sirkeci station) – but only to paddle. The water around the Kızıl Adalar (Princes' Islands) is fairly clean, though the tiny beaches are crammed bottom-to-bottom in summer. The best options, however, are the beach-side towns along the Black Sea coast: Kilyos (a day trip by bus) or Şile (a day trip with a private vehicle). Both these towns and the Kızıl Adalar are covered in the Excursions chapter.

Most of İstanbul's pool facilities are privately owned and expensive. Your best bet is to sweet-talk the reception staff at a three- or four-star hotel with a pool. You may be able to work out a pay-by-swim or a monthly rate. Note, however, that most of the pools will be tiny and indoor. The big, outdoor pools in the five-star hotels charge hefty admission fees. The only hotel in Old İstanbul with a swimming pool is Orient Hotel (see the Places to Stay chapter), though it's not keen on nonguests using the pool. Try charming the staff.

Many of the local gyms are testosterone-no-go-zones for women: They're brimming with ogling gents sporting muscles and attitude. The equipment is usually fairly limited too, so it's probably worth forking out a bit more and joining a hotel gym. Most gyms are on the Beyoğlu side of town. Here are some pool and gym options:

Dorint Park Hotel (☎ 212-254 5100) Topçu Caddesi 23, Taksim. The Dorint has a pool and gym you can use for US$150 a month with unlimited access, or US$99 a month for use between 9am and 5pm. One-day passes costs US$20 during the week, or US$30 on the weekend.

Kuzey Yıldızı Kültür ve Spor Merkezi (☎ 212-252 6716, fax 243 1016) Havyar Sokak 30-2, Cihangir. As well as gym facilities at this female-friendly place east of Sıraselviler Caddesi, you will find aerobics, aikido and yoga. Gym membership cost US$37 per month for visits twice a week. For aerobics you'll pay US$7.50 per class.

The Marmara İstanbul (Map 16, #14; ☎ 212-251 4696, W www.themarmaraistanbul.com). The Marmara hotel on Taksim Meydanı is a pricey option, but it has a sparkling-clean outdoor pool with great views. It's an odd shape if you like doing laps, but you'll cope. A day swim costs US$33; a monthly membership costs US$165. The gym is perfect.

BOSPHORUS NIGHT CRUISES

One of the cheapest, yet most enjoyable, night-time activities in İstanbul is to take a Bosphorus ferry. It doesn't really matter where, as long as you don't end up on the southern coast of the Sea of Marmara or on the Kızıl Adalar because you will find it difficult getting back. Enjoy the view, the twinkling lights, the fishing boats bobbing on the waves, the powerful searchlights of the ferries sweeping the sea lanes. Have a glass of tea (a waiter will offer you some). Get off anywhere, and take a taxi to your hotel if you can't catch a ferry back directly.

Perhaps the easiest ferry to catch for this purpose is the one from Eminönü to Üsküdar. Just go to Eminönü, buy two tokens (for the voyages out and back) at dock one, and walk on board. From Üsküdar, just come back; or wait for one of the frequent ferries to Beşiktaş or Kabataş, from where you can catch a bus or dolmuş back to your part of town.

A similar ride is the one from Karaköy to Haydarpaşa or Kadıköy. Return boats bring you right back to Karaköy. The voyage takes 20 minutes in each direction and costs US$1.20 for a round trip.

COURSES

Two universities conduct classes in English in İstanbul and invite foreign students to join (for a fee). See Courses in the Facts for the Visitor chapter for more details. Some travellers, especially if they've scored a job in İstanbul, want to pick up some of the language. Taking a course can also be a good opportunity to meet other expats.

Berlitz (Map 16, #84; ☎ 212-293 7400, fax 293 7699, W www.berlitz.com.tr) Tütüncü Çıkmazı 1/1, Galatasaray. The Berlitz has small classes of up to nine students, but you pay for the privilege at US$160 for 16, 45-minute classes. There's no strict course term, though, so you can start and end when you wish.

Taksim Dilmer (Map 16, #5; ☎ 212-292 9696, fax 292 9693, W www.dilmer.com) Tarık Zafer Tunaya Sokak 18, Taksim. Taksim Dilmer has courses for 40, 64, 80, 96 or 180 hours over one or two months, with day or evening classes. A 40-hour course costs US$140, an 80-hour class US$280.

Hamams

The joy of a steam bath was passed from the Romans to the Byzantines and on to the Turks, who have relished it ever since. Most homes didn't have washing facilities, and due to Islam's emphasis on personal squeaky-cleanliness, hundreds of hamams were constructed throughout İstanbul. A visit to the hamam was also a social occasion and often an all-day affair. It allowed a prospective mother-in-law to eye off, pinch and prod a prospective daughter-in-law or, as was the custom, a bride-to-be would spend time here as part of her wedding preparations. Now that many people have bathrooms in İstanbul, hamams are nowhere near as popular as they used to be but, nevertheless, visiting a hamam is an experience you should not miss.

The price for the quintessential washing experience varies according to the hamam: Some hamams are dank dives where you may come out dirtier than you went in, others are plain and clean, and a handful are tourist traps. You'll be up for US$3 to US$10 in a local bath if you bring your own soap, shampoo and towel, and bathe yourself – add US$4 to US$6 if an assistant washes and massages you. At the 'historic' touristy baths, prices go from US$15 to US$25, including a massage. Massages yo-yo between being enjoyable, limp-wristed or mortally dangerous. Tips will be expected (give 10% to 20% of total fee) if they're not included in the price; even if they are included, some attendants can be pushy, so stand your ground.

Bath Procedure

Upon entry you are shown to a dressing cubicle. Store your clothes, place the bath-wrap *(peştemal)* that's provided around you, and slip into the clickety wooden sandals. An attendant leads you through the cool room *(frigidarium)* and the warm room *(tepidarium)* to the hot room *(caldarium)*, where you sit and sweat for a while, relaxing and loosening up, perhaps on the central, raised platform *(göbektaşı)* atop the heating source.

Soon you will be half-asleep and as soft as putty from the steamy heat. The cheapest bath is the one you do yourself, having brought your own soap, shampoo and towel. But the real Turkish bath experience is to have an attendant wash and massage you.

If you have opted for the latter, an attendant douses you with warm water and lathers you with a sudsy swab. Next you are scrubbed with a coarse cloth mitten loosening dirt you never suspected you had. Then comes a shampoo, another dousing with warm water, followed by one with cool water.

When the scrubbing is over, head for the cool room, there to be swathed in towels and then led back to your cubicle for a rest or a nap. Here you can order tea, coffee, a soft drink or a bottle of beer. If you want to nap, tell the attendant when to wake you.

Modesty

Traditional Turkish baths have separate sections for men and women, or have only one set of facilities and admit men or women at different times. Bath etiquette requires that men remain clothed with the bath-wrap at all times. In the women's section women usually wear their underwear (but not their bra). During the bathing, everyone washes their private parts themselves, without removing the bath-wrap or underclothes.

In touristy areas, some baths now accept that foreign men and women like to bathe together. No Turkish woman would let a masseur touch her (it must be a masseuse), but masseurs are usually the only massagers available in these foreign-oriented baths. We've received complaints from women

Hamams

readers who have suffered indignities at the hands of sleazy masseurs. Women willing to accept a masseur should have the massage within view of – preferably very near – male companions or other friends, and should protest at the first sign of impropriety.

Fancy Tourist Baths

Although these 'historic' baths are pricey, they are spotlessly clean, the attendants often speak some English or French, and they're set in gorgeous buildings.

Cağaloğlu Hamamı (Map 13, #28; ☎ 212-522 2424, w www.cagalogluhamami.com.tr) Yerebatan Caddesi 34. This hamam is open 7am to 10pm (men) and 8am to 8pm (women) and is 350m northwest of Aya Sofya. Built over three centuries ago, this is one of the city's most beautiful hamams. It boasts (without evidence) that King Edward VIII, Kaiser Wilhelm II, Franz Liszt and Florence Nightingale have enjoyed its pleasures, no doubt at the same time, and with Elvis in attendance. A self-service bath costs US$10, the full treatment US$20, the deluxe 'fit for a sultan' treatment US$30, plus tips.

Çemberlitaş Hamamı (Map 13, #6; ☎ 212-520 1850, w www.cemberlitashamami.com.tr) Vezir Hanı Caddesi 8. This hamam is open 6am to midnight and is just off Divan Yolu near the Kapalı Çarşı. This is perhaps the best place for your first Turkish bath experience. It's a double hamam (twin baths for men and women) designed by Sinan for Nurbanu Sultan, wife of Sultan Selim II, in 1584. It costs US$8 (US$6 for students) to wash yourself, US$15 (US$12 for students) if the attendant washes and massages you.

Tarihi Galatasaray Hamamı (Historic Galatasaray Turkish Bath; Map 16, #63; ☎ 212-292 5712, 249 4332) Turnacıbaşı Sokak 24, Çukurcuma. This hamam is open 5am to midnight (men), 8am to 8pm (women) and is off İstiklal Caddesi just north of Galatasaray Square. It's one of the city's best, with lots of marble decoration, comfy little cubicles for resting and sipping tea after the bath, pretty fountains and even a shoeshine service. The only downside is the complaints we've received from readers about surly and tip-hungry staff. Prepare yourself for the experience; US$25 with massage, US$20 without, plus at least 20% more in tips.

Local Baths

If it's a no-frills bath you're after, ask at your hotel for directions to neighbourhood baths *(mahalli hamam)* where locals go. Neighbourhood baths will treat you much better for much less money than the touristy baths, though as more foreigners patronise them they may suffer the same fate. Here are some suggestions.

Çinili Hamam (Map 19, #31) Çinili Külhan Sokak, Üsküdar. If you're over on the Asian side of town you may want to pop into this very local, cheap and friendly hamam. A wash-only costs US$3; or it's US$5.50 with a massage. It is open 8am to 5pm daily.

Kadırga Hamamı (Map 13, #111) Kadırga Limanı Caddesi 129, Kadırga. The men's entrance is opposite the park, the women's section *(Kadınlar Kısmı)* is on Piyerloti Caddesi up the hill. A one-hour bath costs just US$3 self-service, or US$7 with a massage.

Tarihi Ali Paşa Hamamı (Map 16, #140) Ali Paşa Medresesi Sokak, Tophane. Near the Kılıç Ali Paşa Camii in Beyoğlu, this cheap, clean-enough local bath costs US$3 for do-it-yourself, US$6 for a massage.

Tarihi Gedikpaşa Hamamı (Map 15, #47; ☎ 212-517 8956) Emin Sinan Hamamı Sokak 65-7, Gedik Paşa. This place is over five centuries old and although prices are crawling up – US$12 for the works including a good massage – it's an OK option.

Tarihi Nişancı Hamamı (Map 15, #43; ☎ 212-518 0935) Türkeli Caddesi 45, Kumkapı. It's a little out of the way and it's decent value: US$3 do-it-yourself, or US$6 with a massage.

Places to Stay

Turkey's tourism boom of the 1980s and 1990s saw the construction of hundreds of hotels in İstanbul. The accommodation situation is good. Note: Suggestions for places to stay along the Bosphorus are given in the Excursions chapter.

WHERE TO STAY

The Sultan Ahmet Camii, more commonly known as Blue Mosque, gives its name to the quarter surrounding it. This is the heart of Old İstanbul and the city's premier sightseeing area, so the hotels here, and in the adjoining neighbourhoods to the east (Cankurtaran), west (Küçük Aya Sofya) and north (Binbirdirek), are supremely convenient.

Akbıyık Caddesi in Cankurtaran is the backpacker hub, with thumping bars and drunken carousing by night and street cafes by day. Other streets in the area are low key. Most places in Cankurtaran also have rooftop terraces with views over the Bosphorus. Küçük Aya Sofya is a charming, old-fashioned neighbourhood, just downhill from the south-western end of the Hippodrome; while just uphill and to the west, Binbirdirek is a quiet residential district named after the Byzantine cistern of that name.

The heart of modern İstanbul, Taksim Square and Beyoğlu, are also good places to stay, with lots of restaurants, theatres and shops nearby. Many of the hotels in Beyoğlu and Taksim are mid-range to top-end places.

The small pocket north-west of Taksim Square has nearly a dozen hotels claiming to be modern and swearing they're four-star – don't be fooled. Although most of them are worn around the edges, they're clean enough and OK value for money, if you bargain. It's a convenient position here, in walking distance to the sights of Beyoğlu.

Between Galatasaray Square and Tünel Square, west of İstiklal Caddesi, is Tepebaşı (**teh**-peh-bah-shuh), which was the first luxury hotel district in the city. Today most luxury hotels are just north of Taksim and along the Bosphorus.

TYPES OF ACCOMMODATION

Keep in mind that the appearance of a hotel's lobby tells you little about its rooms. Look at several rooms if possible. If the first one you see won't do, ask *'Başka var mı?'* ('Are there others?')

Budget

İstanbul has camping out near the airport about 20km from Sultanahmet. The Sultanahmet area is the place to head for other budget accommodation: A mattress on a rooftop or dorm beds are reasonably easy to find. Some places also have kitchens where you can do your own cooking for little or no extra fee.

Mid-Range

Mid-range hotels are usually newer buildings constructed during the past two decades. Virtually all of these places have lifts, restaurants and bars (though often empty), and staff who speak a smattering of foreign languages. Many rooms are equipped with TV, and some also have minibars.

The Cankurtaran and Küçük Aya Sofya districts, near Sultanahmet, are the best places to find hotels made from restored Ottoman mansions. Most have been modernised inside, but a handful still retain all their Ottoman charm.

Top End

İstanbul's international-standard, luxury hotels are mostly just north of Taksim in Harbiye, and along the Bosphorus. Often these hotels offer special packages; ask when you make reservations. The big international chains usually allow children of any age to share a double room with their parents at no extra charge or, if two rooms are needed, they charge only the single rate for each room.

Apartments & Long-Term Rentals

A few hotels and guesthouses have apartments with fully furnished kitchens. These are cost-efficient for families and groups for the short term. Try the Galata Konutları Apart Hotel and the Family House, both in Beyoğlu, or the Side Hotel & Pension and Star Guesthouse, both in Cankurtaran in the Sultanahmet area.

It's difficult to find furnished apartments or share accommodation, but you could look for ads in the *Turkish Daily News*, *İstanbull...* magazine, or check the bulletin boards at Yağmur Cybercafe (Map 16, #120; Şeyh Bender Sokak 18, Asmalımescit), Taksim Dilmer (Map 16, #5; Tarık Zafer Tunaya Sokak 18, Taksim) or the cultural centres (for addresses see the Facts for the Visitor chapter). If that fails you're probably going to have to rent an empty flat and furnish it yourself. Look for rental apartments *(kiralık daireler)* in real-estate brokers *(emlakçı)*. Expect to pay around US$400 per month for a basic unfurnished two-bedroom flat or around US$500 for a furnished place. For a deposit you'll need the equivalent of three months' rent. If you've landed a teaching job, ask the school about accommodation options as many provide flats as part of the salary package.

Most foreigners start out in suburbs where there's an existing expat community (ie, Cihangir, Taksim, Beşiktaş, Kadıköy or Bakırköy), which means you'll have fewer difficulties with language, but may pay a premium price for rental.

BOOKING

The city is such a popular tourist destination that many of the best guesthouses and hotels fill up even out of season so book ahead. Try not to pay the 'normal' published rates (rack rates), which are quite high. And some places offer cheaper rates if you book through the Web site. There's also a board with 22 mid-range to top-end hotel listings in the Arrivals hall of the Atatürk Airport and a free phone booking service. They sometimes include free transfers.

PLACES TO STAY – BUDGET

Camping

İstanbul has some good camping options out near the airport, but they are a bit isolated unless you have your own vehicle.

Londra Kamping *(☎ 212-560 4200, fax 559 3438, Çobançeşme-Kuleli Hevkii, Bakırköy)* **Map 11** Camp sites per double US$7. This is on the south side of the Londra Asfaltı Highway between the airport and Topkapı gate across from the milk factory *(süt sanayi)*. Grassy plots with small trees are off the highway, behind a Shell service station. You won't escape the noise and pollution completely here, but it's not an impossible location. To reach it you must be going eastward from the airport towards Topkapı (Cannon Gate) and turn right into the service road *(servis alanı)*; watch carefully for the sign. The camping ground is on the right-hand side, about 500m after the turn.

Ataköy Mokamp *(☎ 212-559 6014, fax 560 0426, Ataköy Sahil Yolu, Bakırköy)* **Map 11** Camp sites per double US$11. This leafy camping ground inside the holiday village Ataköy Tatil Köyü complex, has the use of a bar, restaurant, swimming pools and other services at the hotel nearby. Try to get a site near the shore *(sahile yakın)* and away from the highway. Ataköy is accessible by suburban train line *(banliyö treni)* from Sirkeci and by Eminönü-Ataköy and Taksim-Ataköy buses. Coming from Atatürk Airport, the Havaş bus doesn't stop anywhere near, so it's best to take a 10-minute taxi ride for US$3.

Sultanahmet Area (Map 13)

Sultanahmet is the touristy heart of İstanbul but Cankurtaran, close by, is well geared to the penny-counting traveller. Note that some hotels in this area are run or haunted by carpet-sellers who can be pushy in their efforts to get you into the ground-floor shop to buy a rug.

Hostels Dorm beds and heaps of services keep İstanbul's hostels packed. You generally need to bring your own towel and warm bedding. Sheets are supplied.

Orient Hostel *(☎ 212-518 0789, fax 518 3894, ⓔ orienthostel@superonline.com, Akbıyık Caddesi 13, Cankurtaran)* **Map 13, #74** Beds in 4/8 bed dorm US$8/6, doubles with/without bath US$30/16. Always packed with young Aussies spewing in the bathroom, groping on the Orient Bar dance floor or ogling at the nightly belly-dance show, the Orient has wanton charisma, great breakfasts and clean enough accommodation (get new carpets!). Big nights happen here, which may be exactly what you do – or don't – want.

Sultan Hostel *(☎ 212-516 9260, fax 517 1626,* **W** *www.sultanhostel.com, Terbıyık Sokak 3, Cankurtaran)* **Map 13, #79** Beds in 4-bed/6-bed/8-bed dorm US$7/6/6, singles/doubles without bath US$12/18. Hot on the heels of Orient's infamy, Sultan has an open rooftop restaurant with good views, and cheap food and grog designed to froth up the crowd. The no-frills rooms are cleaner than the Orient's.

Yücelt Interyouth Hostel *(☎ 212-513 6150, fax 512 7628,* **W** *www.yucelthostel.com, Caferiye Sokak 6/1, Sultanahmet)* **Map 13, #52** Beds in 4/8 bed dorm US$8/6, singles/doubles without bath US$15/16. 'Feel the History' writes the hostel card. Here you can see *and* feel the history: See the crusty carpets throughout and feel like you're walking on a pot scourer. The busy place is a warren of basic, clean (get new carpets too!) rooms plus a cheap-eats restaurant, pumping bar (belly dancing) and Internet facilities. Love it or hate it.

Guesthouses These places are smaller than the hostels and usually quieter.

Mavi Guesthouse *(☎ 212-516 5878, fax 517 7287,* **e** *mavipans@hotmail.com, Kutlugün Sokak 3, Cankurtaran)* **Map 13, #69** Beds in 4/8-bed dorm US$8, singles/doubles without bath US$14/22; includes breakfast. Mavi's management is very friendly, which is just as well since some rooms are gruesome and windowless, and the whole place is sagging. Mattresses on the rooftop cost US$5 (including breakfast) or there are light and livable small rooms at the front.

Konya Pansiyon *(☎/fax 212-638 3638,* **e** *aytekinelif@hotmail.com, Terbıyık Sokak 15, Cankurtaran)* **Map 13, #80** Beds in 4-bed dorm US$5, singles/doubles with bath US$25/30, without bath US$10/16. This is a poky family-run place, with a bare (bit grim) courtyard and a tiny kitchen you can use. It's friendly and there's a small library.

Çelik *(☎ 212-518 9675, fax 458 0748, Mimar Mehmet Ağa Caddesi 22, Cankurtaran)* **Map 13, #94** Singles/doubles with bath US$20/25. Six small, light rooms keep this tiny guesthouse busy, plus it has the bonus of a kitchen you can use and a small hang-out spot (no views).

Guesthouse Sunrise *(Şafak Pansiyon, ☎ 212-517 7858, fax 638 6222, Küçük Aya sofya Caddesi 36, Küçük Aya sofya)* **Map 13, #120** Beds in 10-bed dorm US$6, rooms with/without bath US$25/20. Don't get too excited about the cheapish dorm; although the rate includes breakfast, the 'dorm' is an undercover roof garden. The rooms at the front are best, avoid the depressing ones at the back. The shared bathrooms are clean but the rest of the place is a bit worn. The staff are friendly and there's a kitchen you can use.

Star Guesthouse *(☎ 212-638 2302, fax 516 1827, Akbıyık Caddesi 10, Cankurtaran)* **Map 13, #75** Singles/doubles with bath US$25/35, without bath US$15/25, 3-bed apartments US$30. The apartments are the best value here; they're large with a TV, fridge, small kitchen and the bathrooms are immaculate. The rooms are decent value, too, though you may have a little trouble navigating the stairs if you've had a few too many drinks.

Alp Guesthouse *(☎ 212-517 9570, fax 518 5728, Adliye Sokak 4, Cankurtaran)* **Map 13, #47** Singles with bath US$30-35, doubles with bath US$50-60; includes breakfast. Friendly and popular, Alp has basic rooms with earthy colours, kilim wall hangings and fake wooden beams. It's popular decor (ho hum) in Sultanahmet. The rooftop restaurant has uncluttered views of the Bosphorus.

Terrace Guesthouse *(☎ 212-638 9733, fax 638 9734,* **e** *terrace@escortnet.com, Kutlugün Sokak 39, Cankurtaran)* **Map 13, #83** Singles/doubles with bath US$45/60; includes breakfast. The Terrace has only a few rooms, but they're cheerful and two have balconies with sea views. There's a small rooftop dining room and terrace with excellent views. The rooms without views are on the verge of being overpriced.

Hotels There's not much difference between guesthouses and hotels in İstanbul, but the latter are usually larger.

Hotel Ema *(☎ 212-511 7166, fax 512 4878, Salkımsöğüt Sokak 18, Alemdar)* **Map 13, #46** Singles/doubles with bath US$15/25, without bath US$12/20. This place has rooms ranging from depressing dens, to light and simple rooms, so choose carefully before you book in. You won't avoid the cheap and nasty carpets, but it's a friendly spot.

Türkmen Hotel & Pansiyon *(☎ 212-517 1355, fax 638 5546,* **W** *www.turkmenhotel.com.tr, Dizdariye Çeşmesi Sokak 27, Binbirdirek)* **Map 13, #109** Pension: singles/doubles without bath US$8/16; hotel: singles with bath US$20-25, doubles with bath US$25-35. This is a modern, nondescript but friendly place on a quiet back street a bit out of the way. Rooms in the hotel are plain; get one of the rooms at the back which have a small balcony and OK views over the Bosphorus. However, you should avoid staying in the gruesome warren-cum-pension.

Side Hotel & Pension *(☎/fax 212-517 6590,* **W** *www.sidehotel.com, Utangaç Sokak 20, Cankurtaran)* **Map 13, #82** Pension: singles with/without bath US$30/20, doubles with/without bath US$35/25; hotel: singles/doubles with bath US$40/50; apartments US$60. Side has two sections: the older pension with characterless but clean rooms (avoid the back rooms which look out on to the stairs); and the hotel with quaint spotless rooms with wooden floors. Each apartment sleeps four and has a private kitchen – these are great value. All guests can share the rooftop garden-lounge which has good views.

Hotel Şebnem *(☎ 212-517 6623, fax 638 1056,* **W** *www.sebnemhotel.com, Adliye Sokak 1, Cankurtaran)* **Map 13, #73** Singles/doubles with bath US$40/60; includes breakfast. Rooms here have a touch of older-style charm (two-poster beds, wooden floors) and spotless modern bathrooms. The large terrace upstairs has OK views over the Bosphorus. It's a quiet place and the staff are friendly.

Beyoğlu (Maps 16 & 17)

A few inexpensive options exist amid Beyoğlu's banks, pubs, nightclubs and shops. It's a good alternative to Sultanahmet.

Saydam Hotel *(☎ 212-251 8116, fax 244 0366, Sofyalı Sokak 1, Tepebaşı)* **Map 16, #122** Singles/doubles with bath US$15/25; includes breakfast. All rooms here are small, but clean enough and each has a fridge and TV. The bathrooms are fine. It's a quiet spot and very welcoming.

Hotel Plaza *(☎ 212-245 3273, fax 293 7040, Arslanyatağı Sokak 19-21, Cihangir)* **Map 16, #51** Singles with bath US$25-30, doubles with bath US$45-50; includes breakfast. It's worth taking a look at this old-fashioned place, off Sıraselviler Caddesi by the Alman Hastanesi (German Hospital). Although it's a bit difficult to find, it's quiet and has some fine Bosphorus views.

Otel Avrupa *(☎ 212-250 9420, fax 250 7399,* **e** *otelavrupa@superonline.com, Topçu Caddesi 32, Taksim)* **Map 17, #44** Singles/doubles with bath US$30/39, without bath US$26/35; includes breakfast. This place puts many of the mid-range hotels around it to shame. You could eat off the tiled floors, the service is friendly and the rates are very reasonable.

PLACES TO STAY – MID-RANGE

Sultanahmet Area (Map 13)

Mid-range hotels in the Sultanahmet area are usually characterful, historic buildings – even Ottoman-style mansions – or comfortable but characterless modern buildings.

Guesthouses Most guesthouses stay down in the budget scale, but some are taking the step into mid-range prices.

Berk Guesthouse *(☎ 212-516 9671, fax 517 7715,* **e** *reservations@berkguesthouse.com, Kutlugün Sokak 27, Cankurtaran)* **Map 13, #76** Singles with bath US$40-75, doubles with bath US$50-90; includes breakfast. This is a friendly pension with a cute lounge area on top with OK views. The rooms are clean, plain and overpriced for their quality, but breakfasting in the homey kitchen and courtyard should make up for them. Count the family portraits!

Older-Style Hotels These are very popular in the Sultanahmet area with tourists lured into the Ottoman facades. Some of them are quite modern inside, though.

Hotel Turkuaz *(☎ 212-518 1897, fax 517 3380, Cinci Meydanı Sokak 36, Kadırga)* **Map 13, #112** Singles with bath US$30-40, doubles with bath US$40-90; includes breakfast. For maximum Ottoman ambience, the award goes to this hotel, located at the bottom of the hill from the south-western corner of the Hippodrome, somewhat out of the way. The 14 double rooms, furnishings, Turkish bath and Turkish folk-art lounge in this period house are the real thing, not posh modern imitations. When you stay in the 'Sultan's Room', you feel the part.

Hotel Poem *(☎/fax 212-517 6836, W www.hotelpoem.com, Terbıyık Sokak 12, Cankurtaran)* **Map 13, #81** Singles/doubles with bath US$45/65; includes breakfast. Here you'll find two buildings (one an ugly restoration) with a small glass pavilion-bar in between, and a leafy green outlook. The rooms are clean, plain and a few have sea views, but the main drawcard here is the rooftop terrace with superb views.

Hotel Ararat *(☎ 212-516 0411, fax 518 5241, W www.ararathotel.com, Torun Sokak 3, Sultanahmet)* **Map 13, #96** Singles/doubles with bath US$55/60, rooms with bath and views US$70; includes breakfast. Ararat is a carbon copy (wooden floors, murals and so on) of the Empress Zoe (review following), but it's hardly surprising since the same guy decorated both. A couple of the rooms are coffin-like but most are cosy and quaint with spotless, stylish bathrooms. The big plus here is the rooftop terrace-bar with comfy cushions, full views of the Blue Mosque and a fireplace to snuggle by.

Hotel Empress Zoe *(☎ 212-518 2504, fax 518 5699, e info@emzoe.com, Adliye Sokak 10, Cankurtaran)* **Map 13, #71** Singles with bath US$55, doubles with bath small/large US$70/85 (10% discount for cash); includes breakfast. The lobby of this hotel is in a Byzantine cistern next to an old Ottoman *hamam* (steam bath). Upstairs, the rooms are decorated in a style – earth colours, kilims, chunky wooden furniture, murals – that is the prototype for many hotel makeovers in Sultanahmet. The rooftop bar-lounge-terrace has excellent views; the leafy 'secret garden' is flower-bordered heaven. Now, to bring you back down to earth: All the rooms are small and the singles are overpriced.

Hotel Turkoman *(☎ 212-516 2956, fax 516 2957, W www.turkomanhotel.com, Asmalı Çeşme Sokak 2, Sultanahmet)* **Map 13, #105** Singles/doubles with bath US$70/90; includes breakfast. Up the hill a few steps off the Hippodrome, this is a renovated, 19th-century building with the feeling of a private club. The rooms have names, not numbers, and are simply but tastefully decorated (brass beds). Take your breakfast on the roof terrace which has OK views of the Blue Mosque.

Hotel Historia *(☎ 212-517 7472, fax 516 8169, W www.historiahotel.com, Amiral Tafdil Sokak 23, Cankurtaran)* **Map 13, #88** Singles/doubles with bath US$70/90. Historia's pretty green and white facade is its only concession to history: Inside, the mirrored feature walls and gaudy pastiche of genres would make an Otto-man blush. Fear not, the modern rooms are comfortable, though small. Get one of the rooms with a balcony with views.

Grand Hotel Ayasofya *(☎ 212-516 9446, fax 518 0700, W www.ayasofyahotel.com, Demirci Reşit Sokak 28, Küçük Aya Sofya)* **Map 13, #117** Singles/doubles with bath US$75/100. Light, modern rooms with mod cons and small bathrooms attract people to this renovated house. The rooftop has OK views, too. The friendly staff are ready to haggle with you for lower rates.

Ayasofya Pansiyonları *(☎ 212-513 3660, fax 513 3669, Soğukçeşme Sokak, Sultanahmet)* **Map 13, #55** Singles with bath US$80-90, doubles with bath US$100-120; includes breakfast. On the north side of Aya Sofya against the walls of Topkapı Palace, this is a row of Ottoman houses that have now been refitted. The 58 rooms with private baths are in 19th-century Ottoman style with brass or antique wooden beds, glass lamps, Turkish carpets and period wall hangings. The cheaper rooms at the back get less light; front rooms look right onto Aya Sofya.

Konuk Evi *(☎ 212-513 3660, fax 513 3669, Soğukçeşme Sokak, Sultanahmet)* **Map 13, #49** Singles with bath US$80-90, doubles with bath US$100-120; includes breakfast. This place was rebuilt in 1992 to duplicate the historic mansion that stood on this site during the reign of Sultan Abdül Hamit. It now has a garden, and a conservatory-restaurant as well as 20 guest rooms (with only a few mod cons) decorated similarly to those of Ayasofya Pansiyonları.

Best Western Hotel Sokullu Paşa *(☎ 212-518 1790, fax 518 1793, W www.sokullupasahotel.com, Şehit Mehmet Paşa Sokak 5/7, Küçük Aya Sofya)* **Map 13, #116** Rooms with bath US$90/110; includes breakfast. This is a renovated Ottoman house with its own small leafy courtyard and hamam (no massages available). The rooms are nothing special, but they're clean enough. The hotel will cut the price quickly if it's not full.

Sarı Konak Oteli *(☎ 212-638 6258, fax 517 8635, W www.sarikonak.com, Mimar Mehmet Ağa Caddesi 42-46, Cankurtaran)* **Map 13, #89** Singles/doubles with bath US$90/120; includes breakfast. This is a casually classy find with clean rooms (dazzling curtains), twinkling white bathrooms, and Ottoman-style decorations throughout. Other drawcards are the pretty walled courtyard and the roof terrace with excellent views.

Hotel Obelisk & Sümengen *(☎ 212-517 7173, fax 516 8282, W www.obelisksumengen.com, Amiral Tafdil Sokak 17-19, Cankurtaran)* **Map 13, #87** Singles/doubles with bath US$90/120, includes breakfast. Two hotels joined to become this rambling renovated Ottoman town house with its own marble Turkish bath (US$10 extra). There's an airy, light dining room and open-air rooftop terrace with views of the Sea of Marmara. The mixed bag of rooms range from older style charm (with small bathrooms) to rooms with views, but some rooms only face on to corridors.

Mavi Ev *(Blue House; ☎ 212-638 9010, fax 638 9017, e bluehouse@bluehouse.com.tr, Dalbastı Sokak 14, Sultanahmet)* **Map 13, #92** Singles/doubles with bath US$120/140; includes breakfast. The exterior is polished and twee, but inside the spotless older-style rooms have a minibar and satellite TV. Enjoy the morning views of the Blue Mosque from the rooftop restaurant, which is only open in good weather.

Modern Hotels Modern hotels are not in vogue in the Sultanahmet area, but sometimes the Ottoman hotels are dressed-up modern hotels with dressed-up prices. You may be better saving your cash, staying in a 100% modern hotel and visiting the Ottoman-style hotels for a meal.

Hotel Nomade *(☎ 212-511 1296, fax 513 2404, Ticarethane Sokak 15, Alemdar)* **Map 13, #29** Singles/doubles with bath US$50/60; includes breakfast. This friendly place is just a few steps off busy Divan Yolu. The small rooms have countryside decor with wooden floorboards, while the upstairs terrace has good views and plenty of comfy cushions from which to enjoy it.

Hotel Halı *(☎ 212-516 2170, fax 516 2172, W www.halihotel.com, Klodfarer Caddesi 20, Çemberlitaş)* **Map 13, #12** Singles/doubles with bath US$45/75; includes breakfast. In an attempt to lend some character to the place rugs are littered over the floor. They needn't have worried as the rooms speak for themselves: small, but spotless, and some have good views. Scoff the all-you-can-eat breakfast while you enjoy the superb views from the rooftop restaurant.

Sirkeci (Map 15)

This area used to be sleazy a decade ago, but today its convenient location has encouraged some mid-range hotels to open.

Orient Express *(☎ 212-520 7161, fax 526 8446, e info@orientexpresshotel.com, Hüdavendigar Caddesi 34)* **Map 15, #23** Singles/doubles with bath US$100/120; includes breakfast. Cosy, immaculate rooms, each with a sparkling white bathroom, pull the tourists into the Orient Express. There's also an indoor pool – a rarity around here – and a rooftop terrace-bar with good views.

Fener (Map 18)

It's a bit out of the way, but if you're spending time traipsing around the churches and mosques of Balat and Fener then you may want to stay close by.

Hotel Daphnis *(☎ 212-531 4858, fax 532 8992,* W *www.hoteldaphnis.com, Sadrazam Ali Paşa Caddesi 26)* Singles/doubles with bath US$80/100; includes breakfast. The rooms are cute and old fashioned, though the bathrooms are minuscule. Service is good in this homey place.

Beyoğlu (Maps 16 & 17)

Many mid-range options hide in the busy streets of Beyoğlu.

Older-Style Hotels Tepebaşı, in Beyoğlu, was the hub of luxury hotels built in the late 19th century – some of them have barely been touched since.

Büyük Londra Oteli *(☎ 212-293 1619, fax 245 0671, Meşrutiyet Caddesi 117, Tepebaşı)* **Map 16, #99** Singles/doubles with bath US$60/80; includes breakfast. This dates from the same era as the Pera Palas Oteli (see later in this chapter), but has much smaller rooms and bathrooms, and is worse for wear. But it does preserve some of the Victorian-era glory, in the public rooms at least, at a price that includes a significant nostalgia mark-up, but is nonetheless lower than the Pera's. They'll come down in price if business is slow.

Modern Hotels Beyoğlu's modern hotels were mostly built in the 1980s, but they offer good service and decent prices after a bit of bargaining.

Riva Otel *(☎ 212-256 4420, fax 256 2033, Aydede Caddesi 8, Taksim)* **Map 17, #46** Singles/doubles with bath US$50/70; includes breakfast. This is more like it: One of the few hotels in this area that knows it's looking like a has-been and charges accordingly. The rooms are clean and roomy.

Grace Hotel *(☎ 212-293 3955, fax 252 4370, Meşrutiyet Caddesi 38, Tepebaşı)* **Map 16, #83** Singles/doubles with bath US$90/110. Next to the British consulate, this modern, four-star hotel is good value for money. There's a pool, sauna and the rooms are clean, though the grandma floral bedspreads may scare some away.

Hotel Lamartine *(☎ 212-254 6270, fax 256 2776, Lamartin Caddesi 25, Taksim)* **Map 17, #45** Singles/doubles with bath US$110/130; includes breakfast. Don't let the tasteless 'art' on the wall of the foyer put you off. This place has few facilities (no pool or gym) but the rooms are large, clean and quite colourful. The service is good, too.

Feronya Hotel *(☎ 212-238 0901, fax 238 0866,* W *www.feronya.com, Abdülhak Hamit Caddesi 70-72, Taksim)* **Map 17, #42** Singles/doubles with bath US$100/140. No-one would call it stylish – in fact the decor smacks of a cheap '90s fit-out complete with wood veneer finishes. But it's a colourful, clean, friendly spot.

Yenişehir Palas *(☎ 212-252 7160, fax 249 7507,* e *yenisehirpalasotel@ixir.com, Oteller Sokak 1-3, Tepebaşı)* **Map 16, #115** Singles/doubles with bath US$85-110/115-145; includes breakfast. This smallish hotel has no views, but it does have excellent service and small but comfy and spotless rooms. The bathrooms are modern and colourful. There's supposed to be a pool on the way, but we wouldn't count on it.

Hotel Mercure *(☎ 212-251 4646, fax 249 8033,* e *H1342@accor-hotels.com, Meşrutiyet Caddesi, Tepebaşı)* **Map 16, #116** Singles/doubles with bath US$125/145; includes breakfast. This modern 22-storey tower has 192 simple rooms with satellite TV and minibar, and many have splendid views of the Golden Horn, the Old City and the Bosphorus. There's a small rooftop pool and restaurant. It's good value.

The Madison Hotel *(☎ 212-238 5460, fax 238 5151,* W *www.themadisonhotel.com.tr, Recep Paşa Caddesi 23, Taksim)* **Map 17, #40** Singles/doubles with bath US$120/160. The rooms here are clean, plain and roomy. There's a hamam, gym and a small indoor swimming pool.

Apartments If you're staying a few nights, apartments are value-for-money accommodation in İstanbul.

Family House *(☎ 212-249 7351, fax 249 9667,* e *familyhouse@ihlas.net.tr, Kutlu Sokak 53, Gümüşsuyu)* **Map 16, #13** 4-person apartments US$96 nightly, US$600 weekly, US$2400 monthly. Extra beds 10% per person. Family House has five small four-room apartments in a quiet building. The basic, '70s apartments have two single beds and one double bed, telephone, digital TV and a fully furnished kitchen (no food is available). To find Family House, walk down İnönü Caddesi from Taksim, walk beneath the large red Chinese gate and down the steps, then down another flight.

Galata Konutları Apart Hotel *(☎ 212-252 6062, fax 244 2323, Ⓦ www.galataresidence.com, Hacı Ali Sokak, Karaköy)* **Map 16, #153** 4-person apartments US$100 nightly, US$630 weekly; 2-person apartments US$60 nightly, US$350 weekly. Buried in Galata's maze of narrow streets, between the Galata Tower and Karaköy Square, this historic building was once owned by the wealthy Kamondo family. It's now an apartment-hotel. The older-style apartments each have a fully equipped kitchen.

PLACES TO STAY – TOP END

Near the Airport (Map 11)

Atatürk Airport is 24km from Sultanahmet or Taksim. It's far more interesting to stay in the city centre than near the airport and it's easy to get to/from the airport. But if you're still keen, the hotels out this way offer good value for money.

The Holiday Inn has two hotels near its Ataköy beach and Galleria shopping complex 8km south-east of the airport.

Holiday Inn İstanbul Ataköy Marina *(☎ 212-560 4110, fax 559 4905, Ⓔ crowneplaza@superonline.com, Sahil Yolu, Ataköy)* Singles/doubles with bath US$170/192; includes breakfast. This laid-back hotel allows its guests to use the more lavish facilities at the neighbouring Crowne Plaza. There's a free shuttle bus available for trips to Taksim and Sultanahmet.

Holiday Inn Crowne Plaza *(☎ 212-560 8100, fax 560 8155, Ⓦ www.crowneplaza.com, Sahil Yolu, Ataköy)* Singles/doubles with bath US$199/235; includes breakfast. This glitzy five-star place is a 298-room high-rise tower offering all luxury facilities including a free shuttle bus to/from the airport and the city centre.

Polat Renaissance İstanbul Hotel *(☎ 212-663 1700, fax 663 1755, Ⓔ rezervasyon@polatholding.com, Sahil Caddesi 2, Yeşilyurt)* Rooms from US$153. This hotel, 4km south of the airport, is a tall tower of reflective glass with 390 luxury rooms, plus a pool and all other facilities. The free shuttle service takes you to/from the airport only.

Çınar Hotel *(☎ 212-663 2900, fax 663 2917, Ⓔ reservation@cinarhotel.com.tr, Yeşilköy)* Singles/doubles with bath US$225/280, with breakfast. This plush hotel, only 4km from the airport, is designed so you can fully appreciate the views over the water. Plush rooms, sea-water pool, gym and all the other facilities you'd expect for this price tag are here, except there's no shuttle bus to the airport or the centre of town.

Sultanahmet Area (Map 13)

The cramped urban fabric of Old İstanbul doesn't allow for acres of pampering space most top-end hotels require. If you're after swimming pools, fully kitted gyms and tennis courts head to Taksim and beyond. But what Sultanahmet does have is good and, in the case of Four Seasons, it's the best.

Older-Style Hotels Top-end hotels tend to be stylishly renovated Ottoman mansions; less-expensive hotels tend to have cheap, modern fit-outs.

Yeşil Ev *(☎ 212-517 6785, fax 517 6780, Ⓦ www.turing.org.tr, Kabasakal Caddesi 5, Sultanahmet)* **Map 13, #67** Single/doubles with bath US$120/160; Pasha's Room, with private Turkish bath, US$250; includes breakfast. This is an Ottoman house with 22 large rooms furnished in fine taste with period pieces and antiques; each has a modern bathroom. Behind the hotel is a lovely shaded garden-terrace cafe-restaurant – shame about the terrible service.

Four Seasons Hotel İstanbul *(☎ 212-638 8200, fax 638 8210, Ⓦ www.fshr.com, Tevkifhane Sokak 1, Cankurtaran)* **Map 13, #68** Singles with bath US$330-600, doubles with bath US$375-650. This is İstanbul's top hotel in every respect: location, accommodation, style, furnishings and service. With only 65 rooms and a staff of around

200, this immaculate Ottoman building, literally in the shadow of the Blue Mosque and Aya Sofya has only one problem: There aren't enough rooms for everyone who wants one.

Modern Hotels These hotels have all the mod cons but no pools or gym, but you can't complain about the location.

Hotel Arcadia *(☎ 212-516 9696, fax 516 6118, W www.hotelarcadiaistanbul.com, Dr İmran Öktem Caddesi 1, Sultanahmet* **Map 13, #17** Singles/doubles with bath US$135/155; includes breakfast. Situated on the north-west side of the law courts, this is a modern mid-rise hotel with comfortable small rooms. The location is excellent – quiet and convenient – and the afternoon views of the Blue Mosque, Aya Sofya, Topkapı Palace and the Sea of Marmara from the upper-floor rooms and rooftop restaurant are nothing short of spectacular.

Hotel Armada *(☎ 212-638 1370, fax 518 5060, W www.armadahotel.com.tr, Ahırkapı Sokak, Cankurtaran)* **Map 13, #125** Singles/doubles with bath US$145/175. Very near the Cankurtaran suburban train station, this huge hotel is a few steps from the Bosphorus shore and only a 10-minute walk uphill to Sultanahmet. The colourful rooms are not very plush but they're comfy and roomy. The rooftop restaurant-bar has good views.

Aksaray & Laleli (Map 14) & Beyazıt (Map 15)

The district of Beyazıt, 2km west of Sultanahmet, has a handful of top-end options close by shoppers' heaven: Kapalı Çarşı (Grand Bazaar).

Best Western President Hotel *(☎ 212-516 6980, fax 516 6998, W www.thepresidenthotel.com.tr, Tiyatro Caddesi 25, Beyazıt)* **Map 15, #46** Singles/doubles with bath US$130/170; includes breakfast. Only a block from the Kapalı Çarşı, this is the place for inveterate shoppers. Though it's on a narrow street, you're in good company here, with the Ministry of Finance's shiny granite-clad guesthouse directly opposite. The President offers luxury – comfy rooms and a pool – and moderate prices.

Merit Antique Hotel *(☎ 212-513 9300, fax 512 6390, W www.meritantiquehotel.com.tr, Ordu Caddesi* **Map 14** Singles/doubles with bath US$160-190/200-240. In 1918 this building was built for people made homeless by fires, but Merit's only concession to its history is the facade. Inside, the busy hotel is decked out in true '80s (anti) style mixed with a few remnants of Ottoman kitsch. Thankfully the rooms are plain.

Beyoğlu (Map 16) & Harbiye (Map 17)

Except for a handful of options, most of the district's luxury hotels are in Harbiye, a few blocks north of Taksim Square.

Older-Style Hotels The famous Pera Palas fills up with tourists looking to relive the great age of Constantinople. ***Pera Palas Oteli*** *(☎ 212-251 4560, fax 251 4089, Meşrutiyet Caddesi 98-100, Tepebaşı)* **Map 16, #117** Singles/doubles with bath US$100-140/140-220; includes breakfast. The public salons and bar amply fulfil the nostalgia need, though the indifferent service and mediocre restaurant are strong reminders that things were better here a century ago.

The Pera's 145 rooms vary from high-ceilinged chambers, with period furnishings and bathrooms to match, to cramped upper-floor servants' quarters and uninspiring annexe rooms. You're paying a premium for nostalgia here, much of which you can enjoy at huge savings just by having a coffee in the grand salon or a drink at the bar.

The Pera Palas' ingenious promoters claim that Agatha Christie stayed in room 411 when she visited İstanbul, though reliable sources affirm that she stayed at the once prime but now long-gone Tokatliyan Hotel on İstiklal Caddesi. However, there is no disputing that the great Atatürk preferred room 101, a vast suite which, kept just as he used it, is now a museum (ask at the reception desk for admission).

Modern Hotels Often with large grounds, usually with views and always luxurious, İstanbul's top-end modern hotels are world class.

Hotel Richmond *(☎ 212-252 5460, fax 252 9707,* **W** *www.richmondhotels.com.tr, İstiklal Caddesi 445, Tünel)* **Map 16, #114** Singles/doubles with bath US$160/195; includes breakfast. Next to the palatial Russian consulate, this is one of the few hotels on İstiklal. Behind and around its 19th-century facade, the Richmond is all modern, quite comfortable and well run, with 104 full-service rooms.

The Marmara *(☎ 212-251 4696, fax 244 0509,* **W** *www.themarmaraistanbul.com, Taksim Square)* **Map 16, #14** Singles/doubles with bath US$230-315/260-345; includes breakfast. Right beside busy Taksim Square, the Marmara has splendid views of the square on one side and the Old City, Beyoğlu and the Bosphorus on the other. The service is immaculate, plus the rooms are spotless and comfortable, and there's a pool, gym and hamam.

İstanbul Hilton *(☎ 212-315 6000, fax 240 4165,* **W** *www.hilton.com, Cumhuriyet Caddesi, Harbiye)* **Map 17, #27** Singles with bath US$295-350, doubles with bath US$330-380. The Hilton is set in a 5.6-hectare park overlooking the Bosphorus, with tennis courts, swimming pool and large luxurious rooms (possibly the best in İstanbul). Service is also top-notch here.

Hyatt Regency İstanbul *(☎ 212-225 7000, fax 225 7007,* **W** *www.istanbul.hyatt.com, Taşkışla Caddesi, Elmadağ)* **Map 17, #35** Singles/doubles with bath US$240-385/270-385. This 360-room hotel has the feel of a vast Ottoman mansion with modern conveniences (pool, gym etc). It's one of the plushest top hotels. The rooms are modern, large and the bathrooms are huge. The catch? The views are average or nonexistent.

Ceylan Inter-Continental İstanbul *(☎ 212-231 2121, fax 231 2180,* **W** *www.interconti.com, Asker Ocağı Caddesi 1, Elmadağ)* **Map 17, #38** Rooms with bath US$320-460. This hotel has all the embellishments – bubbling foyer waterfall, gym, pool, plush rooms, ear-to-ear smiles – you'd expect in a top hotel. The rooms are large, light and some have excellent views but the standard rooms only look over Taksim Gezi Parkı.

The Bosphorus (Map 6)

There are several luxury hotels north-east of Taksim Square. While they enjoy fine views of the Bosphorus, their location out of the centre requires you to take taxis everywhere as few attractions are within walking distance.

Conrad International Istanbul *(☎ 212-227 3000, fax 259 6667,* **W** *www.conradhotels.com, Yıldız Caddesi, Beşiktaş)* Singles/doubles with bath US$195-295/235-310. Conrad's rooms are light-filled, with floral furnishings, and they are very clean, but nothing special. Views are only good if you're on the top floors, but this place has all the mod cons.

Swissôtel İstanbul The Bosphorus *(☎ 212-259 0101, fax 259 0105, Bayıldım Caddesi 2, Maçka)* Singles with bath US$195-320, doubles with bath US$215-350. This busy place capitalises upon its magnificent Bosphorus views: the lobby, restaurant and 585 rooms all benefit. Lavish use of marble gives it a luxury feel, and all services give it luxury for real.

Çırağan Palace Hotel Kempinski İstanbul *(☎ 212-258 3377, fax 259 6687,* **W** *www.ciragan-palace.com, Çırağan Caddesi 84, Beşiktaş)* Rooms with bath US$350-880. This is a modern 315-room luxury hotel annexe built next to the historic Çırağan Palace, on the shore at the foot of the Yıldız Palace park. Destroyed by fire in 1911, the rebuilt marble palace holds meeting rooms, VIP suites, a ballroom and restaurants. The annexe has east-facing rooms which enjoy fine Bosphorus views, but west-facing 'park-view' rooms look onto a stone wall. All luxury services are available though the rooms aren't İstanbul's finest – you're paying for location and prestige.

Places to Eat

It's worth travelling to İstanbul just to eat. Turkish cuisine is the very heart and soul of eastern Mediterranean cooking, which demands fresh, high-quality ingredients and careful preparation. And if you become kebaped-out on Turkish cuisine, İstanbul has many others – Italian and French, for example – to tantalise your taste buds. Note: Restaurant suggestions for dining on the Bosphorus are given in the Excursions chapter under the heading for the town in which the restaurant is found.

RESTAURANTS

Fast Food

İstanbul has many fast-food restaurants *(hazir yemek lokanta),* which are small places serving 'ready-made food' – soups, stews, rice etc – kept warm in steam tables. Sometimes they have roast meats as well. This food isn't İstanbul's best – it can be a bit oily and sloppy as it may have been lolling around in the steam table for days. Still, much of it is fine and it's a decent, quick fix, and healthier than other fast-food options such as McDonald's. These places don't normally serve alcohol. You can expect to pay between US$2 and US$5 per meal.

Köftecis & Kebapçıs

Köftecis which serve grilled lamb meatballs, and kebapçıs which serve a variety of grilled meats are usually simple places. At an *ocakbaşı* (grill) you can sit and watch the cook at work. Order your main meat course by the portion: *bir porsyon* (one portion) if you're not overly hungry; *bir buçuk porsyon* (one and a half) if you are, and *duble porsyon* (double) if you're ravenous. An order of *köfte* (grilled mince meatballs) or *şiş kebap* (grilled skewered meat), a plate of salad, and a glass of *ayran* (a yogurt drink) usually costs around US$3 to US$6.

If you're a pork devotee you'll have trouble finding it in İstanbul as Muslims don't eat pork, so head to the restaurants serving international cuisine and expect to pay top dollar.

Restaurant Hints

In most restaurants in İstanbul, there is a convenient *lavabo* (sink) so that you can wash your hands before eating. Just say the word and the waiter will point it out.

If you're a woman you may wish to ask for the *aile salonu* (family dining room, often upstairs), which will be free of the all-male atmosphere to be found in some cheap Turkish eateries.

Many Turkish waiters have the annoying habit of snatching your plate away before you're finished with it. This may be due to a rule of Eastern etiquette which holds that it is impolite to leave a finished plate sitting in front of a guest. If a waiter engages in plate-snatching, say *'Kalsın'* (Let it stay).

Cafes

Artsy cafe-bars are in plague proportions in İstanbul. Most of these places offer cuisine and decor – not to mention people – that would be at home in Paris, London or New York. Most cafes are clustered in Beyoğlu, but many are dotted in the suburbs on both sides of the Bosphorus and in other well-heeled neighbourhoods. Good coffee is easily found – though the perfect cappuccino froth poses as much of a challenge in İstanbul as it does anywhere. You should try Turkish coffee *(kahve),* of course; it comes in sugary, potent shots. You'll usually find a variety of teas, including herbal infusions. Most cafes also have European-styled cakes: Cheesecake is very much in vogue and tiramisu is popular, too. Savoury snacks are also available.

The ubiquitous tea garden *(çay bahçesi)* is the saggy cousin of the hip Beyoğlu cafe. It is usually an outdoor, leafy garden serving tea, coffee and occasionally snacks (no alcohol) frequented by clusters of moustached gents playing backgammon, students lazing around a *nargileh* (water pipe), courting couples and families.

Meyhanes

magine an Irish pub meeting a tapas bar, vith a dash of Turkish wedding party hrown in: You've conjured up a *meyhane* tavern) in İstanbul. Carousing at a mey-ane is a must-do. Packed on weekends, a neyhane is where friends gather to spend he night, and probably end up drunk in the isles. Musicians strumming *fasıl* (folk nusic) move from table to table frothing up he punters and playing requests. Revellers ing along, throw their arms around each ther, clap boisterously and break into ance. Food is usually ordered a couple of ishes at a time; it's always meze (starters), ften fish and occasionally meat dishes, too. here are usually no menus so you'll need o look and point. Everyone drinks *rakı* anise alcohol); it's very strong, and al-hough you'll be encouraged with stories hat 'it won't give you a hangover' and 'it ures colds' it's pure fabrication – that stuff s potent.

The musicians, by the way, tend to steer lear of tourists, who are known to be un-ccustomed to meyhane etiquette; which is very polite way of saying they don't tip vell, if at all. The rule is you should give at east US$5 per table, so if there are two of ou at a table tip US$5, if there are three JS$5 is still OK and so on.

Atmosphere is what meyhanes are all bout so they tend to cluster together with treet-side tables spewing out into crammed in streets. Kumkapı and Çiçek Pasajı are ouristy, Nevizade Sokak in Beyoğlu is un-ouristy (for now) – all are lots of fun. See estaurant suggestions under the Meyhane ections later in this chapter.

Vegetarian Restaurants

'ou'll be able to get at least a couple of egetable dishes in any restaurant in İstan-ul but most of the time they'll be cooked vith meat stock. Ask the waiter if they have ny meatless dishes: '*Etsiz yemek var mı?*'. you like your food 100% vegetable, head o Beyoğlu where there is a handful of real egetarian places, where pulses, organic roduce, herbal infusions and tofu can be ound. Otherwise, many cheap restaurants serve pide (Turkish pizza), a long boat-like bready pizza, which can be cooked with just cheese or tomato. These are cheap (US$1 to US$1.50) and filling.

Fish Restaurants

Fish restaurants *(balık restoran)* are popular in İstanbul, and you'll find them near some fish markets (in Kumkapı near Sultanahmet and Galatasaray in Beyoğlu, for example) and especially along the Bosphorus. Fish prices are not usually put on the menu. You must ask the waiter what's fresh and ask to see the fish. A few restaurants may try to cook you up old fish. This trick is not just pulled out for foreigners – most locals ask to check the fish is fresh, so don't be embarrassed to do the same. The eyes should be clear and the flesh under the gill slits near the eyes should be bright red, not burgundy. After your fish has been given the all clear, ask the approximate price. The fish will be weighed, and the price computed at the day's per-kilogram rate. Sometimes you can haggle. Buy fish in season as fish out of season are very expensive.

From March to the end of June is a good time to order delicious turbot, covered in ugly red mumps *(kalkan)*, mackerel *(uskumru)* and fresh anchovies *(hamsi)*, but from July to mid-August is spawning season for many species, and fishing them is prohibited. In July and August, these are the easiest to find in the markets and on the restaurant tables: small bluefish *(çinakop)*, medium-size bluefish *(lüfer)*, bonito *(palamut)*, striped goatfish *(tekir, Mullus surmuletus)*, red mullet *(barbunya, Mullus barbatus)*, and scad or horse mackerel *(istavrit)*.

You'll find the best fish at İstanbul's meyhanes. See the Meyhane sections later in this chapter for suggestions. Şile has excellent fish, too (see the Excursions chapter).

Mixed Cuisine

İstanbul does have some good international cuisine and many mid-range to top-end restaurants serve various world dishes with varying success. North American, Italian and French cuisine is popular; Asian cuisine is a bit harder to find. There are also restaurants in İstanbul which serve meals originating from different areas within Turkey, eg, Urfa kebap, an eggplant dish from Şanlıurfa in Eastern Turkey. Other restaurants serve both international and Turkish regional food.

SELF-CATERING

A few of the guesthouses have communal kitchen facilities you can use for little or no cost. Some mid-range places have apartments to rent out and these have private kitchens. İstanbul also has many small supermarkets (eg, Gima) sprinkled through the streets around Beyoğlu, with giant cousins (eg, Migros) in the suburbs. Then there is the ubiquitous corner shop *(bakkal)*, which has bread, milk and usually fruit and vegetables.

The street markets are the cheapest and most entertaining places to pick up eggs, fruit, vegetables, rice, pulses, cheese and more. Akbıyık Caddesi in Cankurtaran (near Sultanahmet) – backpacker central – has a street market all day Wednesday. Down in Eminönü, the streets around the Mısır Çarşısı (Egyptian Market), sell fish, meats, vegies, spices, sweets and much more. In Beyoğlu, the Balık Pazar (Fish Market) just off İstiklal Caddesi in Galatasaray, is a prime area for picnic assembly, with greengrocers, delicatessens *(şarküteri)* and bakeries offering cheeses, dried meats such as pastrami *(pastırma)*, pickled fish, olives, jams and preserves, and several varieties of bread including wholegrain.

BREAKFAST

The standard breakfast *(komple kahvaltı)* you'll be given in your hotel consists of fresh bread *(ekmek)* with jam or honey, butter, salty black olives, sliced tomatoes and cucumbers, a hard-boiled egg, cheese – white sheep's milk cheese, mild yellow processed cheese *(kaşar peynir)* – and tea *(çay;* **chah**-yee) or coffee. The bread and tea are usually fresh and good, but the other ingredients are often stale or mushy. Bacon is difficult to find as any pork product is forbidden to Muslims, but you may find it in posh hotels.

If the typical breakfast listed above sounds unappealing, your other options are limited, unfortunately. Most restaurants in the Sultanahmet area serve either the standard breakfast or omelettes that can be tast or terrible. French toast is often experimented with; the results sometimes tast like a honey-soaked dishcloth.

Many locals pop into cheap restaurant for soup *(çorba)* for breakfast and dip i heaps of fresh bread. This is a tasty, nutritious and cheap (around US$0.70) option Try a fast-food restaurant (hazır yeme lokanta) or a Turkish pizza restaurant *(pid salonu)* for early-morning soup. Another option is *su börek* (layers of tender noodle-lik pastry with touches of cheese and parsley Get some fresh, first thing in the morning and you'll find this stuff melts in you mouth. One portion costs about US$1.

SWEETS & DESSERTS

Although most restaurants serve Turkis desserts, most locals head to the sweet-toot specialists, the pastry shop *(pastane)* – her the desserts are spot on. Most have tray upo tray of super-sweet biscuits and cookies (tr *kadayıf,* a mix of shredded wheat an sugar); and shelf upon shelf of baked ric pudding *(fırın sütlaç)* and luscious puddin with fruit and nuts *(aşure)*. There are usuall some stools to sit on, and a larger pastr shop may also sell beverages and börek c other savoury pastry treats. Sweets are rea sonably priced; you'll pay around US$1 pe tempting treat. Sticky *baklava* (layered pas try with pistachios), is usually sold too, bu true connoisseurs buy it at a *baklavac* (baklava shop). And, while in İstanbul, yo must try gooey Turkish delight (yum). Se the boxed text 'Turkish Delight'.

DRINKS

Nonalcoholic

Drinking tea is a national pastime and tea i central to every social gathering; it's ofte complimentary, especially when shoppin The cute tulip-shaped glasses come with dainty saucer, and usually two lumps c sugar on the side – milk is never added. A cafes you may be able to get a milky tea b asking *'Sütlu çay var mı?'* ('Do you hav milky tea?'). Apple tea *(alma çay)* is a swe concoction of chemicals, vaguely tasting lik

Turkish Delight

You can't come to İstanbul and not try real *lokum* (Turkish delight). The stuff you get here is the best in the world. And what better place to buy this traditional Ottoman treat than from the original shop of **Ali Muhiddin Hacı Bekir** (☎ 212-522 0666, Hamidiye Caddesi) **(Map 15, #13)** inventor of Turkish delight.

The story goes that Ali Muhiddin came to İstanbul from the Black Sea mountain town of Kastamonu and established himself as a confectioner in the Ottoman capital in the late 18th century. Dissatisfaction with hard candies and traditional sweets led the impetuous Ali Muhiddin to invent a new confection that would be easy to swallow. He called his soft, gummy creation *rahat lokum*, the 'comfortable morsel'. Lokum, as it soon came to be called, was an immediate hit with the denizens of the imperial palace, and anything that goes well with the palace goes well with the populace.

Ali Muhiddin elaborated on his original confection, as did his offspring (the shop is still owned by his descendants), and now you can buy lokum made with various fillings: walnut *(cevizli)*, pistachio *(şam fıstıklı)*, orange-flavoured *(portakkallı)* or almond *(bademli)*. You can also get an assortment *(çeşitli)*. Price is according to weight; 1kg costs US$2 to US$6, depending upon variety. Ask for a free sample by indicating your choice and saying *'Deneyelim!'* ('Let's try it!').

Between November and February a cool-weather speciality is added to the list of treats for sale. Helva, a crumbly sweet block of sesame mash, is flavoured with chocolate or pistachio nuts or sold plain. Ali Muhiddin Hacı Bekir has another, more modern shop at İstiklal Caddesi 129, Beyoğlu **(Map 16, #65)**.

pples. It's popular with tourists, much to the musement of some locals who are too ough' to drink this caffeine-free sugar hit.

Surprisingly, Turkish coffee is not idely consumed. It's a soupy brew, takes uite an art to prepare, and leaves a thick esidue on the bottom of the cup. Many eople have turned to Nescafe, though it's ore expensive and nowhere near as nice.

Many locals don't drink the tap water so you probably shouldn't either. Water in plastic bottles is readily available in shops and *büfes* (buffets) but a better option is the recyclable glass bottles available in restaurants. In fine weather you may see water-sellers kitted up in garish costumes. With their ungainly water jug, complete with jangling glasses, they ostentatiously pour water from a great height – shame it's not bottled.

If you're in İstanbul during the coolest months, from November to February, try the delicious, and unusual taste of *sahlep*, which is hot, sweetened milk flavoured with tasty orchid-root *(Orchis mascula)* powder and a sprinkle of cinnamon.

Alcoholic

Served in long thin glasses, the spirit rakı fires the passions – and loins, in some cases – of the meyhane barflies. It's the darling drink of many locals. The seemingly innocent clear substance is usually mixed with water into a milky brew; too much can turn you into a swaying, teary mess.

Wine *(şarap)* bars are all the rage with the hip, arty crew. Turkish wine isn't bad, either, although the whites are a sickly sweet. All venues serve beer *(bira)*, at about US$2 a glass. A popular and tasty local brew is Efes, which usually comes as light (low alcohol) and dark.

PLACES TO EAT – BUDGET

Sultanahmet Area (Map 13)

Some Sultanahmet restaurants serve up overpriced fodder for tourists and disguise it as Turkish cuisine. These lazy places seem to have a 'tourists won't know if it's good or bad Turkish food' attitude – which unfortunately can end up being true. The best way to get around this is to get out of the touristy areas and wander in to a restaurant busy with locals. But if you've had a long day and you want to eat in Sultanahmet, consider the recommendations listed below.

Fast Food At fast-food restaurants (hazır yemek lokanta), remember to steer clear of dishes that look like they've been sitting there since the beginning of the Republic.

Saving Money

Several tips can save you loads of money on food. Firstly, order as you eat. Turks order appetisers, eat them, then decide what to have next. Often you will be directed to a steam table to select your meal. There can be a tendency to get excited and order too many dishes – don't, you can go and look again.

Secondly, fill up with bread. Turkish sourdough is delicious, fresh and complimentary with all meals.

Thirdly, don't accept food you have not specifically ordered. For example, in the Çiçek Pasajı in Beyoğlu, cheeky waiters may put a dish of fresh almonds on your table. They're not a gift – you can be sure they'll show up on your bill at the end. If you haven't ordered it, ask *'Bedava mı?'* ('Is it free?'). If the answer is no, say *'İstemiyorum'* ('I don't want it').

Finally, always ask prices in advance – especially for fish – and be sure you receive an itemised bill (it's customary), and check it for errors. By the way, the traditional Turkish practice of figuring the bill, then turning it over, folding it in half and writing the total on the back has the look of a rip-off. It's not necessarily so, but you should feel no embarrassment in opening the bill, redoing the addition, and questioning any items, including obscure cover *(kuver)* and service *(servis)* charges.

Tarihi Çeşme Restaurant *(☎ 212-516 3580, Küçük Aya Sofya Camii Sokak 7, Küçük Aya Sofya)* **Map 13, #114** Dishes US$0.50-2.50. Open 7.30am-midnight daily. Popular with locals, this cute little restaurant serves up a limited range of ready-made food plus meat dishes. There's a small outdoor eating area.

Yeni Birlik Lokantası *(☎ 212-517 6465, Peykhane Sokak 46)* **Map 13, #108** Dishes US$1.50-3.50. Open 11am-3.30pm Mon-Fri. Locals have cottoned on to the good, value-for-money food and excellent service which make this one of the best eateries in Sultanahmet. There's no menu, so you have to look and point at the steam trays and discourage the excitable staff from overfilling your plate. Note the opening hours.

Can Restaurant *(☎ 212-527 7030, Divan Yolu 10)* **Map 13, #33** Dishes US$1.50-4 Open 9am-11pm daily. This is a cafeteria style place which has been here for decades and its taste buds seem to have dulled. Still there's a decent range of average food, good for a quick fix. It's a bit overpriced, but it's convenient.

Köftecis & Kebapçıs Divan Yolu's köftecis were traditionally where the district's workers ate cheap, filling, tasty lunches. Now they're famous their prices have risen a bit, but the köfte and şiş kebap are still spot on.

Sultanahmet Köftecisi *(☎ 212-511 3960, Divan Yolu 4)* **Map 13, #35** Dishes US$0.50-2. Open 10.30am-midnight daily. Tiles and more tiles: Despite the like-dining-in-a bathroom experience, this no-frills, no-menu place has delicious köfte. Avoid the chilli and herb condiments that look rather hen-pecked.

Kardeşler Karadeniz Pide Salonu *(☎ 212-518 0000, Peykhane Sokak 41)* **Map 13, #107** Dishes US$1-2. Open 10am-8.30pm daily. This basic eatery with bright lights has a good reputation with locals. The pide and kebaps are appetising, served quickly and very cheap.

Sultanahmet Meşhur Halk Köftecisi Selim Usta *(Chef Selim, Famous Köfte Maker; ☎ 212-513 1438, Divan Yolu 12)* **Map 13, #32** Dishes US$1.50-2. Open 10.30am-midnight daily. With prices clearly marked, this popular spot has two clean shops side-by-side, packed with locals and tourists here for a tasty, quick food fix. Accolades line the walls, but you be the judge.

Karadeniz Aile Pide ve Kebap Salonu *(☎ 212-522 9191, Biçki Yurdu Sokak I)* **Map 13, #27** Dishes US$1.50-4. Open 9am-11pm daily. This place, just off Divan Yolu, is a bit overpriced since it's near the tourist strip but it still has good food. There's a small outdoor eating area. It serves soup, kebaps and excellent pide.

Cafes Sultanahmet's cafes and tea gardens are mostly used by locals who come to enjoy the shade, tea and maybe a nargile

Derviş Aile Çay Bahçesi *(Dervish Family Tea Garden; Kabasakal Caddesi 2/1)* **Map 13, #65** Snacks US$0.80-1. Open 24 hrs (supposedly) May-Sept, 9am-6pm Oct-Apr. If you prefer shade to sun, find this leafy place with comfy chairs, backgammon and good views to the Blue Mosque. Try *peynirli tost* (US$0.80), a cheese sandwich mashed in a vice-like cooker. Tea costs US$0.50.

Sultan Sofrası *(☎ 212-518 1526, Sultanahmet Atmeydanı 40)* **Map 13, #20** Dishes US$1.50-3. Open 24 hrs (supposedly). A part-indoor, part-outdoor cafe-restaurant facing the Hippodrome, this is a good place for a snack, drink and people-watching. The soup (US$1.50) is delicious.

Çiğdem Patisserie *(☎ 212-526 8859, Divan Yolu 62/A)* **Map 13, #25** Dishes US$1-5. Open 7am-11.30pm daily. Busy with a giggling school crowd in the early morning and packed with uni students in the afternoon, this place is a mishmash of mock Roman style that suits the eclectic crowd. The menu (in Turkish) has snacks (US$0.50 to US$2), cakes and drinks including great cappuccino (US$1.50).

Cafe Meşale *(☎ 212-518 9562, Arasta Çarşısı 45)* **Map 13, #97** Dishes US$1.50-5.50. Open 24 hrs (supposedly) Mar-Aug, 9am-6pm Sept-Feb. At the end of Arasta Bazaar, this cafe really turns it on for the tourists: Dervishes whirl on and off between 8pm and 9.45pm nightly; musicians play from 7pm to 11pm daily; and a cluster of squatting women wearing headscarves flap out *gözleme* (crepes). Love it or hate it. There's a huge menu and the food is quite good. You can smoke a nargileh here too, but it's expensive (US$3 to US$4).

Mixed Cuisine Many of the restaurants in Sultanahmet try to cater for everyone by providing a mix of international dishes and Turkish food.

Cennet *(☎ 212-513 1416, Yeniçeriler Caddesi 90)* **Map 13, #7** Dishes US$1.50-2.50. Open 9am-11pm daily. Set in a restored hamam, here you can try on Ottoman costumes, recline 'Ottoman-style' and listen to 'Ottoman' musicians (noon to 9.30pm daily). It's as cheesy as it sounds, but there's more: Scarf-clad 'villagers' sit centre stage rolling gözleme, the restaurant's speciality.

Doy-Doy *(Fill up! Fill up!; ☎ 212-517 1588, Şifa Hamamı Sokak 13)* **Map 13, #119** Dishes US$1.50-3. Open 8am-11pm daily. This simple, cheap restaurant favourite is always busy with backpackers and has a few locals squeezed in too. There's a rooftop dining area with good views. You won't write home about the food, but the service is very good, friendly and the menu is extensive, including a handful of vegetable dishes.

Pudding Shop *(☎ 212-522 2970, Divan Yolu 6)* **Map 13, #34** Dishes US$1.50-3.50. Open 7am-11pm daily. The Pudding Shop, with its recent sparkling glass facelift, has sold out on the drop-out generation of the 1960s who made it famous. Average food and stale bread make a meal taken for nostalgia's sake (which many people like to do) unappealing, but there's a good selection of vegetable dishes.

Sultan Pub *(☎ 212-528 1719, Divan Yolu 2)* **Map 13, #40** Dishes US$1.50-5. Open 9am-midnight daily. This popular spot has a range of dishes such as the sultan pizza, schnitzel with french fries and an assortment of Turkish fare, but the ice-cream sundaes (US$3) draw the crowds. It's a favourite meet, chat and drink spot for over 30s.

And Restaurant *(☎ 212-520 7676, And Hotel, Cami Çıkmazı 40)* **Map 13, #45** Dishes US$3-6. Open noon-midnight daily. Incredible 360-degree views make this a stand-out restaurant; the service and food are good too. There are outdoor (not for those afraid of heights) and indoor (not for those seeking a buzzing atmosphere) eating areas.

Topkapı Palace (Map 3)

Everyone who visits Topkapı Palace has a problem: Since it can take almost a whole day to see the palace properly (including the Harem), where does one eat lunch?

Snacks (biscuits, sweets etc) and drinks are sold from a ***kiosk*** by the entrance to the Harem. But for anything more substantial you must patronise the following place.

Konyalı Restaurant *(☎ 212-513 9696)* **Map 3, #2** Open 10am-6pm Wed-Mon. Find the Mecidiye Köşkü (Kiosk of Sultan

Abdül Mecit) all the way down at the northern end of the palace, and you will find the Konyalı. The food here can be quite good or mediocre; the service is always hectic as there are many mouths to feed. Arrive by 11.30am to beat the lunch rush, or come later in the afternoon.

The restaurant is divided into two sections: The cafeteria, where you shuffle along with a tray and choose your meal, or the pricier a la carte restaurant. The cafe has meals such as döner kebaps (US$3), pastry with cheese (US$2.50) and tea for US$1. It's an outdoor terrace with superb Bosphorus views.

The restaurant is in the Mecidiye Köşkü and in an undercover area (also with good views) beside the cafeteria. Here you'll pay from US$3.50 to US$8 per main, with choices such as spaghetti bolognese and kebaps with yogurt.

Sirkeci & Eminönü (Map 15)

For an authentic Turkish restaurant experience head to Hocapaşa, a district of Eminönü in a workaday area named after its small mosque, as is customary. İbni Kemal Caddesi, the restaurant centre, is lined with over a dozen small manic restaurants with tables out in the narrow, shady pedestrian-only street. These restaurants are jumping at weekday lunch times. Hocapaşa is a 15-minute walk from Sultanahmet.

Et-İş *(☎ 212-513 1910, İbni Kemal Caddesi 25)* **Map 15, #19** Dishes US$0.70-2.50. Open 7am-11.30pm. This busy spot has a seemingly endless supply of meal options. The lunch specials (noon to 2.30pm daily) that pull the crowds include 'meal deals' such as *piliç şiş* (chicken), a salad and an ayran – all for US$2. The food isn't brilliant, but it's certainly cheap and filling. Close by, you can't miss the monster döner kebap on the sign of the ***Kasap Osman İskender***. It also has decent food.

Kardeşler Anadolu Lokantası *(☎ 212-512 1797, İbni Kemal Caddesi 24)* **Map 15, #21** Dishes US$1-2.50. Open 7am-10pm daily. This one isn't as busy as the other two as it is just off the main drag down a little street. The service is better here, though, and so is the food.

Hatay *(☎ 212-522 8513, İbni Kemal Caddesi 9-11)* **Map 15, #33** Dishes US$1-2.50. Open noon-1am daily. Towards the south end of the street, Hatay is more of a sit-down relaxed eatery. It has plain yellow decor and it's clean and popular with tourists. Hatay has superb meze and other good meals.

Borsa Lokantası *(☎ 212-527 2350, Yalı Köşkü Caddesi 60-62, Eminönü)* **Map 15, #17** Dishes US$1.50-3. Open 7.30am-9pm Mon-Sat. For modern surroundings, try this cafeteria, inland from the ferry docks. (Look for it at the inland end of the pedestrian overpass.) Pick and choose as you shuffle along the line: stuffed vine leaves, kebaps, a good selection of vegetable dishes, and plenty more. It's a clean and friendly spot.

Fish Sandwiches The cheapest way to enjoy fresh fish from the waters round İstanbul is to buy a fish sandwich from a boatman. Go to the Eminönü end of the Galata Bridge and you'll see bobbing boats tied to the quay. In each boat, men tend a cooker loaded with fish fillets. The quick-cooked fish is slid into a slit quarter-loaf of bread, and costs about US$1.

Kapalı Çarşı (Map 4)

Fast Food In the Kapalı Çarşı (Grand Bazaar), shoppers and touts are on the same side when it comes to food: both must keep up their energy for the bargaining ahead.

Subaşı Restaurant *(☎ 212-522 4762, Nuruosmaniye Caddesi 48)* **Map 4, #5** Dishes US$1-2.50. Open 8am-4pm Mon-Sat. This ready-food place is chock-a-block with locals. The food is good and the price is right. To find it, leave the bazaar by Çarşı Nuruosmaniye Kapısı and walk downhill one block to this restaurant on the right.

Köşk Restaurant *(☎ 212-513 0072, Keseciler Caddesi 98-100)* **Map 4, #8** Dishes US$1-4. Open 9am-6pm Tues-Sat. Ready-made lunch and sometimes overly attentive service make this small basic eatery a decent choice.

Havuzlu Lokantası *(☎ 212-527 3346, Gani Çelebi Sokak 3)* **Map 4, #20** Dishes US$3-5. Open 8.30am-6pm Mon-Sat. Havuzlu has an indoor area made up of a walled-off bazaar street and another area set out in front of the entrance by a little stone pool. It's a plain place with polite but unhurried waiter service, which is fine until they're busy in which case you'll have to eat your napkin as an appetiser. To find the Havuzlu, ask for the PTT, which is close by.

Colheti Cafe & Restaurant *(☎ 212-512 5094, Sandal Bedesteni 36)* **Map 4, #7** Dishes US$2-6. Open 9am-6.30pm Mon-Sat. This cafe is set up in the former auction hall (Sandal Bedesteni), and it's pleasant and spacious. Tasty kebaps are on offer, but avoid the limp hamburgers at all costs. The food is overpriced though, which means you're paying for the atmosphere, so sit out your money's worth on the comfy cane chairs.

Cafes The cafes in the Kapalı Çarşı serve as gossip dens for buyers and sellers.

Şark Kahvesi *(Oriental Cafe; ☎ 212-512 1144, Yağlıkçılar Caddesi 134)* **Map 4, #18** Open 9am-6pm Mon-Sat. Drinks US$0.30-1.50, snacks US$0.40-1. This smoky, large cafe is always packed with salesmen-on-breaks and tourists, with card-shuffling gents up the back. The arched ceilings betray its former existence as part of a bazaar street; some enterprising *kahveci* (coffee-house owner) walled up several sides and turned it into a cafe. On the grimy walls hang framed portraits of sultans, Atatürk and champion Turkish freestyle wrestlers.

Fez Cafe *(☎ 212-527 3684, Halıcılar Caddesi 62)* **Map 4, #14** Dishes US$3-4. Open 9am-6pm Tues-Sat. Set in a rough-stone den, Fez has a good selection of drinks including herbal teas (US$2.50 per pot), and international eats such as muesli (US$4) and chicken salad (US$4). It's a busy spot, which seems to make some of the waiters pushy.

Cafe İst *(☎ 212-527 9853, Takkeciler Sokak 41-43)* **Map 4, #10** Dishes US$3.50-5. Open 9am-6pm Tues-Sat. This small, friendly spot has pastas and sandwiches, well-frothed cappuccino (US$3) and herbal teas (US$1). It's darkly lit with fake frescoes.

Sülemaniye (Map 15)

Darüzziyafe *(☎ 212-511 8414, Şifahane Caddesi 6)* **Map 15, #1** Dishes US$2-6. Open noon-11pm daily. Constructed as part of the *külliye* (complex) of the Süleymaniye Camii, the building has a pretty courtyard with a fountain surrounded by porches. The court is used for dining in fine weather, though it's worth poking your head in for a coffee (US$1) or a look. The food is Ottoman-style, with Süleymaniye soup for US$2, meze for US$2 to US$4, and meat dishes up to US$6. Check your bill for errors.

Western Districts (Maps 18 & 12)

There are a few pleasant places to find refreshment out in the western suburbs.

Kariye Pembe Köşk *(☎ 212-635 8586)* Dishes US$1.50-2. In the plaza out the front of the Kariye Müzesi (Chora Church) is this tea garden serving standard dishes.

Karadeniz Lahmacun, Pide ve Kebap Salonu *(☎ 212-616 5609, Kalenderhane Caddesi 51, Eyüp)* Dishes US$2-4. Across from the Eyüp Sultan Camii, this is cheap and cheerful with simple, daggy furnishings. There's no menu so choose your meal from the front of the restaurant, and check prices.

Pierre Loti Café *(☎ 212-581 2696, Gümüşsuyu Balmumcu Sokak 1, Eyüp)* Open 8am-midnight daily. Tea US$0.60, Nescafe US$1. This rustic cafe, which today bears the name of a French novelist (see The Walls & Eyüp in the Things to See & Do chapter for directions) offers superb views. However, only drinks are served.

Beyoğlu (Maps 16 & 17)

Fast Food The cheapest eats in Beyoğlu are at the 24-hour büfes right between Sıraselviler and İstiklal Caddesis. These are the last stop for clubbers who come to line their stomachs before heading home. They serve freshly squeezed orange juices (US$1), döner sandwiches (US$1.50) and the Atom drink (US$1.50) 'to give you strength' (going home alone?). You may want to avoid the *dilli* (tongue) sandwiches, yuk.

The local ***McDonald's*** **(Map 17, #58)**, north of Taksim Square, is always packed. It is on the east side of Cumhuriyet Caddesi near the Turkish Airlines office and the PTT, along with ***Pizza Hut*** **(Map 17, #56)**.

Taksim Sütiş *(☎ 212-251 3270, İstiklal Caddesi 7)* **Map 16, #18** Dishes US$1-3. Open 6am-1am daily. Sütiş is a great spot to stop for su börek for breakfast – at this time of the day it's fresh and absolutely divine (US$1 per portion). This place specialises in desserts, but it also has biscuits and other snacks for good prices.

Karadeniz Pide Salonu *(☎ 212-243 3629, Oteller Sokak 24)* **Map 16, #119** Dishes US$1.50-3. Open 24 hrs (supposedly). For a light lunch near the Pera Palas and Mercure hotels, go to this place, behind and to the left of the Mercure, where you can get a fresh pide with butter and cheese for US$1.25.

Afacan Pizza & Burger Restaurant *(☎ 212-249 5692, İstiklal Caddesi 329)* **Map 16, #92** Dishes US$1-4. Open 7am-9pm daily. This is standard Turkish fare, served in a tacky tiled interior, but service here is with a smile and prices are clearly marked.

Borsa Fast Food Kafeteryası *(☎ 212-152 5594, İstiklal Caddesi 87-89)* **Map 16, #44** Dishes US$1.50-4. Open 7.30am-2am daily. This is modern, bright and popular with Turkish youths – especially the *dondurma* (ice cream) kiosk. Grills (US$2 to US$3) are the speciality, and beer (US$1.50) is served.

Köftecis & Kebapçıs Three floors of old-fashioned atmosphere, plus excellent food, have kept this place in business for years.

Musa Usta Adana Kebap Salonu *(☎ 212-245 2932, Küçük Parmakkapı Sokak 14)* **Map 16, #42** Dishes under US$4. Sit around the ocakbaşı and watch your meat grilled to perfection. It's licensed too (beers US$1.50, wine US$7 a bottle).

Cafes The poky side streets leading from İstiklal Caddesi are lined with lively little cafes and bars, each filled with loyal clientele. An evening's stroll here, looking for good music, drinks and snacks, is among this city's best diversions. Low-key arty cafes tend to be down the Tünel end, while cafes-cum-bars and clubs are clustered up the Taksim end.

Nöbonb Cafe & Curio Shop *(☎ 212-244 0038, Çukurlu Çeşme Sokak 12)* **Map 16, #50** Drinks US$1.50-3. Open noon-midnight daily. Treasure, junk, haute fashion, rags – whichever way you look at it Nöbonb has tonnes of it, with piles and piles of second-hand clothing upstairs as well. Out the back, there are musty chairs and comfy couches – it's a refreshingly uncool hang-out. Try the owner's pride and joy; his special brand of herbal tea.

Cafe Kino *(☎ 212-245 0010, Sofyalı Sokak 4)* **Map 16, #121** Dishes US$1-4. Open 10am-11pm daily. With maximum choice of tea (12 varieties) and coffee (nine varieties) and minimum decorations, this cafe is chic, small and inviting. Cream walls, floorboards and high-backed blue chairs fill the picture. There's no alcohol served.

Dulcinea *(☎ 212-245 1039, Meşelik Sokak 20)* **Map 16, #47** Dishes US$2-5. Open 12.30pm-1am daily. Move over try-hards, Dulcinea has its finger firmly in İstanbul's arty pie. Here the low lighting, airiness and white whites inspire lots of peck-pecks on the cheeks. Downstairs, the gallery exhibits contemporary art, while the bar-cafe hosts performers in the New Jazz Line Festival (April) and more. There's also good food, cakes and top-grade coffee.

Cafe Enginar *(☎ 212-293 9697, Şah Kapısı Sokak 4)* **Map 16, #145** Dishes US$2-5. This is a refurbished wine store and the perfect spot for an espresso (US$1.50), a bite to eat, such as a club sandwich or vegetable crepe or, of course, a glass of wine (US$2). There's live music here on Wednesday and Friday night (9pm to midnight).

Meyhanes You could spend a budget night out at the meyhanes along Nevizade Sokak for under US$10 per person, but you'd have to be very careful to limit your food and drink. For info, see Meyhanes under Mid-Range later in this chapter.

Otantik *(☎ 212-293 6515, Balo Sokak 1/3)* **Map 16, #74** Dishes US$1-3. Open 9am-2am daily. On the third floor, this friendly Anatolian restaurant has tear-jerking folk music nightly and village decorations – plus the food is good. This is not the groovy Beyoğlu set: At the next table the moustached chaps sway to the sing-along; families, couples and women in headscarves come out on the town here. On weekends the live music goes from 4pm to 1am, during the week it's from 9pm to 1am. Entry is free. Go.

Vegetarian Restaurants Eating food without meat is still a bewildering concept to many İstanbullus.

Nuh'un ambarı *(☎ 212-292 9272, Yeni Çarşı Caddesi 54)* **Map 16, #91** Dishes US$2-6. Open 9am-7.30pm daily, food available noon-7pm. Both simple and unpretentious, this 'green' eatery has the mandatory natural hues, twinkling wildlife music in the background plus excellent food (without the usual over-lashings of oil you find in some Turkish food). Pick and choose from what has been cooked daily in the kitchen. There are heaps of herbal teas, jams and other natural products for sale, as well as general info about environmental issues.

Zencefil *(☎ 212-244 4082, Kurabiye Sokak 3)* **Map 16, #26** Dishes US$2-6. Open 9am-midnight Mon-Sat. This plain small restaurant has reasonable food (zucchini pie, pesto with spaghetti), herb teas and home-made bread. If you're craving a hearty combo salad, this is the place to come.

Mixed Cuisine The bars in Beyoğlu have spawned all the restaurants, and vice versa. Punters come here to cheaply line their stomachs before the alcoholic onslaught of the night begins. Many of the restaurants continue the tradition of looking to Europe for inspiration and serve tasty world-food dishes.

Hala *(☎ 212-293 7531, Çukurlu Çeşme Sokak 26)* **Map 16, #48** Dishes US$1-3. Open 10am-midnight daily. This students' hang-out serves *mantı* (Turkish ravioli) and other mama-cooked favourites in a colourful, bright setting. It's a spot for a quick, value-for-money feed. There's no alcohol served. Look for the traditionally clad woman rolling out mantı dough in the window.

Mercan *(212-245 5574, Balık Pazarı 18)* **Map 16, #80** Dishes US$1.50-3. Open 11am-2am daily. This is a cheap quick-bite place, if the gaudy white-and-red tiles do not frighten you off. It specialises in greasy but tasty *midye tavası* (mussels deep-fried on a skewer) for US$1.50 and a bit more if they're served in a *sandviçli* (in bread). It's in the Balık Pazar (Fish Market), next door to the Çiçek Pasajı.

Pano *(☎ 212-292 6664, Hamalbaşı Caddesi)* **Map 16, #81** Dishes $1.50-3.50. Open noon-2am daily. Although Pano is really a wine bar (see Beyoğlu under Bars in the Entertainment chapter), this talented spot also has top-notch food. With a selection of over 35 mouth-watering meze dishes, you can't complain about variety! Grab a few – the calamari is superb. Come during the day if you want a quiet meal; at night, especially on the weekends, the place is packed.

Marco Paşa *(☎ 212-252 8080, Sadri Alışık Sokak 8)* **Map 16, #68** Dishes US$1-4. Open 8am-midnight daily. If you thought Cennet restaurant (near Sultanahmet) was cheesy, you haven't seen anything yet. You can't miss the stuffed goats outside, but inside it gets worse. Think hectic mess of 'village' decor, fake trees, more taxidermists' delights and the mandatory 'village' women sweating over the gözleme. Feast your eyes.

Atlas Restaurant & Cafe *(☎ 212-292 4813, İstiklal Caddesi 251/1)* **Map 16, #78** Dishes US$1-4. Open 9am-midnight daily. Built by an Armenian architect in 1815, and once the residence of Mr Fethi Okyar (first prime minister of the Turkish Republic), Atlas is now a favourite lunch place serving fine pizzas, burgers and Turkish food and a good-value set lunch for US$3. Some of the seats at the front have small balconies overlooking İstiklal Caddesi. Don't miss the ornate ceilings.

Zarifi *(☎ 212-293 5480, Çukurlu Çeşme Sokak 13)* **Map 16, #49** Dishes US$2-6. Open 7pm-4am daily. Anyone who's anyone is eating Greek plus Armenian dishes at the modern, stark Zarifi. The staff are unflappable, the food good and the wine list excessive. This place also has a long bar where you can pop in for a drink (US$3 plus) and mingle with the great-looking 30-something set. We don't usually review lavatories, but the bright chunky mosaics in the bathrooms deserve a special mention!

Kaktüs *(☎ 212-249 5979, İmam Adnan Sokak 4)* **Map 16, #33** Dishes US$3-6. Open 9am-2am daily. Delicious food, huge serves and a laid-back atmosphere – one of the only problems with Kaktüs is it's a little cramped. The overgrown Kaktüsburger is a favourite, and the menu is so long you may have trouble choosing. Unfortunately the chef gets creative with the schnitzel's batter – rolled oats just don't cut it.

Urban *(☎ 212-252 1325, Kartal Sokak 6)* **Map 16, #79** Dishes US$3-6. Open noon-11pm daily. This split-level trendy cafe-bistro has classical/jazz/soul background music, with the lowest floor backing onto a Byzantine cistern. The speciality is pasta, but there are other meals too, plus a good choice of teas and coffees (no alcohol). The crowd is 35 plus.

Great Hong Kong Restaurant *(☎ 212-244 4088, İnönü Caddesi 12/B)* **Map 16, #12** Lunch buffet US$4; noon-2.30pm daily. Just out of Taksim near the top of İnönü Caddesi on the right-hand side you'll see a large Chinese gateway. Beyond it, down the stairs, this restaurant serves excellent all-you-can-eat Chinese buffet lunches.

Nişantaşı (Map 17)

The beautiful people of Nişantaşı do eat too; but not in the handful of budget eateries for riffraff.

Kahramanmaraş *(☎ 212-225 2962, Teşvikiye Caddesi 139)* **Map 17, #6** Dishes US$0.80-1.50. Open 11am-7pm daily. Very un-Nişantaşı, with dirt-cheap prices, this eat-and-run eatery is small and busy. The menu is limited – *lahmacun* (Arabic soft pizza) and köfte are the specialities.

Macrocenter *(☎ 212-233 0570, Abdi İpekçi Caddesi 24-26)* **Map 17, #7** Dishes US$2-5. Open 8.30am-9pm daily. This mini food court has cheapish eats on a prime piece of real estate. There is a variety of sandwiches, doughnuts, meze, warm eats and drinks. Pay near the exit on your way out.

Ortaköy & Around (Maps 11 & 12)

Near McDonald's on Köprübası Sokak in Ortaköy, there are two rows of snack stands selling *kumpir* (big baked potatoes topped with various sauces and condiments; US$2.50), gözleme (US$1.50) and *midye tavası* (stuffed mussels which can be the equivalent of gastroenteritic hand grenades; US$0.20 each).

Malta Köşkü *(Malta Kiosk; ☎ 212-258 9493, Yıldız Park)* Snacks US$1.50-2.50, mains US$3-7. Open 9am-10pm daily. Restored in 1979, the kiosk is now an outdoor cafe and restaurant with excellent views. No alcoholic beverages are served. (See under Yıldız Şale & Park in the Dolmabahçe Palace to Ortaköy section of the Things to See & Do chapter for directions.)

Üsküdar (Map 19)

This Asian-side suburb has many local eateries to reward you if you've made the effort to come over.

Kız Kulesi *(☎ 216-342 4747)* **Map 19, #18** The tower, just off the Asian mainland, is now a cafe and restaurant serving meals for all budgets. There's fast food, such as kebaps and sandwiches, for US$2.50 to US$3.50, served between 11.30am and 7pm daily. If you'd prefer to have a sit-down meal, there's also a set Turkish lunch served on an upper level for US$9 (1pm to 6pm daily). After 8.30pm your only option is the lower basement restaurant serving a pricey international cuisine set menu for US$50 excluding drinks; book ahead. Although the basement restaurant is atmospheric and stylish (stone walled, comfy chairs) most tables aren't beside the few small, low windows so don't expect views. For information on getting to Kız Kulesi, see Sights on the Asian Shore in the Things to See & Do chapter.

Niyazibey İskender Kebapçı *(☎ 216-310 4821, Ahmediye Meydanı 2)* **Map 19, #26** Dishes US$1.50-6. Open 10am-11pm daily. Niyazibey is spotless, with good service and a large range of meats, but also pide (US$1.50) if you're budgeting. This place is inland, at the corner of Tavukçu Bakkal Sokak near the Akbank.

Huzur Restaurant *(☎ 216-333 3157, Salacak İskele Caddesi 18)* **Map 19, #20** Dishes US$2-10. Open noon-1am daily. Huzur has inviting laid-back charm, excellent food and the added bonus of uninterrupted views over to Old İstanbul, Beyoğlu and Kız Kulesi. There's a rooftop outdoor dining area, and a frilly-curtained room complete with dusty fake plants. It only has a Turkish menu, but you can look in the kitchen to choose the meats, fish and starters. The calamari is superb. If you continue for 200m south of the Salacak boat stop for the Kız Kulesi, you'll see it on the left, up from the road and overlooking the Bosphorus.

Çamlıca Restaurant (☎ *216-443 2198, Büyük Çamlıca)* Dishes US$1-2.50. Open 10am-11pm daily. This prime position remarkably didn't get snatched up into an exclusive enclave; the lovely restaurant has very reasonable prices. Comfy seating is around large table-trays, in restored Ottoman-styled kiosks. Outside, under the shade, in full enjoyment of the views you'll find a ***tea garden*** with cheap drinks and snacks (US$0.50 to US$1) sold during warm weather. (For directions, see under Büyük Çamlıca in the Sights on the Asian Shore section of Things to See & Do chapter.)

Kadıköy (Map 11)

Kadıköy has a good selection of cafes and restaurants.

Cafe Antre (☎ *216-338 3483, Miralay Nazım Sokak 10)* Dishes US$1.50-3.50. Open 8am-4am daily. If you're craving a sandwich, Antre has a good selection of hot and cold choices. With a small garden outside, the charming old house has been lovingly converted into this friendly cafe. It's inland, just off Bahariye Caddesi, the main pedestrian drag.

Denizatı (☎ *216-414 7643, Tarihi Kadıköy İskelesi)* Dishes US$2-4. Open 8am-4am daily. With a prime position right on the dock above the ferry terminal, this restaurant is a real find. It has delicious food (huge sandwiches, salads and Turkish cuisine), good service, live music some nights and awesome views to the Bosphorus and down on to the ferry commuters buzzing back and forth. There's an old-fashioned indoor eating area, plus sunny, or shaded terraces. The only minus is the menu is in Turkish. You'll find it at the dock for the ferries to/from the Kızıl Adalar (Princes' Islands) and Beşiktaş.

PLACES TO EAT – MID-RANGE

Sultanahmet Area (Map 13)

Meyhanes Old İstanbul isn't renowned for its carousing meyhane ways, but there is at least one good option.

Antique Gallery (☎ *212-512 4262, Salkım Söğüt Sokak 18/B)* **Map 13, #72** Dishes US$3-10. Open 8am-1am daily. With fish, meat and a few vegetable dishes, Antique's real draw card is the nightly live classical Turkish music and the many coloured lamps. The food can be hit and miss, but the village-like decor, service and music make up for it.

Mixed Cuisine Sultanahmet has many international restaurants primed for tourists' palates and purses.

Dubb Indian Restaurant (☎ *212-513 7308, İncili Çavuş Sokak 10)* **Map 13, #41** Dishes US$3.50-7. Open noon-midnight daily. Good service, spot-on food and plenty of vegetable dishes keep people flocking back to Dubb. There's a small outdoor eating area, or inside the rooms are spotless and rustic. There's a great selection of curries, bread, kebaps, lassi, tandoori and more. Book at the weekends.

The Sultanahmet area has a bunch of unoriginal renovated houses-cum-restaurants serving a mixed Ottoman and international cuisine. However, the Ottoman dishes are so Europeanised that the Topkapı Palace chefs would certainly be turning in their graves. These restaurants have the same good service, jazz and classical background music, and florally long-winded menus. They all even sprinkle the same garnishes on the plates. Only go to these if you need a rest from real İstanbul, because this is not it. Oh, and they're all primed for couples. These are the restaurants:

Magnaura Café Restaurant (☎ *212-518 7622, Akbıyık Caddesi 27)* **Map 13, #84** Dishes US$4-7. Open 9am-1am daily. Right in the midst of the Cankurtaran hotel area, this place serves European-American dishes with Ottoman accents. It has three floors, and a terrace and street-side eating area. Its decor is mustard, with wispy murals and floorboards. It's quiet and romantic.

Rumeli Café *(☎ 212-512 0008, Ticarethane Sokak 8)* **Map 13, #30** Dishes US$5-10. Open 8am-2am daily. The Rumeli has cool stone walls for hot days and fireplaces for chilly evenings. The menu lists Ottoman food, seafood, some vegetable dishes and international cuisine. The rooms out the back can be a bit cramped. There's a pleasant outdoor eating area. Book ahead.

Mozaik Café Restaurant *(☎ 212-513 6367, İncili Çavuş Sokak 1)* **Map 13, #31** Dishes US$5-16. Open 9am-1am daily. Mozaik is almost a carbon copy of its neighbour, the Rumeli. The menu lists Ottoman and international food, with some vegetable and seafood dishes. Here the music oscillates between jazz and Latin. The service is excellent. There's an outdoor eating area, and a mellow bar below. Book ahead.

Rami *(☎ 212-517 6593, Utangaç Sokak 6)* **Map 13, #95** Dishes US$10-12. Open noon-midnight daily. This poky restored house has several quaint dining rooms decorated with impressionist-style paintings by Turkish painter Rami Uluer (1913–88), but the favoured spot is the rooftop terrace which has a full view of the Blue Mosque. Ottoman specialities such as *hünkâr beğendi* (grilled lamb and rich aubergine puree) or *kağıt kebap* (lamb and vegetables cooked in a paper pouch) are served. Rami is pricey, but the food is really Ottoman, and really good. Book ahead.

Sirkeci & Eminönü (Map 15)

Mixed Cuisine This area of İstanbul doesn't have a great variety of sit-down restaurants, so your best bet is to go elsewhere.

Pandeli *(☎ 212-527 3909, Mısır Çarşısı 1, Eminönü)* **Map 15, #8** Dishes US$3-10. Open noon-3.30pm daily. Over the main entrance (facing the Galata Bridge) of the Mısır Çarşışı, this famous restaurant was founded decades ago by a Greek chef, now long gone to that great kitchen in the sky. He'd be appalled if he knew how overpriced and shoddy the food is now. The small dining rooms panelled in colourful faience are beautiful, and well worth seeing, but we recommend you only stop by for a beer (US$2), wine (US$4) or a cup of tea (US$0.80).

Kumkapı (Map 15)

Meyhanes In Byzantine times, the fishers' harbour called Kontoscalion was due south of Beyazıt. The gate into the city from that port came to be called Kumkapı (Sand Gate) by the Turks. Though the gate is long gone, the district is still filled with fishers who moor their boats in a more modern version of the old harbour. Each afternoon and evening the streets of the neighbourhood resound to the footsteps of people hungry for fish. In fine weather, restaurant tables crowd the narrow streets, and happy diners clatter plates and cutlery between bolts of pungent rakı.

The scene has become a bit too hectic for some, with touts pushing menus and cheesy smiles at you. Ignore them, find a table, order carefully (and don't accept anything you haven't ordered), and you'll enjoy yourself.

The cheapest way to go is by train from Sirkeci train station, though you can also board the train at Cankurtaran. When you get to the Kumkapı train station, leave the station and walk down the most prominent street, which is Ördekli Bakkal Sokak (Grocer with a Duck St).

A taxi driver will probably cruise all the way along the shore road (Kennedy Caddesi), around the old city, in order to enter this congested district from the sea side; figure on US$5 or so from Sultanahmet, US$7 or US$8 from Taksim.

Restaurants Kumkapı has dozens of seafood restaurants, many operated by Turkish citizens of Greek or Armenian ancestry. Among the favourite fish dishes to order is *kılıç şiş*, chunks of swordfish skewered and grilled over charcoal, but there are also fish soups and stews, fish poached with vegetables, pan-fried fish and pickled fish. Stroll along until you find a restaurant that catches your eye; the cheaper ones are in the side streets. Expect to part with US$20 to US$40 per person for the meal, appetisers, salads, drink, sweet, tax and tip all included. The restaurants are open from noon to midnight daily.

Minas *(☎ 212-522 9646, Samsa Sokak 7)* **Map 15, #49** Minas, facing the square, is not one of the cheaper places; you can dine for a lot less elsewhere, but it has a prime viewing position.

Köşem Cemal Restaurant *(☎ 212-520 1229, Samsa Sokak 1)* **Map 15, #50** Also facing the square, this restaurant has white tablecloths, good careful service and a mixed clientele of Turks and tourists.

Ördekli Bakkal Sokak, which runs from the train station to Kumkapı Square, the neighbourhood square, has another half-dozen good seafood restaurants. In a street off to the left, ***Yengeç Balık Lokantası*** *(☎ 212-516 3227, Telli Odalar Sokak 6)* **(Map 15, #48)** has good fish and service. Further along, on the right, ***Liman Balık Restaurant*** *(☎ 212-517 2318, Çapariz Sokak 3)* **(Map 15, #51)**, has similar fare.

If you arrive by taxi, you may get dropped near Çakmaktaşı Sokak, in which case calamari devotees should head to ***Denizkızı Balık Restaurant*** *(☎ 212-518 8659, Çakmaktaşı Sokak 3/5)* **(Map 15, #52)**.

Western Districts (Maps 14 & 18)

There are a few decent places to eat out in the western suburbs.

Zeyrekhane *(☎ 212-532 2778)* Dishes US$3-10. Open 9am-11pm Tues-Sun. This restaurant, which is near Zeyrek Camii, has an outdoor garden with cushioned couches to soak up the superb views. It has tasty Ottoman food (fancy quail kebap served with eggplant?), and efficient, but curt service.

Asitane Restaurant *(☎ 212-534 8414)* Dishes US$3.50-9. Beneath the Kariye Oteli, near the Kariye Müzesi (Chora Church), this restaurant is set in a pretty garden, and there's a stylish indoor part too. The food is a mix of international and Turkish dishes – the baked goose may tempt you.

Beyoğlu (Map 16)

Meyhanes At Galatasaray, at İstiklal Caddesi 172, is the main entrance to the famous ***Çiçek Pasajı*** (Flower Passage) **(Map 16, #77)**, a cluster of taverna-restaurants open 10am to midnight every day in the courtyard of a historic building.

The Çiçek Pasajı has been tarted up for tourists, but it's still popular with rowdy Turkish groups of fortysomethings who come here on the weekends to hear the fasıl, eat fish, break into dance and, after copious amounts of alcohol, grope each other. It's fun to watch. Overcharging is not uncommon and be cautious with locals who chat you up and propose outings or nightclubs, which may turn into rip-offs (see the boxed text 'Nightlife Rip-Offs' in the Entertainment chapter).

On the weekends the Çiçek Pasajı is packed so you'll probably just have to get a table where you can. ***Stop Restaurant*** serves decent food, the ***Paryon*** close by, is similar. Dishes should cost from US$2 to US$7.

The 20-to-35 set hangs out in the meyhanes deeper in the market. Walk along Sahne Sokak to the first street on the right, Nevizade Sokak. This street is wall-to-wall restaurants with pavement tables; on Thursday, Friday and Saturday nights in fine weather you can barely walk down it. Packs of rakı-swilling young professionals eye each other off, sing to the fasıl, scoff meze and chatter madly. Vendors stroll up and down selling a weird collection of wares and every so often a football chant drowns everything out. It's great fun.

The restaurants charge about US$2 to US$3 for meze, about twice that for kebaps; ask the prices of fish before you order. Alcohol is served enthusiastically. The restaurants are open from noon to midnight daily.

Two restaurants with excellent food and service are ***Ney'le Mey'le*** *(☎ 212-249 8103, Nevizade Sokak 12)* **(Map 16, #75)** and ***İmroz Restaurant*** *(☎ 212-249 9073, Nevizade Sokak 24)* **(Map 16, #75)**.

Vegetarian Beyoğlu is the best place to find vegetarian food.

Nature & Peace *(☎ 212-252 8609, Büyükparmakkapı Sokak 21)* **Map 16, #40** Dishes US$5.50-7. Open 11am-midnight daily. All mains (eg, green lentil balls, vegie cocktail) are served with complimentary soup and salad. Herbal teas cost US$1.50. The decor is strictly old Pera in contrast to the touchy-feely name. The really incredible cheesecake (US$2.50) will leave you feeling neither natural nor peaceful – enjoy every mouthful!

Mixed Cuisine In İstanbul, mid-range cuisine is one step up in price from budget, but often two steps up in quality.

Soho Supper Club *(☎ 212-245 0152, Meşelik Sokak 14)* **Map 16, #46** Dishes US$3.50-8. Open 10am-2am daily. Slick Soho has a Clark Gable breakfast, David Bowie sandwich, and a JR Burger – does anyone want to tell them these folk aren't hip any more? Ignore the try-hard menu, the food is excellent.

Four Seasons *(Dört Mevsim; ☎ 212-293 3941, İstiklal Caddesi 509)* **Map 16, #131** Dishes US$4-8. Open noon-3pm & 6pm-midnight, Mon-Sat. Almost in Tünel Square, this place is popular with the diplomatic set at lunch time. Under Turkish and English management, the food is continental with several delicious concessions to Turkish cuisine; preparation and service are first rate. Delicious starters cost US$1.50 to US$4, and the mains include quail and steak Diane.

Hacı Baba Restaurant *(☎ 212-244 1886, İstiklal Caddesi 49)* **Map 16, #23** Dishes US$3-7. Open noon-12.30am daily. Quaint and vibrant, this 1920s restaurant has four rooms including a pleasant leafy terrace. It's busy with tourists for good reasons: the menu is long and varied, the food is very good, the service is usually competent and some English is spoken. You're welcome to have a look in the kitchen if you need help to choose your meal or you can serve your own plate of cold meze for US$4.50.

Hacı Abdullah *(☎ 212-293 8561, Sakızağacı Caddesi 17)* **Map 16, #69** Dishes US$3-7. Open noon-10.30pm daily. Hacı's is a Beyoğlu institution, having been in business a century. Its dining rooms are simple, service is friendly and single women are welcomed. The Turkish and Ottoman cuisine is outstanding (the desserts superb) with a varied menu of traditional dishes otherwise rarely found in restaurants, all served on Hacı's very own crockery.

Nişantaşı (Map 17)

Nişantaşı has posh restaurants that come and go with the fashions, though at least one has been around for years.

Hasır *(☎ 212-225 4545, Valikonağı Caddesi 65)* **Map 17, #3** Dishes US$4.50-7. Open 10am-midnight daily. The menu here is part Turkish, part international, served in posh but not overdone surroundings. It has jazz background music, good service and tasty food too. The better dining room is the one upstairs.

Ortaköy (Map 11)

If you've made it out to Ortaköy your effort will be amply rewarded with tasty eats.

İlhami'nin Yeri *(İlhami's Place; ☎ 212-260 8080, Osmanzade Sokak 6)* Dishes US$4-8. Open noon-1am daily. This is one of the last true meyhanes playing fasıl music in the area. It's a white-tableclothed affair specialising in seafood, but meze and meat dishes are served too. The musicians usually play nightly from 8pm onwards. You won't be charged an entrance fee but you will be charged US$0.50 to go to the toilet – so don't drink too much! The food is good, but the service is hair-wrenchingly bad.

Down by the water at İskele Meydanı, several restaurants and cafes line the little square beside the Bosphorus and the pretty Ortaköy Camii. This is a very atmospheric spot to eat, drink and people-watch. The places closest to the mosque are cheap cafes with games to play. Those a bit further away from the mosque are cafes with more substantial food (no alcohol), those furthest away are full-blown restaurants with alcohol. (In Turkey alcohol cannot be consumed within 100m of a mosque.)

The ***Çay Bahçesi*** *(İskele Meydanı)* closest to the mosque, has cheap tea (US$0.50), coffee and backgammon. These cafes are popular with uni students.

Cafe First Class *(☎ 212-259 0751, İskele Meydanı 40)* Dishes US$3-5. Open 7.30am-1am daily. Three floors, all with good views over the square, plus an outdoor eating area make this cafe stand out. It has a range of tasty salads, hot and cold sandwiches and more substantial food such as meatballs and pizzas.

Çınaraltı Cafe Restaurant *(☎ 212-261 4616, İskele Meydanı 44-46)* Dishes US$3-9. Open noon-1am Mon-Fri, 7.30am-1am

Sat-Sun. Here the fish prices are clearly marked, but there are also meat dishes (try beefsteak with cream in crepe) and tasty meze all served on fancy white tablecloths. *Çınaraltı* means 'beneath the plane tree', and the resilient tree bursts through the roof of the restaurant to prove it.

PLACES TO EAT – TOP END

Sultanahmet Area (Map 13)

The Sultanahmet area doesn't have a huge range of top-end eateries as this end of the scale is well catered for in the top hotels over in, or near, Beyoğlu.

Sarnıç *(☎ 212-512 4291, Soğukçeşme Sokak)* **Map 13, #53** Dishes US$11-24. Open 8pm-midnight Tues-Sun Aug-June. The baronial fireplace hardly belongs in this sunken stone cistern, but the rosy glow is welcome on rainy evenings. A nightly piano and violin recital help set the mood, but the dark, candle-lit restaurant barely needs more ambience. The menu is a blend of French and Turkish cuisine. Although some have complained that the food is a bit overpriced, none complain about the service or venue.

Hotel Arcadia *(☎ 212-516 9696, Hotel Arcadia, Dr İmran Öktem Caddesi 1)* **Map 13, #17** Dishes US$12-25. Open 9am-midnight daily. The restaurant of the Hotel Arcadia has a truly breathtaking view of the Blue Mosque late in the afternoon, and good meals and service.

Beyoğlu & Beyond (Maps 16 & 12)

Mixed Cuisine Top dollar buys top international cuisine, whipped up by chefs who have often studied overseas.

Great Hong Kong Restaurant *(☎ 212-244 4088, İnönü Caddesi 12/B)* **Map 16, #12** All-you-can-eat lunch buffet US$4, dinner dishes US$10-15. Open noon-2.30pm lunch, 6pm-11.30pm dinner. Just out of Taksim near the top of İnönü Caddesi on the right-hand side you'll see a large Chinese gateway. Beyond it, down the stairs, the restaurant serves good Chinese dishes.

Café du Levant *(☎ 212-250 8938, Hasköy Caddesi 27, Sütlüce)* Dishes US$12-24. Open noon-10.30pm Tues-Sun. This elegant restaurant is on the grounds of the Rahmi M Koç Müzesi in Sütlüce, about 4km west of Taksim Square. The indoor-outdoor French bistro has tasty gourmet food and the service is excellent.

Udonya *(☎ 212-256 9318, Kemankeş Caddesi, Karaköy)* Dishes US$15-55. Open noon-2.30pm & 6.30pm-11pm Mon-Sat. Primed for sushi addicts, Udonya serves up fixes of 14 pieces for US$23, or 24 for US$55 in simple, stark decor. Bargain hunters will like the set meals though: Depending on the daily menu, a set lunch can cost US$15 to US$20, or dinner US$35 to US$40.

Panorama Restaurant *(☎ 212-251 4696, The Marmara, Taksim Square)* **Map 16, #14** Dishes US$12-30. Open 11am-midnight daily. Living up to its name, the Panorama on the 20th floor has panoramic views plus excellent food, plain decor and top service. Make sure you get a table beside the window.

Boğaziçi Borsa Restaurant *(☎ 212-232 4201, Darülbedai Sokak, Harbiye)* **Map 17, #13** Open noon-11.30pm daily. Dishes US$5.50-14. This modern place is just north of the İstanbul Hilton in the Lütfi Kırdar Kongre ve Sergi Salonu (convention centre), and serves superb Ottoman specialities and new-wave Turkish cuisine in simple, but stylish surroundings. Book ahead.

Liman *(☎ 212-292 3992, Rıhtım Caddesi 52/3, Karaköy)* **Map 16, #155** Dishes US$10-15. Open 11am-midnight daily. Classic 1930s, classy Liman has good food, excellent service and exceptional views of the comings and goings of the Eminönü and Karaköy docks. It's well worth splashing out here. Turkish food is the speciality.

Tugra Restaurant *(☎ 212-258 3377, Çırağan Caddesi 84, Beşiktaş)* Dishes US$20-40. Open 7.30pm-11.30pm daily. Set in the original palace part of the Çırağan Palace Hotel, this restaurant specialises in top-notch Ottoman cuisine. With immaculate table settings (crisp white tablecloths, sparkling glasses etc), perfect waiting staff and excellent food, this is a classy find. The Bosphorus views just add to the experience.

Entertainment

In the last decade İstanbul has replaced its festering hang-outs with almost too many funky bars and clubs. From clubbing in stark techno doof dens to catching a world-class band or wobbling your belly to dance, İstanbul now has it all. Nightlife centres on Beyoğlu – take a stroll down İstiklal Caddesi on a Thursday, Friday or Saturday night if you don't believe us. But it doesn't stop there. Along the Bosphorus more joints have opened, with *barlar sokaks* (bar streets) pumping it out till the early morning – try Ortaköy for size.

But İstanbul has much more than bars and clubs. The theatre scene thrives (though unfortunately for travellers it's mostly in Turkish) while massive concert halls, and İstanbul's superb historic venues regularly host world-class international and local orchestras, ballet and more. You can catch folk dance, music and the latest Hollywood flick. And regular international festivals of music, film and dance seem to be on constant rotation.

And then there are the dirt-cheap or free options such as a must-do ferry ride across the Bosphorus or strolling through one of the many charming overgrown parks.

VENUES

İstanbul's major venues for concerts and performances of dance, classic music and opera include the following:

Atatürk Cultural Centre *(AKM, Atatürk Kültür Merkezi;* ☎ *212-245 2590, Taksim Square)* **Map 16, #4** Plonked beside Taksim Square, this late-1960s arts centre – some might call it ugly – hosts a variety of performances: theatre, ballet, opera and more. Sneak a look at the spindly staircase and pop into the box office (*gişeler;* open 10am to 6pm daily) to see what's on.

Aya İrini Kilisesi *(Church of Divine Peace; First Court of Topkapı Palace, Sultanahmet)* **Map 13, #56** Big-name classical events – orchestras, choirs – make the most of the acoustics in this ancient venue. A board outside lists upcoming events and contact details (you usually buy tickets through Biletix – see the boxed text 'Buying Tickets').

Cemal Reşit Rey Konser Salonu *(Cemal Reşit Rey Concert Hall;* ☎ *212-232 9830,* Ⓦ *www.crrks.org, Darülbedai Sokak, Harbiye)* **Map 17, #10** Pop in to pick up one of the monthly guides which lists upcoming events – possibly ballet, folk music, opera – with reviews (in English) and prices. The box office is open 10am to 7.30pm daily, or you can buy tickets from Biletix.

Lütfi Kırdar Concert Hall *(Convention Centre; Lütfi Kırdar Kongre ve Sergi Salonu;* ☎ *212-296 3055, Darülbedai Sokak, Harbiye)* **Map 17, #13** Originally built for the 1948 World Wrestling Championships, this huge refurbished concert hall hosts conferences, the Borusan İstanbul Philharmonic Orchestra, and events for the International İstanbul Music Festival.

Sunken Cistern *(Yerebatan Sarnıçı;* ☎ *212-522 1259, Yerebatan Caddesi 13)* **Map 13, #43** The cistern occasionally hosts low-key Turkish classic music concerts in summer. The venue is certainly original, so get along to a concert if you can. Upcoming events are advertised at the cistern's ticket office.

Tarık Zafer Tunaya Kültür Merkezi *(Tarık Zafer Tunaya Cultural Centre;* ☎ *212-293 1270, Şahkulu Bostanı Sokak 8, Tünel)* **Map 16, #130** With regular Turkish flicks as well as lectures, this place also has Turkish classic music once or twice a week (shows start at 6pm or 7pm). Buy tickets beforehand at the venue.

Outdoor venues for summer performances include the following:

Cemil Topuzlu Açık Hava Tiyatrosu *(Cemil Topuzlu Open-Air Theatre;* ☎ *212-296 3610, Taşkışla Caddesi, Harbiye)* **Map 17, #14** This place packs in 4000 and has international (such as PJ Harvey, Sting) and big-name local acts. It's just north of the İstanbul Hilton.

Buying Tickets

Buying tickets for events in a foreign country can be somewhat daunting when your grasp of the language is limited to 'thank you' and 'sorry, I'm married'. Most venues sell tickets at the box office, which allows you to deal face to face with the seller. This way you can gesticulate (a prerequisite to helping you be understood), and it also means you can check out the advertising literature, photographs and make double-sure the performance (if verbal) is going to be in a language you understand.

If you can't make it to the box office, or there isn't one for the venue, try **Biletix** (*☎ 216-454 555, W www.biletix.com*). It's a major ticket seller for all kinds of events from festivals, big-name concerts (the likes of Madonna, Julio Iglesias – yes, surprisingly his tickets aren't free) to football matches. Biletix outlets are found in many spots throughout the city – in Vakkorama in Akmerkez, at the Raksotek Mağazası in Ortaköy – but the most convenient for travellers is the one in the Vakkorama centre, at İstiklal Caddesi 162, Beyoğlu. Alternatively, you could buy your ticket by credit card on Biletix's Web site and collect the tickets from the venue before the concert, but this usually means standing in long queues.

Tickets for local theatre range from about US$2 to US$3; local opera, dance and ballet tickets cost about US$5 to US$7; international acts, whether part of an international festival or not, start at the US$8 mark, rising to US$18 and occasionally US$50. And don't come to İstanbul thinking you'll save on tickets for your hero Julio Iglesias – concerts like his will set you back US$90.

Rumeli Hisarı (*☎ 212-263 5305, Yahya Kemal Caddesi 42*) **Map 11** Concerts here, usually jazz or Turkish classical music, are set in leafy grounds with the backdrop of Rumeli Hisarı's ancient walls. Rumeli Hisarı is north of Bebek on the Bosphorus.

CLASSICAL MUSIC

İstanbul has a lively classical music scene. Traditional Turkish music, or folk music, is popular, as is European classical music played by groups such as the İstanbul Symphony Orchestra. There are also regular visits by international orchestras and chamber ensembles. Both the Atatürk Cultural Centre and Cemal Reşit Rey Konser Salonu are good starting points for these events (see their contact details under Venues).

Another option is the free concerts held at the ***Italian Cultural Centre*** (*İtalyan Kültür Merkezi; ☎ 212-293 9848, fax 251 0749, Meşrutiyet Caddesi 161, Tepebaşı*). These regular, low-key performances are mainly organised by the Borusan Centre for Culture & Arts (see Art Galleries later in this chapter) and feature piano recitals, ensembles and the Borusan Chamber Orchestra.

Festivals

International İstanbul Music Festival (*☎ 212-293 3133, fax 249 5667, W www.istfest.org, İstiklal Caddesi 146, Beyoğlu*) Tickets US$8-50. Held in early June to early July, this is İstanbul's premier event. World-class performers meet some of the city's finest locations – Aya İrini Kilisesi, Atatürk Cultural Centre – and the mix of soloists, virtuosos, orchestras and dance troupes showcases the classic to the contemporary. Big names have included Philip Glass, Kiri Te Kanawa and the New York Philharmonic Orchestra, but the list changes every year, as does the focus, eg, French or Italian music. Check out the program on the excellent Web site. Tickets can be bought from Biletix.

Yapı Kredi Festival (*☎ 212-252 4700, W www.ykykultur.com.tr*) Tickets US$12-22. This is not really a festival but about 12 bank-backed art events that occur over the course of the year. Concerts include flamenco dancing, ballet or classical music and more. Tickets can be bought between 9am and 5pm Monday to Saturday at the Yapı Kredi Bookshop (Map 16, #86), İstiklal Caddesi 285, Galatasaray. The Web site has a general blurb in English, with the most recent concert (in Turkish) under 'Festival'.

ART GALLERIES

İstanbul has a thriving contemporary art scene and because there isn't a national gallery here, small independent galleries exhibit the work. Most galleries are in Beyoğlu and all exhibitions are free. To see paintings older than a few decades, visit the İstanbul Museum of Painting & Sculpture in Beşiktaş; see the Dolmabahçe Palace to Ortaköy section in the Things to See & Do chapter for details. For more information on Turkish painting see Arts in the Facts about İstanbul chapter.

Asmalımescit Sanat Galerisi *(☎ 212-249 6979, Sofyalı Sokak 5, Tünel)* **Map 16, #123** Open 11am-7pm daily. Set in an older house, this gallery exhibits local artists in the small rooms.

Borusan Sanat Galerisi *(☎ 212-292 0655, **W** www.borusansanat.com, İstiklal Caddesi 421)* Open 9am-7pm Mon-Sat. This gallery, part of the Borusan Centre for Culture & Arts, showcases Turkish work, often as mixed artist exhibitions. It also occasionally has big-name international exhibitions too.

Galeri Artist *(☎ 212-251 9163, Altıpatlar Sokak 26, Çukurcuma)* **Map 16, #58** Open 11am-6.30pm Thur-Tues. Jammed between antique shops, this tiny gallery mostly has local artists showing for the first time.

Schneidertemple Art Centre *(Schneidertempel Sanat Merkezı; ☎ 212-252 5157, Felek Sokak 1)* **Map 16, # 152** Open 10.30am-6.30pm Tues-Sat, noon-6.30pm Sun. Schneidertemple exhibits İstanbul's Jewish art and includes frequent exhibitions from abroad.

Taksim Sanat Galerisi *(☎ 212-245 2068, Cumhuriyet Caddesi 23, Taksim)* **Map 17, #47** Open 10am-7pm Mon-Sat. Pop in on your way past to visit this medium-sized exhibition space. It specialises in local work.

Yapı Kredi Bankası Gallery *(☎ 212-252 4700, İstiklal Caddesi 285, Galatasaray)* **Map 16, #86** Open 10am-7pm Mon-Fri, noon-5pm Sat, 1pm-5pm Sun. The convenient location makes dropping into this gallery easy; international artists often exhibit in this roomy, airy space.

Festivals

International İstanbul Biennial *(☎ 212-293 3133, fax 249 5667, **W** www.istfest.org, İstiklal Caddesi 146, Beyoğlu)* Admission free. İstanbul's biennial brings together over 65 international and local artists from more than 45 countries to explore themes such as cultural differences and art installations in traditional spaces. In 1999 the biennial entitled 'The Passion and The Wave' explored the aftermath of the earthquake in a human context. Venues vary but usually include the Sunken Cistern, Aya İrini Kilisesi at Topkapı Palace and art galleries. In 2003, the biennial will take place in mid-September and last for about a month.

FOLK DANCE & MUSIC

Turks are enthusiastic folklore fans and many are still close enough to their traditions to be able to jump in and dance along at a performance. Unfortunately folklore concerts aren't a regular fixture in İstanbul's entertainment scene; however, a couple of concert halls around town do occasionally have inexpensive performances. Contact the Cemal Reşit Rey Konser Salonu or the Tarık Zafer Tunaya Kültür Merkezi (see Venues earlier in this chapter) to see what's on.

The only other option is the cheesy, touristy 'Turkish Shows' which provide a snapshot of Turkey's traditional dances and belly dancing. These are designed to fleece you, but most people have fun anyway. All three venues listed below provide free pick-up from your hotel. You must book ahead.

Gar *(☎ 212-588 4046, **e** garmusichall@superonline.com, Mustafa Kemal Caddesi 3, Yenikapı)* **Map 14** Gar is one of the cheaper places but its shows get good reviews. The show runs from 9pm to midnight daily and costs US$50 with dinner, or US$35 for just the show.

Orient House *(☎ 212-517 6163, **W** www.orienthouseistanbul.com, Tiyatro Caddesi 27, Beyazıt)* **Map 15, #45** Orient is popular because it's close to Sultanahmet and its publicity peddlers have sprinkled brochures and the promise of attractive commissions to most Sultanahmet hotels – but it also gets good reviews! The five-course meal and performance costs from US$60 to US$75, depending on who you talk to; try bargaining.

Kervansaray *(☎ 212-246 0818, **W** www.kervansaraytr.com, Cumhuriyet Caddesi 30,*

Harbiye) **Map 17, #21** On the north side of the İstanbul Hilton arcade, this is a club of long standing with decent food (five-course meal) and a good show at US$75 per person. The dinner starts at 7.30pm, the show at 9pm.

BELLY DANCE

Although belly dancing has a long, wobbly and undulating history, contrary to popular belief it's not strictly a Turkish dance. It's said to have originated in Egypt as a meditative-erotic dance to entertain the elite in life and death (tomb paintings of dancers have been found). It was brought to Turkey during the Ottoman Empire. Today in İstanbul it's mainly tourist fodder, and although it's entertaining – and pretty sexy – the dancers are usually second-rate, and you won't see a performance of the art at anywhere near its best. Both ***Orient Hostel*** and the ***Yücelt Interyouth Hostel*** have free shows starring 'the best belly dancer in İstanbul' – don't be fooled. See Folk Dance & Music for more belly-dancing venues.

BALLET & OPERA

Ballet and opera have a keen following in İstanbul and there are regular performances by home-grown and international artists. The Atatürk Cultural Centre and the Cemal Reşit Rey Konser Salonu hold most of the performances so make these your first stop for information.

The İstanbul State Opera has a season running from October to May with some extra performances during the International İstanbul Music Festival. Mozart's *Abduction from the Seraglio* is one of its star performances. The İstanbul State Ballet usually performs classic ballets such as the *Nutcracker* at the Atatürk Cultural Centre.

If you miss out on a live performance, the ***Aksanat Kültür Merkezi*** **(Map 16, 27)** *(Aksanat Cultural Centre; ☎ 212-252 3500, İstiklal Caddesi 16, Taksim)* regularly shows DVDs of famous ballets and operas such as the *Nutcracker* and *Swan Lake*.

Festivals

International İstanbul Dance Festival *(Cemal Reşit Rey Konser Salonu; ☎ 212-232 9830, Ⓦ www.crrks.org, Darülbedai Sokak, Harbiye)* Tickets US$4.50-9. This is a small new festival of ballet and modern dance held over a few days in early March with performances each night from Turkey and abroad. Tickets can be bought from the Cemal Reşit Rey Concert Hall or Biletix.

THEATRE

The Turks are enthusiastic theatregoers, and seem to have a special genius for dramatic art. The problem for the foreign visitor, of course, is language. If you're a true theatre buff you might well enjoy a performance of a familiar classic, provided you know the play well enough to follow the action. Stop by the box office at the Atatürk Cultural Centre to see what's on. Your best chance of seeing theatre in a language you understand is at the International İstanbul Theatre Festival.

Festivals

International İstanbul Theatre Festival *(☎ 212-293 3133, fax 249 5667, Ⓦ www.istfest.org, İstiklal Caddesi 146, Beyoğlu)* Tickets US$5-12. The festival takes place from mid-May for about two weeks every two years from 2002. Dominated by local theatre groups, it mixes classic, experimental and musical performances with workshops and exhibitions. The local cast have shared the festival with such names as Marcel Marceau, Indonesian groups and Japanese Noh theatre.

CINEMA

İstiklal Caddesi, between Taksim and Galatasaray, is the heart of İstanbul's cinema *(sinema)* district.

Films are mostly shown in English with Turkish subtitles, but double-check at the box office in case the film has Turkish *(Türkçe)* dubbing. For movie listings, see the *Turkish Daily News*.

When possible, buy your tickets a few hours in advance. Tickets cost US$3.50 for adults, US$2.50 for students – some places offer reduced rates on Monday and Wednesday. Also, the usher will expect a small tip for showing you to your seat.

General Release

Many films shown in İstanbul are Hollywood boy-meets-girl flicks, but tear-jerky Turkish melodramas are also popular.

AFM Fitaş (Map 16, #28; ☎ 212-249 0166) İstiklal Caddesi 24-26, Fitaş Pasajı. AFM is a large complex with five cinemas in one.

Atlas (Map 16, #73; ☎ 212-252 8576) İstiklal Caddesi 209, Kuyumcular Pasajı. Busy and bustling, Atlas shows the standard fare in standard surrounds.

Emek (Map 16, #72; ☎ 212-293 8439) İstiklal Caddesi, Yeşilçam Sokak 5. Emek is a charming cinema, and one of İstanbul's oldest.

Rexx (Map 11; ☎ 216-336 0112) Sakızgülü Sokak 20-22, Kadıköy. This cinema, on the Asian side of İstanbul, has standard flicks, but it does show some films during the İstanbul International Film Festival.

Şafak Sinemaları (Map 13, #4; ☎ 212-516 2660) Divan Yolu 134, Çemberlitaş. This seven-screen cinema is the closest to Sultanahmet, which is only a 10-minute walk along Divan Yolu. Enter via the menswear arcade.

Sinepop (Map 16, #71; ☎ 212-251 1176) İstiklal Caddesi, Yeşilçam Sokak 22. Sinepop lacks the style of Emek, close by, but is more comfortable.

Arthouse Films

If you prefer movies with more brain than Hollywood brawn, head to the following cinemas:

Aksanat Kültür Merkezi (Map 16, #27; Aksanat Cultural Centre; ☎ 212-252 3500) İstiklal Caddesi 16, Taksim. In the Akbank building on İstiklal Caddesi, Aksanat shows movies – mainly classics – as well as DVDs of concerts (Bon Jovi, for example, but don't let that put you off), ballet, opera and theatre.

Alkazar Sinema Merkezi (☎ 212-293 2466) İstiklal Caddesi 179. A good selection of arty movies are screened in Alkazar's plush, cosy interior. It's popular with uni students and expats.

Atatürk Kitaplığı (☎ 212-249 0945) Mete Caddesi 45, Taksim. Classic foreign black-and-whites plus arthouse films are sometimes shown at 6pm or 7pm at this venue. Some movies have Turkish subtitles, others have Turkish dubbing – find out before you buy your ticket.

Bilgi Üniversitesi (☎ 212-293 5010, **W** www.bilgi.edu.tr) İnönü Caddesi 28, Şişli. This student haunt shows an excellent variety of films: shorts, manga, black-and-white classics and more. Check out the Web site for details.

Goethe Institut and **Institut Français d'Istanbul** have films in German and French (respectively), but sometimes in English too. For contact details see Cultural Centres & Libraries in the Facts for the Visitor chapter.

Festivals

International İstanbul Film Festival *(☎ 212-293 3133, fax 249 5667,* **W** *www.istfest.org, İstiklal Caddesi 146, Beyoğlu)* Tickets US$3-5. Last two weeks of April. In 1982 the İstanbul Film Festival meant a handful of film lovers, watching a handful of flicks. Since then the festival has blossomed, and it now shows over 170 films in venues mainly in Beyoğlu. International movies dominate the program, but the highlight for the traveller should be the Turkish films, which all have English subtitles. For film reviews, screening details and other information check out the Web site.

BARS

İstanbul has a plethora of bars, and most of them double as cafes by day. Many of the bars are sleek and modern, with decoration inspired by European interior design, but some are set in renovated Ottoman buildings. As with drinking holes anywhere in the world, each bar tends to attract its own set of regular barflies.

Sultanahmet Area (Map 13)

Cheers Bar *(☎ 0532-409 6369, Akbıyık Caddesi 20, Cankurtaran)* **Map 13, #77** Admission free. Open noon-2am daily. This tourist hang-out is a skinny terrace with two levels decked out mock-renovation style with exposed bricks and chipped plaster. The cheap booze (US$2) is accompanied by 100% foreign music. There's an outdoor seating area.

Orient Bar *(☎ 212-518 0789, Akbıyık Caddesi 13, Cankurtaran)* **Map 13, #74** Admission free. Open noon-2am daily. Bursting with backpackers, the Orient Bar fires up nightly into a boy-meets-girl boozy dance den. A belly dancer performs every night at 9pm; here it's a lot about breasts and little to do with talent, though most people enjoy it. There are nargileh pipes to suck on and beer costs US$2.

ENTERTAINMENT

Ayazma Bar *(☎ 212-516 6185, Akbıyık Caddesi 40, Cankurtaran)* **Map 13, #86** Admission free. Open 6pm-1am daily. Small, packed and popular with twentysomething locals, the chocolate-coloured Ayazma Bar nearly splits at the seams when the football (soccer) is screened. Beer costs US$2.

Sultan Pub *(☎ 212-528 1719, Divan Yolu 2, Sultanahmet)* **Map 13, #40** Admission free. This spot is popular with thirtysomethings who come to chat, sit outdoors and enjoy the views to Aya Sofya and the Blue Mosque. It's a quietish, busy spot.

Theodora Bar *(☎ 212-520 1035, Alemdar Caddesi 2, Sultanahmet)* **Map 13, #51** Admission free. Open 11am-1am daily, happy hour 5pm-7pm. This Brit-style bar has a large, quietish upstairs area and a fake cellar that fires up after 11pm for dancing (with a mix of Turkish and Euro pop). The service can be slow, but upstairs is a good spot for a quiet drink – if you can handle the cheesy cover songs from the musician (from 9.30pm nightly). Drinks start at US$2 and food is available.

Beyoğlu (Map 16)

James Joyce Irish Pub *(☎ 212-244 0241, W www.irishpubjamesjoyce.com, Zambak Sokak 6)* **Map 16, #25** US$9 Fri-Sat. Open 9am-1am Sun-Thur, 9am-3am Fri-Sat, happy hour noon-8pm daily. Decked out in cliched Irish pub paraphernalia, the busy James Joyce has Irish grog (US$7 to US$11) and a lively bunch of foreign and Turkish revellers. On Friday and Saturday nights, live music – a mixture of rock'n'roll and dance – runs from 11pm to 3am. Beers cost US$3 (US$2 during happy hour) and food is available (all-day breakfast US$4.50).

Hayal Kahvesi *(☎ 212-244 2558, Büyükparmakkapı Sokak 19)* **Map 16, #41** Admission US$7 Fri-Sat. Open 10am-2am daily. Check out this place, where gilded local 20- to 35-year-olds cram in to drink, jostle and be merry. Here, Turk pop and one-hit wonders of the '80s are revived (unfortunately) by the band on Friday and Saturday nights.

Rio Bravo *(☎ 212-292 9269, İstiklal Caddesi 303)* **Map 16, #95** Admission free. Open noon-2am daily. This huge bar, overdone with mock Brit-pub decor, has live Latin-'80s-Turk pop music from 9pm to 1.30am Wednesday to Saturday. The live music gets 80% of the 25-and-over crowd up and dancing. Join in because drinks are expensive (US$4 and rising).

Pano *(☎ 212-292 6664, Hamalbaşı Caddesi, Galatasaray)* **Map 16, #81** Admission

Women-Friendly Bars

Going out as a solo woman, or even as a group of women, can be a bit intimidating in a Muslim country. But İstanbul is very relaxed and welcoming and you'll have a great time provided you follow a few simple rules:

- If you leave the bar after 9pm, don't walk to your hotel unless it's very close; ask a member of staff to ring a taxi for you.
- Avoid casual eye contact. If you are groped, say *'Ayıp!'* (ah-**yuhp**) which means 'Shame on you!' and walk away.
- If you want to be left alone in a bar and someone comes up to talk, say: *'Yalnız kalmak istiyorum'* ('I want to be alone'). If that doesn't work, try: *'Beni yalnız bırak'* ('Leave me alone'). If the message still isn't getting through, ask the bar staff to help you out.
- Stick to bars in areas regularly frequented by tourists and/or Turkish women, eg, Sultanahmet and Beyoğlu. Don't enter bars where all the customers are male.
- Read the Women Travellers section in the Facts for the Visitor chapter for tips on how to dress and behave.

All the cafes recommended in this book are female-friendly spaces. For bars in Sultanahmet try **Orient Bar**, **Cheers Bar** and the **Sultan Pub**. All these spots are used to seeing foreign women out on their own and you shouldn't get harassed. In Beyoğlu head to **Bilsak 5 Kat**, **Jazz Cafe**, **Kaktüs** or the **James Joyce Irish Pub**. These places are mostly frequented by locals, including plenty of Turkish women, and each also has a bar, which is a good prop for people sitting on their own.

free. Open noon-2am daily. Pano is on a winning combination: oodles of atmosphere, good service, excellent food and affordability. During the day it's a quiet bar, at night it's standing room only. Everyone's here (uni students, casual business sorts, expats) to enjoy the cheap, tasty wine at US$3.50 a bottle. Check out the ornate ceiling.

Bilsak 5 Kat *(☎ 212-293 3774, Soğancı Sokak 7/5, Cihangir)* **Map 16, #54** Admission free. Open 4.30pm-2am daily. Top views shoot its ratings high, but the Bilsak has more than views: plush maroon retro finishes; picture windows; techno/bebop/fusion music; polished floorboards; and beers for US$3. It's a very slick and unpretentious package enjoyed by a mixed foreigner–Turkish crowd.

Baraka *(☎ 212-292 2979, Balo Sokak 2/3)* **Map 16, #74** Admission free. Open noon-2am daily. Up on the 2nd floor, you'll find this unsigned bar: a grungy, squeaky floorboarded smoke pit with a handful of seats overlooking the goings-on along İstiklal Caddesi. Here your three-day growth is welcome, your black clothing applauded and your social-science degree feels at home. It's friendly and unpretentious, but the toilets are feral.

Yaga *(☎ 212-292 2829, Sıraselviler Caddesi 67, Taksim)* **Map 16, #19** Admission US$5 Fri-Sat. Open 1pm-4am daily. The hulks at the door put up a thick testosterone curtain, but if you smile sweetly and show ID you should get through. This big, split-level place has a billiard table, dance floor, garden (very pleasant in summer) and a couple of bars. It's mostly Western pop, and the band bleats out tunes a la 'Unchain My Heart' on Friday and Saturday nights – but don't let that put you off because it's a fun spot.

Kaktüs *(☎ 212-249 5979, İmam Adnan Sokak 4, Taksim)* **Map 16, #33** Admission free. Open 9am-2am daily. Although a prime place to eat (see the Places to Eat chapter), Kaktüs is also a pleasant place to have a drink. There's street-side seating, as well as the simple (slightly cramped) mellow interior. It draws a mid-30s-plus crowd who may be attracted to the extensive drink list and the cocktails (US$2.50 to US$6).

Soho Supper Club *(☎ 212-245 0152, Meşelik Sokak 14, Taksim)* **Map 16, #46** Admission free. Open 10am-2am daily. Ignore the style police at the door. Soho is minimalist, chic, and it's complemented by a gourmet 20s crowd. Beers cost US$2.50, cocktails US$4.50 to US$7. The food is good (see the Places to Eat chapter).

The Tepe Lounge *(The Marmara; ☎ 212-251 4696, Taksim Square)* **Map 16, #14** Admission free. Open 11am-midnight daily. This is definitely a non-rowdy zone, but you're not here to live it up, you're here for the views. From a height of 20 storeys, people in Taksim Square look like ants; those afraid of heights should stare at the stunning İstanbul horizon. Come just before sunset.

Orient Express Bar *(☎ 212-251 4560, Ground floor, Pera Palas Oteli)* **Map 16, #117** Admission free. Open 10am-2am daily. It really is worthwhile seeing the famous old-world Pera Palas, and if you have a drink in the bar you've got a good excuse to come in. To keep out the riffraff prices are steep – Pera Palas cocktail US$5, beer US$3.50 – but don't let that stop you; it certainly didn't stop us!

Harbiye & Nişantaşı (Map 17)

Pub Avni *(☎ 212-246 1136, American Bar Restaurant, Cumhuriyet Caddesi 239)* **Map**

Late-Night Transport

Getting home after pumpkin hour (midnight) can be a bit difficult in İstanbul, and that's not because you may be drunk. Most ferries turn in at around 11pm, the buses and trains dry up at midnight and the *dolmuşes* (shared minibuses) an hour or so thereafter. You could always walk, and if you're going out locally it's usually fine to do so. But although İstanbul isn't a dangerous city, we wouldn't recommend you set out from Beyoğlu to Sultanahmet at 2am, especially after a few drinks. Taxis are the best option. After midnight, the night *(gece)* rate kicks in until 6am; the base rate starts at US$0.70 – 50% more than the day *(gündüz)* rate. From Beyoğlu to Sultanahmet should cost between US$3 and US$5.

17, #17 Admission free. Open noon-2am daily. Just north-west of the Hilton is this elongated bar with a nightly crowd of middle-aged regulars, American and European recorded music, and a variety of snacks (US$1 to US$3) and full meals (US$2.50 to US$4). Beers cost US$2, imported spirits US$4 to US$5.50.

Ortaköy (Map 11)

Ortaköy is only 6km from Sultanahmet, less from Beyoğlu, and it's worthwhile making the effort to get there to enjoy its pretty Bosphorus-side setting, the market on Sunday (the best day to go) and the live Turk pop at its many tiny bars packed along the narrow lanes. Get there by bus No 25E from Eminönü or bus No 40, 40A or 40T from Taksim Square; a taxi at the end of the night should cost US$3.50 to Beyoğlu and US$5 to Sultanahmet.

The bars are clustered between the square at the edge of the Bosphorus, İskele Meydanı, and the main road along which the bus travels.

The Wall *(☎ 212-236 1903, Kaymakçı Sokak 14)* Admission free. Open noon-3am daily. This basic, dark den with a star lit ceiling and spangled-edged bar attracts gushing couples who schmooze on the makeshift dance floor in front of the vocalist. Others sing along to the Turk pop covers, and everyone has a good time. The nightly live music starts at 9pm. Beers cost US$2.50.

Gulet Cafe-Bar *(☎ 212-227 2092, Yelkovan Sokak 2)* Admission free. Open 3pm-2am daily. Similar to The Wall, this place serves up a singer with backing keyboard (from 9pm onwards, nightly), but it's a bit bigger so groups come along. Drinks cost US$2.50, and you'll end up paying for the nibbles that come with the drinks so ask prices first.

Ceneviz Kahvesi *(☎ 212-227 1400, Osmanzade Sokak 13-15)* Admission free. Open 1pm-2am daily. Verging on groovy, the Ceneviz is part cellar, part cave with raw rock/brick finishes and low lighting. It's popular with expats and locals, probably because of the cheap beer (US$2), mellow tunes and because it's one of the few places around here that doesn't have live Turk pop renditions. It's near the Burger King.

DISCOS & ROCK CLUBS

İstanbul has plenty of rock clubs, and most have a dance floor and live music after 10pm on the weekends. The live music tends to be covers of Turk pop hits mixed with '70s and '80s revival stuff. You may be pleased to hear that the city's discos don't usually have live music, but they do tend to be pricier, which invites a groovy crowd.

Sultanahmet (Map 13)

Teras Pub-Disco *(☎ 212-526 9701, Divan Yolu 66)* **Map 13, #26** Admission free. Open noon-2am daily. Daggy and dark, this bar has an upstairs dance floor pumped with a sweating 20s crowd, strobe, disco ball and steaming gropers in the corners. And you haven't seen anything yet – don't be surprised to see dance moves a la Michael Jackson meets belly dancing. The crowd is mainly Turkish, and the music jolts between Turkish pop, techno and '80s hits. Beer costs US$2.

Beyoğlu (Map 16)

Kemancı *(☎ 212-251 2723, Sıraselviler Caddesi 69, Taksim)* **Map 16, #20** Admission US$6 Thur-Sat. Open 6pm-2am daily. Wear your sunglasses (we kid you not), don black and an airbrushed Slayer T-shirt and you'll fit right in at Kemancı. It's three smoky, packed floors of İstanbul at its grungiest – which isn't saying much since the bands on the 1st and 3rd floors are known to burst into grunge covers of top 10 hits (really, why would you bother?). The 2nd floor is truer hard rock. Either way, this place is definitely worth a visit.

Andon *(☎ 212-251 0222, Sıraselviler Caddesi 89, Taksim)* **Map 16, #21** Admission free. Open 7pm-1am Mon-Sat. Andon has something for everyone: a rooftop restaurant with fine views over the Bosphorus, a *meyhane* (tavern) with live *fasıl* (folk music), a wine bar with a rowdy soloist, and a dance party on the ground floor. It's four floors of variety; pick and choose on the night.

Riddim Cafe & Bar *(☎ 212-249 8333, Büyükparmakkapı Sokak 8, Taksim)* **Map 16, #39** Admission free. Open 4pm-3am daily. This is one of the few spots in İstanbul to play reggae, but not the Bob Marley variety. This is hardcore reggae-techno with a splash of world music played to a sweaty, dancing mix of Turks and foreigners. It's a bit of a pick-up joint, which may, or may not, be exactly what you're after. Beers cost US$2.

Babylon *(☎ 212-292 7368, W www.babylon-ist.com, Şeyhbender Sokak 3, Tünel)* **Map 16, #124** Tickets US$5.50-11. Here you'll get experimental, hip-hop, lounge, world music and more – often played by international names. It's best to get your ticket in advance via Biletix or the box office. Check out the program on the Web site.

Life_Roof *(☎ 212-244 0486, 5th floor, İmam Adnan Sokak 12, Taksim)* **Map 16, #66** Admission free. Open 11am-4am daily. Although this place tries to pull in day crowds for its OK food (mains around US$3), stay away until Wednesday night for live Latin music or Friday, Saturday and Sunday nights for US rock and folk. Beer costs US$2.

Kuruçeşme (Map 11)

Laila *(☎ 212-227 1711, Muallim Naci Caddesi 141-2)* Admission US$25 Fri-Sat. Open 7pm-4am daily June-Oct. This huge outdoor club has cashed-up beautiful people doofing until the wee hours alongside spectacular views of the Bosphorus. Food is available and the dress code is glamour, darlings. The fashionably late arrive just before the serious dance action starts at around 11pm. There's no live music; it's DJs here. Kuruçeşme is about 1km northeast of Ortaköy or 7km from Sultanahmet; get there by taxi.

Festivals

Fuji Film Music Days *(☎ 212-252 5167, W www.pozitif-ist.com)* Tickets US$18. This isn't really a festival but a two-night event in mid-May with one international group playing per night, each supported by DJs. Music is usually jazz/funk/dance/ambient, played by groups such as St Germain and Transglobal Underground. Check the Web site for venues.

Efes Pilsen Blues Festival *(☎ 212-252 5167, W www.pozitif-ist.com)* Tickets US$3.50-8. This is a two-day İstanbul event in October or November which travels around Turkey and beyond. Running since 1990, it has mostly international artists and has included names (along with the typical blues tags of 'red hot' and 'the chief') such as Long John Hunter & the Bad Blues Band, Guitar Shorty and the Zydeco Brothers.

Nightlife Rip-Offs

Foreigners, especially single foreign males, are targets for a classic İstanbul rip-off that works like this:

You're a single male out for a stroll in the afternoon or evening. A well-spoken, well-dressed Turk strikes up a conversation, and says he knows 'a good place where we can have a drink and chat' or 'a great nightspot' etc. You enter, sit down, and immediately several women move to your table and order drinks. When the drinks come, you're asked to pay – anywhere from US$100 to however much money you have with you. It's a mugging, and if you don't pay up they take you into the back office and take it from you.

An exotic variation is a single foreign male having a drink and a meal at the Çiçek Pasajı. Several Turkish friends strike up a conversation, then suggest you all take a taxi to another place. In the taxi, they forcefully relieve you of your wallet.

How do you avoid such rip-offs? As many Turks are generous, hospitable, curious and gregarious, it's difficult to know whether an invitation is genuine (as it most often is) or the prelude to a mugging. Tread carefully if there's any reason for suspicion. As for nightclub recommendations, take them from a trusted source, such as your hotel clerk.

GAY & LESBIAN VENUES

Lambda İstanbul, the gay, lesbian, bisexual and transgender liberation group, has a Web site (W www.qrd.org/qrd/www/world/europe/turkey) with listings of bars, restaurants, *hamams* (steam baths) and details of weekly meetings and monthly parties. See Gay & Lesbian Travellers in the Facts for the Visitor chapter for information about general attitudes in İstanbul.

İstanbul has a number of venues that cater to gay, lesbian and bisexual crowds.

Kemancı *(☎ 212-245 3048, Sıraselviler Caddesi 69, Taksim)* **Map 16, #20** Admission US$6 Thur-Sat. Open 6pm-2am daily. This place attracts a mixed bag of revellers, but the smoky and packed top floor (there are three floors) sways to '80s hits and attracts a gay and lesbian crowd.

Club 14 *(☎ 212-256 2121, Abdülhak Hamit Caddesi 14, Taksim)* **Map 17, #61** Admission US$10. Open 11pm-4am daily. This popular club attracts a 20- to 35-year-old crowd who like to dance. It also runs its own radio station, Radio 2019 at 90.6 MHz.

Club Neo *(☎ 212-254 4526, Lamartin Caddesi 40, Taksim)* **Map 17, #41** Admission Fri US$5, Sat US$7. Open 10pm-2am Tues-Sun. Club Neo is a popular mixed-crowd venue; it's very lesbian friendly. The basement venue gets good raps. It's packed on the weekends.

Bar Bahçe *(☎ 212-243 2879, Soğancı Sokak 7/1, Cihangir)* **Map 16, #54** Admission free Mon-Thur, US$5 Fri-Sat. Open 9pm-2am Mon-Sat. Mostly dance floor plus a small bar, this club is all stark metallic finish with bubble-gum colours. It attracts a mixed crowd of 18s to 35s. Don't turn up until 11.30pm.

Bilsak 5 Kat *(☎ 212-293 3774, Soğancı Sokak 7/5, Cihangir)* **Map 16, #54** Admission free. Open 4.30pm-2am daily. Bilsak, more of a bar than a club, kicks off after 11pm, though you may want to stop by for dinner and the top Bosphorus views beforehand. It's a plush, unpretentious package enjoyed by a mixed 20s to 40s crowd.

JAZZ

Some İstanbul jazz venues have a loose interpretation of jazz, and die-hard jazz junkies may be rattled by their definition: You'll be tapping along to Dave Brubeck or a Miles Davis number to be rudely startled when the ensemble breaks into a cover of Madonna. Luckily most of the time things stay jazz. But jazz is vogue in İstanbul and the to-be-seen-in venues have inflated drink prices (if no cover charge) and a few inflated egos behind the bars. Who cares! Try these venues:

Kehribar *(☎ 212-231 4100, Cumhuriyet Caddesi 2)* **Map 17, #34** Admission free. Open 6pm-1am Mon-Sat. On the ground floor of Divan Oteli, Kehribar is smooth and luxurious, with excellent live music every night and expensive drinks (US$6.50 and upwards).

Kerem Görsev Jazz Bar *(☎ 212-231 3950, Abdi İpekçi Caddesi 61, Milli Reasürans Carşışı, Teşvikiye)* **Map 12** Admission US$13. Open 6pm-2am Mon-Sat Oct-June. Right at home in the posh end of town, this bar is owned by Kerem Görsev, a well-known Turkish jazz player. Live music starts at 10.30pm Monday to Thursday, 11pm Friday to Saturday, with (surprise, surprise) Kerem Görsev's quartet headlining most evenings. Don't disgrace yourself on the Oscar Peterson cocktails (US$6).

Shaft Blues & Jazz Club *(☎ 216-349 9956, W www.shaftclub.com, Osmancık Sokak 13, Kadıköy)* **Map 11** Adult/student US$5/4. Open 11am-2am daily. This club on the Asian side has a mishmash of blues/jazz/funk nights for the student set, but on Sunday night at 8pm the program gets as jazzy as it can.

Cafe Gramofon *(☎ 212-293 0786, Tünel Meydanı 3, Tünel)* **Map 16, #135** Admission US$7. Open 9am-2am daily. For the seriously cool, this chic cafe-bar dishes up jazz on Monday (10.30pm to 1am) with a large dash of drum'n'bass. Check the program before you come because it changes regularly. Beer costs US$3.

Jazz Cafe *(☎ 212-245 0516, Hasnun Galip Sokak 20, Beyoğlu)* **Map 16, #38** Admission free. Open 4pm-2am Mon-Sat. Bathed in mood lighting, the groupies of this mellow place are expats, jazz-heads and mainly 30-somethings. Most nights it's prerecorded jazz (and the music may lurch into an '80s hit at any moment) so check out the live music schedule beforehand. Beers cost US$2.50.

Festivals

International İstanbul Jazz Festival *(☎ 212-293 3133, fax 249 5667, W www.istfest.org, İstiklal Caddesi 146, Beyoğlu)* Tickets US$4-15. This festival was part of the International İstanbul Music Festival but started out on its own in 1994. It runs for two weeks in the beginning of July. Typically, it's a weird hybrid of conventional jazz, electronica, drum'n'bass, world music and rock. Names include Nick Cave, Miles Davis, Lou Reed, Randy Crawford and Massive Attack. Check the Web site for listings and venues.

Akbank Jazz Festival *(☎ 212-252 5167, W www.pozitif-ist.com)* Tickets US$4-10. This 10-day event in October draws more local musicians than the bigger International İstanbul Jazz Festival. Concerts are held at the Atatürk Cultural Centre, Cemal Reşit Rey Konser Salonu and Babylon. Line-ups have included Acid Trippin' Plays Mingus and Art Ensemble of Africa (which should give you an idea of the eclecticism). Check the Web site for listings and venues.

New Jazz Line Festival *(☎ 212-245 1048, W www.yenicaz.com)* Tickets US$4-18. This event runs for over two weeks in early April and attracts international and local musicians exploring new jazz and electronic trends. Names have included Richard Galliano and King Kooba. Many of the performances are held at the cafe Dulcinea (Map 16, #47; ☎ 212-245 1039) at Meşelik Sokak 20, Beyoğlu.

ENTERTAINING THE KIDS

Free Thrills

Most playgrounds in İstanbul are antiquated jerry-built jobs. If you're still keen (or you're getting tired of being nagged), there's a small playground **(Map 13)** near the Cankurtaran train station, east of Sultanahmet, and a bigger one in the park **(Map 13)** along Kadırga Limanı Caddesi in Küçük Ayasofya. Over in Beyoğlu there's a playground **(Map 16)** right beside the Bosphorus near the Fındıklı Molla Çelebı Camii and the Kabataş Ferry Port.

A run in the park could expel those hyperactive juices. Take the kids to Gülhane Park **(Map 15)**, near Sultanahmet, where there's also a decrepit little zoo *(admission free; open 10am-4pm)*. Yıldız Park **(Map 12)**, north-east of Beşiktaş, has more running space and the bonus of ducks to feed.

Cheap Thrills

The eerie darkness of the **Sunken Cistern (Map 13, #43)** in Sultanahmet usually fascinates kids. Another sure winner is to climb aboard any ferry going from Eminönü across the Bosphorus to Kadıköy or Üsküdar. Either trip takes only 15 or 20 minutes each way. Kids will love the boat ride and you'll love the fine city views. Boats leave frequently and cost less than US$1.60 for a round trip.

Another option is to take the **Tünel (Map 16)**, İstanbul's little century-old underground train, from Karaköy at the northern end of Galata Bridge, up to the southern end of İstiklal Caddesi. From there, jump aboard the restored Victorian-era tram that rattles along İstiklal to Taksim Square.

Yedikule (Map 11) (Fortress of the Seven Towers) is along the Sea of Marmara, about 5km west of Sultanahmet. It's easy to get to by train from Sirkeci or Cankurtaran. See the Things to See & Do chapter for details. **Rumeli Hisarı (Map 11)**, on the European shore of the Bosphorus and a 30-minute bus ride north of Taksim, is another castle with crenellated walls, cylindrical towers and ancient cannons. See the Excursions chapter for more information.

The **Askeri Müzesi (Map 17, #11)** (Military Museum), just north of Taksim Square and the İstanbul Hilton, has lots of old swords, suits of armour, military tents, cannons and more. Kids should also enjoy the concerts by the Mehter, the medieval Ottoman military band, which are held between 3pm and 4pm Wednesday to Sunday.

The Shadow Puppet Theatre (Karagöz) mentioned under its own heading later in this chapter should appeal to kids as well.

Not-So-Cheap Thrills

The Play Barn *(☎ 212-299 4803, Kirazlıbağ Sokak 4, Yeniköy)* **Map 11** Open 10am-7pm Tues-Sun. Admission US$6 per hour. This indoor playground provides supervised play with games and crafts.

ENTERTAINMENT

Tatilya *(☎ 212-852 0505, Beylikdüzü Mevkii, Büyükçekmece)* Open noon-11pm Mon-Fri, 11am-11pm Sat-Sun. Admission US$13, free for children under two years. This undercover fun park is in the district of Büyükçekmece, about 25km west of Sultanahmet. There's a rollercoaster, fun rides for all ages, restaurants and more. Free daily service buses pick up throughout the city including Taksim and Aksaray. These buses will take you to and from Tatilya, but the timetable is likely to change, and the services are irregular, so ring first.

SHADOW PUPPET THEATRE (KARAGÖZ)

Although this theatre's 'birthplace' is in Bursa (south of the Sea of Marmara), there are also performances in İstanbul. The puppets (10cm to 50cm tall) are cut from hide pieces, coated with oil to promote translucency, and decorated with colourful paints. Most have movable arms and legs sewn onto the body and some have movable heads. The puppets prance behind a white sheet.

Muammer Karaca Tiyatrosu *(☎ 212-252 4456, Odakule Karşısı, İstiklal Caddesi)* **Map 16, #102** Tickets US$5-9. This theatre has regular concerts starting at 8pm daily, Wednesday to Sunday from Ocober to June.

Festivals

International İstanbul Puppet Festival *(Uluslararası İstanbul Kukla Festivali; ☎ 212-254 2738)* Tickets US$3-10 For eight days in the beginning of May this recent addition to İstanbul's impressive festival list highlights Turkish Karagöz puppetry. International puppeteers come from lands afar including Russia, Italy and Portugal. Many events are held in the Atatürk Cultural Centre. There are 'adults-only' events (don't get too excited) and performances for children.

SPECTATOR SPORTS

There's only one spectator sport that matters to many Turks. What some call soccer, the Turks call soccer.

For 24 hours preceding the big match, scarves are worn, flags are aflutter and hotted-up testosterone-motors bounce up and down at red lights before screeching off and dragging team colours behind them. The victorious team enjoys its colours plastered over the city for another day, or two, or three... At the end of the game, traffic around Beyoğlu crawls to a halt as merrymakers head to Taksim Square. Shoulder to shoulder the crowds sway, chant club anthems and clamber all over each other, while many still find time to ogle passing women (football is strictly a game for blokes, you see).

Eighteen teams from all over Turkey compete from August to May. Each season three move up from the second league into first, and three get demoted. The top team of the first league plays in the European Cup.

İstanbul's three major teams and their colours are:

Beşiktaş (W www.bjk.com/turk) İnönü Stadyumu, Beşiktaş. Black and white.
Fenerbahçe (W www.fenerbahce.org.tr) Rüştü Saraçoğlu Stadyum, Kadıköy. Yellow and blue.
Galatasaray (W www.galatasaray.org.tr) Ali Sami Yen Stadyum, Mecidiyeköy (about 3km north-east of Taksim). Yellow and red.

Matches are usually held on the weekend, often on a Saturday night. Tickets are sold at the clubhouses at the stadium *(stadyum)* or at Biletix, and usually go on sale between Tuesday and Thursday for a weekend game. For open seating you'll pay around US$4.50; for covered seating – which has the best views – around US$13. If you miss out on the tickets you can get them at the door of the stadium, but note that they are outrageously overpriced.

Although violence at home games is not unknown, most matches are fine. If you're worried, avoid the Galatasaray and Fenerbahçe clashes as the supporters of these arch rivals can become overly fired up.

If you can't make it to a live game, you can always try one of the several bars around town that screen the game live, such as ***Ayazma Bar*** *(☎ 212-516 6185, Akbıyık Caddesi 40, Cankurtaran)* **(Map 13, #86)**.

TURKISH CARPETS

Turkey is famous for its beautiful carpets *(halı)* and kilims and wherever you go in İstanbul you'll be spoilt for choice as to what to buy. In shops throughout the city, you will find carpets from all regions of Turkey – and beyond. Unfortunately, the business is very lucrative and the hard-sell antics of some dealers and their shills have tended to bring it into disrepute, putting many visitors off venturing into the shops. Also, with the tourism boom, carpet prices have risen so much that it may actually be cheaper to buy your Turkish carpet at home. Indeed, we've heard one story of a man who bought up old kilims in the Paris flea market, had them cleaned, then brought them to İstanbul to sell to tourists at high prices – creative recycling!

If you have it in mind to buy a carpet, browse in your local shop before coming to İstanbul. This will give you some idea of prices and will acquaint you with the various designs so you can shop more knowledgeably on arrival.

An Age-Old Art

Turkish women have been weaving carpets for a very long time. These beautiful, durable, eminently portable floor coverings were a nomadic family's most valuable and practical 'furniture', warming and brightening the clan's oft-moved homes.

The oldest-known carpet woven in the Turkish double-knotted Gördes style (Gördes is a town in the mountains of north-west Turkey) dates from between the 4th and 1st centuries BC.

It is thought that hand-woven carpet techniques were introduced to Anatolia by the Seljuks in the 12th century. Thus it's not surprising that Konya, the Seljuk capital, was mentioned by Marco Polo as a centre of carpet production in the 13th century.

Traditional Patterns

Traditionally, village women wove carpets for their own family's use, or for their dowry. Knowing they would be judged on their efforts, the women took great care over their handiwork, hand-spinning and dyeing the wool, and choosing what they judged to be the most interesting and beautiful patterns.

The general pattern and colour scheme of old carpets was influenced by local traditions and the availability of certain types of wool and colours of dyes. Patterns were memorised, and women usually worked with no more than 18 inches of the carpet visible. But each artist imbued her work with her own personality, choosing a motif or a colour based on her own artistic preferences, and even events and emotions in her daily life.

Even carpets made today often use the same traditional patterns and incorporate all sorts of symbols that can be 'read' by those in the know. At a glance two carpets might look identical, but closer examination reveals the subtle differences that give each Turkish carpet its individuality and much of its charm.

Inset: Motifs used in carpet designs are often derived from the natural environment in which weavers live. This common motif represents a scorpion or spider.

DIANA MAYFIELD

EDDIE GERALD

ANNA JUDD

Carpets are one of Turkey's most sought-after handicrafts and are made throughout the country, usually by women. Popular designs are mass produced, but the one-off work of art can also still be found. Most carpets are made of wool (top right), but the most expensive are 100% silk.

STUART WASSERMAN

DAVOR PAVICHICH

DAVOR PAVICHICH

DIANA MAYFIELD

Top: You can find rugs from all over Turkey in İstanbul, including these from Dalyan, in the western Mediterranean region.

Middle Left: This 200-year-old prayer rug from the Göreme region is a comparatively modern example of an art that stretches back to the 4th century BC.

Middle Right: This prayer rug from İstanbul's Blue Mosque features a traditional minaret design.

Bottom: Turkish carpets and coffee pots are for sale near Aya Sofya in İstanbul's Sultanahmet area.

In the 19th century, the European rage for Turkish carpets spurred the development of carpet companies. The companies, run by men, would deal with customers, take orders, purchase and dye the wool according to the customers' preferences, and contract local women to produce the finished product. The designs might be left to the women, but more often were provided by the company, based on the customers' tastes. Though well made, these carpets lost some of the originality and spirit of the older work.

Carpet Weaving Today

These days the picture is more complicated. Many carpets are made not according to local traditions, but to the dictates of the market. Weavers in eastern Turkey might make carpets in popular styles native to western Turkey. Long-settled villagers might duplicate the wilder, hairier and more naive *yörük* (nomad) carpets.

Village women still weave carpets but most of them work to fixed contracts for specific shops. Usually they work to a pattern and are paid for their final effort rather than for each hour of work. A carpet made to a fixed contract may still be of great value to its purchaser. However, the selling price should be lower than for a one-off piece.

Other carpets are the product of division of labour, with different individuals responsible for dyeing and weaving. What such pieces lose in individuality and rarity is often more than made up for in quality control. Most silk Hereke carpets (Hereke is a small town near İzmit, about 100km south-east of İstanbul) are mass produced, but to standards that make them some of the most sought-after of all Turkish carpets.

Fearing that old carpet-making methods would be lost, the Ministry of Culture now sponsors a number of projects to revive traditional weaving and dyeing methods in western Turkey. Some carpet shops will have stocks of these 'project carpets', which are usually of high quality with prices reflecting that fact. Some of these carpets are also direct copies of antique pieces in museums.

Kilims, Sumaks & Cicims

Most carpet shops have a range of pieces made by a variety of techniques. Besides the traditional pile carpets, they usually offer double-sided flat-woven mats such as kilims. Some traditional kilim motifs are similar to patterns found at the prehistoric mound of Çatal Höyük, testifying to the very ancient traditions of flat-woven floor coverings in Anatolia. Older, larger kilims may actually be two narrower pieces of similar, but not always identical, design stitched together. As this is now rarely done, any such piece is likely to be fairly old.

Other flat-weave techniques include *sumak*, a style originally from Azerbaijan in which intricate details are woven with coloured thread by wrapping them around the warp. The loose weft ends are left hanging at the back of the rug.

Cicims are kilims with small and lively patterns embroidered on the top of them.

Carpets from Other Countries

As well as Turkish carpets, many carpet shops sell pieces from other countries, especially from Iran, Afghanistan and from the ex-Soviet Republics of Azerbaijan, Turkmenistan and Uzbekistan. If it matters that yours is actually from Turkey, bear in mind that Iran favours the single knot and Turkey the double knot. Turkish carpets also tend to have a higher pile, more dramatic designs and more varied colours than their Iranian cousins. Some Iranian sumaks are decorated with naive animal patterns, encouraging shopkeepers to call them 'Noah's Ark carpets' although they have absolutely nothing to do with the Bible story.

A Carpet-Buyer's Primer

The bad news is that there are no short cuts when it comes to learning about carpets. To ensure you get a good buy, you'll have to spend time visiting several shops and compare prices and quality. You may want to stroll through the government-run ***Haseki Hamam Carpet & Kilim Sales Store*** *(Aya Sofya Meydanı 4, Sultanahmet)* **Map 13, #64**. Although the carpets and kilims here aren't necessarily the best quality or price, it's a good starting point as the prices are fixed and there's no hassle to buy.

When deciding whether to buy a particular carpet, it might help to follow some of the guidelines below.

A good-quality, long-lasting carpet should be 100% wool *(yüz de yüz yün)*: check the warp (the lengthwise yarns), weft (the crosswise yarns) and pile (the vertical yarns knotted into the matrix of warp and weft). Is the wool fine and shiny, with signs of the natural oil? More expensive carpets may be of a silk and wool blend. Cheaper carpets may have warp and weft of mercerised cotton. You can tell by checking the fringes at either end; if the fringe is of cotton or 'flosh' (mercerised cotton) you shouldn't pay for wool. Another way to identify the material of the warp and weft is to turn the carpet over and look for the fine, frizzy fibres common to wool, but not to cotton. But bear in mind that just being made of wool doesn't guarantee a carpet's quality. If the dyes and design are ugly, even a 100% woollen carpet can be a bad buy.

Check the closeness of the weave by turning the carpet over and inspecting the back. In general, the tighter the weave and the smaller the knots, the higher the quality and durability of the carpet. The oldest carpets sometimes had thick knots, so consider the number of knots alongside the colours and the quality of the wool.

Compare the colours on the back with those on the front. Spread the nap with your fingers and look at the bottom of the pile. Are the colours brighter there than on the surface? Slight colour variations could occur in older carpets when a new batch of dye was mixed, but richer colour deep in the pile is often an indication that the surface has faded in the sun. Natural dyes don't fade as readily as chemical dyes. There is nothing wrong with chemical dyes, which have a long history of their own, but natural dyes and colours tend to be preferred and therefore fetch higher prices. Don't pay for natural if you're getting chemical.

New carpets can be made to look old, and damaged or worn carpets can be rewoven (good work, but expensive), patched or even painted. There is nothing wrong with a dealer offering you a patched or repainted carpet, of course, provided they point out these defects and price the piece accordingly. And note that some red Bukhara carpets (Bukhara is a city region in Uzbekistan) will continue to give off colour, even though they're of better quality than cheap woollen carpets which don't.

When you are examining the carpet, look at it from one end, then from the other. The colours will differ because the pile always leans one way or the other. Take the carpet out into the sunlight and look at it there. Imagine where you might put the carpet at home, and how the light will strike it.

It's all very well to pluck some fibres and burn them to see if they smell like wool, silk, or nylon or to rub a wet handkerchief over the carpet to see if the colour comes off, but unless you know what you're doing you're unlikely to learn much from the exercise – and you may well end up with an irate carpet seller to deal with!

In the end the most important consideration should be whether or not you like the carpet.

Pricing & Payment

When it comes to buying, there's no substitute for spending time developing an 'eye' for what you really like. You also need to be realistic about your budget. These days carpets are such big business that true bargains are hard to come by unless there's something (like gigantic size) that makes them hard to sell for their true value.

Prices are determined by age, material, quality, condition, demand in the market, the enthusiasm of the buyer, and the debt load of the seller. Bear in mind that if you do your shopping on a tour or when accompanied by a guide, the price will be hiked by up to 35% to cover somebody's commission.

It may be wiser to go for something small but of high quality rather than for a room-sized cheapie. Another way to make the money stretch further is to opt for one of the smaller items made from carpet materials: old camel bags and hanging baby's cradles opened out to make rugs on which food would be eaten; decorative grain bags; even the bags that once held rock salt for animals. Note that cushion covers, which are all the rage, were made from damaged kilims, but now they're so popular good kilims are getting the chop to make them; by not buying them you won't support this destruction.

Some dealers may take personal cheques, but all prefer cash. Most shops take credit cards but some require you to pay the credit card company's fee and the cost of the phone call to check your creditworthiness. A few dealers will let you pay in instalments.

All of this is a lot to remember, but it will be worth it if you get a carpet you like at a decent price. It will give you pleasure for the rest of your life.

Shopping

İstanbul is a riot of temptations to a shopaholic: must-have colourful carpets and kilims lure everywhere you turn, fashionable clothing is around every corner, and the leather jackets are stylish and mostly well made. Then there are the items – ceramics, jewellery, copper goods etc – that cram every tourist handicraft shop. Sure, they're common here, but they look great when you get them home (speaking from experience). The variety of goods is mind-boggling, the prices reasonable – try as you might, you won't go home empty-handed.

CARPETS

There must be as many carpet shops in İstanbul as there are taxis, and as many carpet touts as carpet shops. Get used to 'Looking for me?', 'You dropped my heart' and other inane lines the hopefuls will drop in an effort to strike up a conversation and lure you into their shop. If you're interested in buying one of these beautiful and durable souvenirs you will have to go along with a bit of hoo-ha, but the special section 'Turkish Carpets' (pp176–9) should help make the ordeal as painless as possible. It also has the lowdown on carpet making, kilims (flat-woven mats) and traditional styles.

Where to Buy Carpets

The following carpet shops have been recommended, but use your judgment and shop around; just because the shop is listed here doesn't mean it's a sound guarantee that you won't get ripped off.

Shopping Hotspots

İstanbul has thousands of shops and many shopping hubs, but a few places will give you a quintessential İstanbul shopping experience.

Kapalı Çarşı (Map 4)

In Beyazıt, and also known as the Grand Bazaar, this is a must-do. It's a one-stop shop where you can buy everything from *nargilehs* (water pipes), carpets and clothes, to leather, silk cushion covers, jewellery, backgammon sets and ceramics. Most find the experience trying as the touts are insistent, but endure if you can.

Mısır Çarşısı (Map 15)

This market in Eminönü, also known as the Egyptian Market or the Spice Bazaar, and the streets surrounding it, have plenty of spices and sweets. It's also a colourful and entertaining browse.

Arasta Bazaar (Map 13)

Set beside the Blue Mosque the Arasta is a long corridor lined with shops. There are plenty of carpet shops and some ceramic and jewellery shops too, but touts abound.

Aznavur Pasajı (Map 16)

This mini-Kapalı Çarşı along İstiklal Caddesi over in Beyoğlu misses the hassle and bustle of its cousin over the Golden Horn, but still has some of the same goods: silver jewellery, ceramics, oils, inlaid woodwork. Upstairs, there are tacky presents plus hippy-ish clothes and handbags. If you can't find what you want here, you may be able to find it at the nearby Avrupa Pasajı (European Passage) leading off the Balık Pazar (Fish Market).

Tahtakale (Map 15)

Finally, no trip to İstanbul would be complete without a stroll through the ancient shopping district of Tahtakale – especially along Uzunçarşı Caddesi and Mahmut Paşa Yokuşu. This is where the locals shop; prepare your elbows and dive in for a look. Although you're not going to find classic tourist souvenirs (unless you think circumcision robes and wedding dresses make great presents) you'll enjoy a walk through this chaotic mess. See The Bazaar District walking tour in the Things to See & Do chapter for sights to watch out for as you stroll through this area.

Anadolu *(☎ 212-519 2341, Çorlulu Alipaşa Medresesi 36/5, Çarşıkapı)* **Map 4, #25** This shop, taking up several rooms of a disused *medrese* (Muslim theological seminary), has a huge variety of cloth, embroidery, kilims and carpets from US$80.

Gallery Natural *(☎ 212-517 0383, Akbıyık Caddesi 31, Sultanahmet)* **Map 13, #85** This simple, small shop has some carpets copied from museum pieces but most are new nomadic works. Prices range from US$60 to US$650.

Halı Evi *(☎ 212-519 2350, Soğukçeşme Sokak 40/A, Sultanahmet)* **Map 13, #48** This small shop has a mixed bag of pieces ranging from US$70 to US$600. Next door, the same family has a full-to-the-brim gift shop (items have price tags), and upstairs there's a guesthouse.

Haseki Hamam Carpet & Kilim Sales Store *(☎ 212-638 0035, 4 Aya Sofya Meydanı, Sultanahmet)* **Map 13, #64** Located in the Baths of Lady Hürrem, this Ministry of Culture carpet shop sells new carpets replicated from museum pieces. There's no hassle to buy here as the prices are set at US$80 or US$100 per sq metre. You can't haggle, but it's a good spot to wander through and get an idea of prices.

Heritage *(☎ 212-528 3256, Caferiye Sokak 6/A, Sultanahmet)* **Map 13, #52** This large shop specialises in natural dyes and charges by the metre with discounts if you buy more than two pieces: US$200 to US$240 per metre for kilims, US$300 to US$350 for carpets.

Sebil *(☎ 212-519 4353, Babıhümayun Caddesi 28, Sultanahmet)* **Map 13, #60** Near Topkapı Palace's Imperial Gate, Sebil is a laid-back shop with lots of carpets and kilims (mostly from eastern Turkey) above a gift shop. Prices range from US$40 to US$2000.

Su-De *(☎/fax 212-516 5488, İletişim Han 7/2, Sultanahmet)* **Map 13, #15** This large shop has a good range of its speciality – rare or antique carpets and kilims. Prices start at around US$100.

Carpet Bait & Switch

If you haggle for a carpet, at least shop around and get to know the price levels a bit. Beware of the following scam.

You make friends with a charming Turk, or perhaps a Turkish-American/European couple. They recommend a friend's shop, so you go and have a look. There's no pressure to buy. Indeed, your new friends wine and dine you (always in a jolly group with others). Before you leave İstanbul you decide to buy a carpet. You go to the shop, choose one you like, and ask the price. So far so good; if you can buy that carpet at a good price, everything's fine. But if the owner strongly urges you to buy a 'better' carpet, more expensive because it's 'old' or 'Persian' or 'rare', or 'makes a good investment', beware. You may return home to find you've paid many times more than it is worth. If the shopkeeper ships the carpet for you, the cheap carpet which arrives may not be the expensive carpet you bought.

To avoid this rip-off, you choose the carpet, inspect it carefully, compare prices for similar work at other shops, then buy and take it with you or ship it yourself; don't have the shopkeeper ship it.

MICK WELDON

LEATHER

On any given Kurban Bayramı (Sacrifice Holiday), more than 2.5 million sheep get the axe in Turkey. Add to that the normal day-to-day needs of a cuisine based on mutton and lamb and you have a huge amount of raw material to be made into leather items.

Shoes, bags, jackets, skirts, vests, hats, gloves and trousers are all made from soft leather. This is a big industry in Turkey; so much leather clothing is turned out that a good deal of it will be badly cut or carelessly made, but there are lots of fine pieces as well.

The best way to be assured of quality is to shop around, trying on garments in several shops. Look especially for quality stitching and lining, sufficient fullness of sleeve and leg, and care taken in the small things such as attaching buttons and zippers.

Made-to-order garments can be excellent or disappointing, as the same tailor who made the ready-made stuff will make the ordered stuff, and will be making it fast because the shopkeeper has already impressed you by saying 'No problem. I can have it for you tomorrow'. It's better to find something off the rack that fits than to order it, unless you can order without putting down a deposit or committing yourself to buy (this is often possible).

Where to Buy Leather

The traditional leather apparel centre is the Kürkçüler Çarşısı section of the Kapalı Çarşı (Grand Bazaar), but there are many other shops on and off Fesçiler Caddesi, the street leading in from the entrance by the Beyazıt Camii. Less touristy (read: cheaper) leather shops also fill street after street in the Beyazıt, Laleli and Aksaray districts and these are worth checking out.

Koç *(☎ 212-527 5553, Kürkçüler Çarşısı 22, Kapalı Çarşı)* **Map 4, #24** This is a small shop, but it's crammed with a good range of jackets. Fashion is big here – there's plenty of coloured leather – but there are also classic styles. It's a busy shop, so they may not be too keen to bargain.

Leko Deri *(☎ 212-518 6900, Mithatpaşa Caddesi 14, Beyazıt)* **Map 15, #42** Leko looks a bit posh from the outside but the prices appear to be OK. It's a large shop crammed with jackets, including plenty of suede. Most of the jackets are classic styles which is just as well since the attempts at 'fashion' are embarrassingly bad.

Tergan *(☎ 212-638 4670, Tatlı Kuyu Hamam Sokak 5/B, Beyazıt)* **Map 15, #44** Specialising in briefcases, wallets and handbags, this large store around the corner

Bagging a Bargain

The prospect of bargaining seems to fire up many travellers and tales rattle around the dorm bunks and the hotel lobbies about so-and-so who saved US$5 on the bargain of the year. In İstanbul many shop items bear price stickers, but when you shop for souvenirs or expensive items, particularly in the bazaars and markets, you'll be able to test out those bargaining skills.

Traditionally, when a customer enters a Turkish shop to make a significant purchase, he or she is offered a comfortable seat and a drink (coffee, tea or a soft drink). There is some getting acquainted chitchat, then some discussion of the goods (carpets, apparel, jewellery etc) in general, then of the customer's tastes, preferences and requirements. Finally, a number of items in the shop are shown for the customer's inspection.

The customer asks the price; the shop owner gives it; the customer looks doubtful and makes a counteroffer 25% to 50% lower. This procedure goes back and forth several times before a price is arrived at. If no price is agreed upon, the customer has absolutely no obligation and may walk out at any time.

To bargain effectively you must not be in a hurry, and you must know something about the items in question and their market price. The best way to do this is to look at similar goods in several shops, asking prices but not making counteroffers. Shopkeepers will give you a quick education about their wares by showing you what's good about them, and telling you what's bad about their competitors' goods. Soon you will discover which shops have the best quality for the lowest asking prices, and you can proceed to bargain.

You can often get a discount by offering to buy several items at once; or to pay in US dollars, or another strong major currency; or to not want a receipt.

If you don't have sufficient time to shop around, follow the age-old rule: Find something you like at a price you're willing to pay, buy it, enjoy it and don't worry about whether or not you received the world's lowest price.

from Leko Deri has a decent range of conventional styles and colours. Come here for your boring mission-brown briefcase, go to the shops along Direkli Camii Sokak for your hot-pink patent leather handbag.

SILK

Bursa, south of the Sea of Marmara, is the silk centre of Turkey. Silkworms are raised, their cocoons are sold in Bursa and there the silk is crafted into scarves and other items. Here in İstanbul you can get your hands on Bursa's beautiful scarves; many have ornate hand-painted patterns and/or marbled colouring.

İpek *(☎ 212-249 8207, İstiklal Caddesi 230/7-8, Galatasaray)* **Map 16, #96** This shop has a massive range of Bursa's silk scarves (US$6 to US$55) and ties (US$5 to US$25), elegantly presented in this boutique spot. But this is İstiklal Caddesi – prime real estate – so top range comes with premium price tags.

Silk & Cashmere *(☎ 212-282 0235, Akmerkez shopping centre, Etiler)* **Map 11** This store sells a blend of silk and cashmere accessories and clothes for men and women. The fashions are conventional, but the selection is good, though prices are high – these are classic pieces.

HANDICRAFTS

The Kapalı Çarşı has oodles of shops flogging touristy handicrafts such as ceramics, copperware and jewellery. Although these pieces are handmade and mostly beautiful in their own right, each is usually just a number in a long production line. This won't probably matter to most travellers, but if you want high-quality, original artwork (and you've a bit of cash to splash) you have to shop around. Artisans making this work are few and far between.

Where to Buy Handicrafts

The Kapalı Çarşı has many shops selling handicrafts. If you're interested in embroidered scarves, Çakmakçılar Yokuşu, north of the bazaar, has a row of shops selling many. To find top-quality original pieces, start your search in Sultanahmet. See Ceramics later in this chapter for good ceramics shop recommendations as well.

Caferağa Medresesi *(☎ 212-513 3601, Caferiye Sokak, Sultanahmet)* **Map 13, #50** The rooms around this pretty medresesi are used as art teaching studios and some of the product – jewellery, marbled paper *(ebru)* – is sold here for reasonable prices. There's not much to choose from, but it's worthwhile wandering in for a peek.

Dösim *(☎ 212-513 3134, Babıhümayun Caddesi, Sultanahmet)* **Map 13, #59** Open 9am-5pm Wed-Mon. This government-run shop, near Topkapı Palace's Imperial Gate, has a quality selection of jewellery, crockery, cooking pots, brass, embroidery and more. All items have price tags (a nice change) plus there's no hassle. Prices range from about US$3 to US$20.

İstanbul Sanatlar Çarşısı *(Handicrafts Market; ☎ 212-517 6782, Kabasakal Caddesi, Sultanahmet)* **Map 13, #66** Set in the small rooms surrounding the leafy courtyard of the 18th-century Cedid Mehmed Efendi Medresesi, beside the Yeşil Ev hotel, the Sanatlar Çarşısı has local artisans working on the spot. You can wander through and watch them at work, and buy their beautiful calligraphy, embroidery, glassware, miniature paintings, ceramics and not-so-beautiful, but interesting, dolls. These are original works, and the prices reflect this.

Sofa *(☎ 212-527 9134, W www.kashifsofa.com, Nuruosmaniye Caddesi 42 & 106B, Beyazıt)* Sofa has a mix of miniature paintings, jewellery, calligraphy and contemporary art. While some of the stock is antique, much has been recently crafted and is inspired by antique works.

ANTIQUES

The grand Ottoman-era houses of İstanbul have given up a lot of fascinating stuff left over from the empire: tacky furniture in the Ottoman baroque style, jewellery, crockery, paintings and more. You'll also see older relics – illuminated manuscripts, Greek and Roman figurines – in antique shops. Prices for antiques are never fixed so you'll always have to bargain hard.

Antiquities & the Law

When shopping for antiques, it's important to remember that antiquities – objects from Turkey's Hittite, Graeco-Roman, Byzantine and classical Ottoman past – may not be sold, bought, or taken out of the country under penalty of law. A century-old painting, lamp-shade or carpet usually poses no problems, but a Roman statuette, Byzantine icon or 17th-century İznik tile means trouble, and quite possibly time in jail.

Where to Buy Antiques

The shops in the so-called Old Bazaar at the centre of the Kapalı Çarşı specialise in antiques and jewellery, but there are other, less obvious places to search for the perfect knick-knack.

Çukurcuma (Map 16) On the prowl for antiques, most İstanbullus in the know will tell you to head for Çukurcuma, a district lost in the maze of backstreet Beyoğlu, south-east of Galatasaray. Start from Galatasaray and follow Turnacıbaşı Sokak south-east off İstiklal Caddesi. When you see the Tarihi Galatasaray Hamamı, go left, then right, around the bath and continue downhill on Çapanoğlu Sokak and Acıçeşme Sokak (lots of steps) to Faik Paşa Sokak (also called Faik Paşa Yokuşu) which has about six antique shops. Just beyond it, Çukurcuma Caddesi has more shops – these mostly stock furniture.

Anadolu Mezat *(☎ 0532-262 5627, Çukurcuma Caddesi 67)* **Map 16, #60** This dark den is so crammed with furniture you can barely get through the door.

Şamdan *(☎ 212-245 4445, Altı Patlar Sokak 20)* **Map 16, #57** There isn't a heap of stuff here but it's well presented. There's a good collection of crockery and furniture.

Semantik *(☎ 212-292 2015, Hayriye Caddesi 11)* **Map 16, #62** A messy mass of dusty cluttered bits and pieces, Semantik certainly has a lot – but no furniture – if you've the energy to dig through it.

Yaman *(☎ 212-249 5188, Faik Paşa Sokak 41)* **Map 16, #59** This gigantic, labyrinthine shop has a huge selection including kilims, calligraphy, furniture and lamps plus a cosy cafe for a pit stop.

Aksaray (Map 14) Rarely seeing tourists, the ***Horhor Bit Pazarı*** *(Kırık Tulumba Sokak 13/22)* has five storeys crammed with antique furniture and bits and pieces. To get there from Sultanahmet catch the street tram along Divan Yolu to the Aksaray junction stop; then walk north for 10 minutes.

Kadıköy (Map 11) You may have more luck with your bargaining here on the less touristy, Asian side of İstanbul. ***Galeri Antik*** *(☎ 216-330 9852, Tellalzade Sokak 1)* is crammed with lights and other collectables. It's one in a row of antique shops along this street, each with a good selection of furniture, light fittings and more.

NEW & SECOND-HAND BOOKS

Books published in Turkish are relatively cheap, those published in Turkey for a foreign audience considerably more expensive, but books imported from abroad (mostly in English) are very pricey. A book which sells for US$20 at home may cost US$35 or US$40 in İstanbul, so don't come here looking for bargains.

Where to Buy New & Second-hand Books

Second-hand nonfiction in foreign languages is hard to find, though you won't have too much trouble finding fiction to buy or swap.

Sultanahmet Area (Map 13) This very touristy area has a surprisingly small number of bookshops.

Galeri Kayseri *(☎ 212-512 0456, Divan Yolu 58, Sultanahmet)* **Map 13, #24** This small shop is packed with an excellent selection of fiction and nonfiction about İstanbul's art, history, religion and more – plus a huge collection of Lonely Planet titles.

Natural Foreign Book Exchange *(☎ 212-517 0384, Akbıyık Caddesi 31, Cankurtaran)* **Map 13, #85** Down the stairs you'll find a good selection of fiction. Most books are in

English but you will find other languages. Prices start at US$4.50, but if you return a book you get 50% off your next buy.

Sahaflar Çarşısı (Map 15, #37) Sahaflar Çarşısı, the Old Book Bazaar, is great fun for browsing, but you'll find more new than old. It's just west of the Kapalı Çarşı, sandwiched between Çadırcılar Caddesi and the Beyazıt Camii. Close by in the flea market you may find English and other foreign-language books.

Dilmen Kitabevi *(☎ 212-527 9934, Sahaflar Çarşısı 20)* This tiny shop is crammed with books on Ottoman and Byzantine art, calligraphy, architecture and carpets.

Gözen Kitap ve Yayınevi *(☎ 212-511 2205, Sahaflar Çarşısı 27)* A good selection of books focusing on the art and architecture of İstanbul and Turkey is stocked here, plus a range of touristy books.

Beyoğlu (Map 16) The largest bookshops are in or near Beyoğlu.

Dünya Aktüel *(☎ 212-249 1006, İstiklal Caddesi 469, Tünel)* **Map 16, #128** This large, stark bookshop has only a handful of guidebooks and a few other foreign-language titles, but it does have a large collection of magazines (some in English).

Eren *(☎ 212-251 2858, Sofyalı Sokak 34, Tünel)* **Map 16, #126** Although you wouldn't think so from the outside, Eren hides an immense range of art, craft and history books about Turkey as well as heaps on İstanbul.

Homer Kitabevi *(☎ 212-249 5902, ⓔ homerkitabevi@superonline.com, Yeniçarşı Caddesi 28/A, Galatasaray)* **Map 16, #88** Homer has an excellent selection of history, architecture and art books – all about Turkey and İstanbul and all in English. There's also a decent stock of Lonely Planet titles. You'll find classic fiction here too.

Metro *(☎ 212-245 2324, İstiklal Caddesi 513, Tünel)* **Map 16, #132** With only a small collection of books about İstanbul, Metro's strong point is its collection of İstanbul maps.

Pandora *(☎ 212-243 3503, ⓔ info@pandora.com.tr, Büyükparmakkapı Sokak 3, Taksim)* **Map 16, #43** Pandora has a good selection of guidebooks and other general English-language books about İstanbul, as well as plenty of fiction.

Robinson Crusoe *(☎ 212-293 6968, ⓔ rob@turk.net, İstiklal Caddesi 389, Tünel)* **Map 16, #105** Behind the posh floor-to-ceiling glass front there's an excellent selection of English-language coffee-table titles about Turkey and İstanbul, plus some history, fiction and a few travel guides.

Remzi Kitabevi *(☎ 212-234 5475, Rumeli Caddesi 44, Nişantaşı)* In Nişantaşı, northeast of Taksim, look for the excellent Remzi, which has a wide selection of English-language books on all subjects. It also has a superb branch in the Akmerkez shopping centre (☎ 212-282 2575).

OLD BOOKS, MAPS & PRINTS

Collectors will have a field day with İstanbul's wealth of antique books – some immaculate, some moth-eaten. The city and its inhabitants have been immortalised in maps, illustrations and engravings throughout the years and many of these are available as prints which make excellent souvenirs.

Where to Buy Old Books, Maps & Prints

You can pick up cheap (US$2 to US$5 each) coloured prints from many of the handicraft shops. The row outside Aya Sofya has a good range. If you want something fancier, plenty of shops sell pricier souvenirs.

Beyoğlu (Tünel) (Map 16) At the southern end of İstiklal Caddesi, directly across from the upper station of the Tünel, is the Tünel Pasajı, one of those old İstanbul shopping passages with sturdy metal gates which could be chained and locked at night. Today it has upmarket antique book/print shops plus an artsy cafe. Sofyalı Sokak, at the northern end of the passage (ie, away from the Tünel station), also has some similar shops.

Artrium *(☎ 212-251 4302, Tünel Geçidi 7)* **Map 16, #127** This large upmarket shop has lots of arty things such as prints, old movie posters, frames, miniature paintings, old postcards and heaps more.

Ottomania *(☎ 212-243 2157, Sofyalı Sokak 30-32)* **Map 16, #125** This is a top-end shop, with good-quality old maps, engravings and prints – many of them framed.

Librairie de Péra *(☎ 212-252 3078, Galipdede Caddesi 22)* **Map 16, #137** This is a good antiquarian shop with old books (and some new) in English with some in German, French, Russian, Greek, Armenian, Arabic and Turkish. You'll find a mixed bag of history, art, politics plus some classic literature. Galipdede Caddesi, which runs down to Galata Tower, starts from Tünel Square.

Beyoğlu (Çukurcuma) (Map 16) Another option is to forage around Çukurcuma (south-east of İstiklal Caddesi) – the antique shop hotbed. Here some shops may also stock old prints, maps and books. See Antiques earlier in this chapter for shop listings.

Galeri Alfa *(☎ 212-251 1672, Faikpaşa Sokak 47)* **Map 16, #61** You must be buzzed in to enter this small, upmarket shop. Though there are heaps of maps and prints, the specialities here are the colourful toy Ottoman soldiers and harem women – even Süleyman the Magnificent has been shrunk to 10cm tall. It's worth popping in just to see them.

COPPER

Copper vessels are another souvenir choice. Some are old – sometimes several centuries old – most are handsome, and some are still eminently useful. The new copperware tends to be of a lighter gauge; that's one of the ways you tell the new from old. But even the new stuff will have been made by hand.

Copper vessels should not be used for cooking in or eating from unless they are tinned inside: that is, washed with molten tin which covers the toxic copper. If you intend to use a copper vessel, make sure the interior layer of tin is intact, or negotiate to have it *kalaylamak* (tinned). If there is a *kalaycı* shop nearby, ask about the price of the tinning in advance, as tin is expensive.

Most souvenir shops sell a few copper items, but Kapalı Çarşı's Old Bazaar has shops crammed with the stuff. You may also find copper goods in the shops at the southern end of Nuruosmaniye Caddesi, just outside the bazaar.

INLAID WOOD

Jewellery boxes, chess and backgammon *(tavla)* boards and other items will be inlaid with different coloured woods, silver or mother-of-pearl. Make sure there is indeed inlay. These days, alarmingly accurate decals exist. Also, check the silver: is it silver, or aluminium or pewter? And what about that mother-of-pearl, is it in fact 'daughter-of-polystyrene'? You'll find these wares in all souvenir shops, though the southern end of Uzunçarşı Caddesi, north of the Kapalı Çarşı, has some wholesalers selling backgammon sets – you may get a better deal here.

JEWELLERY

İstanbul is a wonderful place to buy jewellery, especially antique. New gold work tends to be flashy, yellowy and overdecorated – it won't appeal to some. Silverware is more refined, and there is an incredible variety of styles. Few pieces are what anyone would consider chic-contemporary; the newer designs tend to be inspired by Ottoman and Byzantine jewellery.

Gold shops should have a copy of the newspaper that bears the daily price for unworked gold of so many carats. Serious gold buyers should check this price, watch carefully as the jeweller weighs the piece in question, and then calculate what part of the price is for gold and what part for labour. Silver will also be weighed. There is sterling silver jewellery (look for the hallmark), but nickel silver and pewter-like alloys are much more common. Serious dealers don't try to pass off alloy as silver. Some shops will pass off plastic, glass and other stones as real gemstones – if you don't know what you're looking for, steer clear.

Where to Buy Jewellery

Gold shoppers should head to Kuyumcular Caddesi (Jewellers St) or Kalpakçılarbaşı Caddesi in the Kapalı Çarşı where there are a plethora of gold shops. Silver shoppers should head to the Old Bazaar, also in the

Grand Bazaar. Bileyciler Sokak, south of the bazaar, has silver wholesalers bursting with goodies. And don't forget the Sunday market at Ortaköy, which has heaps of silver jewellery too.

Eller *(☎ 212-249 2364, Postacılar Sokak 12, Tünel)* **Map 16, #110** This airy gallery/jewellery shop has handmade replicas of ancient Anatolian jewellery, as well as unusual modern pieces. The artist works up the back. It's a very friendly place, so feel free to wander through.

Hematit *(☎ 212-249 5634, Aznavur Pasajı 10, İstiklal Caddesi 212, Galatasaray)* **Map 16, #85** Hematit has a good selection of silver jewellery and you can have a good hassle-free browse here.

Traditional Silver *(☎ 212-513 4893, Old Bazaar, 126-7, Kapalı Çarşı)* **Map 4, #11** This place is just one of many in the Old Bazaar, but it has all new wares and the staff seem to be friendly and willing to bargain.

MEERSCHAUM

If you smoke a pipe, you know about meerschaum. For those who don't, meerschaum ('sea foam' in German; *lületaşı* in Turkish) is a hydrous magnesium silicate, a white, soft stone which is porous but heat-resistant. When carved into a pipe, it smokes cool and sweet.

Over time, it absorbs residues from the tobacco and turns a nut-brown colour. Devoted meerschaum pipe smokers even have special gloves for holding the pipe as they smoke, so that oil from their fingers won't sully the fine, even patina of the pipe.

The world's largest and finest beds of meerschaum are found in Turkey, near the city of Eskişehir. Miners climb down shafts in the earth to bring up buckets of mud, some of which contain chunks of the mineral. Artful carving of this soft stone has always been done, and blocks of meerschaum were exported to be carved abroad as well.

Malls & Markets (Map 11)

With one foot planted in the East, and another in the West, İstanbul has more than its fair share of contradictions: Ritzy shopping plazas dot posh suburbs, while the mass of shoppers elbow for goods at the weekly street markets.

Street Markets

Kadıköy, on the Asian side, has a massive **Tuesday market**. It's a tent-city sheltering too many clothes, lingerie, toys and household goods, and it's a good excuse to get yourself over to the Asian side. See Sights on the Asian Shore in the Things to See & Do chapter for getting there and away information.

Ironically, there's a **Thursday morning market** beside Akmerkez that sells cheap fakes of the designer labels sold next door.

Shopping Centres

The anarchy of a market is a lot more fun than visiting another same-same shopping centre, but we've listed the malls in case it's wet, cold and you just want to stay inside.

Akmerkez shopping centre *(☎ 212-282 0170, Nisbetiye Caddesi, Etiler)* Open 10am-10pm daily. This place gets top buzz among İstanbul's upmarket shoppers. Located in Etiler, well north of Taksim and west of Bebek, it's an authentic posh US-style shopping mall with all the well-known, world-class names (Polo-Ralph Lauren, Pierre Cardin, Benetton) and the best of the Turkish chains (Beymen, Tiffany & Tomato, Yargıcı) as well as numerous boutiques. When you get tired of shopping, take sustenance in any of the cafes or restaurants, or from the supermarket, or relax in one of the cinemas. You can get here by the Taksim metro (get off at the Levent station), by bus No 58A from Eminönü, or by taxi in around 15 minutes (US$10) from Taksim.

Galleria *(☎ 212-559 9560, Rauf Orbay Caddesi, Ataköy)* Open 10am-10pm daily. İstanbul's first US-style shopping mall is on the Marmara shore road at Ataköy, west of the city walls. Now upstaged by its sibling Akmerkez, Galleria is nonetheless still fairly busy with plenty of shopping options.

These days, however, the export of block meerschaum is prohibited because the government realised that exporting uncarved blocks was the same as exporting the jobs to carve them. So any carved pipe will have been carved in Turkey.

You'll marvel at the artistry of the Eskişehir carvers. Pipes portraying turbaned *paşas* (powerful officials), wizened old men, and mythological beasts, as well as bracelets, pendants, eggs and cigarette holders, will be on view in any souvenir shop.

When buying, look for purity and uniformity in the stone. Carving is often used to cover up flaws in a piece of meerschaum. For pipes, check that the bowl walls are uniform in thickness, and that the hole at the bottom of the bowl is centred. Purists buy uncarved, plain pipe-shaped meerschaums that are simply but perfectly made.

Prices for pipes vary, but should be between US$15 and US$25 for average-quality carving and stone, or US$25 to US$60 for better quality.

Meerschaum Pipes *(☎ 212-516 4142, Arasta Çarşısı 63, Sultanahmet)* **Map 13, #98** Here is a good selection of well-crafted pipes and some other meerschaum objects such as figurines and eggs. Pipes start at US$25, though the plain pipes go for US$40 to US$60.

Yerliexport *(☎ 212-526 2619, Old Bazaar, 59, Kapalı Çarşı)* **Map 4, #12** This shoebox-sized shop is packed with a good range of quality pipes plus other items. Prices range from US$20.

CLOTHES

In İstanbul you can buy clothes you'd be able to find in department stores all over the world – but some of the gaudy stuff, fortunately, you'll only find here. Either way, clothing is decently priced, usually good quality, and it's the kind of gear you know you'll actually wear when you get home.

Where to Buy Clothes

Nişantaşı (Map 17) Fashion victims head to Abdi İpekçi Caddesi, Nişantaşı. Here it's bumper to bumper Mercs. Hugo Boss, Gucci and Emporio Armani rub shoulders, while well-dressed glamour-pusses totter from one shop to the next. Top Shop (club-wear plus latest fashions and OK prices) and Esprit have outlets along Valikonağı Caddesi. More affordable are the shops a bit further north, along and around Rumeli Caddesi. Here you'll find jam-packed blocks of shops with women's fashion, upmarket infant apparel, lingerie, sportswear, and shoes for both men and women. Don't miss Baytar Ahmet Efendi Sokak, which leads off Rumeli Caddesi. It has shoulder-to-shoulder women's fashion stores, with prices ranging from US$5 to US$25.

İstiklal Caddesi (Map 16) İstiklal Caddesi also has many clothing stores worth looking at.

Tiffany & Tomato *(☎ 212-292 6872, İstiklal Caddesi 305, Galatasaray)* **Map 16, #94** Here you will find basic fashions: cotton pants, tops and T-shirts for men and women. Prices range from US$5 to US$20.

Vakko *(☎ 212-251 4092, İstiklal Caddesi 123-5, Taksim)* **Map 16, #37** If you're intimidated by the uninviting double-doored entrance you've failed the test! Vakko has been in business for at least half a century, and that's not by inviting in those who can't afford its high style and quality.

Roxy *(☎ 212-244 3363, Aznavur Pasajı 11, İstiklal Caddesi 212, Galatasaray)* **Map 16, #85** Second-hand clothes of 1950s to 1970s ilk are very vogue in İstanbul and often have to be imported. This boosts up the prices to make this fashion unfashionably pricey. If you're still keen try Roxy.

Levi's and other jean labels are sold at Kapalı Çarşı. Although cheap – starting at US$25 – these are invariably fakes. Make sure you try them on, as some of the crutches seem to be a bit low, lopsided or excruciatingly tight. Save embarrassing yourself and consider buying cheap (US$25 to US$50) legitimate jeans from local labels such as ***Mavi*** *(☎ 212-249 3758, İstiklal Caddesi 117, Beyoğlu)* **(Map 16, #36)**.

İstanbul has heaps of super-cheap clothes, though you usually need to scavenge through mounds of never-been-in-fashion wear to find something you're happy to be seen in (why are leopard prints perennially fashionable in İstanbul?).

Ortave Alt Çarşı *(Cnr İstiklal Caddesi & Nuruziya Sokak)* **Map 16, #103** Open 10am-7pm Mon-Sat. This is an ageing shopping mall gone trash. With three levels of mega-cheap bargains you'll find bras for US$3, knickers for US$1, tops, skirts and leggings for US$1 to US$3. There's heaps of children's wear too.

Beyazıt & Eminönü (Map 15) Over in Old İstanbul the place to look for fashion is in Beyazıt along Yeniçeriler Caddesi, but you'll find nonfashion in many spots. If you're after a new handbag, Beyazıt also has row upon row of shops churning out top fashion items – usually patent leather or vinyl – for bottom-dollar prices. Handbag central is Direkli Camii Sokak, and here you'll pick one up for US$8 to US$20.

An average-quality men's off-the-rack three-piece suit should cost between US$50 and US$150. For a local designer label, or if you buy from a department store or large popular store, you'll pay over US$150. Sports jackets and shirts are also good buys. Men's wear – canvas trousers and jeans – are available at stores in the street bazaar along Yeni Cami Meydanı Sokak beside Yeni Cami in Eminönü. Expect to pay around US$10 for trousers.

Gülüm Giyim Sanayı *(☎ 212-522 3675, Aşirefendi Caddesi 61, Sultanhamam)* A reader recommends this shop, near Eminönü, which sells suits and shirts.

Vakko's Sale Store *(Vakko İndirim Mağazası; ☎ 212-522 8941, Şeyhülislam Hayri Efendi Caddesi 7/12-14, Eminönü)* **Map 15, #14** If you like Vakko's style, but not the price tags, then this poor-cousin store is for you. There's a good selection of women's, men's and children's clothing and shoes for about a quarter of the presale price. And it's not all daggy stuff, either.

SPICES, POTIONS & TURKISH DELIGHT

Where to Buy

Eminönü (Map 15) The Mısır Çarşısı was once the centre of the spice and medicinal herb trade in İstanbul. It's still an important outlet, though these days locals are more likely to shop in the surrounding streets, leaving the market for tourists. Do what the locals do and shop along Hasırcılar Caddesi for spices, tea, herbs and sweets. Prices are clearly marked and you should taste goods before you buy.

Mehmet Kalmaz Baharatçı *(☎ 212-522 6604, Mısır Çarşısı 41)* One of the few shops here that specialises in potions and lotions, this old-fashioned place sells remedies to make women younger, another to make men stronger, and a Royal love potion that, we guess, is supposed to combine the two. At around US$3 per potion, what are you waiting for?

Kurukahveci Mehmet Efendi Mahtumları *(☎ 212-511 4262, Hasırcılar Caddesi 1-5)* **Map 15, #9** Considered by many to sell the best brew in town, Turkish coffee here costs US$1.70 per 250g, Colombian US$2 per 250g.

Ali Muhiddin Hacı Bekir *(☎ 212-522 0666, Hamidiye Caddesi)* **Map 15, #13** It's best to buy Turkish delight in specialist shops and you can't get better than this. Turkish delight here ranges from US$2 to US$5 per kilogram, and this is the original shop of the comfortable morsel's inventor (see the boxed text 'Turkish Delight' in the Places to Eat chapter).

Hafız Mustafa Şekerlemeleri *(☎ 212-526 5627, Hamidiye Caddesi 84-86)* **Map 15, #12** Close by, this shop also has Turkish delight, plus all sorts of other sweet temptations.

Kapalı Çarşı (Map 4) The bazaar has a handful of spice and potion dealers too.

Abdulla Natural Products *(☎ 212-522 9078, Halıcılar Caddesi 53)* **Map 4, #13** Well seated on the natural product bandwagon, Abdulla has Turkish oil blend mixes, natural soaps (US$4.50) and herbal teas – all wrapped in hessian and paper. The best buy here is the soap.

Beyoğlu (Map 16) Over in Beyoğlu, head to İstiklal Caddesi and look around the Balık Pazarı (Fish Market) for spices and herbs.

Mystical Parfümevi *(☎ 212-292 9290, Aznavur Pasajı 3, İstiklal Caddesi 212)* **Map 16, #85** This aromatic booth has a range of perfumes made from essential oil blends.

Ali Muhiddin Hacı Bekir *(☎ 212-244 2804, İstiklal Caddesi 129)* **Map 16, #65** If huge chunks of helva aren't enough to draw your sweet teeth in, then the Turkish delight (US$2 to US$5 per kilogram) and the crunchy biscuits should do the trick. There's tasty stuff and plenty of it.

GLASSWARE

İstanbul produces some unique glasswork, a legacy of the Ottoman Empire's affection for this delicate and intricate art. Paşabahçe, a large factory on the Asian side, has been producing glass for 150 years and still churns out some good stuff. If you're after tea sets, the Kapalı Çarşı has many shops selling plain, colourful and ugly, heavily gilded sets. Note that most of the ornate, curvy perfume bottles you see in the touristy shops are Egyptian, despite what the seller might say.

Paşabahçe *(☎ 212-244 0544, İstiklal Caddesi 314, Tepebaşı)* **Map 16, #106** This outlet has a good range of contemporary (nothing special) and older-style (some gilded and colourful) pieces. Prices are high: Each glass costs US$6 and up, though you can get half-dozen sets from US$28. The factory outlet, over in Paşabahçe, has a larger selection but the prices are the same and it's an ordeal to get to.

İstanbul Sanatlar Çarşısı *(Handicrafts Market; ☎ 212-517 6782; Kabasakal Caddesi, Sultanahmet)* **Map 13, #66** At this handicraft market, an artisan makes glassware reminiscent of ancient traditional Ottoman styles.

CERAMICS

After carpets and kilims, ceramics would have to be Turkey's most successful souvenir industry. And for good reason: The ceramics are beautiful and the standard fare fits within most budgets. Many of the tiles you see in the tourist shops have been painted using a silkscreen printing method and this is why they're cheap at US$2 per 20cm by 20cm. One step up are the ubiquitous hand-painted bowls, plates and other pieces (US$5 to US$40); these are made by rubbing a patterned carbon paper on the raw ceramic, tracing the black outline, and filling in the holes with colour. The most expensive ceramics for sale are hand-painted – without the use of a carbon paper pattern – and derived from original design. Note that many of the ceramics have lead in the glaze so it's probably safest to use them as ornaments.

Where to Buy Ceramics

Unsurprisingly, the Kapalı Çarşı has heaps of stores selling ceramics, but for original artworks you have to shop around.

İznik Classics & Tiles *(☎ 212-517 1705, Arasta Çarşısı 67 & 73, Sultanahmet)* **Map 13, #99** These two shops (same owners) have a small selection of plates, vases and tiles – all hand-painted originals. As you're not getting mass-produced work, the prices are steep at US$300 and rising. The shop opposite has a large range of mass-produced stock, which is still beautiful.

MZK Hediyelik Eşya *(☎ 212-234 4005, Cumhuriyet Caddesi 83, Elmadağ)* **Map 17, #31** This shop specialises in hand-painted Ottoman-style baroque porcelain vases, bowls and more. It's the kind of stuff you may see in Dolmabahçe Palace. Some pieces are over the top, with florally decorations and splashes of gold and silver, but others are subdued. Prices range from US$8 to US$70.

Selvi El Sanatları *(☎ 212-527 0997, Yağlıkçılar Caddesi 54, Kapalı Çarşı)* **Map 4, #1** The speciality here is Kütahya faience; the small range of hand-painted (20cm by 20cm) tiles cost US$18 to US$55 each. There is also a selection of the standard tourist ware: vases, plates, cups and bowls.

Yıldız Ceramics *(☎ 212-261 1354, Yıldız Park, Beşiktaş)* **Map 12** This small shop has goods from the famous Yıldız Porselen Fabrikası which used to supply the palaces with porcelain. If you like the florally Ottoman-style baroque look, you'll like these pieces starting from US$2. The shop is at the entrance to the factory (see Yıldız Şale & Park under Dolmabahçe Palace to Ortaköy in the Things to See & Do chapter for more information).

MUSIC & MUSICAL INSTRUMENTS

If you dig Turkish folk music, then İstanbul is a great place to pick up an instrument. Percussion, wind and string instruments can all be purchased here and as these aren't top-ticket tourist souvenirs, you should be able to bargain and pay a reasonable price. For names and information about folk instruments see Arts in the chapter Facts about İstanbul chapter.

Where to Buy Musical Instruments

Elvis *(☎ 212-293 8752, Galipdede Caddesi 35, Tünel)* **Map 16, #138** If you thought Elvis was hiding in the Bahamas you're wrong. He's here selling a good range of traditional string instruments.

Kıvılcım Music *(☎ 212-252 3558, Galipdede Caddesi 10, Tünel)* **Map 16, #136** Here you'll find electric guitars and İstanbul's famous cymbals.

Mega Music Centre *(☎ 212-521 3855, Atatürk Bulvarı, Vefa)* **Map 14** Over in Old İstanbul you will find bigger shops such as this one stocking Turkish CDs and traditional stringed instruments; these are wholesale establishments but you'll be able to buy here too. Close by, and south-east of Şehzade Mehmet Camii along Şehzade Caddesi, there's another clutch of instrument shops. These specialise in percussion instruments.

Where to Buy Music

CDs aren't particularly cheap in İstanbul, though you will find a few pirate copies being sold around Sultanahmet. Foreign performers' CDs usually cost from US$10 to US$20, while local artists' CDs go for around US$9.

Lale Plak *(☎ 212-293 7739, Galipdede Caddesi 1, Tünel)* **Map 16, #133** Open 9am-7pm Mon-Sat, noon-6pm Sun. This small shop is crammed with CDs of jazz, Western classical, Turkish classical (not much contemporary) and Latin music ranging from US$9 to US$18.

Mephisto *(☎ 212-293 1909, İstiklal Caddesi 173 & 197, Beyoğlu)* Both these stores have a huge CD collection of Turkish popular music, but there's some Turkish folk and classic music here too, plus books and a cafe.

Excursions

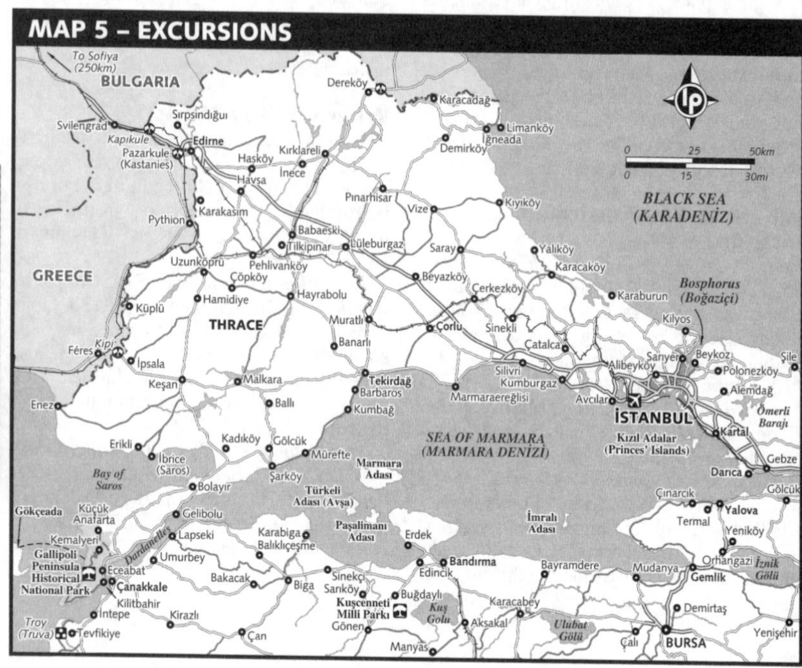

İstanbul makes an excellent base for day trips and overnight excursions to several places in Thrace, the Black Sea and Marmara region, and even further afield to Gallipoli and Troy.

For more detailed information on all of these excursions, refer to Lonely Planet's *Turkey,* which covers the entire country in detail. Travel agencies in İstanbul can arrange any of these excursions for you (see Travel Agencies under Organised Tours in the Getting Around chapter).

The Bosphorus (Map 6)

The forces of history have travelled up and down the Bosphorus, affecting empires and the great imperial capital of İstanbul as they came and went. The strait, which connects the Black Sea (Karadeniz) and the Sea of Marmara (Marmara Denizi), is 32km long, from 500m to 3km wide and 50m to 120m (average 60m) deep. An excursion up the Bosphorus is an essential part of any visit to İstanbul.

In Turkish the strait is the Boğaziçi (*iç,* inside or interior: 'within the strait') or İstanbul Boğazı, from *boğaz,* throat or strait.

The Bosphorus provides a convenient boundary for geographers. As it was a military bottleneck, armies marching from the east tended to stop on the eastern side, and those from the west on the western. So the western side was always more like Europe, the eastern more like Asia. Though the modern Turks think of themselves as Europeans, it is still common to say that Europe ends and Asia begins at the Bosphorus.

Except for the few occasions when the Bosphorus froze, until 1973 crossing it always meant going by boat. Late in that year, the Bosphorus Bridge, the fourth-longest suspension bridge in the world, was opened. For the first time there was a firm physical link across the straits from Europe to Asia.

Traffic was so heavy over the new bridge that it paid for itself in less than a decade. Now there is a second bridge, the Fatih Bridge (named after Mehmet the Conqueror, Mehmet Fatih), just north of Rumeli Hisarı. A third bridge, even further north, is planned.

History

Ancient myth lives on in the name of the Bosphorus. *Bous* is cow in ancient Greek, and *poros* is crossing place, so 'Bosphorus' is the place where the cow crossed. The cow was Io, a beautiful lady with whom Zeus, king of the gods, had an affair. When his wife Hera discovered his infidelity, Zeus tried to make up for it by turning his erstwhile lover into a cow. Hera, for good measure, provided a horsefly to sting Io on the rump and drive her across the strait. (Notice that Zeus got off with no punishment!)

From earliest times the Bosphorus has been a maritime road to adventure. It is thought that Ulysses' travels brought him through the Bosphorus. Byzas, founder of Byzantium, explored these waters before the time of Jesus. Mehmet the Conqueror built two mighty fortresses at the strait's narrowest point so as to close it off to allies of the Byzantines. Each spring, enormous Ottoman armies would take several days to cross the Bosphorus on their way to campaigns in Asia. At the end of WWI, the defeated Ottoman capital cowered under the guns of Allied frigates anchored in the strait. When the republic was proclaimed, the last sultan of the Ottoman Empire snuck quietly down to the Bosphorus shore, boarded a British man-of-war and sailed away to exile.

TOURING THE BOSPHORUS

You could spend several days exploring the sights of the Bosphorus: there are four Ottoman palaces, three castles, plenty of tempting fish restaurants and several pretty towns. However, one day will do in a pinch.

The essential feature of any Bosphorus tour is a cruise along the strait. If you only have a day, a trip combining travel by both land and sea is best. Begin your explorations with a ferry cruise, then visit selected sites by bus, *dolmuş* (shared taxi or minibus) and taxi.

A Bosphorus Cruise (Map 15)

The ferry used by most tourists is the Eminönü-Kavaklar Boğaziçi Özel Gezi

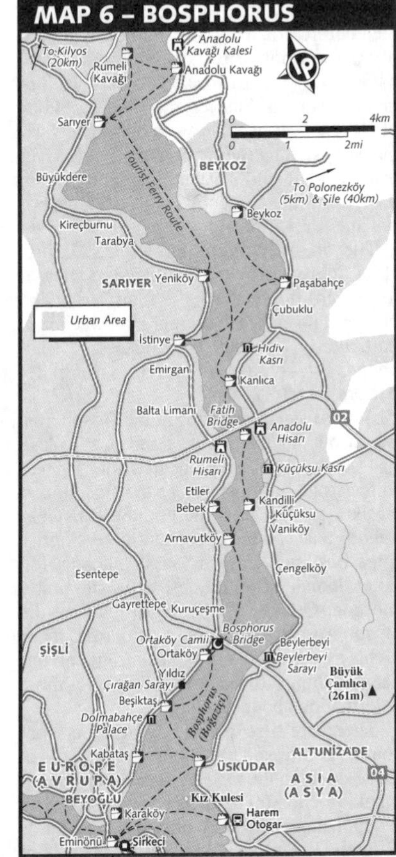

Seferleri (Eminönü-Kavaklar Bosphorus Special Touristic Excursions) up the Bosphorus. These ferries depart from the Boğaz Hattı dock (number three; Map 15) at Eminönü (daily at 10.35am and 1.35pm), stop at Beşiktaş on the European shore, Kanlıca on the Asian shore, Yeniköy, Sarıyer and Rumeli Kavağı on the European shore, and Anadolu Kavağı on the Asian shore (the turnaround point). Times are subject to change and there are sometimes more trips added during summer.

The ferries take 1¾ hours to get all the way to pretty Anadolu Kavağı where you may want to take a fish lunch and stroll up to the castle which looks out to the Black Sea, before you catch the 3pm or 5pm boat back. The whole trip takes six hours. If you haven't the time to spare, you may want to go only as far as Sarıyer, then take a dolmuş or bus No 25E back down, stopping at various sights along the way. Arrival at Sarıyer is at 11.50am and 2.50pm. Departures from Sarıyer for the trip back down the Bosphorus are at 3.15pm and 5.15pm.

The one-way/return fare is US$2.50/1. Hold onto your ticket; you need to show it to reboard the boat for the return trip. The boats fill up early in summer – on weekends particularly – so buy your ticket and walk aboard at least 30 or 45 minutes prior to departure to get a seat.

As you start your trip up the Bosphorus, watch out for the small island Kız Kulesi, just off the Asian shore near Üsküdar. Eyes to the front, and just before the first stop at Beşiktaş, you'll pass the grandiose Dolmabahçe Palace on the European shore. Shortly after Beşiktaş, Çırağan Sarayı, now a top hotel, looms up on the left while the pretty mosque, Ortaköy Camii, is just before the Bosphorus Bridge. You could tour these sights by bus on your way back from Sarıyer; see the Things to See & Do chapter for more information about each sight.

There are also private Bosphorus boat tours. The ticket touts buzz around dock three flogging the tickets. These tours are on smaller boats (60 to 100 people), each with a small sun deck. They only travel as far as Rumeli Hisarı (without stopping) where they stop for lunch for an hour before returning. The whole trip takes about three hours and costs US$9 (try bargaining). The advantage of these trips is they're shorter and the boat goes closer to the shore; the disadvantages are the price, plus you don't get to see the whole of the Bosphorus. These boats leave on the half-hour starting at around 10.30am and finishing at 6pm from May to September (4pm at other times).

Cross-Bosphorus Ferries

At several points along the Bosphorus, passenger ferries run between the European and Asian shores, allowing you to cross easily from one side to the other. Southernmost are the routes from Eminönü, Kabataş and Beşiktaş in Europe to Üsküdar in Asia.

Another ring route is from Kanlıca to Anadolu Hisarı and Kandilli on the Asian shore, then across the Bosphorus to Arnavutköy and Bebek on the European shore. Departures from Kanlıca are at 7.15am, 8.30am, 9.40am, 10.50am, 12.35pm, 2.05pm, 3.45pm, 5.05pm and 6.15pm. The Kanlıca-Bebek voyage takes 25 minutes and costs US$0.50. If you miss the ferry at Kanlıca, you can hire a tiny boat from beside the dock to motor you across the Bosphorus for US$3 (per boat). In fact you can do this at many spots along the Bosphorus and it's a mini-adventure that shouldn't be missed.

Other ring ferries run from İstinye on the European side to Beykoz and Paşabahçe on the Asian side. Yet another ring ferry operates between Sarıyer in Europe and Anadolu Kavağı in Asia, with 16 ferries a day from 7am to 10.45pm; nine of these ferries stop at Rumeli Kavağı (in Europe) on the way.

Touring by Land

Many of the Bosphorus sights can be seen by ferry but for others you'll have to tour by land.

European Shore Bus No 25E travels along the Bosphorus shore between Eminönü and Sarıyer, stopping at Dolmabahçe Palace, Beşiktaş, Çırağan Sarayı, Ortaköy, Rumeli Hisarı and other places along the way. If you'd like to see the sights on land as well as by ferry you can catch the excursion ferry up to Sarıyer and return by bus No 25E, or you could start by bus and catch the ferry back. The shore road traffic can be slow (particularly on weekends) so allow several hours for the trip.

Asian Shore Bus No 15A runs from Üsküdar all the way to Anadolu Kavağı. You could do a joint ferry and bus trip along the Asian side but bus No 15A is infrequent. Still, if you're interested, you could catch the 10.35am excursion ferry, which arrives at 12.25pm at Anadolu Kavağı, then the bus back. Buses leave Anadolu Kavağı at 12.30pm, 3pm and 5.30pm.

SIGHTS ON THE EUROPEAN SHORE

Here are some sights to look out for as you head north up the shore from Ortaköy. For information on the sights along the Bosphorus before Ortaköy (ie, Dolmabahçe Palace), see the Things to See & Do chapter.

Bebek

Bebek is a glamorous suburb of İstanbul with a strong foreign and academic presence because of nearby **Boğaziçi Üniversitesi** (Bosphorus University). Its shops surround a small park and a mosque, with the Bosphorus and ferry dock on the east side and the **Egyptian consulate** on the south side. The consulate is an Art Nouveau, waterside mini-palace built by the khedive of Egypt, Abbas Hilmi, who also later built Hıdiv Kasrı on the Asian side (see Hıdiv Kasrı under Kanlıca later in the chapter for more information). A ring ferry service joins Bebek with Kanlıca and Anadolu Hisarı on the Asian shore; another weekday morning and evening service heads south to Arnavutköy, Ortaköy and Beşiktaş.

Above Bebek you'll notice the New England 19th-century-style architecture of the Boğaziçi Üniversitesi. Founded as Robert College in the mid-19th century by the American Board of Foreign Missions, the college had an important influence on the modernisation of political, social, economic and scientific thought in Turkey. Though donated by the board to the Turkish Republic in the early 1970s, instruction is still in English.

If you fancy a bite to eat, Bebek has a handful of oh-so-trendy places.

Mellow Le Fer Forge *(☎ 212-257 0984, Cevdetpaşa Caddesi 125/1)* This is overflowing with wrought-iron furniture, but it has a plum Bosphorus-side spot.

New Yorker *(☎ 212-287 5295)* Dishes from US$5-12. Open 9am to midnight daily. Opposite Mellow Le Fer Forge on the main road, this is for those tiring of Turkish food. This flashy modern restaurant has an international blend of Italian dishes (risotto with scallops), US dishes (New York sirloin steak), fish and really yummy desserts (warm apple crisp).

Rumeli Hisarı

About 1.5km north of Bebek centre is **Rumeli Hisarı** *(Fortress of Europe; ☎ 212-263 5305, Yahya Kemal Caddesi 42; adult/student US$2/1; open 9.30am-6pm Thur-Tues)*. Within the walls are park-like grounds, an open-air theatre and the minaret of a ruined mosque. Stairs lead up to the ramparts and towers where you can get beautiful views of the Bosphorus.

Here at the narrowest part of the Bosphorus, Mehmet the Conqueror had this fortress built in a mere four months during 1452, in preparation for his planned siege of Byzantine Constantinople. To speed its completion in line with his impatience to conquer Constantinople, Mehmet ordered each of his three viziers to take responsibility for one of the three main towers. If the tower's construction was not completed on schedule, the vizier would pay with his life, or so legend has it. Not surprisingly, the work was completed on time, with Mehmet's three generals competing fiercely with one another to finish.

Once completed, Rumeli Hisarı, in concert with Anadolu Hisarı on the Asian shore just opposite, controlled all traffic on the Bosphorus, and cut the city off from resupply by sea from the north.

The mighty fortress's useful military life lasted less than one year. After the conquest of Constantinople, it was used as a glorified

Bosphorus toll booth for a while, then as a barracks, later as a prison, and finally as an open-air theatre, but never again as a fortress.

Places to Eat Between Rumeli Hisarı and the bus stop to the north, there are several fish restaurants and tea gardens.

Cafe Kale & Pastane *(☎ 212-265 0097, Yahya Kemal Caddesi 16)* Dishes US$1.50-3.50. Open 6am-11.30pm daily. This is a low-key, friendly, cute little place serving kebaps, omelettes and salads. It has great views of the Bosphorus.

Karaca Fish Restaurant *(☎ 212-263 3468, Yahya Kemal Caddesi 10)* Dishes US$4-11. Open noon-midnight daily. The restaurant has a rooftop with OK Bosphorus views; downstairs a tree staked its claim to the territory, and the restaurant just had to build around it. There's excellent fish and a plethora of meze choices.

Rumeli İskele *(☎ 212-263 2997, Yahya Kemal Caddesi 1)* Mains US$4-19. Open noon-1am daily. This is right near the bus stop and has top Bosphorus viewing as the restaurant sits right by the water. The service and food is impeccable.

Emirgan & İstinye

Emirgan is a wealthy suburb north of the Fatih Bridge. In late April to early May, Emirgan Park, just above the town, gets decked out in tulips. North of Emirgan, there's a ferry dock near the small yacht-lined cove of İstinye; a ring ferry service runs from İstinye to Beykoz and Paşabahçe on the Asian shore.

If you're feeling flush with cash you may want to indulge at İstinye's famous restaurant. ***Süreyya*** *(☎ 212-277 5886, İstinye Caddesi 26)* Dishes US$12-20. Open noon-3pm & 8pm-midnight daily, except Sunday. This has superb and varied cuisine, with Russian, Turkish and continental dishes. Chicken Kiev is a favourite here, but there's also good borscht and various French-inspired dishes. Reservations are essential.

Yeniköy

Just north of İstinye, Yeniköy is on a point jutting out from the European shore. It was first settled in classical times and later became a favourite summer resort, as indicated by the lavish 19th-century Ottoman *yalı* (seaside villa) of the one-time grand vizier, Sait Halim Paşa. Not too many of these luxurious wooden villas survive. Fire destroyed a lot. Economics and the desire for modern conveniences caused many others to be torn down before preservation laws were promulgated. Today it is against the law to remove a yalı from the Bosphorus – it must either be repaired or rebuilt.

Yeniköy has options for the hungry. ***Tribeca*** *(☎ 212-223 9919, Kapalı Bakkal Sokak 5)* Snacks US$2.50-5. Open 9am-11pm daily. Bagels in İstanbul have taken off at Tribeca – which has several other outlets around town – and these tasty bagels just may be the snack you're after. The chicken salad bagel is especially good.

Tarabya

Originally called Therapeia for its healthy climate, the little cove of Tarabya has been a favourite summer watering place for İstanbul's well-to-do for centuries, though unfortunately the concrete monster hotel perched on the north mouth of the cove has poisoned some of its charm.

North of the village are some of the old summer embassies of foreign powers. When the heat and fear of disease increased in the warm months, foreign ambassadors and their staff would retire to palatial residences, complete with lush gardens, on this shore. The region for such embassy residences extended north to the village of Büyükdere.

Büyükdere

Tarabya leads in to Büyükdere, notable for a number of churches, summer embassies and the **Sadberk Hanım Müzesi** *(Sadberk Hanım Museum; ☎ 212-242 3813, Piyasa Caddesi 25-29; adult/student US$2/0.50; open 10.30am-6pm Thur-Tues Apr-Sept, 10am-5pm Thur-Tues Oct-Mar)*. The museum is on the shore road just north of the Surp Boğos Armenian Catholic Church (1885), or 200m north of the Büyükdere ferry dock.

Named after the wife of the late Mr Vehbi Koç, founder of Turkey's foremost commercial empire in 1926, the museum is her private collection of Anatolian antiquities and Ottoman heirlooms. Plaques are in English and Turkish.

The original museum building, reached after a 12- to 15-minute walk south from the ferry docks in Sarıyer, is a graceful old Bosphorus yalı, once the summer residence of Manuk Azaryan Efendi, an Ottoman Armenian who was speaker of the upper house in the Ottoman parliament. It houses the most interesting of the museum's collections, which are artefacts and exhibits from Turkey's Islamic past such as worry beads of solid gold; golden, bejewelled tobacco boxes and watches (one bears the sultan's monogram in diamonds); beautiful İznik and Kütahya pottery; and even a table that once belonged to Napoleon (he's pictured on it, surrounded by his generals). A number of rooms in the great old house have been arranged and decorated in Ottoman style – the style of the ruling class, obviously. There's a sumptuous maternity room with embroidered cloth, a henna party room and a room set up for circumcisions. A display case holds a fine collection of Ottoman spoons (the prime dining utensil) made from tortoiseshell, ebony, ivory.

The collections in the new building, beside the original, include choice artefacts dating from as early as the 6th century BC, and continuing through Roman and Byzantine times. There is also a well-chosen collection of Chinese celadon ware from the 14th to 16th centuries, later Chinese blue-and-white porcelain and some 18th-century Chinese porcelain made specifically for the Ottoman market.

Sarıyer

The villagers of Sarıyer have occupied themselves for most of their history by fishing in the currents of the Bosphorus. Fishing is still a pastime and the main livelihood here, and Sarıyer is justly noted for its several good fish restaurants. It's a busy place.

Turn right as you leave the ferry dock, stay as close to the shore as possible, and you will pass the seabus terminal and several fish restaurants before coming to the **Tarihi Balıkçılar Çarşısı**, the village's historic fish market.

Places to Eat Outside the Tarihi Balıkçılar Çarşısı there are some busy tea gardens serving snacks. Look out for the ***Sarıyer Spor Kulübü*** which has kebaps, Turkish omelette and prime views.

To the south there are several small fish restaurants. The bobbing ***Balık Ekmek İzgara*** is a little boat restaurant moored beside the quay. It dishes up fish for US$2 to US$3 from April to October.

Dolphin Class *(☎ 212-242 8705, Balıkpazarı Yanı 5)* Mains US$2-5. Open 9am-midnight daily. This place has one of the best positions of the many restaurants here. Its upstairs terrace has good Bosphorus views, while the fish is good and the mezes are tasty.

Aquarius *(☎ 212-271 3434, Cami Arkası Sokak 11-13)* Fish meals US$4-15. Open 9am-midnight daily. Close to Dolphin Class, but a bit posher with a vine-covered outdoor eating area and crisp white tablecloths. Choose your fish from one of the many tanks – you can't complain about freshness!

Getting There & Away The Bosphorus excursion ferries from Eminönü (see Touring the Bosphorus at the beginning of this chapter) stop at Sarıyer on both the outbound and return voyages. There is a seabus service to Karaköy as well.

From 7am to 10.45pm, 16 ferries a day cross the Bosphorus (US$0.50) from Sarıyer to Anadolu Kavağı on the Asian side (see Sights on the Asian Shore later in this chapter), with some stopping at Rumeli Kavağı as well.

Heading to Kilyos, 10km north, dolmuşes and the İETT bus No 151 (US$0.60) leave from a stop about 1km inland from the seabus stop. To find it, head inland along Sular Caddesi for about 700m until you come to the *belediye* (town hall). Turn right into Eski Kilyos Caddesi soon after the belediye and you'll see the Kilyos bus stand 100m or so ahead. The bus to Kilyos takes about 20 minutes. Dolmuşes for Rumeli Kavağı leave from Sular Caddesi, also.

If you are heading south you can catch buses from the same bus stop. It's easy enough to get to Taksim Square by bus No 25T, which doesn't follow the coast all the way, or bus No 25E which follows the coast all the way to Eminönü; there are also dolmuşes here which follow the same routes.

Rumeli Kavağı

This, the village furthest north on the European shore, is a sleepy place that gets most of its excitement from the arrival and departure of the ferry. There is a little public beach named **Altınkum** near the village. North of Rumeli Kavağı is a military zone, off limits to casual visitors.

Kilyos

İstanbul's coastal resort of Kilyos is a favourite place for a swim in the chilly waters of the Black Sea, or a leisurely meal at any time of year. You can even stay overnight if you like.

Dolmuşes and buses from Sarıyer make the trip over the hills to Kilyos in about 20 minutes, passing little impromptu open-air roadside restaurants featuring *kuzu çevirme* (spit-roasted lamb) and clusters of Lego-like holiday homes.

Kilyos' best beach is the fenced one in front of the Turban Kilyos Moteli, open daily in warm weather from 9am to 6pm for US$3.50 per person. It gets very crowded on summer weekends, but it's not bad during the week. Parking costs US$2; if you drive, park elsewhere in the village and walk to the beach.

Note that there can be a deadly undertow in the Black Sea. Swim only in protected areas or where there is an attentive lifeguard. Don't swim alone and be on guard against both the undertow and the riptide.

Places to Stay & Eat On summer weekends all Kilyos' lodgings fill up: Plan your visit for the middle of the week, reserve ahead, or visit outside the high season (which lasts from mid-July to the end of August). Most hotels have restaurants attached. From the bus and dolmuş stand, walk uphill through the intersection and continue uphill along Kale Caddesi to find the string of hotels. All the following hotels have rooms with private bathrooms.

Yonca Hotel *(☎ 212-201 1045, Kale Caddesi 32)* Rooms US$18. The quaint seafood restaurant here is popular which is just as well since some of the rooms – windowless coffins – are depressing; others are OK. Check out the room before you check in.

Yuva Motel & Restaurant *(☎ 212-201 1043, fax 201 2128, Kale Caddesi 28)* Singles/doubles US$15/22. Rooms here are nothing fancy but they're OK. The restaurant on the rooftop has partly obscured views of the sea.

Gurup Hotel *(☎ 212-201 1194, fax 201 1266, Kale Caddesi 21/1)* Singles/doubles US$21/28. Though its name means 'abundance' in Turkish, this two-star 42-room hotel is also often filled by British holiday groups (its other Turkish meaning) who like its swimming pool and Jacuzzi. All the fun has worn out the rooms, but they're clean enough; the price includes breakfast.

Kilyos Kale Hotel *(☎ 212-201 1818, fax 201 1823, Kale Caddesi 78)* Singles/doubles US$22/30. Here the rooms are clean, and there's also a swimming pool. The suites are the best value, though: US$44 to sleep four in a two-room apartment (no kitchen).

Erzurumlu Otel Restaurant *(☎ 212-201 1003, fax 201 2254, Kale Caddesi 77)* Singles/doubles US$28/35. Rooms here are also clean and have sea views. There's a tiny pool, a bar beside it and even the restaurant (mains US$3 to US$5.50) has excellent views. This is the pick of the bunch, and it charges accordingly.

For other restaurants, look down in the village or you will find the following near the shore.

Motel Mehtup Restaurant *(☎ 212-201 1016, Plaj Yolu 31)* Dishes US$2-8. This large restaurant has a rooftop with great views over the water. There is also a handful of basic twin-bed rooms for US$18 each.

Tayfun Cafe & Bar *(☎ 212-201 1710, Plaj Yolu 35)* Open 8am-2am daily. Drinks from US$1.50. Right by the beach entrance, this tiny basic bar serves beer and not much else. At night the pop gets cranked up, which may or may not be just what you're after.

Getting There & Away Kilyos is 35km north of the Galata Bridge, and can take two to three hours to reach by bus in moderately heavy traffic. All public transport comes through Sarıyer. The last bus and dolmuş leave from Kilyos for Sarıyer at about 9pm daily.

SIGHTS ON THE ASIAN SHORE

The Asian shore has a number of possibilities for sightseeing. You'll probably need to start your adventure at Üsküdar (see the Things to See & Do chapter for more information).

Beylerbeyi Sarayı

Both shores of the Bosphorus have their Ottoman palaces. The grandest on the Asian side is Beylerbeyi Sarayı *(☎ 216-321 9320, Abdullah Ağa Caddesi; admission US$3; open 9.30am-5pm Tues & Wed, Fri-Sun).* It's a few kilometres north of Üsküdar. Catch bus No 15A or a dolmuş north along the shore road from Üsküdar's main square, and get out at the Çayırbaşı stop, just north of Beylerbeyi and the Asian pylons of the Bosphorus Bridge.

The fee for a camera permit (no flash or tripod) is US$4.50, for a video it's US$9, and is a waste of money. Admission includes a guided tour.

Today the palace, for all its grandeur, is musty but still impressive, particularly on a sunny afternoon when golden light floods the rooms. The tour goes too fast. Soon you are overwhelmed by Bohemian crystal chandeliers, French (Sèvres) and Ming vases, and sumptuous carpets.

Every sultan needs some little place to get away to, and 30-room Beylerbeyi Sarayı was the place for Abdülaziz (r. 1861–76). Mahmut II had built a wooden palace here, but like so many others, it burned down. Abdülaziz wanted stone and marble, so he ordered the architect of the time, Serkis Balyan, to get to work on Beylerbeyi Sarayı. Balyan came up with an Ottoman gem, complete with a fountain in the entrance hall and two little tent-like kiosks in the sea wall. The sultan provided much of the woodwork himself.

Abdülaziz spent a lot of time here, as did other monarchs and royal guests, for this was, in effect, the sultan's guest quarters. Empress Eugénie of France stayed here on a long visit in 1869. Other royal guests included Nasruddin, shah of Persia; Nicholas, grand duke of Russia; and Nicholas, king of Montenegro. The palace's last imperial 'guest' was none other than the former sultan, Abdül Hamit II, who was brought here to spend the remainder of his life (from 1913 to 1918) under house arrest, having spent the four years immediately following his deposition in 1909 in Ottoman Salonika. He had the dubious pleasure of gazing across the Bosphorus at Yıldız and watching the great empire he had ruled with an iron fist for over 30 years crumble before his eyes.

Çengelköy

The gorgeous village of Çengelköy, north of Beylerbeyi, is a good place for a break.

Çengelköy Tarihi Çınaraltı Çay Bahçesi *(Historic Anchor Village Tea Garden Beneath the Plane Tree; ☎ 216-422 1036, Camii Sokak 5)* Dishes $1-3. Open 6am-midnight daily. This busy cafe lives up to its name; it's clustered around the trunk of a gigantic plane tree behind a little mosque at the edge of the Bosphorus. Light meals and beverages are served as well as tea (US$0.40).

Küçüksu Kasrı

The Büyük Göksu Deresi (Great Heavenly Stream) and Küçük Göksu Deresi (Small Heavenly Stream) are two brooks that descend from the Asian hills into the Bosphorus. Between them is a flat, fertile delta, grassy and shady, and just perfect for picnics, which the Ottoman upper classes enjoyed here frequently. Foreign residents, referring to the place as 'The Sweet Waters of Asia', would often join them.

If the weather was good, the sultan was there, and in style. Sultan Abdül Mecit's answer to a simple picnic blanket was the Küçüksu Kasrı *(☎ 216-332 0237, Küçüksu Caddesi; adult/student US$2/0.50; open 9.30am-5pm Tues & Wed, Fri-Sun),* an ornate lodge built in 1856. Earlier sultans had wooden kiosks here, but architect Nikogos Balyan, son of the designer of Dolmabahçe, produced a rococo gem in marble for his monarch. The standout feature here is the stunning parquetry floors, with a different design in every room. You'll pay US$4.50 to take your camera in (no tripod or flash) or US$9 for a video – don't bother.

Take bus No 15A or a dolmuş along the shore road north from Beylerbeyi to reach the Küçüksu Kasrı bus stop, then walk the 300m to the shore to find it.

Anadolu Hisarı

About 1km north of Küçüksu, in the shadow of the Fatih Bridge, is the castle and village of Anadolu Hisarı. This small castle built by Sultan Beyazıt I in 1391 was repaired and strengthened as the Asian strongpoint in Mehmet the Conqueror's stranglehold on Byzantine Constantinople in the mid-15th century. Anadolu Hisarı is a fraction the size of its great European counterpart, Rumeli Hisarı. You're free to wander about the ruined walls.

Kanlıca

The Fatih Bridge soars across the Bosphorus just north of Anadolu Hisarı. North of the bridge are more small Asian Bosphorus towns, including Kanlıca, famous for its yogurt. The **mosque** in the shady town square dates from 1560. You could catch a ferry or small boat from Kanlıca across the Bosphorus to Arnavutköy and Bebek on the European shore (see Cross-Bosphorus Ferries earlier in this chapter for details).

If you've worked up an appetite, Kanlıca has a few eateries around or near the town square.

Havuzbaşı Restaurant *(☎ 216-413 0948, Kanlıca İskelesi)* Dishes US$2-8. Open 10am-midnight daily. You won't find anything quainter than this tiny, lollypop-pink restaurant complete with frilly-edged chairs. It's right beside the Kanlıca ferry stop on the water's edge, and it looks like it may tip in at any moment. The food is good, mainly seafood, and on Friday and Saturday nights there's low-key live music.

Körfez Restaurant *(☎ 216-413 4314, Körfez Caddesi 78)* Dishes US$15-22. Lunch noon-3pm, dinner 7pm-midnight Tues-Sun. This is a glamorous waterside place perfect for special occasions. Call for reservations; you can also book the restaurant's boat to bring you over from the European side. The speciality here is sea bass baked in salt, and it also does a famous and delicious zucchini salad.

Hıdiv Kasrı High on a promontory above the town, overlooking the Bosphorus, is this Art Nouveau villa *(Khedive's Villa; ☎ 216-413 9644, Çubuklu Yolu 32; admission free; open 9am-10pm daily)*, built by the khedive of Egypt as a summer cottage during visits to İstanbul.

Having ruled Egypt for centuries, the Ottomans lost control to an adventurer named Muhammed Ali (also known as Mehmet Ali), who took over the government of Egypt in 1805 and defied the sultan in İstanbul to dislodge him. The sultan, unable to do so, gave him quasi-independence and had to be satisfied with reigning over Egypt rather than ruling. This was left to Muhammed Ali and his line, and the ruler of Egypt was styled *hıdiv*, 'khedive' (not 'king', as that would be unbearably independent). The khedives of Egypt kept up the pretence of Ottoman suzerainty by paying tribute to İstanbul.

The Egyptian royal family, which looked upon itself as Turkish (and spoke Turkish rather than Arabic as the court language), often spent its summers in a traditional yalı on the Bosphorus shore. In 1906, Khedive Abbas Hilmi built himself a palatial villa on the most dramatic promontory on the Bosphorus, a place commanding a magnificent view. The Egyptian royal family occupied it into the 1930s, after which it became the property of the municipality.

Restored after decades of neglect, the Hıdiv Kasrı serves as a restaurant (no alcoholic beverages) and tea garden, much to the delight of İstanbullus and tourists alike. The villa is a gem and the view from the gardens is superb.

The villa is a few minutes by taxi (US$2) uphill from Kanlıca or Çubuklu. To walk here, go north from Kanlıca's main square and mosque and turn right at the first street (Kafadar Sokak), which winds up to the villa car park (15 or 20 minutes by foot).

Paşabahçe & Beykoz

North of Çubuklu, the bland town of Paşabahçe has a large glassware factory whose products you will no doubt use in Turkey's restaurants.

From Beykoz, a road heads about 10km eastward towards the Polish village of Polonezköy and the Black Sea beach resort of Şile (see the Polonezköy and Şile entries later in this chapter). Much of the land along the Bosphorus shore north of Beykoz is in a military zone.

Anadolu Kavağı

Anadolu Kavağı is the final stop on the Bosphorus excursion ferry route. Surrounded by countryside, it's a pleasant town in which to spend the 2½ hours before the 3pm or 5pm ferry heads back to Eminönü.

Perched above the village are the ruins of Anadolu Kavağı Kalesi *(admission free),* a medieval castle with eight massive towers in its walls. First built by the Byzantines, it was restored and reinforced by the Genoese in 1350, and later by the Ottomans. As the strait is narrow here, it was a good choice for a defensive site to control traffic. Two more fortresses put up by Sultan Murat IV in the 17th century are north of here; beyond, the land to the north is a military zone. It'll take you 30 to 50 minutes to walk up to the fortress from the town. Alternatively, taxis wait near the fountain in the town square just east of the ferry dock; they charge US$5 for the return trip with 30 minutes waiting time. Whichever way you get there, it's worth the effort for the spectacular Black Sea views.

No prizes for guessing what the food speciality is here: seafood. Most restaurants are found around the ferry pier, hoping to lure you in as you disembark. Many of the cheap fish restaurants have a fixed menu for US$5 including beer or wine, calamari, fish, mussels, salad and bread. Don't get too excited – it's passable, but at that price you can't expect too much. Try the ***Sahil,*** or ***Altın Balık,*** both north of the ferry dock.

Kavak & Doğanay Restaurant *(☎ 216-320 2036, Yalı Caddesi 13)* Dishes US$3.50-9. Open noon-11pm daily. A notch above the cheapies, and right on the waterfront, this is the place to enjoy a leisurely lunch. Beers cost US$1.50.

You can reach Anadolu Kavağı by bus No 15A or ferry, either on the Bosphorus excursion tour from Eminönü or from Sarıyer and Rumeli Kavağı on the European shore.

Polonezköy

What's a Polish village doing about 25km from Taksim Square? Founded in 1842, it was originally named Adampol after Prince Adam Jerzy Czartoryski (1770–1861), who was once the Imperial Russian foreign minister and later head of a short-lived Polish revolutionary government (1830–31). When the revolution failed, he bought land in the Ottoman Empire for some of his former soldiers. In 1853 Russia provoked war with the Ottoman Empire; Britain, France and Sardinia joined the Ottomans in battling the Russians in the Crimea. The men of Adampol organised a regiment of Ottoman Cossacks and fought with such bravery that Sultan Abdül Mecit exempted them and their heirs from taxation.

A generation ago, Polish was still the lingua franca in the village, but the language and customs of old Poland are dying out. Even so, the 'Polish Pope', John Paul II, visited the village in 1979.

For more than a century, city people would come here for authentic Polish farm food: wild mushrooms, wild boar, omelettes with eggs from free-range chickens and excellent fruit. Farmhouses provided simple lodgings as well as meals, and this attracted another, nonculinary clientele: lovers who, unable to show a marriage licence, could not shack up in İstanbul's hotels.

Alas, Polonezköy has lost some of its charm but simple meals, fresh produce and lodgings are still available. Lovers still make up a hefty segment of the trade. Their weekends are aided by home-grown pollen potions sold in the town to 'increase sexual power' with 'alive sex hormones' – the mind boggles. Polonezköy is only reached if you have your own vehicle.

Places to Stay & Eat Polonezköy has just a small selection of places to stay and eat.

Melis *(☎ 216-432 3063, fax 432 3130, Polonezköy 26)* Singles/doubles US$9/18. Right in the centre of town, this modern place has clean, basic rooms and a pretty garden out the front. Book ahead.

Leonardo *(☎ 216-432 3082, Köyiçi Sokak 32)* Dishes US$5-7 Mon-Fri; open buffet US$13, US$6 for children noon-6pm Sat & Sun. The all-you-can-eat on the weekends seems pricey, but if you feel like a feast the variety and quality won't disappoint you. Leonardo also has a children's playground, a swimming pool, and lovely gardens to eat in. It's right in the centre of town.

Şile

Şile, a small fishing town 72km north-east of Üsküdar on the Black Sea coast, has long sand beaches and a fairly laid-back atmosphere – at least on weekdays.

Buses (US$2.50) depart from the western side of Üsküdar's main square on the hour from 7am to 7pm for the two-hour journey.

Known as Kalpe in classical times, Şile was a port of call for ships sailing east from the Bosphorus. It was visited by Xenophon and his Ten Thousand on their way back to Greece from their disastrous campaign against Artaxerxes II of Persia in the 4th century BC. Unable to find ships to sail them to Greece, Xenophon and his men marched to Chrysopolis (Üsküdar) along the route now followed by the modern road.

Şile's other claim to fame is *Şile bezi*, an open-weave cotton cloth with hand embroidery, usually made into shirts and skirts, which are cool in the summer heat.

Places to Stay & Eat Şile has many hotels, but all are dated and worn around the edges. Still, you didn't come here to spend time in your hotel (or did you?).

Değirmen Hotel *(☎ 216-711 5048, fax 711 5248, Plaj Yolu 24)* Singles/doubles US$18/35. Don't get excited when you see the groomed exterior – inside Değirmen has seen better days. The rooms are clean enough, all have a bathroom, the price includes breakfast and it has a plum position.

Kumbaba Hotel *(☎ 216-711 5038, fax 711 4851, Kumbaba)* Doubles US$50-70. Located 2km south of town, you cross a froggy creek by pontoon to get to Kumbaba. And it gets better: beachside location, rambling garden, sand dunes and wildlife surrounds. Here's the catch: bare and overpriced rooms.

Grand Şile *(☎ 216-711 4676, fax 711 4680, Plaj Yolu 19)* Singles/doubles US$60/100. The baby-poo coloured Grand is an eyesore on the outside and the inside isn't better. But it does have prime water viewing, a pool, hamam and billiard tables. The rooms are clean enough and each has a bathroom and small balcony – which you might sit out on if you like being conspicuous. Bargain hard.

Unsurprisingly, Şile's restaurants specialise in fish but check it is fresh before you order it. Down on the harbour several floating ***fish boat restaurants*** are moored. These serve fish and drinks from 9am to 9pm Monday to Friday, and 9am to midnight Saturday and Sunday. They have great views to Şile and cute little tables and chairs, but as there are no menus, watch for bill fiddling. A meal should cost about US$2 to US$4.

Anamın Yeri Beyti Kebap & Lahmacun Salonu *(☎ 216-711 5755, Üsküdar Caddesi 72)* Dishes US$2-3. Open 11am-10pm daily. This basic, friendly eatery has views over the harbour and quick eats such as soup, kebaps and bread. Ignore the two kitsch fountains inside if you can. It's right near the bus station.

Restaurant Vira *(☎ 216-712 0553)* Dishes US$1-7. Drinks from US$1.50. Open noon-midnight daily. Nothing else around here comes close to Vira with its rustic charm, great service and excellent food. The barn-like interior is crammed with fishing paraphernalia, the floating pontoon has good views over the harbour, and then there's the cute bar – oh, and an open fire in winter. Vira is down by the harbour.

Kızıl Adalar (Map 11)

Most İstanbullus shorten the Kızıl Adalar (Princes' Island or Red Islands) to Adalar (The Islands) as it's the only archipelago around. The islands lie about 20km southeast of the city in the Sea of Marmara.

In Byzantine times, refractory princes, deposed monarchs and others whose bodies had outlived their roles were interned here. A Greek Orthodox monastery and seminary on the island of Heybeliada turned out Orthodox priests until the 1970s.

In the 19th century the Ottoman business community of Greeks, Jews and Armenians favoured the islands as summer resorts. Many of the fine Victorian villas built by these wealthy Ottomans survive, and make the larger islands, Büyükada and Heybeliada, charming places.

Only a few minutes after landing, you'll realise Kızıl Adalar's surprise: there are no cars! Except for the necessary police, fire and sanitation vehicles, transportation is by bicycle, horse-drawn carriage and foot, as in centuries past.

When you visit the islands, bear in mind that there's no naturally occurring fresh water here. Use water sparingly as all water must be brought from the mainland.

Touring the Islands

At least 13 ferries run to the islands each day from 7am to 11.30pm, departing from Sirkeci's 'Adalar İskelesi' dock, east of the dock for car ferries to Harem. On summer weekends, board the vessel and seize a seat at least half an hour before departure time unless you want to stand the whole way. It costs US$1.30 each way.

You can also take a fast catamaran from Eminönü or Kabataş to Bostancı on the Asian shore, then another from Bostancı to Büyükada, but you save little time, and the cost is much higher.

The ferry steams away from Sirkeci, out of the Golden Horn and around Saray Burnu, offering fine views of Topkapı Sarayı, Aya Sofya and the Blue Mosque on the right, and Üsküdar and Haydarpaşa to the left. It'll make a quick stop at Kadıköy on the Asian side. After about 50 minutes, the ferry reaches Kınalıada, the first small island; then it's another 15 minutes to Burgazada; another 15 minutes to Heybeliada, the second-largest island; and another 15 minutes to Büyükada, the largest. Some express ferries go directly to Büyükada, from which there are occasional ferries to Heybeli, and fast catamarans to Bostancı.

You can get off at the first island or Heybeliada and catch the next ferry along (no extra charge) so don't limit yourself to visiting one island.

Kınalıada & Burgazada

These two small islands offer little reward for the trouble of getting off the ferry.

Kınalıada, flat and fairly featureless except for a forest of cell-phone antennas, is a collection of summer villas, and is favoured by Armenian families. If you stop here to have a meal (there are no hotels), you'll probably be the only foreigner in sight.

Burgazada has a church, a synagogue, and the home of the late writer Sait Faik, now a museum.

Heybeliada

Called Heybeli for short, this island is home to the Turkish Naval Academy (to the left of the ferry dock). Within the academy grounds is the grave of Sir Edward Barton (died 1598), ambassador of Queen Elizabeth I to the Sublime Porte. Much less touristy than Büyükada, it's a delightful place for walking in the pine groves and swimming from the tiny (but crowded) beaches. There's not much accommodation, but there are several restaurants with good food and decent prices.

A 50-minute carriage tour (horse-drawn carriage: *fayton;* long tour: *büyük tur*) of the island costs US$12, the 25-minute tour *(küçük tur)* is US$7. Battered bicycles are for rent *(kiralık bisiklet)* at several shops.

Merit Halki Palace *(☎ 216-351 0025, fax 351 8483, Refah Şehitler Caddesi 88)* Singles/doubles US$90/100. Prime lodging here is at a restored Ottoman Victorian gingerbread villa with 45 modern rooms all with bathroom; the price includes breakfast and there is a pool and all pampering comforts. Book ahead.

For picnic supplies, on arrival at the ferry docks turn right onto Ayyıldız Caddesi, behind and parallel to the waterfront restaurant street. Along Ayyıldız Caddesi you'll find the ***Mehtap Pasta ve Unlu Mamülleri***, a bakery selling pastries and bread. Close by, the ***Gül Market*** at Ayyıldız Caddesi 13 can provide other picnic necessities such as preserved meats, olives, pickles and drinks.

Ada Restaurant *(☎ 216-351 9438, Rıhtım Caddesi 47)* Dishes US$0.50-2.50. Open 9am-1am daily. Ada is one of the restaurants lining the waterfront to the right of the ferry dock. It's probably the cheapest, serving *lahmacun* (Arabic soft pizza; US$0.50), pide (US$1.50 to US$2.50) and meat dishes up to US$2.50. Other ***restaurants*** along this strip dish up seafood for about US$2.50 to US$4 per main.

Büyükada

The 'Great Island's' splendid Victoriana greets you as you approach by sea, its gingerbread villas climbing up the slopes of the hill and the bulbous twin domes of the Splendid Otel providing an unmistakable landmark.

Walk from the ferry to the clock tower in İskele Meydanı (Dock Square). The market district (with restaurants) is to the left along Recep Koç Sokak. For a stroll up the hill and through the lovely old houses, bear right onto 23 Nisan Caddesi. If you need a goal for your wanderings, head along Kadıyoran Caddesi to the Greek Monastery of St George, in the 'saddle' between Büyükada's two highest hills. When you get there the monastery restaurant has good food. Bicycles are available for rent in several shops, and shops on the market street can provide picnic supplies, though food is cheaper on the mainland.

Just to the left of the square by the clock tower is the waiting area for horse-drawn carriages. Hire one for a long tour of about an hour for US$16, or a short tour of mostly the town, not the shores or hills, for US$12. Prices are set by the city government, and are prominently posted, though you may be able to haggle out of season.

Places to Stay & Eat ***Hotel Princess*** *(☎ 216-382 1628, fax 382 1949, İskele Meydanı 2)* Singles/doubles US$60/70. This hotel is right next to the clock tower and behind its old-fashioned front lurks modern motel-like rooms. Some rooms are too small, others are OK, but all have good bathrooms. Breakfast is included and there is a small swimming pool.

Splendid Otel *(☎ 216-382 6950, fax 382 6775, 23 Nisan Caddesi 71)* Singles/doubles US$60/80. To the right and about 200m up the hill from the clock tower, this is a perfect, if faded, Ottoman Victorian period piece, complete with *grande dames* taking tea on the terrace each afternoon. Rooms are simple and some have a little balcony overlooking the sea. The modern bathrooms are spotless. Breakfast is included.

İskele Meydanı is surrounded by restaurants. To the left as you come up from the dock are several small places featuring *kokoreç* (lambs' intestines).

Taş Fırın *(Stone Oven; ☎ 216-382 1720, Recep Koç Sokak 48)* Dishes US$1-3. This local, small eatery serves cheap lahmacun (US$0.60) and pide (US$2) as well as more substantial plates.

Altın Fıçı *(☎ 216-382 6545, Recep Koç Sokak 8)* Dishes US$1-3.50. Open 10am-midnight. This friendly restaurant serves good food and beer (US$1.50) on outdoor stools and barrels.

More expensive restaurants are along Gülistan Caddesi, along the waterfront to the east of the ferry docks. Try ***Birtat Restaurant*** with mains from US$4 to US$10, or ***Hamdi Baba***.

Edirne (Map 7)

Edirne, 235km (2½ hours) north-west of İstanbul, is the traditional way-station on the road from the Bosphorus to Europe. It was the second capital city (after Bursa) of the Ottoman Empire, and an important staging post for the sultan's annual military campaigns in Europe. As such it was graced with fine mosques, baths and caravanserais, including the serene Selimiye Camii, masterwork of the great Sinan.

Edirne is famous for the Kırkpınar oil wrestling festival. Hundreds of leather-clad hulks gather in Sarayiçi, which is about

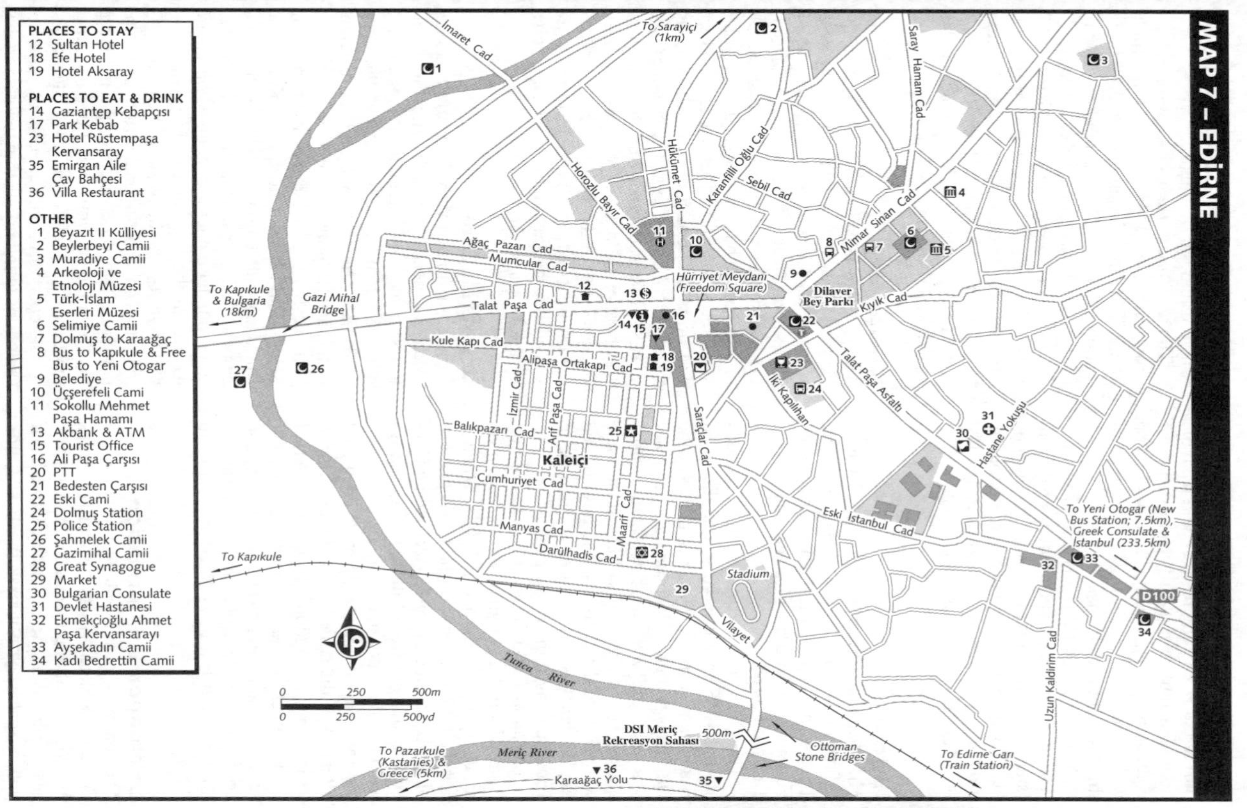
MAP 7 – EDİRNE
PLACES TO STAY
12 Sultan Hotel
18 Efe Hotel
19 Hotel Aksaray
PLACES TO EAT & DRINK
14 Gaziantep Kebapçısı
17 Park Kebab
23 Hotel Rüstempaşa Kervansaray
35 Emirgan Aile Çay Bahçesi
36 Villa Restaurant
OTHER
1 Beyazıt II Külliyesi
2 Beylerbeyi Camii
3 Muradiye Camii
4 Arkeoloji ve Etnoloji Müzesi
5 Türk-İslam Eserleri Müzesi
6 Selimiye Camii
7 Dolmuş to Karaağaç
8 Bus to Kapıkule & Free Bus to Yeni Otogar
9 Belediye
10 Üçşerefeli Cami
11 Sokollu Mehmet Paşa Hamamı
13 Akbank & ATM
15 Tourist Office
16 Ali Paşa Çarşısı
20 PTT
21 Bedesten Çarşısı
22 Eski Cami
24 Dolmuş Station
25 Police Station
26 Şahmelek Camii
27 Gazimihal Camii
28 Great Synagogue
29 Market
30 Bulgarian Consulate
31 Devlet Hastanesi
32 Ekmekçioğlu Ahmet Paşa Kervansarayı
33 Ayşekadın Camii
34 Kadı Bedrettin Camii
İmaret Cad
To Sarayiçi (1km)
Saray Hamam Cad
Hükümet Cad
Karanfilli Oğlu Cad
Sebil Cad
Horozlu Bayır Cad
Mimar Sinan Cad
Ağaç Pazarı Cad
Mumcular Cad
Hürriyet Meydanı (Freedom Square)
Dilaver Bey Parkı
Kıyık Cad
To Kapıkule & Bulgaria (18km)
Gazi Mihal Bridge
Talat Paşa Cad
Kule Kapı Cad
Alipaşa Ortakapı Cad
İzmir Cad
Arif Paşa Cad
Balıkpazarı Cad
Kaleiçi
Cumhuriyet Cad
Maarif Cad
Manyas Cad
Darülhadis Cad
Saraçlar Cad
İki Kapılıhan
Talat Paşa Asfaltı
Hastane Yokuşu
Eski İstanbul Cad
To Yeni Otogar (New Bus Station; 7.5km), Greek Consulate & İstanbul (233.5km)
D100
Uzun Kaldirim Cad
Stadium
Vilayet
To Kapıkule
Tunca River
Meriç River
DSI Meriç Rekreasyon Sahası
Ottoman Stone Bridges
To Edirne Garı (Train Station)
To Pazarkule (Kastanies) & Greece (5km)
Karaağaç Yolu
0 250 500m
0 250 500yd

EXCURSIONS

1km north-east of Edirne, and battle it out during the week-long festival held from the middle of June to early July (for exact dates contact the tourist office). The town fills up with spectators so if you want to come at this time book well ahead.

At other times Edirne is untouristy, unrushed and it makes a pleasant day trip from İstanbul. You can do the return day trip by bus, though you'll want to leave İstanbul by around 9am to make a full day of it. The last bus from Edirne heads back to İstanbul at 8.30pm.

History

The Roman emperor Hadrian founded Edirne in the 2nd century as Hadrianopolis. The town's name was later shortened by Europeans to Adrianople, and later by the Turks to Edirne.

The Ottoman state, an emirate founded around 1288 in north-west Anatolia, used Bursa as its capital. By the mid-1300s, the Ottomans had grown substantially in power and size, and were looking for new conquests. The mighty walls of Constantinople were beyond their powers, but they crossed the Dardanelles and captured Adrianople in 1362, making it their new capital.

For almost 100 years, this was the city from which the Ottoman sultan set out on his campaigns to Europe and Asia. When at last the time was ripe for the final conquest of the Byzantine Empire, Mehmet the Conqueror rode out from Edirne on the Via Ignatia to Constantinople.

When the Ottoman Empire disintegrated after WWI, the Allies granted all of Thrace to the Greek kingdom. In the summer of 1920, Greek armies occupied Edirne, but several years later Atatürk's republican armies drove them out, and the Treaty of Lausanne left Edirne and eastern Trakya to the Turks.

Orientation & Information

The centre of town is Hürriyet Meydanı, or Freedom Square. All the important sights are within walking distance of this square. Just north-east is the Üçşerefeli Cami, but if you head east you'll pass the Eski Cami, and soon see Sinan's masterpiece, the Selimiye Camii, up on the hill.

The *yeni otogar* (new bus station) is 9km south-east of the Eski Cami near the highway (TEM) to İstanbul. The main dolmuş station (Map 7, #24) is behind (south-east of) the Hotel Rüstempaşa Kervansaray.

The helpful tourist office (Map 7, #15; ☎/fax 284-213 9208) is just west of Hürriyet Meydanı. It's open 8.30am to 5pm Monday to Friday. The bar in the Hotel Rüstempaşa Kervansaray (Map 7, #23; see Places to Eat & Drink) has Internet facilities.

Kaleiçi (Map 7)

The Old Town called Kaleiçi (Within the Fortress) was the original medieval town with streets laid out on a grid plan. Walk south along Maarif Caddesi, the street beside the tourist office, to pass some fine old Ottoman wooden houses, designed in an ornate style known as Edirnekâri. At the southern end of Maarif Caddesi you will come to what's left of Edirne's great synagogue (Map 7, #28). There are other fine houses along Cumhuriyet Caddesi, which crosses Maarif Caddesi north of the synagogue.

Fragments of Byzantine city walls are still visible on the edges of Kaleiçi, down by the Tunca River.

Üçşerefeli Cami

Üçşerefeli Cami **(Map 7, #10)** *(Hükümet Caddesi)* means 'mosque with three galleries (balconies)'. Actually it's one of the mosque's four minarets that has the three balconies. The minarets, built at different times, are all quite different.

Its design shows the transition from the Selçuk Turkish-style mosques of Konya and Bursa to a truly Ottoman style, which would be perfected later in İstanbul. In the Selçuk style, smaller domes are mounted on square rooms. At the Üçşerefeli, which was completed in 1447, the wide (24m) dome is mounted on a hexagonal drum and supported by two walls and two pillars. Keep this in mind as you visit Edirne's other mosques which reflect earlier or later styles.

The courtyard, with its central *şadırvan* (ablutions fountain), was an innovation that came to be standard in the great Ottoman mosques. At the time of research it was closed for restoration, and the mosque itself will continue to be filled with scaffolding for years to come.

Across the street from the mosque is the **Sokollu Mehmet Paşa Hamamı (Map 7, #11)** *(Turkish baths; ☎ 284-213 4512; open 6am-5pm),* built in the late 1500s and looking a bit run-down today. Designed by the great Mimar Sinan for Grand Vizier Sokollu Mehmet Paşa, it is a *çifte hamam* (twin baths). Simple admission costs US$2, washing by an attendant US$3.50, a massage US$5.50.

Eski Cami (Map 7, #22)

From Hürriyet Meydanı, walk east on Talat Paşa Caddesi to the Eski Cami or Old Mosque. On your way you'll pass the *bedesten* (covered market for the sale of valuable goods) across the park on your right. Dating from 1418, it's now known as the **Bedesten Çarşısı**, or Bedesten Bazaar, and is still filled with shops.

The Eski Cami *(Talat Paşa Caddesi),* built in 1414, exemplifies one of two principal mosque styles used by the Ottomans in their earlier capital, Bursa. The Eski Cami has rows of arches and pillars supporting a series of small domes. Inside, there's a marvellous mihrab. Huge calligraphic inscriptions adorn the walls, both inside and out. Look out for the Roman columns at the front of the mosque; incorporating architectural remnants was a common practice over the centuries. The mosque is currently under restoration but you can still enter.

Selimiye Camii (Map 7, #6)

This mosque *(☎ 284-213 9735, Mimar Sinan Caddesi)* is the finest work of the great Ottoman architect Mimar Sinan, or so the architect himself believed (see the special section 'Architecture' pp29–35). Constructed for Sultan Selim II between 1569 and 1575, this mosque is smaller than Sinan's earlier (1557) tremendous Süleymaniye Camii in İstanbul, but more elegant and harmonious. It crowns its small hill and was meant to dominate the town and be easily visible from all approaches across the rolling Thracian landscape. To fully appreciate its excellence you should enter it from the west, as the architect intended. Walk up the street and through the courtyard rather than through the park and the *arasta* (shops), a financially necessary but obtrusive later addition made during the reign of Murat III.

The harmony and serenity of this most symmetrical of mosques surrounds you as you enter. The broad, lofty dome – at 31.5m wider than that of İstanbul Aya Sofya by a few centimetres – is supported by eight pillars, as well as arches and external buttresses. The interior is surprisingly spacious and the walls, because they bear only a portion of the dome's weight, can be filled with windows, thus admitting plentiful light. Beneath the main dome is the *kürsü,* or prayer-reader's platform, and beneath that is a fountain.

As you might expect, the interior furnishings of the Selimiye Camii are exquisite, from the delicately carved marble *mimber* (pulpit) to the outstanding İznik faïence.

In contrast to its many 'twinnings' (pairs of windows, columns etc), the north side of the mosque has playful groupings of three arches, domes, niches etc; and even triads of pairs (windows).

Part of the Selimiye's excellent effect comes from its four slender, very tall (71m) minarets, fluted to emphasise their height. You'll notice that each is *üçşerefeli,* or built with three balconies – Sinan's respectful acknowledgment, perhaps, to his predecessor, the architect of the Üçşerefeli Cami.

Museums

The Selimiye's *medrese* (theological seminary) now houses the **Türk-İslam Eserleri Müzesi (Map 7, #5)** *(Turkish & Islamic Arts Museum; ☎ 284-225 1120; adult/student US$1/0.50; open 9am-1pm & 2.30pm-6.30pm Tues-Sun).* The collection, labelled in Turkish only, is eclectic. Here you'll see weapons and chain mail, dervish arts and crafts, artefacts from the Balkan Wars, locally made stockings and kitchen utensils.

The **Arkeoloji ve Etnoloji Müzesi (Map 7, #4)** *(Archaeological & Ethnological*

Museum; adult/student US$1/0.50; open 9am-1pm & 2.30pm-6.30pm Tues-Sun) has a mixed bag of exhibits, including sculpture and textiles, spanning prehistoric to Ottoman times. To find it cross the parking lot north-east of Selimiye Camii.

River Walks (Map 7)

Follow Saraçlar Caddesi south and out of town, under the railway line and across an Ottoman stone humpback bridge spanning the Tunca River. A longer Ottoman bridge crosses the Meriç to the south. On the south side of the Meriç bridge take a break at the tea garden or restaurant (see Places to Eat & Drink for recommendations).

Muradiye Camii (Map 7, #3)

A short walk (10 to 15 minutes) north-east of the Selimiye along Mimar Sinan Caddesi brings you to the Muradiye Camii *(open during prayer times only)*, a mosque built on the orders of Sultan Murat II. Finished in 1436, it was once the centre of a Mevlevi (Whirling Dervish) lodge. The small cupola atop the main dome is unusual. The mosque has a T-shaped plan with twin *eyvans* (niche-like rooms) and exquisite İznik tiles, especially in the mihrab.

Beyazıt II Külliyesi (Map 7, #1)

Building mosque complexes on the outskirts of populated areas was the way the Ottomans expanded their cities. The scheme seems not to have worked for the Beyazıt II Külliyesi, built from 1484 to 1488, which remains on Edirne's outskirts, unpopulated and little used.

The mosque's *külliye* (mosque complex) is extensive and includes a *tabhane* (hostel for travellers), medrese, bakery, *imaret* (soup kitchen), *tımarhane* (insane asylum) and *darüşşifa* (hospital). These buildings were fully restored in the late 1970s, though time has obviously been at work since then.

Places to Stay

Hotel Aksaray *(☎ 284-212 6035, Alipaşa Ortakapı Caddesi 14)* **Map 7, #19** Double with/without bath US$13/9. Aksaray is a charming old Edirnekâri, but before you get too excited, some of the rooms are depressing shoe boxes, others have horrible brown cheap carpet – only a handful are livable. There is no food served and hot water is available usually only in the evenings and mornings – but the staff are friendly.

Efe Hotel *(☎ 284-213 6166, fax 213 6080, Maarif Caddesi 13)* **Map 7, #18** Singles/doubles US$20/30. Clean, colourful and modern, Efe is well set up for tourists and good value for money. The price includes breakfast. Each room has a bathroom with 24-hour hot water, air-con plus a TV. There are also two roomy suite rooms (singles/doubles US$25/40) and a Brit-style pub downstairs.

Sultan Hotel *(☎ 284-225 1372, fax 225 5763, Talat Paşa Caddesi 170)* **Map 7, #12** Singles/doubles US$25/35. Although the hotel is a daggy 1970s construction, the rooms are plain, clean and each has hot-water shower and a TV. The price includes breakfast. There's plentiful parking in the hotel's rear car park.

Places to Eat & Drink

Edirne has many small eateries, especially *köftecis* (serving grilled lamb meatballs) and *ciğercis* (serving fried liver).

Gaziantep Kebapçısı *(☎ 284-225 4078, Hürriyet Meydanı Kirişçiler İşhanı 2)* **Map 7, #14** Dishes US$0.50-1.50. Open 6am-11pm daily. Next to the tourist office, this is a bright, clean spot with tasty grilled kebaps and salads (no alcohol).

Park Kebab *(☎ 284-225 5657, Maarif Caddesi 9)* **Map 7, #17** Dishes US$1-4. Open 11.30am-11pm daily. Just around the corner, this modern restaurant with mock cistern decor has good service. It's a leisurely spot to have a feed.

For atmosphere and views the eateries out by the Meriç River, south of the town, win hands down.

Emirgan Aile Çay Bahçesi *(☎ 284-212 2906, Karaağaç Yolu)* **Map 7, #35** Snacks US$1-1.50. Open 8.30am-11pm daily. This tea garden, opposite the restored Ottoman *çeşme* (fountain) of Hacı Adil Bey, has welcome shade and fine sunset views of the river and bridge.

VERITY CAMPBELL

MARTIN MOOS

MARTIN MOOS

Top: Anadolu Kavağı, on the Bosphorus, offers stunning views from its medieval castle.
Bottom Left: Two of Edirne's Üçşerefeli Cami's four minarets, all of which are quite different in style
Bottom Right: The Selimiye Camii, Edirne, was the masterwork of Sinan, the 16th-century architect.

ANNA JUDD

IZZET KERIBAR

BRETT SHEARER

Top: Gallipoli's Anzac Cove is the site of the ill-fated Allied landing of 25 April 1915.
Bottom Left: Trench warfare played a large part in the brutal nine-month campaign.
Bottom Right: This memorial is to the thousands of soldiers who died at Gallipoli during WWI.

***Villa** (☎ 284-225 4077, Karaağaç Yolu)* **Map 7, #36** Set menu US$9. Open 6pm-11pm daily. This six-course set menu isn't as good value as it sounds, but the outdoor eating area has superb views. Restaurants along here are seasonal and cater to wedding parties, so book first and make sure it's open.

If you'd like to have a drink (beer US$1) or play billiards, head to the ***Hotel Rüstempaşa Kervansaray** (☎ 284-225 7195, İki Kapılıhan Caddesi 57)* **(Map 7, #23)** Set in a caravanserai built by Sinan, the leafy courtyards make a gorgeous setting for an afternoon drink. It's open 10am to 2pm daily. Don't be tempted to stay here; the rooms are grotty, small and terribly overpriced.

Another more rowdy bar option is the Efe Hotel's ***pub** (open 6pm-2am daily)*; see Places to Stay.

Getting There & Away

From İstanbul, the quickest way to get to Edirne is to take a bus from the otogar. Buses depart for Edirne from office *(peron)* 103–104 at 7am, 7.45am and 8.30am then every half-hour until 5.30pm (and a few more until 10.30pm). It takes about 2½ hours to make the 235km journey. Tickets cost US$6. Once you reach Edirne's yeni otogar, take a dolmuş (US$0.40) to the Eski Cami, near Hürriyet Meydanı in the city centre. Leaving Edirne, catch one of the regular free minibuses to the yeni otogar from the bus stop along Mimar Sinan Caddesi (in the centre of town). Buses to İstanbul leave Edirne's yeni otogar about every half-hour from 5.15am to 8.30pm.

Trains between Edirne and İstanbul are slow and inconvenient – don't bother.

Gallipoli & Troy

The slender peninsula that forms the northwestern side of the Dardanelles (Çanakkale Boğazı), across the water from the town of Çanakkale, is called Gallipoli (Gelibolu in Turkish). The Gallipoli battlefields, a raging hell during WWI, are now hills covered in scrubby brush, pine forests and farmers' fields.

It's possible to visit the battlefields of Gallipoli, the Dardanelles strait, Çanakkale and the ruins of Troy from İstanbul in a very long day by public transport. It'll be quicker if you hire a car. The most relaxed option, however, is to stay the night in Çanakkale and make it a two-day excursion. You could combine this excursion with a trip to Edirne, making it a comfortable three-day trip.

GALLIPOLI (Maps 8 & 9)

History

With the intention of capturing the Ottoman capital and the road to Eastern Europe during WWI, Winston Churchill, British First Lord of the Admiralty, organised a naval assault on the Dardanelles. A strong Franco-British fleet tried first to force them in March 1915 but failed. Then, in April, British, Australian, New Zealand and Indian troops were landed on Gallipoli, and French troops near Çanakkale. Both Turkish and Allied troops fought desperately and fearlessly, and devastated one another. After months of ferocious combat with little progress, the Allied forces were withdrawn.

The Turkish success at Gallipoli was partly due to bad luck and bad leadership on the Allied side, and partly due to the timely provision of reinforcements coming to the aid of the Turkish side under the command of General Liman von Sanders. But a crucial element in the defeat was that the Allied troops happened to land in a sector where they faced Lieutenant-Colonel Mustafa Kemal (Atatürk).

He was a relatively minor officer, but he had General von Sanders' confidence. He guessed the Allied battle plan correctly when his commanders did not, and stalled the invasion by bitter fighting that wiped out his division. Though suffering from malaria, he commanded in full view of his troops and of the enemy, and miraculously escaped death several times. His brilliant performance made him a folk hero and paved the way for his promotion to pasha (general).

The Gallipoli campaign lasted for nine months, until January 1916, and resulted in a total of more than half a million Allied and Turkish casualties.

Touring the Battlefields

Gallipoli is a fairly large area to tour: It's over 35km as the crow flies from the northernmost battlefield to the southern tip of the peninsula. The principal battles took place on the western shore of the peninsula near Anzac Cove and Arıburnu Cemetery, and in the hills just to the east.

With a car you can easily tour the major battlefields in a day and be in a Çanakkale hotel by nightfall. If you're in a hurry, a morning or afternoon will be enough time to see the main sites.

If you're a hiker, and you have lots of time, take a ferry from Çanakkale to Eceabat and a dolmuş or taxi to Kabatepe, and follow the trail around the sites described in an excellent map sold at the visitor centre (Kabatepe Tanıtma Merkezi) there.

Gallipoli tours on Anzac Day are a major money-spinner, but everyone wants a piece of the action year-round. Hotels or pensions will put pressure on you to take a tour (they receive commission) from either of two companies: TJ Tours or Hassle Free. Most tours you book through guesthouses or other tour agencies – even in İstanbul – will join you up with Hassle Free's tours.

The daily tours are by minibus, take five to six hours (usually in the afternoon) and include a small, so-so packed lunch. Anzac Day tours are package tours – see the boxed text 'Anzac Day Tours'.

Hassle Free *(☎ 286-213 5969, 🆆 www.anzachouse.com, Cumhuriyet Meydanı 61, Çanakkale)* **Map 10, #12** In Anzac House hostel, Hassle Free runs Gallipoli tours for US$21, as well as Troy tours for US$14. These tours tend to be large – sometimes up to three minibuses trail along – but the guides are good. Hassle Free also organises a round-trip Gallipoli tour from İstanbul (US$59) including a Troy tour and one night's accommodation in Çanakkale.

TJ Tours *(☎ 286-814 3121, fax 8143122, 🆆 www.anzacgallipolitours.com, Cumhuriyet Caddesi 5/A, Eceabat)* TJ also has Gallipoli tours for US$19, as well as walking tours on the peninsula for US$19. If you take both tours you'll pay US$29. TJ's tours tend to be smaller and they include prerecorded national anthems. TJ also has a busy, clean hostel at Eceabat.

Anzac Day Tours

Anzac Day (25 April) draws Australians and New Zealanders to Gallipoli to commemorate the battles of WWI at a dawn service. At this time of the year potential visitors can become sitting targets for tour operators. The two-day tours on offer include all food, transport and accommodation. Here's what one traveller had to say:

Imagine 20,000 Turkish backpackers travelling to Bega to see the 'Big Cheese'...on the same day. Sure, the Big Cheese doesn't hold the same place in Turkish hearts as Anzac Cove does to Australians and New Zealanders, but in terms of the crowds, lack of accommodation and chaos the event would produce, the analogy works. If you book ahead, you'll pay three times too much (I paid US$140 for two days), if you don't, you may miss out all together. The accommodation was poor, the organisation was minimal (40 busloads of tourists crammed into the house-sized museum), and the food was ordinary. What I can say is, they got me there and it was a moving, eye-opening experience. I was glad I went but I wouldn't go again.

Matthew Williamson

If you want to avoid the crowds, you won't, but you could avoid the tours by booking your own accommodation (at least two months in advance) for the night of the 24th, and touring by rental car. You'll need to get to the ceremony site hours before the service starts at 5.30am. The Çanakkale-Eceabat ferries are packed from 3am onwards. Ring the tourist office in Çanakkale for more advice.

Troy-Anzac Tours *(☎ 286-217 5849, fax 217 0196, Saat Kulesi Meydanı 6)* **Map 10, #18** Troy-Anzac faces the clock tower in Çanakkale and charges US$21 for Gallipoli tours.

Gallipoli National Historic Park (Maps 8 & 9)

Gallipoli National Historic Park **(Map 8)** (Gelibolu Yarımadası Tarihi Milli Parkı)

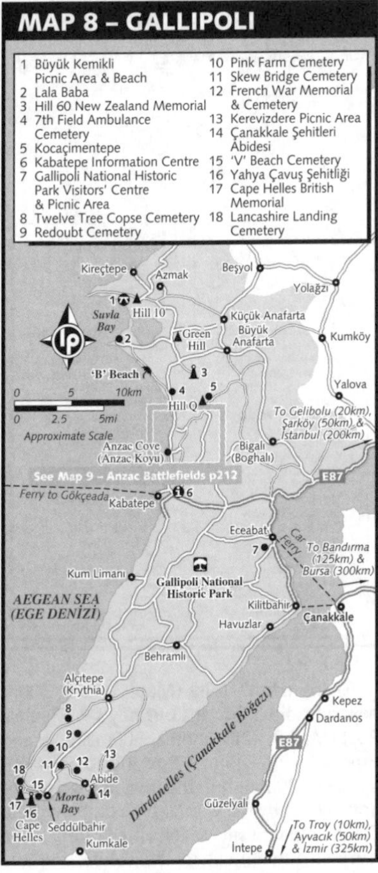

covers much of the peninsula and all of the significant battle sites. Your first stop should be the **Kabatepe Information Centre (Map 8)** *(Kabatepe Tanıtma Merkezi; ☎ 286-814; open 9am-1pm & 2pm-6pm daily)*. To get there, head north of Eceabat and after about 3km you'll see a road marked for Kabatepe; follow this until you come to the information centre, just east of the village of Kabatepe. The small **museum** *(adult/student US$1/0.50)*, in the information centre, is worth seeing. It has period uniforms, soldiers' letters and other battlefield finds. An excellent map (US$2) is sold here, too.

Anzac Cove & Beaches (Map 9) Head west from the information centre, then north for 3km to the **Beach (Hell Spit) Cemetery (Map 9, #29)**; shortly after a road goes inland to the Shrapnel Valley and **Plugge's Plateau Cemeteries (Map 9, #24)**.

Further north from the inland turn-off is Anzac Cove (Anzac Koyu). The ill-fated Allied landing was made here on 25 April 1915, beneath and just south of the Arıburnu cliffs. The Allied forces were ordered to advance inland, but met with fierce resistance from the Ottoman forces under Mustafa Kemal (Atatürk), who had foreseen the landing here and, disobeying an order from his commanders to send his troops south to Cape Helles, was prepared for it. After this first failed effort, the Anzacs concentrated on consolidating the beachhead, which they did until June while awaiting reinforcements.

In August a major offensive was staged in an attempt to advance beyond the beachhead and up to the ridges of Chunuk Bair (Conkbayırı) and Sarı Bair. It resulted in the bloodiest battles of the campaign, but little progress was made.

As a memorial reserve, the beach here is off limits to swimmers and picnickers.

A few hundred metres beyond Anzac Cove is the **Arıburnu Cemetery (Map 9, #23)** and, further along, the **Canterbury Cemetery (Map 9, #22)**. Less than 1km further along the seaside road are the cemeteries at **No 2 Outpost (Map 9, #14)**, set back inland from the road, and the **New Zealand No 2 Outpost (Map 9, #13)**, right next to the road. The **Embarkation Pier Cemetery (Map 9, #12)** is shortly beyond them.

Anzac Cove to Lone Pine (Map 9) Retrace your steps and follow the signs up the hill for **Lone Pine (Kanlı Sırt) Cemetery (Map 9, #27)**. It's along the same inland road that passes Shrapnel Valley. Another 3km uphill will take you to the **Chunuk Bair New Zealand Memorial (Map 9, #2)**.

This area, which saw the most bitter fighting of the campaign, was later cloaked in pines, but a disastrous forest fire in 1994 denuded the hills. Reforestation efforts are under way.

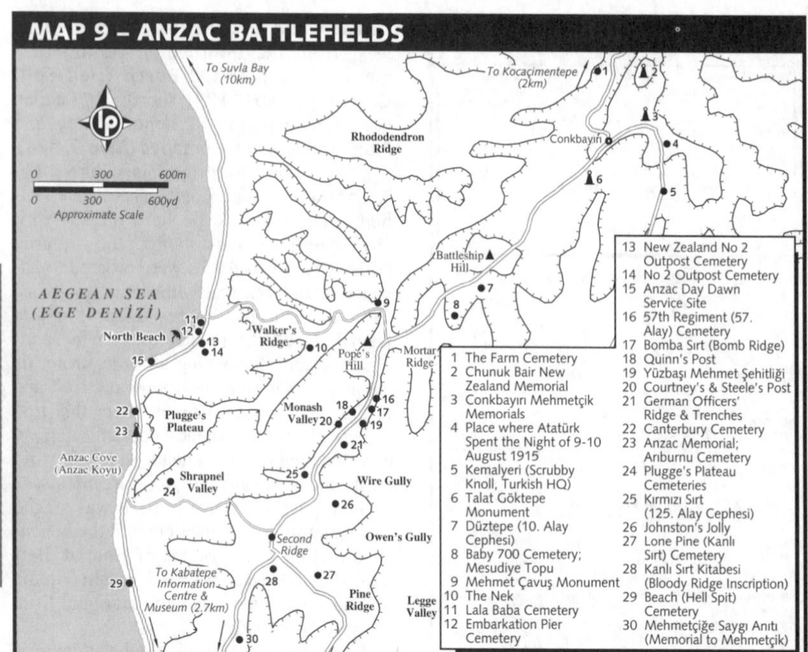

At Lone Pine, 400m uphill from the **Kanlı Sırt Kitabesi (Bloody Ridge Inscription) (Map 9, #28)**, Australian forces captured the Turkish positions on the evening of 6 August. In the few days of the August assault 4000 men died here. The trees that shaded the cemetery were swept away by the 1994 fire, leaving only one: a lone pine planted as a memorial years ago from the seed of the original tree that had stood here during the battle. The small tombstones carry touching epitaphs: 'Only son', 'He died for his country' and 'If I could hold your hand once more just to say well done'.

Lone Pine to Quinn's Post (Map 9) As you progress up the hill, you quickly come to understand the ferocity of the battles. At some points the trenches were only a few metres apart. The order to attack meant certain death to all who followed it, and virtually all on both the Ottoman and Allied sides did as they were ordered.

At **Johnston's Jolly (Map 9, #26)**, 300m beyond Lone Pine, at **Courtney's & Steele's Post (Map 9, #20)**, another 300m along, and especially at **Quinn's Post (Map 9, #18)**, another 400m uphill, the trenches were separated only by the width of the modern road. On the western side at Johnston's Jolly is the Turkish monument to the soldiers of the 125th Regiment who died here on 'Red Ridge' (Kırmızı Sırt/125 Alay Cephesi). At Quinn's Post is the memorial to Sergeant Mehmet, who fought with rocks and his fists after he ran out of ammunition; and the Captain Mehmet Cemetery.

57th Regiment (57. Alay) (Map 9) Just over 1km uphill from Lone Pine is another monument to 'Mehmetçik' **(Map 9, #30)** (the Turkish equivalent of GI Joe) on the west side of the road and, on the east side, the cemetery and monument for officers and soldiers of the Ottoman 57th Regiment **(Map 9, #16)**. As the Anzac troops made their way up the scrub-covered slopes towards Chunuk Bair on 25 April, divisional commander Mustafa Kemal (Atatürk) brought up the 57th Infantry Regiment and gave them his famous order: 'I order you not just to attack, but to die. In the time it takes us to die, other troops and commanders will arrive to take our places'. The 57th was wiped out, but held the line and inflicted equally heavy casualties on the Anzacs below.

The statue of an old man showing his granddaughter the battle sites portrays veteran Hüseyin Kaçmaz, who fought in the Balkan Wars, in the Gallipoli campaign and in the War of Independence at the fateful Battle of Dumlupınar. He died in 1994 at the age of 110.

Mehmet Çavuş & the Nek (Map 9) A few hundred metres past the 57th Regiment Cemetery, a road goes west to the monument to **Mehmet Çavuş (Map 9, #9)** (another Sergeant Mehmet) and **the Nek (Map 9, #10)**. It was at the Nek on 7 August 1915 that the 8th (Victorian) and 10th (West Australian) regiments of the 3rd Light Horse Brigade vaulted out of their trenches into withering fire and certain death. They were doomed but utterly courageous.

Baby 700 Cemetery (Map 9, #8), on the site of the other object of the assault, is 300m further uphill from Mehmet Çavuş.

Chunuk Bair (Map 9) At the top of the hill, past the monument to Talat Göktepe **(Map 9, #6)**, is a 'T' intersection. A right turn takes you east to the spot where, having stayed awake for four days straight, Atatürk spent the night of 9 to 10 August **(Map 9, #4)**, and to **Kemalyeri (Scrubby Knoll) (Map 9, #5)**, his command post. A left turn leads after 100m to Chunuk Bair, the first objective of the Allied landing in April 1915, and now the site of the New Zealand memorial.

Chunuk Bair was also at the heart of the struggle from 6 to 9 August 1915, when 28,000 men died on this ridge. The peaceful pine grove of today makes it difficult to imagine the blasted wasteland of almost a century ago, when bullets, bombs and shrapnel mowed down men and trees as the fighting went on with huge numbers of casualties. The Anzac attack on 6 to 7 August, which included the New Zealand Mounted Rifle Brigade and a Maori contingent, was deadly, but the attack on the following day was of a ferocity which, according to Atatürk, 'could scarcely be described'.

On the eastern side of the road is the **New Zealand Memorial (Map 9, #2)** and some reconstructed **Turkish trenches**. Signs indicate the spots at which Mustafa Kemal stood on 8 August 1915: where he gave the order for the crucial attack at 4.30am *(Atatürk'ün taarruz emrini verdiği yer);* where he watched the progress of the battle *(Savaş gözetleme yeri);* and the spot where shrapnel would have hit his heart, but was stopped by his pocket watch.

To the east a side road leads up to the **Turkish Conkbayırı Mehjmetçik Memorial (Map 9, #3)**. Here you will find five gigantic tablets with inscriptions (in Turkish) describing the progress of the battle.

Beyond Chunuk Bair the road leads to Kocaçimentepe, less than 2km along.

Southern Peninsula (Map 8) A road goes south from near the Kabatepe information centre past the side road to **Kum Limanı**, where there is a good swimming beach and the ***Hotel Kum and Kum Camping*** *(☎ 286-814 1466, fax 814 1917)*. It has camp sites US$4 per person and comfy rooms with bath US$50.

From Kabatepe it's about 18km to the village of **Alçıtepe**, formerly known as Krythia or Kirte. In the village, signs point out the road south-west to the cemeteries of **Twelve Tree Copse (Map 8, #8)** and **Pink Farm (Map 8, #10)**, and north to the Turkish cemetery **Sargı Yeri** and **Nuri Yamut monument.**

Heading south, the road passes the **Redoubt Cemetery (Map 8, #9)**. About 5.5km south of Alçıtepe, just south of the **Skew Bridge Cemetery**, the road divides, the right fork leading to the village of **Seddülbahir** and several Allied memorials. Seddülbahir, 1.5km from the intersection, is a sleepy farming village with a PTT, a ruined Ottoman/Byzantine fortress, army post and a small harbour.

The initial Allied attack was two-pronged, with the southern landing taking place here at the tip of the peninsula on **'V' Beach (Map 8, #15)**. Yahya Çavuş (Sergeant Yahya) was the Turkish officer who led the first resistance to the Allied landing on 25 April 1915, causing heavy casualties. The cemetery named after him, **Yahya Çavuş Şehitliği (Map 8, #16)**, is between the Helles Memorial and 'V' Beach.

Follow the signs for Yahya Çavuş Şehitliği to reach the **Cape Helles British Memorial (Map 8, #17)**, 1km beyond the Seddülbahir village square. From the Helles Memorial there are very fine views of the Dardanelles, with ships cruising placidly up and down. A half-million men were killed, wounded or lost in the dispute over which ships should (or should not) go through this strait.

Lancashire Landing Cemetery (Map 8, #18) is off to the north along a road marked by a sign; another sign points south to 'V' Beach, 550m downhill.

East of Seddülbahir Retrace your steps to the road division and go east. For Abide and/or Çanakkale Şehitleri Abidesi follow signs east at Morto Bay. Along the way you pass the **French War Memorial and Cemetery (Map 8, #12)**. French troops, including a regiment of Africans, attacked Kumkale on the Asian shore in March 1915 with complete success, then re-embarked and landed in support of their British comrades-in-arms at Cape Helles.

Çanakkale Şehitleri Abidesi (Çanakkale Martyrs' Memorial) **(Map 8, #14)** commemorates all of the Turkish soldiers who fought and died at Gallipoli. It's a gigantic four-legged stone table (almost 42m high and surrounded by landscaped grounds) standing above a war museum *(Şehitleri Abidesi Müzesi; ☎ 286-862 0082; admission US$0.80; open 9am-5pm daily)*. At the foot of the Turkish monument hill is a fine pine-shaded picnic area.

Getting There & Away

See Getting There & Away under Çanakkale for full transport details.

ÇANAKKALE (Map 10)

Çanakkale is a hub for transport to Troy and across the Dardanelles to Gallipoli. It was here that Leander swam across what was then called the Hellespont to his lover Hero, and here too that Lord Byron did his romantic bit and duplicated the feat. The defence of the Dardanelles during WWI led to a Turkish victory over Anzac forces on 18 March 1916, now a major local holiday.

Çanakkale is not a pretty town, so don't plan to stay too long.

Orientation & Information

The bus station (otogar) (Map 10, #8) is 1km inland from the ferry docks, but many buses also stop at ticket offices nearer to the docks. The helpful tourist office (Map 10, #14; ☎/fax 286-217 1187) and many cheap hotels and cafes are within a few steps of the docks, near the landmark clock tower.

For Internet, try Micronet (Map 10, #20; ☎ 286-213 9613), at Kemalyeri Sokak 6/3. It's open 10.30am to 11.30pm daily, and charges US$0.60 per hour.

Things to See

The Ottoman castle of Çimenlik Kalesi, built by Sultan Mehmet the Conqueror in 1452, is now the **Askeri Müzesi (Map 10, #29)** *(Military Museum; ☎ 286-213 1730, Yalı Sokak; adult/student US$0.50/0.20, open 9am-noon, 1.30pm-5pm Tues & Wed, Fri-Sun)*. It's set in a nice park beside the water. One of the highlights is a replica of the *Nusrat* minelayer ship, which played a pivotal role in the Gallipoli campaign.

Just over 2km south-east of the clock tower, the **Arkeoloji Müzesi (Map 10, #35)** *(Archaeological Museum; ☎ 286-217 3252, 100 Yil Caddesi; adult/student US$1.30/0.70; open 10am-5pm Tues-Sun)* holds artefacts found at Troy, Dardonos (near Çanakkale) and Assos.

Places to Stay

All hotels and guesthouses are heavily booked in summer; the town is insanely crowded around Anzac Day (25 April).

Hotel Kervansaray *(☎ 286-217 8192, Fetvane Sokak 13)* **Map 10, #22** Doubles

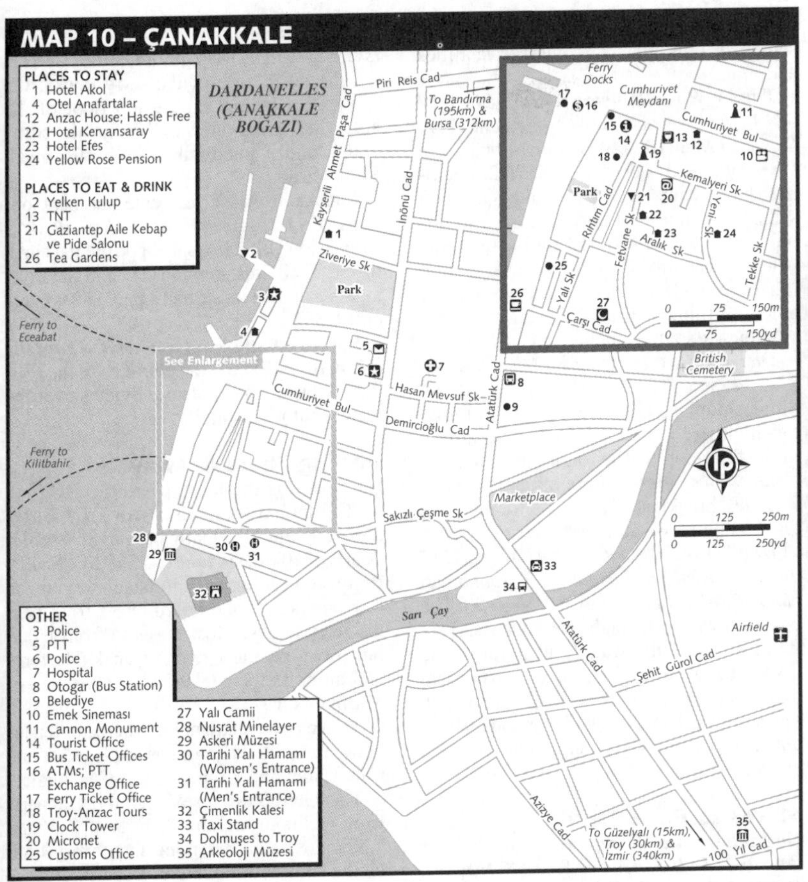

with/without bath US$7/6. From the outside, this gorgeous old house looks promising. Inside, the rooms are run-down, dark and the shared toilets are grotty – it's just as well it has a perversely alluring decrepit charm and a pretty leafy garden. Don't believe the '24 hour hot shower' on the business card, nor (women take note) the 'As comfortable as your home' – unless you have a team of ogling moustached gents in your lounge this won't be true.

Hotel Efes *(☎/fax 286-217 3256, Aralık Sokak 5)* **Map 10, #23** Singles/doubles US$5/10-24. This is one of the few places in Turkey run by a woman and is excellent value for money. Sure, the rooms are characterless and the echo of your feet on the tiled floors may drive you insane but you won't be complaining about the cleanliness. There's a small courtyard and some extra-long beds built for long-legged travellers.

Anzac House *(☎ 286-213 5969, fax 217 2906, W www.anzachouse.com, Cumhuriyet Meydanı 61)* **Map 10, #12** Bed in 4- to 6-bed dorm US$5, singles/doubles US$9/14. This tourist hotspot has echoey soulless rooms, some minuscule, others windowless, but all are spotless with immaculate shared bathrooms. Nightly *Gallipoli* videos are screened, plus there are Internet facilities and more.

Yellow Rose Pension *(☎/fax 286-217 3343, W www.yellowrose.4mg.com, Yeni Sokak 5)* **Map 10, #24** Bed in 14-bed dorm US$4.50, singles/doubles US$7/12. Facilities (table tennis, laundry, nightly *Gallipoli* screenings, Internet) may draw you to this old house now converted into a rambling pension. The mixed bag of rooms (bargaining is invited) includes some with crazy coloured tiling – not for the faint-hearted. All singles/doubles include a bathroom.

Otel Anafartalar *(☎ 286-217 4454, fax 217 4457, İskele Meydanı)* **Map 10, #4** Singles/doubles US$18/30. You can't miss this high-rise monstrosity on the north side of the ferry docks. The rooms are dated, but clean, with spotless bathrooms and the price includes breakfast. The front rooms have Dardanelle views at no extra cost.

Hotel Akol *(☎ 286-217 9456, fax 217 2897, W www.hotelakol.com, Kordonboyu)* **Map 10, #1** Singles/doubles US$60/90. The best in town is this high-rise, four-star 138-room hotel on the waterfront north of the docks. Each room is clean, with bathroom and air-con, plus many have a balcony with water views. There's a pool, bar and restaurant. It's popular with tour groups so book ahead.

Places to Eat & Drink

Gaziantep Aile Kebap ve Pide Salonu *(☎ 286-217 1193, Fetvane Sokak 8)* **Map 10, #21** Dishes US$0.50-2. Near the clock tower, this friendly no-frills place serves huge tasty pide, a range of soups and kebaps.

The most enjoyable places to dine are those facing the water, to the north and south of the ferry docks. Be sure to ask prices as bill fiddling is not unknown.

Yelken Kulup *(Sailing Club; ☎ 286-213 2335)* **Map 10, #2** Dishes US$2-3. Open 4pm-midnight. The Sailing Club is north of the ferry dock, out on a marina. It's a pleasant, laid-back spot with good food (meze, kebaps and more), but better views over the water. Ignore, if you can, the elevator-style music and the pink walls.

Otel Anafartalar *(☎ 286-217 4454, İskele Meydanı)* **Map 10, #4** Buffet US$12. On the north side of the ferry docks, the spotless restaurant on the top floor of the hotel has great views, live music some nights and a good-value set-buffet meal. Book ahead.

Çanakkale has a few entertainment options. ***TNT*** *(Fetvane Sokak)* **Map 10, #13** Admission US$2 Fri-Sat. Opposite the clock tower, TNT fires up on Friday and Saturday nights with live music and a pool table. Beers cost US$2.

For something less feral, the ***tea gardens*** **(Map 10, #26)** near the entrance to the Military Museum have pleasant views over the water (but no alcohol).

Getting There & Away

Çanakkale is the logical base for visits to the Gallipoli battlefields and/or Troy. Buses depart İstanbul's main otogar at Esenler hourly (340km, six hours, US$9 to US$12). If you're heading back to İstanbul, you can buy bus tickets and board buses from near the ferry docks. Most buses to/from İstanbul travel on the Eceabat-Çanakkale ferry and along the Thracian side of the Sea of Marmara coast.

To cross the Dardanelles, there are ferries between Gelibolu and Lapseki; Eceabat and Çanakkale; and Kilitbahir and Çanakkale.

The Gelibolu-Lapseki car ferry departs from Gelibolu at 1am, 3am, 5am, 6.30am, 7.30am, 8.15am, 9am and then every hour on the hour until midnight. Departures from Lapseki are at 2am, 4am, 5.45am, 6.30am, 7.30am, 8.15am and 9am, then every hour on the hour until midnight. The fare is US$0.80 per person, US$4 for a car. If you miss this boat, you can go south-west to Eceabat (45km, one hour) and catch the similar car ferry, or to Kilitbahir 7km beyond Eceabat and catch the small private ferry, which takes about 10 cars, and charges slightly less than the other ferries.

TROY (Map 5)

The approach to Troy (Truva), 30km from Çanakkale, is across low, rolling grain fields, with villages here and there. This is the ancient Troad, all but lost to legend until German-born Californian treasure-seeker and amateur archaeologist Heinrich Schliemann (1822–90) excavated it in 1871. He uncovered four superimposed ancient towns, destroying three others in the process.

Troy won't bamboozle you with well-preserved remains or immaculate carvings, but if you're interested in history you'll enjoy it. The views around the countryside and over to the Dardanelles are a bonus.

History

In Homer's *Iliad,* Troy was the town of Ilium. The Trojan War took place in the 13th century BC, with Agamemnon, Achilles, Odysseus (Ulysses), Patroclus and Nestor on the Achaean (Greek) side, and Priam with his sons Hector and Paris on the Trojan side. Rather than suggesting commercial rivalries as a cause for the war, Homer claimed that Paris had kidnapped the beautiful Helen from her husband Menelaus, King of Sparta (his reward for giving the golden apple for most beautiful woman to Aphrodite, goddess of love), and the king asked the Achaeans to help him get her back.

During the decade-long war, Hector killed Patroclus and Achilles killed Hector. Paris knew that Achilles' mother had dipped her son in the River Styx to make him invincible. However, to do so she had had to hold him by his heel, the one part of his body that remained unprotected. Hence Paris shot Achilles in the heel and bequeathed a phrase to the English language.

When 10 years of carnage couldn't end the war, Odysseus came up with the idea of the wooden horse filled with soldiers, against which Cassandra warned the Trojans in vain. It was left outside the west gate for the Trojans to wheel inside the walls.

One theory has it that the earthquake of 1250 BC gave the Achaeans the break they needed, bringing down Troy's formidable walls and allowing them to battle their way into the city. In gratitude to Poseidon, the earth-shaker, they built a monumental wooden statue of his horse. So there may well have been a real Trojan horse, even though Homer's account is not historical.

Excavations by Schliemann and others have revealed nine ancient cities, one on top of another, dating back to 3000 BC. The first people lived here during the early Bronze Age. The cities called Troy I to Troy V (3000–1700 BC) had a similar culture, but Troy VI (1700–1250 BC) took on a different character, with a new population of Indo-European stock related to the Mycenaeans. The town doubled in size and carried on a prosperous trade with Mycenae.

Troy VII lasted from 1250 to 1050 BC, then sank into a torpor for four centuries. It was revived as a Greek city (Troy VIII, 700–85 BC) and then as a Roman one (Troy IX, 85 BC–AD 500).

The Ruins of Troy

Half a kilometre before the archaeological site *(☎ 286-283 0536; adult/student US$3.50/2 plus US$1.50 per car; open 8.30am-5pm*

MICK WELDON

An eye-catching replica of the famous Trojan horse can be seen as you approach Troy.

Nov-May, 8am-8pm June-Oct), the village of Tevfikiye has a hotel, restaurants and souvenir shops. The window *(gişe)* where you buy your admission ticket is just past Tevfikiye, 500m before the site.

A huge replica of the wooden Trojan horse catches your eye as you approach Troy. The Kazı Evi (Excavation House) to the right of the path was used by earlier archaeological teams. Today it holds exhibits on work in progress. The models and illustrations should help you understand what Troy looked like at different points in its history. The main structures at Troy are well signed. Notice the oldest still-standing wall in the world; the **bouleuterion** (council chamber) built circa 800 BC; the **stone ramp** from Troy II; and the **Temple of Athena** from Troy VIII, rebuilt by the Romans.

Getting There & Away

In Çanakkale, walk straight inland from the ferry docks and turn right onto Atatürk Caddesi, the Troy road; the dolmuş station for minibuses to Tevfikiye and Troy is several hundred metres along it under a small bridge. Dolmuşes go to Troy (30km, 35 minutes, US$1.50) every 30 to 60 minutes in high summer.

If you'd prefer to take a tour, Troy-Anzac and Hassle Free run tours for US$14 (see Gallipoli earlier in this chapter). The tours start at 8.30am so you could do both a Troy and Gallipoli tour in one day.

The taxi office near the dolmuş stop in Çanakkale has a fixed price of US$35 for the return taxi trip to Troy with an hour's wait at Troy. You should be able to haggle this down to around US$20.

Language

Turkish is the dominant language in the Turkic language group which also includes such less-than-famous tongues as Kirghiz, Kazakh and Azerbaijani. Once thought to be related to Finnish and Hungarian, the Turkic languages are now seen as comprising their own unique language group. You can find people who speak Turkish, in one form or another, from Belgrade all the way to Xinjiang in China.

In 1928, Atatürk did away with the Arabic alphabet and adopted a Latin-based alphabet much better suited to easy learning and correct pronunciation. He also instituted a language reform to purge Turkish of obscure Arabic and Persian borrowings, in order to rationalise and simplify it. The result is a logical, systematic and expressive language which has only one irregular noun (*su*, 'water'), one irregular verb (*etmek*, 'to be') and no genders. It's so logical, in fact, that Turkish grammar formed the basis for the development of Esperanto, an artificial international language.

Grammar

Word order and verb formation in Turkish are very different from what you'll find in Indo-European languages like English. This makes it somewhat difficult to learn at first, despite its elegant simplicity. A few hints will help you comprehend road and shop signs, schedules and menus. For a more comprehensive guide to Turkish, get a copy of Lonely Planet's *Turkish phrasebook*.

Suffixes

A Turkish word consists of a root and one or more suffixes added to it. While English has only a few suffixes (*-'s* for possessive, *-s/-es* for plural), Turkish has loads of them. Not only that, these suffixes are subject to an unusual system of 'vowel harmony' whereby most of the vowel sounds within individual words are made in a similar manner. What this means is that the suffix might be *-lar* when attached to one word, but *-ler* when attached to another; the suffix retains the same meaning, though. In some cases these suffixes are preceded by a 'buffer letter', a 'y' or an 'n'.

Here are some of the noun suffixes you'll encounter most frequently:

-a, -e	'to'
-dan, -den	'from'
-dır, -dir, -dur, -dür	emphatic (ignore it!)
-(s)ı, -(s)i, -(s)u, -(s)ü	object-nouns (ignore it!)
-(n)ın, -(n)in	possessive
-lar, -ler	plural
-lı, -li, -lu, -lü	'with'
-sız, -siz, -suz, -süz	'without'

Here are some of the common verb suffixes:

-ar, -er, -ır, -ir, -ur, -ür	simple present tense
-acak, -ecek, -acağ-, -eceğ	future tense
-dı, -di, -du, -dü	simple past tense
-ıyor-, -iyor-	continuous (like English '-ing', eg, '... is eating')
-mak, -mek	infinitive ending

Nouns

Suffixes can be added to nouns to modify them. The two you'll come across most frequently are *-ler* and *-lar*, which form the plural: *otel* (hotel), *oteller* (hotels); *araba* (car), *arabalar* (cars).

Other suffixes modify in other ways: *ev* (house), *Ahmet*, but *Ahmet'in evi* (Ahmet's house). Similarly with *İstanbul* and *banka*: it's *İstanbul Bankası* when the two are used together. You may see *-i*, *-ı*, *-u* or *-ü*, *-si*, *-sı*, *-su* or *-sü* added to any noun. A *cami* is a mosque; but the *cami* built by Mehmet Pasha is the *Mehmet Paşa Camii*, with a double 'i'. Ask for a *bira* and the waiter will bring you a bottle of whatever type is available; ask for an *Efes Birası* and that's the brand you'll get.

Yet other suffixes on nouns tell you about direction: *-a* or *-e* means 'to': *otobüs* (bus), *otobüse* (to the bus) and *Bodrum'a* (to Bodrum). The suffix *-dan* or *-den* means 'from': *Ankara'dan* (from Ankara), *köprüden*, (from the bridge). Stress is on these final syllables (*-a* or *-dan*) whenever they are used.

Verbs

Verbs consist of a root plus any number of modifying suffixes. Verbs can be so complex that they constitute whole sentences in themselves, although this is rare. The standard example for blowing your mind is *Afyonkarahisarlılaştıramadıklarımızdanmı-sınız?* (Aren't you one of those people whom we tried, unsuccessfully, to make resemble the citizens of Afyonkarahisar?). Luckily it's not the sort of word you see every day!

The infinitive verb form is with *-mak* or *-mek*, as in *gitmek* (to go) or *almak* (to take). The stress in the infinitive is always on the last syllable ('geet-**mehk**', 'ahl-**mahk**').

The simple present form is with -r, as in *gider* (he/she/it goes), *giderim* (I go). The suffix *-iyor* has a similar meaning: *gidiyorum* (I'm going). For the future, there's *-ecek* or *-acak*, as in *alacak* (ah-lah-**jahk**), he will take (it).

Word Order

The nouns and adjectives usually come first, then the verb; the final suffix on the verb is the subject of the sentence:

I'll go to Istanbul.	*İstanbul'a gideceğim.*
I want to buy (take) a carpet.	*Halı almak istiyorum.* (lit: 'carpet to buy want I')

Pronunciation

Once you learn a few basic rules, you'll find Turkish pronunciation quite simple to master. Despite oddities such as the soft 'g' (*ğ*) and undotted 'i' (*ı*), it's a phonetically consistent language – there's generally a clear one-letter/one-sound relationship.

It's important to remember that each letter is pronounced; vowels don't combine to form diphthongs and consonants don't combine to form other sounds (such as 'th', 'gh' or 'sh' in English). Watch out for this. Your eye will keep seeing familiar English double-letter sounds in Turkish – where they don't exist. It therefore follows that h in Turkish is always pronounced as a separate letter; in English, we're used to pronouncing it only when it occurs before a vowel, but in Turkish it can appear in the middle or at the end of a word as well. Always pronounce it; your Turkish friend Ahmet is 'ahh-meht' not 'aa-meht', and the word rehber (guide) is pronounced 'rehh-behr' not 're-behr'.

Here are some of the letters in Turkish which may cause initial confusion:

A, a	as in 'art' or 'bar'
â	a faint 'y' sound in the preceding consonant
E, e	as in 'fell' or as the first vowel in 'ever'
İ, i	a short 'i', as in 'hit' or 'sit'
I, ı	a neutral vowel; as the 'a' in 'ago'
O, o	between the 'o' in 'hot' and the 'aw' in 'awe'
Ö, ö	as the 'e' in 'her' said with pursed lips
U, u	as the 'oo' in 'moo'
Ü, ü	an exaggerated rounded-lip 'yoo'
C, c	as the 'j' in 'jet'
Ç, ç	as the 'ch' in 'church'
G, g	always hard as in 'get' (not as in 'gentle')
ğ	silent; lengthens preceding vowel
H, h	always pronounced; a weak 'h' as in 'half'
J, j	as the 'z' in 'azure'
S, s	always as in 'stress' (not as in 'ease')
Ş, ş	as the 'sh' in 'show'
V, v	soft, almost like a 'w'
W, w	same as Turkish 'v' (only found in foreign words)

Greetings & Civilities

Hello.	*Merhaba.*
Good morning/ Good day.	*Günaydın.*
Good evening.	*İyi akşamlar.*
Good night.	*İyi geceler.*
Goodbye. (said by one departing)	*Allaha ısmarladık.*
Goodbye. (said by one staying)	*Güle güle.*
Stay happy. (alternative for 'goodbye')	*Hoşça kalın.*
How are you?	*Nasılsınız?*
I'm fine, thank you.	*İyiyim, teşekkür ederim.*
Very well.	*Çok iyiyim.*
What's your name?	*İsminiz ne?*
My name is ...	*İsmim ...*

Useful Words & Phrases

Yes.	*Evet.*
No.	*Hayır.*
Please.	*Lütfen.*
Thanks.	*Teşekkürler.*
Thank you very much.	*Çok teşekkür ederim.*
You're welcome.	*Bir şey değil.*
Pardon me.	*Affedersiniz.*
Help yourself.	*Buyurun(uz).*
What?	*Ne?*
How?	*Nasıl?*
Who?	*Kim?*
Why?	*Niçin, neden?*
How many lira?	*Kaç lira?*
large	*büyük*
medium	*orta*
small	*küçük*
not ...	*... değil*
and	*ve*
or	*veya*
good	*iyi*
bad	*fenah*
beautiful	*güzel*

Language Difficulties

Do you speak English?	*İnglizce konuşuyormusunuz?*
Do you understand?	*Anlıyormusunuz?*
I understand.	*Anlıyorum.*
I don't understand.	*Anlamıyorum.*
Please write it down.	*Lütfen yazınız.*
How do you say ...?	*... nasıl söylüyorsun?*
What does ... mean?	*... ne demek?*

Countries

Where are you from?	*Nerelisiniz?*
Australia	*Avustralya*
Austria	*Avusturya*
Belgium	*Belçika*
Canada	*Kanada*
Denmark	*Danimarka*
France	*Fransa*
Germany	*Almanya*
Greece	*Yunanistan*
India	*Hindistan*
Israel	*İsrail*
Italy	*Italya*
Japan	*Japonya*
Netherlands	*Holanda*
New Zealand	*Yeni Zelanda*
Norway	*Norveç*
South Africa	*Güney Afrika*
Sweden	*İsveç*
Switzerland	*İsviçre*
UK	*İngiltere*
USA	*Amerika*

Getting Around

Where is a/the ...?	*... nerede?*
airport	*havaalanı*
bus station	*otogar*
dock	*iskele*
left-luggage office	*emanetçi*
railway station	*gar/istasyon*
When does it ...?	*Ne zaman ...?*
leave	*kalkar*
arrive	*gelir*
aeroplane	*uçak*
flight	*uçuş*
gate	*kapı*
bus	*otobüs/araba*
direct (bus)	*direk(t)*
indirect (bus)	*aktarmalı*
train	*tren*
couchette	*kuşet*

sleeping car	*yataklı vagon*
dining car	*yemekli vagon*
no-smoking car	*sigara içilmeyen vagon*
ship	*gemi*
boat	*tekne/motor*
ferry	*feribot*
cabin	*kamara*
berth	*yatak*
class	*mevki/sınıf*

ticket	*bilet*
a ticket to (...)	*(...'a) bir bilet*
timetable	*tarife*
reserved seat	*numaralı yer*
1st class	*birinci sınıf*
2nd class	*ikinci sınıf*
one-way	*gidiş*
return	*gidiş-dönüş*
student (ticket)	*öğrenci (bileti)*
full fare (ticket)	*tam (bileti)*

early	*erken*
late	*geç*
fast	*çabuk*
slow	*yavaş*
next	*gelecek*
last	*son*
daily	*hergün*

car	*araba*
diesel (fuel)	*mazot, motorin*
highway	*otoyol*
motor oil	*motor yağı*
petrol (gasoline)	*benzin*
regular/super (fuel)	*normal/süper*

map	*harita*
street/avenue	*sokak/cadde(si)*
left	*sol*
right	*sağ*
straight on	*doğru*
here	*burada*
there	*şurada*
over there	*orada*
near	*yakın*
far	*uzak*

Accommodation

Where is ...?	*... nerede?*
Where is a clean, cheap hotel?	*Ucuz, temiz bir otel nerede?*

Signs

Giriş	**Entrance**
Çikiş	**Exit**
Açik	**Open**
Kapali	**Closed**
Danişma	**Information**
Boş Oda Var	**Rooms Available**
Dolu	**Full/No Vacancies**
Polis/Emniyet	**Police**
Polis Karakolu/ Emniyet Müdürlüğü	**Police Station**
Yasak(tir)	**Prohibited**
Tuvalet	**Toilets**

Do you have any rooms available?	*Odanızvar mı?*

I'd like a room ...	*Bir ... oda istiyorum.*
with one bed	*tek yataklı*
with two beds	*iki yataklı*
with a double bed	*geniş yatak*
with a shower	*duşlu*

What does it cost for (three) nights?	*Kaç lira (üç) gece için?*
Is a hot shower included?	*Sıcak duş dahıl mi?*
Does it include breakfast?	*Kahvaltı dahil mi?*
Is there a cheaper room?	*Daha ucuzu var mı?*
May I see the room?	*Odayı görebilir miyim?*
It's too small.	*Çok küçük.*
It's very noisy.	*Çok gürültülü.*
It's fine. I'll take it.	*İyi, tutuyorum.*
Where's the toilet?	*Tuvalet nerede?*

air-conditioning	*klima*
bath	*banyo*
cold water	*soğuk su*
hot water	*sıcak su*
light(s)	*ışık(lar)*
light bulb	*ampül*
shower	*duş*
soap	*sabun*
toilet paper	*tuvalet kağıdı*
towel	*havlu*

Around Town

Where is (a/the) ...?	... *nerede?*
customs	*gümrük*
exchange	*kambiyo*
post office (PTT)	*postane/postahane*
poste restante	*postrestant*
restaurant	*lokanta*
toilet	*tuvalet*
Turkish bath	*hamam*
Is there a local Internet cafe?	*Civarda Internet cafe var mı?*
I want to look at my email.	*E-mailime bakmak istiyorum.*
open	*açık*
closed	*kapalı*
(by) air mail	*uçakla or uçak ile*
cash	*efektif*
cheque	*çek*
commission	*komisyon*
dollars	*dolar*
exchange rate	*kur*
foreign currency	*döviz*
identification	*kimlik*
postage stamp	*pul*
telephone token	*jeton*
working hours	*çalışma saatleri*

Shopping

Where is (a) ...?	.... *nerede?*
bookshop	*bir kitapçı*
covered bazaar	*kapalı çarşı*
market/shopping district	*çarşı*
newsagent	*haber ajansı*
shop	*dükkan*
I want to buy ...	... *satın almak istiyorum.*
Do you have ...?	... *var mı?*
We don't have ...	... *yok.*
Give me ...	... *bana verin.*
I want ...	... *istiyorum.*
Which?	*Hangi?*
this one	*bunu*
How much/many?	*Kaç/Kaç tane?*
this much	*bu kadar*
It's (very) cheap.	*(Çok) ucuz.*
It's (very) expensive.	*(Çok) pahalı.*
I'll give you ...	... *vereceğim.*
price	*fiyat*
service charge	*servis ücreti*
tax	*vergi*

Food

I can't eat any meat.	*Hiç et yiyemiyorum.*
I eat only fruit and vegetables.	*Yalnız meyve ve sebze yiyorum.*
restaurant	*lokanta*
pastry shop	*pastane*
'oven' (bakery)	*fırın*
Turkish pizza shop	*pideci*
köfte restaurant	*köfteci*
kebap restaurant	*kebapçı*
snack shop	*büfe*
alcohol served	*içkili*
no alcohol served	*içkisiz*
breakfast	*kahvahltı*
lunch	*öğle yemeği*
supper	*akşam yemeği*
portion/serving	*porsyon*
fork	*çatal*
knife	*bıçak*
spoon	*kaşık*
plate	*tabak*
glass	*bardak*
bill/cheque	*hesap*
service charge	*servis ücreti*
tip	*bahşiş*

Health

I'm ill.	*Hastayım.*
Please call a doctor.	*Doktor/Hekim çağırın.*
Please call an ambulance.	*Cankurtaran çağırın.*
Where's the nearest ...?	*En yakın ... nerede?*
doctor	*doktor*
hospital	*hastane*
chemist/pharmacy	*eczane*
dentist	*diş hekimi*
diarrhoea	*ishalim*
fever	*ateşim*
handicapped	*özürlü/sakat*
headache	*ibaş ağrısı*
nausea	*mide bulantısı*
stomachache	*mide ağrısı*

Emergencies

Help!	*İmdat!*
It's an emergency.	*Acil durum.*
I'm ill.	*Hastayım.*
Call the police!	*Polisi çağırın!*
Find a doctor!	*Doktoru arayın!*
(There's a) fire!	*Yangın var!*
There's been an accident.	*Bir kaza oldu.*
Go away!	*Gidin!* (polite)
	Git! (informal)
I've been raped/ assaulted.	*Tecavüze/Saldırıya uğradım.*
I've been robbed.	*Soyuldum.*
I'm lost.	*Kayboldum.*
Where are the toilets?	*Tuvalet nerede?*

condom	*kondom*
medicine	*ilaç*
mosquito repellent	*sivrisineğe karşı ilaç*
sanitary pad	*hijenik kadın bağı*
tampon	*tampon*

Time & Dates

What time is it?	*Saat kaç?*
It's (8) o'clock.	*Saat (sekiz).*
It's half past three.	*Saat üç buçuk.* ('hour three-one half')
At what time?	*Saat kaçta?*
When?	*Ne zaman?*
day	*gün*
week	*hafta*
month	*ay*
year	*sene/yıl*

Sunday	*Pazar*
Monday	*Pazartesi*
Tuesday	*Salı*
Wednesday	*Çarşamba*
Thursday	*Perşembe*
Friday	*Cuma*
Saturday	*Cumartesi*

January	*Ocak*
February	*Şubat*
March	*Mart*
April	*Nisan*
May	*Mayıs*
June	*Haziran*
July	*Temmuz*
August	*Ağustos*
September	*Eylül*
October	*Ekim*
November	*Kasım*
December	*Aralık*

Numbers

0	*sıfır*
1	*bir*
2	*iki*
3	*üç*
4	*dört*
5	*beş*
6	*altı*
7	*yedi*
8	*sekiz*
9	*dokuz*
10	*on*
11	*on bir*
12	*on iki*
13	*on üç*
20	*yirmi*
30	*otuz*
40	*kırk*
50	*elli*
60	*altmış*
70	*yetmiş*
80	*seksen*
90	*doksan*
100	*yüz*
200	*iki yüz*
1000	*bin*
2000	*iki bin*
10,000	*on bin*

one million	*milyon*

-½ *(yarım)* – used alone, as in 'I want half'
-½ *(buçuk)* – always used with a whole number, eg, '1½', *bir buçuk*

Ordinal numbers consist of the number plus the suffix *-inci*, *-ıncı*, *-uncu* or *-üncü*, depending upon 'vowel harmony'.

first	*birinci*
second	*ikinci*
sixth	*altıncı*
13th	*onüçüncü*

Glossary

Here, with definitions, are some useful words and abbreviations. For **architectural terms**, see the special section 'Architecture' on pp29–35.

ada(sı) – island
aile salonu – family room; for couples, families and women in a Turkish restaurant
altgeçidi – pedestrian subway/underpass
arabesque – Arabic-style Turkish music
Asya – Asian İstanbul
Avrupa – European İstanbul
ayran – a yogurt drink

bahçe(si) – garden
balık – fish
banliyö treni (s), **banliyö trenleri** (pl) – suburban (or commuter) train
belediye – town hall
bey – 'Mr'; follows the name
birahane – beer hall
boğaz – strait
bordro – exchange receipt
börek – flaky pastry stuffed with white cheese and parsley
büfe – snack bar
bulvarı – often abbreviated to 'bul'; boulevard or avenue
büyük tur – long tour

caddesi – often abbreviated to 'cad'; street
caïque – long, thin rowboat
çalışma vizesi – work visa
çamaşır – laundry; underwear
çarşı(sı) – market, bazaar
çay bahçesi – tea garden
cicim – embroidered mat
çift – pair
çorba – soup

darüşşifa – hospital
deniz – sea
deniz otobüsü – catamaran; sea bus
Dikkat! Yavaş! – Careful! Slow!
dolmuş – shared taxi (or minibus)
döner kebap – meat roasted on a revolving, vertical spit
dondurma – ice cream
döviz bürosu – currency exchange office

eczane – chemist/pharmacy
ekmek – bread
emanet – left luggage
emniyet – security
eyvan – vaulted hall opening onto a central court in a medrese or mosque
ezan – the Muslim call to prayer

fasıl – energetic folk music played in taverns or *meyhanes*
fayton – horse-drawn carriage
feribot – ferry
fiş – electricity plug

gazino – open-air Turkish nightclub (not for gambling)
gece – night
gişe – ticket booth
göbektaşı – hot platform in Turkish bath
gözleme – Turkish pancake
gündüz – daytime

hamam(ı) – Turkish steam bath
harem – family/women's quarters of a residence
hat(tı) – route
hazır yemek lokanta – ready-made-food restaurant
hısar(ı) – fortress or citadel

ikamet tezkeresi – residence permit, known as 'pink book'
imam – prayer leader; Muslim cleric; teacher
imaret – soup kitchen
iskele(si) – landing-place, wharf, quay

jeton – token (for telephones)

kadın – wife
kale(si) – fortress, citadel
kapı(sı) – door, gate
Karagöz – shadow-puppet theatre
kat – storey (of a building)

KDV – katma değer vergisi; value-added tax (VAT)
kebapçı – place selling kebaps
kilim – pileless woven run
köfte – Turkish meatballs
köprü – bridge
köy(ü) – village
küçük tur – short tour
kürsü – prayer-reader's platform
kuru temizleme – dry cleaning

lahmacun –Arabic soft pizza
liman(ı) – harbour
lokanta – restaurant
lokum – Turkish delight

mahalli hamam – neighbourhood Turkish bath
mahfil – high, elaborate chair
Maşallah – Wonder of God! (said in admiration or to avert the evil eye)
menba suyu – spring water
merkez postane – central post office
mescit – prayer room/small mosque
mevlevi – whirling dervish
meydan(ı) – public square, open place
meyhanes – wine shops, taverns
müezzin – the official who sings the *ezan,* or call to prayer
müze(si) – museum

nargileh – water pipe

ocakbaşı – grill
oda(sı) – room
otel – hotel
otogar – bus station
otostop – hitch
otoyol – multilane toll highway

padişah – Ottoman emperor, sultan
pansiyon – pension, B&B, guesthouse
pastane – also pastahane; pastry shop, patisserie
pazar(ı) – weekly market, bazaar
pide –Turkish pizza
polis – police
PTT – Posta, Telefon, Telğraf; post, telephone and telegraph office

rakı – aniseed-flavoured grape brandy

saz – traditional Turkish long-necked string instrument
sebil – fountain
sedir – low sofa
şehir – city; municipal area
sema – Sufic religious ceremony
servis ücreti – service charge
servis yolu – service road
sıcak şarap – mulled wine
şile bezi – an open-weave cotton cloth with hand embroidery
sinema – cinema
şiş kebap – grilled, skewered meat
sokak, sokağı – often abbreviated to 'sk' or 'sok'; street or lane
su – water
Sufi – Muslim mystic, member of a mystic ('dervish') brotherhood
sultan – sovereign
sumak – flat-woven rug with intricate detail
sünnet odası – circumcision room

tabhane – hostel
tarikat – a Sufic order
TC – Türkiye Cumhuriyeti (Turkish Republic); designates an official office or organisation
telekart – telephone debit card
tuğra – sultan's monogram, imperial signature
ücretsiz servis – free service

valide sultan – queen mother

yardımcı – assistant
yeni otogar – new bus station
yıldız – star
yol(u) – road, way

Thanks

Many thanks to the travellers who used the last edition and wrote to us with helpful hints, useful advice and interesting anecdotes:

Terry Adby, Prof Etienne Aernoudt, Jefley Aitken, Sheila Aly, Nancy Anderson, Hiroyuki Asakuno, Paul Augenbroe, Mike Baker, Melangell Bakker, Cheryl Barnett, Ezster Blaskovics, Cindy & Maggie Blick, David Bolster, Lars Brannwall, Dorothy Brier Cohen, Evan Brinder, James Brock, Adam Brozek, Janet M Bryan, Roger Burrows, Andrew Cameron, Tui Cameron, Gilly Carr, N & C Carter, Elizabeth Centeno, Karen Chakmakian, Vinod Chandra, Kathleen Cherry, Phillip Chladek, Serhat Ciddi, Mike Clark, Ian Coggin, John & Susan Coote, Sue Counter, Michael Cowling, Liza Cragg, John Curry, Jeannie & Keith de Jong, Simona Decina, Karen Deetz, Graeme Dempster, Arati Desai, Joel Didomizio, Matjaz Dolenc, Jason Dore, Jason Dressler, Carl DuBee, Gertjan Duiker, Tim Evans, Deborah Filcoff, Robert G Finkel, Lawrence Forrester, Garry Garrard, Gaelen Gates, Terry Geisecke, Murat Germen, Sebrina Gibson, John L Goodman, Wynand Goyarts, Raphael Gruener, Pierre-Michel Guyot, Shelly Habel, John Hanks, Jean L Hardy, Julie Hartman, Tony Hayman, Phil Heinecke, Hilary Hepkiunsa, Kym Hirst, Sara-Jane Hodge, G Hoover, Fran Hopkins, Eric Horsenyi, Stephen Howse, Barbara C Hunt, Carol Huston, Tony Hylton, Mohammed Ally Islam, Rok Jarc, Karl Jeffery, Peter Jowett, Kristin Joynt, Ann Kennedy, Simon Kennedy, Pete Kesting, Carlo Krusich, Tone Larssen, Goss Lauren, Goerge Lechner, Caroline Lees, Juha Levo, Daniel Lieberfeld, Kristina Lindberg, Man-Sum Liu, Christina Lowe, Jenny MacPherson, Sally Marquigny, Massimo Marrella, Wendy McCarty, Kathryn McClurg, Bonnie McMillon, Karen Mickle, Lois & Art Morriss, Ted & Brenda Mouritz, Ann Mullen, Karen Myhill-Jones, T Nelson, Debby Nieuwenhuizen, Debbie O'Bray, Ryan & Peter Olwagen, Louise Otto, Kate Overheu, Tracey Parker, Davor Pavicic, Monica Pearl, Sean Plamondon, Jim Potter, Carlo Pozzi, MH Pratley, Scott Prysi, Thomas Reber, Melinda Reidinger, Dick Richards, Patrick Robin, Manel Roca, Cornelius Rost, Esa Ruotsalainen, Dave Russell, Krzysztof Rybak, Vera Di SanVito, Suzanne Sataline, Christian Schmidt, Carl Schwartzman, Paul Sebastianelli, Andrew & Ingrid Shepherd, J & B Skerritt, Valerie Slemeck, Yolanthe Smit, Alex Smith, Andrew Smith, Bill Smith, Eduardo Spaccasassi, Dieter Spreen, Peter Sumner, Sue Swarin, Yoel Swartz, Mark Tague, Luciano Tallone, Joshua Taylor Barnes, David & Evonne Templeton, Gordon Thomas, Rinaldo Tomaselli, Bern Toomey, KJ Troy, John Udy, Yusuf Usul, Cecile van der Herten, Elina Varmola, Thomas Vaughan, Reinfrid Vergeiner, Paul Waldman, Kerry & John Wallace, Nick Walmsley, Craig & Shannon Watts, Philip Weld, Kian White, Bryan Whitman, Roger Williams, Roger AC Williams, Karen Wilson, Ian Wright, William Yates, Yoram Yom-Tov, Genevieve Zalatorius

Lonely Planet Guides by Region

Lonely Planet is known worldwide for publishing practical, reliable and no-nonsense travel information in our guides and on our Web site. The Lonely Planet list covers just about every accessible part of the world. Currently there are 16 series: Travel guides, Shoestring guides, Condensed guides, Phrasebooks, Read This First, Healthy Travel, Walking guides, Cycling guides, Watching Wildlife guides, Pisces Diving & Snorkeling guides, City Maps, Road Atlases, Out to Eat, World Food, Journeys travel literature and Pictorials.

AFRICA Africa on a shoestring • Botswana • Cairo • Cairo City Map • Cape Town • Cape Town City Map • East Africa • Egypt • Egyptian Arabic phrasebook • Ethiopia, Eritrea & Djibouti • Ethiopian Amharic phrasebook • The Gambia & Senegal • Healthy Travel Africa • Kenya • Malawi • Morocco • Moroccan Arabic phrasebook • Mozambique • Namibia • Read This First: Africa • South Africa, Lesotho & Swaziland • Southern Africa • Southern Africa Road Atlas • Swahili phrasebook • Tanzania, Zanzibar & Pemba • Trekking in East Africa • Tunisia • Watching Wildlife East Africa • Watching Wildlife Southern Africa • West Africa • World Food Morocco • Zambia • Zimbabwe, Botswana & Namibia
Travel Literature: Mali Blues: Traveling to an African Beat • The Rainbird: A Central African Journey • Songs to an African Sunset: A Zimbabwean Story

AUSTRALIA & THE PACIFIC Aboriginal Australia & the Torres Strait Islands •Auckland • Australia • Australian phrasebook • Australia Road Atlas • Cycling Australia • Cycling New Zealand • Fiji • Fijian phrasebook • Healthy Travel Australia, NZ & the Pacific • Islands of Australia's Great Barrier Reef • Melbourne • Melbourne City Map • Micronesia • New Caledonia • New South Wales • New Zealand • Northern Territory • Outback Australia • Out to Eat – Melbourne • Out to Eat – Sydney • Papua New Guinea • Pidgin phrasebook • Queensland • Rarotonga & the Cook Islands • Samoa • Solomon Islands • South Australia • South Pacific • South Pacific phrasebook • Sydney • Sydney City Map • Sydney Condensed • Tahiti & French Polynesia • Tasmania • Tonga • Tramping in New Zealand • Vanuatu • Victoria • Walking in Australia • Watching Wildlife Australia • Western Australia
Travel Literature: Islands in the Clouds: Travels in the Highlands of New Guinea • Kiwi Tracks: A New Zealand Journey • Sean & David's Long Drive

CENTRAL AMERICA & THE CARIBBEAN Bahamas, Turks & Caicos • Baja California • Belize, Guatemala & Yucatán • Bermuda • Central America on a shoestring • Costa Rica • Costa Rica Spanish phrasebook • Cuba • Cycling Cuba • Dominican Republic & Haiti • Eastern Caribbean • Guatemala • Havana • Healthy Travel Central & South America • Jamaica • Mexico • Mexico City • Panama • Puerto Rico • Read This First: Central & South America • Virgin Islands • World Food Caribbean • World Food Mexico • Yucatán
Travel Literature: Green Dreams: Travels in Central America

EUROPE Amsterdam • Amsterdam City Map • Amsterdam Condensed • Andalucía • Athens • Austria • Baltic States phrasebook • Barcelona • Barcelona City Map • Belgium & Luxembourg • Berlin • Berlin City Map • Britain • British phrasebook • Brussels, Bruges & Antwerp • Brussels City Map • Budapest • Budapest City Map • Canary Islands • Catalunya & the Costa Brava • Central Europe • Central Europe phrasebook • Copenhagen • Corfu & the Ionians • Corsica • Crete • Crete Condensed • Croatia • Cycling Britain • Cycling France • Cyprus • Czech & Slovak Republics • Czech phrasebook • Denmark • Dublin • Dublin City Map • Dublin Condensed • Eastern Europe • Eastern Europe phrasebook • Edinburgh • Edinburgh City Map • England • Estonia, Latvia & Lithuania • Europe on a shoestring • Europe phrasebook • Finland • Florence • Florence City Map • France • Frankfurt City Map • Frankfurt Condensed • French phrasebook • Georgia, Armenia & Azerbaijan • Germany • German phrasebook • Greece • Greek Islands • Greek phrasebook • Hungary • Iceland, Greenland & the Faroe Islands • Ireland • Italian phrasebook • Italy • Kraków • Lisbon • The Loire • London • London City Map • London Condensed • Madrid • Madrid City Map • Malta • Mediterranean Europe • Milan, Turin & Genoa • Moscow • Munich • Netherlands • Normandy • Norway • Out to Eat – London • Out to Eat – Paris • Paris • Paris City Map • Paris Condensed • Poland • Polish phrasebook • Portugal • Portuguese phrasebook • Prague • Prague City Map • Provence & the Côte d'Azur • Read This First: Europe • Rhodes & the Dodecanese • Romania & Moldova • Rome • Rome City Map • Rome Condensed • Russia, Ukraine & Belarus • Russian phrasebook • Scandinavian & Baltic Europe • Scandinavian phrasebook • Scotland • Sicily • Slovenia • South-West France • Spain • Spanish phrasebook • Stockholm • St Petersburg • St Petersburg City Map • Sweden • Switzerland • Tuscany • Ukrainian phrasebook • Venice • Vienna • Wales • Walking in Britain • Walking in France • Walking in Ireland • Walking in Italy • Walking in Scotland • Walking in Spain • Walking in Switzerland • Western Europe • World Food France • World Food Greece • World Food Ireland • World Food Italy • World Food Spain **Travel Literature:** After Yugoslavia • Love and War in the Apennines • The Olive Grove: Travels in Greece • On the Shores of the Mediterranean • Round Ireland in Low Gear • A Small Place in Italy

Lonely Planet Mail Order

Lonely Planet products are distributed worldwide. They are also available by mail order from Lonely Planet, so if you have difficulty finding a title please write to us. North and South American residents should write to 150 Linden St, Oakland, CA 94607, USA; European and African residents should write to 10a Spring Place, London NW5 3BH, UK; and residents of other countries to Locked Bag 1, Footscray, Victoria 3011, Australia.

INDIAN SUBCONTINENT & THE INDIAN OCEAN Bangladesh • Bengali phrasebook • Bhutan • Delhi • Goa • Healthy Travel Asia & India • Hindi & Urdu phrasebook • India • India & Bangladesh City Map • Indian Himalaya • Karakoram Highway • Kathmandu City Map • Kerala • Madagascar • Maldives • Mauritius, Réunion & Seychelles • Mumbai (Bombay) • Nepal • Nepali phrasebook • North India • Pakistan • Rajasthan • Read This First: Asia & India • South India • Sri Lanka • Sri Lanka phrasebook • Tibet • Tibetan phrasebook • Trekking in the Indian Himalaya • Trekking in the Karakoram & Hindukush • Trekking in the Nepal Himalaya • World Food India **Travel Literature:** The Age of Kali: Indian Travels and Encounters • Hello Goodnight: A Life of Goa • In Rajasthan • Maverick in Madagascar • A Season in Heaven: True Tales from the Road to Kathmandu • Shopping for Buddhas • A Short Walk in the Hindu Kush • Slowly Down the Ganges

MIDDLE EAST & CENTRAL ASIA Bahrain, Kuwait & Qatar • Central Asia • Central Asia phrasebook • Dubai • Farsi (Persian) phrasebook • Hebrew phrasebook • Iran • Israel & the Palestinian Territories • Istanbul • Istanbul City Map • Istanbul to Cairo • Istanbul to Kathmandu • Jerusalem • Jerusalem City Map • Jordan • Lebanon • Middle East • Oman & the United Arab Emirates • Syria • Turkey • Turkish phrasebook • World Food Turkey • Yemen **Travel Literature:** Black on Black: Iran Revisited • Breaking Ranks: Turbulent Travels in the Promised Land • The Gates of Damascus • Kingdom of the Film Stars: Journey into Jordan

NORTH AMERICA Alaska • Boston • Boston City Map • Boston Condensed • British Columbia • California & Nevada • California Condensed • Canada • Chicago • Chicago City Map • Chicago Condensed • Florida • Georgia & the Carolinas • Great Lakes • Hawaii • Hiking in Alaska • Hiking in the USA • Honolulu & Oahu City Map • Las Vegas • Los Angeles • Los Angeles City Map • Louisiana & the Deep South • Miami • Miami City Map • Montreal • New England • New Orleans • New Orleans City Map • New York City • New York City City Map • New York City Condensed • New York, New Jersey & Pennsylvania • Oahu • Out to Eat – San Francisco • Pacific Northwest • Rocky Mountains • San Diego & Tijuana • San Francisco • San Francisco City Map • Seattle • Seattle City Map • Southwest • Texas • Toronto • USA • USA phrasebook • Vancouver • Vancouver City Map • Virginia & the Capital Region • Washington, DC • Washington, DC City Map • World Food New Orleans **Travel Literature**: Caught Inside: A Surfer's Year on the California Coast • Drive Thru America

NORTH-EAST ASIA Beijing • Beijing City Map • Cantonese phrasebook • China • Hiking in Japan • Hong Kong & Macau • Hong Kong City Map • Hong Kong Condensed • Japan • Japanese phrasebook • Korea • Korean phrasebook • Kyoto • Mandarin phrasebook • Mongolia • Mongolian phrasebook • Seoul • Shanghai • South-West China • Taiwan • Tokyo • Tokyo Condensed • World Food Hong Kong • World Food Japan **Travel Literature:** In Xanadu: A Quest • Lost Japan

SOUTH AMERICA Argentina, Uruguay & Paraguay • Bolivia • Brazil • Brazilian phrasebook • Buenos Aires • Buenos Aires City Map • Chile & Easter Island • Colombia • Ecuador & the Galapagos Islands • Healthy Travel Central & South America • Latin American Spanish phrasebook • Peru • Quechua phrasebook • Read This First: Central & South America • Rio de Janeiro • Rio de Janeiro City Map • Santiago de Chile • South America on a shoestring • Trekking in the Patagonian Andes • Venezuela **Travel Literature**: Full Circle: A South American Journey

SOUTH-EAST ASIA Bali & Lombok • Bangkok • Bangkok City Map • Burmese phrasebook • Cambodia • Cycling Vietnam, Laos & Cambodia • East Timor phrasebook • Hanoi • Healthy Travel Asia & India • Hill Tribes phrasebook • Ho Chi Minh City (Saigon) • Indonesia • Indonesian phrasebook • Indonesia's Eastern Islands • Java • Lao phrasebook • Laos • Malay phrasebook • Malaysia, Singapore & Brunei • Myanmar (Burma) • Philippines • Pilipino (Tagalog) phrasebook • Read This First: Asia & India • Singapore • Singapore City Map • South-East Asia on a shoestring • South-East Asia phrasebook • Thailand • Thailand's Islands & Beaches • Thailand, Vietnam, Laos & Cambodia Road Atlas • Thai phrasebook • Vietnam • Vietnamese phrasebook • World Food Indonesia • World Food Thailand • World Food Vietnam

ALSO AVAILABLE: Antarctica • The Arctic • The Blue Man: Tales of Travel, Love and Coffee • Brief Encounters: Stories of Love, Sex & Travel • Buddhist Stupas in Asia: The Shape of Perfection • Chasing Rickshaws • The Last Grain Race • Lonely Planet ... On the Edge: Adventurous Escapades from Around the World • Lonely Planet Unpacked • Lonely Planet Unpacked Again • Not the Only Planet: Science Fiction Travel Stories • Ports of Call: A Journey by Sea • Sacred India • Travel Photography: A Guide to Taking Better Pictures • Travel with Children • Tuvalu: Portrait of an Island Nation

Index

Text

A

Abdül Hamit II 16
accommodation 138-47, *see* Places to Stay index
activities, *see* individual entries
Ahmet III's Dining Room 33
air travel 61-4
  airline offices 64
airport 72
  travel to/from 72-3
Akbıyık Camii 90
Akmerkez shopping centre 34, 187
Aksaray 99, **Map 14**
Alay Köşkü 88
alcohol 151
Altınkum 198
Anadolu Hisarı 200
Anadolu Kavağı 201
antiques 183-4
Anzac Cove 211
apartments 138-9
Aqueduct of Valens 30, 102-3
Arap Camii 116
Arasta Bazaar 180
Archaeology Museum 87, **86**
architecture 22, 29-35
  Byzantine 29
  glossary 34-5
  highlights 29
  Ottoman 31
area codes 46
Arkeoloji Müzeleri, *see* İstanbul Archaeology Museums
Arkeoloji Müzesi, Çanakkale 214
Armenian Church of Three Altars, *see* Üç Horan Ermeni Kilisesi
Armenians 21
art
  festivals 166
  galleries 115, 165-6
arts, *see* individual entries
Asian İstanbul 36
Askeri Müzesi
  İstanbul 109-10, 214
  Çanakkale 214
Atatürk 17, 206, 209, 211, 213
Atatürk Cultural Centre 34, 109
Atatürk Kültür Merkezi, *see* Atatürk Cultural Centre
Atik Valide Camii 124
Atmeydanı, *see* Hippodrome
ATMs 43
Avrupa Pasajı 111
Aya İrini Kilisesi 92
Aya Sofya 30, 78, 80-3, **81**
Aya Triyada Kilisesi 110
Aynalıkavak Kasrı 133-4
Ayoub al-Ansari 132
Azapkapı Sokollu Mehmet Paşa Camii 116-17
Aznavur Pasajı 180

B

backgammon 134
Balat 129
Balık Pazar 111-12
ballet 25, 167
bargaining, *see* money
bars 168-75
  women-friendly 169
Basın Müzesi 100
Baths of Lady Hürrem 88-9
Bebek 195
Bedesten Çarşısı 207
Belediye Sarayı, *see* İstanbul City Hall
belly dance 167
Beyazıt Camii 101
Beyazıt II Külliyesi 208
Beyazıt Square 30, 101
Beykoz 201
Beylerbeyi Sarayı 199
Beyoğlu 36, 108-16, **Map 16**
billiards 134
Binbirdirek 100
Blue Mosque 78, 89-90
boat travel 70-1, 76-7,
  Bosphorus night cruises 135
  Bosphorus tours 193-5
  islands tours 203
  to/from Kadıköy 124-5
  to/from Üsküdar 122
body language 26
books 47-8, *see also* literature
  where to buy 184-6
Bosphorus 36-7, 78, 192-202
bowling 134
Bozdoğan Kemeri, *see* Aqueduct of Valens
Bucoleon Palace 30, 85
Burgazada 203
bus travel
  to/from İstanbul 64-6,
  within İstanbul 73
business hours 57
business travellers 59-60
Büyük Çamlıca 124
Büyük Valide Han 105-6
Büyük Yeni Han 105-6
Büyükada 204-6
Büyükdere 196-7
Büyüksaray Mozaik Müzesi, *see* Great Palace Mosaics Museum
Byzantine Church of St Polyeuchtos 103

C

Çadır Köşkü 120
Caferağa Medresesi 35, 88
Cağaloğlu Square 99
calligraphy 21-2, 101
camping 139
Çanakkale 214-16
car travel 56, 69-70, 75
  driving licence 41
  rental 75
  to/from İstanbul 69-70
  within İstanbul 75
Carpet & Kilim Museum 90
carpets 176-9, 180-1
Cartoon & Humour Museum 103
Cağaloğlu Square 99
Çemberlitaş 30, 100
Çengelköy 199
central post office 33
cheap thrills 174
children, travel with 54
  entertainment 174-5
Chora Church, *see* Kariye Müzesi
Church of Divine Peace, *see* Aya İrini Kilisesi
Church of the Pantocrator, *see* Zeyrek Camii
churches & cathedrals
  Aya İrini Kilisesi 92
  Aya Triyada Kilisesi 110

Byzantine Church of St Polyeuchtos 103
Christ Church 113
Dutch Chapel 112
Hagios Phocas 121
Panaya Isodyon 112
St George 129
St Mary Draperis 112
St Stephen of the Bulgars 129
SS Peter & Paul 115
San Antonio di Padua 112
Çiçek Pasajı 111
cicims, *see* carpets
cinemas 167-8, *see also* films
Çinili Cami 124
Çinili Köşk, *see* Tiled Kiosk
Çırağan Sarayı 119
circumcision 106, 132
Cistern of Aspar, *see* Çukur Bostan
classical music 24-5, 165
climate 18
conduct, *see* cultural considerations
Conqueror Monument Park, *see* Fatih Anıtı Parkı
consulates 41-2
copper 186
costs, *see* money
courses 135
Covered Market, *see* Kapalı Çarşı
credit cards, *see* money
cruises, *see* boat travel
Çukur Bostan 127
cultural centres 54-5
cultural considerations 26-7
Cumhuriyet Anıtı 109
currency, *see* money
customs regulations 42
cybercafes, *see* Internet
cycling 203-4

D

dance 24
festivals 167
Dandolo, Enrico 83
Deniz Müzesi 118
dentist 52
digital resources, *see* Internet
disabled travellers 54
discos 171-2
Divan Edebiyatı Müzesi, *see* Museum of Court Literature
Divan Yolu 99-100

Bold indicates maps.

documents 40-1
Dolmabahçe Palace 33, 117-18
dolmuş travel 76
drinks 150-1
driving, *see* car travel
drugs 56
Dutch Chapel 112

E

earthquakes 17-18
economy 19-20
Ecumenical Orthodox Patriarchate 128-9
Edirne 204-9
Edirnekapı 125-6
Egyptian Market, *see* Mısır Çarşısı
electricity 50
email services 46-7
embassies 41-2
emergencies 57
Eminönü 103-8
Emirgan 196
entertainment 164-75
environmental issues 18-19, 37
Eski Cami 31, 207-9
etiquette, *see also* cultural considerations
mosque etiquette 27
exchange rates, *see* money
excursions 192-218
Bosphorus 192-202
Edirne 204-9
Gallipoli & Troy 209-18
Kızıl Adalar 202-4
Eyüp 131-3
Eyüp Ensari, *see* Ayoub al-Ansari
Eyüp Sultan Camii 131

F

faience 22
Fatih Anıtı Parkı 103
Fatih Camii 130
fax services 46
Fener 128-9
festivals, *see also* special events
art 166
dance 167
film 168
jazz 174
music 165
puppet 175
theatre 167
Fethiye Camii 127-8
films 25-6, 48, *see also* cinemas
festivals 168
Firuz Ağa Camii 99

fish market, *see* Balık Pazar
folk dance & music 23-4, 166-7
food 148-63, *see also* Places to Eat index
breakfast 150
cafes 148
fast food 148
fish restaurants 149, 160-1
fish sandwiches 154
kebapçıs 148
köftecis 148
meyhanes 149
mixed cuisine 149-50
self-catering 150
sweets 150
Turkish delight 151
vegetarian restaurants 149
Fortress of the Seven Towers, *see* Yedikule
Fountain of Sultan Ahmet III 33, 91-9
French Consulate General 111

G

Galata, *see* Karaköy
Galata Bridge (Kulesi) 108-9
Galata Tower 115
Galatasaray Lycée 111, 112
Galatasaray Square 111
Galipdede Caddesi 113-14
Gallipoli 209-14
gay & lesbian travellers 53-4
entertainment venues 172-3
geography 17, 36
geology 17-18
Golden Gate, *see* Yedikule
Golden Horn 10, 108
golf 134
government 19
Grand Bazaar, *see* Kapalı Çarşı
Great Byzantine Palace 30, 80, 85
Bucoleon Palace 85
Great Palace Mosaics Museum 79
Great School 128
Greek Lycee of Fener, *see* Great School
Greek Orthodox Church of the Holy Trinity, *see* Aya Triyada Kilisesi
Greeks 21
Gülhane Park 88
gyms 134

H

Hacı Bedel Mustafa Efendi Camii 124

Halı ve Kilim Müzesi, *see* Carpet & Kilim Museum
hamams 136-7
Baths of Lady Hürrem 88-9
Cağaloğlu Hamamı 100
Çemberlitaş Hamamı 100
Çinili Hamam 124
Mahmut Paşa Hamamı 105
Sokollu Mehmet Paşa Hamamı, Edirne 207
Tarihi Galatasaray Hamamı 111
Hamamzade İsmail Dede Efendi Evi Müzesi 90
handicrafts 183
hans 107
harem life 94
Hasırcılar Caddesi 107
Haseki Hürrem Hamamı, *see* Baths of Lady Hürrem
Hasköy 133-4
Haydarpaşa train station 74, 125
health 50-3
Heybeliada 203-4
Hıdiv Kasrı 200
Hippodrome 30, 78, 83-4
history 10-17
Byzantium 10
Crusades 12-13
founding of Constantinople 10-11
Justinian, Emperor 11
Ottoman Conquest 13-15
Ottoman decline 15
Republican İstanbul 17-20
hitching 70
holidays 57-60
hospitals 53
hostels 139-40
hotels, *see* Places to Stay index
hünkar mahfili, *see* imperial loge
Hürrem Sultan 15

I

Ihlamur Kasrı 118-19
imperial loge 34, 82
inlaid wood 186
insurance 41
Internet
access 46-7
resources 47
İskele Camii 122
Islam 27-8
mosque etiquette 27
İstanbul Archaeology Museums 78, 86-8, **86**
İstanbul City Hall 34, 102-3
İstanbul City Museum, *see* İstanbul Şehir Müzesi
İstanbul Karikatür ve Mizah Müzesi, *see* Cartoon & Humour Museum
İstanbul Museum of Painting & Sculpture 118
İstanbul Şehir Müzesi 121
İstanbul University 101
İstiklal Caddesi 110-13, **Map 16**
İstinye 196
itineraries 36, 38-9

J

Janissaries 92, 96, 100
jazz 173-4
festivals 174
jewellery 186-7
Jews 20-1
Justinian, Emperor 11

K

Kadıköy 125
Kaiser Wilhelm's Fountain 84
Kaleiçi 206-9
Kamondo Stairs 115
Kanlıca 200
Kapalı Çarşı 78, 104-5, 180, *see map opposite p105*
Kara Davut Paşa Camii 123-4
Karagöz puppet theatre 175
Karaköy 114-17
Kariye Müzesi 30, 78, 126-7
Kemal, Mustafa, *see* Atatürk
Khedive's Villa, *see* Hıdiv Kasrı
kilims, *see* carpets
Kilyos 198-9
Kınalıada 203
Kiosk of the Linden Tree, *see* Ihlamur Kasrı
Kış Bahçesi 120
Kız Kulesi 123
Kızıl Adalar 202-4
Koca Sinan Paşa Medresesi 101
Köprülü library 100
Küçük Aya Sofya Camii 30, 85
Küçük Çamlıca 124
Küçüksu Kasrı 33, 199-200
Kurban Bayramı 57-8
Kurds 20

L

laundry 50
leather goods 181-3
legal matters 57
lesbian travellers 53-4
lese-majesty 55
libraries 54-5
Light of Osman Mosque, *see* Nuruosmaniye Camii
literature 26, *see also* books
Lone Pine 211-12
Loti, Pierre 133
luggage storage 50

M

magazines 48-9
Mahmut Paşa Yokuşu 105
Maiden's Tower, *see* Kız Kulesi
Maiyet Köşkü 119
malls 187
maps 36-7, 185-6
Maritime Museum, *see* Deniz Müzesi
markets 187, *see also* Kapalı Çarşı
Arasta Bazaar 180
Aznavur Pasajı 180
Balık Pazar 111-12
Mısır Çarşısı 32, 107, 180
Tahtakale 106, 180
measures, *see* weights & measures
medical treatment, *see* health, hospitals
meerschaum 187-8
Mehmet II, Sultan 13-14
Merasim Köşkü 119, *see* İstanbul Şehir Müzesi
metro travel 74
Mihrimah Sultan Camii 125-6
Milion 30, 99
Military Museum, *see* Askeri Müzesi
Mimar Sinan Çarşısı 123
Mısır Çarşısı 32, 107, 180
money 42-5
mosaics 79, 80-3, 126
mosque etiquette 27
Mosque of the Conqueror, *see* Fatih Camii
Mosque of the Conquest, *see* Fethiye Camii
Mosque of the Prince, *see* Şehzade Mehmet Camii
Mosque of Yavuz Selim, *see* Sultan Selim Camii
mosques
Akbıyık Camii 90
Arap Camii 116
Beyazıt Camii 101

Blue Mosque 78, 89-90
Çinili Cami 124
Eski Cami 31, 207-9
Eyüp Sultan Camii 131
Fatih Camii 130
Fethiye Camii 127-9
Firuz Ağa Camii 99
Küçük Aya Sofya Camii 30, 85
Mihrimah Sultan Camii 125-6
Muradiye Camii 208
Nuruosmaniye Camii 103
Ortaköy Camii 121
Rüstem Paşa Camii 106
Şehzade Mehmet Camii 102
Selimiye Camii 29, 31, 125, 207-9
Şemsi Paşa Camii 122
Sokollu Mehmet Paşa Camii 90
Süleymaniye Camii 32, 78, 10, **32**
Sultan Selim Camii 128
Üçşerefeli Cami 31, 206-7
Valide Camii 33, 103
Yeni Cami 32, 107
Yeni Valide Camii 123
Zeyrek Camii 30, 130
motorcycle travel 69-70
museums
Archaeology Museum 87, **86**
Arkeoloji Müzesi (Çanakkale) 214
Askeri Müzesi (Çanakkale) 214
Askeri Müzesi (İstanbul) 109-10, 214
Basın Müzesi 100
Carpet & Kilim Museum 90
Cartoon & Humour Museum 103
Deniz Müzesi 118
Great Palace Mosaics Museum 79
Hamazade İsmail Dede Efendi Evi Müzesi 90
İstanbul Archaeology Museums 78, 86-8, **88**
İstanbul Museum of Painting & Sculpture 118
İstanbul Şehir Müzesi 121
Kariye Müzesi 30, 78, 126-7
Museum of Court Literature 113-15
Museum of the Ancient Orient 86, **86**
Museum of Turkish & Islamic Arts 78, 90-1
Museum of Turkish Calligraphic Art 101-2
Museum of Turkish Musical Instruments 133
Rahmi M Koç Müzesi 134
Sadberk Hanım Müzesi 196
Tanzimat Müzesi 88
Tiled Kiosk 87-8, **86**
Yıldız Şale Müzesi 121
music 23-5
classical 24-5, 165
festivals 165
folk 23-4, 166-7
jazz 173-4
popular 24
musical instruments 23

N

nargileh 134
Netherlands Consulate General 112
New Queen Mother's Mosque, *see* Yeni Valide Camii
newspapers 48-9
nightclubs 171-2
Nightingale, Florence 16
Nişantaşı 109
Nuruosmaniye Camii 103

O

Obelisk of Theodosius 84
Old Book Bazaar 105
Old İstanbul 36
opera 25, 167
Opera House, *see* Atatürk Cultural Centre
organised tours 77
Orhan 13
Osman 13
Orient Express 69
Ortaköy 121-2
Ortaköy Camii 121

P

painting 22
Palace of Antiochus 99
Palace of Constantine Porphyrogenetus, *see* Tekfur Sarayı
Palais de France 112
Palazzo di Venezia 112
Paşabahçe 201
Patrikhane, *see* Ecumenical Orthodox Patrairchate
people 20-1
Pera 108
Pera Palas Oteli 113
Pharos lighthouse 85
photography & video 49-50
planning 36
politics 19
pollution 57
Polonezköy 201-3
popular music 24
population 20-1
postal services 45
Press Museum, *see* Basın Müzesi
puppet theatre 175
festivals 175

R

racism 56-7
radio 49
Rahmi M Koç Müzesi 134
Ramazan 58
religion 27-8
religious holidays 57-8
Republic Monument, *see* Cumhuriyet Anıtı
Resim ve Heykel Müzesi, *see* İstanbul Museum of Painting & Sculpture
restaurants 148-50, *see also* Places to Eat index
Retinue Kiosk, *see* Maiyet Köşkü
Rough-Stone Obelisk 84
Roxelana, *see* Hürrem Sultan
Royal Swedish Consulate 113
Rumeli Hisarı 195-6
Rumeli Kavağı 198
Russian Consulate General 112
Rüstem Paşa Camii 106

S

Sadberk Hanım Müzesi 196
safety 55-7, 172
Sahaflar Çarşısı, *see* Old Book Bazaar
St John of Studius 29
St Mary of the Mongols 128
Sancta Sophia, *see* Aya Sofya
Sarıyer 197-8
Sarnıç 35
scams 172, 181
Schneidertemple Art Centre 115
sculpture 22
Şehzade Mehmet Camii 102
Şeker Bayramı 57-8
Selim III 15
Selim 'the Grim' 128

Bold indicates maps.

Selimiye Camii 29, 31, 125, 207-9
Selimiye Kışlası 125
Şemsi Paşa Camii 122
senior travellers 54
Şerefiye Sarnıçı 100
shopping 180-91
Şile 202-3
silk goods 183
Sirkeci train station 33
Soğukçeşme Sokak 88
Sokollu Mehmet Paşa Camii 90
special events 57-60
Sphendoneh 84
Spice Bazaar, *see* Mısır Çarşısı
Spiral Column 84
sports 175
Sublime Porte 88
Süleyman the Magnificent 14-15
Süleymaniye Camii 32, 78, 10, **32**
Sultan Ahmet Camii, *see* Blue Mosque
Sultan Selim Camii 128
Sultanahmet 79-91, **Map 13**
sumaks, *see* carpets
Sunken Cistern 30, 83-4
synagogues
  Ahrida 129
  Etz Ahayim 121
  Neve Shalom 115
  Yanbol 129

T

taboos,
  see cultural considerations
Tahtakale 106, 180
Taksim Gezi Yeri 109
Taksim Square 109
Tanzimat Müzesi 88
Tarabya 196
taxes, *see also* money
  departure tax 61
taxi travel 75-6, 170
Tekfur Sarayı 30, 127
telephone services 45-6
Tersane Sarayı,
  see Aynalıkavak Kasrı
textiles 22
theatre 25, 167
  festivals 167
theft 55
Theodora 11
Theodora, Empress 12, 82-3
Theodosius Cistern,
  see Şerefiye Sarnıçı
Tiled Kiosk 87-8, **86**
Tiled Mosque, *see* Çinili Cami
time 50
tipping, *see* money
toilets 50
tomb of Valide Sultan Turhan Hatice 107
Topkapı Palace 78, 91-9
  see map opposite p97
tourist offices 37
Tower of Sultan Ahmet III 131
traffic accidents 56
train travel
  to/from İstanbul 66-9
  within İstanbul 73-4
tram travel 74
travel
  agencies 40
  insurance 41
  with children 54, 174-5
travellers cheques, *see* money
Troy 216-18
tulips 98
Tünel 113-14
Tünel underground train 74-5
Türk Vakıf Hat Sanatları Müzesi, *see* museums, Turkish Calligraphic Art
Türk ve İslam Eserleri Müzesi, *see* Museum of Turkish & Islamic Arts
Turkish baths, *see* hamams
Turkish carpets, *see* carpets
Turkish delight 151
Turks 20
TV 49

U

Üç Horan Ermeni Kilisesi 111
Üçşerefeli Cami 31, 206-7
universities 55
US Consulate General 113
Üsküdar 122-4, **Map 19**
Uzunçarşı Caddesi 106

V

Valide Camii 33, 103
video, *see* photography & video
visas 40-1
  extensions 40-1
  work 40-1
Voyvoda Caddesi 116

W

walking tours 78-137
  Byzantine Sultanahmet 79-85
  Ottoman Sultanahmet 85-91
  Palace of the Sultans 91-9
  Path of Empires 99-103
  The Bazaar District 103-8
  Beyoğlu 108-16
  Dolmabahçe Palace to Ortaköy 116-21
  Üsküdar 121-5
  Western Districts 125-30
Walls, the 130-1
weights & measures 50
whirling dervishes 113-14
women travellers 53
  health 52
  women-friendly bars 169
work 60

Y

Yedikule 30, 130-1
Yeni Cami 32, 107
Yeni Valide Camii 123
Yeniköy 196
Yerebatan Sarnıçı, *see* Sunken Cistern
Yeşil Sera 120
Yıldız Park 119-21
Yıldız Porselen Fabrikası 120
Yıldız Şale 120-1
Yıldız Şale Müzesi 121

Z

Zeyrek Camii 30, 130
Zoe, Empress 12, 82-3
zoo 88

Places to Stay

Alp Guesthouse 140
Ataköy Mokamp 139
Ayasofya Pansiyonları 142
Berk Guesthouse 141
Best Western Hotel Sokullu Paşa 143
Best Western President Hotel 146
Büyük Londra Oteli 144
Çelik 140
Ceylan Inter-Continental İstanbul 147
Çınar Hotel 145
Çırağan Palace Hotel Kempinski İstanbul 147
Conrad International Istanbul 147
Family House 144-5
Feronya Hotel 144
Four Seasons Hotel İstanbul 145-6
Galata Konutları Apart Hotel 145
Grace Hotel 144
Grand Hotel Ayasofya 142
Guesthouse Sunrise 140
Holiday Inn Crowne Plaza 145
Holiday Inn İstanbul Ataköy Marina 145
Hotel Ararat 142
Hotel Arcadia 146
Hotel Armada 146
Hotel Daphnis 144
Hotel Ema 141
Hotel Empress Zoe 142
Hotel Halı 143
Hotel Historia 142
Hotel Lamartine 144
Hotel Mercure 144
Hotel Nomade 143
Hotel Obelisk & Sümengen 143
Hotel Plaza 141
Hotel Poem 142
Hotel Richmond 147
Hotel Şebnem 141
Hotel Turkoman 142
Hotel Turkuaz 142
Hyatt Regency İstanbul 147
İstanbul Hilton 147
Konuk Evi 143
Konya Pansiyon 140
Londra Kamping 139
Madison Hotel, The 144
Mavi Ev 143
Mavi Guesthouse 140
Merit Antique Hotel 146
Orient Express 143
Orient Hostel 139-40
Otel Avrupa 141
Pera Palas Oteli 146
Polat Renaissance İstanbul Hotel 145
Riva Otel 144
Şafak Pansiyon, *see* Guesthouse Sunrise
Sarı Konak Oteli 143
Saydam Hotel 141
Side Hotel & Pension 141
Star Guesthouse 140
Sultan Hostel 140
Swissôtel İstanbul The Bosphorus 147
Terrace Guesthouse 140
The Marmara 147
Türkmen Hotel & Pansiyon 141
Yenişehir Palas 144
Yeşil Ev 145
Yücelt Interyouth Hostel 140

Places to Eat

Afacan Pizza & Burger Restaurant 156
And Restaurant 153
Andon 171
Antique Gallery 159
Asitane Restaurant 127, 161
Atlas Restaurant & Cafe 157
Beydağı 102
Boğaziçi Borsa Restaurant 163
Borsa Fast Food Kafeteryası 156
Borsa Lokantası 154
Cafe Antre 159
Café du Levant 134, 163
Cafe Enginar 115, 156
Cafe First Class 162
Cafe İst 155
Cafe Kino 156
Cafe Meşale 153
Çamlıca Restaurant 124, 159
Can Restaurant 152
Çay Bahçesi 162
Cennet 100, 153
Chef Selim, *see* Sultanahmet Meşhur Halk Köftecisi Selim Usta
Çiçek Pasajı 161
Çınaraltı Cafe Restaurant 162
Çiğdem Patisserie 153
Colheti Cafe & Restaurant 104, 155
Darüzziyafe 102, 155
Denizatı 159
Denizkızı Balık Restaurant 161
Derviş Aile Çay Bahçesi 153
Dervish Family Tea Garden, *see* Karadeniz Aile Pide ve Kebap Salonu
Doy-Doy 153
Dubb Indian Restaurant 159
Dulcinea 156
Et-İş 154
Famous Köfte-Maker, *see* Sultanahmet Meşhur Halk Köftecisi Selim Usta
Fez Cafe 155
Fill Up! Fill Up!, *see* Doy-Doy
Four Seasons 162
Great Hong Kong Restaurant 158, 163
Hacı Abdullah 162
Hacı Baba Restaurant 162
Hala 157
Hasır 162
Hatay 154
Havuzlu Lokantası 154-5
Hotel Arcadia 163
Huzur Restaurant 123, 158-9
İmroz Restaurant 161
James Joyce Irish Pub 169
Kahramanmaraş 158
Kaktüs 157-8, 170
Karadeniz Aile Pide ve Kebap Salonu 152
Karadeniz Lahmacun, Pide ve Kebap Salonu 132, 155
Karadeniz Pide Salonu 156
Kardeşler Anadolu Lokantası 154
Kardeşler Karadeniz Pide Salonu 152
Kariye Pembe 127
Kariye Pembe Köşk 155
Kasap Osman İskender 154
Kız Kulesi 158
Konyalı Restaurant 98, 153-4
Köşem Cemal Restaurant 161
Köşk Restaurant 154
Laila 172
Ihami'nin Yeri 162

Life_Roof 172
Liman 163
Liman Balık Restaurant 161
Macrocenter 158
Magnaura Café Restaurant 159
Malta Köşkü 120, 158
Marco Paşa 157
McDonald's 155
Mercan 157
Minas 160-1
Mozaik Café Restaurant 160
Musa Usta Adana Kebap Salonu 156
Nature & Peace 161
Ney'le Mey'le 161
Niyazibey İskender Kebapçı 123, 158
Nöbonb Cafe & Curio Shop 156
Nuh'un ambarı 157
Otantik 156-7
Pandeli 160
Pano 157
Panorama Restaurant 163
Paryon 161
Pierre Loti Café 132, 155
Pizza Hut 155
Pub Avni 170-1
Pudding Shop 153
Rami 160
Rejans Lokantası 112
Rumeli Café 160
Şark Kahvesi 105, 155
Sarnıç 163
Set Üstü Çay Bahçesi 88
Soho Supper Club 162, 170
Stop Restaurant 161
Subaşı Restaurant 154
Sultan Pub 153
Sultan Sofrası 153
Sultanahmet Köftecisi 152
Sultanahmet Meşhur Halk Köftecisi Selim Usta 152
Taksim Sütiş 156
Tarihi Çeşme Restaurant 152
Theodora Bar 169
Tugra Restaurant 163
Udonya 163
Urban 158
Yengeç Balık Lokantası 161
Yeni Birlik Lokantası 152
Zarifi 157
Zencefil 157
Zeyrekhane 130, 161

Boxed Text

Akbil Fare Savings 74
Antiquities & the Law 184
Anzac Day Tours 210
Ayoub al-Ansari 132
Bagging a Bargain 182
Buses to/from İstanbul 65
Buying Tickets 165
Carpet Bait & Switch 181
Dandolo the Doge 83
Dolmabahçe Palace to Ortaköy 116
Glossary of Architecture 35
Great Byzantine Palace 80
Hamams 137
Hans 107
Hassle-Free Service Buses 73
İstanbul in 48 Hours 39
İstanbul's Highlights 78
İstanbul's Must-See Architecture 29
Janissaries, The 96
Late-Night Transport 170
Life in the Cage 94
Mad about Tulips 98
Major Islamic Holidays 58
Malls & Markets 187
Maşallah! 106
Nightlife Rip-Offs 172
Old Book Bazaar 105
Orient Express, The 69
Pera in History 108
Pera Palas Oteli 113
Pierre Loti 133
Restaurant Hints 148
Saving Money 152
Selim 'the Grim' 128
Shopping Hotspots 180
Topkapı Palace 91
Traditional Musical Instruments 23
Turkish Body Language 26
Turkish Delight 151
Turkish Lira Crash 42
Turkish Top of the Pops 24
Üsküdar 122
Whirling Dervishes, The 114
Women-Friendly Bars 169

MAP 11 – GREATER İSTANBUL

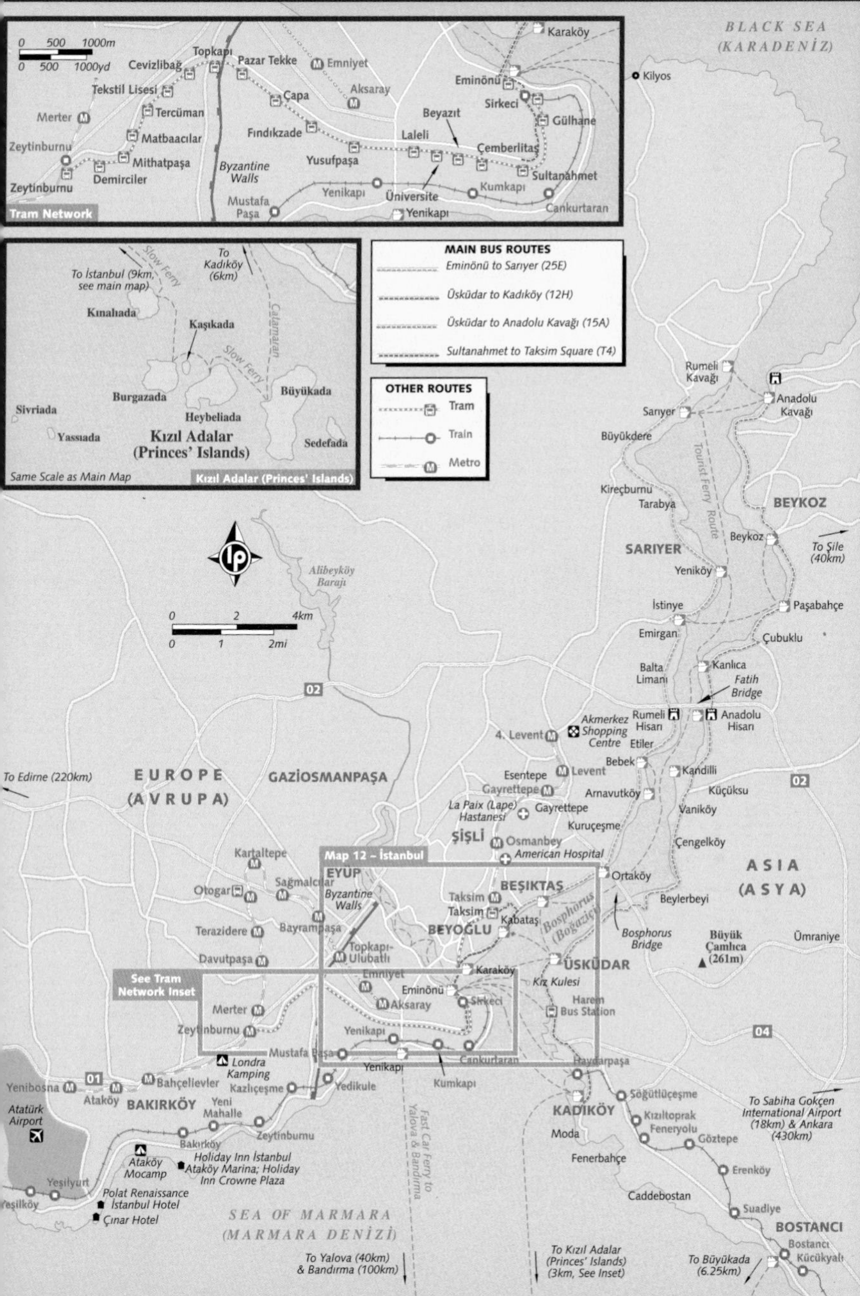

MAP 12 – İSTANBUL

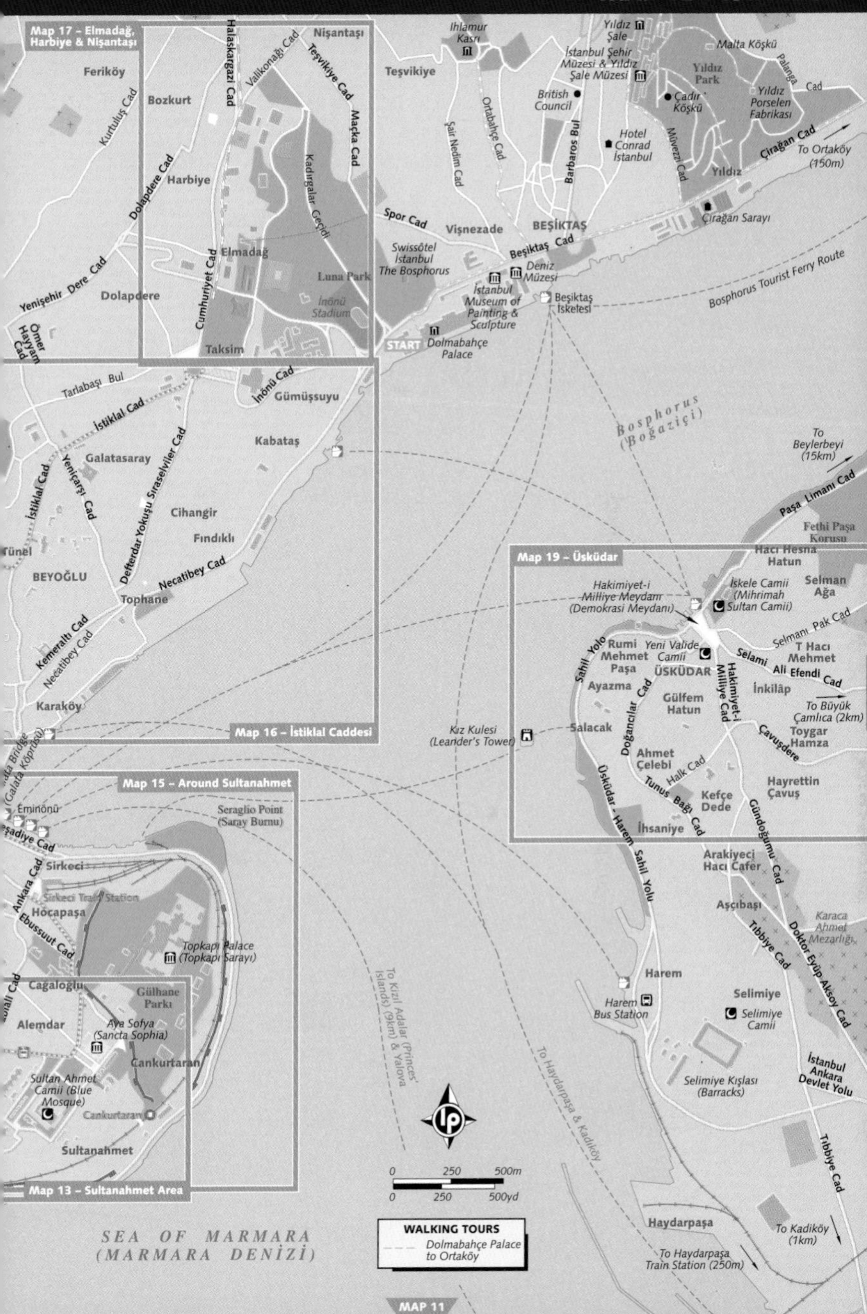

Map 17 – Elmadağ, Harbiye & Nişantaşı
Feriköy
Kurtuluş Cad
Bozkurt
Halaskargazi Cad
Vallkonağı Cad
Nişantaşı
Teşvikiye Cad
Maçka Cad
Harbiye
Dolapdere Cad
Kadırgalar Geçidi
Elmadağ
Cumhuriyet Cad
Luna Park
İnönü Stadium
Yenişehir Dere Cad
Dolapdere
Ömer Hayyam Cad
Taksim
Teşvikiye
Ihlamur Kasrı
Şair Nedim Cad
Ortabahçe Cad
Yıldız Şale
İstanbul Şehir Müzesi & Yıldız Şale Müzesi
British Council
Barbaros Bul
Hotel Conrad İstanbul
Çadır Köşkü
Müvezzi Cad
Yıldız Park
Malta Köşkü
Palanga Cad
Yıldız Porselen Fabrikası
Çırağan Cad
To Ortaköy (150m)
Yıldız
Çırağan Sarayı
Spor Cad
Vişnezade
BEŞİKTAŞ
Beşiktaş Cad
Swissôtel İstanbul The Bosphorus
Deniz Müzesi
İstanbul Museum of Painting & Sculpture
Beşiktaş İskelesi
Bosphorus Tourist Ferry Route
START
Dolmabahçe Palace
Tarlabaşı Bul
İnönü Cad
Gümüşsuyu
İstiklal Cad
Galatasaray
Yeniçarşı Cad
Defterdar Yokuşu Sıraselviler Cad
Kabataş
Cihangir
Fındıklı
Tünel
BEYOĞLU
Necatibey Cad
Tophane
Kemeraltı Cad
Karaköy
Bosphorus (Boğaziçi)
To Beylerbeyi (15km)
Paşa Limanı Cad
Fethi Paşa Korusu
Map 16 – İstiklal Caddesi
Map 19 – Üsküdar
Hacı Hesna Hatun
Hakimiyet-i Milliye Meydanı (Demokrasi Meydanı)
İskele Camii (Mihrimah Sultan Camii)
Selman Ağa
Selmanı Pak Cad
Sahil Yolu
Rumi Mehmet Paşa
Yeni Valide Camii
ÜSKÜDAR
Selami Ali Efendi Cad
T Hacı Mehmet
Ayazma
Hakimiyet-i Milliye Cad
Gülfem Hatun
İnkilâp
To Büyük Çamlıca (2km)
Kız Kulesi (Leander's Tower)
Salacak
Doğancılar Cad
Toygar Hamza
Çavuşdere
Ahmet Çelebi
Halk Cad
Tunus Bağı Cad
Hayrettin Çavuş
Kefçe Dede
Üsküdar - Harem Sahil Yolu
İhsaniye
Gündoğumu Cad
Arakiyeci Hacı Cafer
Aşçıbaşı
Karaca Ahmet Mezarlığı
Tıbbiye Cad
Doktor Eyüp Aksoy Cad
Harem
Harem Bus Station
Selimiye
Selimiye Camii
Selimiye Kışlası (Barracks)
İstanbul Ankara Devlet Yolu
Galata Bridge (Galata Köprüsü)
Map 15 – Around Sultanahmet
Eminönü
Seraglio Point (Saray Burnu)
Reşadiye Cad
Sirkeci
Ankara Cad
Sirkeci Train Station
Hocapaşa
Ebussuut Cad
Topkapı Palace (Topkapı Sarayı)
Cagaloglu
Gülhane Parkı
Alemdar
Aya Sofya (Sancta Sophia)
Cankurtaran
Sultan Ahmet Camii (Blue Mosque)
Sultanahmet
Map 13 – Sultanahmet Area
To Kızıl Adalar (Princes' Islands) (9km) & Yalova
To Haydarpaşa & Kadıköy
0 250 500m
0 250 500yd
SEA OF MARMARA (MARMARA DENİZİ)
WALKING TOURS
Dolmabahçe Palace to Ortaköy
Haydarpaşa
To Haydarpaşa Train Station (250m)
To Kadıköy (1km)
Tıbbiye Cad
MAP 11

MAP 13 – SULTANAHMET AREA

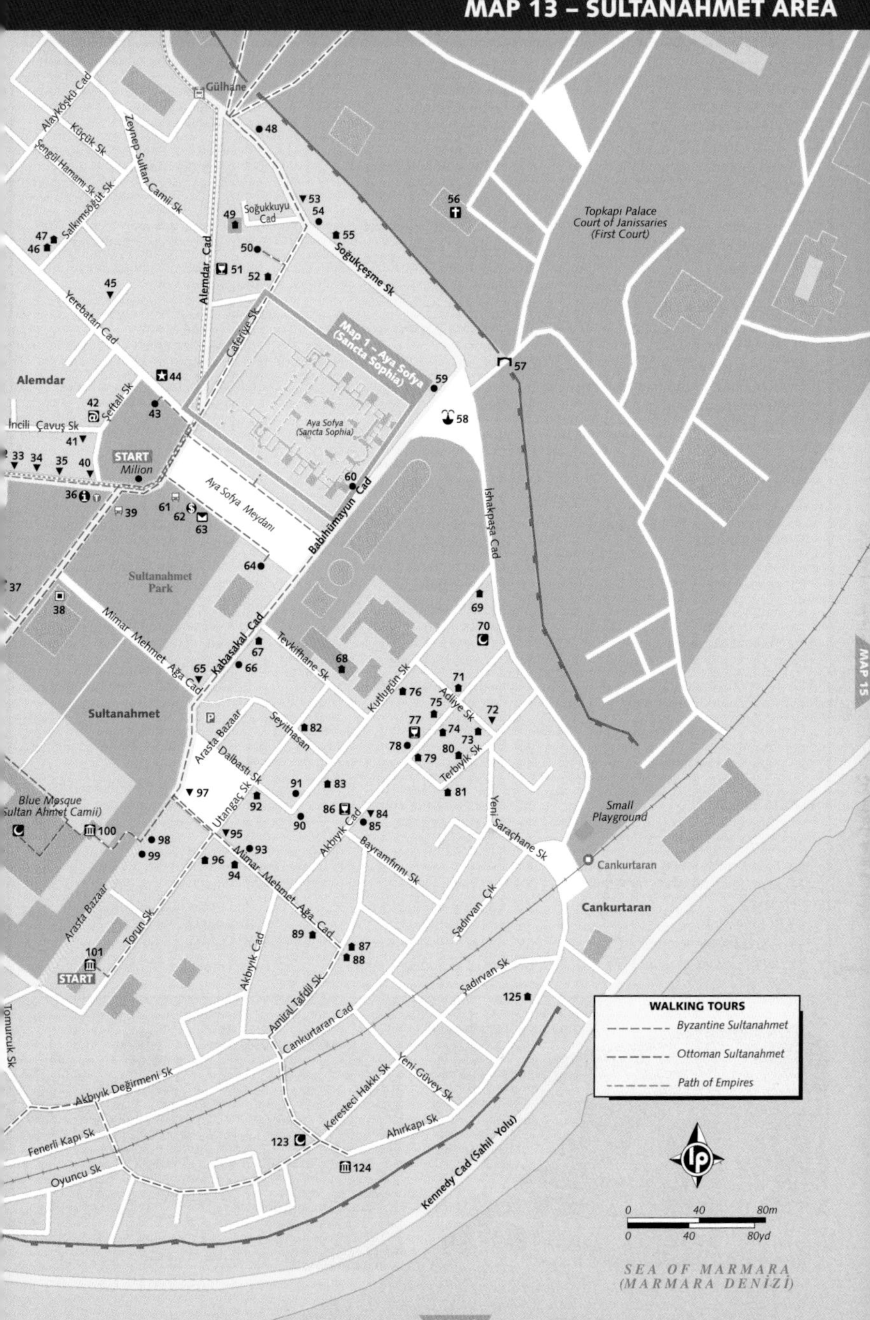

Gülhane
Alayköşkü Cad
Küçük Sk
Şengül Hamamı Sk
Salkımsöğüt Sk
Zeynep Sultan Camii Sk
Alemdar Cad
Soğukkuyu Cad
Soğukçeşme Sk
Yerebatan Cad
Caferiye Sk
Map 1 – Aya Sofya (Sancta Sophia)
Aya Sofya (Sancta Sophia)
Alemdar
Şeftali Sk
İncili Çavuş Sk
START
Milion
Aya Sofya Meydanı
Babıhümayun Cad
Sultanahmet Park
Mimar Mehmet Ağa Cad
Kabasakal Cad
Tevkifhane Sk
Kutlugün Sk
Adliye Sk
İshakpaşa Cad
Topkapı Palace Court of Janissaries (First Court)
Sultanahmet
Arasta Bazaar
Seyithasan
Dalbastı Sk
Terbıyık Sk
Blue Mosque (Sultan Ahmet Camii)
Utangaç Sk
Akbıyık Cad
Bayramfırını Sk
Yeni Saraçhane Sk
Small Playground
Cankurtaran
Mimar Mehmet Ağa Cad
Şadırvan Çık
Arasta Bazaar
Torun Sk
START
Akbıyık Cad
Amiral Tafdil Sk
Şadırvan Sk
Cankurtaran Cad
Tomurcuk Sk
Akbıyık Değirmeni Sk
Keresteci Hakkı Sk
Yeni Güvey Sk
Ahırkapı Sk
Fenerli Kapı Sk
Oyuncu Sk
Kennedy Cad (Sahil Yolu)
WALKING TOURS
Byzantine Sultanahmet
Ottoman Sultanahmet
Path of Empires
0 40 80m
0 40 80yd
SEA OF MARMARA (MARMARA DENİZİ)

MAP 15

MAP 12

MAP 13 – SULTANAHMET AREA

PLACES TO STAY

12 Hotel Halı
17 Hotel Arcadia
29 Hotel Nomade
46 Hotel Ema
47 Alp Guesthouse
49 Konuk Evi
52 Yücelt Interyouth Hostel; Heritage
55 Ayasofya Pansiyonları
67 Yeşil Ev
68 Four Seasons Hotel İstanbul
69 Mavi Guesthouse
71 Hotel Empress Zoe
73 Hotel Şebnem
74 Orient Hostel; Orient Bar
75 Star Guesthouse; Star Laundry
76 Berk Guesthouse
79 Sultan Hostel
80 Konya Pansiyon
81 Hotel Poem
82 Side Hotel & Pansiyon
83 Terrace Guesthouse
87 Hotel Obelisk & Sümengen
88 Hotel Historia
89 Sarı Konak Oteli
92 Mavi Ev
94 Çelik
96 Hotel Ararat
105 Hotel Turkoman
109 Türkmen Hotel & Pansiyon
112 Hotel Turkuaz
116 Best Western Hotel Sokullu Paşa
117 Grand Hotel Ayasofya
120 Guesthouse Sunrise
125 Hotel Armada

PLACES TO EAT

7 Cennet
20 Sultan Sofrası
25 Çiğdem Patisserie
27 Karadeniz Aile Pide ve Kebap Salonu
30 Rumeli Café
31 Mozaik Café Restaurant
32 Sultanahmet Meşhur Halk Köftecisi Selim Usta
33 Can Restaurant
34 Pudding Shop
35 Sultanahmet Köftecisi
40 Sultan Pub
41 Dubb Indian Restaurant
45 And Restaurant
53 Sarnıç
65 Derviş Aile Çay Bahçesi
72 Antique Gallery
84 Magnaura Café Restaurant
95 Rami
97 Cafe Meşale
107 Kardeşler Karadeniz Pide Salonu
108 Yeni Birlik Lokantası
114 Tarihi Çeşme Restaurant
119 Doy-Doy

OTHER

1 Nuruosmaniye Camii
2 Atik Ali Paşa Camii
3 Çemberlitaş
4 Şafak Sinemaları
5 Köprülü Tomb & Mosque
6 Çemberlitaş Hamamı
8 Basın Müzesi
9 Köprülü Library
10 Tombs
11 Yapı Kredi
13 Şerefiye Sarnıçı
14 Keçicizade Fuat Paşa Camii
15 Su-De
16 Binbirdirek
18 PTT
19 Museum of Turkish & Islamic Arts
21 Palace of Antiochus
22 Firuz Ağa Camii
23 Marco Polo
24 Galeri Kayseri
26 Teras Pub-Disco
28 Cağaloğlu Hamamı
36 Tourist Office
37 Kaiser Wilhelm's Fountain
38 Tomb of Sultan Ahmet I
39 'T4' Bus to Taksim Square
42 Anatolia Internet Cafe
43 Sunken Cistern
44 Tourism Police
48 Halı Evi
50 Caferağa Medresesi
51 Theodora Bar
54 İstanbul Library
56 Aya İrini Kilisesi
57 Imperial Gate, Topkapı Palace
58 Fountain of Sultan Ahmet III
59 Dösim
60 Sebil
61 İstanbul Vision
62 Yapı Kredi ATM
63 PTT Booth
64 Baths of Lady Hürrem; Haseki Hamam Carpet & Kilim Sales Store
66 İstanbul Sanatlar Çarşısı
70 İshak Paşa Camii
77 Cheers Bar
78 Backpackers
85 Natural Foreign Book Exchange; Gallery Natural
86 Ayazma Bar
90 Magnaura Palace Restoration
91 Kirkit Voyage
93 Aypa Bookshop
98 Meerschaum Pipes
99 İznik Classics & Tiles
100 Carpet & Kilim Museum
101 Great Palace Mosaics Museum
102 Obelisk of Theodosius
103 Spiral Column
104 Rough-Stone Obelisk
106 Doğu Expres
110 Sokolu Mehmet Paşa Camii
111 Kadırga Hamamı
113 Küçük Aya Sofya Camii
115 Çardaklı Hamamı
118 Sphendoneh
121 Bucoleon Palace
122 Pharos Lighthouse
123 Akbıyık Camii
124 Hamamzade İsmail Dede Efendi Evi Müzesi

BOTH PHOTOS BY GREG ELMS

A typical 24-hour *büfe* (fast-food buffet)

A sandwich stand in the Eminönü District

Fatih Camii
Tombs
Fatih
Zeyrek
Zeyrek Camii
Zeyrekhane
Vefa
Cartoon & Humour Museum
Fatih Anıtı Parkı
Saraçhane
Saraçhane Parkı
Kalenderhane
Şehzade Mehmet Camii
Byzantine Church of St Polyeuchtos
İstanbul City Hall
Aksaray
Aksaray
Valide Camii
Murat Paşa Camii
Yusufpaşa
Fındıkzade
Haseki
Aksaray Square
Laleli Camii
Laleli
FINISH
Merit Antique Hotel
Balaban Ağa
MAP 15
Nişanca
Yenikapı
Gar
Havaş Airport Bus Stop
Yenikapı
Samatya
SEA OF MARMARA (MARMARA DENİZİ)
Yenikapı Fast Car Ferry & Seabus Port
MAP 12
WALKING TOURS
Path of Empires
0 100 200m
0 100 200yd
Adnan Menderes Bulvarı
Atatürk Bulvarı
Turgut Özal Cad (Millet Cad)
Ordu Cad
Macar Kardeşler Cad
Akdeniz Cad
Horhor Cad
Şehzadebaşı Cad
Namık Kemal Cad
Mustafa Kemal Cad
Küçük Langa Cad
Hayriye Tüccarı Cad
Cerrahpaşa Cad
Haseki Cad
Samatya Cad
Kennedy Cad
Türkeli Cad
Gençtürk Cad
Aqueduct of Valens

MAP 15 – AROUND SULTANAHMET

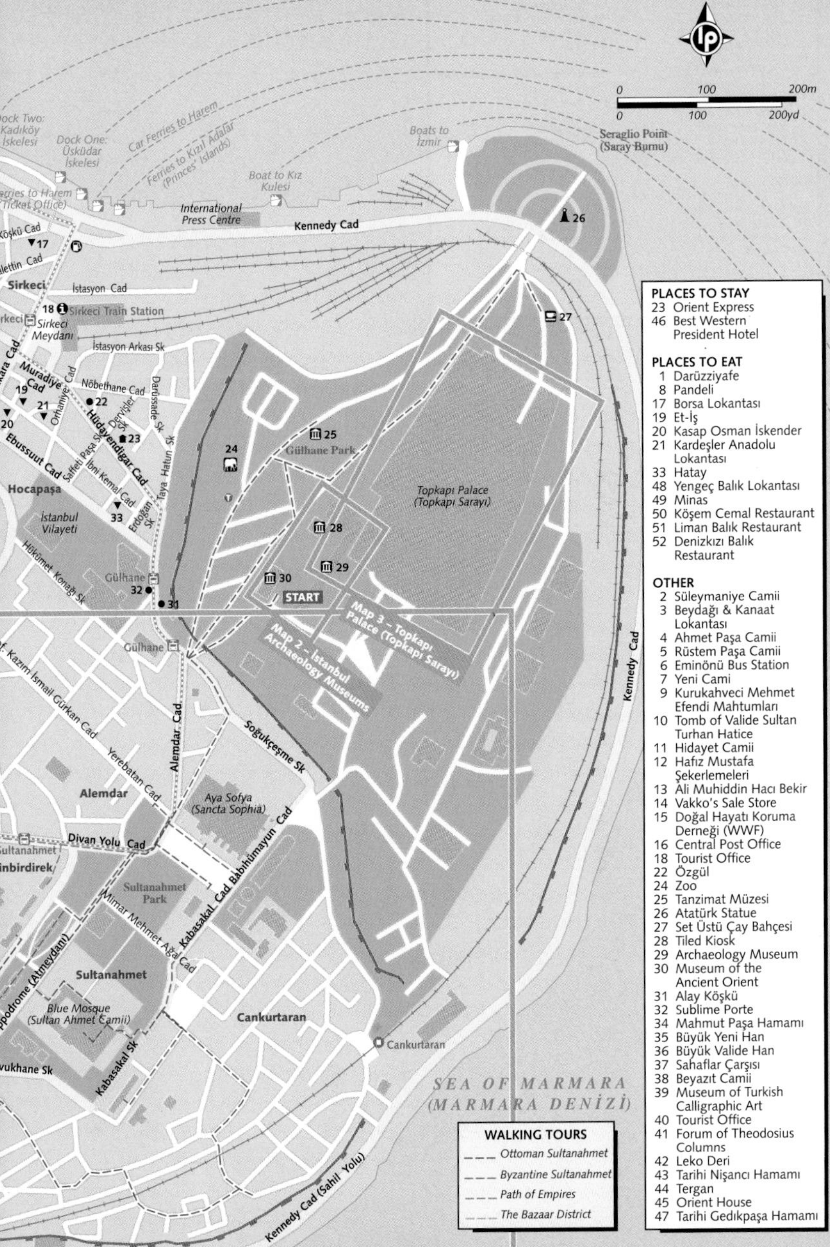
0
100
200m
0
100
200yd
Seraglio Point
(Saray Burnu)
Dock Two:
Kadıköy
İskelesi
Dock One:
Üsküdar
İskelesi
Car Ferries to Harem
Ferries to Kızıl Adalar
(Princes' Islands)
Boat to Kız
Kulesi
Boats to
İzmir
International
Press Centre
Kennedy Cad
Sirkeci
İstasyon Cad
Sirkeci Train Station
Sirkeci
Meydanı
İstasyon Arkası Sk
Muradiye Cad
Nöbethane Cad
Hüdavendigar Cad
Ebussuut Cad
Hocapaşa
İstanbul
Vilayeti
Hükümet Konağı Sk
Gülhane Park
Topkapı Palace
(Topkapı Sarayı)
START
Map 3 – Topkapı Palace (Topkapı Sarayı)
Map 2 – İstanbul Archaeology Museums
Gülhane
Alemdar Cad
Soğukçeşme Sk
Yerebatan Cad
Alemdar
Aya Sofya
(Sancta Sophia)
Babıhümayun Cad
Divan Yolu Cad
Sultanahmet
Park
Kabasakal Cad
Mimar Mehmet Ağa Cad
Sultanahmet
Blue Mosque
(Sultan Ahmet Camii)
Cankurtaran
Kabasakal Sk
SEA OF MARMARA
(MARMARA DENİZİ)
Kennedy Cad (Sahil Yolu)
PLACES TO STAY
23 Orient Express
46 Best Western President Hotel
PLACES TO EAT
1 Darüzziyafe
8 Pandeli
17 Borsa Lokantası
19 Et-İş
20 Kasap Osman İskender
21 Kardeşler Anadolu Lokantası
33 Hatay
48 Yengeç Balık Lokantası
49 Minas
50 Köşem Cemal Restaurant
51 Liman Balık Restaurant
52 Denizkızı Balık Restaurant
OTHER
2 Süleymaniye Camii
3 Beydağı & Kanaat Lokantası
4 Ahmet Paşa Camii
5 Rüstem Paşa Camii
6 Eminönü Bus Station
7 Yeni Cami
9 Kurukahveci Mehmet Efendi Mahtumları
10 Tomb of Valide Sultan Turhan Hatice
11 Hidayet Camii
12 Hafız Mustafa Şekerlemeleri
13 Ali Muhiddin Hacı Bekir
14 Vakko's Sale Store
15 Doğal Hayatı Koruma Derneği (WWF)
16 Central Post Office
18 Tourist Office
22 Özgül
24 Zoo
25 Tanzimat Müzesi
26 Atatürk Statue
27 Set Üstü Çay Bahçesi
28 Tiled Kiosk
29 Archaeology Museum
30 Museum of the Ancient Orient
31 Alay Köşkü
32 Sublime Porte
34 Mahmut Paşa Hamamı
35 Büyük Yeni Han
36 Büyük Valide Han
37 Sahaflar Çarşısı
38 Beyazıt Camii
39 Museum of Turkish Calligraphic Art
40 Tourist Office
41 Forum of Theodosius Columns
42 Leko Deri
43 Tarihi Nişancı Hamamı
44 Tergan
45 Orient House
47 Tarihi Gedikpaşa Hamamı
WALKING TOURS
Ottoman Sultanahmet
Byzantine Sultanahmet
Path of Empires
The Bazaar District
MAP 12

MAP 16 – İSTİKLAL CADDESİ

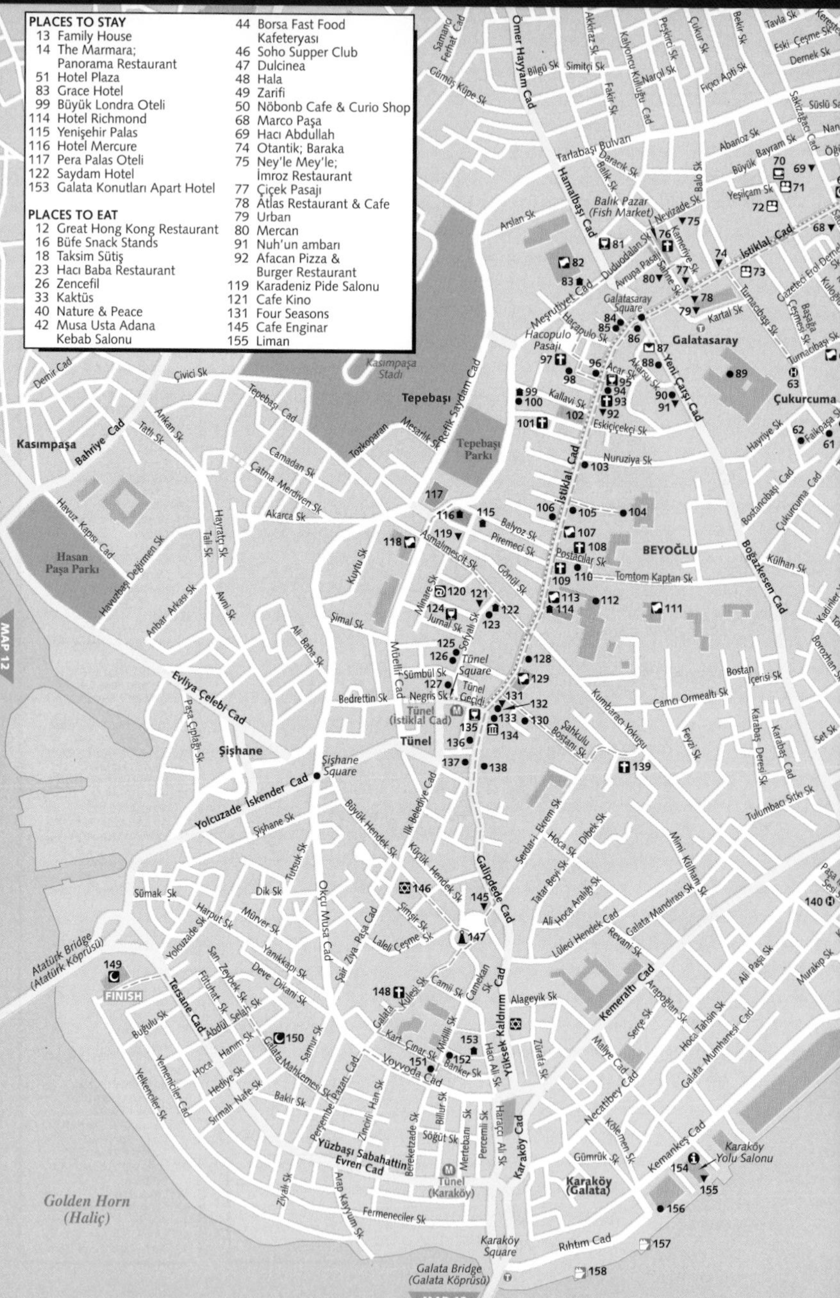

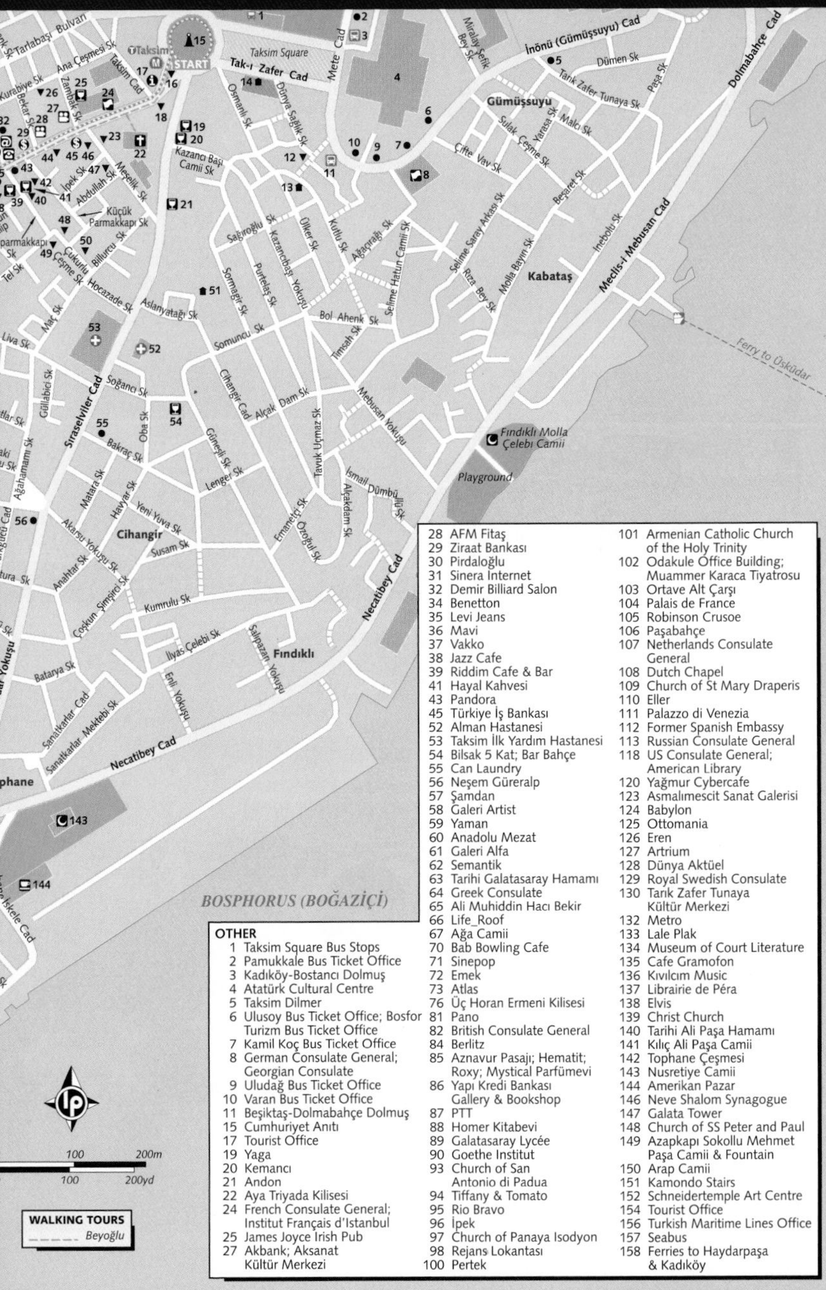
OTHER
1 Taksim Square Bus Stops
2 Pamukkale Bus Ticket Office
3 Kadıköy-Bostancı Dolmuş
4 Atatürk Cultural Centre
5 Taksim Dilmer
6 Ulusoy Bus Ticket Office; Bosfor Turizm Bus Ticket Office
7 Kamil Koç Bus Ticket Office
8 German Consulate General; Georgian Consulate
9 Uludağ Bus Ticket Office
10 Varan Bus Ticket Office
11 Beşiktaş-Dolmabahçe Dolmuş
15 Cumhuriyet Anıtı
17 Tourist Office
19 Yaga
20 Kemancı
21 Andon
22 Aya Triyada Kilisesi
24 French Consulate General; Institut Français d'Istanbul
25 James Joyce Irish Pub
27 Akbank; Aksanat Kültür Merkezi
28 AFM Fitaş
29 Ziraat Bankası
30 Pirdaloğlu
31 Sinera Internet
32 Demir Billiard Salon
34 Benetton
35 Levi Jeans
36 Mavi
37 Vakko
38 Jazz Cafe
39 Riddim Cafe & Bar
41 Hayal Kahvesi
43 Pandora
45 Türkiye İş Bankası
52 Alman Hastanesi
53 Taksim İlk Yardım Hastanesi
54 Bilsak 5 Kat; Bar Bahçe
55 Can Laundry
56 Neşem Güreralp
57 Şamdan
58 Galeri Artist
59 Yaman
60 Anadolu Mezat
61 Galeri Alfa
62 Semantik
63 Tarihi Galatasaray Hamamı
64 Greek Consulate
65 Ali Muhiddin Hacı Bekir
66 Life_Roof
67 Ağa Camii
70 Bab Bowling Cafe
71 Sinepop
72 Emek
73 Atlas
76 Üç Horan Ermeni Kilisesi
81 Pano
82 British Consulate General
84 Berlitz
85 Aznavur Pasajı; Hematit; Roxy; Mystical Parfümevi
86 Yapı Kredi Bankası Gallery & Bookshop
87 PTT
88 Homer Kitabevi
89 Galatasaray Lycée
90 Goethe Institut
93 Church of San Antonio di Padua
94 Tiffany & Tomato
95 Rio Bravo
96 İpek
97 Church of Panaya Isodyon
98 Rejans Lokantası
100 Pertek
101 Armenian Catholic Church of the Holy Trinity
102 Odakule Office Building; Muammer Karaca Tiyatrosu
103 Ortave Alt Çarşı
104 Palais de France
105 Robinson Crusoe
106 Paşabahçe
107 Netherlands Consulate General
108 Dutch Chapel
109 Church of St Mary Draperis
110 Eller
111 Palazzo di Venezia
112 Former Spanish Embassy
113 Russian Consulate General
118 US Consulate General; American Library
120 Yağmur Cybercafe
123 Asmalımescit Sanat Galerisi
124 Babylon
125 Ottomania
126 Eren
127 Artrium
128 Dünya Aktüel
129 Royal Swedish Consulate
130 Tarık Zafer Tunaya Kültür Merkezi
132 Metro
133 Lale Plak
134 Museum of Court Literature
135 Cafe Gramofon
136 Kıvılcım Music
137 Librairie de Péra
138 Elvis
139 Christ Church
140 Tarihi Ali Paşa Hamamı
141 Kılıç Ali Paşa Camii
142 Tophane Çeşmesi
143 Nusretiye Camii
144 Amerikan Pazar
146 Neve Shalom Synagogue
147 Galata Tower
148 Church of SS Peter and Paul
149 Azapkapı Sokollu Mehmet Paşa Camii & Fountain
150 Arap Camii
151 Kamondo Stairs
152 Schneidertemple Art Centre
154 Tourist Office
156 Turkish Maritime Lines Office
157 Seabus
158 Ferries to Haydarpaşa & Kadıköy
WALKING TOURS
Beyoğlu
100
200m
100
200yd
Taksim Square
Taksim
START
Tak-ı Zafer Cad
İnönü (Gümüşsuyu) Cad
Dümen Sk
Tarık Zafer Tunaya Sk
Dolmabahçe Cad
Gümüşsuyu
Kabataş
Meclis-i Mebusan Cad
Ferry to Üsküdar
Fındıklı Molla Çelebi Camii
Playground
Necatibey Cad
Fındıklı
Cihangir
Sıraselviler Cad
BOSPHORUS (BOĞAZİÇİ)
Tarlabaşı Bulvarı
Taksim Cad
Mete Cad
Osmanlı Sk
Dünya Sağlık Sk
Kazancı Başı Camii Sk
Sağıroğlu Sk
Kazancıbaşı Yokuşu
Ülker Sk
Kutlu Sk
Ağaçrağlı Sk
Selime Hatun Camii Sk
Selime Saray Arkası Sk
Molla Bayırı Sk
Rıza Bey Sk
Bol Ahenk Sk
Somuncu Sk
Sormagir Sk
Purtelaş Sk
Aslanyatağı Sk
Hocazade Sk
Soğancı Sk
Cihangir Cad
Alçak Dam Sk
Mebusan Yokuşu
Tavuk Uçmaz Sk
Güneşli Sk
Lenger Sk
Bakraç Sk
Oba Sk
Akarsu Yokuşu Sk
Susam Sk
Yeni Yuva Sk
Havyar Sk
Matara Sk
Kumrulu Sk
İlyas Çelebi Sk
Salıpazarı Yokuşu
Emil Yokuşu
Necatibey Cad
Batarya Sk
Sanatkarlar Cad
Sanatkarlar Mektebi Sk
Tophane İskele Cad

MAP 12
MAP 12

VERITY CAMPBELL

ADINA TOVY AMSEL

Top: Kız Kulesi (Maiden's Tower), a toll booth and defence point in ancient times, as seen from Salacak on the Asian side of İstanbul
Bottom: The entrance to İstanbul University, built in the 19th century for the Ottoman War Ministry

MAP 17 – ELMADAĞ, HARBİYE & NİŞANTAŞI

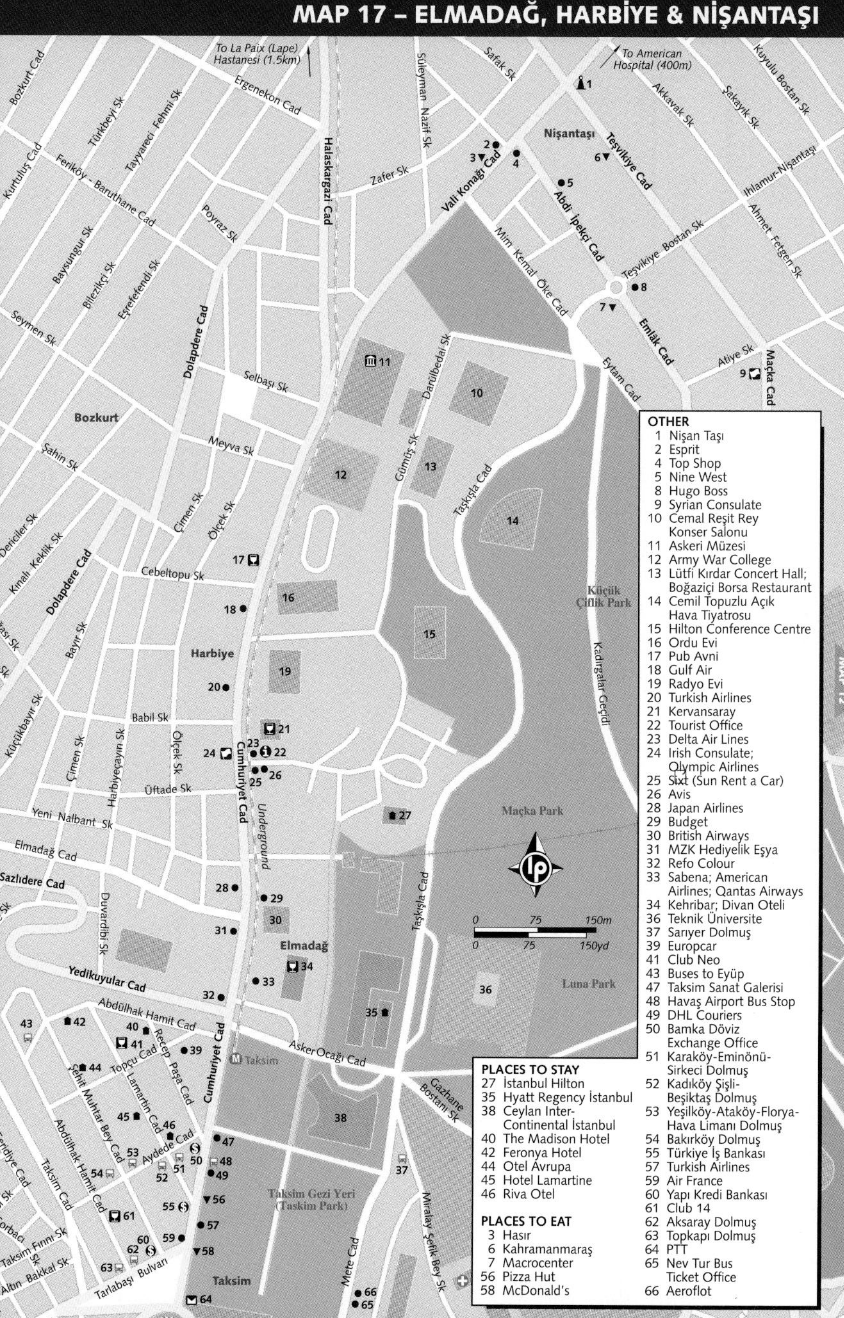

OTHER
1 Nişan Taşı
2 Esprit
4 Top Shop
5 Nine West
8 Hugo Boss
9 Syrian Consulate
10 Cemal Reşit Rey Konser Salonu
11 Askeri Müzesi
12 Army War College
13 Lütfi Kırdar Concert Hall; Boğaziçi Borsa Restaurant
14 Cemil Topuzlu Açık Hava Tiyatrosu
15 Hilton Conference Centre
16 Ordu Evi
17 Pub Avni
18 Gulf Air
19 Radyo Evi
20 Turkish Airlines
21 Kervansaray
22 Tourist Office
23 Delta Air Lines
24 Irish Consulate; Olympic Airlines
25 Sixt (Sun Rent a Car)
26 Avis
28 Japan Airlines
29 Budget
30 British Airways
31 MZK Hediyelik Eşya
32 Refo Colour
33 Sabena; American Airlines; Qantas Airways
34 Kehribar; Divan Oteli
36 Teknik Üniversite
37 Sarıyer Dolmuş
39 Europcar
41 Club Neo
43 Buses to Eyüp
47 Taksim Sanat Galerisi
48 Havaş Airport Bus Stop
49 DHL Couriers
50 Bamka Döviz Exchange Office
51 Karaköy-Eminönü-Sirkeci Dolmuş
52 Kadıköy Şişli-Beşiktaş Dolmuş
53 Yeşilköy-Ataköy-Florya-Hava Limanı Dolmuş
54 Bakırköy Dolmuş
55 Türkiye İş Bankası
57 Turkish Airlines
59 Air France
60 Yapı Kredi Bankası
61 Club 14
62 Aksaray Dolmuş
63 Topkapı Dolmuş
64 PTT
65 Nev Tur Bus Ticket Office
66 Aeroflot
PLACES TO STAY
27 İstanbul Hilton
35 Hyatt Regency İstanbul
38 Ceylan Inter-Continental İstanbul
40 The Madison Hotel
42 Feronya Hotel
44 Otel Avrupa
45 Hotel Lamartine
46 Riva Otel
PLACES TO EAT
3 Hasır
6 Kahramanmaraş
7 Macrocenter
56 Pizza Hut
58 McDonald's
To La Paix (Lape) Hastanesi (1.5km)
To American Hospital (400m)
Nişantaşı
Bozkurt
Harbiye
Elmadağ
Taksim
Küçük Çiftlik Park
Maçka Park
Luna Park
Taksim Gezi Yeri (Taskim Park)
Taksim
Underground
MAP 12
MAP 16
0 75 150m
0 75 150yd
Bozkurt Cad
Türkbeyi Sk
Tayyareci Fehmi Sk
Ergenekon Cad
Halaskargazi Cad
Süleyman Nazif Sk
Şafak Sk
Kuyulu Bostan Sk
Akkavak Sk
Sakayık Sk
Teşvikiye Cad
Vali Konağı Cad
Zafer Sk
Abdi İpekçi Cad
Ihlamur-Nişantaşı
Ahmet Fetgeri Sk
Teşvikiye Bostan Sk
Mim Kemal Öke Cad
Emlâk Cad
Eytam Cad
Atiye Sk
Maçka Cad
Kurtuluş Cad
Feriköy - Baruthane Cad
Poyraz Sk
Baysungur Sk
Bilezikçi Sk
Eşrefefendi Sk
Seymen Sk
Dolapdere Cad
Selbaşı Sk
Darülbedai Sk
Meyva Sk
Şahin Sk
Gümüş Sk
Taşkışla Cad
Çimen Sk
Ölçek Sk
Dericiler Sk
Kınalı Keklik Sk
Cebeltopu Sk
Bayır Sk
Kadırgalar Geçidi
Küçükbayır Sk
Babil Sk
Harbiyeçayırı Sk
Cumhuriyet Cad
Üftade Sk
Yeni Nalbant Sk
Elmadağ Cad
Sazlıdere Cad
Duvardibi Sk
Yedikuyular Cad
Abdülhak Hamit Cad
Recep Paşa Cad
Topçu Cad
Asker Ocağı Cad
Şehit Muhtar Bey Cad
Lamartin Cad
Aydede Cad
Gazhane Bostanı Sk
Feridiye Cad
Taksim Cad
Taksim Fırını Sk
Altın Bakkal Sk
Tarlabaşı Bulvarı
Mete Cad
Miralay Şefik Bey Sk

MAP 18 – WESTERN DISTRICTS

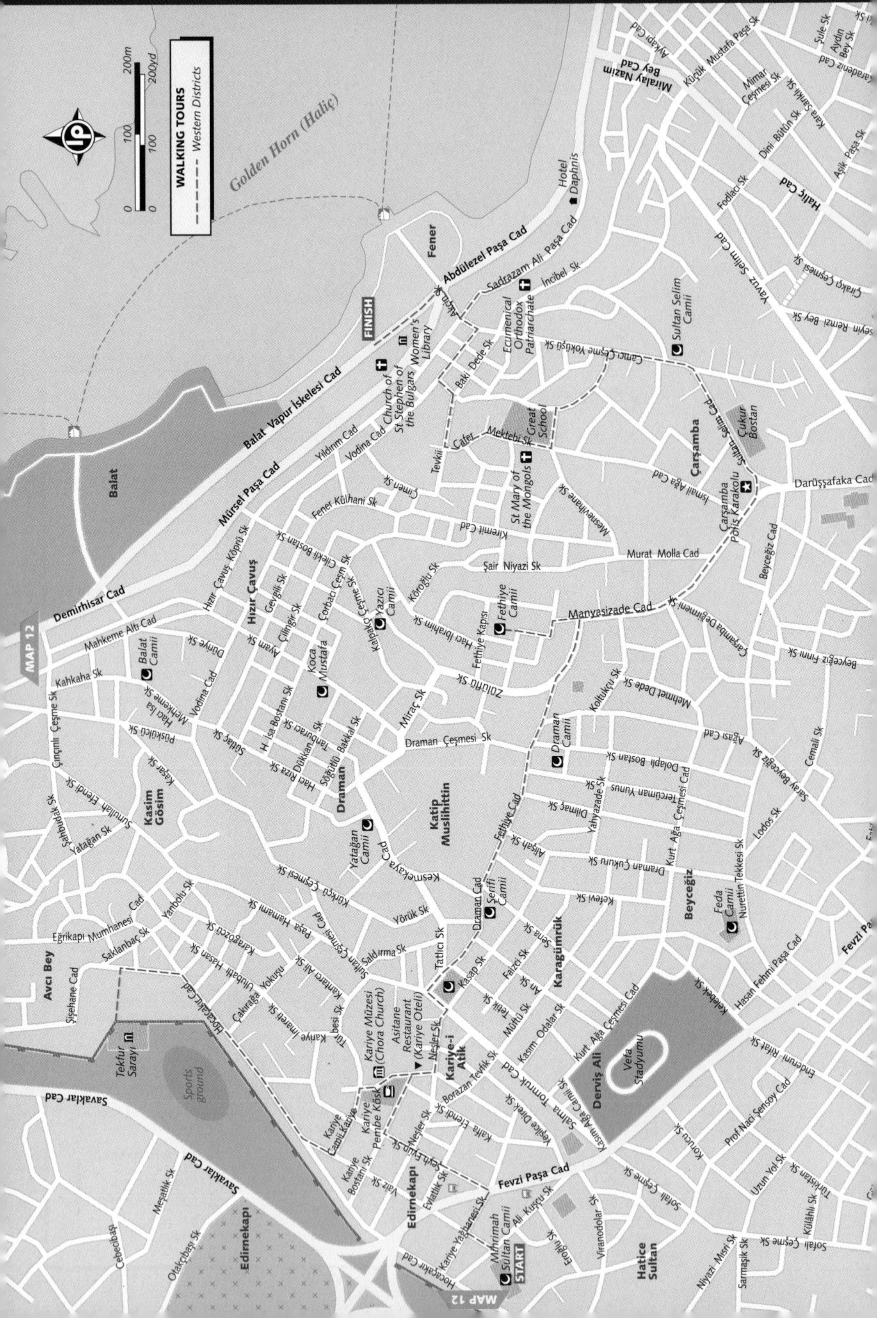

0
100
200m
0
100
200yd
WALKING TOURS
Western Districts
Golden Horn (Haliç)
Balat
Fener
FINISH
START
MAP 12
MAP 12
Hotel Daphnis
Abdülezel Paşa Cad
Balat Vapur İskelesi Cad
Mürsel Paşa Cad
Demirhisar Cad
Church of St Stephen of the Bulgars
Women's Library
Ecumenical Orthodox Patriarchate
Sadrazam Ali Paşa Cad
İncibel Sk
Great School
St Mary of the Mongols
Mektebi Sk
Sultan Selim Camii
Sultan Selim Cad
Yavuz Selim Cad
Çukur Bostan
Çarşamba
Çarşamba Polis Karakolu
Darüşşafaka Cad
Miralay Nazım Bey Cad
Ayvansaray Cad
Küçük Mustafa Paşa Sk
Mimar Çeşmesi Sk
Dini Bütün Sk
Fodlacı Sk
Haliç Cad
Aşık Paşa Sk
Kara Sarıklı Sk
Şule Sk
Aydın Bey Sk
Karadeniz Cad
Çırakçı Çeşmesi Sk
Hüseyin Remzi Bey Sk
Camcı Çeşme Yokuşu Sk
İsmail Ağa Cad
Baki Dede Sk
Yıldırım Cad
Vodina Cad
Fener Külhani Sk
Çimen Sk
Kiremit Cad
Mesnevihane Sk
Murat Molla Cad
Şair Niyazi Sk
Köroğlu Sk
Fethiye Camii
Fethiye Kapısı
Hacı İbrahim Sk
Manyasizade Cad
Çarşamba Değirmeni Sk
Beyceğiz Cad
Beyceğiz Fırını Sk
Mehmet Dede Sk
Koltukçu Sk
Zülüflü Sk
Yazıcı Camii
Kalpakçı Çeşme Sk
Çorbacı Çeşm Sk
Çilekli Bostan Sk
Hızır Çavuş
Hızır Çavuş Köprü Sk
Gevgili Sk
Çilingir Sk
Ayan Sk
Koca Mustafa
Mahkeme Altı Cad
Dünya Sk
Balat Camii
Kahkaha Sk
Vodina Cad
Mirac Sk
Draman Çeşmesi Sk
Draman Camii
Ağası Cad
Dolaplı Bostan Sk
Saray Beyceğiz Sk
Cemali Sk
Hacı İsa Mektebe Sk
Püskülcü Sk
Çinçinli Çeşme Sk
H İsa Bostanı Sk
Tanburacı Sk
Dükkan Sk
Bakkal Sk
Söğütlü
Hacı Rıza Sk
Sıddıs Sk
Kaşar Sk
Draman
Katip Muslihittin
Kasım Gösim
Sunullah Efendi Sk
Şahbudak Sk
Yatağan Sk
Yatağan Camii
Fethiye Cad
Yahyazade Sk
Dilmaç Sk
Tercüman Yunus
Kurt Ağa Çeşmesi Cad
Alişah Sk
Draman Çukuru Sk
Nurettin Tekkesi Sk
Lodos Sk
Kesmekaya Cad
Küfecü Çeşmesi Sk
Yörük Sk
Draman Cad
Şerifi Camii
Kefevi Sk
Beyceğiz
Feda Camii
Fevzi Paşa Cad
Hasan Fehmi Paşa Cad
Kelebek Sk
Sena Sk
Karagümrük
Faizci Sk
Kasap Sk
Arı Sk
Tatlıcı Sk
Saldırma Sk
Sultan Çeşmesi Cad
Paşa Hamamı Sk
Kantarcı Ali Sk
Karagözcü Sk
Yanbolu Sk
Eğrikapı Mumhanesi Cad
Saklanbaç Sk
Avcı Bey
Şişehane Cad
Hasan Sk
Unbatlı
Çakırağa Yokuşu
Hoca Çakır Cad
Tekfur Sarayı
Sports ground
Kariye İmareti Sk
Tur... besi Sk
Kariye Müzesi (Chora Church)
Asitane Restaurant (Kariye Oteli)
Nesler Sk
Kariye-i Atik
Tetik Sk
Müftü Sk
Kasım Odalar Sk
Kurt Ağa Çeşmesi Cad
Derviş Ali
Vefa Stadyumu
Enderuni Rifat Sk
Prof Naci Şensoy Cad
Borazan Tevfik Sk
Tomruk Cad
Salma Tomruk Cad
Kasım Ağa Camii Sk
Kariye Pembe Köşk
Kariye Camii Kariye
Kalfa Efendi Sk
Yeşilce Direk Sk
Koncu Sk
Savaklar Cad
Savaklar Cad
Kariye Bostanı Sk
Neşter Sk
Şeyh Eyüp Sk
Vaiz Sk
Edirnekapı
Evlatlık Sk
Kariye Yağhanesi Sk
Mihrimah Sultan Camii
Ali Kuşçu Sk
Sofalı Çeşme Sk
Uzun Yol Sk
Türkistan Sk
Külâhlı Sk
Sofalı Çeşme Sk
Mesatlık Sk
Cebecibaşı
Otakçıbaşı Sk
Edirnekapı
Hocaçakır Cad
Eroğlu Sk
Viranodalar Sk
Hatice Sultan
Niyazi Mısri Sk
Sarmaşık Sk

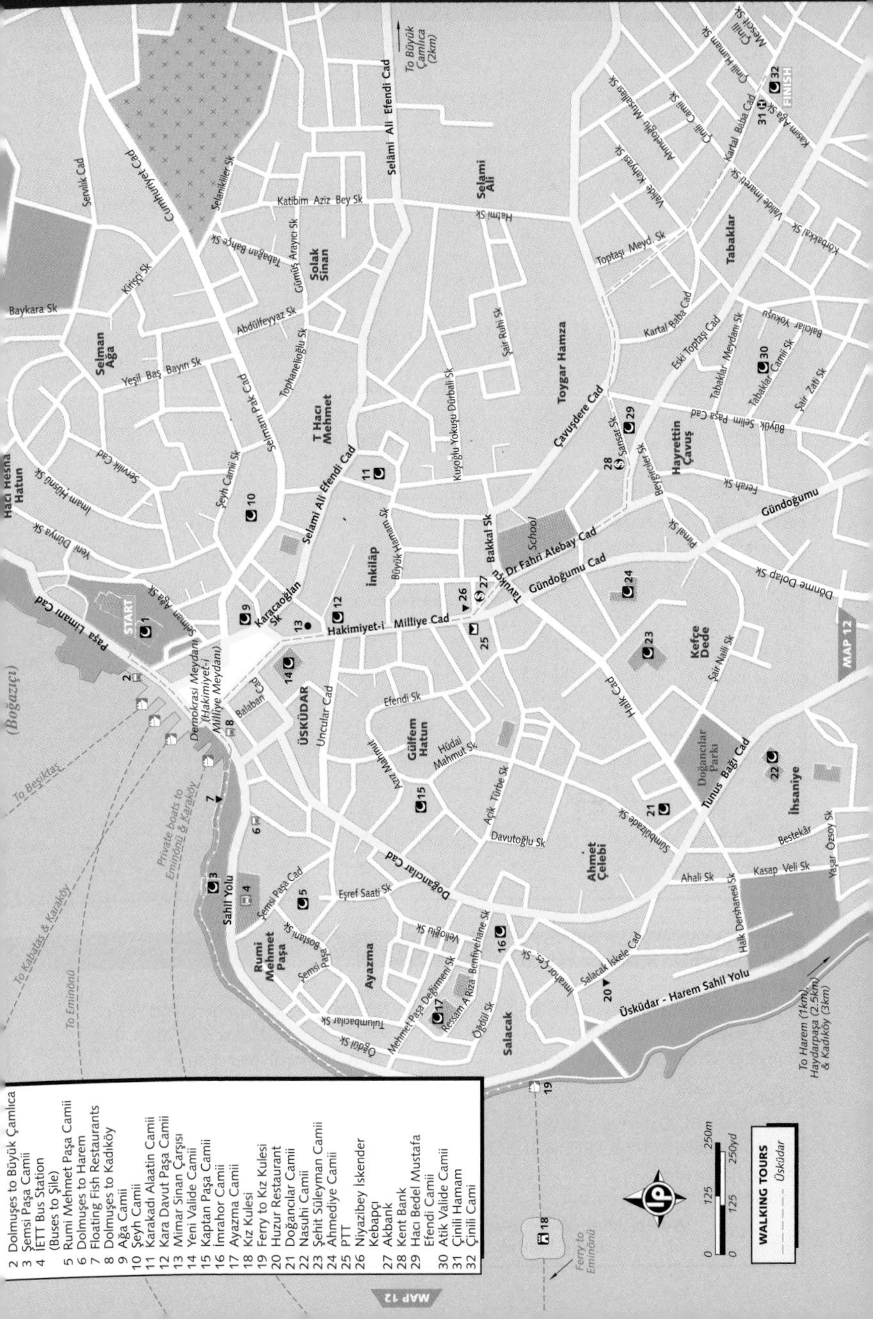

MAP 19 – ÜSKÜDAR

2 Dolmuşes to Büyük Çamlıca
3 Şemsi Paşa Camii
4 İETT Bus Station (Buses to Şile)
5 Rumi Mehmet Paşa Camii
6 Dolmuşes to Harem
7 Floating Fish Restaurants
8 Dolmuşes to Kadıköy
9 Ağa Camii
10 Şeyh Camii
11 Karakadı Alaatin Camii
12 Kara Davut Paşa Camii
13 Mimar Sinan Çarşısı
14 Yeni Valide Camii
15 Kaptan Paşa Camii
16 İmrahor Camii
17 Ayazma Camii
18 Kız Kulesi
19 Ferry to Kız Kulesi
20 Huzur Restaurant
21 Doğancılar Camii
22 Nasuhi Camii
23 Şehit Süleyman Camii
24 Ahmediye Camii
25 PTT
26 Niyazibey İskender Kebapçı
27 Akbank
28 Kent Bank
29 Hacı Bedel Mustafa Efendi Camii
30 Atik Valide Camii
31 Çinili Hamam
32 Çinili Cami

WALKING TOURS

Üsküdar

MAP LEGEND

CITY ROUTES

Freeway	Freeway		Unsealed Road
Highway	Primary Road		One Way Street
Road	Secondary Road		Pedestrian Street
Street	Street		Stepped Street
Lane	Lane		Tunnel
	On/Off Ramp		Footbridge

REGIONAL ROUTES

Tollway, Freeway
Primary Road
Secondary Road
Minor Road

BOUNDARIES

International
State
Disputed
Fortified Wall

HYDROGRAPHY

River, Creek · Dry Lake; Salt Lake
Canal · Spring; Rapids
Lake · Waterfalls

TRANSPORT ROUTES & STATIONS

Train · Ferry
Underground Metro · Walking Trail
Metro · Walking Tour
Tramway · Path
Cable Car, Chairlift · Pier or Jetty

AREA FEATURES

Building · Market · Beach · Campus
Park, Gardens · Sports Ground · Cemetery · Plaza

POPULATION SYMBOLS

CAPITAL	National Capital	**CITY**	City	Village	Village
CAPITAL	State Capital	**Town**	Town		Urban Area

MAP SYMBOLS

Place to Stay · Place to Eat · Point of Interest

Airport	Embassy	Monument	Post Office
Bank	Fort	Mosque	Pub or Bar
Border Crossing	Fountain	Museum	Ruins
Bus Station (Otogar)	Hamam	National Park; Zoo	Shopping Centre
Bus/Dolmuş Stop	Hospital	Palace	Synagogue
Cafe/Tea Garden	Information	Parking	Taxi
Cave	Internet Cafe	Petrol	Telephone
Church	Lighthouse	Picnic	Tomb
Cinema; Theatre	Lookout	Police Station	Tourist Information

Note: not all symbols displayed above appear in this book

LONELY PLANET OFFICES

Australia
Locked Bag 1, Footscray, Victoria 3011
☎ 03 8379 8000 fax 03 8379 8111
email: talk2us@lonelyplanet.com.au

USA
150 Linden St, Oakland, CA 94607
☎ 510 893 8555 TOLL FREE: 800 275 8555
fax 510 893 8572
email: info@lonelyplanet.com

UK
10a Spring Place, London NW5 3BH
☎ 020 7428 4800 fax 020 7428 4828
email: go@lonelyplanet.co.uk

France
1 rue du Dahomey, 75011 Paris
☎ 01 55 25 33 00 fax 01 55 25 33 01
email: bip@lonelyplanet.fr
www.lonelyplanet.fr

World Wide Web: www.lonelyplanet.com *or* AOL keyword: lp
Lonely Planet Images: lpi@lonelyplanet.com.au